THE WRITINGS OF HERMAN MELVILLE

The Northwestern-Newberry Edition

VOLUME TWELVE

Clarel

This volume edited by
HARRISON HAYFORD
ALMA A. MacDOUGALL
HERSHEL PARKER
G. THOMAS TANSELLE

Historical and Critical Note by
WALTER E. BEZANSON

Historical Supplement by
HERSHEL PARKER

Executive Editor
LYNN HORTH

Associates
RICHARD COLLES JOHNSON
ROBERT C. RYAN

Contributing Scholar
MARK NIEMEYER

Clarel

*A Poem and Pilgrimage
in the Holy Land*

HERMAN MELVILLE

NORTHWESTERN UNIVERSITY PRESS
and
THE NEWBERRY LIBRARY
Evanston and Chicago
1991

PUBLICATION *of this edition of* THE WRITINGS OF HERMAN MELVILLE *has been made possible through the financial support of Northwestern University and its Research Committee and The Newberry Library. The research necessary to establish the text was initially undertaken under the Cooperative Research Program of the U.S. Office of Education, and preparation of this volume has been supported by the National Endowment for the Humanities, a federal agency which supports the study of such fields as history, philosophy, literature, and languages. Northwestern University Press produced and published this edition and reserves all rights.*

LIBRARY OF CONGRESS CATALOG CARD NUMBER 90-60361

PRINTED IN THE UNITED STATES OF AMERICA

Cloth Edition, ISBN 0-8101-0906-9
Paper Edition, ISBN 0-8101-0907-7

By

A SPONTANEOUS ACT,

NOT VERY LONG AGO,

MY KINSMAN, THE LATE

Peter Gansevoort,

OF ALBANY, N. Y.,

IN A PERSONAL INTERVIEW PROVIDED FOR THE PUBLICATION
OF THIS POEM, KNOWN TO HIM BY REPORT,
AS EXISTING IN MANUSCRIPT.

JUSTLY AND AFFECTIONATELY THE PRINTED BOOK IS

Inscribed with his name.

Contents

PART ONE · JERUSALEM

Canto 1 · *The Hostel*	3
Canto 2 · *Abdon*	8
Canto 3 · *The Sepulchre*	12
Canto 4 · *Of the Crusaders*	17
Canto 5 · *Clarel*	18
Canto 6 · *Tribes and Sects*	23
Canto 7 · *Beyond the Walls*	25
Canto 8 · *The Votary*	27
Canto 9 · *Saint and Student*	29
Canto 10 · *Rambles*	31
Canto 11 · *Lower Gihon*	33
Canto 12 · *Celio*	36
Canto 13 · *The Arch*	40
Canto 14 · *In the Glen*	43
Canto 15 · *Under the Minaret*	47
Canto 16 · *The Wall of Wail*	50
Canto 17 · *Nathan*	55
Canto 18 · *Night*	64
Canto 19 · *The Fulfillment*	67
Canto 20 · *Vale of Ashes*	68

ix

Canto 21 · *By-Places*   70

Canto 22 · *Hermitage*   71

Canto 23 · *The Close*   74

Canto 24 · *The Gibe*   77

Canto 25 · *Huts*   79

Canto 26 · *The Gate of Zion*   82

Canto 27 · *Matron and Maid*   84

Canto 28 · *Tomb and Fountain*   87

Canto 29 · *The Recluse*   91

Canto 30 · *The Site of the Passion*   92

Canto 31 · *Rolfe*   95

Canto 32 · *Of Rama*   103

Canto 33 · *By the Stone*   105

Canto 34 · *They Tarry*   108

Canto 35 · *Arculf and Adamnan*   110

Canto 36 · *The Tower*   113

Canto 37 · *A Sketch*   115

Canto 38 · *The Sparrow*   118

Canto 39 · *Clarel and Ruth*   120

Canto 40 · *The Mounds*   121

Canto 41 · *On the Wall*   123

Canto 42 · *Tidings*   127

Canto 43 · *A Procession*   130

Canto 44 · *The Start*   131

PART TWO · THE WILDERNESS

Canto 1 · *The Cavalcade*   133

Canto 2 · *The Skull Cap*   140

Canto 3 · *By the Garden*   141

Canto 4 · *Of Mortmain*   146

Canto 5 · *Clarel and Glaucon*   150

Canto 6 · *The Hamlet*   153

Canto 7 · *Guide and Guard*   154

Canto 8 · *Rolfe and Derwent*   157

Canto 9 · *Through Adommin*   158

Canto 10 · *A Halt*   161

Canto 11 · *Of Deserts*   168

Canto 12 · *The Banker*   170
Canto 13 · *Flight of the Greeks*   172
Canto 14 · *By Achor*   176
Canto 15 · *The Fountain*   180
Canto 16 · *Night in Jericho*   182
Canto 17 · *In Mid-Watch*   186
Canto 18 · *The Syrian Monk*   187
Canto 19 · *An Apostate*   192
Canto 20 · *Under the Mountain*   194
Canto 21 · *The Priest and Rolfe*   197
Canto 22 · *Concerning Hebrews*   201
Canto 23 · *By the Jordan*   205
Canto 24 · *The River-Rite*   210
Canto 25 · *The Dominican*   213
Canto 26 · *Of Rome*   219
Canto 27 · *Vine and Clarel*   224
Canto 28 · *The Fog*   229
Canto 29 · *By the Marge*   230
Canto 30 · *Of Petra*   235
Canto 31 · *The Inscription*   237
Canto 32 · *The Encampment*   240
Canto 33 · *Lot's Sea*   243
Canto 34 · *Mortmain Reappears*   246
Canto 35 · *Prelusive*   248
Canto 36 · *Sodom*   249
Canto 37 · *Of Traditions*   253
Canto 38 · *The Sleep-Walker*   255
Canto 39 · *Obsequies*   257

PART THREE · MAR SABA

Canto 1 · *In the Mountain*   263
Canto 2 · *The Carpenter*   268
Canto 3 · *Of the Many Mansions*   270
Canto 4 · *The Cypriote*   272
Canto 5 · *The High Desert*   276
Canto 6 · *Derwent*   282
Canto 7 · *Bell and Cairn*   286

Canto 8 · *Tents of Kedar*   289
Canto 9 · *Of Monasteries*   293
Canto 10 · *Before the Gate*   295
Canto 11 · *The Beaker*   298
Canto 12 · *The Timoneer's Story*   306
Canto 13 · *Song and Recitative*   311
Canto 14 · *The Revel Closed*   314
Canto 15 · *In Moonlight*   318
Canto 16 · *The Easter Fire*   321
Canto 17 · *A Chant*   329
Canto 18 · *The Minster*   331
Canto 19 · *The Masque*   333
Canto 20 · *Afterwards*   338
Canto 21 · *In Confidence*   339
Canto 22 · *The Medallion*   348
Canto 23 · *Derwent with the Abbot*   350
Canto 24 · *Vault and Grotto*   354
Canto 25 · *Derwent and the Lesbian*   357
Canto 26 · *Vine and the Palm*   361
Canto 27 · *Man and Bird*   363
Canto 28 · *Mortmain and the Palm*   368
Canto 29 · *Rolfe and the Palm*   371
Canto 30 · *The Celibate*   373
Canto 31 · *The Recoil*   378
Canto 32 · *Empty Stirrups*   380

PART FOUR · BETHLEHEM

Canto 1 · *In Saddle*   383
Canto 2 · *The Ensign*   388
Canto 3 · *The Island*   395
Canto 4 · *An Intruder*   398
Canto 5 · *Of the Stranger*   400
Canto 6 · *Bethlehem*   405
Canto 7 · *At Table*   406
Canto 8 · *The Pillow*   409
Canto 9 · *The Shepherds' Dale*   410
Canto 10 · *A Monument*   415
Canto 11 · *Disquiet*   420

Canto 12 · *Of Pope and Turk* 421

Canto 13 · *The Church of the Star* 424

Canto 14 · *Soldier and Monk* 431

Canto 15 · *Symphonies* 434

Canto 16 · *The Convent Roof* 436

Canto 17 · *A Transition* 442

Canto 18 · *The Hillside* 444

Canto 19 · *A New-Comer* 448

Canto 20 · *Derwent and Ungar* 453

Canto 21 · *Ungar and Rolfe* 457

Canto 22 · *Of Wickedness the Word* 461

Canto 23 · *Derwent and Rolfe* 463

Canto 24 · *Twilight* 465

Canto 25 · *The Invitation* 466

Canto 26 · *The Prodigal* 468

Canto 27 · *By Parapet* 477

Canto 28 · *David's Well* 478

Canto 29 · *The Night Ride* 482

Canto 30 · *The Valley of Decision* 486

Canto 31 · *Dirge* 490

Canto 32 · *Passion Week* 491

Canto 33 · *Easter* 494

Canto 34 · *Via Crucis* 496

Canto 35 · *Epilogue* 498

EDITORIAL APPENDIX

HISTORICAL AND CRITICAL NOTE · *By Walter E. Bezanson* 505

HISTORICAL SUPPLEMENT · *By Hershel Parker* 639

TEXTUAL RECORD

Note on the Text 675

Discussions 703

List of Emendations 841

RELATED DOCUMENTS

Melville's Annotated Copy of *Clarel* 849

Elizabeth Shaw Melville's Copies of *Clarel* 865

The "Ditty of Aristippus" Manuscript 867

Parallel Passages in *Clarel* and Melville's 1856-57 Journal 871

Melville's "Monody": For Hawthorne? 883

If during the period in which this work has remained unpublished, though not undivulged, any of its properties have by a natural process exhaled; it yet retains, I trust, enough of original life to redeem it at least from vapidity. Be that as it may, I here dismiss the book—content beforehand with whatever future awaits it.

Clarel

Part 1

Jerusalem

1. THE HOSTEL

IN CHAMBER low and scored by time,
  Masonry old, late washed with lime—
  Much like a tomb new-cut in stone;
Elbow on knee, and brow sustained
All motionless on sidelong hand,   5
A student sits, and broods alone.
    The small deep casement sheds a ray
Which tells that in the Holy Town
It is the passing of the day—
The Vigil of Epiphany.   10
Beside him in the narrow cell
His luggage lies unpacked; thereon
The dust lies, and on him as well—
The dust of travel. But anon
His face he lifts—in feature fine,   15
Yet pale, and all but feminine
But for the eye and serious brow—
Then rises, paces to and fro,
And pauses, saying, "Other cheer
Than that anticipated here,   20

3

By me the learner, now I find.
Theology, art thou so blind?
What means this naturalistic knell
In lieu of Siloh's oracle
Which here should murmur? Snatched from grace,   25
And waylaid in the holy place!
Not thus it was but yesterday
Off Jaffa on the clear blue sea;
Nor thus, my heart, it was with thee
Landing amid the shouts and spray;   30
Nor thus when mounted, full equipped,
Out through the vaulted gate we slipped
Beyond the walls where gardens bright
With bloom and blossom cheered the sight.
    "The plain we crossed. In afternoon,   35
How like our early autumn bland—
So softly tempered for a boon—
The breath of Sharon's prairie land!
And was it, yes, her titled Rose,
That scarlet poppy oft at hand?   40
Then Ramleh gleamed, the sail-white town
At even. There I watched day close
From the fair tower, the suburb one:
Seaward and dazing set the sun:
Inland I turned me toward the wall   45
Of Ephraim, stretched in purple pall.
Romance of mountains! But in end
What change the near approach could lend.
    "The start this morning—gun and lance
Against the quarter-moon's low tide;   50
The thieves' huts where we hushed the ride;
Chill day-break in the lorn advance;
In stony strait the scorch of noon,
Thrown off by crags, reminding one
Of those hot paynims whose fierce hands   55
Flung showers of Afric's fiery sands
In face of that crusader-king,
Louis, to wither so his wing;
And, at the last, aloft for goal,

Like the ice-bastions round the Pole,   60
Thy blank, blank towers, Jerusalem!"

    Again he droops, with brow on hand.
But, starting up, "Why, well I knew
Salem to be no Samarcand;
'Twas scarce surprise; and yet first view   65
Brings this eclipse. Needs be my soul,
Purged by the desert's subtle air
From bookish vapors, now is heir
To nature's influx of control;
Comes likewise now to consciousness   70
Of the true import of that press
Of inklings which in travel late
Through Latin lands, did vex my state,
And somehow seemed clandestine. Ah!
These under-formings in the mind,   75
Banked corals which ascend from far,
But little heed men that they wind
Unseen, unheard—till lo, the reef—
The reef and breaker, wreck and grief.
But here unlearning, how to me   80
Opes the expanse of time's vast sea!
Yes, I am young, but Asia old.
The books, the books not all have told.
    "And, for the rest, the facile chat
Of overweenings—what was that   85
The grave one said in Jaffa lane
Whom there I met, my countryman,
But new-returned from travel here;
Some word of mine provoked the strain;
His meaning now begins to clear: 90
Let me go over it again:—
    "Our New World's worldly wit so shrewd
Lacks the Semitic reverent mood,
Unworldly—hardly may confer
Fitness for just interpreter   95
Of Palestine. Forego the state
Of local minds inveterate,

Tied to one poor and casual form.
To avoid the deep saves not from storm.
    "Those things he said, and added more;   100
No clear authenticated lore
I deemed. But now, need now confess
My cultivated narrowness,
Though scarce indeed of sort he meant?
'Tis the uprooting of content!"   105
    So he, the student. 'Twas a mind,
Earnest by nature, long confined
Apart like Vesta in a grove
Collegiate, but let to rove
At last abroad among mankind,   110
And here in end confronted so
By the true genius, friend or foe,
And actual visage of a place
Before but dreamed of in the glow
Of fancy's spiritual grace.   115
    Further his meditations aim,
Reverting to his different frame
Bygone. And then: "Can faith remove
Her light, because of late no plea
I've lifted to her source above?"   120
Dropping thereat upon the knee,
His lips he parted; but the word
Against the utterance demurred
And failed him. With infirm intent
He sought the house-top. Set of sun: 125
His feet upon the yet warm stone,
He, Clarel, by the coping leant,
In silent gaze. The mountain town,
A walled and battlemented one,
With houseless suburbs front and rear,   130
And flanks built up from steeps severe,
Saddles and turrets the ascent—
Tower which rides the elephant.
Hence large the view. There where he stood,
Was Acra's upper neighborhood.   135
The circling hills he saw, with one

Excelling, ample in its crown,
Making the uplifted city low
By contrast—Olivet. The flow
Of eventide was at full brim;   140
Overlooked, the houses sloped from him—
Terraced or domed, unchimnied, gray,
All stone—a moor of roofs. No play
Of life; no smoke went up, no sound
Except low hum, and that half drowned.   145
     The inn abutted on the pool
Named Hezekiah's, a sunken court
Where silence and seclusion rule,
Hemmed round by walls of nature's sort,
Base to stone structures seeming one   150
E'en with the steeps they stand upon.
     As a three-decker's stern-lights peer
Down on the oily wake below,
Upon the sleek dark waters here
The inn's small lattices bestow   155
A rearward glance. And here and there
In flaws the languid evening air
Stirs the dull weeds adust, which trail
In festoons from the crag, and veil
The ancient fissures, overtopped   160
By the tall convent of the Copt,
Built like a light-house o'er the main.
     Blind arches showed in walls of wane,
Sealed windows, portals masoned fast,
And terraces where nothing passed   165
By parapets all dumb. No tarn
Among the Kaatskills, high above
Farm-house and stack, last lichened barn
And log-bridge rotting in remove—
More lonesome looks than this dead pool   170
In town where living creatures rule.
     Not here the spell might he undo;
The strangeness haunted him and grew.
     But twilight closes. He descends
And toward the inner court he wends.   175

2. ABDON

A lamp in archway hangs from key—
A lamp whose sidelong rays are shed
On a slim vial set in bed
Of door-post all of masonry.
    That vial hath the Gentile vexed;   5
Within it holds Talmudic text,
Or charm. And there the Black Jew sits,
Abdon the host. The lamp-light flits
O'er reverend beard of saffron hue
Sweeping his robe of Indian blue.   10
    Disturbed and troubled in estate,
Longing for solacement of mate,
Clarel in court there nearer drew,
As yet unnoted, for the host
In meditation seemed engrossed,   15
Perchance upon some line late scanned
In leathern scroll that drooped from hand.
    Ere long, without surprise expressed,
The lone man marked his lonelier guest,
And welcomed him. Discourse was bred;   20
In end a turn it took, and led
To grave recital. Here was one
(If question of his word be none)
Descended from those dubious men,
The unreturning tribes, the Ten   25
Whom shout and halloo wide have sought,
Lost children in the wood of time.
    Yes, he, the Black Jew, stinting naught,
Averred that ancient India's clime
Harbored the remnant of the Tribes,   30
A people settled with their scribes
In far Cochin. There was he born
And nurtured, and there yet his kin,
Never from true allegiance torn,
Kept Moses' law.
               Cochin, Cochin   35
(Mused Clarel), I have heard indeed

Of those Black Jews, their ancient creed
And hoar tradition. Esdras saith
The Ten Tribes built in Arsareth—
Eastward, still eastward. That may be.   40
    But look, the scroll of goat-skin, see
Wherein he reads, a wizard book;
It is the Indian Pentateuch
Whereof they tell. Whate'er the plea
(And scholars various notions hold   45
Touching these missing clans of old),
This seems a deeper mystery;
How Judah, Benjamin, live on—
Unmixed into time's swamping sea
So far can urge their Amazon.   50
    He pondered. But again the host,
Narrating part his life-time tossed,
Told how, long since, with trade in view,
He sailed from India with a Jew
And merchant of the Portuguese   55
For Lisbon. More he roved the seas
And marts, till in the last event
He pitched in Amsterdam his tent.
    "There had I lived my life," he said,
"Among my kind, for good they were;   60
But loss came—loss, and I was led
To long for Judah—only her.
But see." He rose, and took the light
And led within: "There ye espy
What prospect's left to such as I—   65
Yonder!"—a dark slab stood upright
Against the wall; a rude grave-stone
Sculptured, with Hebrew ciphers strown.
    "Under Moriah it shall lie—
No distant date, for very soon,   70
Ere yet a little, and I die.
From Ind to Zion have I come,
But less to live, than end at home.
One other last remove!" he sighed,
And meditated on the stone,   75

Lamp held aloft. That magnified
The hush throughout the dim unknown
Of night—night in a land how dead!
    Thro' Clarel's heart the old man's strain
Dusky meandered in a vein   80
One with the revery it bred;
His eyes still dwelling on the Jew
In added dream—so strange his shade
Of swartness like a born Hindoo,
And wizened visage which betrayed   85
The Hebrew cast. And subtile yet
In ebon frame an amulet
Which on his robe the patriarch wore—
And scroll, and vial in the door,
These too contributed in kind.   90
    They parted. Clarel sought his cell
Or tomb-like chamber, and—with mind
To break or intermit the spell,
At least perplex it and impede—
Lighted the lamp of olive oil,   95
And, brushing from a trunk the soil—
'Twas one late purchased at his need—
Opened, and strove to busy him
With small adjustments. Bootless cheer!
While wavering now, in chanceful skim   100
His eyes fell on the word JUDÆA
In paper lining of the tray,
For all was trimmed, in cheaper way,
With printed matter. Curious then
To know this faded denizen,   105
He read, and found a piece complete,
Briefly comprised in one poor sheet:

    "The World accosts—

    "Last one out of Holy Land,
What gift bring'st thou? Sychem grapes?   110
Tabor, which the Eden drapes,
Yieldeth garlands. I demand

Something cheery at thy hand.
Come, if Solomon's Song thou singest,
Haply Sharon's rose thou bringest."   115

    "The Palmer replies:

    "Nay, naught thou nam'st thy servant brings,
Only Judæa my feet did roam;
And mainly there the pilgrim clings
About the precincts of Christ's tomb.   120
These palms I bring—from dust not free,
Since dust and ashes both were trod by me."

    O'er true thy gift (thought Clarel). Well,
Scarce might the world accept, 'twould seem.
But I, shall *I* my feet impel   125
Through road like thine and naught redeem?
Rather thro' brakes, lone brakes, I wind:
As I advance they close behind.—
    Thought's burden! on the couch he throws
Himself and it—rises, and goes   130
To peer from casement. 'Twas moonlight,
With stars, the Olive Hill in sight,
Distinct, yet dreamy in repose,
As of Katahdin in hot noon,
Lonely, with all his pines in swoon.   135
    The nature and evangel clashed,
Rather, a double mystery flashed.
Olivet, Olivet do I see?
The ideal upland, trod by *Thee?*
    Up or reclined, he felt the soul   140
Afflicted by that noiseless calm,
Till sleep, the good nurse, deftly stole
The bed beside, and for a charm
Took the pale hand within her own,
Nor left him till the night was gone.   145

3. The Sepulchre

In Crete they claimed the tomb of Jove
In glen over which his eagles soar;
But thro' a peopled town ye rove
To Christ's low urn, where, nigh the door,
Settles the dove. So much the more   5
The contrast stamps the human God
Who dwelt among us, made abode
With us, and was of woman born;
Partook our bread, and thought no scorn
To share the humblest, homeliest hearth,   10
Shared all of man except the sin and mirth.
Such, among thronging thoughts, may stir
In pilgrim pressing thro' the lane
That dusty wins the reverend fane,
Seat of the Holy Sepulchre,   15
And naturally named therefrom.
        What altars old in cluster rare
And grotto-shrines engird the Tomb:
Caves and a crag; and more is there;
And halls monastic join their gloom.   20
To sum in comprehensive bounds
The Passion's drama with its grounds,
Immense the temple winds and strays
Finding each storied precinct out—
Absorbs the sites all roundabout—   25
Omnivorous, and a world of maze.
        And yet time was when all here stood
Separate, and from rood to rood,
Chapel to shrine, or tent to tent,
Unsheltered still the pilgrim went   30
Where now enroofed the whole coheres—
Where now thro' influence of years
And spells by many a legend lent,
A sort of nature reappears—
Sombre or sad, and much in tone   35
Perhaps with that which here was known
Of yore, when from this Salem height,
Then sylvan in primeval plight,

Down came to Shaveh's Dale, with wine
And bread, after the four Kings' check, 40
The Druid priest Melchizedek,
Abram to bless with rites divine.
    What rustlings here from shadowy spaces,
Deep vistas where the votary paces,
Will, strangely intermitting, creep 45
Like steps in Indian forest deep.
How bird-like steals the singer's note
Down from some rail or arch remote:
While, glimmering where kneelers be,
Small lamps, dispersed, with glow-worm light 50
Mellow the vast nave's azure night,
And make a haze of mystery:
The blur is spread of thousand years,
And Calvary's seen as through one's tears.
    In cloistral walks the dome detains 55
Hermits, which during public days
Seclude them where the shadow stays,
But issue when charmed midnight reigns,
Unshod, with tapers lit, and roam,
According as their hearts appoint, 60
The purlieus of the central Tomb
In round of altars; and anoint
With fragrant oils each marble shelf;
Or, all alone, strange solace find
And oratory to their mind 65
Lone locked within the Tomb itself.
    Cells note ye as in bower a nest
Where some sedate rich devotee
Or grave guest-monk from over sea
Takes up through Lent his votive rest, 70
Adoring from his saintly perch
Golgotha and the guarded Urn,
And mysteries everywhere expressed;
Until his soul, in rapt sojourn,
Add one more chapel to the Church. 75
    The friars in turn which tend the Fane,
Dress it and keep, a home make there,
Nor pass for weeks the gate. Again

Each morning they ascend the stair
Of Calvary, with cloth and broom,   80
For dust thereon will settle down,
And gather, too, upon the Tomb
And places of the Passion's moan.
Tradition, not device and fraud
Here rules—tradition old and broad.   85
Transfixed in sites the drama's shown—
Each given spot assigned; 'tis here
They scourged Him; soldiers yonder nailed
The Victim to the tree; in jeer
There stood the Jews; there Mary paled;   90
The vesture was divided here.
     A miracle-play of haunted stone—
A miracle-play, a phantom one,
With power to give pause or subdue.
So that whatever comment be—   95
Serious, if to faith unknown—
Not possible seems levity
Or aught that may approach thereto.
     And, sooth, to think what numbers here,
Age after age, have worn the stones   100
In suppliance or judgment fear;
What mourners—men and women's moans,
Ancestors of ourselves indeed;
What souls whose penance of remorse
Made poignant by the elder creed,   105
Found honest language in the force
Of chains entwined that ate the bone;
How here a'Becket's slayers clung
Taking the contrite anguish on,
And, in release from fast and thong,   110
Buried upon Moriah sleep;
With more, much more; such ties, so deep,
Endear the spot, or false or true
As an historic site. The wrong
Of carpings never may undo   115
The nerves that clasp about the plea
Tingling with kinship through and through—
Faith child-like and the tried humanity.

But little here moves hearts of some;
Rather repugnance grave, or scorn 120
Or cynicism, to mark the dome
Beset in court or yard forlorn
By pedlars versed in wonted tricks,
Venders of charm or crucifix;
Or, on saint-days, to hark the din 125
As during market day at inn,
And polyglot of Asian tongues
And island ones, in interchange
Buzzed out by crowds in costumes strange
Of nations divers. Are these throngs 130
Merchants? Is this Cairo's bazar
And concourse? Nay, thy strictures bar.
It is but simple nature, see;
None mean irreverence, though free.
    Unvexed by Europe's grieving doubt 135
Which asks *And can the Father be?*
Those children of the climes devout,
On festival in fane installed,
Happily ignorant, make glee
Like orphans in the play-ground walled. 140
    Others the duskiness may find
Imbued with more than nature's gloom;
These, loitering hard by the Tomb,
Alone, and when the day's declined—
So that the shadow from the stone 145
Whereon the angel sat is thrown
To distance more, and sigh or sound
Echoes from place of Mary's moan,
Or cavern where the cross was found;
Or mouse-stir steals upon the ear 150
From where the soldier reached the spear—
Shrink, much like Ludovico erst
Within the haunted chamber. Thou,
Less sensitive, yet haply versed
In everything above, below— 155
In all but thy deep human heart;
Thyself perchance mayst nervous start
At thine own fancy's final range

Who here wouldst mock: with mystic smart
The subtile Eld can slight avenge.   160
But gibe—gibe on, until there crawl
About thee in the scorners' seat,
Reactions; and pride's Smyrna shawl
Plague-strike the wearer. Ah, retreat!
    But how of some which still deplore   165
Yet share the doubt? Here evermore
'Tis good for such to turn afar
From the Skull's place, even Golgotha,
And view the cedarn dome in sun
Pierced like the marble Pantheon: 170
No blurring pane, but open sky:
In there day peeps, there stars go by,
And, in still hours which these illume,
Heaven's dews drop tears upon the Tomb.
    Nor lack there dreams romance can thrill: 175
In hush when tides and towns are still,
Godfrey and Baldwin from their graves
(Made meetly near the rescued Stone)
Rise, and in arms. With beaming glaives
They watch and ward the urn they won.   180
    So fancy deals, a light achiever:
Imagination, earnest ever,
Recalls the Friday far away,
Re-lives the crucifixion day—
The passion and its sequel proves,   185
Sharing the three pale Marys' frame;
Thro' the eclipse with these she moves
Back to the house from which they came
To Golgotha. O empty room,
O leaden heaviness of doom—   190
O cowering hearts, which sore beset
Deem vain the promise now, and yet
Invoke him who returns no call;
And fears for more that may befall.
O terror linked with love which cried   195
"Art gone? is't o'er? and crucified?"
    Who might foretell from such dismay
Of blank recoilings, all the blest

Lilies and anthems which attest
The floral Easter holiday?   200

4. OF THE CRUSADERS

When sighting first the towers afar
Which girt the object of the war
And votive march—the Saviour's Tomb,
What made the red-cross knights so shy?
And wherefore did they doff the plume   5
And baldrick, kneel in dust, and sigh?
   Hardly it serves to quote Voltaire
And say they were freebooters—hence,
Incapable of awe or sense
Pathetic; no, for man is heir   10
To complex moods; and in that age
Belief devout and bandit rage
Frequent were joined; and e'en to-day
At shrines on the Calabrian steep—
Not insincere while feelings sway—   15
The brigand halts to adore, to weep.
Grant then the worst—is all romance
Which claims that the crusader's glance
Was blurred by tears?
            But if that round
Of disillusions which accrue   20
In this our day, imply a ground
For more concern than Tancred knew,
Thinking, yet not as in despair,
Of Christ who suffered for him there
Upon the crag; then, own it true,   25
Cause graver much than his is ours
At least to check the hilarious heart
Before these memorable towers.
   But wherefore this? such theme why start?
Because if here in many a place   30
The rhyme—much like the knight indeed—
Abjure brave ornament, 'twill plead
Just reason, and appeal for grace.

5. CLAREL

Upon the morrow's early morn
Clarel is up, and seeks the Urn.
    Advancing towards the fane's old arch
Of entrance—curved in sculptured stone,
Dim and defaced, he saw thereon   5
From rural Bethany the march
Of Christ into another gate—
The golden and triumphal one,
Upon Palm Morn. For porch to shrine
On such a site, how fortunate   10
That adaptation of design.
Well might it please.
                    He entered then.
Strangers were there, of each degree,
From Asian shores, with island men,
Mild guests of the Epiphany.   15
    As when to win the Paschal joy
And Nisan's festal month renew,
The Nazarenes to temple drew,
Even Joseph, Mary, and the BOY,
Whose hand the mother's held; so here   20
To later rites and altars dear,
Domestic in devotion's flame
Husbands with wives and children came.
    But he, the student, under dome
Pauses; he stands before the Tomb.   25
Through open door he sees the wicks
Alight within, where six and six
For Christ's apostles, night and day,
Lamps, olden lamps do burn. In smoke
Befogged they shed no vivid ray,   30
But heat the cell and seem to choke.
    He marked, and revery took flight:
"These burn not like those aspects bright
Of starry watchers when they kept
Vigil at napkined feet and head   35
Of Him their Lord.—Nay, is He fled?

Or tranced lies, tranced nor unbewept
With Dorian gods? or, fresh and clear,
A charm diffused throughout the sphere,
Streams in the ray through yonder dome?   40
Not hearsed He is. But hath ghost home
Dispersed in soil, in sea, in air?
False Pantheism, false though fair!"
    So he; and slack and aimless went,
Nor might untwine the ravelment   45
Of doubts perplexed. For easement there
Halting awhile in pillared shade,
A friar he marked, in robe of blue
And round Greek cap of sable hue:
Poor men he led; much haste he made,   50
Nor sequence kept, but dragged them so
Hither and thither, to and fro,
To random places. Might it be
That Clarel, who recoil did here,
Shared but that shock of novelty   55
Which makes some Protestants unglad
First viewing the mysterious cheer
In Peter's fane? Beheld he had,
In Rome beneath the Lateran wall,
The Scala Santa—watched the knees   60
Of those ascending devotees,
Who, absolution so to reap,
Breathe a low prayer at every step.
    Nay, 'twas no novelty at all.
Nor was it that his nature shrunk   65
But from the curtness of the monk:
Another influence made swerve
And touched him in profounder nerve.
    He turned, and passing on enthralled,
Won a still chapel; and one spake   70
The name. Brief Scripture, here recalled,
The context less obscure may make:
'Tis writ that in a garden's bound
Our Lord was urned. On that green ground
He reappeared, by Mary claimed.   75

The place, or place alleged, is shown—
Arbors congealed to vaults of stone—
The Apparition's chapel named.
This was the spot where now, in frame
Hard to depict, the student came—   80
The spot where in the dawning gray,
His pallor with night's tears bedewed,
Restored the Second Adam stood—
Not as in Eden stood the First
All ruddy. Yet, in leaves immersed   85
And twilight of imperfect day,
Christ seemed the gardener unto her
Misjudging, who in womanhood
Had sought him late in sepulchre
Embowered, nor found.
                Here, votive here—   90
Here by the shrine that Clarel won—
A wreath shed odors. Scarce that cheer
Warmed some poor Greeks recumbent thrown,
Sore from late journeying far and near,
To hallowed haunts without the town;   95
So wearied, that no more they kneeled,
But over night here laid them down,
Matrons and children, yet unhealed
Of ache. And each face was a book
Of disappointment. "Why weep'st thou?   100
Whom seekest?"—words, which chanceful now
Recalled by Clarel, he applied
To these before him; and he took,
In way but little modified,
Part to himself; then stood in dream   105
Of all which yet might hap to them.
He saw them spent, provided ill—
Pale, huddled in the pilgrim fleet,
Back voyaging now to homes afar.
Midnight, and rising tempests beat—   110
Such as St. Paul knew—furious war,
To meet which, slender is the skill.
The lamp that burnt upon the prow

In wonted shrine, extinct is now—
Drowned out with Heaven's last feeble star.   115
Panic ensues; their course is turned;
Toward Tyre they drive—Tyre undiscerned:
A coast of wrecks which warping bleach
On wrecks of piers where eagles screech.
     How hopeful from their isles serene   120
They sailed, and on such tender quest;
Then, after toils that came between,
They re-embarked; and, tho' distressed,
Grieved not, for Zion had been seen;
Each wearing next the heart for charm   125
Some priestly scrip in leaf of palm.
     But these, ah, these in Dawn's pale reign
Asleep upon beach Tyrian!
Or is it sleep? no, rest—that rest
Which naught shall ruffle or molest.   130
     In gliding turn of dreams which mate
He saw from forth Damascus' gate
Tall Islam in her Mahmal go—
Elected camel, king of all,
In mystic housings draped in flow,   135
Silk-fringed, with many a silver ball,
Worked ciphers on the Koran's car
And Sultan's cloth. He hears the jar
Of janizaries armed, a throng
Which drum barbaric, shout and gong   140
Invest. And camels—robe and shawl
Of riders which they bear along—
Each sheik a pagod on his tower,
Cross-legged and dusky. Therewithal,
In affluence of the opal hour,   145
Curveting troops of Moslem peers
And flash of scimeters and spears
In groves of grass-green pennons fair,
(Like Feiran's palms in fanning air,)
Wherefrom the crescent silvery soars.   150
     Then crowds pell-mell, a concourse wild,
Convergings from Levantine shores;

On foot, on donkeys; litters rare—
Whole families; twin panniers piled;
Rich men and beggars—all beguiled   155
To cheerful trust in Allah's care;
Allah, toward whose prophet's urn
And Holy City, fond they turn
As forth in pilgrimage they fare.
    But long the way. And when they note,   160
Ere yet they pass wide suburbs green,
Some camp in field, nor far remote,
Inviting, pastoral in scene;
Some child shall leap, and trill in glee
"Mecca, 'tis Mecca, mother—see!"   165
    Then first she thinks upon the waste
Whither the Simoom maketh haste;
Where baskets of the white-ribbed dead
Sift the fine sand, while dim ahead
In long, long line, their way to tell,   170
The bones of camels bleaching dwell,
With skeletons but part interred—
Relics of men which friendless fell;
Whose own hands, in last office, scooped
Over their limbs the sand, but drooped: 175
Worse than the desert of the Word,
El Tih, the great, the terrible.
    Ere town and tomb shall greet the eye
Many shall fall, nor few shall die
Which, punctual at set of sun,   180
Spread the worn prayer-cloth on the sand,
Turning them toward the Mecca stone,
Their shadows ominously thrown
Oblique against the mummy land.
    These pass; they fade. What next comes near?   185
The tawny peasants—human wave
Which rolls over India year by year,
India, the spawning place and grave.
    The turbaned billow floods the plains,
Rolling toward Brahma's rarer fanes—   190

His Compostel or brown Loret
Where sin absolved, may grief forget.
But numbers, plague-struck, faint and sore,
Drop livid on the flowery shore—
Arrested, with the locusts sleep,   195
Or pass to muster where no man may peep.
    That vision waned. And, far afloat,
From eras gone he caught the sound
Of hordes from China's furthest moat,
Crossing the Himalayan mound,   200
To kneel at shrine or relic so
Of Buddha, the Mongolian Fo
Or Indian Saviour. What profound
Impulsion makes these tribes to range?
Stable in time's incessant change   205
Now first he marks, now awed he heeds
The intersympathy of creeds,
Alien or hostile tho' they seem—
Exalted thought or groveling dream.
    The worn Greek matrons mark him there: 210
Ah, young, our lassitude dost share?
Home do thy pilgrim reveries stray?
Art *thou* too, weary of the way?—
    Yes, sympathies of Eve awake;
Yet do but err. For how might break   215
Upon those simple natures true,
The complex passion? might they view
The apprehension tempest-tossed,
The spirit in gulf of dizzying fable lost?

6. TRIBES AND SECTS

He turned to go; he turned, but stood:
In many notes of varying keys,
From shrines like coves in Jordan's wood
Hark to the rival liturgies,

Which, rolling underneath the dome,   5
Resound about the patient Tomb
And penetrate the aisles. The rite
Of Georgian and Maronite,
Armenian and fervid Greek,
The Latin organ, and wild clash   10
Of cymbals smitten cheek to cheek
Which the dark Abyssinian sways;
These like to tides together dash
And question of their purport raise.
    If little of the words he knew,   15
Might Clarel's fancy forge a clue?
A malediction seemed each strain—
Himself the mark: O heart profane,
O pilgrim-infidel, begone!
Nor here the sites of Faith pollute,   20
Thou who misgivest we enthrone
A God untrue, in myth absurd
As monstrous figments blabbed of Jove,
Or, worse, rank lies of Islam's herd:
We know thee, thou there standing mute.   25
Out, out—begone! try Nature's reign
Who deem'st the super-nature vain:
To Lot's Wave by black Kedron rove;
On, by Mount Seir, through Edom move;
There crouch thee with the jackall down—   30
Crave solace of the scorpion!
    'Twas fancy, troubled fancy weaved
Those imputations half believed.
The porch he neared; the chorus swelled;
He went forth like a thing expelled.   35
    Yet, going, he could but recall
The wrangles here which oft befall:
Contentions for each holy place,
And jealousies how far from grace:
O, bickering family bereft,   40
Was feud the heritage He left?

7. BEYOND THE WALLS

In street at hand a silence reigns
Which Nature's hush of loneness feigns.
Few casements, few, and latticed deep,
High raised above the head below,
That none might listen, pry, or peep,   5
Or any hint or inkling know
Of that strange innocence or sin
Which locked itself so close within.
The doors, recessed in massy walls,
And far apart, as dingy were   10
As Bastile gates. No shape astir
Except at whiles a shadow falls
Athwart the way, and key in hand
Noiseless applies it, enters so
And vanishes. By dry airs fanned,   15
The languid hyssop waveth slow,
Dusty, on stones by ruin rent.
'Twould seem indeed the accomplishment
Whereof the greater prophet tells
In truth's forecasting canticles   20
Where voice of bridegroom, groom and bride
Is hushed.
              Each silent wall and lane—
The city's towers in barren pride
Which still a stifling air detain,
So irked him, with his burden fraught,   25
Timely the Jaffa Gate he sought,
Thence issued, and at venture went
Along a vague and houseless road
Save narrow houses where abode
The Turk in man's last tenement   30
Inearthed. But them he heeded not,
Such trance his reveries begot:
    "Christ lived a Jew: and in Judæa
May linger any breath of Him?
If nay, yet surely it is here   35
One best may learn if all be dim."

Sudden it came in random play
"Here to Emmaus is the way;"
And Luke's narration straight recurred,
How the two falterers' hearts were stirred   40
Meeting the Arisen (then unknown)
And listening to his lucid word
As here in place they traveled on.
    That scene, in Clarel's temper, bred
A novel sympathy, which said—   45
I too, I too; could I but meet
Some stranger of a lore replete,
Who, marking how my looks betray
The dumb thoughts clogging here my feet,
Would question me, expound and prove,   50
And make my heart to burn with love—
Emmaus were no dream to-day!
    He lifts his eyes, and, outlined there,
Saw, as in answer to the prayer,
A man who silent came and slow   55
Just over the intervening brow
Of a nigh slope. Nearer he drew
Revealed against clear skies of blue;
And—in that Syrian air of charm—
He seemed, illusion such was given,   60
Emerging from the level heaven,
And vested with its liquid calm.
    Scarce aged like time's wrinkled sons,
But touched by chastenings of Eld,
Which halloweth life's simpler ones;   65
In wasted strength he seemed upheld
Invisibly by faith serene—
Paul's evidence of things not seen.
    No staff he carried; but one hand
A solitary Book retained.   70
Meeting the student's, his mild eyes
Fair greeting gave, in faint surprise.
But, noting that untranquil face,
Concern and anxiousness found place
Beyond the occasion and surmise: 75

"Young friend in Christ, what thoughts molest
That here ye droop so? Wanderest
Without a guide where guide should be?
Receive one, friend: the book—take ye."
  From man to book in startled way   80
The youth his eyes bent. Book how gray
And weather-stained in woeful plight—
Much like that scroll left bare to blight,
Which poet pale, when hope was low,
Bade one who into Libya went,   85
Fling to the wasteful element,
Yes, leave it there, let wither so.
  Ere Clarel ventured on reply
Anew the stranger proffered it,
And in such mode he might espy   90
It was the page of—Holy Writ.
Then unto him drew Clarel nigher:
"Thou art?" "The sinner Nehemiah."

8. THE VOTARY

Sinner?—So spake the saint, a man
Long tarrying in Jewry's court.
With him the faith so well could sort
His home he'd left, nor turned again,
His home by Narraganset's marge,   5
Giving those years on death which verge
Fondly to that enthusiast part
Oft coming of a stricken heart
Unselfish, which finds solace so.
  Though none in sooth might hope to know, 10
And few surmise his forepast bane,
Such needs have been; since seldom yet
Lone liver was, or wanderer met,
Except he closeted some pain
Or memory thereof. But thence,   15
May be, was given him deeper sense
Of all that travail life can lend,

Which man may scarce articulate
Better than herds which share. What end?
How hope? turn whither? where was gate   20
For expectation, save the one
Of beryl, pointed by St. John?
That gate would open, yea, and Christ
Thence issue, come unto His own,
And earth be re-imparadised.   25
     Passages, presages he knew:
Zion restore, convert the Jew,
Reseat him here, the waste bedew;
Then Christ returneth: so it ran.
     No founded mission chartered him;   30
Single in person as in plan,
Absorbed he ranged, in method dim,
A flitting tract-dispensing man:
Tracts in each text scribe ever proved
In East which he of Tarsus roved.   35
     Though well such heart might sainthood claim,
Unjust alloy to reverence came.
In Smyrna's mart (sojourning there
Waiting a ship for Joppa's stair)
Pestered he passed thro' Gentile throngs   40
Teased by an eddying urchin host,
His tracts all fluttering like tongues
The fire-flakes of the Pentecost.
     Deep read he was in seers devout,
The which forecast Christ's second prime,   45
And on his slate would cipher out
The mystic days and dates sublime,
And *"Time and times and half a time"*
Expound he could; and more reveal;
Yet frequent would he feebly steal   50
Close to one's side, asking, in way
Of weary age—the hour of day.
But how he lived, and what his fare,
Ravens and angels, few beside,
Dreamed or divined. His garments spare   55
True marvel seemed, nor unallied

To clothes worn by that wandering band
Which ranged and ranged the desert sand
With Moses; and for forty years,
Which two-score times re-clad the spheres   60
In green, and plumed the birds anew,
One vesture wore. From home he brought
The garb which still met sun and dew,
Ashen in shade, by rustics wrought.
　　Latin, Armenian, Greek, and Jew   65
Full well the harmless vagrant kenned,
The small meek face, the habit gray:
In him they owned our human clay.
The Turk went further: let him wend;
Him Allah cares for, holy one: 70
A *Santon* held him; and was none
Bigot enough scorn's shaft to send.
For, say what cynic will or can,
Man sinless is revered by man
Thro' all the forms which creeds may lend.   75
　　And so, secure, nor pointed at,
Among brave Turbans freely roamed the Hat.

9. Saint and Student

"Nay, take it, friend in Christ," and held
The book in proffer new; the while
His absent eyes of dreamy Eld
Some floating vision did beguile
(Of heaven perchance the wafted hem),   5
As if in place of earthly wight
A haze of spirits met his sight,
And Clarel were but one of them.
　　"Consult it, heart; wayfarer you,
And this a friendly guide, the best;   10
No ground there is that faith would view
But here 'tis rendered with the rest;
The way to fields of Beulah dear
And New Jerusalem is here."

"I know that guide," said Clarel, "yes;"   15
And mused awhile in bitterness;
Then turned and studied him again,
Doubting and marveling. A strain
Of trouble seamed the elder brow:
"A pilgrim art thou? pilgrim thou?"   20
Words simple, which in Clarel bred
More than the simple saint divined;
And, thinking of vocation fled,
Himself he asked: or do I rave,
Or have I left now far behind   25
The student of the sacred lore?
Direct he then this answer gave:
"I am a traveler—no more."
      "Come then with me, in peace we'll go;
These ways of Salem well I know;   30
Me let be guide whose guide is this,"
And held the Book in witness so,
As 'twere a guide that could not miss:
"Heart, come with me; all times I roam,
Yea, everywhere my work I ply,   35
In Salem's lanes, or down in gloom
Of narrow glens which outer lie:
Ever I find some passer-by.
But thee I'm sent to; share and rove,
With me divide the scrip of love."   40
      Despite the old man's shattered ray,
Won by his mystic saintly way,
Revering too his primal faith,
And grateful for the human claim;
And deeming he must know each path,   45
And help him so in languid frame—
The student gave assent, and caught
Dim solacement to previous thought.

10. RAMBLES

Days fleet. They rove the storied ground—
Tread many a site that rues the ban
Where serial wrecks on wrecks confound
Era and monument and man;
Or rather, in stratifying way   5
Bed and impact and overlay.
The Hospitalers' cloisters shamed
Crumble in ruin unreclaimed
On shivered Fatimite palaces
Reared upon crash of Herod's sway—   10
In turn built on the Maccabees,
And on King David's glory, they;
And David on antiquities
Of Jebusites and Ornan's floor,
And hunters' camps of ages long before.   15
So Glenroy's tiers of beaches be—
Abandoned margins of the Glacial Sea.
      Amid that waste from joy debarred,
How few the islets fresh and green;
Yet on Moriah, tree and sward   20
In Allah's courts park-like were seen
From roof near by; below, fierce ward
Being kept by Mauritanian guard
Of bigot blacks. But of the reign
Of Christ did no memento live   25
Save soil and ruin? Negative
Seemed yielded in that crumbling fane,
Erst gem to Baldwin's sacred fief,
The chapel of our Dame of Grief.
      But hard by Ophel's winding base,   30
Well watered by the runnel led,
A spot they found, not lacking grace,
Named Garden of King Solomon,
Tho' now a cauliflower-bed
To serve the kitchens of the town.   35
      One day as here they came from far,
The saint repeated with low breath,

"Adonijah, Adonijah—
The stumbling-stone of Zoheleth."
He wanders, Clarel thought—but no,   40
For text and chapter did he show
Narrating how the prince in glade,
This very one, the banquet made,
The plotters' banquet, long ago,
Even by the stone named Zoheleth;   45
But startled by the trump that blew,
Proclaiming Solomon, pale grew
With all his guests.
                    From lower glen
They slanted up the steep, and there
Attained a higher terraced den,   50
Or small and silent field, quite bare.
The mentor breathed: "Come early here
A sign thou'lt see."—Clarel drew near;
"What sign?" he asked. Whereto with sighs:
"Abashed by morning's holy eyes   55
This field will crimson, and for shame."
      Struck by his fantasy and frame,
Clarel regarded him for time,
Then noted that dull reddish soil,
And caught sight of a thing of grime   60
Whose aspect made him to recoil—
A rotting charnel-house forlorn
Midway inearthed, caved in and torn.
And Clarel knew—one scarce might err—
The field of blood, the bad Aceldama.   65
      By Olivet in waning day
The saint in fond illusion went,
Dream mixed with legend and event;
And as with reminiscence fraught,
Narrated in his rambling way   70
How here at eve was Christ's resort,
The last low sheep-bell tinkling lone—
Christ and the dear disciple—John.
      Oft by the Golden Gate that looks
On Shaveh down, and far across   75

Toward Bethany's secluded nooks—
That gate which sculptures rare emboss
In arches twin; the same where rode
Christ entering with secret load—
Same gate, or on or near the site—   80
When palms were spread to left and right
Before him, and with sweet acclaim
Were waved by damsels under sway
Of trees wherefrom those branches came—
Over and under palms He went   85
Unto that crown how different!
The port walled up by Moslem hands
In dread of that predicted day
When pealing hymns, armed Christian bands—
So Islam seers despondent vouch—   90
Shall storm it, wreathed in Mary's May:
By that sealed gate, in languor's slouch,
How listless in the golden day,
Clarel the mentor frequent heard
The time for Christ's return allot: 95
A dream, and like a dream it blurred
The sense—faded, and was forgot.
Moved by some mystic impulse, far
From motive known or regular,
The saint would thus his lore unfold,   100
Though inconclusive; yes, half told
The theme he'd leave, then nod, droop, doze—
Start up and prattle—sigh, and close.

11. LOWER GIHON

Well for the student, might it last,
This dreamful frame which Lethe bred:
Events obtruded, and it passed.
For on a time the twain were led
From Gihon's upper pool and glade   5
Down to the deeper gulf. They strayed
Along by many silent cells

Cut in the rock, void citadels
Of death. In porch of one was seen
A mat of tender turf, faint green;   10
And quiet standing on that sward
A stranger whom they overheard
Low murmuring—"Equivocal!
Woo'st thou the weary to thee—tell,
Thou tomb, so winsome in thy grace?   15
To me no reassuring place."
    He saw them not; and they, to shun
Disturbing him, passed, and anon
Met three demoniacs, sad three
Ranging those wasteful limits o'er   20
As in old time. That look they wore
Which in the moody mad bids flee;
'Tis—What have I to do with thee?
    Two shunned approach. But one did sit
Lost in some reminiscence sore   25
Of private wrong outrageous. He,
As at the larger orb of it,
Looming through mists of mind, would bound,
Or cease to pore upon the ground
As late; and so be inly riven   30
By arrows of indignant pain:
Convulsed in face, he glared at heaven
Then lapsed in sullenness again.
    Dire thoughts the pilgrim's mind beset:
"And did Christ come? in such a scene   35
Encounter the poor Gadarene
Long centuries ago? and yet—
Behold!"
        But here came in review—
Though of their nearness unaware—
The stranger, downward wending there,   40
Who marking Clarel, instant knew—
At least so might his start declare—
A brother that he well might own
In tie of spirit. Young he was,
With crescent forehead—but alas,   45

Of frame mis-shaped. Word spake he none,
But vaguely hovered, as may one
Not first who would accost, but deep
Under reserve the wish may keep.
Ere Clarel, here embarrassed grown,   50
Made recognition, the Unknown
Compressed his lips, turned and was gone.
Mutely for moment, face met face:
But more perchance between the two
Was interchanged than e'en may pass   55
In many a worded interview.
    The student in his heart confessed
A novel sympathy impressed;
And late remissness to retrieve
Fain the encounter would renew.   60
And yet—if oft one's resolution
Be overruled by constitution—
Herein his heart he might deceive.
    Ere long, retracing higher road,
Clarel with Nehemiah stood   65
By David's Tower, without the wall,
Where black the embattled shadows fall
At morn over Hinnom. Groups were there
Come out to take the evening air,
Watching a young lord Turk in pride,   70
With fez and sash as red as coral,
And on a steed whose well-groomed hide
Was all one burnished burning sorrel,
Scale the lit slope; then veering wide,
Rush down into the gloomful gorge,   75
The steel hoof showering sparks as from a forge.
Even Nehemiah, in senile tone
Of dreamy interest, was won
That shooting star to gaze upon.
    But rallying, he bent his glance   80
Toward the opposing eminence;
And turning, "Seest thou not," he said,
"As sinks the sun beyond this glen
Of Moloch, how clouds intervene

And hood the brightness that was shed?   85
But yet few hours and he will rise
In better place, and beauty get;
Yea, friend in Christ, in morning skies
Return he will over Olivet:
And we shall greet him. Say ye so?   90
Betimes then will we up and go.
Farewell. At early dawn await
Christ's bondman old at Stephen's Gate."

12. CELIO

But ere they meet in place assigned,
It needs—to make the sequel clear—
A crossing thread be first entwined.
    Within the Terra-Santa's wall
(A prefix dropped, the Latins here   5
So the Franciscan Convent call),
Commended to the warden's care,
The mitred father-warden there,
By missives from a cardinal,
It chanced an uncompanioned youth,   10
By birth a Roman, shelter found.
In casual contact, daily round,
Mixed interest the stranger won.
Each friar, the humblest, could but own
His punctual courtesy, in sooth,   15
Though this still guarded a reserve
Which, not offending, part estranged.
Sites, sites and places all he ranged
Unwearied, but would ever swerve
From escort such as here finds place,   20
Or cord-girt guide, or chamberlain
Martial in Oriental town,
By gilt-globed staff of office known,
Sword by his side, in golden lace,
Tall herald making clear the van.   25

But what most irked each tonsured man,
Distrust begat, concern of heart,
Was this: though the young man took part
In chapel service, 'twas as guest
Who but conformed; he showed no zest   30
Of faith within, faith personal.
Ere long the warden, kindly all,
Said inly with himself: Poor boy,
Enough hast thou of life-annoy;
Let be reproach. Tied up in knot   35
Of body by the fleshly withes,
Needs must it be the spirit writhes
And takes a warp. But Christ will blot
Some records in the end.
                        And own,
So far as *in* by *out* is shown,   40
Not idle was the monk's conceit.
Fair head was set on crook and lump,
Absalom's locks but Æsop's hump.
Deep in the grave eyes' last retreat,
One read thro' guarding feint of pride,   45
Quick sense of all the ills that gride
In one contorted so. But here,
More to disclose in bearing chief,
More than to monks might well appear,
There needs some running mention brief.   50
    Fain had his brethren have him grace
Some civic honorable place;
And interest was theirs to win
Ample preferment; he as kin
Was loved, if but ill understood: 55
At heart they had his worldly good;
But he postponed, and went his way
Unpledged, unhampered. So that still
Leading a studious life at will,
And prompted by an earnest mind,   60
Scarce might he shun the fevered sway
Of focused question in our day.
Overmuch he shared, but in that kind

Which marks the Italian turn of thought,
When, counting Rome's tradition naught,   65
The mind is coy to own the rule
Of sect replacing, sect or school.
At sea, in brig which swings no boat,
To founder is to sink.
                    On day
When from St. Peter's balcony,   70
The raised pontific fingers bless
The city and the world; the stress
He knew of fate: Blessest thou *me,*
One wave here in this heaving sea
Of heads? how may a blessing be?   75
Luckless, from action's thrill removed,
And all that yields our nature room;
In courts a jest; and, harder doom,
Never the hunchback may be loved.
Never! for Beatrice—*Bice*—O,   80
Diminutive once sweet, made now
All otherwise!—didst thou but fool?
Arch practice in precocious school?
Nay, rather 'twas ere thou didst bud
Into thy riper womanhood.   85
        Since love, arms, courts, abjure—why then
Remaineth to me what? the pen?
Dead feather of ethereal life!
Nor efficacious much, save when
It makes some fallacy more rife.   90
My kin—I blame them not at heart—
Would have me act some routine part,
Subserving family, and dreams
Alien to me—illusive schemes.
        This world clean fails me: still I yearn.   95
Me then it surely does concern
Some other world to find. But where?
In creed? I do not find it there.
That said, and is the emprise o'er?
Negation, is there nothing more?   100
This side the dark and hollow bound

Lies there no unexplored rich ground?
Some other world: well, there's the *New*—
Ah, joyless and ironic too!
    They vouch that virgin sphere's assigned   105
Seat for man's re-created kind:
Last hope and proffer, they protest.
Brave things! sun rising in the west;
And bearded centuries but gone
For ushers to the beardless one.   110
Nay, nay; your future's too sublime:
The Past, the Past is half of time,
The proven half.—Thou Pantheon old,
Two thousand years have round thee rolled:
Yet thou, in Rome, thou bid'st me seek   115
Wisdom in something more antique
Than thou thyself. Turn then: what seer,
The senior of this Latian one,
Speaks from the ground, transported here
In Eastern soil? Far buried down—   120
For consecration and a grace
Enlocking Santa Croce's base—
Lies earth of Jewry, which of yore
The homeward bound Crusaders bore
In fleet from Jaffa.—Trajan's hall,   125
That huge ellipse imperial,
Was built by Jews. And Titus' Arch
Transmits their conqueror in march
Of trophies which those piers adorn.
There yet, for an historic plea,   130
In heathen triumph's harlotry
The Seven-Branched Candlestick is borne.
    What then? Tho' all be whim of mine,
Yet by these monuments I'm schooled,
Arrested, strangely overruled;   135
Methinks I catch a beckoning sign,
A summons as from Palestine.
Yea, let me view that pontiff-land
Whose sway occult can so command;
Make even Papal Rome to be   140

Her appanage or her colony.
Is Judah's mummy quite unrolled?
To pluck the talisman from fold!
    But who may well indeed forecast
The novel influence of scenes   145
Remote from his habitual Past?
The unexpected supervenes;
Which Celio proved. 'Neath Zion's lee
His nature, with that nature blent,
Evoked an upstart element,   150
As do the acid and the alkali.

13. THE ARCH

Blue-lights sent up by ship forlorn
Are answered oft but by the glare
Of rockets from another, torn
In the same gale's inclusive snare.

    'Twas then when Celio was lanced   5
By novel doubt, the encounter chanced
In Gihon, as recited late,
And at a time when Clarel too,
On his part, felt the grievous weight
Of those demoniacs in view;   10
So that when Celio advanced
No wonder that the meeting eyes
Betrayed reciprocal surmise
And interest. 'Twas thereupon
The Italian, as the eve drew on,   15
Regained the gate, and hurried in
As he would passionately win
Surcease to thought by rapid pace.
Eastward he bent, across the town,
Till in the Via Crucis lone   20
An object there arrested him.
    With gallery which years deface,
Its bulk athwart the alley grim,

The arch named Ecce Homo threw;
The same, if child-like faith be true,   25
From which the Lamb of God was shown
By Pilate to the wolfish crew.
And Celio—in frame how prone
To kindle at that scene recalled—
Perturbed he stood, and heart-enthralled.   30
    No raptures which with saints prevail,
Nor trouble of compunction born
He felt, as there he seemed to scan
Aloft in spectral guise, the pale
Still face, the purple robe, and thorn;   35
And inly cried—*Behold the Man!*
Yon Man it is this burden lays:
Even he who in the pastoral hours,
Abroad in fields, and cheered by flowers,
Announced a heaven's unclouded days;   40
And, ah, with such persuasive lips—
Those lips now sealed while doom delays—
Won men to look for solace there;
But, crying out in death's eclipse,
When rainbow none his eyes might see,   45
Enlarged the margin for despair—
My God, my God, forsakest me?
    Upbraider! we upbraid again;
Thee we upbraid; our pangs constrain
Pathos itself to cruelty.   50
Ere yet thy day no pledge was given
Of homes and mansions in the heaven—
Paternal homes reserved for us;
Heart hoped it not, but lived content—
Content with life's own discontent,   55
Nor deemed that fate ere swerved for us:
The natural law men let prevail;
Then reason disallowed the state
Of instinct's variance with fate.
But thou—ah, see, in rack how pale   60
Who did the world with throes convulse;
Behold him—yea—behold the Man

Who warranted if not began
The dream that drags out its repulse.
    Nor less some cannot break from thee;   65
Thy love so locked is with thy lore,
They may not rend them and go free:
The head rejects; so much the more
The heart embraces—what? the love?
If true what priests avouch of thee,   70
The shark thou mad'st, yet claim'st the dove.
    Nature and thee in vain we search:
Well urged the Jews within the porch—
"How long wilt make us still to doubt?"
How long?—'Tis eighteen cycles now—   75
Enigma and evasion grow;
And shall we never find thee out?
What isolation lones thy state
That all we else know cannot mate
With what thou teachest? Nearing thee   80
All footing fails us; history
Shows there a gulf where bridge is none!
In lapse of unrecorded time,
Just after the apostles' prime,
What chance or craft might break it down?   85
Served this a purpose? By what art
Of conjuration might the heart
Of heavenly love, so sweet, so good,
Corrupt into the creeds malign,
Begetting strife's pernicious brood,   90
Which claimed for patron thee divine?
    Anew, anew,
For this thou bleedest, Anguished Face;
Yea, thou through ages to accrue,
Shalt the Medusa shield replace: 95
In beauty and in terror too
Shalt paralyze the nobler race—
Smite or suspend, perplex, deter—
Tortured, shalt prove a torturer.
Whatever ribald Future be,   100

Thee shall these heed, amaze their hearts with thee—
Thy white, thy red, thy fairness and thy tragedy.

    He turned, uptorn in inmost frame,
Nor weened he went the way he came,
Till meeting two there, nor in calm—   105
A monk and layman, one in creed,
The last with novice-ardor warm,
New-comer, and devout indeed,
To whom the other was the guide,
And showed the Places. "Here," he cried,   110
At pause before a wayside stone,
"Thou mark'st the spot where that bad Jew
His churlish taunt at Jesus threw
Bowed under cross with stifled moan:
Caitiff, which for that cruel wrong   115
Thenceforth till Doomsday drives along."
    Starting, as here he made review,
Celio winced—Am *I* the Jew?
Without delay, afresh he turns
Descending by the Way of Thorns,   120
Winning the Proto-Martyr's gate,
And goes out down Jehoshaphat.
Beside him slid the shadows flung
By evening from the tomb-stones tall
Upon the bank far sloping from the wall.   125
Scarce did he heed, or did but slight
The admonishment the warder rung
That with the setting of the sun,
Now getting low and all but run,
The gate would close, and for the night.   130

14. In the Glen

If Savonarola's zeal devout
But with the fagot's flame died out;
If Leopardi, stoned by Grief,

A young St. Stephen of the Doubt,
Might merit well the martyr's leaf;   5
In these if passion held her claim,
Let Celio pass, of breed the same,
Nor ask from him—not found in them—
The Attic calm, or Saxon phlegm.
    Night glooming now in valley dead,   10
The Italian turned, regained the gate,
But found it closed, the warder fled,
And strange hush of an Eastern town
Where life retreats with set of sun.
Before the riveted clamped wood   15
Alone in outer dark he stood.
A symbol is it? be it so:
Harbor remains, I'll thither go.
    A point there is where Kedron's shore
Narrowing, deepening, steepening more,   20
Shrinks to an adamantine pass
Flanked by three tombs, from base to head
Hewn from the cliff in cubic mass,
One quite cut off and islanded,
And one presents in Petra row   25
Pillars in hanging portico
Or balcony, here looking down
Vacantly on the vacant glen:
A place how dead, hard by a town.
'Twas here that Celio made his den   30
Where erst, as by tradition held,
St. James from hunters lay concealed,
Levites and bigots of the thong.
    Hour after hour slow dragged along.
The glen's wall with night roundabout   35
Blended as cloud with cloud-rack may.
But lo—as when off Tamura
The splash of north-lights on the sea
Crimsons the bergs—so here start out
Some crags aloft how vividly.   40
    Apace he won less narrow bound.
From the high gate, behold, a stream

Of torches. Lava-like it wound
Out from the city locked in dream,
And red adown the valley flowed.   45
Was it his friends the friars? from height
Meet rescue bringing in that light
To one benighted? Yes, they showed
A file of monks. But—how? their wicks
Invest a shrouded crucifix;   50
And each with flambeau held in hand,
Craped laymen mingle with the band
Of cord-girt gowns. He looks again:
Yes, 'tis the Terra Santa's train.
Nearer they come. The warden goes,   55
And other faces Celio knows.
Upon an office these are bound
Consolatory, which may stem
The affliction, or relieve the wound
Of those which mute accompany them   60
In mourners' garb.
                    Aside he shrunk
Until had passed the rearmost monk;
Then, cloaked, he followed them in glade
Where fell the shadow deeper made.
Kedron they cross. Much so might move—   65
If legend hold, which none may prove,—
The remnant of the Twelve which bore
Down thro' this glen in funeral plight
The Mother of our Lord by night
To sepulcher. Nay, just before   70
Her tomb alleged, the monks and they
Which mourn, pause and uplift a lay;
Then rise, pass on, and bow the knee
In dust beside Gethsemane.
    One named the Bitter Cup, and said: 75
"Saviour, thou knowest: it was here
The angels ministered, thy head
Supported, kissed thy lidded eyes
And pale swooned cheek till thou didst rise;
Help these then, unto these come near!"   80

Out sobbed the mourners, and the tear
From Celio trickled; but he mused—
Weak am I, by a myth abused.
　　Up Olivet the torch-light train
Filed slowly, yielding tribute-strain   85
At every sacred place they won;
Nor tarried long, but journeyed on
To Bethany—thro' stony lane
Went down into the narrow house
Or void cave named from Lazarus.   90
The flambeaux redden the dark wall,
Their shadows on that redness fall.
To make the attestation rife,
The resurrection and the life
Through Him the lord of miracle—   95
The warden from the page doth bruit
The story of the man that died
And lived again—bound hand and foot
With grave-clothes, rose—electrified;
Whom then they loosed, let go; even he   100
Whom many people came to see,
The village hinds and farm-house maids,
Afterward, at the supper given
To Jesus in the balmy even,
Who raised him vital from the shades.   105
The lesson over, well they sang
"O death, where is thy sting? O grave,
Where is thy victory?" It rang,
And ceased. And from the outward cave
These tones were heard: "But died he twice?   110
He comes not back from Paradise
Or Hades now. A vacant tomb
By Golgotha they show—a cell,
A void cell here. And is it well?
Raiser and raised divide one doom;   115
Both vanished now."
　　　　　　　　No thrills forewarn
Of fish that leaps from midnight tarn;
The very wave from which it springs

Is startled and recoils in rings.
So here with Celio and the word   120
Which from his own rash lips he heard.
He, hastening forth now all unseen,
Recrossed the mountain and ravine,
Nor paused till on a mound he sate
Biding St. Stephen's opening gate.   125
      Ere long in gently fanning flaws
An odoriferous balmy air
Foreruns the morning, then withdraws,
Or—westward heralding—roves there.
The startled East a tremor knows—   130
Flushes—anon superb appears
In state of housings, shawls and spears,
Such as the Sultan's vanguard shows.
      Preceded thus, in pomp the sun
August from Persia draweth on,   135
Waited by groups upon the wall
Of Judah's upland capital.

15. UNDER THE MINARET

"Lo, shoot the spikes above the hill:
Now expectation grows and grows;
Yet vain the pageant, idle still:
When one would get at Nature's will—
To be put off by purfled shows!   5
      "He breaks. Behold, thou orb supreme,
'Tis Olivet which thou ascendest—
The hill and legendary chapel;
Yet how indifferent thy beam!
Awe nor reverence pretendest: 10
Dome and summit dost but dapple
With gliding touch, a tinging gleam:
Knowest thou the Christ? believest in the dream?"
      'Twas Celio—seated there, as late,
Upon the mound. But now the gate,   15
Flung open, welcomes in the day,

And lets out Clarel with the guide;
These from the wall had hailed the ray;
And Celio heard them there aside,
And turning, rose. Was it to greet?   20
    But ere they might accost or meet,
From minaret in grounds hard by
Of Omar, the muezzin's cry—
Tardy, for Mustapha was old,
And age a laggard is—was rolled,   25
Announcing Islam's early hour
Of orison. Along the walls
And that deep gulf over which these tower—
Far down toward Rogel, hark, it calls!
Can Siloa hear it, yet her wave   30
So listless lap the hollow cave?
Is Zion deaf? But, promptly still,
Each turban at that summons shrill,
Which should have called ere perfect light,
Bowed—hands on chest, or arms upright;   35
While over all those fields of loss
Where now the Crescent rides the Cross,
Sole at the marble mast-head stands
The Islam herald, his two hands
Upon the rail, and sightless eyes   40
Turned upward reverent toward the skies.
And none who share not this defect
The rules to function here elect;
Since, raised upon the lifted perch
What leave for prying eyes to search   45
Into the privacies that lurk
In courts domestic of the Turk,
Whose tenements in every town
Guard well against the street alone.
    But what's evoked in Clarel's mien—   50
What look, responsive look is seen
In Celio, as together there
They pause? Can these a climax share?
Mutual in approach may glide
Minds which from poles adverse have come,   55

Belief and unbelief? may doom
Of doubt make such to coincide—
Upon one frontier brought to dwell
Arrested by the Ezan high
In summons as from out the sky   60
To matins of the infidel?
The God alleged, here in abode
Ignored with such impunity,
Scarce true is writ a jealous God.
    Think ye such thoughts? If so it be,   65
Yet these may eyes transmit and give?
Mere eyes? so quick, so sensitive?
    Howbeit Celio knew his mate:
Again, as down in Gihon late,
He hovered with his overture—   70
An overture that scorned debate.
But inexperienced, shy, unsure—
Challenged abrupt, or yea or nay,
Again did Clarel hesitate;
When quick the proud one with a look   75
Which might recoil of heart betray,
And which the other scarce might brook
In recollection, turned away.
    Ah, student, ill thy sort have sped:
The instant proffer—it is fled!   80
    When, some days after, for redress
Repentant Clarel sought access,
He learned the name, with this alone—
From convent Celio was gone,
Nor knew they whither.
                Here in press   85
To Clarel came a dreamy token:
What speck is that so far away
That wanes and wanes in waxing day?
Is it the sail ye fain had spoken
Last night when surges parted ye?   90
But on, it is a boundless sea.

16. The Wall of Wail

Beneath the toppled ruins old
In series from Moriah rolled
Slips Kedron furtive? underground
Peasants avouch they hear the sound.
In aisled lagunes and watery halls   5
Under the temple, silent sleep
What memories elder? Far and deep
What ducts and chambered wells and walls
And many deep substructions be
Which so with doubt and gloom agree,   10
To question one is borne along—
Based these the Right? subserved the Wrong?
    'Twas by an all-forgotten way,
Whose mouth in outer glen forbid
By heaps of rubbish long lay hid,   15
Cloaca of remotest day;
'Twas by that unsuspected vault
With outlet in mid city lone,
A spot with ruin all bestrown—
The peasants in sedition late   20
Captured Jerusalem in strait,
Took it by underground assault.
    Go wander, and within the walls,
Among the glades of cactus trees
Where no life harbors, peers or calls—   25
Wild solitudes like shoals in seas
Unsailed; or list at still sundown,
List to the hand-mills as they drone,
Domestic hand-mills in the court,
And groups there in the dear resort,   30
Mild matron pensive by her son,
The little prattler at her knee:
Under such scenes abysses be—
Dark quarries where few care to pry,
Whence came those many cities high—   35
Great capitals successive reared,
And which successive disappeared

On this same site. To powder ground,
Dispersed their dust blows round and round.
    No shallow gloss may much avail   40
When these or kindred thoughts assail:
Which Clarel proved, the more he went
A rover in their element.
For—trusting still that in some place
Where pilgrims linger he anew   45
The missing stranger yet would face
And speak with—never he withdrew
His wandering feet.
             In aimless sort
Passing across the town amort,
They came where, camped in corner waste,   50
Some Edomites were at repast—
Sojourners mere, and of a day—
Dark-hued, nor unlike birds of prey
Which on the stones of Tyre alight.
While Clarel fed upon that sight—   55
The saint repeating in his ear
Meet text applying to the scene—
As liberated from ravine,
Voices in choral note they hear;
And, strange as lilies in morass,   60
At the same moment, lo, appear
Emerging from a stony pass,
A lane low-vaulted and unclean,
Damsels in linen robes, heads bare,
Enlinked with matrons pacing there,   65
And elders gray; the maids with book:
Companions would one page o'erlook;
And vocal thus they wound along,
No glad procession, spite the song.
For truth to own, so downcast they—   70
At least the men, in sordid dress
And double file—the slim array,
But for the maidens' gentleness
And voices which so bird-like sang,
Had seemed much like a coffle gang.   75

But Nehemiah a key supplied:
"Alas, poor misled Jews," he sighed,
"Ye do but dirge among your dead.—
The Hebrew quarter here we tread;
And this is Friday; Wailing Day: 80
These to the temple wend their way.
And shall we follow?" Doing so
They came upon a sunken yard
Obscure, where dust and rubbish blow.
Felonious place, and quite debarred   85
From common travel. On one side
A blind wall rose, stable and great—
Massed up immense, an Ararat
Founded on beveled blocks how wide,
Reputed each a stone august   90
Of Solomon's fane (else fallen to dust)
But now adopted for the wall
To Islam's courts. There, lord of all,
The Turk permits the tribes to creep
Abject in rear of those dumb stones,   95
To lean or kneel, lament and weep;
Sad mendicants shut out from gate
Inexorable. Sighs and groans:
To be restored! we wait, long wait!
They call to count their pristine state   100
On this same ground: the lifted rows
Of peristyles; the porticoes
Crown upon crown, where Levite trains
In chimes of many a silver bell
(Daintily small as pearls in chain)   105
Hemming their mantles musical—
Passed in procession up and down,
Viewing the belt of guarding heights,
And march of shadows there, and flights
Of pigeon-pets, and palm leaves blown;   110
Or heard the silver trumpets call—
The priestly trumps, to festival.
So happy they; such Judah's prime.
But we, the remnant, lo, we pale;

Cast from the Temple, here we wail—   115
Yea, perish ere come Shiloh's time.
    Hard by that joyless crew which leant
With brows against the adamant—
Sad buttresses thereto—hard by—
The student marks the Black Jew bowed;   120
His voice he hears amid the crowd
Which supplicate stern Shaddai.
And earnest, too, he seeth there
One scarcely Hebrew in his dress
Rural, and hard cheek's swarthiness,   125
With nothing of an Eastern air.
His eyes met Clarel's unremoved—
In end a countryman he proved,
A strange apostate. On the twain
Contrasted so—the white, the black—   130
Man's earliest breed and latest strain—
Behind the master Moslem's back
Skulking, and in great Moses' track—
Gazed Clarel with the wonderment
Of wight who feels the earth upheave   135
Beneath him, and learns, ill-content,
That terra firma can deceive.
    When now those Friday wails were done,
Nehemiah, sidling with his book
Unto a lorn decrepit one,   140
Proferred a tract: "'Tis Hebrew, look,"
Zealous he urged; "it points the way,
Sole way, dear heart, whereby ye may
Rebuild the Temple." Answer none
Gat he from Isaac's pauper son,   145
Who, turning, part as in disdain,
Crept toward his squalid home. Again
Enrapt stood Clarel, lost awhile:
"Yon Jew has faith; can faith be vain?
But *is* it faith? ay, faith 's the word—   150
What else? Faith then can thus beguile
Her faithfulest. Hard, that is hard!"
So doubts invaded, found him out.

He strove with them; but they proved stout,
Nor would they down.
              But turn regard.   155
Among the maids those rites detained,
One he perceived, as it befell,
Whose air expressed such truth unfeigned,
And harmonies inlinked which dwell
In pledges born of record pure—   160
She looked a legate to insure
That Paradise is possible
Now as hereafter. 'Twas the grace
Of Nature's dawn: an Eve-like face
And Nereid eyes with virgin spell   165
Candid as day, yet baffling quite
Like day, through unreserve of light.
A dove she seemed, a temple dove,
Born in the temple or its grove,
And nurtured there. But deeper viewed,   170
What was it that looked part amiss?
A bit impaired? what lack of peace?
Enforced suppression of a mood,
Regret with yearning intertwined,
And secret protest of a virgin mind.   175
    Hebrew the profile, every line;
But as in haven fringed with palm,
Which Indian reefs embay from harm,
Belulled as in the vase the wine—
Red budded corals in remove,   180
Peep coy through quietudes above;
So through clear olive of the skin,
And features finely Hagarene;
Its way a tell-tale flush did win—
A tint which unto Israel's sand   185
Blabbed of the June in some far clover land.
    Anon by chance the damsel's eye
Fell on Nehemiah, and the look
A friendly recognition spoke,
Returned in kind. When by-and-by   190
The groups brake up and homeward bent;

Then, nor unnoted by the youth,
That maiden with the apostate went,
Whose voice paternal called her—"Ruth!"
    "Tell, friend," said Clarel eagerly,   195
As from the wall of wail they passed;
"Father and daughter? Who may be
That strange pervert?" No willing haste
The mentor showed; awhile he fed
On anxious thoughts; then grievingly   200
The story gave—a tangled thread,
Which, cleared from snarl and ordered so,
Follows transferred, with interflow
Of much Nehemiah scarce might add.

17. NATHAN

Nathan had sprung from worthy stock—
Austere, ascetical, but free,
Which hewed their way from sea-beat rock
Wherever woods and winter be.
    The pilgrim-keel in storm and stress   5
Had erred, and on a wilderness.
But shall the children all be schooled
By hap which their forefathers ruled?
Those primal settlers put in train
New emigrants which inland bore;   10
From these too, emigrants again
Westward pressed further; more bred more;
At each remove a goodlier wain,
A heart more large, an ampler shore,
With legacies of farms behind;   15
Until in years the wagons wind
Through parks and pastures of the sun,
Warm plains as of Esdraleon:
'Tis nature in her best benign.
Wild, wild in symmetry of mould,   20
With freckles on her tawny gold,
The lily alone looks pantherine—

The libbard-lily. Never broods
The gloom here of grim hemlock woods
Breeding the witchcraft-spell malign;   25
But groves like isles in Grecian seas,
Those dotting isles, the Sporades.
But who the gracious charm may tell—
Long rollings of the vast serene—
The prairie in her swimming swell   30
Of undulation.
            Such glad scene
Was won by venturers from far
Born under that severer star
The landing patriarchs knew. In fine,
To Illinois—a turf divine   35
Of promise, how auspicious spread,
Ere yet the cities rose thereon—
From Saco's mountain wilds were led
The sire of Nathan, wife and son;
Life's lot to temper so, and shun   40
Mountains whose camp withdrawn was set
Above one vale he would forget.
    After some years their tale had told,
He rested; lay forever stilled
With sachems and mound-builders old.   45
The son was grown; the farm he tilled;
A stripling, but of manful ways,
Hardy and frugal, oft he filled
The widow's eyes with tears of praise.
An only child, with her he kept   50
For *her* sake part, the Christian way,
Though frequent in his bosom crept
Precocious doubt unbid. The sway
He felt of his grave life, and power
Of vast space, from the log-house door   55
Daily beheld. Three Indian mounds
Against the horizon's level bounds
Dim showed across the prairie green
Like dwarfed and blunted mimic shapes
Of Pyramids at distance seen   60

From the broad Delta's planted capes
Of vernal grain. In nearer view
With trees he saw them crowned, which drew
From the red sagamores of eld
Entombed within, the vital gum 65
Which green kept each mausoleum.
    Hard by, as chanced, he once beheld
Bones like sea corals; one bleached skull
A vase vined round and beautiful
With flowers; felt, with bated breath 70
The floral revelry over death.
    And other sights his heart had thrilled;
Lambs had he known by thunder killed,
Innocents—and the type of Christ
Betrayed. Had not such things sufficed 75
To touch the young pure heart with awe,
Memory's mint could move him more.
In prairie twilight, summer's own,
The last cow milked, and he alone
In barn-yard dreamy by the fence, 80
Contrasted, came a scene immense:
The great White Hills, mount flanked by mount,
The Saco and Ammonoosuc's fount;
Where, in September's equinox
Nature hath put such terror on 85
That from his mother man would run—
Our mother, Earth: the founded rocks
Unstable prove: the Slide! the Slide!
Again he saw the mountain side
Sliced open; yet again he stood 90
Under its shadow, on the spot—
Now waste, but once a cultured plot,
Though far from village neighborhood—
Where, nor by sexton hearsed at even,
Somewhere his uncle slept; no mound, 95
Since not a trace of him was found,
So whelmed the havoc from the heaven.
    This reminiscence of dismay,
These thoughts unhinged him. On a day

Waiting for monthly grist at mill   100
In settlement some miles away,
It chanced, upon the window-sill
A dusty book he spied, whose coat,
Like the Scotch miller's powdered twill,
The mealy owner might denote.   105
Called off from reading, unaware
The miller e'en had left it there.
A book all but forsaken now
For more advanced ones not so frank,
Nor less in vogue and taking rank;   110
And yet it never shall outgrow
That infamy it first incurred,
Though—viewed in light which moderns know—
Capricious infamy absurd.
    The blunt straightforward Saxon tone,   115
Work-a-day language, even his own,
The sturdy thought, not deep but clear,
The hearty unbelief sincere,
Arrested him much like a hand
Clapped on the shoulder. Here he found   120
Body to doubt, rough standing-ground.
After some pages brief were scanned,
"Wilt loan me this?" he anxious said.
The shrewd Scot turned his square, strong head—
The book he saw, in troubled trim,   125
Fearing for Nathan, even him
So young, and for the mill, may be,
Should his unspoken heresy
Get bruited so. The lad but part
Might penetrate that senior heart.   130
Vainly the miller would dissuade;
Pledge gave he, and the loan was made.
    Reclined that night by candle dim
He read, then slept, and woke afraid:
The White Hill's slide! the Indian skull!   135
But this wore off; and unto him
Came acquiescence, which tho' dull
Was hardly peace. An altered earth

Sullen he tilled, in Adam's frame
When thrust from Eden out to dearth   140
And blest no more, and wise in shame.
The fall! nor aught availed at need
To Nathan, not each filial deed
Done for his mother, to allay
This ill. But tho' the Deist's sway,   145
Broad as the prairie fire, consumed
Some pansies which before had bloomed
Within his heart; it did but feed
To clear the soil for upstart weed.
　　　Yes, ere long came replacing mood.   150
The god, expelled from given form,
Went out into the calm and storm.
Now, ploughing near the isles of wood
In dream he felt the loneness come,
In dream regarded there the loam   155
Turned first by him. Such mental food
Need quicken, and in natural way,
Each germ of Pantheistic sway,
Whose influence, nor always drear,
Tenants our maiden hemisphere;   160
As if, dislodged long since from cells
Of Thracian woodlands, hither stole—
Hither, to renew their old control—
Pan and the pagan oracles.
　　　How frequent when Favonius low   165
Breathed from the copse which mild did wave
Over his father's sylvan grave,
And stirred the corn, he stayed the hoe,
And leaning, listening, felt a thrill
Which heathenized against the will.   170

　　　Years sped. But years attain not truth,
Nor length of life avails at all;
But time instead contributes ruth:
His mother—her the garners call:
When sicklemen with sickles go,   175
The churl of nature reaps her low.

Let now the breasts of Ceres swell—
In shooks, with golden tassels gay,
The Indian corn its trophies ray
About the log-house; is it well   180
With death's ripe harvest?—To believe,
Belief to win nor more to grieve!
But how? a sect about him stood
In thin and scattered neighborhood;
Uncanny, and in rupture new;   185
Nor were all lives of members true
And good. For them who hate and heave
Contempt on rite and creed sublime,
Yet to their own rank fable cleave—
Abject, the latest shame of time;   190
These quite repelled, for still his mind
Erring, was of no vulgar kind.
Alone, and at Doubt's freezing pole
He wrestled with the pristine forms
Like the first man. By inner storms   195
Held in solution, so his soul
Ripened for hour of such control
As shapes, concretes. The influence came,
And from a source that well might claim
Surprise.
            'Twas in a lake-port new,   200
A mart for grain, by chance he met
A Jewess who about him threw
Else than Nerea's amorous net
And dubious wile. 'Twas Miriam's race:
A sibyl breathed in Agar's grace—   205
A sibyl, but a woman too;
He felt her grateful as the rains
To Rephaim and the Rama plains
In drought. Ere won, herself did woo:
"Wilt join my people?" Love is power;   210
Came the strange plea in yielding hour.
Nay, and turn Hebrew? But why not?
If backward still the inquirer goes
To get behind man's present lot

Of crumbling faith; for rear-ward shows   215
Far behind Rome and Luther——what?
The crag of Sinai. Here then plant
Thyself secure: 'tis adamant.
    Still as she dwelt on Zion's story
He felt the glamour, caught the gleam;   220
All things but these seemed transitory—
Love, and his love's Jerusalem.
And interest in a mitred race,
With awe which to the fame belongs,
These in receptive heart found place   225
When Agar chanted David's songs.
    'Twas passion. But the Puritan—
Mixed latent in his blood—a strain
How evident, of Hebrew source;
'Twas that, diverted here in force,   230
Which biased—hardly might do less.
Hereto append, how earnestness,
Which disbelief for first-fruits bore,
Now, in recoil, by natural stress
Constrained to faith—to faith in more   235
Than prior disbelief had spurned;
As if, when he toward credence turned,
Distance therefrom but gave career
For impetus that shot him sheer
Beyond. Agar rejoiced; nor knew   240
How such a nature, charged with zeal,
Might yet overpass that limit due
Observed by her. For woe or weal
They wedded, one in heart and creed.
Transferring fields with title-deed,   245
From rustic life he quite withdrew—
Traded, and throve. Two children came:
Sedate his heart, nor sad the dame.
But years subvert; or he outgrew
(While yet confirmed in all the myth)   250
The mind infertile of the Jew.
His northern nature, full of pith,
Vigor and enterprise and will,

Having taken thus the Hebrew bent,
Might not abide inactive so   255
And but the empty forms fulfill:
Needs utilize the mystic glow—
For nervous energies find vent.

    The Hebrew seers announce in time
The return of Judah to her prime;   260
Some Christians deemed it then at hand.
Here was an object: Up and do!
With seed and tillage help renew—
Help reinstate the Holy Land.

    Some zealous Jews on alien soil   265
Who still from Gentile ways recoil,
And loyally maintain the dream,
Salute upon the Paschal day
With *Next year in Jerusalem!*
Now Nathan turning unto her,   270
Greeting his wife at morning ray,
Those words breathed on the Passover;
But she, who mutely startled lay,
In the old phrase found import new,
In the blithe tone a bitter cheer   275
That did the very speech subdue.
She kenned her husband's mind austere,
Had watched his reveries grave; he meant
No flourish mere of sentiment.
Then what to do? or how to stay?   280
Decry it? that would faith unsay.
Withstand him? but she gently loved.
And so with Agar here it proved,
As oft it may, the hardy will
Overpowered the deep monition still.   285

    Enough; fair fields and household charms
They quit, sell all, and cross the main
With Ruth and a young child in arms.
A tract secured on Sharon's plain,
Some sheds he built, and ground walled in   290

Defensive; toil severe but vain.
The wandering Arabs, wonted long
(Nor crime they deemed it, crime nor sin)
To scale the desert convents strong—
In sly foray leaped Nathan's fence   295
And robbed him; and no recompense
Attainable where law was none
Or perjured. Resolute hereon,
Agar, with Ruth and the young child,
He lodged within the stronghold town   300
Of Zion, and his heart exiled
To abide the worst on Sharon's lea.
Himself and honest servants three
Armed husbandmen became, as erst
His sires in Pequod wilds immersed.   305
Hittites—foes pestilent to God
His fathers old those Indians deemed:
Nathan the Arabs here esteemed
The same—slaves meriting the rod;
And out he spake it; which bred hate   310
The more imperiling his state.
      With muskets now his servants slept;
Alternate watch and ward they kept
In grounds beleaguered. Not the less
Visits at stated times he made   315
To them in Zion's walled recess.
Agar with sobs of suppliance prayed
That he would fix there: "Ah, for good
Tarry! abide with us, thine own;
Put not these blanks between us; should   320
Such space be for a shadow thrown?
Quit Sharon, husband; leave to brood;
Serve God by cleaving to thy wife,
Thy children. If come fatal strife—
Which I forebode—nay!" and she flung   325
Her arms about him there, and clung.
      She plead. But tho' his heart could feel,
'Twas mastered by inveterate zeal.

Even the nursling's death ere long
Balked not his purpose tho' it wrung.   330

    But Time the cruel, whose smooth way
Is feline, patient for the prey
That to this twig of being clings;
And Fate, which from her ambush springs
And drags the loiterer soon or late   335
Unto a sequel unforeseen;
These doomed him and cut short his date;
But first was modified the lien
The husband had on Agar's heart;
And next a prudence slid athwart—   340
After distrust. But be unsaid
That steep toward which the current led.
Events shall speak.
                And now the guide,
Who did in sketch this tale begin,
Parted with Clarel at the inn;   345
And ere long came the eventide.

18. NIGHT

Like sails convened when calms delay
Off the twin forelands on fair day,
So, on Damascus' plain behold
Mid groves and gardens, girdling ones,
White fleets of sprinkled villas, rolled   5
In the green ocean of her environs.
    There when no minaret receives
The sun that gilds yet St. Sophia,
Which loath and later it bereaves,
The peace fulfills the heart's desire.   10
In orchards mellowed by eve's ray
The prophet's son in turban green,
Mild, with a patriarchal mien,
Gathers his fruity spoil. In play
Of hide-and-seek where alleys be,   15

The branching Eden brooks ye see
Peeping, and fresh as on the day
When haply Abram's steward went—
Mild Eliezer, musing, say—
By those same banks, to join the tent   20
In Canaan pitched. From Hermon stray
Cool airs that in a dream of snows
Temper the ardor of the rose;
While yet to moderate and reach
A tone beyond our human speech,   25
How steals from cloisters of the groves
The *ave* of the vesper-doves.
Such notes, translated into hues,
Thy wall, Angelico, suffuse,
Whose tender pigments melt from view—   30
Die down, die out, as sunsets do.
     But rustling trees aloft entice
To many a house-top, old and young:
Aerial people! see them throng;
And the moon comes up from Paradise.   35

     But in Jerusalem—not there
Loungers at eve to roof repair
So frequent. Haply two or three
Small quiet groups far off you see,
Or some all uncompanioned one   40
(Like ship-boy at mast-head alone)
Watching the star-rise. Silently
So Clarel stands, his vaulted room
Opening upon a terrace free,
Lifted above each minor dome   45
On grade beneath. Glides, glides away
The twilight of the Wailing Day.
The apostate's story fresh in mind,
Fain Clarel here had mused thereon,
But more upon Ruth's lot, so twined   50
With clinging ill. But every thought
Of Ruth was strangely underrun
By Celio's image. Celio—sought

Vainly in body—now appeared
As in the spiritual part,   55
Haunting the air, and in the heart.
    Back to his chamber Clarel veered,
Seeking that alms which unrest craves
Of slumber: alms withheld from him;
For midnight, rending all her graves,   60
Showed in a vision far and dim
Still Celio—and in pallid stress
Fainting amid contending press
Of shadowy fiends and cherubim.
Later, anew he sought the roof;   65
And started, for not far aloof,
He caught some dubious object dark,
Huddled and hooded, bowed, and set
Under the breast-high parapet,
And glimmering with a dusky spark.   70
It moved, it murmured. In deep prayer
'Twas Abdon under *talith*. Rare
That scarf of supplication—old,
Of India stuff, with braid of gold
In cipher. Did the Black Jew keep   75
The saying—*Prayer is more than sleep?*
Islam says that. The Hebrew rose,
And, kindled by the starry sky,
In broidered text that mystic flows
The *talith* gleams. Divested then   80
He turned, not knowing Clarel nigh,
And would have passed him all unseen.
But Clarel spake. It roused annoy—
An Eastern Jew in rapt employ
Spied by the Gentile. But a word   85
Dispelled distrust, good-will restored.
    "Stay with me," Clarel said; "go not.
A shadow, but I scarce know what—
It haunts me. Is it presage?—Hark!
That piercing cry from out the dark!"   90
"'Tis for some parted spirit—gone,
Just gone. The custom of the town

That cry is; yea, the watcher's breath
Instant upon the stroke of death."
    "Anew! 'Tis like a tongue of flame   95
Shot from the fissure;" and stood still:
"Can fate the boding thus fulfill?
First ever I, first to disclaim
Such premonitions.—Thrillest yet
'Tis over, but we might have met?—   100
Hark, hark; again the cry is sped;
For *him* it is—found now—nay, fled!"

19. THE FULFILMENT

Such passion!—But have hearts forgot
That ties may form where words be not?
The spiritual sympathy
Transcends the social. Which appears
In that presentiment, may be,   5
Of Clarel's inquietude of fears
Proved just.
        Yes, some retreat to win
Even more secluded than the court
The Terra Santa locks within:
Celio had found withdrawn resort   10
And lodging in the deeper town.
There, by a gasping ill distressed—
Such as attacks the hump-bowed one—
After three days the malady pressed:
He knew it, knew his course was run,   15
And, turning toward the wall, found rest.
    'Twas Syrians watched the parting hour—
And Syrian women shrilled the cry
That wailed it. This, with added store,
Learned Clarel, putting all else by   20
To get at items of the dead.
Nor, in the throb that casts out fear,
Aught recked he of a scruple here;
But, finding leaves that might bestead,

The jotted journaled thoughts he read.   25
A second self therein he found,
But stronger—with the heart to brave
All questions on that primal ground
Laid bare by faith's receding wave.
But lo, arrested in event—   30
Hurried down Hades' steep descent;
Cut off while in progressive stage
Perchance, ere years might more unfold:
Who young dies, leaves life's tale half told.
How then? Is death the book's fly-page?   35
Is no hereafter? If there be,
Death foots what record? how forestalls
Acquittance in eternity?
Advance too, and through age on age?
Here the tree lies not as it falls;   40
For howsoe'er in words of man
The word and will of God be feigned,
No incompletion's heaven ordained.
    Clarel, through him these reveries ran.

20. VALE OF ASHES

Beyond the city's thin resort
And northward from the Ephraim port
The Vale of Ashes keepeth place.
If stream it have which showeth face,
Thence Kedron issues when in flood: 5
A pathless dell men seldom trace;
The same which after many a rood
Down deepens by the city wall
Into a glen, where—if we deem
Joel's wild text no Runic dream—   10
An archangelic trump shall call
The nations of the dead from wreck,
Convene them in one judgment-hall
The hollow of Melchizedek.

That upper glade by quarries old   15
Reserves for weary ones a seat—
Porches of caves, stone benches cold,
Grateful in sultry clime to meet.
To this secluded spot austere,
Priests bore—Talmudic records treat—   20
The ashes from the altar; here
They laid them, hallowed in release,
Shielded from winds in glade of peace.

From following the bier to end
Hitherward now see Clarel tend;   25
A dell remote from Celio's mound,
As he for time would shun the ground
So freshly opened for the dead,
Nor linger there while aliens stray
And ceremonious gloom is shed.   30
Withdrawing to this quiet bay
He felt a natural influence glide
In lenitive through every vein,
And reach the heart, lull heart and brain.
The comrade old was by his side,   35
And solace shared. But this would pass,
Or dim eclipse would steal thereon,
As over autumn's hill-side grass
The cloud. Howbeit, in freak anon
His Bible he would muttering con,   40
Then turn, and brighten with a start—
"I hear them, hear them in my heart;
Yea, friend in Christ, I hear them swell—
The trumpets of Immanuel!"
Illusion. But in other hour   45
When oft he would foretell the flower
And sweets that time should yet bring in,
A happy world, with peace for dower—
This more of interest could win;
For he, the solitary man   50
Who such a social dream could fan,
What had he known himself of bliss?

And—nearing now his earthly end—
Even that he pledged he needs must miss.
    To Clarel now, such musings lend   55
A vague disturbance, as they wend
Returning thro' the noiseless glade.
But in the gate Nehemiah said,
"My room in court is pleasant, see;
Not yet you've been there—come with me."   60

21. By-Places

On Salem's surface undermined,
Lo, present alley, lane or wynd
Obscure, which pilgrims seldom gain
Or tread, who wonted guides retain.
Humble the pilots native there: 5
Following humbly need ye fare:
Afoot; for never camels pass—
Camels, which elsewhere in the town,
Stalk through the street and brush the gown;
Nor steed, nor mule, nor smaller ass.   10
Some by-paths, flanked by wall and wall,
Affect like glens. Dismantled, torn,
Disastrous houses, ripe for fall—
Haggard as Horeb, or the rock
Named Hermit, antler of Cape Horn—   15
Shelter, in chamber grimed, or hall,
The bearded goat-herd's bearded flock;
Or quite abandoned, sold to fear,
Yawn, and like plundered tombs appear.
Here, if alone, strive all ye can,   20
Needs must ye start at meeting man.
Yet man here harbors, even he—
Harbors like lizard in dry well,
Or stowaway in hull at sea
Down by the keelson; criminal,   25
Or penitent, or wretch undone,
Or anchorite, or kinless one,

Or wight cast off by kin; or soul
Which anguished from the hunter stole—
Like Emim Bey the Mamaluke.   30
He—armed, and, happily, mounted well—
Leaped the inhuman citadel
In Cairo; fled—yea, bleeding, broke
Through shouting lanes his breathless way
Into the desert; nor at bay   35
Even there might stand; but, fox-like, on,
And ran to earth in Zion's town;
Here maimed, disfigured, crouched in den,
And crouching died—securest then.
    With these be hearts in each degree   40
Of craze, whereto some creed is key;
Which, mastered by the awful myth,
Find here, on native soil, the pith;
And leaving a shrewd world behind—
To trances open-eyed resigned—   45
As visionaries of the Word
Walk like somnambulists abroad.

22. HERMITAGE

Through such retreats of dubious end
Behold the saint and student wend,
Stirring the dust that here may keep
Like that on mummies long asleep
In Theban tomb. Those alleys passed,   5
A little square they win—a waste
Shut in by towers so hushed, so blind,
So tenantless and left forlorn
As seemed—an ill surmise was born
Of something prowling there behind.   10
    An arch, with key-stone slipped half down
Like a dropped jaw—they enter that;
Repulse nor welcome in the gate:
Climbed, and an upper chamber won.
It looked out through low window small   15

On other courts of bale shut in,
Whose languishment of crumbling wall
Breathed that despair alleged of sin.
Prediction and fulfillment met
In faint appealings from the rod: 20
Wherefore forever dost forget—
For so long time forsake, O God?

    But Clarel turned him, heedful more
To note the place within. The floor
Rudely was tiled; and little there   25
A human harbor might express
Save a poor chest, a couch, a chair;
A hermitage how comfortless.
The beams of the low ceiling bare
Were wreck-stuff from the Joppa strand: 30
Scant the live timber in that land.
Upon the cot the host sat down,
Short breathing, with late travel spent;
And wiping beads from brow and crown,
Essayed a smile, in kindness meant.   35
    But now a little foot was heard
Light coming. On the hush it fell
Like tinkling of the camel-bell
In Uz. "Hark! yea, she comes—my bird!"
Cried Nehemiah who hailed the hap;   40
"Yea, friend in Christ, quick now ye'll see
God's messenger which feedeth me;"
And rising to the expected tap,
He oped the door. Alone was seen
Ruth with a napkin coarse yet clean,   45
Folding a loaf. Therewith she bore
A water-pitcher, nothing more.
These alms, the snowy robe and free,
The veil which hid each tress from sight,
Might indicate a vestal white   50
Or priestess of sweet charity.
    The voice was on the lip; but eyes
Arrested in their frank accost,

Checked speech, and looked in opening skies
Upon the stranger. Said the host,   55
Easing her hands, "Bird, bird, come in:
Well-doing never was a sin—
God bless thee!" In suffusion dim
His eyes filled. She eluding him,
Retreated. "What, and flown?" breathed he: 60
"Daily this raven comes to me;
But what should make it now so shy?"
The hermit motioned here to share
The loaf with Clarel; who put by
The proffer. So, with Crusoe air   65
Of castaway on isle in sea
Withdrawn, he broke the unshared bread—
But not before a blessing said:
Loaf in left hand, the right hand raised
Higher, and eyes which heavenward gazed.   70
    Ere long—refection done—the youth
Lured him to talk of things, in range
Linking themselves at last with Ruth.
Her sire he spake of. Here 'twas strange
How o'er the enthusiast stole a change—   75
A meek superior look in sooth:
"Poor Nathan, did man ever stray
As thou? to Judaize to-day!
To deem the crook of Christ shall yield
To Aaron's staff! to till thy field   80
In hope that harvest time shall see
Solomon's hook in golden glee
Reaping the ears. Well, well! meseems—
Heaven help him; dreams, but dreams—dreams, dreams!"
"But thou, thou too, with faith sincere   85
Surely believ'st in Jew restored."
"Yea, as forerunner of our Lord.—
Poor man, he's weak; 'tis even here"
Touching his forehead—"he's amiss."
    Clarel scarce found reply to this,   90
Conjecturing that Nathan too
Must needs hold Nehemiah in view

The same; the which an after-day
Confirmed by proof. But now from sway
Of thoughts he would not have recur,   95
He slid, and into dream of her
Who late within that cell shed light
Like the angel succorer by night
Of Peter dungeoned. But apace
He turned him, for he heard the breath,   100
The old man's breath, in sleep. The face
Though tranced, struck not like trance of death
All rigid; not a masque like that,
Iced o'er, which none may penetrate,
Conjecturing of aught below.   105
Death freezes, but sleep thaws. And so
The inmate lay, some lines revealed—
Effaced, when life from sleep comes back.
And what their import? Be it sealed.
But Clarel felt as in affright   110
Did Eliphaz the Temanite
When passed the vision ere it spake.

    He stole forth, striving with his thought,
Leaving Nehemiah in slumber caught—
Alone, and in an unlocked room,   115
Safe as a stone in vacant tomb,
Stone none molest, for it is naught.

23. THE CLOSE

Next day the wanderer drawing near
Saluting with his humble cheer,
Made Clarel start. Where now the look
That face but late in slumber took?
Had he but dreamed it? It was gone.   5
    But other thoughts were stirring soon,
To such good purpose, that the saint
Through promptings scarce by him divined,
Anew led Clarel thro' constraint
Of inner bye-ways, yet inclined   10

Away from his peculiar haunt,
And came upon a little close,
One wall whereof a creeper won.
On casement sills, small pots in rows
Showed herb and flower, the shade and sun—   15
Surprise how blest in town but sere.
Low breathed the guide, "They harbor here—
Agar, and my young raven, Ruth.
And, see, there's Nathan, nothing loath,
Just in from Sharon, 'tis his day;   20
And, yes—the Rabbi in delay."—
        The group showed just within the door
Swung open where the creeper led.
In lap the petting mother bore
The half reclining maiden's head—   25
The stool drawn neighboring the chair;
In front, erect, the father there,
Hollow in cheek, but rugged, brown—
Sharon's red soil upon his shoon—
With zealot gesture urged some plea   30
Which brought small joy to Agar's eyes,
Whereto turned Ruth's. In scrutiny
Impassive, wrinkled, and how wise
(If wisdom be but craft profound)
Sat the hoar Rabbi. This his guise: 35
In plaits a head-dress agate-bound,
A sable robe with mystic hem—
Clasps silver, locked in monogram.

        An unextinguished lamp they view
Whose flame scarce visibly did sway,   40
Which having burned till morning dew
Might not be quenched on Saturday
The unaltered sabbath of the Jew.
Struck by the attitudes, the scene,
And loath, a stranger, to advance   45
Obtrusive, coming so between;
While, in emotion new and strange,
Ruth thrilled him with life's first romance;

Clarel abashed and faltering stood,
With cheek that knew a novel change.   50
    But Nehemiah with air subdued
Made known their presence; and Ruth turned,
And Agar also, and discerned
The stranger, and a settle placed:
Matron and maid with welcome graced   55
Both visitors, and seemed to find
In travel-talk which here ensued
Relief to burdens of the mind.
But by the sage was Clarel viewed
With stony and unfriendly look—   60
Fixed inquisition, hard to brook.
And that embarrassment he raised
The Rabbi marked, and colder gazed.
But in redemption from his glance—
For a benign deliverance—   65
On Clarel fell the virgin's eyes,
Pure home of all we seek and prize,
And crossing with their humid ray
The Levite's arid eyes of gray—
But skill is none to word the rest: 70
To Clarel's heart there came a swell
Like the first tide that ever pressed
Inland, and of a deep did tell.

    Thereafter, little speech was had
Save syllables which do but skim;   75
Even in these, the zealot—made
A slave to one tyrannic whim—
Was scant; while still the sage unkind
Sat a torpedo-fish, with mind
Intent to paralyze, and so   80
Perchance, make Clarel straight forego
Acquaintance with his flock, at least
With two, whose yearnings—he the priest
More than conjectured—oft did flow
Averse from Salem. None the less   85
A talismanic gentleness

Maternal welled from Agar faint;
Thro' the sad circle's ill constraint
Her woman's way could yet instill
Her prepossession, her good will;   90
And when at last they bade good-bye—
The visitors—another eye
Spake at the least of amity.

24. THE GIBE

In the south wall, where low it creeps
Crossing the hollow down between
Moriah and Zion, by dust-heaps
Of rubbish in a lonely scene,
A little door there is, and mean—   5
Such as a stable may befit;
'Tis locked, nor do they open it
Except when days of drought begin,
To let the water-donkeys in
From Rogel. 'Tis in site the gate   10
Of Scripture named the dung-gate—that
Also (the legends this instill)
Through which from over Kedron's rill—
In fear of rescue should they try
The way less roundabout and shy—   15
By torch the tipstaves Jesus led,
And so thro' back-street hustling sped
To Pilate. Odor bad it has
This gate in story, and alas,
In fact as well, and is in fine   20
Like ancient Rome's port Esquiline
Wherefrom the scum was cast.—
                               Next day
Ascending Zion's rear, without
The wall, the saint and Clarel stay
Their feet, being hailed, and by a shout   25
From one who nigh the small gate stood:
"Ho, ho there, worthy pilgrims, ho!

Acquainted in this neighborhood?
What city's this? town beautiful
Of David? I'm a stranger, know.   30
'Tis heavy prices here must rule;
Choice house-lot now, what were it worth?
How goes the market?" and more mirth.
    Down there into the place unclean
They peer, they see the man therein,   35
An iron-gray, short, rugged one,
Round shouldered, and of knotty bone;
A hammer swinging in his hand,
And pouch at side, by the ill door.
Him had they chanced upon before   40
Or rather at a distance seen
Upon the hills, with curious mien
And eyes that—scarce in pious dream
Or sad humility, 'twould seem—
Still earthward bent, would pry and pore.   45
Perceiving that he shocked the twain,
His head he wagged, and called again,
"What city's this? town beautiful——"
No more they heard; but to annul
The cry, here Clarel quick as thought   50
Turned with the saint and refuge sought
Passing an angle of the wall.
    When now at slower pace they went
Clarel observed the sinless one
Turning his Bible-leaves content;   55
And presently he paused: "Dear son,
The Scripture is fulfilled this day;
Note what these *Lamentations* say;
The doom the prophet doth rehearse
In chapter second, fifteenth verse: 60
'All that pass by clap their hands
At thee; they hiss, and wag the head,
Saying, Is this the city'—read,
Thyself here read it where it stands."
    Inquisitive he quick obeyed,   65
Then dull relapsed, and nothing said,

Tho' more he mused, still laboring there
Upward, by arid gullies bare:—
What object sensible to touch
Or quoted fact may faith rely on, 70
If faith confideth overmuch
That here's a monument in Zion:
Its substance ebbs—see, day and night
The sands subsiding from the height;
In time, absorbed, these grains may help 75
To form new sea-bed, slug and kelp.
    "The gate," cried Nehemiah, "the gate
Of David!" Wending thro' the strait,
And marking that, in common drought,
'Twas yellow waste within as out, 80
The student mused: The desert, see,
It parts not here, but silently,
Even like a leopard by our side,
It seems to enter in with us—
At home amid men's homes would glide. 85
But hark! that wail how dolorous:
So grieve the souls in endless dearth;
Yet sounds it human—of the earth!

25. HUTS

The stone huts face the stony wall
Inside—the city's towering screen—
Leaving a reptile lane between;
And streetward not a window small,
Cranny nor loophole least is seen: 5
Through excess of biting sympathies
So hateful to the people's eyes
Those lepers and their evil nook,
No outlook from it will they brook:
None enter; condolence is none. 10
That lava glen in Luna's sphere,
More lone than any earthly one—
Whereto they Tycho's name have given—

Not more from visitant is riven
Than this stone lane.
                    But who crouch here?   15
Have these been men? these did men greet
As fellows once? It is a scene—
Illusion of time's mirage fleet:
On dry shard-heaps, and things which rot—
Scarce into weeds, for weeds are green—   20
Backs turned upon their den, they squat,
Some gossips of that tribe unclean.
    Time was when Holy Church did take,
Over lands then held by Baldwin's crown,
True care for such for Jesu's sake,   25
Who (so they read in ages gone)
Even as a leper was foreshown;
And, tho' apart their lot she set,
It was with solemn service yet,
And forms judicial lent their tone: 30
The sick-mass offered, next was shed
Upon the afflicted human one
The holy water. He was led
Unto the house aloof, his home
Thenceforth. And here, for type of doom,   35
Some cemetery dust was thrown
Over his head: "Die to the world:
Her wings of hope and fear be furled:
Brother, live now to God alone."
And from the people came the chant: 40
"My soul is troubled, joy is curbed,
All my bones they are disturbed;
God, thy strength and mercy grant!"
And next, in order due, the priest
Each habit and utensil blessed—   45
Hair-cloth and barrel, clapper, glove;
And one by one as these were given,
With law's dread charge pronounced in love,
So, link by link, life's chain was riven—
The leper faded in remove.   50
    The dell of isolation here

To match, console, and (could man prove
More than a man) in part endear,
How well had come that smothered text
Which Julian's pagan mind hath vexed—   55
And ah, for soul that finds it clear:
"He lives forbid;
From him our faces have we hid;
No heart desires him, none redress,
He hath nor form nor comeliness;   60
For a transgressor he's suspected,
Behold, he is a thing infected,
Smitten of God, by men rejected."
    But otherwise the ordinance flows.
For, moving toward the allotted cell,   65
Beside the priest the leper goes:
"I've chosen it, here will I dwell."
He's left. At gate the priest puts up
A cross, a can; therein doth drop
The first small alms, which laymen swell.   70
To aisles returned, the people kneel;
Heart-piercing suppliance—appeal.
    But not the austere maternal care
When closed the ritual, ended there
With benediction. Yet to heal,   75
Rome did not falter, could not faint;
She prompted many a tender saint,
Widow or virgin ministrant.
But chiefly may Sybella here
In chance citation fitly show,   80
Countess who under Zion's brow
In house of St. John Almoner
Tended the cripples many a year.
    Tho' long from Europe's clime be gone
That pest which in the perished age   85
Could tendance such in love engage,
Still in the East the rot eats on.
Natheless the Syrian leper goes
Unfriended, save that man bestows
(His eye averting) chanceful pence   90

Then turns, and shares disgust of sense.
    Bonds sympathetic bind these three—
Faith, Reverence, and Charity.
If Faith once fail, the faltering mood
Affects—needs must—the sisterhood.   95

26. The Gate of Zion

As Clarel entered with the guide,
Beset they were by that sad crew—
With inarticulate clamor plied;
And faces, yet defacements too,
Appealed to them; but could not give   5
Expression. There, still sensitive,
Our human nature, deep inurned
In voiceless visagelessness, yearned.
    Behold, proud worm (if such can be),
What yet may come, yea, even to thee.   10
Who knoweth? canst forecast the fate
In infinite ages? Probe thy state:
Sinless art thou? Then these sinned not.
These, these are men; and thou art—what?
    For Clarel, turning in affright,   15
Fain would his eyes renounce the light.
But Nehemiah held on his path
Mild and unmoved—scarce seemed to heed
The suitors, or deplore the scath—
His soul pre-occupied and freed   20
From actual objects thro' the sway
Of visionary scenes intense—
The wonders of a mystic day
And Zion's old magnificence.
Nor hither had he come to show   25
The leper-huts, but only so
To visit once again the hill
And gate Davidic.
                    In ascent
They win the port's high battlement,

And thence in sweep they view at will 30
That theatre of heights which hold
As in a Coliseum's fold
The guarded Zion. They command
The Mount of Solomon's Offense,
The Crag of Evil Council, and 35
Iscariot's gallows-eminence.
  Pit too they mark where long ago
Dull fires of refuse, shot below,
The city's litter, smouldering burned,
Clouding the glen with smoke impure, 40
And griming the foul shapes obscure
Of dismal chain-gangs in their shame
Raking the garbage thither spurned:
Tophet the place—transferred, in name,
To penal Hell.
    But shows there naught 45
To win here a redeeming thought?
Yes: welcome in its nearer seat
The white Cœnaculum they greet,
Where still an upper room is shown—
In dream avouched the very one 50
Wherein the Supper first was made
And Christ those words of parting said,
Those words of love by loved St. John
So tenderly recorded. Ah,
They be above us like a star, 55
Those Paschal words.
    But they descend;
And as within the wall they wend,
A Horror hobbling on low crutch
Draws near, but still refrains from touch.
Before the saint in low estate 60
He fawns, who with considerate
Mild glance regards him. Clarel shrank:
And he, is *he* of human rank?—
"Knowest thou him?" he asked.—"Yea, yea,"
And beamed on that disfeatured clay: 65
"Toulib, to me? to Him are due

These thanks—the God of me and you
And all; to whom His own shall go
In Paradise and be re-clad,
Transfigured like the morning glad.—   70
Yea, friend in Christ, this man I know,
This fellow-man."—And afterward
The student from true sources heard
How Nehemiah had proved his friend,
Sole friend even of that trunk of woe,   75
When sisters failed him in the end.

27. MATRON AND MAID

Days fleet. No vain enticements lure
Clarel to Agar's roof. Her tact
Prevailed: the Rabbi might not act
His will austere. And more and more
A prey to one devouring whim,   5
Nathan yet more absented him.
Welcome the matron ever had
For Clarel. Was the youth not one
New from the clime she doated on?
And if indeed an exile sad   10
By daisy in a letter laid
Reminded be of home-delight,
Tho' there first greeted by the sight
Of that transmitted flower—how then
Not feel a kin emotion bred   15
At glimpse of face of countryman
Tho' stranger? Yes, a Jewess—born
In Gentile land where nature's wreath
Exhales the first creation's breath—
The waste of Judah made her lorn.   20
The student, sharing not her blood,
Nearer in tie of spirit stood
Than he she called Rabboni. So
In Agar's liking did he grow—
Deeper in heart of Ruth; and learned   25

The more how both for freedom yearned;
And much surmised, too, left unsaid
By the tried mother and the maid.
    Howe'er dull natures read the signs
Where untold grief a hermit pines—   30
The anxious, strained, weak, nervous air
Of trouble, which like shame may wear
Her gaberdine; though soul in feint
May look pathetic self-restraint,
For ends pernicious; real care,   35
Sorrow made dumb where duties move,
Never eluded love, true love,
A deep diviner.
             Here, for space
The past of wife and daughter trace.
Of Agar's kin for many an age   40
Not one had seen the heritage
Of Judah; Gentile lands detained.
So, while they clung to Moses' lore
Far from the land his guidance gained,
'Twas Eld's romance, a treasured store   45
Like plate inherited. In fine
It graced, in seemly way benign,
That family feeling of the Jew,
Which hallowed by each priestly rite,
Makes home a temple—sheds delight   50
Naomi ere her trial knew.
    Happy was Agar ere the seas
She crossed for Zion. Pride she took—
Pride, if in small felicities—
Pride in her little court, a nook   55
Where morning-glories starred the door:
So sweet without, so snug within.
At sunny matin meal serene
Her damask cloth she'd note. It bore
In Hebrew text about the hem,   60
Mid broidered cipher and device,
"IF I FORGET THEE, O JERUSALEM!"
And swam before her humid eyes,

In rainbowed distance, Paradise.
Faith, ravished, followed Fancy's path   65
In more of bliss than nature hath.
But ah, the dream to test by deed,
To seek to handle the ideal
And make a sentiment serve need:
To try to realize the unreal!   70
'Twas not that Agar reasoned—nay,
She did but feel, true woman's way.
What solace from the desert win
Far from known friends, familiar kin?
How nearer God? The chanted Zion   75
Showed graves, but graves to gasp and die on.
     Nathan, her convert, for his sake
Grief had she stifled long; but now,
The nursling one lay pale and low.
Oft of that waxen face she'd think   80
Beneath the stones; her heart would sink
And in hard bitterness repine,
"Slim grass, poor babe, to grave of thine!"

     Ruth, too, when here a child she came,
Would blurt in reckless childhood's way,   85
"'Tis a bad place." But the sad dame
Would check; and, as the maiden grew,
Counsel she kept—too much she knew.
But how to give her feelings play?
With cherished pots of herbs and flowers   90
She strove to appease the hungry hours;
Each leaf bedewed with many a tear
For Gentile land, how green and dear!
What tho' the dame and daughter both
In synagogue, behind the grate   95
Dividing sexes, oftimes sat?
It was with hearts but chill and loath;
Never was heaven served by that
Cold form.—With Clarel seemed to come
A waftage from the fields of home,   100

Crossing the wind from Judah's sand,
Reviving Agar, and of power
To make the bud in Ruth expand
With promise of unfolding hour.

28. TOMB AND FOUNTAIN

Clarel and Ruth—might it but be
That range they could green uplands free
By gala orchards, when they fling
Their bridal favors, buds of Spring;
And, dreamy in her morning swoon,   5
The lady of the night, the moon,
Looks pearly as the blossoming;
And youth and nature's fond accord
Wins Eden back, that tales abstruse
Of Christ, the crucified, Pain's Lord,   10
Seem foreign—forged—incongruous.

    Restrictions of that Eastern code
Immured the maiden. From abode
Frequent nor distant she withdrew
Except with Jewess, scarce with Jew.   15
So none the less in former mode,
Nehemiah still with Clarel went,
Who grew in liking and content
In company of one whose word
Babbled of Ruth——"My bird—God's bird."   20

    The twain were one mild morning led
Out to a waste where beauty clings,
Vining a grot how doubly dead:
The rifled *Sepulcher of Kings*.
    Hewn from the rock a sunken space   25
Conducts to garlands—fit for vase—
In sculptured frieze above a tomb:
Palm leaves, pine apples, grapes. These bloom,

Involved in death—to puzzle us—
As 'twere thy line, Theocritus,   30
Dark Joel's text of terror threading:
Yes, strange that Pocahontas-wedding
Of contraries in old belief—
Hellenic cheer, Hebraic grief.
The homicide Herods, men aver,   35
Inurned behind that wreathage were.

    But who is he uncovered seen,
Profound in shadow of the tomb
Reclined, with meditative mien
Intent upon the tracery?   40
A low wind waves his Lydian hair:
A funeral man, yet richly fair—
Fair as the sabled violets be.
    The frieze and this secluded one,
Retaining each a separate tone,   45
Beauty yet harmonized in grace
And contrast to the barren place.
    But noting that he was discerned,
Salute the stranger made, then turned
And shy passed forth in obvious state   50
Of one who would keep separate.

    Those cells explored, thro' dale they paced
Downward, and won Moriah's walls
And seated them. Clarel recalls
The colonnades that Herod traced—   55
Herod, magnific Idumæan—
In marble along the mountain flank:
Column on column, rank on rank
Above the valley Tyropœon.
    Eastward, in altitude they view   60
Across Jehoshaphat, a crag
Of sepulchers and huts. Thereto
They journey. But awhile they lag
Beneath, to mark the tombs in row
Pierced square along the gloomy steep   65
In beetling broadside, and with show

Of port-holes in black battle-ship.
  They climb; and Clarel turning saw
Their late resort, the hill of law—
Moriah, above the Kedron's bed;   70
And, turreting his aged head,
The angle of King David's wall—
Acute seen here, here too best scanned,
As 'twere that cliff, tho' not so tall,
Nor tempest-sculptured therewithal,   75
Envisaged in Franconian land,
The marvel of the Pass.
        Anon
A call he hears behind, in note
Familiar, being man's; remote
No less, and strange in hollowed tone   80
As 'twere a voice from out the tomb.
A tomb it is; and he in gloom
Of porch there biddeth them begone.
Clings to his knee a toddling one
Bewildered poising in wee hand   85
A pictured page—Nehemiah's boon—
He passive in the sun at stand.
Morosely then the Arab turns,
Snatches the gift, and drops and spurns.
  As down now from the crag they wend   90
Reverted glance see Clarel lend:
Thou guest of Death, which in his house
Sleep'st nightly, mayst thou not espouse
His daughter, Peace?
      Aslant they come
Where, hid in shadow of the rocks,   95
Stone steps descend unto Siloam.
Proof to the fervid noon-day tide
Reflected from the glen's steep side,
Moist ledge with ledge here interlocks,
Vaulting a sunken grotto deep.   100
  Down there, as quiet as in sleep,
Anew the stranger they descried
Sitting upon a step full low,
Watching the fountain's troubled tide

Which after ebb began to flow,   105
Gurgling from viewless caves. The lull
Broke by the flood is wonderful.
Science explains it. Bides no less
The true, innate mysteriousness.
Through him there might the vision flit   110
Of angel in Bethesda's pool
With porches five, so troubling it
That whoso bathed then was made whole?
Or, by an equal dream beguiled,
Did he but list the fountain moan   115
Like Ammon's in the Libyan wild,
For muse and oracle both gone?
      By chance a jostled pebble there
Slipped from the surface down the stair.
It jarred—it broke the brittle spell: 120
Siloam was but a rural well.

      Clarel who could again but shun
To obtrude on the secluded one,
Turned to depart.—"Ere yet we go,"
Said Nehemiah, "I will below: 125
Dim be mine eyes, more dim they grow:
I'll wash them in these waters cool,
As did the blind the Master sent,
And who came seeing from this pool;"
And down the grotto-stairs he went.   130
      The stranger, just ascending, stood;
And, as the votary laved his eyes,
He marked, looked up, and Clarel viewed,
And they exchanged quick sympathies
Though but in glance, moved by that act   135
Of one whose faith transfigured fact.
A bond seemed made between them there;
And presently the trio fare
Over Kedron, and in one accord
Of quietude and chastened tone   140
Approach the spot, tradition's own,
For ages held the garden of Our Lord.

29. THE RECLUSE

Ere yet they win that verge and line,
Reveal the stranger. Name him—Vine.
His home to tell—kin, tribe, estate—
Would naught avail. Alighting grow,
As on the tree the mistletoe,   5
All gifts unique. In seeds of fate
Borne on the winds these emigrate
And graft the stock.
            Vine's manner shy
A clog, a hindrance might imply;
A lack of parlor-wont. But grace   10
Which is in substance deep and grain
May, peradventure, well pass by
The polish of veneer. No trace
Of passion's soil or lucre's stain,
Though life was now half ferried o'er.   15
If use he served not, but forbore—
Such indolence might still but pine
In dearth of rich incentive high:
Apollo slave in Mammon's mine?
Better Admetus' shepherd lie.   20
    A charm of subtle virtue shed
A personal influence coveted,
Whose source was difficult to tell
As ever was that perfumed spell
Of Paradise-flowers invisible   25
Which angels round Cecilia bred.
    A saint then do we here unfold?
Nay, the ripe flush, Venetian mould
Evinced no nature saintly fine,
But blood like swart Vesuvian wine.   30
What cooled the current? Under cheer
Of opulent softness, reigned austere
Control of self. Flesh, but scarce pride,
Was curbed: desire was mortified;
But less indeed by moral sway   35
Than doubt if happiness thro' clay

Be reachable. No sackclothed man;
Howbeit, in sort Carthusian
Tho' born a Sybarite. And yet
Not beauty might he all forget,   40
The beauty of the world, and charm:
He prized it tho' it scarce might warm.
    Like to the nunnery's denizen
His virgin soul communed with men
But thro' the wicket. Was it clear   45
This coyness bordered not on fear—
Fear or an apprehensive sense?
Not wholly seemed it diffidence
Recluse. Nor less did strangely wind
Ambiguous elfishness behind   50
All that: an Ariel unknown.
It seemed his very speech in tone
Betrayed disuse. Thronged streets astir
To Vine but ampler cloisters were.
Cloisters? No monk he was, allow;   55
But gleamed the richer for the shade
About him, as in sombre glade
Of Virgil's wood the Sibyl's Golden Bough.

30. The Site of the Passion

And wherefore by the convents be
Gardens? Ascetics roses twine?
Nay, but there is a memory.
Within a garden walking see
The angered God. And where the vine   5
And olive in the darkling hours
Inweave green sepulchers of bowers—
Who, to defend us from despair,
Pale undergoes the passion there
In solitude? Yes, memory   10
Links Eden and Gethsemane;

So that not meaningless in sway
Gardens adjoin the convents gray.

On Salem's hill in Solomon's years
Of gala, O the happy town!　　　　　　　　　15
In groups the people sauntered down,
And, Kedron crossing, lightly wound
Where now the tragic grove appears,
Then palmy, and a pleasure-ground.

The student and companions win　　　　　　20
The wicket—pause, and enter in.
By roots strapped down in fold on fold—
Gnarled into wens and knobs and knees—
In olives, monumental trees,
The Pang's survivors they behold.　　　　　　25
A wizened blue fruit drops from them,
Nipped harvest of Jerusalem.
Wistful here Clarel turned toward Vine,
And would have spoken; but as well
Hail Dathan swallowed in the mine—　　　　30
Tradition, legend, lent such spell
And rapt him in remoteness so.
　　Meanwhile, in shade the olives throw,
Nehemiah pensive sat him down
And turned the chapter in St John.　　　　　35
　　What frame of mind may Clarel woo?
He the night-scene in picture drew—
The band which came for sinless blood
With swords and staves, a multitude.
They brush the twigs, small birds take wing,　40
The dead boughs crackle, lanterns swing,
Till lo, they spy them thro' the wood.
"Master!"—'Tis Judas. Then the kiss.
And He, He falters not at this—
Speechless, unspeakably submiss:　　　　　45
The fulsome serpent on the cheek
Sliming: endurance more than meek—

Endurance of the fraud foreknown,
And fiend-heart in the human one.
Ah, now the pard on Clarel springs: 50
The Passion's narrative plants stings.
    To break away, he turns and views
The white-haired under olive bowed
Immersed in Scripture; and he woos—
"Whate'er the chapter, read aloud."   55
The saint looked up, but with a stare
Absent and wildered, vacant there.
    As part to kill time, part for task
Some shepherd old pores over book—
Shelved farm-book of his life forepast   60
When he bestirred him and amassed;
If chance one interrupt, and ask—
What read you? he will turn a look
Which shows he knows not what he reads,
Or knowing, he but weary heeds,   65
Or scarce remembers; here much so
With Nehemiah, dazed out and low.
And presently—to intercept—
Over Clarel, too, strange numbness crept.
    A monk, custodian of the ground,   70
Drew nigh, and showed him by the steep
The rock or legendary mound
Where James and Peter fell asleep.
Dully the pilgrim scanned the spot,
Nor spake.—"Signor, and think'st thou not   75
'Twas sorrow brought their slumber on?
St. Luke avers no sluggard rest:
Nay, but excess of feeling pressed
Till ache to apathy was won."
To Clarel 'twas no hollow word.   80
Experience did proof afford.
For Vine, aloof he loitered—shrunk
In privity and shunned the monk.
Clarel awaited him. He came—
The shadow of his previous air   85
Merged in a settled neutral frame—

Assumed, may be. Would Vine disclaim
All sympathy the youth might share?

    About to leave, they turn to look
For him but late estranged in book: 90
Asleep he lay; the face bent down
Viewless between the crossing arms,
One slack hand on the good book thrown
In peace that every care becharms.
Then died the shadow off from Vine: 95
A spirit seemed he not unblest
As here he made a quiet sign
Unto the monk: Spare to molest;
Let this poor dreamer take his rest,
His fill of rest.
               But now at stand   100
Who there alertly glances up
By grotto of the Bitter Cup—
Spruce, and with volume light in hand
Bound smartly, late in reference scanned?
Inquisitive Philistine: lo,   105
Tourists replace the pilgrims so.
    At peep of that brisk dapper man
Over Vine's face a ripple ran
Of freakish mockery, elfin light;
Whereby what thing may Clarel see?   110
O angels, rescue from the sight!
Paul Pry? and in Gethsemane?
He shrunk the thought of it to fan;
Nor liked the freak in Vine that threw
Such a suggestion into view;   115
Nor less it hit that fearful man.

31. ROLFE

The hill above the garden here
They rove; and chance ere long to meet
A second stranger, keeping cheer

Apart. Trapper or pioneer
He looked, astray in Judah's seat—   5
Or one who might his business ply
On waters under tropic sky.
Perceiving them as they drew near,
He rose, removed his hat to greet,
Disclosing so in shapely sphere   10
A marble brow over face embrowned:
So Sunium by her fane is crowned.
One read his superscription clear—
A genial heart, a brain austere—
And further, deemed that such a man   15
Though given to study, as might seem,
Was no scholastic partisan
Or euphonist of Academe,
But supplemented Plato's theme
With dædal life in boats and tents,   20
A messmate of the elements;
And yet, more bronzed in face than mind,
Sensitive still and frankly kind—
Too frank, too unreserved, may be,
And indiscreet in honesty.   25
      But what implies the tinge of soil—
Like tarnish on Pizarro's spoil,
Precious in substance rudely wrought,
Peruvian plate—which here is caught?
What means this touch of the untoward   30
In aspect hinting nothing froward?

      From Baalbec, for a new sojourn,
To Jewry Rolfe had made return;
To Jewry's inexhausted shore
Of barrenness, where evermore   35
Some lurking thing he hoped to gain—
Slip quite behind the parrot-lore
Conventional, and——what attain?
      Struck by each clear or latent sign
Expressive in the stranger's air,   40
The student glanced from him to Vine:

Peers, peers—yes, needs that these must pair.
Clarel was young. In promise fine,
To him here first were brought together
Exceptional natures, of a weather   45
Strange as the tropics with strange trees,
Strange birds, strange fishes, skies and seas,
To one who in some meager land
His bread wins by the horny hand.
What now may hap? what outcome new   50
Elicited by contact true—
Frank, cordial contact of the twain?
Crude wonderment, and proved but vain.
If average mortals social be,
And yet but seldom truly meet,   55
Closing like halves of apple sweet—
How with the rarer in degree?
      The informal salutation done,
Vine into his dumb castle went—
Not as all parley he would shun,   60
But looking down from battlement,
Ready, if need were, to accord
Reception to the other's word,—
Nay, far from wishing to decline,
And neutral not without design,   65
May be.—
              "Look, by Christ's belfry set,
Appears the Moslem minaret!"
So—to fill trying pause alone—
Cried Rolfe; and o'er the deep defile
Of Kedron, pointed toward the Town,   70
Where, thronged about by many a pile
Monastic, but no vernal bower,
The Saracen shaft and Norman tower
In truce stand guard beside that Dome
Which canopies the Holy's home: 75
"The tower looks lopped; it shows forlorn—
A stunted oak whose crown is shorn;
But see, palm-like the minaret stands
Superior, and the tower commands."

"Yon shaft," said Clarel, "seems ill-placed."   80
"Ay, *seems;* but 'tis for memory based.
The story's known: how Omar there
After the town's surrender meek—
Hallowed to him, as dear to Greek—
Clad in his clouts of camel's hair,   85
And with the Patriarch robed and fine
Walking beneath the dome divine,
When came the Islam hour for prayer
Declined to use the carpet good
Spread for him in the church, but stood   90
Without, even yonder where is set
The monumental minaret;
And, earnest in true suppliance cried,
Smiting his chest: 'Me overrule!
Allah, to me be merciful!'   95
'Twas little shared he victor-pride
Though victor. So the church he saved
Of purpose from that law engraved
Which prompt transferred to Allah sole
Each fane where once his rite might roll.   100
Long afterward, the town being stormed
By Christian knights, how ill conformed
The butchery then to Omar's prayer
And heart magnanimous. But spare."

Response they looked; and thence he warmed: 105
"Yon gray Cathedral of the Tomb,
Who reared it first? a woman weak,
A second Mary, first to seek
In pagan darkness which had come,
The place where they had laid the Lord: 110
Queen Helena, she traced the site,
And cleared the ground, and made it bright
With all that zeal could then afford.
But Constantine—there falls the blight!
The mother's warm emotional heart,   115
Subserved it still the son's cold part?
Even he who, timing well the tide,

Laced not the Cross upon Rome's flag
Supreme, till Jove began to lag
Behind the new religion's stride.   120
And Helena—ah, may it be
The saint herself not quite was free
From that which in the years bygone,
Made certain stately dames of France,
Such as the fair De Maintenon,   125
To string their rosaries of pearl,
And found brave chapels—sweet romance:
Coquetry of the borrowed curl?—
You let me prate."
           "Nay, nay—go on,"
Cried Clarel, yet in such a tone   130
It showed disturbance.—
            "Laud the dame:
Her church, admit, no doom it fears.
Unquelled by force of battering years—
Years, years and sieges, sword and flame;
Fallen—rebuilt, to fall anew;   135
By armies shaken, earthquake too;
Lo, it abides—if not the same,
In self-same spot. Last time 'twas burnt
The Rationalist a lesson learnt.
But you know all."—
          "Nay, not the end,"   140
Said Vine. And Clarel, "We attend."
  "Well, on the morrow never shrunk
From wonted rite the steadfast monk,
Though hurt and even maimed were some
By crash of the ignited dome.   145
Staunch stood the walls. As friars profess
(And not in fraud) the central cell—
Christ's tomb and faith's last citadel—
The flames did tenderly caress,
Nor harm; while smoking, smouldering beams,   150
Fallen across, lent livid gleams
To Golgotha. But none the less
In robed procession of his God

The mitred one the cinders trod;
Before the calcined altar there   155
The host he raised; and hymn and prayer
Went up from ashes. These, ere chill,
Away were brushed; and trowel shrill
And hod and hammer came in place.
'Tis now some three score years ago.   160
   "In Lima's first convulsion so,
When shock on shock had left slim trace
Of hundred temples; and—in mood
Of malice dwelling on the face
Itself has tortured and subdued   165
To uncomplaint—the cloud pitch-black
Lowered o'er the rubbish; and the land
Not less than sea, did countermand
Her buried corses—heave them back;
And flocks and men fled on the track   170
Which wins the Andes; then went forth
The prelate with intrepid train
Rolling the anthem 'mid the rain
Of ashes white. In rocking plain
New boundaries staked they, south and north,   175
For ampler piles. These stand. In cheer
The priest reclaimed the quaking sphere.
Hold it he shall, so long as spins
This star of tragedies, this orb of sins."
   "That," Clarel said, "is not my mind.   180
Rome's priest forever rule the world?"
   "The priest, I said. Though some be hurled
From anchor, nor a haven find;
Not less religion's ancient port,
Till the crack of doom, shall be resort   185
In stress of weather for mankind.
Yea, long as children feel affright
In darkness, men shall fear a God;
And long as daisies yield delight
Shall see His footprints in the sod.   190
Is't ignorance? This ignorant state
Science doth but elucidate—

Deepen, enlarge. But though 'twere made
Demonstrable that God is not—
What then? it would not change this lot: 195
The ghost would haunt, nor could be laid."
    Intense he spake, his eyes of blue
Altering, and to eerie hue,
Like Tyrrhene seas when overcast;
The which Vine noted, nor in joy,   200
Inferring thence an ocean-waste
Of earnestness without a buoy:
An inference which afterward
Acquaintance led him to discard
Or modify, or not employ.   205
    Clarel ill-relished.
                Rolfe, in tone
Half elegiac, thus went on:
"Phylæ, upon thy sacred ground
Osiris' broken tomb is found:
A god how good, whose good proved vain—   210
In strife with bullying Python slain.
For long the ritual chant or moan
Of pilgrims by that mystic stone
Went up, even much as now ascend
The liturgies of yearning prayer   215
To one who met a kindred end—
Christ, tombed in turn, and worshiped *there,*"
And pointed.—"Hint you," here asked Vine,
"In Christ Osiris met decline
Anew?"—"Nay, nay; and yet, past doubt,   220
Strange is that text St. Matthew won
From gray Hosea in sentence: *Out*
Of Egypt have I called my son."
    Here Clarel spake, and with a stir
Not all assured in eager plight: 225
"But does not Matthew there refer
Only to the return from flight,
Flight into Egypt?"—"May be so,"
Said Rolfe; "but then Hosea?—Nay,
We'll let it pass."—And fell delay   230

Of talk; they mused.—
                              "To Cicero,"
Rolfe sudden said, "is a long way
From Matthew; yet somehow he comes
To mind here—he and his fine tomes,
Which (change the gods) would serve to read   235
For modern essays. And indeed
His age was much like ours: doubt ran,
Faith flagged; negations which sufficed
Lawyer, priest, statesman, gentleman,
Not yet being popularly prized,   240
The augurs hence retained some state—
Which served for the illiterate.
Still, the decline so swiftly ran
From stage to stage, that *To Believe,*
Except for slave or artisan,   245
Seemed heresy. Even doubts which met
Horror at first, grew obsolete,
And in a decade. To bereave
Of founded trust in Sire Supreme,
Was a vocation. Sophists throve—   250
Each weaving his thin thread of dream
Into the shroud for Numa's Jove.
Cæsar his atheism avowed
Before the Senate. But why crowd
Examples here: the gods were gone.   255
Tully scarce dreamed they could be won
Back into credence; less that earth
Ever could know yet mightier birth
Of deity. He died. Christ came.
And, in due hour, that impious Rome,   260
Emerging from vast wreck and shame,
Held the fore front of Christendom.
The inference? the lesson?—come:
Let fools count on faith's closing knell—
Time, God, are inexhaustible.—   265
But what? so earnest? ay, again."
     "Hard for a fountain to refrain,"
Breathed Vine. Was that but irony?

At least no envy in the strain.
Rolfe scarce remarked, or let go by.   270
    For Clarel—when ye, meeting, scan
In waste the Bagdad caravan,
And solitude puts on the stir,
Clamor, dust, din of Nineveh,
As horsemen, camels, footmen all,   275
Soldier and merchant, free and thrall,
Pour by in tide processional;
So to the novice streamed along
Rolfe's filing thoughts, a wildering throng.
Their sway he owned. And yet how Vine—   280
Who breathed few words, or gave dumb sign—
Him more allured, suggestive more
Of choicer treasure, rarer store
Reserved, like Kidd's doubloons long sought
Without the wand.
                    The ball of thought   285
And chain yet dragging, on they strained
Oblique along the upland—slow
And mute, until a point they gained
Where devotees will pause, and know
A tenderness, may be. Here then,   290
While tarry now these pilgrim men,
The interval let be assigned
A niche for image of a novel mind.

32. Of Rama

That Rama whom the Indian sung—
A god he was, but knew it not;
Hence vainly puzzled at the wrong
Misplacing him in human lot.
Curtailment of his right he bare   5
Rather than wrangle; but no less
Was taunted for his tameness there.
A fugitive without redress,
He never the Holy Spirit grieved,

Nor the divine in him bereaved,   10
Though what that was he might not guess.

    Live they who, like to Rama, led
Unspotted from the world aside,
Like Rama are discredited—
Like him, in outlawry abide?   15
May life and fable so agree?—
    The innocent if lawless elf,
Etherial in virginity,
Retains the consciousness of self.
Though black frost nip, though white frost chill,   20
Nor white frost nor the black may kill
The patient root, the vernal sense
Surviving hard experience
As grass the winter. Even that curse
Which is the wormwood mixed with gall—   25
Better dependent on the worse—
Divine upon the animal—
That can not make such natures fall.
    Though yielding easy rein, indeed,
To impulse which the fibers breed,   30
Nor quarreling with indolence;
Shall these the cup of grief dispense
Deliberate to any heart?
Not craft they know, nor envy's smart.
Theirs be the thoughts that dive and skim,   35
Theirs the spiced tears that overbrim,
And theirs the dimple and the lightsome whim.
    Such natures, and but such, have got
Familiar with strange things that dwell
Repressed in mortals; and they tell   40
Of riddles in the prosiest lot.
    Mince ye some matter for faith's sake
And heaven's good name? 'Tis these shall make
Revolt there, and the gloss disclaim.
    They con the page kept down with those   45
Which Adam's secret frame disclose,
And Eve's; nor dare dissent from truth
Although disreputable, sooth.

The riches in them be a store
Unmerchantable in the ore.   50
No matter: "'Tis an open mine:
Dig; find ye gold, why, make it thine.
The shrewder knack hast thou, the gift:
Smelt then, and mold, and good go with thy thrift."

    Was ever earth-born wight like this?   55
Ay—in the verse, may be, he is.

33. BY THE STONE

Over against the Temple here
A monastery unrestored—
Named from Prediction of Our Lord—
Crumbled long since. Outlying near,
Some stones remain, which seats afford: 5
And one, the fond traditions state,
Is that whereon the Saviour sate
And prophesied, and sad became
To think, what, under sword and flame,
The proud Jerusalem should be,   10
Then spread before him sunnily—
Pillars and palms—the white, the green—
Marble enfoliaged, a fair scene;
But *now*—a vision here conferred
Pale as Pompeii disinterred.   15

    Long Rolfe, on knees his elbows resting
And head enlocked in hands upright,
Sat facing it in steadfast plight
And brooded on that town slow wasting.
"And here," he said, "here did He sit—   20
In leafy covert, say—*Beheld*
The city, and wept over it:
Luke's words, and hard to be excelled,
So just the brief expression there:
Truth's rendering."—With earnest air,   25
More he threw out, in kind the same,

The which did Clarel ponder still;
For though the words might frankness claim,
With reverence for site and name;
No further went they, nor could fill   30
Faith's measure—scarce her dwindled gill
Now standard. On the plain of Troy
(Mused Clarel) as one might look down
From Gargarus with quiet joy
In verifying Homer's sites,   35
Yet scarce believe in Venus' crown
And rescues in those Trojan fights
Whereby she saved her supple son;
So Rolfe regards from these wan heights
Yon walls and slopes to Christians dear.   40
Much it annoyed him and perplexed:
Than free concession so sincere—
Concession due both site and text—
Dissent itself would less appear
To imply negation.
                        But anon   45
They mark in groups, hard by the gate
Which overlooks Jehoshaphat,
Some Hebrew people of the town.
"Who marvels that outside they come
Since few within have seemly home,"   50
Said Rolfe; "they chat there on the seats,
But seldom gossip in their streets.
Who here may see a busy one?
Where's naught to do not much is done.
How live they then? what bread can be?   55
In almost every country known
Rich Israelites these kinsmen own:
The hat goes round the world. But see!"
    Moved by his words, their eyes more reach
Toward that dull group. Dwarfed in the dream   60
Of distance sad, penguins they seem
Drawn up on Patagonian beach.

    "O city," Rolfe cried; "house on moor,
With shutters burst and blackened door—

Like that thou showest; and the gales 65
Still round thee blow the Banshee-wails:
Well might the priest in temple start,
Hearing the voice—'*Woe, we depart!*' "

    Clarel gave ear, albeit his glance
Diffident skimmed Vine's countenance, 70
As mainly here he interest took
In all the fervid speaker said,
Reflected in the mute one's look:
A face indeed quite overlaid
With tremulous meanings, which evade 75
Or shun regard, nay, hardly brook
Fraternal scanning.
              Rolfe went on:
"The very natives of the town
Methinks would turn from it and flee
But for that curse which is its crown— 80
That curse which clogs so, poverty.
See them, but see yon cowering men:
The brood—the brood without the hen!"—

    "City, that dost the prophets stone,
How oft against the judgment dread, 85
How often would I fain have spread
My wings to cover thee, mine own;
And ye would not! Had'st thou but known
The things which to thy peace belong!"
    Nehemiah it was, rejoining them— 90
Gray as the old Jerusalem
Over which how earnestly he hung.
But him the seated audience scan
As he were sole surviving man
Of tribe extinct or world. The ray 95
Which lit his features, died away;
He flagged; and, as some trouble moved,
Apart and aimlessly he roved.

34. They Tarry

"How solitary on the hill
Sitteth the city; and how still—
How still!" From Vine the murmur came—
A cadence, as it were compelled
Even by the picture's silent claim.   5
That said, again his peace he held,
Biding, as in a misty rain
Some motionless lone fisherman
By mountain brook. But Rolfe: "Thy word
Is Jeremiah's, and here well heard.   10
Ay, seer of Anathoth, behold,
Yon object tallies with thy text.
How then? Stays reason quite unvexed?
Fulfillment here but falleth cold.
That stable proof which man would fold,   15
How may it be derived from things
Subject to change and vanishings?
But let that pass. All now's revised:
Zion, like Rome, is Niebuhrized.
Yes, doubt attends. Doubt's heavy hand   20
Is set against us; and his brand
Still warreth for his natural lord—
King Common-Place—whose rule abhorred
Yearly extends in vulgar sway,
Absorbs Atlantis and Cathay;   25
Ay, reaches toward Diana's moon,
Affirming it a clinkered blot,
Deriding pale Endymion.
Since thus he aims to level all,
The Milky Way he'll yet allot   30
For Appian to his Capital.
Then tell, tell then, what charm may save
Thy marvel, Palestine, from grave
Whereto winds many a bier and pall
Of old Illusion? What for earth?   35
Ah, change irreverent,—at odds
With goodly customs, gracious gods;

New things elate so thrust their birth
Up through dejection of the old,
As through dead sheaths; is here foretold   40
The consummation of the past,
And gairish dawning of a day
Whose noon not saints desire to stay—
And hardly I? Who brake love's fast
With Christ—with what strange lords may sup?   45
The reserves of time seem marching up.
But, nay: what novel thing may be,
No germ being new? By Fate's decree
Have not earth's vitals heaved in change
Repeated? some wild element   50
Or action been evolved? the range
Of surface split? the deeps unpent?
Continents in God's caldrons cast?
And this without effecting so
The neutralizing of the past,   55
Whose rudiments persistent flow,
From age to age transmitting, own,
The evil with the good—the taint
Deplored in Solomon's complaint.
Fate's pot of ointment! Wilt have done,   60
Lord of the fly, god of the grub?
Need'st foul all sweets, thou Beelzebub?"

    He ended.—To evade or lay
Deductions hard for tender clay,
Clarel recalled each prior word   65
Of Rolfe which scarcely kept accord,
As seemed, with much dropped latterly.
For Vine, he twitched from ground a weed,
Apart then picked it, seed by seed.
    Ere long they rise, and climbing greet   70
A thing preëminent in seat,
Whose legend still can touch the heart:
It prompted one there to impart
A chapter of the Middle Age—
Which next to give. But let the page   75

The narrator's rambling way forget,
And make to run in even flow
His interrupted tale. And let
Description brief the site foreshow.

35. ARCULF AND ADAMNAN

In spot revered by myriad men,
Whence, as alleged, Immanuel rose
Into the heaven—receptive then—
A little plastered tower is set,
Pale in the light that Syria knows,   5
Upon the peak of Olivet.
'Tis modern—a replacement, note,
For ample pile of years remote,
Nor yet ill suits in dwindled bound,
Man's faith retrenched. 'Twas Hakeem's deed,   10
Mad Caliph (founder still of creed
Long held by tribes not unrenowned)
Who erst the pastoral hight discrowned
Of Helena's church. Woe for the dome,
And many a goodly temple more,   15
Which hither lured from Christendom
The child-like pilgrim throngs of yore.
'Twas of that church, so brave erewhile—
Blest land-mark on the Olive Hight—
Which Arculf told of in the isle   20
Iona. Shipwrecked there in sight,
The palmer dragged they from the foam,
The Culdees of the abbey fair—
Him shelter yielding and a home.
In guerdon for which love and care   25
Received in Saint Columba's pile,
With travel-talk he did beguile
Their eve of Yule.
                    The tempest beat;
It shook the abbey's founded seat,
Rattling the crucifix on wall;   30

And thrice was heard the clattering fall
Of gable-tiles. But host and guest,
Abbot and palmer, took their rest
Inside monastic ingle tall.
What unto them were those lashed seas?   35
Or Patmos or the Hebrides,
The isles were God's.
                It was the time
The church in Jewry dwelt at ease
Tho' under Arabs—Omar's prime—
Penultimate of pristine zeal,   40
While yet throughout faith's commonweal
The tidings had not died away—
Not yet had died into dismay
Of dead, dead echoes that recede:
Glad tidings of great joy indeed,   45
Thrilled to the shepherds on the sward—
"Behold, to you is born this day
A Saviour, which is Christ the Lord;"
While yet in chapel, altar, shrine,
The mica in the marble new   50
Glistened like spangles of the dew.
One minster then was Palestine,
All monumental.
              Arculf first
The wonders of the tomb rehearsed,
And Golgotha; then told of trees,   55
Olives, which in the twilight breeze
Sighed plaintive by the convent's lee—
The convent in Gethsemane—
Perished long since. Then: "On the hill—
In site revealed thro' Jesu's grace"—   60
(Hereat both cross themselves apace)
"A great round church with goodly skill
Is nobly built; and fragrant blows
Morning thro' triple porticoes.
But over that blest place where meet   65
The last prints of the Wounded Feet,
The roof is open to the sky;

'Tis there the sparrows love to fly.
Upon Ascension Day—at end
Of mass—winds, vocal winds descend   70
Among the worshipers." Amain
The abbot signs the cross again;
And Arculf on: "And all that night
The mountain temple's western flank—
The same which fronts Moriah's hight—   75
In memory of the Apostles' light
Shows twelve dyed fires in oriels twelve.
Thither, from towers on Kedron's bank
And where the slope and terrace shelve,
The gathered townsfolk gaze afar;   80
And those twelve flowers of flame suffuse
Their faces with reflected hues
Of violet, gold, and cinnabar.
Much so from Naples (in our sail
We touched there, shipping jar and bale)   85
I saw Vesuvius' plume of fire
Redden the bay, tinge mast and spire.
But on Ascension Eve, 'tis then
A light shows—kindled not by men.
Look," pointing to the hearth; "dost see   90
How these dun embers here by me,
Lambent are licked by flaky flame?
Olivet gleams then much the same—
Caressed, curled over, yea, encurled
By fleecy fires which typic be: 95
O lamb of God, O light o' the world!"
     In fear, and yet a fear divine,
Once more the Culdee made the sign;
Then fervid snatched the palmer's hand—
Clung to it like a very child   100
Thrilled by some wondrous story wild
Of elf or fay, nor could command
His eyes to quit their gaze at him—
Him who had seen it. But how grim
The Pictish storm-king sang refrain,   105

Scoffing about those gables high
Over Arculf and good Adamnan.

The abbot and the palmer rest:
The legends follow them and die—
Those legends which, be it confessed,   110
Did nearer bring to them the sky—
Did nearer woo it to their hope
Of all that seers and saints avow—
Than Galileo's telescope
Can bid it unto prosing Science now.   115

36. THE TOWER

The tower they win. Some Greeks at hand,
Pilgrims, in silence view the land.
One family group in listless tone
Are just in act of faring down.
All leave at last. And these remain   5
As by a hearthstone on the plain
When roof is gone. But can they shame
To tell the evasive thought within?
Does intellect assert a claim
Against the heart, her yielding kin?   10
    But he, the wanderer, the while—
See him; and what may so beguile?
Images he the ascending Lord
Pale as the moon which dawn may meet,
Convoyed by a serene accord   15
And swoon of faces young and sweet—
Mid chaplets, stars, and halcyon wings,
And many ministering things?
    As him they mark enkindled so,
What inklings, negatives, they know!   20
But leaving him in silence due,
They enter there, the print to view—
Affirmed of Christ—the parting foot:

They mark it, nor a question moot;
Next climb the stair and win the roof;   25
Thence on Jerusalem look down,
And Kedron cringing by the town,
Whose stony lanes map-like were shown.
      "Is yon the city Dis aloof?"
Said Rolfe; "nay, liker 'tis some print,   30
Old blurred, bewrinkled mezzotint.
And distant, look, what lifeless hills!
Dead long for them the hymn of rills
And birds. Nor trees, nor ferns they know;
Nor lichen there hath leave to grow   35
In baleful glens which blacked the blood
O' the son of Kish."
                        Far peep they gain
Of waters which in caldron brood,
Sunk mid the mounts of leaden bane:
The Sodom Wave, or Putrid Sea,   40
Or Sea of Salt, or Cities Five,
Or Lot's, or Death's, Asphaltite,
Or Asafœtida; all these
Being names indeed with which they gyve
That site of foul iniquities   45
Abhorred.
            With wordless look intent,
As if the scene confirmed some thought
Which in heart's lonelier hour was lent,
Vine stood at gaze. The rest were wrought
According unto kind. The Mount   50
Of Olives, and, in distance there
The charnel wave—who may recount?
Hope's hill descries the pit Despair:
Flitted the thought; they nothing said;
And down they drew. As ground they tread,   55
Nehemiah met them: "Pleaseth ye,
Fair stroll awaits; if all agree,
Over the hill let us go on—
Bethany is a pleasant town.
I'll lead, for well the way I know."   60

He gazed expectant: Would they go?
Before that simpleness so true
Vine showed embarrassed (Clarel too)
Yet thanked him with a grateful look
Benign; and Rolfe the import took,   65
And whispered him in softened key,
"Some other day."
                And might it be
Such influence their spirits knew
From all the tower had given to view,
Untuned they felt for Bethany?   70

37. A SKETCH

Not knowing them in very heart,
Nor why to join him they were loth,
He, disappointed, moved apart,
With sad pace creeping, dull, as doth
Along the bough the nerveless sloth.   5

   For ease upon the ground they sit;
And Rolfe, with eye still following
Where Nehemiah slow footed it,
Asked Clarel: "Know you anything
Of this man's prior life at all?"   10
"Nothing," said Clarel.—"I recall,"
Said Rolfe, "a mariner like him."
"A mariner?"—"Yes; one whom grim
Disaster made as meek as he
There plodding." Vine here showed the zest   15
Of a deep human interest:
"We crave of you his history."
   And Rolfe began: "Scarce would I tell
Of what this mariner befell—
So much is it with cloud o'ercast—   20
Were he not now gone home at last
Into the green land of the dead,
Where he encamps and peace is shed.

Hardy he was, sanguine and bold,
The master of a ship. His mind   25
In night-watch frequent he unrolled—
As seamen sometimes are inclined—
On serious topics, to his mate,
A man to creed austere resigned.
The master ever spurned at fate,   30
Calvin's or Zeno's. Always still
Man-like he stood by man's free will
And power to effect each thing he would,
Did reason but pronounce it good.
The subaltern held in humble way   35
That still heaven's over-rulings sway
Will and event.
                    "On waters far,
Where map-man never made survey,
Gliding along in easy plight,
The strong one brake the lull of night   40
Emphatic in his willful war—
But staggered, for there came a jar
With fell arrest to keel and speech:
A hidden rock. The pound—the grind—
Collapsing sails o'er deck declined—   45
Sleek billows curling in the breach,
And nature with her neutral mind.
A wreck. 'Twas in the former days,
Those waters then obscure; a maze;
The isles were dreaded—every chain;   50
Better to brave the immense of sea,
And venture for the Spanish Main,
Beating and rowing against the trades,
Than float to valleys 'neath the lee,
Nor far removed, and palmy shades.   55
So deemed he, strongly erring there.
To boats they take; the weather fair—
Never the sky a cloudlet knew;
A temperate wind unvarying blew
Week after week; yet came despair;   60
The bread tho' doled, and water stored,

Ran low and lower—ceased. They burn—
They agonize till crime abhorred
Lawful might be. O trade-wind, turn!
　　"Well may some items sleep unrolled—   65
Never by the one survivor told.
Him they picked up, where, cuddled down,
They saw the jacketed skeleton,
Lone in the only boat that lived—
His signal frittered to a shred.   70
　　" 'Strong need'st thou be,' the rescuers said,
'Who has such trial sole survived.'
'I *willed* it,' gasped he. And the man,
Renewed ashore, pushed off again.
How bravely sailed the pennoned ship   75
Bound outward on her sealing trip
Antarctic. Yes; but who returns
Too soon, regaining port by land
Who left it by the bay? What spurns
Were his that so could countermand?   80
Nor mutineer, nor rock, nor gale
Nor leak had foiled him. No; a whale
Of purpose aiming, stove the bow:
They foundered. To the master now
Owners and neighbors all impute   85
An inauspiciousness. His wife—
Gentle, but unheroic—she,
Poor thing, at heart knew bitter strife
Between her love and her simplicity:
A Jonah is he?—And men bruit   90
The story. None will give him place
In a third venture. Came the day
Dire need constrained the man to pace
A night patrolman on the quay
Watching the bales till morning hour   95
Through fair and foul. Never he smiled;
Call him, and he would come; not sour
In spirit, but meek and reconciled;
Patient he was, he none withstood;
Oft on some secret thing would brood.   100

He ate what came, though but a crust;
In Calvin's creed he put his trust;
Praised heaven, and said that God was good,
And his calamity but just.
So Silvio Pellico from cell-door   105
Forth tottering, after dungeoned years,
Crippled and bleached, and dead his peers:
'Grateful, I thank the Emperor.' "

  There ceasing, after pause Rolfe drew
Regard to Nehemiah in view: 110
"Look, the changed master, roams he there?
I mean, is such the guise, the air?"
  The speaker sat between mute Vine
And Clarel. From the mystic sea
Laocoon's serpent, sleek and fine,   115
In loop on loop seemed here to twine
His clammy coils about the three.
Then unto them the wannish man
Draws nigh; but absently they scan;
A phantom seems he, and from zone   120
Where naught is real tho' the winds aye moan.

38. THE SPARROW

After the hint by Rolfe bestowed,
Redoubled import, one may ween,
Had Nehemiah's submissive mien
For Clarel. Nay, his poor abode—
And thither now the twain repair—   5
A new significance might bear.
  Thin grasses, such as sprout in sand,
Clarel observes in crannies old
Along the cornice. Not his hand
The mower fills with such, nor arms   10
Of him that binds the sheaf, enfold.
Now mid the quiet which becharms

That mural wilderness remote,
Querulous came the little note
Of bird familiar—one of them   15
So numerous in Jerusalem,
Still snared for market, it is told,
And two were for a farthing sold—
The sparrow. But this single one
Plaining upon a terrace nigh,   20
Was like the Psalmist's making moan
For loss of mate—forsaken quite,
Which on the house-top doth alight
And watches, and her lonely cry
No answer gets.—In sunny hight   25
Like dotting bees against the sky
What twitterers o'er the temple fly!
    But now the arch and stair they gain,
And in the chamber sit the twain.
Clarel in previous time secure,   30
From Nehemiah had sought to lure
Some mention of his life, but failed.
Rolfe's hintful story so prevailed,
Anew he thought to venture it.
But while in so much else aside   35
Subject to senile lapse of tide,
In this hid matter of his past
The saint evinced a guardful wit;
His waning energies seemed massed
Here, and but here, to keep the door.   40
At present his reserve of brow
Reproach in such sort did avow,
That Clarel never pressed him more.
Nay, fearing lest he trespass might
Even in tarrying longer now,   45
He parted. As he slow withdrew,
Well pleased he noted in review
The hermitage improved in plight.
    Some one had done a friendly thing:
Who? Small was Clarel's wondering.   50

39. CLAREL AND RUTH

In northern clime how tender show
The meads beneath heaven's humid Bow
When showers draw off and dew-drops cling
To sunset's skirt, and robins sing
Though night be near. So did the light   5
Of love redeem in Ruth the trace
Of grief, though scarce might it efface.
    From wider rambles which excite
The thought, or study's lone repose,
Daily did Clarel win the close.   10
With interest feminine and true
The matron watched that love which grew;
She hailed it, since a hope was there
Made brighter for the grief's degree:
How shines the gull ye watch in air   15
White, white, against the cloud at sea.
    Clarel, bereft while still but young,
Mother or sister had not known;
To him now first in life was shown,
In Agar's frank demeanor kind,   20
What charm to woman may belong
When by a natural bent inclined
To goodness in domestic play:
On earth no better thing than this—
It canonizes very clay: 25
Madonna, hence thy worship is.
    But Ruth: since Love had signed with Fate
The bond, and the first kiss had sealed,
Both for her own and Agar's state
Much of her exile-grief seemed healed: 30
New vistas opened; and if still
Forebodings might not be forgot
As to her sire's eventual lot,
Yet hope, which is of youth, could thrill.
That frame to foster and defend,   35
Clarel, when in her presence, strove
The unrest to hide which still could blend

With all the endearings of their love.
Ruth part divined the lurking care,
But more the curb, and motive too: 40
It made him but love's richer heir;
So much the more attachment grew.
She could not think but all would prove
Subject in end to mighty Love.
That cloud which in the present reigned,   45
By flushful hope's aurora stained,
At times redeemed itself in hues
Of shell, and humming-bird, and flower.
Could heaven two loyal hearts abuse?
The death-moth, let him keep his bower.   50

40. THE MOUNDS

Ere twilight and the shadow fall
On Zion hill without the wall
In place where Latins set the bier
Borne from the gate—who lingers here,
Where, typing faith exempt from loss,   5
By sodless mound is seen a cross?
Clarel it is, at Celio's grave.
For him, the pale one, ere yet cold,
Assiduous to win and save,
The friars had claimed as of their fold;   10
Lit by the light of ritual wicks,
Had held to unprotesting lips
In mistimed zeal the crucifix;
And last, among the fellowships
Of Rome's legitimate dead, laid one   15
Not saved through faith, nor Papal Rome's true son.
Life's flickering hour they made command
Faith's candle in Doubt's dying hand.
So some, who other forms did hold,
Rumored, or criticised, or told   20
The tale.

        Not this did Clarel win
To visit the hermit of the mound.
Nay, but he felt the appeal begin—
The poor petition from the ground:
Remember me! for all life's din   25
Let not my memory be drowned.
And thought was Clarel's even for one
Of tribe not his—to him unknown
Through vocal word or vital cheer:
A stranger, but less strange made here,   30
Less distant. Whom life held apart—
Life, whose cross-purposes make shy—
Death yields without reserve of heart
To meditation.
                With a sigh
Turning, he slow pursued the steep   35
Until he won that leveled spot,
Terraced and elevated plot
Over Gihon, where yet others keep
Death's tryst—afar from kindred lie:
Protestants, which in Salem die.   40
      There, fixed before a founded stone
With Bible mottoes part bestrown,
Stood one communing with the bier.
'Twas Rolfe. "Him, him I knew," said he,
Down pointing; "but 'twas far from here—   45
How far from here!" A pause. "But see,
Job's text in wreath, what trust it giveth;
'I KNOW THAT MY REDEEMER LIVETH.'
Poor Ethelward! Thou didst but grope;
I knew thee, and thou hadst small hope.   50
But if at this spent man's death-bed
Some kind soul kneeled and chapter read—
Ah, own! to moderns death is drear,
So drear: we die, we make no sign,
We acquiesce in any cheer—   55
No rite we seek, no rite decline.
Is't nonchalance of languid sense,
Or the last, last indifference?

With some, no doubt, 'tis peace within;
In others, may be, care for kin: 60
Exemplary thro' life, as well
Dying they'd be so, nor repel."
     He let his eyes half absent move
About the mound: "One's thoughts will rove:
This minds me that in like content,   65
Other forms were kept without dissent
By one who hardly owned their spell.
He, in fulfillment of pledged work,
Among Turks having passed for Turk,
Sickened among them. On death-bed   70
Silent he heard the Koran read:
They shrilled the Islam wail for him,
They shawled him in his burial trim;
And now, on brinks of Egypt's waste,
Where the buried Sultans' chapels rise,   75
Consistently toward Mecca faced,
The blameless simulator lies:
The turbaned Swiss, Sheik Ibrahim—
Burckhardt.—But home the sparrow flees.
Come, move we ere the gate they quit,   80
And we be shut out here with these
Who never shall re-enter it."

41. ON THE WALL

They parted in the port. Near by,
Long stone stairs win the battlement
Of wall, aërial gallery;
And thither now the student bent
To muse abroad.
               The sun's last rays   5
Shed round a nearing train the haze
Of mote and speck. Advanced in view
And claiming chief regard, came two
Dismounted, barefoot; one in dress
Expressive of deep humbleness   10

Of spirit, scarce of social state—
His lineaments rebutted that,
Tho' all was overcast with pain—
The visage of a doom-struck man
Not idly seeking holy ground.   15
Behind, his furnished horse did bound
Checked by a groom in livery fair.
The master paced in act of prayer
Absorbed—went praying thro' the gate.
The attentive student, struck thereat,   20
The wall crossed—from the inner arch,
Viewed him emerging, while in starch
Of prelate robes, some waiting Greeks
Received him, kissed him on both cheeks,
Showing that specializing love   25
And deference grave, how far above
What Lazarus in grief may get;
Nor less sincere those priests were yet.
        Second in the dismounted list
Was one, a laic votarist,   30
The cross and chaplet by his side,
Sharing the peace of eventide
In frame devout. A Latin he,
But not, as seemed, of high degree.
Such public reverence profound   35
In crossing Salem's sacred bound
Is not so common, in late day,
But that the people by the way
In silent-viewing eyes confessed
The spectacle had interest.   40
        Nazarene Hebrews twain rode next,
By one of the escort slyly vexed.
In litter borne by steady mules
A Russian lady parts the screen;
A rider, as the gate is seen,   45
Dismounts, and her alighting rules—
Her husband. Checkered following there,
Like envoys from all Adam's race,
Mixed men of various nations pace,

Such as in crowded steamer come   50
And disembark at Jaffa's stair.
   Mute mid the buzz of chat and prayer,
Plain-clad where others sport the plume,
What countrymen are yonder three?
The critic-coolness in their eyes   55
Disclaims emotion's shallow sea;
Or misapply they precept wise,
Nil admirari? Or, may be,
Rationalists these riders are,
Men self-sufficing, insular.   60
Nor less they show in grave degree
Tolerance for each poor votary.

   Now when the last rays slanting fall,
The last new comer enters in:
The gate shuts after with a din.   65
Tarries the student on the wall.
Dubieties of recent date—
Scenes, words, events—he thinks of all.
As, when the autumn sweeps the down,
And gray skies tell of summer gone,   70
The swallow hovers by the strait—
Impending on the passage long;
Upon a brink and poise he hung.
The bird in end must needs migrate
Over the sea: shall Clarel too   75
Launch o'er *his* gulf, e'en Doubt, and woo
Remote conclusions?
               Unresigned,
He sought the inn, and tried to read
The Fathers with a filial mind.
In vain; heart wandered or repined.   80
The Evangelists may serve his need:
Deep as he felt the beauty sway,
Estrangement there he could but heed,
Both time and tone so far away
From him the modern. Not to dwell,   85
Rising he walked the floor, then stood

Irresolute. His eye here fell
Upon the blank wall of the cell,
The wall before him, and he viewed
A place where the last coat of lime—   90
White flakes whereof lay dropped below—
Thin scaling off, laid open so
Upon the prior coat a rhyme
Pale penciled. In one's nervous trance
Things near will distant things recall,   95
And common ones suggest romance:
He thought of her built up in wall,
Cristina of Coll'alto; yes,
The verse here breaking from recess—
Tho' immaterial, but a thought   100
In some sojurning traveler wrought—
Scribbled, overlaid, again revealed—
Seemed like a tragic fact unsealed:
So much can mood possess a man.
　　He read: obscurely thus it ran:—   105

　　"For me who never loved the stride,
Triumph and taunt that shame the winning side—
Toward Him over whom, in expectation's glow,
Elate the advance of rabble-banners gleam—
Turned from a world that dare renounce Him so,   110
My unweaned thoughts in steadfast trade-wind stream.
If Atheists and Vitriolists of doom
Faith's gathering night with rockets red illume—
So much the more in pathos I adore
The low lamps flickering in Syria's Tomb."—   115

　　"What strain is this?—But, here, in blur:—
'After return from Sepulcher:
B. L.' "—On the ensuing day
He plied the host with question free:
Who answered him, "A pilgrim—nay,   120
How to remember! English, though—
A fair young Englishman. But stay:"
And after absence brief he slow

With volumes came in hand: "These, look—
He left behind by chance."—One book,   125
With portrait of a mitered man,
Treated of high church Anglican,
Confession, fast, saint-day—deplored
That rubric old was not restored.
But under *Finis* there was writ   130
A comment that made grief of it.
　　The second work had other cheer—
Started from Strauss, disdained Renan—
By striding paces up to Pan;
Nor rested, but the goat-god here   135
Capped with the red cap in the twist
Of Proudhon and the Communist.
But random jottings in the marge
Disclosed some reader of the text
Whose fervid comments did discharge   140
More dole than e'en dissent. Annexed,
In either book was penciled small:
"B. L.: Oxford: St. Mary's Hall."

　　Such proved these volumes—such, as scanned
By Clarel, wishful to command   145
Some hint that might supply a clew
Better enabling to construe
The lines their owner left on wall.

42. Tidings

Some of the strangers late arrived
Tarried with Abdon at the inn;
And, ere long, having viewed the town
Would travel further, and pass on
To Siddim, and the Dead Sea win   5
And Saba. And would Clarel go?
'Twas but for days. They would return
By Bethlehem, and there sojourn

Awhile, regaining Zion so.
But Clarel undetermined stood,   10
And kept his vacillating mood,
Though learning, as it happed, that Vine
And Rolfe would join the journeying band.
        Loath was he here to disentwine
Himself from Ruth. Nor less Lot's land,   15
And sea, and Judah's utmost drought
Fain would he view, and mark their tone:
And prove if, unredeemed by John,
John's wilderness augmented doubt.
As chanced, while wavering in mind,   20
And threading a hushed lane or wynd
Quick warning shout he heard behind
And clattering hoofs. He hugged the wall,
Then turned; in that brief interval
The dust came on him, powdery light,   25
From one who like a javelin flew
Spectral with dust, and all his plight
Charged with the desert and its hue;
A courier, and he bent his flight—
(As Clarel afterward recalled)   30
Whither lay Agar's close inwalled.
        The clank of arms, the clink of shoe,
The cry admonitory too,
Smote him, and yet he scarce knew why;
But when, some hours having flitted by,   35
Nearing the precincts of the Jew
His host, he did Nehemiah see
Waiting in arch, and with a look
Which some announcement's shadow took,
His heart stood still—Fate's herald, he?   40
        "What is it? what?"—The saint delayed.—
"Ruth?"—"Nathan;" and the news conveyed.
The threat, oft hurled, as oft reviled
By one too proud to give it heed,
The menace of stern foemen wild,   45
No menace now was, but a deed:
Burned was the roof on Sharon's plain;
And timbers charred showed clotted stain:

But, spirited away, each corse
Unsepulchered remained, or worse. 50

    Ah, Ruth—woe, Agar! Ill breeds ill;
The widow with no future free,
Without resource perhaps, or skill
To steer upon grief's misty sea.
    To grieve with them and lend his aid, 55
Straight to the house see Clarel fare,
The house of mourning—sadder made
For that the mourned one lay not there—
But found it barred. He, waiting so,
Doubtful to knock or call them—lo, 60
The rabbi issues, while behind
The door shuts to. The meeting eyes
Reciprocate a quick surprise,
Then alter; and the secret mind
The rabbi bears to Clarel shows 65
In dark superior look he throws:
Censorious consciousness of power:
Death—and it is the Levite's hour.
No word he speaks, but turns and goes.
    The student lingered. He was told 70
By one without, a neighbor old,
That never Jewish modes relent:
Sealed long would be the tenement
To all but Hebrews—of which race
Kneeled comforters by sorrow's side. 75
So both were cared for. Clogged in pace
He turned away. How pass the tide
Of Ruth's seclusion? Might he gain
Relief from dull inaction's pain?
Yes, join he would those pilgrims now 80
Which on the morrow would depart
For Siddim, by way of Jericho.
    But first of all, he letters sent,
Brief, yet dictated by the heart—
Announced his plan's constrained intent 85
Reluctant; and consigned a ring
For pledge of love and Ruth's remembering.

43. A PROCESSION

But what!—nay, nay: without adieu
Of vital word, dear presence true,
Part shall I?—break away from love?
But think: the circumstances move,
And warrant it. Shouldst thou abide,   5
Cut off yet wert thou from her side
For time: tho' she be sore distressed,
Herself would whisper: "Go—'tis best."

    Unstable! It was in a street,
Half vault, where few or none do greet,   10
He paced. Anon, encaved in wall
A fount arrests him, sculpture wrought
After a Saracen design—
Ruinous now and arid all
Save dusty weeds which trail or twine.   15
While lingering in way that brought
The memory of the Golden Bowl
And Pitcher broken, music rose—
Young voices; a procession shows:
A litter rich, with flowery wreath,   20
Singers and censers, and a veil.
She comes, the bride; but, ah, how pale:
Her groom that Blue-Beard, cruel Death,
Wedding his millionth maid to-day;
She, stretched on that Armenian bier,   25
Leaves home and each familiar way—
Quits all for him. Nearer, more near—
Till now the ineffectual flame
Of burning tapers borne he saw:
The westering sun puts these to shame.   30

    But, hark: responsive marching choirs,
Robed men and boys, in rhythmic law
A contest undetermined keep:
Ay, as the bass in dolings deep
The serious, solemn thought inspires—   35
In unconcern of rallying sort

The urchin-treble shrills retort;
But, true to part imposed, again
The beards dirge out. And so they wind
Till thro' the city gate the train   40
Files forth to sepulcher.
                                Behind
Left in his hermitage of mind,
What troubles Clarel? See him there
As if admonishment in air
He heard. Can love be fearful so?   45
Jealous of fate? the future? all
Reverse—mischance? nay, even the pall
And pit?—No, I'll not leave her: no,
'Tis fixed; I waver now no more.—
    But yet again he thought it o'er,   50
And self-rebukeful, and with mock:
Thou superstitious doubter—own,
Biers need be borne; why such a shock
When passes this Armenian one?
The word's dispatched, and wouldst recall?   55
'Tis but for fleeting interval.

44. The Start

The twilight and the starlight pass,
And breaks the morn of Candlemas.
    The pilgrims muster; and they win
A common terrace of the inn,
Which, lifted on Mount Acra's cope,   5
Looks off upon the town aslope
In gray of dawn. They hear the din
Of mongrel Arabs—the loud coil
And uproar of high words they wage
Harnessing for the pilgrimage.   10
'Tis special—marks the Orient life,
Which, roused from indolence to toil,
Indignant starts, enkindling strife.
Tho' spite the fray no harm they share,
How fired they seem by burning wrong;   15

And small the need for strenuous care,
And languor yet shall laze it long.
  Wonted to man and used to fate
A pearl-gray ass there stands sedate
While being saddled by a clown   20
And buffeted. Of her anon.

  Clarel regards; then turns his eye
Away from all, beyond the town,
Where pale against the tremulous sky
Olivet shows in morning shy;   25
Then on the court again looks down.
The mountain mild, the wrangling crew—
In contrast, why should these indue
With vague unrest, and swell the sigh?
Add to the burden? tease the sense   30
With unconfirmed significance?
  To horse. And, passing one by one
Their host the Black Jew by the gate,
His grave salute they take, nor shun
His formal God-speed. One, elate   35
In air Auroral, June of life,
With quick and gay response is rife.
But he, the Israelite alone,
'Tis he reflects Jehovah's town;
Experienced he, the vain elation gone;   40
While flit athwart his furrowed face
Glimpses of that ambiguous thought
Which in some aged men ye trace
When Venture, Youth and Bloom go by;
Scarce cynicism, though 'tis wrought   45
Not all of pity, since it scants the sigh.

  They part. Farewell to Zion's seat.
Ere yet anew her place they greet,
In heart what hap may Clarel prove?
Brief term of days, but a profound remove.   50

END OF PART FIRST

Part 2

The Wilderness

1. The Cavalcade

ADOWN THE Dolorosa Lane
   The mounted pilgrims file in train
   Whose clatter jars each open space;
Then, muffled in, shares change apace
As, striking sparks in vaulted street,   5
Clink, as in cave, the horses' feet.
   Not from brave Chaucer's Tabard Inn
They pictured wend; scarce shall they win
Fair Kent, and Canterbury ken;
Nor franklin, squire, nor morris-dance   10
Of wit and story good as then:
Another age, and other men,
And life an unfulfilled romance.

   First went the turban—guide and guard
In escort armed and desert trim;   15
The pilgrims next: whom now to limn.
One there the light rein slackly drew,
And skimming glanced, dejected never—
While yet the pilgrimage was new—

133

On sights ungladsome howsoever.   20
Cordial he turned his aspect clear
On all that passed; man, yea, and brute
Enheartening by a blithe salute,
Chirrup, or pat, in random cheer.
This pleasantness, which might endear,   25
Suffused was with a prosperous look
That bordered vanity, but took
Fair color as from ruddy heart.
    A priest he was—though but in part;
For as the Templar old combined   30
The cavalier and monk in one;
In Derwent likewise might you find
The secular and cleric tone.
Imported or domestic mode,
Thought's last adopted style he showed;   35
Abreast kept with the age, the year,
And each bright optimistic mind,
Nor lagged with Solomon in rear,
And Job, the furthermost behind—
Brisk marching in time's drum-corps van   40
Abreast with whistling Jonathan.
Tho' English, with an English home,
His spirits through Creole cross derived
The light and effervescent foam;
And youth in years mature survived.   45
At saddle-bow a book was laid
Convenient—tinted in the page
Which did urbanely disengage
Sadness and doubt from all things sad
And dubious deemed. Confirmed he read: 50
A priest o' the club—a taking man,
And rather more than Lutheran.
A cloth cape, light in air afloat,
And easy set of cleric coat,
Seemed emblems of that facile wit,   55
Which suits the age—a happy fit.

    Behind this good man's stirrups, rode
A solid stolid Elder, shod

With formidable boots. He went
Like Talus in a foundry cast;   60
Furrowed his face, with wrinkles massed.
He claimed no indirect descent
From Grampian kirk and covenant.
    But recent sallying from home,
Late he assigned three days to Rome.   65
He saw the host go by. The crowd,
Made up from many a tribe and place
Of Christendom, kept seemly face:
Took off the hat, or kneeled, or bowed;
But he the helm rammed down apace: 70
Discourteous to the host, agree,
Tho' to a parting soul it went;
Nor deemed that, were it mummery,
'Twas pathos too. This hard dissent—
Transferred to Salem in remove,—   75
Led him to carp, and try disprove
Legend and site by square and line:
Aside time's violet mist he'd shove—
Quite disenchant the Land Divine.
So fierce he hurled zeal's javelin home,   80
It drove beyond the mark—pierced Rome,
And plunged beyond, thro' enemy
To friend. Scarce natural piety
Might live, abiding such a doom.
Traditions beautiful and old   85
Which with maternal arms enfold
Millions, else orphaned and made poor,
No plea could lure him to endure.
Concerned, meek Christian ill might bear
To mark this worthy brother rash,   90
Deeming he served religion there,
Work up the fag end of Voltaire,
And help along faith's final crash—
If that impend.
         His fingers pressed
A ferule of black thorn: he bore   95
A pruning-knife in belt; in vest
A measuring-tape wound round a core;

And field-glass slung athwart the chest;
While peeped from holsters old and brown,
Horse-pistols—and they were his own.   100

    A hale one followed, good to see,
English and Greek in pedigree;
Of middle-age; a ripe gallant,
A banker of the rich Levant;
In florid opulence preserved   105
Like peach in syrup. Ne'er he swerved
From morning bath, and dinner boon,
And velvet nap in afternoon,
And lounge in garden with cigar.
His home was Thessalonica,   110
Which views Olympus. But, may be,
Little he weened of Jove and gods
In synod mid those brave abodes;
Nor, haply, read or weighed Paul's plea
Addressed from Athens o'er the sea   115
Unto the Thessalonians old:
His bonds he scanned, and weighed his gold.
    Parisian was his garb, and gay.
Upon his saddle-pommel lay
A rich Angora rug, for shawl   120
Or pillow, just as need might fall;
Not the Brazilian leopard's hair
Or toucan's plume may show more fair;
Yet, serving light convenience mere,
Proved but his heedless affluent cheer.   125
    Chief exercise this sleek one took
Was toying with a tissue book
At intervals, and leaf by leaf
Gently reducing it. In brief,
With tempered yet Capuan zest,   130
Of cigarettes he smoked the best.
This wight did Lady Fortune love:
Day followed day in treasure-trove.
Nor only so, but he did run
In unmistrustful reveries bright   135

Beyond his own career to one
Who should continue it in light
Of lineal good times.
                              High walled,
An Eden owned he nigh his town,
Which locked in leafy emerald   140
A frescoed lodge. There Nubians armed,
Tall eunuchs virtuous in zeal,
In shining robes, with glittering steel,
Patrolled about his daughter charmed,
Inmost inclosed in nest of bowers,   145
By gorgons served, the dread she-powers,
Duennas: maiden more than fair:
How fairer in his rich conceit—
An Argive face, and English hair
Sunny as May in morning sweet: 150
A damsel for Apollo meet;
And yet a mortal's destined bride—
Bespoken, yes, affianced late
To one who by the senior's side
Rode rakishly deliberate—   155
A sprig of Smyrna, Glaucon he.
His father (such ere long to be)
Well loved him, nor that sole he felt
That fortune here had kindly dealt
Another court-card into hand—   160
The youth with gold at free command;—
No, but he also liked his clan,
His kinsmen, and his happy way;
And over wine would pleased repay
His parasites: Well may ye say   165
The boy's the bravest gentleman!—
    From Beyrout late had come the pair
To further schemes of finance hid,
And for a pasha's favor bid
And grave connivance. That affair   170
Yet lingered. So, dull time to kill,
They wandered, anywhere, at will.
Scarce through self-knowledge or self-love

They ventured Judah's wilds to rove,
As time, ere long, and place, may prove.   175

Came next in file three sumpter mules
With all things needful for the tent,
And panniers which the Greek o'errules;
For there, with store of nourishment,
Rosoglio pink and wine of gold   180
Slumbered as in the smugglers' hold.

Viewing those Levantines in way
Of the snared lion, which from grate
Marks the light throngs on holiday,
Nor e'er relaxes in his state   185
Of rigorous gloom; rode one whose air
Revealed—but, for the nonce, forbear.
Mortmain his name, or so in whim
Some moral wit had christened him.

Upon that creature men traduce   190
For patience under their abuse;
For whose requital there's assigned
No heaven; that thing of dreamful kind—
The ass—elected for the ease,
Good Nehemiah followed these;   195
His Bible under arm, and leaves
Of tracts still fluttering in sheaves.
In pure good will he bent his view
To right and left. The ass, pearl-gray,
Matched well the rider's garb in hue,   200
And sorted with the ashy way;
Upon her shoulders' jointed play
The white cross gleamed, which the untrue
Yet innocent fair legends say,
Memorializes Christ our Lord   205
When Him with palms the throngs adored
Upon the foal. Many a year
The wanderer's heart had longed to view
Green banks of Jordan dipped in dew;
Oft had he watched with starting tear   210

Pack-mule and camel, horse and spear,
Monks, soldiers, pilgrims, helm and hood,
The variegated annual train
In vernal Easter caravan,
Bound unto Gilgal's neighborhood.   215
Nor less belief his heart confessed
Not die he should till knees had pressed
The Palmers' Beach. Which trust proved true:
'Twas charity gave faith her due:
Without publicity or din   220
It was the student moved herein.

    He, Clarel, with the earnest face
Which fitful took a hectic dye,
Kept near the saint. With equal pace
Came Rolfe in saddle pommeled high,   225
Yet e'en behind that peaked redoubt
Sat Indian-like, in pliant way,
As if he were an Osage scout,
Or Gaucho of the Paraguay.

    Lagging in rear of all the train   230
As hardly he pertained thereto
Or his right place therein scarce knew,
Rode one who frequent turned again
To pore behind. He seemed to be
In reminiscence folded ever,   235
Or some deep moral fantasy;
At whiles in face a dusk and shiver,
As if in heart he heard amazed
The sighing of Ravenna's wood
Of pines, and saw the phantom knight   240
(Boccaccio's) with the dagger raised
Still hunt the lady in her flight
From solitude to solitude.
'Twas Vine. Nor less for day dream, still
The rein he held with lurking will.   245

    So filed the muster whose array
Threaded the Dolorosa's way.

2. The Skull-Cap

"See him in his uncheerful head-piece!
Libertad's on the Mexic coin
Would better suit me for a shade-piece:
Ah, had I known he was to join!"—
    So chid the Greek, the banker one   5
Perceiving Mortmain there at hand,
And in allusion to a dun
Skull-cap he wore. Derwent light reined
The steed; and thus: "Beg pardon now,
It looks a little queer, concede;   10
Nor less the cap fits well-shaped brow;
It yet may prove the wishing-cap
Of Fortunatus."
                "No indeed,
No, no, for *that* had velvet nap
Of violet with silver tassel—   15
Much like my smoking-cap, you see,"
Light laughed the Smyrniote, that vassal
Of health and young vivacity.
    "Glaucon, be still," the senior said
(And yet he liked to hear him too);   20
"I say it doth but ill bestead
To have a black cap in our crew."
    "Pink, pink," cried Glaucon, "pink's the hue:—

    "Pink cap and ribbons of the pearl,
            A Paradise of bodice,   25
        The Queen of Sheba's laundry girl—

    "Hallo, what now? They come to halt
Down here in glen! Well, well, we'll vault."
His song arrested, so he spake
And light dismounted, wide awake.—   30

    "A sprightly comrade have you here,"
Said Derwent in the senior's ear.
The banker turned him: "Folly, folly—
But good against the melancholy."

3. BY THE GARDEN

Sheep-tracks they'd look, at distance seen,
Did any herbage border them,
Those slender foot-paths slanting lean
Down or along waste slopes which hem
The high-lodged, walled Jerusalem.   5
    Slipped from Bethesda's Pool leads one
Which by an arch across is thrown
Kedron the brook. The Virgin's Tomb
(Whence the near gate the Latins name—
St. Stephen's, as the Lutherans claim—   10
Hard by the place of martyrdom),
Time-worn in sculpture dim, is set
Humbly inearthed by Olivet.
    'Tis hereabout now halt the band,
And by Gethsemane at hand,   15
For few omitted trifles wait
And guardsman whom adieus belate.
Some light dismount.
                But hardly here,
Where on the verge they might foretaste
Or guess the flavor of the waste,   20
Greek sire and son took festive cheer.
    Glaucon not less a topic found
At venture. One old tree becharmed
Leaned its decrepit trunk deformed
Over the garden's wayside bound: 25
"See now: this yellow olive wood
They carve in trinkets—rosary—rood:
Of these we must provide some few
For travel-gifts, ere we for good
Set out for home. And why not too   30
Some of those gems the nuns revere—
In hands of veteran venders here,
Wrought from the Kedron's saffron block
In the Monk's Glen, Mar Saba's rock;
And cameos of the Dead Sea stone?"   35
    "Buy what ye will, be it Esau's flock,"
The other said: "but for that stone—

Avoid, nor name!"
                    "*That* stone? what one?"
And cast a look of grieved surprise
Marking the senior's ruffled guise;   40
"Those cameos of Death's Sea—"
                              "Have done,
I beg! Unless all joy you'd cripple,
Both noun omit and participle."
        "Dear sir, what noun? strange grammar's this."
"Have I expressed myself amiss?   45
Oh, don't you think it is but spleen:
A well-bred man counts it unclean
This name of—boy, and can't you guess?
Last bankruptcy without redress!"
        "For heaven's sake!"
                          "With that ill word   50
Whose first is D and last is H,
No matter what be in regard,
Let none of mine ere crape his speech,
But shun it, ay, and shun the knell
Of each derivative."
                    "Oh, well—   55
I see, I see; with all my heart!
Each conjugation will I curb,
All moods and tenses of the verb;
And, for the noun, to save from errors
I'll use instead—the '*King of Terrors.*' "   60
        "Sir, change the topic.—Would 'twere done,
This scheme of ours, and we clean gone
From out this same dull land so holy
Which breeds but blues and melancholy.
To while our waiting I thought good   65
To join these travelers on their road;
But there's a bird in saucy glee
Trills—*Fool, retreat; 'tis not for thee.*
Had I fair pretext now, I'd turn.
But yonder—*he* don't show concern,"   70
Glancing toward Derwent, lounging there

Holding his horse with easy air
Slack by the rein.
                    With morning zest,
In sound digestion unoppressed,
The clergyman's good spirits made   75
A Tivoli of that grim glade.
And turning now his cheery eyes
Toward Salem's towers in solemn guise
Stretched dumb along the Mount of God,
He cried to Clarel waiting near   80
In saddle-seat and gazing drear:
"A canter, lad, on steed clean-shod
Didst ever take on English sod?
The downs, the downs! Yet even here
For a fair matin ride withal   85
I like the run round yonder wall.
Hight have you, outlook; and the view
Varies as you the turn pursue."—
So he, thro' inobservance, blind
To that preoccupied young mind,   90
In frame how different, in sooth—
Pained and reverting still to Ruth
Immured and parted from him there
Behind those ramparts of despair.
        Mortmain, whose wannish eyes declared   95
How ill thro' night-hours he had fared,
By chance overheard, and muttered—"Brass,
A sounding brass and tinkling cymbal!
Who he that with a tongue so nimble
Affects light heart in such a pass?"   100
And full his cloud on Derwent bent:
"Yea, and but thou seem'st well content.
But turn, another thing's to see:
Thy back's upon Gethsemane."
        The priest wheeled short: What kind of man   105
Was this? The other re-began:
"'Tis *Terra Santa*—Holy Land:
Terra Damnata though's at hand

Within."—"You mean where Judas stood?
Yes, monks locate and name that ground;   110
They've railed it off. Good, very good:
It minds one of a vacant pound.—
We tarry long: why lags our man?"
And rose; anew glanced toward the hight.
    Here Mortmain from the words and plight   115
Conjecture drew; and thus he ran:
"Be some who with the god will sup,
Happy to share his paschal wine.
'Tis well. But the ensuing cup,
The bitter cup?"
                "Art a divine?"   120
Asked Derwent, turning that aside;
"Methinks, good friend, too much you chide.
I know these precincts. Still, believe—
And let's discard each idle trope—
Rightly considered, they can give   125
A hope to man, a cheerful hope."
    "Not for this world. The Christian plea—
What basis has it, but that here
Man is not happy, nor can be?
There it confirms philosophy: 130
The compensation of its cheer
Is reason why the grass survives
Of verdurous Christianity,
Ay, trampled, lives, tho' hardly thrives
In these mad days."—
             Surprised at it,   135
Derwent intently viewed the man,
Marked the unsolaced aspect wan;
And fidgeted; yet matter fit
Had offered; but the other changed
In quick caprice, and willful ranged   140
In wild invective: "O abyss!
Here, upon what was erst the sod,
A man betrayed the yearning god;
A man, yet with a woman's kiss.

'Twas *human*, that unanimous cry,   145
'We're fixed to hate him—crucify!'
The which they did. And hands, nailed down,
Might not avail to screen the face
From each head-wagging mocking one.
This day, with some of earthly race,   150
May passion similar go on?"—
    Inferring, rightly or amiss,
Some personal peculiar cause
For such a poignant strain as this,
The priest disturbed not here the pause   155
Which sudden fell. The other turned,
And, with a strange transition, burned
Invokingly: "Ye trunks of moan—
Gethsemane olives, do ye hear
The trump of that vain-glorious land   160
Where human nature they enthrone
Displacing the divine?" His hand
He raised there—let it fall, and fell
Himself, with the last syllable,
To moody hush. Then, fierce: "Hired band   165
Of laureates of man's fallen tribe—
Slaves are ye, slaves beyond the scribe
Of Nero; he, if flatterer blind,
Toadied not total human kind,
Which ye kerns do. But Bel shall bow   170
And Nebo stoop."
                    "Ah, come, friend, come,"
Pleaded the charitable priest
Still bearing with him, anyhow,
By fate unbidden to joy's feast:
"Thou'rt strong; yield then the weak some room.   175
Too earnest art thou;" and with eye
Of one who fain would mollify
All frowardness, he looked a smile.
    But not that heart might he beguile:
"Man's vicious: snaffle him with kings;   180
Or, if kings cease to curb, devise

Severer bit. This garden brings
Such lesson. Heed it, and be wise
In thoughts not new."
                    "Thou'rt ill to-day,"
Here peering, but in cautious way,   185
"Nor solace find in valley wild."
    The other wheeled, nor more would say;
And soon the cavalcade defiled.

4. OF MORTMAIN

"Our friend there—he's a little queer,"
To Rolfe said Derwent riding on;
"Beshrew me, there is in his tone
Naught of your new world's chanticleer.
Who's the eccentric? can you say?"   5
    "Partly; but 'tis at second hand.
At the Black Jew's I met with one
Who, in response to my demand,
Did in a strange disclosure run
Respecting him."—"Repeat it, pray."—   10
And Rolfe complied. But here receive
Less the details of narrative
Than what the drift and import may convey.

    A Swede he was—illicit son
Of noble lady, after-wed,   15
Who, for a cause over which be thrown
Charity of oblivion dead,—
Bore little love, but rather hate,
Even practiced to ensnare his state.
His father, while not owning, yet   20
In part discharged the natural debt
Of duty; gave him liberal lore
And timely income; but no more.
    Thus isolated, what to bind
But the vague bond of human kind?   25
The north he left, to Paris came—

Paris, the nurse of many a flame
Evil and good. This son of earth,
This Psalmanazer, made a hearth
In warm desires and schemes for man: 30
Even *he* was an Arcadian.
Peace and good will was his acclaim—
If not in words, yet in the aim:
Peace, peace on earth: that note he thrilled,
But scarce in way the cherubs trilled   35
To Bethlehem and the shepherd band.
Yet much his theory could tell;
And he expounded it so well,
Disciples came. He took his stand.
    Europe was in a decade dim: 40
Upon the future's trembling rim
The comet hovered. His a league
Of frank debate and close intrigue:
Plot, proselyte, appeal, denounce—
Conspirator, pamphleteer, at once,   45
And prophet. Wear and tear and jar
He met with coffee and cigar:
These kept awake the man and mood
And dream. That uncreated Good
He sought, whose absence is the cause   50
Of creeds and Atheists, mobs and laws.
Precocities of heart outran
The immaturities of brain.
    Along with each superior mind
The vain, foolhardy, worthless, blind,   55
With Judases, are nothing loath
To clasp pledged hands and take the oath
Of aim, the which, if just, demands
Strong hearts, brows deep, and priestly hands.
Experience with her sharper touch   60
Stung Mortmain: Why, if men prove such,
Dote I? love theory overmuch?
Yea, also, whither will advance
This Revolution sprung in France
So many years ago? where end?   65

That current takes me. Whither tend?
Come, thou who makest such hot haste
To forge the future—weigh the past.
    Such frame he knew. And timed event
Cogent a further question lent: 70
Wouldst meddle with the state? Well, mount
Thy guns; how many men dost count?
Besides, there's more that here belongs:
Be many questionable wrongs:
By yet more questionable war,   75
Prophet of peace, these wouldst thou bar?
The world's not new, nor new thy plea.
Tho' even shouldst thou triumph, see,
Prose overtakes the victor's songs:
Victorious right may need redress: 80
No failure like a harsh success.
Yea, ponder well the historic page:
Of all who, fired with noble rage,
Have warred for right without reprieve,
How many spanned the wings immense   85
Of Satan's muster, or could cheat
His cunning tactics of retreat
And ambuscade? Oh, now dispense!
The world is portioned out, believe:
The good have but a patch at best,   90
The wise their corner; for the rest—
Malice divides with ignorance.
And what is stable? find one boon
That is not lackey to the moon
Of fate. The flood ebbs out—the ebb   95
Floods back; the incessant shuttle shifts
And flies, and weaves and tears the web.
Turn, turn thee to the proof that sifts:
What if the kings in Forty-eight
Fled like the gods? even as the gods   100
Shall do, return they made; and sate
And fortified their strong abodes;
And, to confirm them there in state,
Contrived new slogans, apt to please—

Pan and the tribal unities. 105
Behind all this still works some power
Unknowable, thou'lt yet adore.
That steers the world, not man. States drive;
The crazy rafts with billows strive.—
Go, go—absolve thee. Join that band 110
That wash them with the desert sand
For lack of water. In the dust
Of wisdom sit thee down, and rust.

So mused he—solitary pined.
Tho' his apostolate had thrown 115
New prospects ope to Adam's kind,
And fame had trumped him far and free—
Now drop he did—a clod unknown;
Nay, rather, he would not disown
Oblivion's volunteer to be; 120
Like those new-world discoverers bold
Ending in stony convent cold,
Or dying hermits; as if they,
Chastised to Micah's mind austere,
Remorseful felt that ampler sway 125
Their lead had given for old career
Of human nature.
            But this man
No cloister sought. He, under ban
Of strange repentance and last dearth,
Roved the gray places of the earth. 130
And what seemed most his heart to wring
Was some unrenderable thing:
'Twas not his bastardy, nor bale
Medean in his mother pale,
Nor thwarted aims of high design; 135
But deeper—deep as nature's mine.
   Tho' frequent among kind he sate
Tranquil enough to hold debate,
His moods he had, mad fitful ones,
Prolonged or brief, outbursts or moans; 140
And at such times would hiss or cry:

"Fair Circe—goddess of the sty!"
More frequent this: "Mock worse than wrong:
The Syren's kiss—the Fury's thong!"

Such he. Tho' scarce as such portrayed   145
In full by Rolfe, yet Derwent said
At close: "There's none so far astray,
Detached, abandoned, as might seem,
As to exclude the hope, the dream
Of fair redemption. One fine day   150
I saw at sea, by bit of deck—
Weedy—adrift from far away—
The dolphin in his gambol light
Through showery spray, arch into sight:
He flung a rainbow o'er that wreck."   155

5. CLAREL AND GLAUCON

Now slanting toward the mountain's head
They round its southern shoulder so;
That immemorial path they tread
Whereby to Bethany you go
From Salem over Kedron's bed   5
And Olivet. Free change was made
Among the riders. Lightly strayed,
With overtures of friendly note,
To Clarel's side the Smyrniote.
Wishful from every one to learn,   10
As well his giddy talk to turn,
Clarel—in simpleness that comes
To students versed more in their tomes
Than life—of Homer spake, a man
With Smyrna linked, born there, 'twas said.   15
But no, the light Ionian
Scarce knew that singing beggar dead,
Though wight he'd heard of with the name;

"Homer? yes, I remember me;
Saw note-of-hand once with his name: 20
A fig for him, fig-dealer he,
The veriest old nobody:"
Then lightly skimming on: "Did you
By Joppa come? I did, and rue
Three dumpish days, like Sundays dull   25
Such as in London late I knew;
The gardens tho' are bountiful.
But Bethlehem—beyond compare!
Such roguish ladies! Tarried there?
You know it is a Christian town,   30
Decreed so under Ibrahim's rule
The Turk." E'en thus he rippled on,
Way giving to his spirits free,
Relieved from that disparity
Of years he with the banker felt,   35
Nor noted Clarel's puzzled look,
Who, novice-like, at first mistook,
Doubting lest satire might be dealt.
      Adjusting now the sporting gun
Slung to his back with pouch and all: 40
"Oh, but to sight a bird, just one,
An eagle say, and see him fall."
And, chatting still, with giddy breath,
Of hunting feats over hill and dale:
"Fine shot was mine by Nazareth;   45
But birding's best in Tempe's Vale:
From Thessalonica, you know,
'Tis thither that we fowlers stray.
But you don't talk, my friend.—Heigh-ho,
Next month I wed; yes, so they say.   50
Meantime do sing a song or so
To cheer one. Won't? Must I?—Let's see:
Song of poor-devil dandy: he:—

      "She's handsome as a jeweled priest
            In ephod on the festa,   55

And each poor blade like me must needs
    Idolize and detest her.

"With rain-beads on her odorous hair
    From gardens after showers,
All bloom and dew she trips along,   60
    Intent on selling flowers.

"She beams—the rainbow of the bridge;
    But, ah, my blank abhorrence,
She buttonholes me with a rose,
    This flower-girl of Florence.   65

"My friends stand by; and, 'There!' she says—
    An angel arch, a sinner:
I grudge to pay, but pay I must,
    Then—dine on half a dinner!—

"Heigh-ho, next month I marry: well!"   70
With that he turned aside, and went
Humming another air content.
And Derwent heard him as befell.
"This lad is like a land of springs,"
He said, "he gushes so with song."—   75
"Nor heeds if Olivet it wrong,"
Said Rolfe; "but no—he sings—he rings;
His is the guinea, fiddle-strings
Of youth too—which may heaven make strong!"
    Meanwhile, in tetchy tone austere   80
That reprobated song and all,
Lowering rode the presbyter,
A cloud whose rain ere long must fall.

6. The Hamlet

In silence now they pensive win
A slope of upland over hill
Eastward, where heaven and earth be twin
In quiet, and earth seems heaven's sill.
About a hamlet there full low,   5
Nor cedar, palm, nor olive show—
Three trees by ancient legend claimed
As those whereof the cross was framed.
Nor dairy white, nor well-curb green,
Nor cheerful husbandry was seen,   10
Though flinty tillage might be named:
Nor less if all showed strange and lone
The peace of God seemed settled down:
Mary and Martha's mountain-town.
      To Rolfe the priest said, breathing low: 15
"How placid! Carmel's beauty here,
If added, could not more endear."—
Rolfe spake not, but he bent his brow.
      Aside glanced Clarel on the face
Of meekness; and he mused: In thee   20
Methinks similitude I trace
To Nature's look in Bethany.
But, ah, and can one dream the dream
That hither thro' the shepherds' gate,
Even by the road we traveled late,   25
Came Jesus from Jerusalem,
Who pleased him so in fields and bowers,
Yes, crowned with thorns, still loved the flowers?
Poor gardeners here that turned the sod
Friends were they to the Son of God?   30
And shared He e'en their humble lot?
The sisters here in pastoral plot
Green to the door—did they yield rest,
And bathe the feet, and spread the board
For Him, their own and brother's guest,   35
The kindly Christ, even man's fraternal Lord?
But see: how with a wandering hand,

In absent-mindedness afloat,
And dreaming of his fairy-land,
Nehemiah smooths the ass's coat.   40

7. GUIDE AND GUARD

Descending by the mountain side
When crags give way to pastures wide,
And lower opening, ever new,
Glades, meadows, hamlets meet the view,
Which from above did coyly hide—   5
And with re-kindled breasts of spring
The robins thro' the orchard wing;
Excellent then—as *there* bestowed—
And true in charm the downward road.
Quite other spells an influence throw   10
Down going, down, to Jericho.
    Here first on path so evil-starred
Their guide they scan, and prize the guard.

    The guide, a Druze of Lebanon,
Was rumored for an Emir's son,   15
Or offspring of a lord undone
In Ibrahim's time. Abrupt reverse
The princes in the East may know:
Lawgivers are outlaws at a blow,
And Crœsus dwindles in the purse.   20
Exiled, cut off, in friendless state,
The Druze maintained an air sedate;
Without the sacrifice of pride,
Sagacious still he earned his bread,
E'en managed to maintain the head,   25
Yes, lead men still, if but as guide
To pilgrims.
                Here his dress to mark:
A simple woolen cloak, with dark
Vertical stripes; a vest to suit;
White turban like snow-wreath; a boot   30

Exempt from spur; a sash of fair
White linen, long-fringed at the ends:
The garb of Lebanon. His mare
In keeping showed: the saddle plain:
Head-stall untasseled, slender rein.   35
But nature made her rich amends
For art's default: full eye of flame
Tempered in softness, which became
Womanly sometimes, in desire
To be caressed; ears fine to know   40
Least intimation, catch a hint
As tinder takes the spark from flint
And steel. Veil-like her clear attire
Of silvery hair, with speckled show
Of grayish spots, and ample flow   45
Of milky mane. Much like a child
The Druze she'd follow, more than mild.
Not less, at need, what power she'd don,
Clothed with the thunderbolt would run
As conscious of the Emir's son   50
She bore; nor knew the hireling's lash,
Red rowel, or rebuke as rash.
Courteous her treatment. But deem not
This tokened a luxurious lot:
Her diet spare; sole stable, earth;   55
Beneath the burning sun she'd lie
With mane disheveled, whence her eye
Would flash across the fiery dearth,
As watching for that other queen,
Her mate, a beauteous Palmyrene,   60
The pride of Tadmore's tented scene.
    Athwart the pommel-cloth coarse-spun
A long pipe lay, and longer gun,
With serviceable yataghan.
But prized above these arms of yore,   65
A new revolver bright he bore
Tucked in the belt, and oft would scan.
Accoutered thus, thro' desert-blight
Whose lord is the Amalekite,

And proffering or peace or war, 70
The swart Druze rode his silvery Zar.

Behind him, jogging two and two,
Came troopers six of tawny hue,
Bewrinkled veterans, and grave
As Carmel's prophets of the cave: 75
Old Arab Bethlehemites, with guns
And spears of grandsires old. Weird ones,
Their robes like palls funereal hung
Down from the shoulder, one fold flung
In mufflement about the head, 80
And kept there by a fillet's braid.

Over this venerable troop
Went Belex doughty in command,
Erst of the Sultan's saucy troop
Which into death he did disband— 85
Politic Mahmoud—when that clan
By fair pretence, in festive way,
He trapped within the Artmedan—
Of old, Byzantium's circus gay.
But Belex a sultana saved— 90
His senior, though by love enslaved,
Who fed upon the stripling's May—
Long since, for now his beard was gray;
Tho' goodly yet the features fine,
Firm chin, true lip, nose aquiline— 95
Type of the pure Osmanli breed.
But ah, equipments gone to seed—
Ah, shabby fate! his vesture's cloth
Hinted the Jew bazaar and moth:
The saddle, too, a cast-off one, 100
An Aga's erst, and late was sown
With seed-pearl in the seat; but now
All that, with tag-work, all was gone—
The tag-work of wee bells in row
That made a small, snug, dulcet din 105
About the housings Damascene.

But mark the bay: his twenty years
Still showed him pawing with his peers.
Pure desert air, doled diet pure,
Sleek tendance, brave result insure.   110
Ample his chest; small head, large eye—
How interrogative with soul—
Responsive too, his master by:
Trim hoof, and pace in strong control.
    Thy birth-day well they keep, thou Don,   115
And well thy birth-day ode they sing;
Nor ill they named thee Solomon,
Prolific sire. Long live the king.

8. ROLFE AND DERWENT

They journey. And, as heretofore,
Derwent invoked his spirits bright
Against the wilds expanding more:
    "Do but regard yon Islamite
And horse: equipments be but lean,   5
Nor less the nature still is rife—
Mettle, you see, mettle and mien.
Methinks fair lesson here we glean:
The inherent vigor of man's life
Transmitted from strong Adam down,   10
Takes no infirmity that's won
By institutions—which, indeed,
Be as equipments of the breed.
God bless the marrow in the bone!
What's Islam now? does Turkey thrive?   15
Yet Islamite and Turk they wive
And flourish, and the world goes on."
    "Ay. But all qualities of race
Which make renown—these yet may die,
While leaving unimpaired in grace   20
The virile power," was Rolfe's reply;
"For witness here I cite a Greek—
God bless him! who tricked me of late

In Argos. What a perfect beak
In contour,—oh, 'twas delicate;   25
And hero-symmetry of limb:
Clownish I looked by side of him.
Oh, but it does one's ardor damp—
That splendid instrument, a scamp!
These Greeks indeed they wear the kilt   30
Bravely; they skim their lucid seas;
But, prithee, where is Pericles?
Plato is where? Simonides?
No, friend: much good wine has been spilt:
The rank world prospers; but, alack!   35
Eden nor Athens shall come back:—
And what's become of Arcady?"
    He paused; then in another key:
"Prone, prone are era, man and nation
To slide into a degradation?   40
With some, to age is that—but that."

    "Pathetic grow'st thou," Derwent said:
And lightly, as in leafy glade,
Lightly he in the saddle sat.

9. THROUGH ADOMMIN

In order meet they take their way
Through Bahurim where David fled;
And Shimei like a beast of prey
Prowled on the side-cliff overhead,
And flung the stone, the stone and curse,   5
And called it just, the king's reverse:
Still grieving grief, as demons may.

    In flanking parched ravine they won,
The student wondered at the bale
So arid, as of Acheron   10
Run dry. Alert showed Belex hale,
Uprising in the stirrup, clear
Of saddle, outlook so to gain,

Rattling his piece and scimeter.
    "Dear me, I say," appealing ran   15
From the sleek Thessalonian.
    "Say on!" the Turk, with bearded grin;
"This is the glen named Adommin!"
    Uneasy glance the banker threw,
Tho' first now of such name he knew   20
Or place. Nor was his flutter stayed
When Belex, heading his brigade,
Drew sword, and with a summons cried:
"Ho, rout them!" and his cohort veered,
Scouring the dens on either side,   25
Then all together disappeared
Amid wild turns of ugly ground
Which well the sleuth-dog might confound.
    The Druze, as if 'twere nothing new—
The Turk doing but as bid to do—   30
A higher stand-point would command.
    But here across his shortened rein
And loosened, shrewd, keen yataghan,
Good Nehemiah laid a hand:
"Djalea, stay—not long I'll be;   35
A word, one Christian word with ye.
I've just been reading in the place
How, on a time, carles far from grace
Left here half dead the faring man:
Those wicked thieves. But heaven befriends,   40
Still heaven at need a rescue lends:
Mind ye the Good Samaritan?"—
    In patient self-control high-bred,
Half of one sense, an ear, the Druze
Inclined; the while his grave eye fed   45
Afar; his arms at hand for use.
    "He," said the meek one going on,
Naught heeding but the tale he spun,
"He, when he saw him in the snare,
He had compassion; and with care   50
Him gently wakened from the swound
And oil and wine poured in the wound;
Then set him on his own good beast,

And bare him to the nighest inn—
A man not of his town or kin—   55
And tended whom he thus released;
Up with him sat he all that night,
Put off he did his journey quite;
And on the morrow, ere he went,
For the mistrustful host he sent,   60
And taking out his careful purse,
He gave him pence; and thus did sue:
'Beseech ye now that well ye nurse
This poor man whom I leave with you;
And whatsoe'er thou spendest more,   65
When I again come, I'll restore.'—
Ye mind the chapter? Well, this day
Were some forlorn one here to bleed,
Aid would be meted to his need
By good soul traveling this way.   70
Speak I amiss? an answer, pray?"—
    In deference the armed man,
O'er pistols, gun, and yataghan,
The turban bowed, but nothing said;
Then turned—resumed his purpose. Led   75
By old traditionary sense,
A liberal, fair reverence,
The Orientals homage pay,
And license yield in tacit way
To men demented, or so deemed.   80

    Derwent meanwhile in saddle there
Heard all, but scarce at ease he seemed,
So ill the tale and time did pair.

    Vine whispered to the saint aside:
"There was a Levite and a priest."   85
    "Whom God forgive," he mild replied,
"As I forget;" and there he ceased.

    Touching that trouble in advance,
Some here, much like to landsmen wise

At sea in hour which tackle tries,   90
The adventure's issue left to chance.
    In spent return the escort wind
Reporting they had put to flight
Some prowlers.—"Look!" one cried. Behind
A lesser ridge just glide from sight—   95
Though neither man nor horse appears—
Steel points and hair-tufts of five spears.
Like dorsal fins of sharks they show
When upright these divide the wave
And peer above, while down in grave   100
Of waters, slide the body lean
And charnel mouth.
                   With thoughtful mien
The student fared, nor might withstand
The something dubious in the Holy Land.

10. A Halt

In divers ways which vary it
Stones mention find in hallowed Writ:
Stones rolled from well-mouths, altar stones,
Idols of stone, memorial ones,
Sling-stones, stone tables; Bethel high   5
Saw Jacob, under starry sky,
On stones his head lay—desert bones;
Stones sealed the sepulchers—huge cones
Heaved there in bulk; death too by stones
The law decreed for crime; in spite   10
As well, for taunt, or type of ban,
The same at place were cast, or man;
Or piled upon the pits of fight
Reproached or even denounced the slain:
So in the wood of Ephraim, some   15
Laid the great heap over Absalom.
    Convenient too at willful need,
Stones prompted many a ruffian deed
And ending oft in parting groans;

By stones died Naboth; stoned to death   20
Was Stephen meek: and Scripture saith,
Against even Christ they took up stones.
     Moreover, as a thing profuse,
Suggestive still in every use,
On stones, still stones, the gospels dwell   25
In lesson meet or happier parable.

     Attesting here the Holy Writ—
In brook, in glen, by tomb and town
In natural way avouching it—
Behold the stones! And never one   30
A lichen greens; and, turn them o'er—
No worm—no life; but, all the more,
Good witnesses.
         The way now led
Where shoals of flints and stones lay dead.
The obstructed horses tripped and stumbled,   35
The Thessalonian groaned and grumbled.
     But Glaucon cried: "Alack the stones!
Or be they pilgrims' broken bones
Wherewith they pave the turnpikes here?
Is this your sort of world, Mynheer?   40

     "Not on your knee—no no, no no;
       But sit you so: verily and verily
     Paris, are you true or no?
       I'll look down your eyes and see.

     "Helen, look—and look and look;   45
       Look me, Helen, through and through;
     Make me out the only rake:
       Set down one and carry two."—

     "Have done, sir," roared the Elder out;
"Have done with this lewd balladry."—   50
     Amazed the singer turned about;
But when he saw that, past all doubt,
The Scot was in dead earnest, he,

"Oh now, monsieur—monsieur, monsieur!"
Appealing there so winningly—   55
Conceding, as it were, his age,
Station, and moral gravity,
And right to be morose indeed,
Nor less endeavoring to assuage
At least. But scarce did he succeed.   60

    Rolfe likewise, if in other style,
Here sought that hard road to beguile;
"The stone was man's first missile; yes,
Cain hurled it, or his sullen hand
Therewith made heavy. Cain, confess,   65
A savage was, although he planned
His altar. Altars such as Cain's
Still find we on far island-chains
Deep mid the woods and hollows dark,
And set off like the shittim Ark.   70
Refrain from trespass; with black frown
Each votary straight takes up his stone—
As once against even me indeed:
I see them now start from their rocks
In malediction."
            "Yet concede,   75
They were but touchy in their creed,"
Said Derwent; "but did you succumb?
These irritable orthodox!"—
    Thereat the Elder waxed more glum.

    A halt being called now with design   80
Biscuit to bite and sip the wine,
The student saw the turbaned Druze
A courtesy peculiar use
In act of his accosting Vine,
Tho' but in trifle—as to how   85
The saddle suited. And before,
In little things, he'd marked the show
Of like observance. How explore
The cause of this, and understand?

The pilgrims were an equal band: 90
Why this preferring way toward one?
    But Rolfe explained in undertone:
"But few, believe, have nicer eye
For the cast of aristocracy
Than Orientals. Well now, own,   95
Despite at times a manner shy,
Shows not our countryman in mold
Of a romanced nobility?
His chary speech, his rich still air
Confirm them in conjecture there.   100
I make slim doubt these people hold
Vine for some lord who fain would go
For delicate cause, incognito.—
What means Sir Crab?"—
                        In smouldering ire
The Elder, not dismounting, views   105
The nearer prospect; ill content,
The distance next his glance pursues,
A land of Eblis burned with fire;
Recoils; then, with big eyebrows bent,
Lowers on the comrades—Derwent most,   110
With luncheon now and flask engrossed;
His bridle turns, adjusts his seat
And holsters where the pistols be,
Nor taking leave like Christian sweet,
(Quite mindless of Paul's courtesy)   115
With dumb indomitable chin
Straight back he aims thro' Adommin,
Alone, nor blandly self-sustained—
Robber and robber-glen disdained.
    As stiff he went, his humor dark   120
From Vine provoked a vivid spark—
Derisive comment, part restrained.
    He passes. Well, peace with him go.
If truth have painted heart but grim,
None here hard measure meant for him;   125
Nay, Haytian airs around him blow,
And woo and win to cast behind

The harsher and inclement mind.
But needs narrate what followed now.
    "Part from us," Derwent cried, "that way?   130
I fear we have offended. Nay,
What other cause?"—
                "The desert, see:
He and the desert don't agree,"
Said Rolfe; "or rather, let me say
He can't provoke a quarrel here   135
With blank indifference so drear:
Ever the desert waives dispute,
Cares not to argue, bides but mute.
Besides, no topographic cheer:
Surveyor's tape don't come in play;   140
The same with which upon a day
He upon all fours soused did roam
Measuring the sub-ducts of Siloam.
Late asking him in casual way
Something about the Tomb's old fane,   145
These words I got: 'Sir, I don't know;
But once I dropped in—not again;
'Tis monkish, 'tis a raree-show—
A raree-show. Saints, sites, and stuff.
Had I my will I'd strip it, strip!'   150
I knew 'twere vain to try rebuff;
But asked, 'Did Paul, embarked in ship
With Castor and Pollux for a sign
Deem it incumbent there to rip
From stern and prow the name and shrine?'   155
'Saint Paul, sir, had not zeal enough;
I always thought so;' and went on:
'Where stands this fane, this Calvary one
Alleged? why, sir, *within* the site
Of Herod's wall? Can *that* be right?'   160
But why detail. Suffice, in few,
Even Zion's hill, he doubts that too;
Nay, Sinai in his dry purview
He's dubious if, as placed, it meet
Requirements."

          "Why then do his feet   165
Tread Judah? no good end is won;"
Said Derwent.
             "Curs need have a bone
To mumble, though but dry nor sweet.
Nay, that's too harsh and overdone.
'Tis still a vice these carpers brew—   170
They try us—us set carping too."
   "Ah well, quick then in thought we'll shun him,
And so foreclose all strictures on him.
Howbeit, this confess off-hand:
Amiss is robed in gown and band   175
A disenchanter.—Friend, the wine!"
   The banker passed it without word.
Sad looked he: Why, these fools are stirred
About a nothing!—Plain to see
Such comradeship did ill agree: 180
Pedants, and poor! nor used to dine
In ease of table-talk benign—
Steeds, pictures, ladies, gold, Tokay,
Gardens and baths, the English news,
Stamboul, the market—gain or lose?   185
   He turned to where young Glaucon lay,
Who now to startled speech was won:
"Look, is he crazy? see him there!"
The saint it was with busy care
Flinging aside stone after stone,   190
Yet feebly, nathless as he wrought
In charge imposed though not unloved;
While every stone that he removed
Laid bare but more. The student sighed,
So well he kenned his ways distraught   195
At influx of his eldritch tide.
   But Derwent, hastening to the spot,
Exclaimed, "How now? surely, 'tis not
To mend the way?"
             With patient look,
Poising a stone as 'twere a clod: 200
"All things are possible with God;

The humblest helper will he brook."
    Derwent stood dumb; but quick in heart
Conjecturing how it was, addressed
Some friendly words, and slid apart;   205
And, yet while by that scene impressed,
Came, as it chanced, where unbecalmed
Mortmain aloof sat all disarmed—
Legs lengthwise crossed, head hanging low,
The skull-cap pulled upon the brow,   210
Hands groping toward the knees: "Then where?
A Thug, the sword-fish roams the sea—
The falcon's pirate in the air;
Betwixt the twain, where shalt thou flee,
Poor flying-fish? whither repair?   215
What other element for thee?
Whales, mighty whales have felt the wound—
Plunged bleeding thro' the blue profound;
But where their fangs the sand-sharks keep
Be shallows worse than any deep."—   220
    Hardly that chimed with Derwent's bell:
Him too he left.
          When it befell
That new they started on their way;
To turn the current or allay,
He talked with Clarel, and first knew   225
Nehemiah's conceit about the Jew:
The ways prepared, the tilth restored
For the second coming of Our Lord.
    Rolfe overheard: "And shall we say
That this is craze? or but, in brief,   230
Simplicity of plain belief?
The early Christians, how did they?
For His return looked any day."

    From dwelling on Rolfe's thought, ere long
On Rolfe himself the student broods: 235
Surely I would not think a wrong;
Nor less I've shrunk from him in moods.
A bluntness is about him set:

Truth's is it? But he winneth yet
Through taking qualities which join.   240
Make these the character? the rest
But rim? On Syracusan coin
The barbarous letters shall invest
The relievo's infinite of charm.—
I know not. Does he help, or harm?   245

11. OF DESERTS

Tho' frequent in the Arabian waste
The pilgrim, up ere dawn of day,
Inhale thy wafted musk, Cathay;
And Adam's primal joy may taste,
Beholding all the pomp of night   5
Bee'd thick with stars in swarms how bright;
And so, rides on alert and braced—
Tho' brisk at morn the pilgrim start,
Ere long he'll know in weary hour
Small love of deserts, if their power   10
Make to retreat upon the heart
Their own forsakenness.
                             Darwin quotes
From Shelley, that forever floats
Over all desert places known,
Mysterious doubt—an awful one.   15
He quotes, adopts it. Is it true?
Let instinct vouch; let poetry
Science and instinct here agree,
For truth requires strong retinue.

Waste places are where yet is given   20
A charm, a beauty from the heaven
Above them, and clear air divine—
Translucent æther opaline;
And some in evening's early dew
Put on illusion of a guise   25
Which Tantalus might tantalize

Afresh; ironical unrolled
Like Western counties all in grain
Ripe for the sickleman and wain;
Or, tawnier than the Guinea gold,   30
More like a lion's skin unfold:
Attest the desert opening out
Direct from Cairo by the Gate
Of Victors, whence the annual rout
To Mecca bound, precipitate   35
Their turbaned frenzy.—
                Sands immense
Impart the oceanic sense:
The flying grit like scud is made:
Pillars of sand which whirl about
Or arc along in colonnade,   40
True kin be to the water-spout.
Yonder on the horizon, red
With storm, see there the caravan
Straggling long-drawn, dispirited;
Mark how it labors like a fleet   45
Dismasted, which the cross-winds fan
In crippled disaster of retreat
From battle.—
            Sinai had renown
Ere thence was rolled the thundered Law;
Ever a terror wrapped its crown;   50
Never did shepherd dare to draw
Too nigh (Josephus saith) for awe
Of one, some ghost or god austere—
Hermit unknown, dread mountaineer.—

When comes the sun up over Nile   55
In cloudlessness, what cloud is cast
O'er Lybia? Thou shadow vast
Of Cheops' indissoluble pile,
Typ'st thou the imperishable Past
In empire posthumous and reaching sway   60
Projected far across to time's remotest day?
     But curb.—Such deserts in air-zone

Or object lend suggestive tone,
Redeeming them.
           For Judah here—
Let Erebus her rival own: 65
'Tis horror absolute—severe,
Dead, livid, honey-combed, dumb, fell—
A caked depopulated hell;
Yet so created, judged by sense,
And visaged in significance   70
Of settled anger terrible.
    Profoundly cloven through the scene
Winds Kedron—word (the scholar saith)
Importing anguish hard on death.
And aptly may such named ravine   75
Conduct unto Lot's mortal Sea
In cleavage from Gethsemane
Where it begins.
             But why does man
Regard religiously this tract
Cadaverous and under ban   80
Of blastment? Nay, recall the fact
That in the pagan era old
When bolts, deemed Jove's, tore up the mound,
Great stones the simple peasant rolled
And built a wall about the gap   85
Deemed hallowed by the thunder-clap.
So here: men here adore this ground
Which doom hath smitten. 'Tis a land
Direful yet holy—blest tho' banned.

    But to pure hearts it yields no fear;   90
And John, he found wild honey here.

12. THE BANKER

Infer the wilds which next pertain.
Though travel here be still a walk,
Small heart was theirs for easy talk.

Oblivious of the bridle-rein
Rolfe fell to Lethe altogether,   5
Bewitched by that uncanny weather
Of sultry cloud. And home-sick grew
The banker. In his reverie blue
The cigarette, a summer friend,
Went out between his teeth—could lend   10
No solace, soothe him nor engage.
And now disrelished he each word
Of sprightly, harmless persiflage
Wherewith young Glaucon here would fain
Evince a jaunty disregard.   15
But hush betimes o'ertook the twain—
The more impressive, it may be,
For that the senior, somewhat spent,
Florid overmuch and corpulent,
Labored in lungs, and audibly.   20
    Rolfe, noting that the sufferer's steed
Was far less easy than his own,
Relieved him in his hour of need
By changing with him; then in tone
Aside, half musing, as alone,   25
"Unwise he is to venture here,
Poor fellow; 'tis but sorry cheer
For Mammon. Ill would it accord
If nabob with asthmatic breath
Lighted on Holbein's Dance of Death   30
Sly slipped among his prints from Claude.
Cosmetic-users scarce are bold
To face a skull. That sachem old
Whose wigwam is man's heart within—
How taciturn, and yet can speak,   35
Imparting more than books can win;
Not Pleasure's darling cares to seek
Such counselor: the worse he fares;
Since—heedless, taken unawares—
Arrest he finds.—Look: at yon ground   40
How starts he now! So Abel's hound,
Snuffing his prostrate master wan,

Shrank back from earth's first murdered man.—
But friend, how thrivest?" turning there
To Derwent. He, with altered air,   45
Made vague rejoinder, nor serene:
His soul, if not cast down, was vexed
By Nature in this dubious scene:
His theory she harsh perplexed—
The more so for wild Mortmain's mien: 50
And Nehemiah in eldritch cheer:
"Lord, now Thou goest forth from Seir;
Lord, now from Edom marchest Thou!"—

    Shunning the Swede—disturbed to know
The saint in strange clairvoyance so,   55
Clarel yet turned to meet the grace
Of one who not infected dwelt—
Yes, Vine, who shared his horse's pace
In level sameness, as both felt
At home in dearth.
              But unconcern   60
That never knew Vine's thoughtful turn
The venerable escort showed:
True natives of the waste abode,
They moved like insects of the leaf—
Tint, tone adapted to the fief.   65

13. Flight of the Greeks

"King, who betwixt the cross and sword
On ashes died in cowl and cord—
In desert died; and, if thy heart
Betrayed thee not, from life didst part
A martyr for thy martyred Lord;   5
Anointed one and undefiled—
O warrior manful, tho' a child
In simple faith—St. Louis! rise,

And teach us out of holy eyes
Whence came thy trust."

              So Rolfe, and shrank,   10
Awed by that region dread and great;
Thence led to take to heart the fate
Of one who tried in such a blank,
Believed—and died.
              Lurching was seen
An Arab tall, on camel lean,   15
Up laboring from a glen's remove,
His long lance upright fixed above
The gun across the knee in guard.
So rocks in hollow trough of sea
A wreck with one gaunt mast, and yard   20
Displaced and slanting toward the lee.
Closer he drew; with visage mute,
Austere in passing made salute.
Such courtesy may vikings lend
Who through the dreary Hecla wend.   25
   Under gun, lance, and scabbard hacked
Pressed Nehemiah; with ado
High he reached up an Arab tract
From the low ass—"Christ's gift to you!"
With clatter of the steel he bore   30
The lofty nomad bent him o'er
In grave regard. The camel too
Her crane-like neck swerved round to view;
Nor more to camel than to man
Inscrutable the ciphers ran.   35
But wonted unto arid cheer,
The beast, misjudging, snapped it up,
And would have munched, but let it drop;
Her master, poling down his spear
Transfixed the page and brought it near,   40
Nor stayed his travel.
              On they went
Through solitudes, till made intent

By small sharp shots which stirred rebound
In echo. Over upland drear
On tract of less obstructed ground   45
Came fairly into open sight
A mounted train in tulip plight:
Ten Turks, whereof advanced rode four,
With leveled pistols, left and right
Graceful diverging, as in plume   50
Feather from feather. So brave room
They make for turning toward each shore
Ambiguous in nooks of blight,
Discharging shots; then reunite,
And, with obeisance bland, adore   55
Their prince, a fair youth, who, behind—
'Tween favorites of equal age,
Brilliant in paynim equipage—
With Eastern dignity how sweet,
Nods to their homage, pleased to mind   60
Their gallant curvets. Still they meet,
Salute and wheel, and him precede,
As in a pleasure-park or mead.

    The escorts join; and some would take
To parley, as is wont. The Druze,   65
Howbeit, hardly seems to choose
The first advances here to make;
Nor does he shun. Alert is seen
One in voluminous turban green,
Beneath which in that barren place   70
Sheltered he looks as by the grace
Of shady palm-tuft. Vernal he
In sacerdotal chivalry:
That turban by its hue declares
That the great Prophet's blood he shares: 75
Kept as the desert stallions be,
'Tis an attested pedigree.
But ah, the bigot, he could lower
In mosque on the intrusive Giaour.
To make him truculent for creed   80
Family-pride joined personal greed.

Tho' foremost here his word he vents—
Officious in the conference,
In rank and sway he ranged, in sooth,
Behind that fine sultanic youth   85
Which held his place apart, and, cool,
In lapse or latency of rule
Seemed mindless of the halting train
And pilgrims there of Franquestan
Or land of Franks. Remiss he wore   90
An indolent look superior.
His grade might justify the air:
The viceroy of Damascus' heir.
His father's jurisdiction sweeps
From Lebanon to Ammon's steeps.   95
Return he makes from mission far
To independent tribes of war
Beyond the Hauran. In advance
Of the main escort, gun and lance,
He aims for Salem back.
                This learned,   100
In anxiousness the banker yearned
To join; nor Glaucon seemed averse.
'Twas quick resolved, and soon arranged
Through fair diplomacy of purse
And Eastern compliments exchanged.   105
    Their wine, in pannier of the mule,
Upon the pilgrims they bestow:
"And pledge us, friends, in valley cool,
If such this doleful road may know:
Farewell!" And so the Moslem train   110
Received these Christians, happy twain.

    They fled. And thou? The way is dun;
Why further follow the Emir's son?
Scarce yet the thought may well engage
To lure thee thro' these leafless bowers,   115
That little avails a pilgrimage
Whose road but winds among the flowers.
Part here, then, would ye win release
From ampler dearth; part, and in peace.

Nay, part like Glaucon, part with song: 120
The note receding dies along:

> "Tarry never there
> Where the air
> Lends a lone Hadean spell—
> Where the ruin and the wreck   125
> Vine and ivy never deck,
> And wizard wan and sibyl dwell:
> There, oh, beware!

> "Rather seek the grove—
> Thither rove,   130
> Where the leaf that falls to ground
> In a violet upsprings,
> And the oracle that sings
> Is the bird above the mound:
> There, tarry there!"   135

14. By Achor

Jerusalem, the mountain town
Is based how far above the sea;
But down, a lead-line's long reach down,
A deep-sea lead, beneath the zone
Of ocean's level, heaven's decree   5
Has sunk the pool whose deeps submerged
The doomed Pentapolis fire-scourged.
    Long then the slope, though varied oft,
From Zion to the seats abject;
For rods and roods ye wind aloft   10
By verges where the pulse is checked;
And chief both hight and steepness show
Ere Achor's gorge the barrier rends
And like a thunder-cloud impends
Ominous over Jericho.   15

    Hard by the brink the Druze leads on,
But halts at a projecting crown

Of cliff, and beckons them. Nor goat
Nor fowler ranging far and high
Scales such a steep; nor vulture's eye   20
Scans one more lone. Deep down in throat
It shows a sooty black.
                "A forge
Abandoned," Rolfe said, "thus may look."
    "Yea," quoth the saint, "and read the Book:
Flames, flames have forked in Achor's gorge."   25
    His wizard vehemence surprised:
Some new illusion they surmised;
Not less authentic text he took:
"Yea, after slaughter made at Ai
When Joshua's three thousand fled,   30
Achan the thief they made to die—
They stoned him in this hollow here—
They burned him with his children dear;
Among them flung his ingot red
And scarlet robe of Babylon: 35
Meet end for Carmi's wicked son
Because of whom they failed at Ai:
'Twas meet the trespasser should die;
Yea, verily."—His visage took
The tone of that uncanny nook.   40
    To Rolfe here Derwent: "Study him;
Then weigh that most ungenial rule
Of Moses and the austere school
Which e'en our saint can make so grim—
At least while Achor feeds his eyes."   45
"But here speaks Nature otherwise?"
Asked Rolfe; "in region roundabout
She's Calvinistic if devout
In all her aspect."—
              Vine, o'ercast,
Estranged rode in thought's hid repast.   50
Clarel, receptive, saw and heard,
Learning, unlearning, word by word.
    Erelong the wilds condense the ill—
They hump it into that black Hill
Named from the Forty Days and Nights,   55

The Quarantania's sum of blights.
Up from the gorge it grows, it grows:
Hight sheer, sheer depth, and death's repose.
Sunk in the gulf the wave disowns,
Stranded lay ancient torrent-stones.   60
These Mortmain marks: "Ah, from your deep
Turn ye, appeal ye to the steep?
But that looks off, and everywhere
Descries but worlds more waste, more bare."

    Flanked by the crag and glen they go.   65
Ahead, erelong in greeting show
The mounts of Moab, o'er the vale
Of Jordan opening into view,
With cloud-born shadows sweeping thro'.
    The Swede, intent: "Lo, how they trail,   70
The mortcloths in the funeral
Of gods!"
        Although he naught confessed,
In Derwent, marking there the scene,
What interference was expressed
As of harsh grit in oiled machine—   75
Disrelish grating interest:
Howbeit, this he tried to screen.
"Pisgah!" cried Rolfe, and pointed him.
    "Peor, too—ay, long Abarim
The ridge. Well, well: for thee I sigh,   80
Poor Moses. Saving Jericho
And her famed palms in Memphian row,
No cheerful landscape met thine eye;
Unless indeed (yon Pisgah's high)
Was caught, beyond each mount and plain,   85
The blue, blue Mediterranean."
    "And might he then for Egypt sigh?"
Here prompted Rolfe; but no reply;
And Rolfe went on: "Balboa's ken
Roved in fine sweep from Darien: 90
The woods and waves in tropic meeting,

Bright capes advancing, bays retreating—
Green land, blue sea in charm competing!"

    Meantime, with slant reverted eyes
Vine marked the Crag of Agonies.   95
Exceeding high (as Matthew saith)
It shows from skirt of that wild path
Bare as an iceberg seamed by rain
Toppling awash in foggy main
Off Labrador. Grottoes Vine viewed   100
Upon the flank—or cells or tombs—
Void as the iceberg's catacombs
Of frost. He starts. A form endued
With living guise, from ledges dim
Leans as if looking down toward him.   105
Not pointing out the thing he saw
Vine watched it, but it showed no claw
Of hostile purpose; tho' indeed
Robbers and outlaws armed have dwelt
Vigilant by those caves where knelt   110
Of old the hermits of the creed.

    Beyond, they win a storied fount
Which underneath the higher mount
Gurgles, clay-white, and downward sets
Toward Jericho in rivulets,   115
Which—much like children whose small mirth
Not funerals can stay—through dearth
Run babbling. One old humpbacked tree,
Sad grandam whom no season charms,
Droops o'er the spring her withered arms;   120
And stones as in a ruin laid,
Like penitential benches be
Where silent thickets fling a shade
And gather dust. Here halting, here
Awhile they rest and try the cheer.   125

15. THE FOUNTAIN

It brake, it brake how long ago,
That morn which saw thy marvel done,
Elisha—healing of the spring!
A good deed lives, the doer low:
See how the waters eager run   5
With bounty which they chiming bring:
So out of Eden's bounds afar
Hymned Pison through green Havilah!
    But ill those words in tone impart
The simple feelings in the heart   10
Of Nehemiah—full of the theme,
Standing beside the marge, with cup,
And pearls of water-beads adroop
Down thinnish beard of silvery gleam.
    "Truly," said Derwent, glad to note   15
That Achor found her antidote,
"Truly, the fount wells grateful here."
Then to the student: "For the rest,
The site is pleasant; nor unblest
These thickets by their shade endear."   20
    Assent half vacant Clarel gave,
Watching that miracle the wave.
    Said Rolfe, reclining by the rill,
"Needs life must end or soon or late:
Perchance set down it is in fate   25
That fail I must ere we fulfill
Our travel. Should it happen true—
Attention, pray—I mend my will,
And name executors in you:
Bury me by the road, somewhere   30
Near spring or brook. Palms plant me there,
And seats with backs to them, all stone:
In peace then go. The years shall run,
And green my grave shall be, and play
The part of host to all that stray   35
In desert: water, shade, and rest
Their entertainment. So I'll win
Balm to my soul by each poor guest

That solaced leaves the Dead Man's Inn.
But charges, mind, yourselves defray—   40
Seeing I've naught."
                        Where thrown he lay,
Vine, sensitive, suffused did show,
Yet looked not up, but seemed to weigh
The nature of the heart whose trim
Of quaint goodfellowship could so   45
Strike on a chord long slack in him.
        But how may spirit quick and deep
A constancy unfreakish keep?
A reed there shaken fitfully
He marks: "Was't this we came to see   50
In wilderness?" and rueful smiled.
        The meek one, otherwise beguiled,
Here chancing now the ass to note
Languidly munching straw and bran,
Drew nigh, and smoothed the roughened coat,   55
And gave her bread, the wheaten grain.
        Vine watches; and his aspect knows
A flush of diffident humor: "Nay,
Me too, me too let wait, I pray,
On our snubbed kin here;" and he rose.   60

        Erelong, alert the escort show:
'Tis stirrups. But the Swede moved not,
Aloof abiding in dark plot
Made by the deeper shadow: "Go—
My horse lead; but for me, I stay;   65
Some bread—there, that small loaf will do:
It is my whim—my whim, I say;
Mount, heed not me."—"And how long, pray?"
Asked Derwent, startled: "eve draws on:
Ye would not tarry here alone?"   70
        "Thou man of God, nor desert here,
Nor Zin, nor Obi, yieldeth fear
If God but be—but be! This waste—
Soon shall night fold the hemisphere;
But safer then to lay me down,   75
Here, by yon evil Summit faced—

Safer than in the cut-throat town
Though on the church-steps. Go from me—
Begone! To-morrow or next day
Jordan ye greet, then round ye sway   80
And win Lot's marge. In sight ye'll be:
I'll intercept. Ride on, go—nay,
Bewitched, why gape ye so at me?
Shall man not take the natural way
With nature? Tut, fling me the cloak!"   85
    Away, precipitate he broke,
The skull-cap glooming thro' the glade:
They paused, nor ventured to invade.

    While so, not unconcerned, they stood,
The Druze said, "Well, let be. Why chafe?   90
Nights here are mild; one's pretty safe
When fearless.—Belex! come, the road!"

16. NIGHT IN JERICHO

Look how a pine in luckless land
By fires autumnal overrun,
Abides a black extinguished brand
Gigantic—killed, not overthrown;
And high upon the horny bough   5
Perches the bandit captain-crow
And caws unto his troop afar
Of foragers: much so, in scar
Of blastment, looms the Crusaders' Tower
On the waste verge of Jericho: 10
So the dun sheik in lawless power
Kings it aloft in sombre robe,
Lord of the tawny Arab mob
To which, upon the plains in view,
He shouts down his wild hullabaloo.   15

    There on the tower, through eve's delay
The pilgrims tarry, till for boon,

Launched up from Nebo far away,
Balloon-like rose the nibbled moon—
Nibbled, being after full one day.   20
Intent they watched the planet's rise—
Familiar, tho' in strangest skies.
The ascending orb of furrowed gold,
Contracting, changed, and silvery rolled
In violet heaven. The desert brown,   25
Dipped in the dream of argent light,
Like iron plated, took a tone
Transmuting it; and Ammon shone
In peaks of Paradise—so bright.
  They gazed. Rolfe brake upon the calm: 30
"O haunted place, O powerful charm!
Were now Elijah's chariot seen
(And yonder, read we writ aright,
He went up—over against this site)
Soaring in that deep heaven serene,   35
To me 'twould but in beauty rise;
Nor hair-clad John would now surprise—
But Volney!"
    "Volney?" Derwent cried;
"Ah, yes; he came to Jordan's side
A pilgrim deist from the Seine."   40
  "Ay, and Chateaubriand, he too,
The Catholic pilgrim, hither drew—
Here formed his purpose to assert
Religion in her just desert
Against the Red Caps of his time.   45
The book he wrote; it dies away;
But those Septemberists of crime
Enlarge in Vitriolists to-day.
Nor while we dwell upon this scene
Can one forget poor Lamartine—   50
A latter palmer. Oh, believe
When, his fine social dream to grieve,
Strode Fate, that realist how grim,
Displacing, deriding, hushing him,
Apt comment then might memory weave   55

In lesson from this waste.—That cry!
And would the jackal testify
From Moab?"
                    Derwent could but sway:
"Omit ye in citation, pray,
The healthy pilgrims of times old?   60
Robust they were; and cheery saw
Shrines, chapels, castles without flaw
Now gone. That river convent's fold,
By willows nigh the Pilgrims' Strand
Of Jordan, was a famous hold.   65
Prince Sigurd from the Norseman land,
Quitting his keel at Joppa, crossed
Hither, with Baldwin for his host,
And Templars for a guard. Perchance
Under these walls the train might prance   70
By Norman warder eyed."
                    "Maybe,"
Responded Vine; "but why disown
The Knight of the Leopard—even he,
Since hereabout that fount made moan,
Named Diamond of the Desert?"—"Yes,"   75
Beamed Rolfe, divining him in clue;
"Such shadows we, one need confess
That Scott's dreamed knight seems all but true
As men which history vouches. She—
Tasso's Armida, by Lot's sea,   80
Where that enchantress, with sweet look
Of kindliest human sympathy,
Such webs about Rinaldo wove
That all the hero he forsook—
Lost in the perfidies of love—   85
Armida—starts at fancy's bid
Not less than Rahab, lass which hid
The spies here in this Jericho."

    A lull. Their thoughts, mute plunging, strayed
Like Arethusa under ground;   90
While Clarel marked where slumber-bound
Lay Nehemiah in screening shade.

Erelong, in reappearing tide,
Rolfe, gazing forth on either side:
"How lifeless! But the annual rout   95
At Easter here, shall throng and shout,
Far populate the lonely plain,
(Next day a solitude again,)
All pressing unto Jordan's dew;
While in the saddle of disdain   100
Skirr the Turk guards with fierce halloo,
Armed herdsmen of the drove." He ceased;
And fell the silence unreleased
Till yet again did Rolfe round peer
Upon that moonlit land of fear: 105
     "Man sprang from deserts: at the touch
Of grief or trial overmuch,
On deserts he falls back at need;
Yes, 'tis the bare abandoned home
Recalleth then. See how the Swede   110
Like any rustic crazy Tom,
Bursting through every code and ward
Of civilization, masque and fraud,
Takes the wild plunge. Who so secure,
Except his clay be sodden loam,   115
As never to dream the day may come
When *he* may take it, foul or pure?
What in these turns of mortal tides—
What any fellow-creature bides,
May hap to any."
                    "Pardon, pray,"   120
Cried Derwent—"but 'twill quick away:
Yon moon in pearl-cloud: look, her face
Peers like a bride's from webs of lace."
They gazed until it faded there:
When Rolfe with a discouraged air   125
Sat as rebuked. In winning strain,
As 'twere in penitence urbane,
Here Derwent, "Come, we wait thee now."
     "No matter," Rolfe said; "let it go.
My earnestness myself decry;   130
But as heaven made me, so am I."

"You spake of Mortmain," breathed Vine low.
As embers, not yet cold, will catch
Quick at the touch of smallest match,
Here Rolfe: "In gusts of lonely pain   135
Beating upon the naked brain—"
     "God help him, ay, poor realist!"
So Derwent, and that theme dismissed.

     When Ashtoreth her zenith won,
Sleep drugged them and the winds made moan.   140

17. IN MID-WATCH

Disturbed by topics canvassed late,
Clarel, from dreams of like debate,
Started, and heard strange muffled sounds,
Outgivings of wild mountain bounds.
He rose, stood gazing toward the hight—   5
Bethinking him that thereaway
Behind it o'er the desert lay
The walls that sheltered Ruth that night—
When Rolfe drew near. With motion slight,
Scarce conscious of the thing he did,   10
Partly aside the student slid;
Then, quick as thought, would fain atone.
     Whence came that shrinking start unbid?
But from desire to be alone?
Or skim or sound him, was Rolfe one   15
Whom honest heart would care to shun?
By spirit immature or dim
Was nothing to be learned from him?
How frank seemed Rolfe. Yet Vine could lure
Despite reserve which overture   20
Withstood—e'en Clarel's—late repealed,
Finding that heart a fountain sealed.

     But Rolfe: however it might be—
Whether in friendly fair advance

Checked by that start of dissonance, 25
Or whether rapt in revery
Beyond—apart he moved, and leant
Down peering from the battlement
Upon its shadow. Then and there
Clarel first noted in his air 30
A gleam of oneness more than Vine's—
The irrelation of a weed
Detached from vast Sargasso's mead
And drifting where the clear sea shines.
    But Clarel turned him; and anew 35
His thoughts regained their prior clew;
When, lo, a fog, and all was changed.
Crept vapors from the Sea of Salt,
Overspread the plain, nor there made halt,
But blurred the heaven.
                As one estranged 40
Who watches, watches from the shore,
Till the white speck is seen no more,
The ship that bears his plighted maid,
Then turns and sighs as fears invade;
See here the student, repossessed 45
By thoughts of Ruth, with eyes late pressed
Whither lay Salem, close and wynd—
The mist before him, mist behind,
While intercepting memories ran
Of chant and bier Armenian. 50

18. THE SYRIAN MONK

At early hour with Rolfe and Vine
Clarel ascends a minor hight;
They overtake in lone recline
A strange wayfarer of the night
Who, 'twixt the small hour and the gray, 5
With cruze and scrip replenished late
In Jericho at the wattled gate,
Had started on the upland way:

A young strange man of aspect thin
From vigils which in fast begin.   10
Though, pinned together with the thorn,
His robe was ragged all and worn—
Pure did he show as mountain-leaf
By brook, or coral washed in reef.
Contrasting with the bleached head-dress   15
His skin revealed such swarthiness,
And in the contour clear and grace
So all unworldly was the face,
He looked a later Baptist John.
They start; surprise perforce they own: 20
Much like De Gama's men, may be,
When sudden on their prow at sea
Lit the strange bird from shores unknown.
      Although at first from words he shrunk,
He was, they knew, a Syrian monk.   25
They so prevailed with him and pressed,
He longer lingered at request.
They won him over in the end
To tell his story and unbend.

      He told how that for forty days,   30
Not yet elapsed, he dwelt in ways
Of yonder Quarantanian hight,
A true recluse, an anchorite;
And only came at whiles below,
And ever in the calm of night,   35
To beg for scraps in Jericho.
'Twas sin, he said, that drove him out
Into the desert—sin of doubt.
Even he it was upon the mount
By chance perceived, untold, by Vine,   40
From Achor's brink. He gave account
Of much besides; his lonely mine
Of deep illusion; how the night,
The first, was spent upon the hight,
And way he climbed:

                        "Up cliff, up crag—   45
Cleft crag and cliff which still retard,
Goat-like I scrambled where stones lag
Poised on the brinks by thunder marred.
A ledge I reached which midway hung
Where a hut-oratory clung—   50
Rude stones massed up, with cave-like door,
Eremite work of days of yore.
White bones here lay, remains of feast
Dragged in by bird of prey or beast.
Hence gazed I on the wilds beneath,   55
Dengadda and the coasts of death.
But not a tremor felt I here:
It was upon the summit fear
First fell; there first I saw this world;
And scarce man's place it seemed to be;   60
The mazed Gehennas so were curled
As worm-tracks under bark of tree.
I ween not if to ye 'tis known—
Since few do know the crag aright,
Years left unvisited and lone—   65
That a wrecked chapel marks the site
Where tempter and the tempted stood
Of old. I sat me down to brood
Within that ruin; and—my heart
Unwaveringly to set apart   70
In meditation upon Him
Who here endured the evil whim
Of Satan—steadfast, steadfast down
Mine eyes fixed on a flinty stone
Which lay there at my feet. But thought   75
Would wander. Then the stone I caught,
Convulsed it in my hand till blood
Oozed from these nails. Then came and stood
The Saviour there—the Imp and He:
Fair showed the Fiend—foul enemy;   80
But, ah, the Other pale and dim:
I saw but as the shade of Him.

That passed. Again I was alone—
Alone—ah, no—not long alone:
As glides into dead grass the snake   85
Lean rustling from the bedded brake,
A spirit entered me. 'Twas he,
The tempter, in return; but *me*
He tempted now. He mocked: 'Why strife?
Dost hunger for the bread of life?   90
Thou lackest faith: faith would be fed;
True faith could turn that stone to bread,
That stone thou hold'st.'—Mute then my face
I lifted to the starry space;
But the great heaven it burned so bright,   95
It cowed me, and back fell my sight.
Then he: 'Is yon the Father's home?
And thou His child cast out to night?
'Tis bravely lighted, yonder dome.'—
'Part speak'st thou true: yea, He is there.'—   100
'Yea, yea, and He is everywhere—
Now and for aye, Evil and He.'—
'Is there no good?'—'Ill to fulfill
Needful is good: good salts the ill.'—
'He's just.'—'Goodness is justice. See,   105
Through all the pirate-spider's snare
Of silken arcs of gossamer,
'Tis delicate geometry:
Adorest the artificer?'—
No answer knew I, save this way: 110
'Faith bideth.'—'Noon, and wait for day?
The sand's half run! Eternal, He:
But aye with a futurity
Which not exceeds his past. Agree,
Full time has lapsed. What ages hoar,   115
What period fix, when faith no more,
If unfulfilled, shall fool?'—I sat;
Sore quivered I to answer that,
Yet answered naught; but lowly said—
'And death?'—'Why beat the bush in thee?   120
It is the cunningest mystery:

Alive thou know'st not death; and, dead,
Death thou'lt not know.'—'The grave will test;
But He, He *is,* though doubt attend;
Peace will He give ere come the end.'—   125
'Ha, *thou* at peace? Nay, peace were best—
Could the unselfish yearner rest!
At peace to be, here, here on earth,
Where peace, heart-peace, how few may claim,
And each pure nature pines in dearth—   130
Fie, fie, thy soul might well take shame.'—
There sunk my heart—he spake so true
In that. O God (I prayed), come through
The cloud; hard task Thou settest man
To know Thee; take me back again   135
To nothing, or make clear my view!—
Then stole the whisper intermitting;
Like tenon into mortice fitting
It slipped into the frame of me:
'Content thee: in conclusion caught   140
Thou'lt find how thought's extremes agree,—
The forethought clinched by afterthought,
The firstling by finality.'—
There close fell, and therewith the stone
Dropped from my hand.—His will be done!"   145
    And skyward patient he appealed,
Raising his eyes, and so revealed
First to the pilgrims' waiting view
Their virginal violet of hue.

    Rolfe spake: "Surely, not all we've heard: 150
Peace—solace—was in end conferred?"—
His head but fell. He rose in haste,
The rough hair-girdle tighter drew
About the hollow of the waist,
Departing with a mild adieu.   155

    They sat in silence. Rolfe at last:
"And this but ecstasy of fast?
Construe then Jonah in despair."—

The student turned, awaiting Vine;
Who answered nothing, plaiting there   160
A weed from neighboring ground uptorn,
Plant common enough in Palestine,
And by the peasants named Christ's Thorn.

19. AN APOSTATE

"Barque, Easter barque, with happier freight
Than Leon's spoil of Inca plate;
Which vernal glidest from the strand
Of statues poised like angels fair;
On March morn sailest—starting, fanned   5
Auspicious by Sardinian air;
And carriest boughs thro' Calpe's gate
To Norman ports and Belgian land,
That the Green Sunday, even there,
No substituted leaf may wear,   10
Holly or willow's lither wand,
But sprays of Christ's canonic tree,
Rome's Palma-Christi by decree,
The Date Palm; ah, in bounty launch,
Thou blessed Easter barque, to me   15
Hither one consecrated branch!"

So Rolfe in burst, and turned toward Vine;
But he the thorn-wreath still did twine.
Rolfe watched him busy there and dumb,
Then cried: "Did gardens favor it,   20
How would I match thee here, and sit
Wreathing Christ's flower, chrysanthemum."

Erelong the Syrian they view
In slow ascent, and also two
Between him and the peak,—one wight   25
An Arab with a pouch, nor light,
A desert Friday to the one
Who went before him, coming down,

Shagged Crusoe, by the mountain spur.
This last, when he the votary meets   30
Sad climbing slow, him loudly greets,
Stopping with questions which refer
In some way to the crag amort—
The crag, since thitherward his hand
Frequent he waves, as with demand   35
For some exact and clear report
Touching the place of his retreat
Aloft. As seemed, in neutral plight
Submiss responds the anchorite,
The wallet dropped beside his feet.   40
These part. Master and man now ply
Yet down the slope; and he in van—
Round-shouldered, and tho' gray yet spry—
A hammer swung.
        I've met that man
Elsewhere (thought Clarel)—he whose cry   45
And gibe came up from the dung-gate
In hollow, when we scarce did wait
His nearer speech and wagging head,
The saint and I.—But naught he said
Hereof.
      The stranger closer drew;   50
And Rolfe breathed "This now is a Jew,—
German, I deem—but readvised—
An Israelite, say, Hegelized—
Convert to science, for but see
The hammer: yes, geology."   55
As now the other's random sight
On Clarel mute and Vine is thrown,
He misinterprets their grave plight;
And, with a banter in the tone,
Amused he cries: "Now, now, yon hight—   60
Come, let it not alarm: a mount
Whereof I've taken strict account
(Its first geologist, believe),
And, if my eyes do not deceive,
'Tis Jura limestone, every spur;   65

Yes, and tho' signs the rocks imprint
Which of Plutonic action hint,
No track is found, I plump aver,
Of Pluto's footings—Lucifer."

    The punning mock and manner stirred   70
Repugnance in fastidious Vine;
But Rolfe, who tolerantly heard,
Parleyed, and won him to define
At large his rovings on the hight.
    The yester-afternoon and night   75
He'd spent there, sleeping in a cave—
Part for adventure, part to spite
The superstition, and outbrave.
'Twas a severe ascent, he said;
In bits a ladder of steep stone   80
With toe-holes cut, and worn, each one
By eremites long centuries dead.
And of his cullings too he told:
His henchman here, the Arab wight,
Bare solid texts from Bible old—   85
True Rock of Ages, he averred.
To read before a learned board,
When home regained should meet his sight,
A monograph he would indite—
The theme, that crag.
              He went his way,   90
To win the tower. Little they say;
But Clarel started at the view
Which showed opposed the anchorite
Ascetical and—such a Jew.

20. UNDER THE MOUNTAIN

From Ur of the Chaldees roved the man—
Priest, shepherd, prince, and pioneer—
Swart Bedouin in time's dusky van;
Even he which first, with mind austere,

Arrived in solitary tone   5
To think of God as One—alone;
The first which brake with hearth and home
For conscience' sake; whom piety ruled,
Prosperity blest, longevity schooled,
And time in fullness brought to Mamre's tomb   10
Arch founder of the solid base of Christendom.
    Even this. For why disown the debt
When vouchers be? Yet, yet and yet
Our saving salt of grace is due
All to the East—nor least the Jew.   15
    Perverse, if stigma then survive,
Elsewhere let such in satire thrive—
Not here. Quite other end is won
In picturing Margoth, fallen son
Of Judah. Him may Gabriel mend.   20

    Little for love, or to unbend,
But swayed by tidings, hard to sift,
Of robbers by the river-drift
In force recruited; they suspend
Their going hence to Jordan's trees.   25
Released from travel, in good hour
Nehemiah dozed within the tower.
    Uplands they range, and woo the breeze
Where crumbled aqueducts and mounds
Override long slopes and terraces,   30
And shattered pottery abounds—
Or such would seem, yet may but be
The shards of tile-like brick dispersed
Binding the wall or bulwark erst,
Such as in Kent still serve that end   35
In Richborough castle by the sea—
A Roman hold. What breadth of doom
As of the worlds in strata penned—
So cosmic seems the wreck of Rome.
    Not wholly proof to natural sway   40
Of serious hearts and manners mild,
Uncouthly Margoth shared the way.

He controverted all the wild,
And in especial, Sodom's strand
Of marl and clinker: "Sirs, heed me: 45
This total tract," and Esau's hand
He waved; "the plain—the vale—Lot's sea—
It needs we scientists remand
Back from old theologic myth
To geologic hammers. Pray,   50
Let me but give ye here the pith:
As the Phlegræan fields no more
Befool men as the spookish shore
Where Jove felled giants, but are known—
The Solfatara and each cone   55
Volcanic—to be but on a par
With all things natural; even so
Siddim shall likewise be set far
From fable."
                    Part overhearing this,
Derwent, in rear with Rolfe: "Old clo'!   60
We've heard all that, and long ago:
Conceit of vacant emphasis:
Well, well!"—Here archly, Rolfe: "But own,
How graceful your concession—won
A score or two of years gone by.   65
Nor less therefrom at need ye'll fly,
Allow. Scarce easy 'tis to hit
Each slippery turn of cleric wit."
Derwent but laughed; then said—"But *he:*
Intelligence veneers his mien   70
Though rude: unprofitably keen:
Sterile, and with sterility
Self-satisfied." "But this is odd!
Not often do we hear you rail:
The gown it seems does yet avail,   75
Since from the sleeve you draw the rod.
But look, they lounge."
                         Yes, all recline,
And on the site where havoc clove
The last late palm of royal line,
Sad Montezuma of the grove.   80

The mountain of the Imp they see
Scowl at the freedom which they take
Relaxed beneath his very lee.
    The bread of wisdom here to break,
Margoth holds forth: the gossip tells   85
Of things the prophets left unsaid—
With master-key unlocks the spells
And mysteries of the world unmade;
Then mentions Salem: "Stale is she!
Lay flat the walls, let in the air,   90
That folk no more may sicken there!
Wake up the dead; and let there be
Rails, wires, from Olivet to the sea,
With station in Gethsemane."
    The priest here flushed. Rolfe rose: and, "How—   95
You go too far!" "A long Dutch mile
Behind the genius of our time."
"Explain that, pray." "And don't you know?
Mambrino's helmet is sublime—
The barber's basin may be vile: 100
Whether this basin is that helm
To vast debate has given rise—
Question profound for blinking eyes;
But common sense throughout her realm
Has settled it."
        There, like vain wight   105
His fine thing said, bidding friends good night,
He, to explore a rift they see,
Parted, bequeathing, as might be,
A glance which said—Again ye'll pine
Left to yourselves here in decline,   110
Missing my brave vitality!

21. THE PRIEST AND ROLFE

Derwent fetched breath: "A healthy man:
His lungs are of the soundest leather."
"Health's insolence in a Saurian,"
Said Rolfe. With that they fell together

Probing the purport of the Jew   5
In last ambiguous words he threw.
But Derwent, and in lenient way,
Explained it.
                "Let him have his say,"
Cried Rolfe; "for one I spare defiance
With such a kangaroo of science."   10
    "Yes; qualify though," Derwent said,
"For science has her eagles too."
    Here musefully Rolfe hung the head;
Then lifted: "Eagles? ay; but few.
And search we in their æries lone   15
What find we, pray? perchance, a bone."
    "A very cheerful point of view!"
"'Tis as one takes it. Not unknown
That even in Physics much late lore
But drudges after Plato's theme;   20
Or supplements—but little more—
Some Hindoo's speculative dream
Of thousand years ago. And, own,
Darwin is but his grandsire's son."
    "But Newton and his gravitation!"   25
"Think you that system's strong persuasion
Is founded beyond shock? O'ermuch
'Twould seem for man, a clod, to clutch
God's secret so, and on a slate
Cipher all out, and formulate   30
The universe." "You Pyrrhonist!
Why, now, perhaps you do not see—
Your mind has taken such a twist—
The claims of stellar chemistry."
    "What's that?" "No matter. Time runs on   35
And much that's useful, grant, is won."
    "Yes; but more's claimed. Now first they tell
The human mind is free to range.
Enlargement—ay; but where's the change?
We're yet within the citadel—   40
May rove in bounds, and study out
The insuperable towers about."

"Come; but there's many a merry man:
How long since these sad times began?"
    That steadied Rolfe: "Where's no annoy   45
I too perchance can take a joy—
Yet scarce in solitude of thought:
Together cymbals need be brought
Ere mirth is made. The wight alone
Who laughs, is deemed a witless one.   50
And why? But that we'll leave unsought."
    "By all means!—O ye frolic shapes:
Thou Dancing Faun, thou Faun with Grapes!
What think ye of them? tell us, pray."
    "Fine mellow marbles."
                        "But their hint?"   55
"A mine as deep as rich the mint
Of cordial joy in Nature's sway
Shared somewhere by anterior clay
When life was innocent and free:
Methinks 'tis this they hint to me."   60
    He paused, as one who makes review
Of gala days; then—warmly too—
"Whither hast fled, thou deity
So genial? In thy last and best,
Best avatar—so ripe in form—   65
Pure as the sleet—as roses warm—
Our earth's unmerited fair guest—
A god with peasants went abreast:
Man clasped a deity's offered hand;
And woman, ministrant, was then   70
How true, even in a Magdalen.
Him following through the wilding flowers
By lake and hill, or glad detained
In Cana—ever out of doors—
Ere yet the disenchantment gained   75
What dream they knew, that primal band
Of gipsy Christians! But it died;
Back rolled the world's effacing tide:
The 'world'—by Him denounced, defined—
Him first—set off and countersigned,   80

Once and for all, as opposite
To honest children of the light.
But worse came—creeds, wars, stakes. Oh, men
Made earth inhuman; yes, a den
Worse for Christ's coming, since his love   85
(Perverted) did but venom prove.
In part that's passed. But what remains
After fierce seethings? golden grains?
Nay, dubious dregs: be frank, and own.
Opinion eats; all crumbles down: 90
Where stretched an isthmus, rolls a strait:
Cut off, cut off! Can'st feel elate
While all the depths of Being moan,
Though luminous on every hand,
The breadths of shallow knowledge more expand?   95
Much as a light-ship keeper pines
Mid shoals immense, where dreary shines
His lamp, we toss beneath the ray
Of Science' beacon. This to trim
Is now man's barren office.—Nay,"   100
Starting abrupt, "this earnest way
I hate. Let doubt alone; best skim,
Not dive."
            "No, no," cried Derwent gay,
Who late, upon acquaintance more,
Took no mislike to Rolfe at core,   105
And fain would make his knell a chime—
Being pledged to hold the palmy time
Of hope—at least, not to admit
That serious check might come to it:
"No, sun doubt's root—'twill fade, 'twill fade!   110
And for thy picture of the Prime,
Green Christianity in glade—
Why, let it pass; 'tis good, in sooth:
Who summons poets to the truth?"

    How Vine sidelong regarded him   115
As 'twere in envy of his gift
For light disposings: so to skim!

    Clarel surmised the expression's drift,
Thereby anew was led to sift
Good Derwent's mind. For Rolfe's discourse—   120
Prior recoil from Margoth's jeer
Was less than startled shying here
At earnest comment's random force.
He shrunk; but owned 'twas weakness mere.
Himself he chid: No more for me   125
The petty half-antipathy:
This pressure it need be endured:
Weakness to strength must get inured;
And Rolfe is sterling, though not less
At variance with that parlor-strain   130
Which counts each thought that borders pain
A social treason. Sterling—yes,
Despite illogical wild range
Of brain and heart's impulsive counterchange.

22. CONCERNING HEBREWS

As by the wood drifts thistle-down
And settles on soft mosses fair,
Stillness was wafted, dropped and sown;
Which stillness Vine, with timorous air
Of virgin tact, thus brake upon,   5
Nor with chance hint: "One can't forbear
Thinking that Margoth is—a *Jew*."
    Hereat, as for response, they view
The priest.
            "And, well, why me?" he cried;
"With one consent why turn to *me*?   10
Am I professional? Nay, free!
I grant that here by Judah's side
Queerly it jars with frame implied
To list this geologic Jew
His way Jehovah's world construe: 15
In Gentile 'twould not seem so odd.
But here may preconceptions thrall?

Be many Hebrews we recall
Whose contrast with the breastplate bright
Of Aaron flushed in altar-light,   20
And Horeb's Moses, rock and rod,
Or closeted alone with God,
Quite equals Margoth's in its way:
At home we meet them every day.
The Houndsditch clothesman scarce would seem   25
Akin to seers. For one, I deem
Jew banker, merchant, statesman—these,
With artist, actress known to fame,
All strenuous in each Gentile aim,
Are Nature's off-hand witnesses   30
There's nothing mystic in her reign:
Your Jew's like wheat from Pharaoh's tomb:
Sow it in England, what will come?
The weird old seed yields market grain."

    Pleased by his wit while some recline,   35
A smile uncertain lighted Vine,
But died away.
        "Jews share the change,"
Derwent proceeded: "Range, they range—
In liberal sciences they roam;
They're leavened, and it works, believe;   40
Signs are, and such as scarce deceive:
From Holland, that historic home
Of erudite Israel, many a tome
Talmudic, shipped is over sea
For antiquarian rubbish."
        "Rest!"   45
Cried Rolfe; "e'en that indeed may be,
Nor less the Jew keep fealty
To ancient rites. Aaron's gemmed vest
Will long outlive Genevan cloth—
Nothing in Time's old camphor-chest   50
So little subject to the moth.
But Rabbis have their troublers too.
Nay, if thro' dusty stalls we look,
Haply we disinter to view
More than one bold freethinking Jew   55

That in his day with vigor shook
Faith's leaning tower."
                    "Which stood the throe,"
Here Derwent in appendix: "look,
Faith's leaning tower was founded so:
Faith leaned from the beginning; yes,   60
If slant, she holds her steadfastness."
    "May be;" and paused: "but wherefore clog?—
Uriel Acosta, he was one
Who troubled much the synagogue—
Recanted then, and dropped undone: 65
A suicide. There's Heine, too,
(In lineage crossed by blood of Jew,)
Pale jester, to whom life was yet
A tragic farce; whose wild death-rattle,
In which all voids and hollows met,   70
Desperately maintained the battle
Betwixt the dirge and castanet.
But him leave to his Paris stone
And rail, and friendly wreath thereon.
Recall those Hebrews, which of old   75
Sharing some doubts we moderns rue,
Would fain Eclectic comfort fold
By grafting slips from Plato's palm
On Moses' melancholy yew:
But did they sprout? So *we* seek balm   80
By kindred graftings. Is that true?"
    "Why ask? But see: there lived a Jew—
No Alexandrine Greekish one—
You know him—Moses Mendelssohn."
    "Is't him you cite? True spirit staid,   85
He, though his honest heart was scourged
By doubt Judaic, never laid
His burden at Christ's door; he urged—
'Admit the mounting flames enfold
My basement; wisely shall my feet   90
The attic win, for safe retreat?' "
    "And *he* said that? Poor man, he's cold.
But was not this that Mendelssohn
Whose Hebrew kinswoman's Hebrew son,

Baptized to Christian, worthily won   95
The good name of Neander so?"
    "If that link were, well might one urge
From such example, thy strange flow,
Conviction! Breaking habit's tether,
Sincerest minds will yet diverge   100
Like chance-clouds scattered by mere weather;
Nor less at one point still they meet:
The self-hood keep they pure and sweet."

    "But Margoth," in reminder here
Breathed Vine, as if while yet the ray   105
Lit Rolfe, to try his further cheer:
"But Margoth!"
                "He, poor sheep astray,
The Levitic cipher quite erased,
On what vile pig-weed hath he grazed.
Not his Spinosa's starry brow   110
(A non-conformer, ye'll allow),
A lion in brain, in life a lamb,
Sinless recluse of Amsterdam;
Who, in the obscure and humble lane,
Such strangers seemed to entertain   115
As sat by tent beneath the tree
On Mamre's plain—mysterious three,
The informing guests of Abraham.
But no, it had but ill beseemed
If God's own angels so could list   120
To visit one, Pan's Atheist.
That high intelligence but dreamed—
Above delusion's vulgar plain
Deluded still. The erring twain,
Spinosa and poor Margoth here,   125
Both Jews, which in dissent do vary:
In these what parted poles appear—
The blind man and the visionary."
    "And whose the eye that sees aright,
If any?" Clarel eager asked.   130
Aside Rolfe turned as overtasked;

And none responded. 'Twas like night
Descending from the seats of light,
Or seeming thence to fall. But here
Sedate a kindly tempered look   135
Private and confidential spoke
From Derwent's eyes, Clarel to cheer:
Take heart; something to fit thy youth
Instill I may, some saving truth—
Not best just now to volunteer.   140
    Thought Clarel: Pray, and what wouldst prove?
Thy faith an over-easy glove.

    Meanwhile Vine had relapsed. They saw
In silence the heart's shadow draw—
Rich shadow, such as gardens keep   145
In bower aside, where glow-worms peep
In evening over the virgin bed
Where dark-green periwinkles sleep—
Their bud the Violet of the Dead.

23. By the Jordan

On the third morn, a misty one,
Equipped they sally for the wave
Of Jordan. With his escort brown
The Israelite attendance gave
For that one day and night alone.   5
Slung by a cord from saddle-bow,
Is it the mace of Ivanhoe?
    Rolfe views, and comments: "Note, I pray,"
He said to Derwent on the way,
"Yon knightly hammer. 'Tis with that   10
He stuns, and would exterminate
Your creeds as dragons."
                 With light fire
Of wit, the priest rejoinder threw;
But turned to look at Nehemiah:
The laboring ass with much ado   15

Of swerving neck would, at the sight
Of bramble-tops, snatch for a bite;
And though it bred him joltings ill—
In patience that did never tire,
Her rider let her have her will.   20
    The apostate, ready with his sneer:
"Yes, you had better—'tis a *she*."
    To Rolfe said Derwent: "There, you see:
It is these infidels that jeer
At everything."
              The Jew withheld   25
His mare, and let Nehemiah pass:
"Who is this Balaam on the ass?"
But none his wonderment dispelled.

    Now skies distill a vaporous rain;
So looked the sunken slimy plain—   30
Such semblance of the vacuum shared,
As 'twere the quaking sea-bed bared
By the Caracas. All was still:
So much the more their bosoms thrill
With dream of some withdrawn vast surge   35
Its timed return about to urge
And whelm them.
            But a cry they hear:
The steed of Mortmain, led in rear,
Broke loose and ran. "Horse too run mad?"
Cried Derwent; "shares his rider's mind—   40
His rider late? shun both their kind?
Poor Swede! But where was it he said
We should rejoin?" "'Tis by Lot's sea,
Remember. And, pray heaven, it be!—
Look, the steed's caught."
              Suspicious ground   45
They skirt, with ugly bushes crowned;
And thereinto, against surprise,
The vigilant Spahi throws his eyes;
To take of distant chance a bond,
Djalea looks forward, and beyond.   50

At this, some riders feel that awe
Which comes of sense of absent law,
And irreligious human kind,
Relapsed, remanded, reassigned
To chaos and brute passions blind.   55
    But is it Jordan, Jordan dear,
That doth that evil bound define
Which borders on the barbarous sphere—
Jordan, even Jordan, stream divine?
In Clarel ran such revery here.   60

    Belex his flint adjusts and rights,
Sharp speaks unto his Bethlehemites;   ·
Then, signaled by Djalea, through air
Surveys the further ridges bare.
Foreshortened 'gainst a long-sloped hight   65
Beyond the wave whose wash of foam
Beats to the base of Moab home,
Seven furious horsemen fling their flight
Like eagles when they launching rush
To snatch the prey that hies to bush.   70
Dwarfed so these look, while yet afar
Descried. But trusting in their star,
Onward a space the party push;
But halt is called; the Druze rides on,
Bids Belex stand, and goes alone.   75
    Now, for the nonce, those speeders sink
Viewless behind the arborous brink.
Thereto the staid one rides—peers in—
Then waves a hand. They gain his side,
Meeting the river's rapid tide   80
Here sluicing through embowered ravine
Such as of yore was Midian's screen
For rites impure. Facing, and near,
Across the waves which intervene,
In shade the robbers reappear: 85
Swart, sinuous men on silvery steeds—
Abreast, save where the copse impedes.
At halt, and mute, and in the van

Confronting them, with lengthy gun
Athwart the knee, and hand thereon,   90
Djalea waits. The mare and man
Show like a stone equestrian
Set up for homage. Over there
'Twas hard for mounted men to move
Among the thickets interwove,   95
Which dipped the stream and made a snare.
But, undeterred, the riders press
This way and that among the branches,
Picking them lanes through each recess,
Till backward on their settling haunches   100
The steeds withstand the slippery slope,
While yet their outflung fore-feet grope;
Then, like sword-push that ends in lunge,
The slide becomes a weltering plunge:
The willows drip, the banks resound;   105
They halloo, and with spray are crowned.
The torrent, swelled by Lebanon rains,
The spirited horses bravely stem,
Snorting, half-blinded by their manes,
Nor let the current master them.   110
As the rope-dancer on the hair
Poises the long slim pole in air;
Twirling their slender spears in pride,
Each horseman in imperiled seat
Blends skill and grace with courage meet.   115
    Soon as they win the hither side,
Like quicksilver to beach they glide,
Dismounting, and essay the steep,
The horses led by slackened rein:
Slippery foothold ill they keep.   120
To help a grim one of the band
Good Nehemiah with mickle strain
Down reaches a decrepit hand:
The sheik ignores it—bandit dun,
Foremost in stride as first in rank—   125
Rejects it, and the knoll is won.

Challengingly he stares around,
Then stakes his spear upon the bank
As one reclaiming rightful ground.
Like otters when to land they go,
Riders and steeds how sleekly show.   130
    The first inquiring look they trace
Is gun by gun, as face by face:
Salute they yield, for arms they view
Inspire respect sincere and true.   135
    Meantime, while in their bearing shows
The thought which still their life attends,
And habit of encountering foes—
The thought that strangers scarce are friends—
What think the horses? Zar must needs   140
Be sociable; the robber steeds
She whinnies to; even fain would sway
Neck across neck in lovesome way.
Great Solomon, of rakish strain,
Trumpets—would be Don John again.   145
    The sheik, without a moment's doubt,
Djalea for captain singles out;
And, after parley brief, would fain
Handle that pistol of the guide,
The new revolver at his side.   150
The Druze assents, nor shows surprise.
Barrel, cap, screw, the Arab tries;
And ah, the contrast needs he own:
Alack, for his poor lance and gun,
Though heirlooms both: the piece in stock   155
Half honeycombed, with cumbrous lock;
The spear like some crusader's pole
Dropped long ago when death-damps stole
Over the knight in Richard's host,
Then left to warp by Acre lost: 160
Dry rib of lance. But turning now
Upon his sweetheart, he was cheered:
Her eye he met, the violet-glow,
Peaked ear, the mane's redundant flow;

It heartened him, and round he veered;   165
Elate he shot a brigand glare:
I, Ishmael, have my desert mare!

    Elicited by contact's touch,
Tyrannous spleen vexed Belex much,
Misliking in poor tribe to mark   170
Freedom unawed and nature's spark.
With tutoring glance, a tempered fire,
The Druze repressed the illiberal ire.
    The silvered saint came gently near,
Meekly intrepid, tract in hand,   175
And reached it with a heart sincere
Unto the sheik, whose fingers spanned
The shrewd revolver, loath to let
That coveted bauble go as yet.
"Nay," breathed the Druze, and gently here: 180
"The print he likes not; let him be;
Pray now, he deems it sorcery."
They drew him back. In rufflement
The sheik threw round a questioning eye;
Djalea explained, and drew more nigh,   185
Recalling him to old content;
Regained the weapon; and, from stores
Kept for such need, wary he pours
A dole of powder.
             So they part—
Recrossing Jordan, horse and gun,   190
With warrior cry and brandished dart,
Where, in the years whose goal is won,
The halcyon Teacher waded in with John.

24. THE RIVER-RITE

And do the clear sands pure and cold
At last each virgin elf enfold?
Under what drift of silvery spar
Sleeps now thy servant, Holy Rood,

Which in the age of brotherhood 5
Approaching here Bethabara
By wilds the verse depicted late,
Of Jordan caught a fortunate
Fair twinkle starry under trees;
And, with his crossed palms heartward pressed, 10
Bowed him, or dropped on reverent knees,
Warbling that hymn of beauty blest—
The *Ave maris stella?*—Lo,
The mound of him do field-mice know?
Nor less the rite, a rule serene, 15
Appropriate in tender grace,
Became the custom of the place
With each devouter Frank.
                              A truce
Here following the din profuse
Of Moab's swimming robbers keen, 20
Rolfe, late enamored of the spell
Of rituals olden, thought it well
To observe the Latin usage: "Look,"
Showing a small convenient book
In vellum bound; embossed thereon, 25
'Tween angels with a rosy crown,
Viols, Cecilia on a throne:
"Thanks, friar Benignus Muscatel;
Thy gift I prize, given me in cell
Of St. John's convent.—Comrades, come! 30
If heaven delight in spirits glad,
And men were all for brothers made,
Grudge not, beseech, to joy with Rome;"
And launched the hymn. Quick to rejoice,
The liberal priest lent tenor voice; 35
And marking them in cheery bloom
On turf inviting, even Vine,
Ravished from his reserve supine,
Drew near and overlooked the page—
All self-surprised he overlooked, 40
Joining his note impulsively;
Yet, flushing, seemed as scarce he brooked

This joy. Was joy a novelty?
Fraternal thus, the group engage—
While now the sun, obscured before,   45
Illumed for time the wooded shore—
In tribute to the beach and tide.
    The triple voices blending glide,
Assimilating more and more,
Till in the last ascriptive line   50
Which thrones the Father, lauds the Son,
Came concord full, completion fine—
Rapport of souls in harmony of tone.

    Meantime Nehemiah, eager bent,
Instinctive caught the sentiment;   55
But checked himself; and, in mixed mood,
Uncertain or relapsing stood,
Till ere the singers cease to thrill,
His joy is stayed. How cometh this?
True feeling, steadfast faith are his,   60
While they at best do but fulfill
A transient, an esthetic glow;
Knew he at last—could he but know—
The rite was alien? that no form
Approved was his, which here might warm   65
Meet channel for emotion's tide?
Apart he went, scarce satisfied;
But presently slipped down to where
The river ran, and tasting spare,
Not quaffing, sighed, "As sugar sweet!"   70
Though unsweet was it from the flow
Of turbid, troubled waters fleet.
    Now Margoth—who had paced the strand
Gauging the level of the land,
Computing part the Jordan's fall   75
From Merom's spring, and therewithal
Had ended with a river-sip,
Which straight he spewed—here curled the lip
At hearing Nehemiah: The fool!
Fool meek and fulsome like to this—   80

Too old again to go to school—
Was never! wonder who he is:
I'll ask himself.—"Who art thou, say?"
"The chief of sinners."—"Lack-a-day,
I think so too;" and moved away,   85
Low muttering in his ill content
At that so Christian bafflement;
And hunted up his sumpter mule
Intent on lunch. A pair hard by
He found. The third some person sly   90
In deeper shade had hitched—more cool.
This was that mule whose rarer wine,
In pannier slung and blushing shy,
The Thessalonian did decline
Away with him in flight to take,   95
And friendly gave them when farewell he spake.

25. The Dominican

"Ah Rome, your tie! may child clean part?
Nay, tugs the mother at the heart!"

  Strange voice that was which three there heard
Reclined upon the bank. They turned;
And he, the speaker of the word,   5
Stood in the grass, with eyes that burned
How eloquent upon the group.
  "Here urging on before our troop,"
He said, "I caught your choral strains—
Spurred quicker, lighted, tied my mule   10
Behind yon clump; and, for my pains,
Meet—three, I ween, who slight the rule
Of Rome, yet thence do here indeed,
Through strong compulsion of the need,
Derive fair rite: or may I err?"   15
  Surprise they knew, yet made a stir
Of welcome, gazing on the man
In white robe of Dominican,

Of aspect strong, though cheek was spare,
Yellowed with tinge athlete may wear　　　　　　　20
Whom rigorous masters overtrain
When they with scourge of more and more
Would macerate him into power.
Inwrought herewith was yet the air
And open frontage frankly fair　　　　　　　　　25
Of one who'd moved in active scene
And swayed men where they most convene.
His party came from Saba last,
Camping by Lot's wave overnight—
French pilgrims. So he did recite　　　　　　　30
Being questioned. Thereupon they passed
To matters of more pith. Debate
They held, built on that hymning late;
Till in reply to Derwent's strain
Thus warmed he, that Dominican:　　　　　　　35
　　　"Crafty is Rome, you deem? Her art
Is simple, quarried from the heart.
Rough marbles, rudiments of worth
Ye win from ledges under earth;
Ye trim them, fit them, make them shine　　　　40
In structures of a fair design.
Well, fervors as obscure in birth—
Precious, though fleeting in their dates—
Rome culls, adapts, perpetuates
In ordered rites. 'Tis these supply　　　　　　　45
Means to the mass to beautify
The rude emotion; lend meet voice
To organs which would fain rejoice
But lack the song; and oft present
To sorrow bound, an instrument　　　　　　　50
Which liberates. Each hope, each fear
Between the christening and the bier
Still Rome provides for, and with grace
And tact which hardly find a place
In uninspired designs."
　　　　　　　　　　"Let be　　　　　　　55
Thou Paul! shall Festus yield to thee?"

Cried Rolfe; "and yet," in altered tone,
"Even these fair things—ah, change goes on!"
  "Change? yes, but not with us. In rout
Sword-hilts rap at the Vatican,   60
And, lo, an old, old man comes out:
'What would ye?' 'Change!' 'I never change.' "
  "Things changing not when all things change
Need perish then, one might retort,
Nor err."
    "Ay, things of human sort." 65
 "Rome superhuman?"
       "As ye will.
Brave schemes these boyish times instill;
But Rome has lived a thousand years:
Shall not a thousand years know more
Than nonage may?" "Then all the cheers 70
Which hail the good time deemed at door
Are but the brayings which attest
The foolish, many-headed beast!"
"Hardly that inference I own.
The people once elected me   75
To be their spokesman. In this gown
I sat in legislative hall
A champion of true liberty—
God's liberty for one and all—
Not Satan's license. Mine's the state 80
Of a staunch Catholic Democrat."
  Indulgent here was Derwent's smile,
Incredulous was Rolfe's. But he:
"Hardly those terms ye reconcile.
And yet what is it that we see?   85
Before the Church our human race
Stand equal. None attain to place
Therein through claim of birth or fee.
No monk so mean but he may dare
Aspire to sit in Peter's chair."   90
  "Why, true," said Derwent; "but what then?
That sums not all. And what think men?"
And, briefly, more, about the rot

Of Rome in Luther's time, the canker spot.
    "Well," said the monk, "I'll not gainsay   95
Some things you put: I own the shame:
Reform was needed, yes, and came—
Reform *within*. But let that go—
That era's gone: how fares it *now?*—
Melancthon! was forecast by thee,   100
Who fain had tempered Luther's mind,
This riot of reason quite set free:
Sects—sects bisected—sects disbanded
Into plain deists underhanded?
Against all this stands Rome's array: 105
Rome is the Protestant to-day:
The Red Republic slinging flame
In Europe—she's your Scarlet Dame.
Rome stands; but who may tell the end?
Relapse barbaric may impend,   110
Dismission into ages blind—
Moral dispersion of mankind.
Ah, God," and dropped upon the knee:
"These flocks which range so far from Thee,
Ah, leave them not to be undone: 115
Let them not cower as 'twixt the sea
And storm—in panic crowd and drown!"
He rose, resumed his previous cheer
With something of a bearing sweet.
    "Brother," said Derwent friendly here,   120
"I'm glad to know ye, glad to meet,
Even though, in part, your Rome seeks ends
Not mine. But, see, there pass your friends:
Call they your name?"
                  "Yes, yes" he said,
And rose to loose his mule; "you're right;   125
We go to win the further bed
Of Jordan, by the convent's site.
A parting word: Methinks ye hold
Reserved objections. I'll unfold
But one:—Rome being fixed in form,   130
Unyielding there, how may she keep

Adjustment with new times? But deep
Below rigidities of form
The invisible nerves and tissues change
Adaptively. As men that range 135
From clime to clime, from zone to zone
(Say Russian hosts that menace Ind)
Through all vicissitudes still find
The body acclimate itself
While form and function hold their own— 140
Again they call:—Well, you are wise;
Enough—you can analogize
And take my meaning: I have done.
No, one more point:—Science but deals
With Nature; Nature is not God; 145
Never she answers our appeals,
Or, if she do, but mocks the clod.
Call to the echo—it returns
The word you send; how thrive the ferns
About the ruined house of prayer 150
In woods; one shadow falleth yet
From Christian spire—Turk minaret:
Consider the indifference there.
'Tis so throughout. Shall Science then
Which solely dealeth with this thing 155
Named Nature, shall she ever bring
One solitary hope to men?
'Tis Abba Father that we seek,
Not the Artificer. I speak,
But scarce may utter. Let it be. 160
Adieu; remember—Oh, not me;
But if with years should fail delight
As things unmask abroad and home;
Then, should ye yearn in reason's spite,
Remember hospitable Rome." 165

He turned, and would have gone; but, no,
New matter struck him: "Ere I go
Yet one word more; and bear with me:
Whatever your belief may be—

If well ye wish to human kind,   170
Be not so mad, unblest, and blind
As, in such days as these, to try
To pull down Rome. If Rome could fall
'Twould not be Rome alone, but all
Religion. All with Rome have tie,   175
Even the railers which deny,
All but the downright Anarchist,
Christ-hater, Red, and Vitriolist.
Could libertine dreams true hope disable,
Rome's tomb would prove Abaddon's cradle.   180
Weigh well the Pope. Though he should be
Despoiled of Charlemagne's great fee—
Cast forth, and made a begging friar,
That would not quell him. No, the higher
Rome's *In excelsis* would extol   185
Her God—her *De profundis* roll
The deeper. Let destructives mind
The reserves upon reserves behind.
Offence I mean not. More's to tell:
But frigates meet—hail—part. Farewell."   190
      And, going, he a verse did weave,
Or hummed in low recitative:

      "Yearly for a thousand years
         On Christmas Day the wreath appears,
            And the people joy together: 195
         Prithee, Prince or Parliament,
         An equal holiday invent
            Outlasting centuries of weather.

      "Arrested by a trembling shell,
         Wee tinkle of the small mass-bell,   200
            A giant drops upon the knee.
         Thou art wise—effect as much;
         Let thy wisdom by a touch
            Reverence like this decree."

26. OF ROME

"Patcher of the rotten cloth,
  Pickler of the wing o' the moth,
  Toaster of bread stale in date,
  Tinker of the rusty plate,
  Botcher of a crumbling tomb,   5
  Pounder with the holy hammer,
  Gaffer-gammer, gaffer-gammer—
  Rome!
The broker take your trumpery pix,
Paten and chalice! Turn ye—lo,   10
Here's bread, here's wine. In Mexico
Earthquakes lay flat your crucifix:
All, all's geology, I trow.
Away to your Pope Joan—go!"

  As he the robed one decorous went,   15
From copse that doggerel was sent
And after-cry. Half screened from view
'Twas Margoth, who, reclined at lunch,
Had overheard, nor spared to munch,
And thence his contumely threw.   20
Rolfe, rising, had replied thereto,
And with some heat, but Derwent's hand
Caught at his skirt: "Nay, of what use?
But wind, foul wind."—Here fell a truce,
Which Margoth could but understand;   25
Wiping his mouth he hied away.
The student who apart though near
Had heard the Frank with tingling cheer,
Awaited now the after-play
Of comment; and it followed: "Own,"   30
Said Rolfe, "he took no shallow tone,
That new St. Dominick. Who'll repay?
Wilt thou?" to Derwent turning.—"No,
Not I! But had our Scot been near
To meet your Papal nuncio!   35
Fight fire with fire. But for me here,

You must have marked I did abstain.—
Odd, odd: this man who'd make our age
To Hildebrand's an appanage—
So able too—lit by our light—   40
Curious, he should so requite!
And, yes, lurked somewhat in his strain—"
    "And in his falling on the knee?"
"Those supple hinges I let be."
    "Is the man false?"
                    "No, hardly that.   45
'Tis difficult to tell. But see:
Doubt late was an aristocrat;
But now the barbers' clerks do swell
In cast clothes of the infidel;
The more then one can now *believe,*   50
The more one's differenced, perceive,
From ribald commonplace. Here Rome
Comes in. This intellectual man—
Half monk, half tribune, partisan—
Who, as he hints—'tis troublesome   55
To analyze, and thankless too:
Much better be a dove, and coo
Softly. Come then, I'll e'en agree
His manner has a certain lure,
Disinterested, earnest, pure   60
And liberal. 'Tis such as he
Win over men."
                    "There's Rome, her camp
Of tried instruction. She can stamp,
On the recruit that's framed aright,
The bearing of a Bayard knight   65
Ecclesiastic. I applaud
Her swordsmen of the priestly sword
Wielded in spiritual fight."
"Indeed? take care! Rome lacks not charm
For fervid souls. Arm ye, forearm!   70
For syrens has she too,—her race
Of sainted virgin ones, with grace
Beyond the grace of Grecian calm,

For this is chill, but that how warm."
"A frank concession." "To be sure!   75
Since Rome may never *me* allure
By her enticing arts; since all
The bias of the days that be
Away leans from Authority,
And most when hierarchical;   80
So that the future of the Pope
Is cast in no fair horoscope;
In brief, since Rome must still decay;
Less care I to disown or hide
Aught that she has of merit rare: 85
Her legends—some are sweet as May;
Ungarnered wealth no doubt is there,
(Too long ignored by Luther's pride)
But which perchance in days divine
(Era, whereof I read the sign)   90
When much that sours the sects is gone,
Like Dorian myths the bards shall own—
Yes, prove the poet's second mine."
　　"All that," said Rolfe, "is very fine;
But Rome subsists, she lives to-day,   95
She re-affirms herself, her sway
Seductive draws rich minds away;
Some pastures, too, yield many a rover:
Sheep, sheep and shepherd running over."
　　"Such sheep and shepherds, let them go;   100
They are not legion: and you know
What draws. Little imports it all
Overbalanced by that tidal fall
Of Rome in Southern Europe. Come."
　　"If the tide fall or here or there,   105
Be sure 'tis rolling in elsewhere."
　　"So oceanic then is Rome?"
"Nay, but there's ample sea-verge left:
A hemisphere invites.—When reft
From Afric, and the East its home,   110
The church shot out through wild and wood—
Germany, Gaul and Britain, Spain—

Colonized, Latinized, and made good
Her loss, and more—resolved to reign."
  "Centuries, centuries long ago!   115
What's that to us? I am surprised.
Rome's guns are spiked; and they'll stay so.
The world is now too civilized
For Rome. Your noble Western soil—
What! *that* be given up for spoil   120
To—to—"
          "There is an Unforeseen.
Fate never gives a guarantee
That she'll abstain from aught. And men
Get tired at last of being free—
Whether in states—in states or creeds.   125
For what's the sequel? Verily,
Laws scribbled by law-breakers, creeds
Scrawled by the freethinkers, and deeds
Shameful and shameless. Men get sick
Under that curse of Frederick   130
The cynical: For punishment
This rebel province I present
To the philosophers. But, how?
Whole nations now philosophize,
And do their own undoing now.—   135
Who's gained by all the sacrifice
Of Europe's revolutions? who?
The Protestant? the Liberal?
I do not think it—not at all:
Rome and the Atheist have gained: 140
These two shall fight it out—these two;
Protestantism being retained
For base of operations sly
By Atheism."
          Without reply
Derwent low whistled—twitched a spray   145
That overhung: "What tree is this?"
  "The tree of knowledge, I dare say;
But you don't eat."—"That's not amiss,"

The good man laughed; but, changing, "O,
That a New-Worlder should talk so!"   150
    "'Tis the New World that mannered me,
Yes, gave me this vile liberty
To reverence naught, not even herself."
    "How say you? you're the queerest elf!
But here's a thought I still pursue—   155
A thought I dreamed each thinker knew:
No more can men be what they've been;
All's altered—earth's another scene."
    "Man's heart is what it used to be."
"I don't know that."
                "But Rome does, though: 160
And hence her stout persistency.
What mean her re-adopted modes
Even in the enemy's abodes?
Their place old emblems reassume.
She bides—content to let but blow   165
Among the sects that peak and pine,
Incursions of her taking bloom."
    "The censer's musk?—'Tis not the vine,
Vine evangelic, branching out
In fruitful latitude benign,   170
With all her bounty roundabout—
Each cluster, shaded or in sun,
Still varying from each other one,
But all true members, all with wine
Derived from Christ their stem and stock;   175
'Tis scarce *that* vine which doth unlock
The fragrance that you hint of. No,
The Latin plant don't flourish so;
Of sad distemper 'tis the seat;
Pry close, and startled you shall meet   180
Parasite-bugs—black swarming ones."
"The monks?"—"You jest: thinned out, those drones."
    Considerate uncommitted eyes
Charged with things manifold and wise,
Rolfe turned upon good Derwent here;   185

Then changed: "Fall back we must. Yon mule
With pannier: Come, in stream we'll cool
The wine ere quaffing.—Muleteer!"

27. VINE AND CLAREL

While now, to serve the pilgrim train,
The Arabs willow branches hew,
(For palms they serve in dearth of true),
Or, kneeling by the margin, stoop
To brim memorial bottles up;   5
And the Greek's wine entices two:
Apart see Clarel here incline,
Perplexed by that Dominican,
Nor less by Rolfe—capricious man:
"I cannot penetrate him.—Vine?"   10
    As were Venetian slats between,
He espied him through a leafy screen,
Luxurious there in umbrage thrown,
Light sprays above his temples blown—
The river through the green retreat   15
Hurrying, reveling by his feet.
    Vine looked an overture, but said
Nothing, till Clarel leaned—half laid—
Beside him: then "We dream, or be
In sylvan John's baptistery: 20
May Pisa's equal beauty keep?—
But how bad habits persevere!
I have been moralizing here
Like any imbecile: as thus:
Look how these willows over-weep   25
The waves, and plain: 'Fleet so from us?
And wherefore? whitherward away?
Your best is here where wildings sway
And the light shadow's blown about;
Ah, tarry, for at hand's a sea   30
Whence ye shall never issue out
Once in.' They sing back: 'So let be!

We mad-caps hymn it as we flow—
Short life and merry! be it so!' "
    Surprised at such a fluent turn,   35
The student did but listen—learn.

    Putting aside the twigs which screened,
Again Vine spake, and lightly leaned
"Look; in yon vault so leafy dark,
At deep end lit by gemmy spark   40
Of mellowed sunbeam in a snare;
Over the stream—ay, just through there—
The sheik on that celestial mare
Shot, fading.—Clan of outcast Hagar,
Well do ye come by spear and dagger!   45
Yet in your bearing ye outvie
Our western Red Men, chiefs that stalk
In mud paint—whirl the tomahawk.—
But in these Nimrods noted you
The natural language of the eye,   50
Burning or liquid, flame or dew,
As still the changeable quick mood
Made transit in the wayward blood?
Methought therein one might espy,
For all the wildness, thoughts refined   55
By the old Asia's dreamful mind;
But hark—a bird?"
                Pure as the rain
Which diamondeth with lucid grain,
The white swan in the April hours
Floating between two sunny showers   60
Upon the lake, while buds unroll;
So pure, so virginal in shrine
Of true unworldliness looked Vine.
Ah, clear sweet ether of the soul
(Mused Clarel), holding him in view.   65
Prior advances unreturned
Not here he recked of, while he yearned—
O, now but for communion true
And close; let go each alien theme;
Give me thyself!

         But Vine, at will   70
Dwelling upon his wayward dream,
Nor as suspecting Clarel's thrill
Of personal longing, rambled still;
"Methinks they show a lingering trace
Of some quite unrecorded race   75
Such as the Book of Job implies.
What ages of refinings wise
Must have forerun what there is writ—
More ages than have followed it.
At Lydda late, as chance would have,   80
Some tribesmen from the south I saw,
Their tents pitched in the Gothic nave,
The ruined one. Disowning law,
Not lawless lived they; no, indeed;
Their chief—why, one of Sydney's clan,   85
A slayer, but chivalric man;
And chivalry, with all that breed
Was Arabic or Saracen
In source, they tell. But, as men stray
Further from Ararat away   90
Pity it were did they recede
In carriage, manners, and the rest;
But no, for ours the palm indeed
In bland amenities far West!
Come now, for pastime let's complain;   95
Grudged thanks, Columbus, for thy main!
Put back, as 'twere—assigned by fate
To fight crude Nature o'er again,
By slow degrees we re-create.
But then, alas, in Arab camps   100
No lack, they say, no lack of scamps."
    Divided mind knew Clarel here;
The heart's desire did interfere.
Thought he, How pleasant in another
Such sallies, or in thee, if said   105
After confidings that should wed
Our souls in one:—Ah, call me *brother!*—
So feminine his passionate mood

Which, long as hungering unfed,
All else rejected or withstood.   110
     Some inklings he let fall. But no:
Here over Vine there slid a change—
A shadow, such as thin may show
Gliding along the mountain-range
And deepening in the gorge below.   115
     Does Vine's rebukeful dusking say—
Why, on this vernal bank to-day,
Why bring oblations of thy pain
To one who hath his share? here fain
Would lap him in a chance reprieve?   120
Lives none can help ye; that believe.
Art thou the first soul tried by doubt?
Shalt prove the last? Go, live it out.
But for thy fonder dream of love
In man toward man—the soul's caress—   125
The negatives of flesh should prove
Analogies of non-cordialness
In spirit.—E'en such conceits could cling
To Clarel's dream of vain surmise
And imputation full of sting.   130
But, glancing up, unwarned he saw
What serious softness in those eyes
Bent on him. Shyly they withdraw.
Enslaver, wouldst thou but fool me
With bitter-sweet, sly sorcery,   135
Pride's pastime? or wouldst thou indeed,
Since things unspoken may impede,
Let flow thy nature but for bar?—
Nay, dizzard, sick these feelings are;
How findest place within thy heart   140
For such solicitudes apart
From Ruth?—Self-taxings.
                But a sign
Came here indicative from Vine,
Who with a reverent hushed air
His view directed toward the glade   145
Beyond, wherein a niche was made

Of leafage, and a kneeler there,
The meek one, on whom, as he prayed,
A golden shaft of mellow light,
Oblique through vernal cleft above,   150
And making his pale forehead bright,
Scintillant fell. By such a beam
From heaven descended erst the dove
On Christ emerging from the stream.
It faded; 'twas a transient ray;   155
And, quite unconscious of its sheen,
The suppliant rose and moved away,
Not dreaming that he had been seen.

     When next they saw that innocent,
From prayer such cordial had he won   160
That all his aspect of content
As with the oil of gladness shone.
Less aged looked he. And his cheer
Took language in an action here:
The train now mustering in line,   165
Each pilgrim with a river-palm
In hand (except indeed the Jew),
The saint the head-stall need entwine
With wreathage of the same. When new
They issued from the wood, no charm   170
The ass found in such idle gear
Superfluous: with her long ear
She flapped it off, and the next thrust
Of hoof imprinted it in dust.
Meek hands (mused Vine), vainly ye twist   175
Fair garland for the realist.
     The Hebrew, noting whither bent
Vine's glance, a word in passing lent:
"Ho, tell us how it comes to be
That thou who rank'st not with beginners   180
Regard have for yon chief of sinners."
     "Yon chief of sinners?"
                              "So names he
Himself. For one I'll not express
How I do loathe such lowliness."

28. The Fog

Southward they file. 'Tis Pluto's park
Beslimed as after baleful flood:
A nitrous, filmed and pallid mud,
With shrubs to match. Salt specks they mark
Or mildewed stunted twigs unclean   5
Brushed by the stirrup, Stygean green,
With shrivelled nut or apple small.
     The Jew plucked one. Like a fuzz-ball
It brake, discharging fetid dust.
     "Pippins of Sodom? they've declined!"   10
Cried Derwent: "where's the ruddy rind?"
     Said Rolfe: "If Circe tempt one thus,
A fig for vice—I'm virtuous.
Who but poor Margoth now would lust
After such fruitage. See, but see   15
What makes our Nehemiah to be
So strange. That look returns to him
Which late he wore by Achor's rim."

     Over pale hollows foully smeared
The saint hung with an aspect weird: 20
"Yea, here it was the kings were tripped,
These, these the slime-pits where they slipped—
Gomorrah's lord and Sodom's, lo!"

     "What's that?" asked Derwent.
                         "You should know,"
Said Rolfe: "your Scripture lore revive: 25
The four kings strove against the five
In Siddim here."
                 "Ah,—Genesis.
But turn; upon this other hand
See here another not remiss."
     'Twas Margoth raking there the land.   30
Some minerals of noisome kind
He found and straight to pouch consigned.
     "The chiffonier!" cried Rolfe; "e'en grim
Milcom and Chemosh scowl at him—

Here nosing underneath their lee   35
Of pagod hights."
                        In deeper dale
What canker may their palms assail?
Spotted they show, all limp they be.
Is it thy bitter mist, Bad Sea,
That, sudden driving, northward comes   40
Involving them, that each man roams
Half seen or lost?
                        But in the dark
Thick scud, the chanting saint they hark:

    "Though through the valley of the shade
            I pass, no evil do I fear;   45
    His candle shineth on my head:
            Lo, he is with me, even here."

    The rack drove by: and Derwent said—
"How apt he is!" then pause he made:
"This palm has grown a sorry sight;   50
A palm 'tis not, if named aright:
I'll drop it.—Look, the lake ahead!"

                    29. BY THE MARGE

The legend round a Grecian urn,
The sylvan legend, though decay
Have wormed the garland all away,
And fire have left its Vandal burn;
Yet beauty inextinct may charm   5
In outline of the vessel's form.
Much so with Sodom, shore and sea.
Fair Como would like Sodom be
Should horror overrun the scene
And calcine all that makes it green,   10
Yet haply sparing to impeach
The contour in its larger reach.
In graceful lines the hills advance,

The valley's sweep repays the glance,
And wavy curves of winding beach;   15
But all is charred or crunched or riven,
Scarce seems of earth whereon we dwell;
Though framed within the lines of heaven
The picture intimates a hell.
    That marge they win. Bides Mortmain there?   20
No trace of man, not anywhere.
    It was the salt wave's northern brink.
No gravel bright nor shell was seen,
Nor kelpy growth nor coralline,
But dead boughs stranded, which the rout   25
Of Jordan, in old freshets born
In Libanus, had madly torn
Green from her arbor and thrust out
Into the liquid waste. No sound
Nor motion but of sea. The land   30
Was null: nor bramble, weed, nor trees,
Nor anything that grows on ground,
Flexile to indicate the breeze;
Though hitherward by south winds fanned
From Usdum's brink and Bozrah's site   35
Of bale, flew gritty atoms light.
Toward Karek's castle lost in blur,
And thence beyond toward Aroer
By Arnon where the robbers keep,
Jackal and vulture, eastward sweep   40
The waters, while their western rim
Stretches by Judah's headlands grim,
Which make in turns a sea-wall steep.
There, by the cliffs or distance hid,
The Fount or Cascade of the Kid   45
An Eden makes of one high glen,
One vernal and contrasted scene
In jaws of gloomy crags uncouth—
Rosemary in the black boar's mouth.
Alike withheld from present view   50
(And, until late, but hawk and kite
Visited the forgotten site),

The Maccabees' Masada true;
Stronghold which Flavian arms did rend,
The Peak of Eleazer's end,   55
Where patriot warriors made with brides
A martyrdom of suicides.
There too did Mariamne's hate
The death of John accelerate.
A crag of fairest, foulest weather—   60
Famous, and infamous together.
      Hereof they spake, but never Vine,
Who little knew or seemed to know
Derived from books, but did incline
In docile way to each one's flow   65
Of knowledge bearing anyhow
In points less noted.
                        Southernmost
The sea indefinite was lost
Under a catafalque of cloud.
      Unwelcome impress to disown   70
Or light evade, the priest, aloud
Taking an interested tone
And brisk, "Why, yonder lies Mount Hor,
E'en thereaway—that southward shore."
      "Ay," added Rolfe, "and Aaron's cell   75
Thereon. A mountain sentinel,
He holds in solitude austere
The outpost of prohibited Seir
In cut-off Edom."
                  "God can sever!"
Brake in the saint, who nigh them stood;   80
"The satyr to the dragon's brood
Crieth! God's word abideth ever:
None there pass through—no, never, never!"
      "My friend Max Levi, he passed through."
They turned. It was the hardy Jew.   85
Absorbed in vision here, the saint
Heard not. The priest in flushed constraint
Showed mixed emotion; part he winced
And part a humor pleased evinced—

Relish that would from qualms be free—   90
Aversion involved with sympathy.
But changing, and in formal way—
"Admitted; nay, 'tis tritely true;
Men pass thro' Edom, through and through.
But surely, few so dull to-day   95
As not to make allowance meet
For Orientalism's display
In Scripture, where the chapters treat
Of mystic themes."
           With eye askance,
The apostate fixed no genial glance: 100
"Ay, Keith's grown obsolete. And, pray,
How long will these last glosses stay?
The agitating influence
Of knowledge never will dispense
With teasing faith, do what ye may.   105
Adjust and readjust, ye deal
With compass in a ship of steel."
    "Such perturbations do but give
Proof that faith's vital: sensitive
Is faith, my friend."
           "Go to, go to: 110
Your black bat! how she hangs askew,
Torpid, from wall by claws of wings:
Let drop the left—sticks fast the right;
Then this unhook—the other swings;
Leave—she regains her double plight."   115
    "Ah, look," cried Derwent; "ah, behold!"
From the blue battlements of air,
Over saline vapors hovering there,
A flag was flung out—curved in fold—
Fiery, rosy, violet, green—   120
And, lovelier growing, brighter, fairer,
Transfigured all that evil scene;
And Iris was the standard-bearer.
    None spake. As in a world made new,
With upturned faces they review   125
That oriflamme, the which no man

Would look for in such clime of ban.
'Twas northern; and its home-like look
Touched Nehemiah. He, late with book
Gliding from Margoth's dubious sway,   130
Was standing by the ass apart;
And when he caught that scarf of May
How many a year ran back his heart:
Scythes hang in orchard, hay-cocks loom
After eve-showers, the mossed roofs gloom   135
Greenly beneath the homestead trees;
He tingles with these memories.
    For Vine, over him suffusive stole
An efflorescence; all the soul
Flowering in flush upon the brow.   140
But 'twas ambiguously replaced
In words addressed to Clarel now—
"Yonder the arch dips in the waste;
Thither! and win the pouch of gold."
    Derwent reproached him: "ah, withhold!   145
See, even death's pool reflects the dyes—
The rose upon the coffin lies!"
    "Brave words," said Margoth, plodding near;
"Brave words; but yonder bow's forsworn.
The covenant made on Noah's morn,   150
Was that well kept? why, hardly here,
Where whelmed by fire and flood, they say,
The townsfolk sank in after day,
Yon sign in heaven should reappear."
    They heard, but in such torpid gloom   155
Scarcely they recked, for now the bloom
Vanished from sight, and half the sea
Died down to glazed monotony.
    Craved solace here would Clarel prove,
Recalling Ruth, her glance of love.   160
But nay; those eyes so frequent known
To meet, and mellow on his own—
Now, in his vision of them, swerved;
While in perverse recurrence ran
Dreams of the bier Armenian.   165

Against their sway his soul he nerved:
"Go, goblins; go, each funeral thought—
Bewitchment from this Dead Sea caught!"

 Westward they move, and turn the shore
Southward, till, where wild rocks are set,   170
Dismounting, they would fain restore
Ease to the limb. But haunts them yet
A dumb dejection lately met.

30. OF PETRA

"The City Red in cloud-land lies
Yonder," said Derwent, quick to inter
The ill, or light regard transfer:
"But Petra must we leave unseen—
Tell us"—to Rolfe—"there hast thou been."   5
 "With dragons guarded roundabout
'Twas a new Jason found her out—
Burckhardt, you know." "But tell." "The flume
Or mountain corridor profound
Whereby ye win the inner ground   10
Petræan; this, from purple gloom
Of cliffs—whose tops the suns illume
Where oleanders wave the flag—
Winds out upon the rosy stain,
Warm color of the natural vein,   15
Of porch and pediment in crag.
One starts. In Esau's waste are blent
Ionian form, Venetian tint.
Statues salute ye from that fane,
The warders of the Horite lane.   20
They welcome, seem to point ye on
Where sequels which transcend them dwell;
But tarry, for just here is won
Happy suspension of the spell."
 "But expectation's raised."

                                    "No more!   25
'Tis then when bluely blurred in shore,
It looms through azure haze at sea—
Then most 'tis Colchis charmeth ye.
So ever, and with all! But, come,
Imagine us now quite at home   30
Taking the prospect from Mount Hor.
Good. Eastward turn thee—skipping o'er
The intervening craggy blight:
Mark'st thou the face of yon slabbed hight
Shouldered about by hights? what Door   35
Is that, sculptured in elfin freak?
The portal of the Prince o' the Air?
Thence will the god emerge, and speak?
El Deir it is; and Petra's there,
Down in her cleft. Mid such a scene   40
Of Nature's terror, how serene
That ordered form. Nor less 'tis cut
Out of that terror—does abut
Thereon: there's Art."
                        "Dare say—no doubt;
But, prithee, turn we now about   45
And closer get thereto in mind;
That portal lures me."
                        "Nay, forbear;
A bootless journey. We should wind
Along ravine by mountain-stair,—
Down which in season torrents sweep—   50
Up, slant by sepulchers in steep,
Grotto and porch, and so get near
Puck's platform, and thereby El Deir.
We'd knock. An echo. Knock again—
Ay, knock forever: none requite: 55
The live spring filters through cell, fane,
And tomb: a dream the Edomite!"
    "And dreamers all who dream of him—
Though Sinbad's pleasant in the skim.
Pæstum and Petra: good to use   60
For sedative when one would muse.

But look, our Emir.—Ay, Djalea,
We guess why thou com'st mutely here
And hintful stand'st before us so."
    "Ay, ay," said Rolfe; "stirrups, and go!"   65
"But first," the priest said, "let me creep
And rouse our poor friend slumbering low
Under yon rock—queer place to sleep."

    "*Queer?*" muttered Rolfe as Derwent went;
"*Queer* is the furthest he will go   70
In phrase of a disparagement.
But—ominous, with haggard rent—
To me yon crag's brow-beating brow
Looks horrible—and I *say* so."

31. THE INSCRIPTION

While yet Rolfe's foot in stirrup stood,
Ere the light vault that wins the seat,
Derwent was heard: "What's this we meet?
A Cross? and—if one could but spell—
Inscription Sinaitic? Well,   5
Mortmain is nigh—*his* crazy freak;
Whose else? A closer view I'll seek;
I'll climb."
    In moving there aside
The rock's turned brow he had espied;
In rear this rock hung o'er the waste   10
And Nehemiah in sleep embraced
Below. The forepart gloomed Lot's wave
So nigh, the tide the base did lave.
Above, the sea-face smooth was worn
Through long attrition of that grit   15
Which on the waste of winds is borne.
And on the tablet high of it—
Traced in dull chalk, such as is found
Accessible in upper ground—
Big there between two scrawls, below   20

And over—a cross; three stars in row
Upright, two more for thwarting limb
Which drooped oblique.
               At Derwent's cry
The rest drew near; and every eye
Marked the device.—Thy passion's whim,   25
Wild Swede, mused Vine in silent heart.
"Looks like the *Southern Cross* to me,"
Said Clarel; "so 'tis down in chart."
"And so," said Rolfe, "'tis set in sky—
Though error slight of place prevail   30
In midmost star here chalked. At sea,
Bound for Peru, when south ye sail,
Startling that novel cluster strange
Peers up from low; then as ye range
Cape-ward still further, brightly higher   35
And higher the stranger doth aspire,
'Till off the Horn, when at full hight
Ye slack your gaze as chilly grows the night.
But Derwent—see!"
               The priest having gained
Convenient lodge the text below,   40
They called: "What's that in curve contained
Above the stars? Read: we would know."
"Runs thus: *By one who wails the loss,*
This altar to the Slanting Cross."
"Ha! under that?" "Some crow's-foot scrawl."   45
"Decipher, quick! we're waiting all."
"Patience: for ere one try rehearse,
'Twere well to make it out. 'Tis verse."
"Verse, say you? Read." "'Tis mystical:

    " 'Emblazoned bleak in austral skies—   50
        A heaven remote, whose starry swarm
        Like Science lights but cannot warm—
        Translated Cross, hast thou withdrawn,
        Dim paling too at every dawn,
        With symbols vain once counted wise,   55
        And gods declined to heraldries?
        Estranged, estranged: can friend prove so?

Aloft, aloof, a frigid sign:
How far removed, thou Tree divine,
Whose tender fruit did reach so low—   60
Love apples of New-Paradise!
About the wide Australian sea
The planted nations yet to be—
When, ages hence, they lift their eyes,
Tell, what shall they retain of thee?   65
But class thee with Orion's sword?
In constellations unadored,
Christ and the Giant equal prize?
The atheist cycles—*must* they be?
Fomentors as forefathers we?'   70

"Mad, mad enough," the priest here cried,
Down slipping by the shelving brinks;
"But 'tis not Mortmain," and he sighed.
      "Not Mortmain?" Rolfe exclaimed. "Methinks,"
The priest, "'tis hardly in his vein."   75
"How? fraught with feeling is the strain?
His heart's not ballasted with stone—
He's crank." "Well, well, e'en let us own
That Mortmain, Mortmain is the man.
We've then a pledge here at a glance   80
Our comrade's met with no mischance.
Soon he'll rejoin us." "There, amen!"
"But now to wake Nehemiah in den
Behind here.—But kind Clarel goes.
Strange how he naps nor trouble knows   85
Under the crag's impending block,
Nor fears its fall, nor recks of shock."

      Anon they mount; and much advance
Upon that chalked significance.
The student harks, and weighs each word,   90
Intent, he being newly stirred.

      But tarries Margoth? Yes, behind
He lingers. He placards his mind:
Scaling the crag he rudely scores

With the same chalk (how here abused!)   95
Left by the other, after used,
A sledge or hammer huge as Thor's;
A legend lending—this, to wit:
"I, Science, I whose gain's thy loss,
I slanted thee, thou Slanting Cross."   100
     But sun and rain, and wind, with grit
Driving, these haste to cancel it.

32. THE ENCAMPMENT

Southward they find a strip at need
Between the mount and marge, and make,
In expectation of the Swede,
Encampment there, nor shun the Lake.
'Twas afternoon. With Arab zest   5
The Bethlehemites their spears present,
Whereon they lift and spread the tent
And care for all.
                    As Rolfe from rest
Came out, toward early eventide,
His comrades sat the shore beside,   10
In shadow deep, which from the west
The main Judæan mountains flung.
That ridge they faced, and anxious hung
Awaiting Mortmain, some having grown
The more concerned, because from stone   15
Inscribed, they had indulged a hope:
But now in ill surmise they grope.
Anew they question grave Djalea.
But what knows *he?*
                    Their hearts to cheer,
"Trust," Derwent said, "hope's silver bell;   20
Nor dream he'd do his life a wrong—
No, never!"
                    "Demons here which dwell,"
Cried Rolfe, "riff-raff of Satan's throng,
May fetch him steel, rope, poison—well,

He'd spurn them, hoot their scurvy hell: 25
There's nobler.—But what *other* knell
Of hap—" He turned him toward the sea.
    Like leagues of ice which slumberous roll
About the pivot of the pole—
Vitreous—glass it seemed to be.   30
Beyond, removed in air sublime,
As 'twere some more than human clime,
In flanking towers of Ætna hue
The Ammonitish mounts they view
Enkindled by the sunset cast   35
Over Judah's ridgy headlands massed
Which blacken baseward. Ranging higher
Where vague glens pierced the steeps of fire,
Imagination time repealed—
Restored there, and in fear revealed   40
Lot and his daughters twain in flight,
Three shadows flung on reflex light
Of Sodom in her funeral pyre.
    Some fed upon the natural scene,
Deriving many a wandering hint   45
Such as will ofttimes intervene
When on the slab ye view the print
Of perished species.—Judge Rolfe's start
And quick revulsion, when, apart,
Derwent he saw at ease reclined,   50
With page before him, page refined
And appetizing, which threw ope
New parks, fresh walks for Signor Hope
To saunter in.
                    "And read you here?
Scarce suits the ground with bookish cheer.   55
Escaped from forms, enlarged at last,
Pupils we be of wave and waste—
Not books; nay, nay!"
                    "Book-comment, though,"—
Smiled Derwent—"were it ill to know?"
    "But how if nature vetoes all   60
Her commentators? Disenthrall

Thy heart. Look round. Are not here met
Books and that truth no type shall set?"—
Then, to himself in refluent flow:
"Earnest again!—well, let it go."   65
      Derwent quick glanced from face to face,
Lighting upon the student's hue
Of pale perplexity, with trace
Almost of twinge at Rolfe: "Believe,
Though here I random page review,   70
Not books I let exclusive cleave
And sway. Much too there is, I grant,
Which well might Solomon's wisdom daunt—
Much that we mark. Nevertheless,
Were it a paradox to confess   75
A book's a man? If this be so,
Books be but part of nature. Oh,
'Tis studying nature, reading books:
And 'tis through Nature each heart looks
Up to a God, or whatsoe'er   80
One images beyond our sphere.
Moreover, Siddim's not the world:
There's Naples. Why, yourself well know
What breadths of beauty lie unfurled
All round the bays where sailors go.   85
So, prithee, do not be severe,
But let me read."
                Rolfe looked esteem:
"You suave St. Francis! Him, I mean,
Of Sales, not that soul whose dream
Founded the bare-foot Order lean.   90
Though wise as serpents, Sales proves
The throbbings sweet of social doves.
I like you."
                Derwent laughed; then, "Ah,
From each Saint Francis am I far!"
And grave he grew.
                It was a scene   95
Which Clarel in his memory scored:
How reconcile Rolfe's wizard chord

And forks of esoteric fire,
With common-place of laxer mien?
May truth be such a spendthrift lord?   100
Then Derwent: he reviewed in heart
His tone with Margoth; his attire
Of tolerance; the easy part
He played. Could Derwent, having gained
A certain slant in liberal thought,   105
Think there to bide, like one detained
Half-way adown the slippery glacier caught?
Was honesty his, with lore and art
Not to be fooled?—But if in vain
One tries to comprehend a man,   110
How think to sound God's deeper heart!

33. LOT'S SEA

Roving along the winding verge
Trying these problems as a lock,
Clarel upon the further marge
Caught sight of Vine. Upon a rock
Low couchant there, and dumb as that,   5
Bent on the wave Vine moveless sat.
The student after pause drew near:
Then, as in presence which though mute
Did not repel, without salute
He joined him.
        Unto these, by chance   10
In ruminating slow advance
Came Rolfe, and lingered.
        At Vine's feet
A branchless tree lay lodged ashore,
One end immersed. Of form complete—
Half fossilized—could this have been,   15
In ages back, a palm-shaft green?
Yes, long detained in depths which store
A bitter virtue, there it lay,
Washed up to sight—free from decay

But dead.
                    And now in slouched return   20
From random prowlings, brief sojourn
As chance might prompt, the Jew they espy
Coasting inquisitive the shore
And frequent stooping. Ranging nigh,
In hirsute hand a flint he bore—   25
A flint, or stone, of smooth dull gloom:
"A jewel? not asphaltum—no:
Observe it, pray. Methinks in show
'Tis like the flagging round that Tomb
Ye celebrate."
                    Rolfe, glancing, said,   30
"I err, or 'twas from Siddim's bed
Or quarry here, those floor-stones came:
'Tis Stone-of-Moses called, they vouch;
The Arabs know it by that name."
        "Moses? who's Moses?" Into pouch   35
The lump he slipped; while wistful here
Clarel in silence challenged Vine;
But not responsive was Vine's cheer,
Discharged of every meaning sign.
        With motive, Rolfe the talk renewed: 40
"Yes, here it was the cities stood
That sank in reprobation. See,
The scene and record well agree."
        "Tut, tut—tut, tut. Of aqueous force,
Vent igneous, a shake or so,   45
One here perceives the sign—of course;
All's mere geology, you know."
        "Nay, how should one know that?"
                              "By sight,
Touch, taste—all senses in assent
Of common sense their parliament.   50
Judge now; this lake, with outlet none
And into which five streams discharge
From south; which east and west is shown
Walled in by Alps along the marge;
North, in this lake, the waters end   55

Of Jordan—end here, or dilate
Rather, and so evaporate
From surface. But do you attend?"
    "Most teachably."
                "Well, now: assume
This lake was formed, even as they tell,   60
Then first when the Five Cities fell;
Where, I demand, ere yet that doom,
Where emptied Jordan?"
                "Who can say?
Not I."
        "No, none. A point I make:
Coeval are the stream and lake!   65
I say no more."
            As came that close
A hideous hee-haw horrible rose,
Rebounded in unearthly sort
From shore to shore, as if retort
From all the damned in Sodom's Sea   70
Out brayed at him. "Just God, what's that?"
"The ass," breathed Vine, with tropic eye
Freakishly impish, nor less shy;
Then, distant as before, he sat.
    Anew Rolfe turned toward Margoth then;   75
"May not these levels high and low
Have undergone derangement when
The cities met their overthrow?
Or say there was a lake at first—
A supposition not reversed   80
By Writ—a lake enlarged through doom
Which overtook the cities? Come!"—
    The Jew, recovering from decline
Arising from late asinine
Applause, replied hereto in way   85
Eliciting from Rolfe—"Delay:
What knowest thou? or what know I?
Suspect you may ere yet you die
Or afterward perchance may learn,
That Moses' God is no mere Pam   90

With painted clubs, but true I AM."
    "Hog-Latin," was the quick return;
"Plague on that ass!" for here again
Brake in the pestilent refrain.
    Meanwhile, as if in a dissent   95
Not bordering their element,
Vine kept his place, aloof in air.
They could but part and leave him there;
The Hebrew railing as they went—
"Of all the dolorous dull men!   100
He's like a poor nun's pining hen.
And *me* too: should I let it pass?
Ass? did he say it was the ass?"
Hereat, timed like the clerk's *Amen*
Yet once more did the hee-haw free   105
Come in with new alacrity.

    Vine tarried; and with fitful hand
Took bits of dead drift from the sand
And flung them to the wave, as one
Whose race of thought long since was run—   110
For whom the spots enlarge that blot the golden sun.

34. Mortmain Reappears

While now at poise the wings of shade
Outstretched overhang each ridge and glade,
Mortmain descends from Judah's hight
Through sally-port of minor glens:
Against the background of black dens   5
Blacker the figure glooms enhanced.
    Relieved from anxious fears, the group
In friendliness would have advanced
To greet, but shrank or fell adroop.
    Like Hecla ice inveined with marl   10
And frozen cinders showed his face
Rigid and darkened. Shunning parle
He seated him aloof in place,
Hands clasped about the knees drawn up

As round the cask the binding hoop—   15
Condensed in self, or like a seer
Unconscious of each object near,
While yet, informed, the nerve may reach
Like wire under wave to furthest beach.
    By what brook Cherith had he been,   20
Watching it shrivel from the scene—
Or voice aerial had heard,
That now he murmured the wild word;
"But, hectored by the impious years,
What god invoke, for leave to unveil   25
That gulf whither tend these modern fears,
And deeps over which men crowd the sail?"
    Up, as possessed, he rose anon,
And crying to the beach went down:
"Repent! repent in every land   30
Or hell's hot kingdom is at hand!
Yea, yea,
In pause of the artillery's boom,
While now the armed world holds its own,
The comet peers, the star dips down;   35
Flicker the lamps in Syria's tomb,
While Anti-Christ and Atheist set
On Anarch the red coronet!"

    "Mad John," sighed Rolfe, "dost there betray
The dire *Vox Clamans* of our day?"   40
    "Why heed him?" Derwent breathed: "alas!
Let him alone, and it will pass.—
What would he now?" Before the bay
Low bowed he there, with hand addressed
To scoop. "Unhappy, hadst thou best?"   45
Djalea it was; then calling low
Unto a Bethlehemite whose brow
Was wrinkled like the bat's shrunk hide—
"Your salt-song, Beltha: warn and chide."

    "Would ye know what bitter drink   50
        They gave to Christ upon the Tree?
    Sip the wave that laps the brink

Of Siddim: taste, and God keep ye!
It drains the hills where alum's hid—
Drains the rock-salt's ancient bed;   55
   Hither unto basin fall
   The torrents from the steeps of gall—
Here is Hades' water-shed.
   Sinner, would ye that your soul
   Bitter were and like the pool?   60
Sip the Sodom waters dead;
   But never from thy heart shall haste
   The Marah—yea, the after-taste."

He closed.—Arrested as he stooped,
Did Mortmain his pale hand recall?   65
No; undeterred the wave he scooped,
And tried it—madly tried the gall.

35. Prelusive

In Piranesi's rarer prints,
Interiors measurelessly strange,
Where the distrustful thought may range
Misgiving still—what mean the hints?
Stairs upon stairs which dim ascend   5
In series from plunged Bastiles drear—
Pit under pit; long tier on tier
Of shadowed galleries which impend
Over cloisters, cloisters without end;
The hight, the depth—the far, the near;   10
Ring-bolts to pillars in vaulted lanes,
And dragging Rhadamanthine chains;
These less of wizard influence lend
Than some allusive chambers closed.
   Those wards of hush are not disposed   15
In gibe of goblin fantasy—
Grimace—unclean diablery:
Thy wings, Imagination, span
Ideal truth in fable's seat:

The thing implied is one with man,   20
His penetralia of retreat—
The heart, with labyrinths replete:
In freaks of intimation see
Paul's "mystery of iniquity:"
Involved indeed, a blur of dream;   25
As, awed by scruple and restricted
In first design, or interdicted
By fate and warnings as might seem;
The inventor miraged all the maze,
Obscured it with prudential haze;   30
Nor less, if subject unto question,
The egg left, egg of the suggestion.
    Dwell on those etchings in the night,
Those touches bitten in the steel
By aqua-fortis, till ye feel   35
The Pauline text in gray of light;
Turn hither then and read aright.

    For ye who green or gray retain
Childhood's illusion, or but feign;
As bride and suit let pass a bier—   40
So pass the coming canto here.

36. SODOM

Full night. The moon has yet to rise;
The air oppresses, and the skies
Reveal beyond the lake afar
One solitary tawny star—
Complexioned so by vapors dim,   5
Whereof some hang above the brim
And nearer waters of the lake,
Whose bubbling air-beads mount and break
As charged with breath of things alive.

    In talk about the Cities Five   10
Engulfed, on beach they linger late.

And he, the quaffer of the brine,
Puckered with that heart-wizening wine
Of bitterness, among them sate
Upon a camel's skull, late dragged   15
From forth the wave, the eye-pits slagged
With crusted salt.—"What star is yon?"
And pointed to that single one
Befogged above the sea afar.
"It might be Mars, so red it shines,"   20
One answered; "duskily it pines
In this strange mist."—"It is the star
Called Wormwood. Some hearts die in thrall
Of waters which yon star makes gall;"
And, lapsing, turned, and made review   25
Of what that wickedness might be
Which down on these ill precincts drew
The flood, the fire; put forth new plea,
Which not with Writ might disagree;
Urged that those malefactors stood   30
Guilty of sins scarce scored as crimes
In any statute known, or code—
Nor now, nor in the former times:
Things hard to prove: decorum's wile,
Malice discreet, judicious guile;   35
Good done with ill intent—reversed:
Best deeds designed to serve the worst;
And hate which under life's fair hue
Prowls like the shark in sunned Pacific blue.
         He paused, and under stress did bow,   40
Lank hands enlocked across the brow.
         "Nay, nay, thou sea,
'Twas not all carnal harlotry,
But sins refined, crimes of the spirit,
Helped earn that doom ye here inherit: 45
Doom well imposed, though sharp and dread,
In some god's reign, some god long fled.—
Thou gaseous puff of mineral breath
Mephitical; thou swooning flaw
That fann'st me from this pond of death;   50

Wert thou that venomous small thing
Which tickled with the poisoned straw?
Thou, stronger, but who yet couldst start
Shrinking with sympathetic sting,
While willing the uncompunctious dart!   55
Ah, ghosts of Sodom, how ye thrill
About me in this peccant air,
Conjuring yet to spare, but spare!
Fie, fie, that didst in formal will
Plot piously the posthumous snare.   60
And thou, the mud-flow—evil mass
Of surest-footed sluggishness
Swamping the nobler breed—art there?
Moan, Burker of kind heart: all's known
To Him; with thy connivers, moan.—   65
Sinners—expelled, transmuted souls
Blown in these airs, or whirled in shoals
Of gurgles which your gasps send up,
Or on this crater marge and cup
Slavered in slime, or puffed in stench—   70
Not ever on the tavern bench
Ye lolled. Few dicers here, few sots,
Few sluggards, and no idiots.
'Tis *thou* who servedst Mammon's hate
Or greed through forms which holy are—   75
Black slaver steering by a star,
'Tis *thou*—and all like thee in state.
Who knew the world, yet varnished it;
Who traded on the coast of crime
Though landing not; who did outwit   80
Justice, his brother, and the time—
These, chiefly these, to doom submit.
But who the manifold may tell?
And sins there be inscrutable,
Unutterable."
            Ending there   85
He shrank, and like an osprey gray
Peered on the wave. His hollow stare
Marked then some smaller bubbles play

In cluster silvery like spray:
"Be these the beads on the wives'-wine,   90
Tofana-brew?—O fair Medea—
O soft man-eater, furry-fine:
Oh, be thou Jael, be thou Leah—
Unfathomably shallow!—No!
Nearer the core than man can go   95
Or Science get—nearer the slime
Of nature's rudiments and lime
In chyle before the bone. Thee, thee,
In thee the filmy cell is spun—
The mould thou art of what men be: 100
Events are all in thee begun—
By thee, through thee!—Undo, undo,
Prithee, undo, and still renew
The fall forever!"
               On his throne
He lapsed; and muffled came the moan   105
How multitudinous in sound,
From Sodom's wave. He glanced around:
They all had left him, one by one.
Was it because he open threw
The inmost to the outward view?   110
Or did but pain at frenzied thought,
Prompt to avoid him, since but naught
In such case might remonstrance do?
But none there ventured idle plea,
Weak sneer, or fraudful levity.   115

   Two spirits, hovering in remove,
Sad with inefficacious love,
Here sighed debate: "Ah, Zoima, say;
Be it far from me to impute a sin,
But may a sinless nature win   120
Those deeps he knows?"—"Sin shuns that way;
Sin acts the sin, but flees the thought
That sweeps the abyss that sin has wrought.
Innocent be the heart and true—
Howe'er it feed on bitter bread—   125

That, venturous through the Evil led,
Moves as along the ocean's bed
Amid the dragon's staring crew."

37. OF TRADITIONS

Credit the Arab wizard lean,
And still at favoring hour are seen
(But not by Franks, whom doubts debar)
Through waves the cities overthrown:
Seboym and Segor, Aldemah,   5
With two whereof the foul renown
And syllables more widely reign.
    Astarte, worshiped on the Plain
Ere Terah's day, her vigil keeps
Devoted where her temple sleeps   10
Like moss within the agate's vein—
A ruin in the lucid sea.
The columns lie overlappingly—
Slant, as in order smooth they slid
Down the live slope. Her ray can bid   15
Their beauty thrill along the lane
Of tremulous silver. By the marge
(If yet the Arab credence gain)
At slack wave, when midsummer's glow
Widens the shallows, statues show—   20
He vouches; and will more enlarge
On sculptured basins broad in span,
With alum scurfed and alkatran.
Nay, further—let who will, believe—
As monks aver, on holy eve,   25
Easter or John's, along the strand
Shadows Corinthian wiles inweave:
Voluptuous palaces expand,
From whose moon-lighted colonnade
Beckons Armida, deadly maid: 30
Traditions; and their fountains run
Beyond King Nine and Babylon.

But disenchanters grave maintain
That in the time ere Sodom's fall
'Twas shepherds here endured life's pain: 35
Shepherds, and all was pastoral
In Siddim; Abraham and Lot,
Blanketed Bedouins of the plain;
Sodom and her four daughters small—
For Sodom held maternal reign—   40
Poor little hamlets, such as dot
The mountain side and valley way
Of Syria as she shows to-day;
The East, where constancies indwell,
Such hint may give: 'tis plausible.   45

     Hereof the group—from Mortmain's blight
Withdrawn where sands the beach embayed
And Nehemiah apart was laid—
Held curious discourse that night.
They chatted; but 'twas underrun   50
By heavier current. And anon,
After the meek one had retired
Under the tent, the thought transpired,
And Mortmain was the theme.
                         "If mad,
'Tis indignation at the bad,"   55
Said Rolfe; "most men somehow get used
To seeing evil, though not all
They see; 'tis sympathetical;
But never some are disabused
Of first impressions which appal."   60
     "There, there," cried Derwent, "let it fall.
Assume that some are but so-so,
They'll be transfigured. Let suffice:
Dismas he dwells in Paradise."
"Who?" "Dismas the Good Thief, you know.   65
Ay, and the Blest One shared the cup
With Judas; e'en let Judas sup
With him, at the Last Supper too.—
But see!"

It was the busy Jew
With chemic lamp aflame, by tent   70
Trying some shrewd experiment
With minerals secured that day,
Dead unctuous stones.
                    "Look how his ray,"
Said Rolfe, "too small for stars to heed,
Strange lights him, reason's sorcerer,   75
Poor Simon Magus run to seed.
And, yes, 'twas here—or else I err—
The legends claim, that into sea
The old magician flung his book
When life and lore he both forsook: 80
The evil spell yet lurks, may be.—
But yon strange orb—can be the moon?
These vapors: and the waters swoon."

Ere long the tent received them all;
They slumber—wait the morning's call.   85

38. THE SLEEP-WALKER

Now Nehemiah with wistful heart
Much heed had given to myths which bore
Upon that Pentateuchal shore;
Him could the wilder legend thrill
With credulous impulse, whose appeal,   5
Oblique, touched on his Christian vein.
Wakeful he bode. With throbbing brain
O'erwrought by travel, long he lay
In febrile musings, life's decay,
Begetting soon an ecstasy   10
Wherein he saw arcade and fane
And people moving in the deep;
Strange hum he heard, and minstrel-sweep.
Then, by that sleight each dreamer knows,
Dream merged in dream: the city rose—   15
Shrouded, it went up from the wave;

Transfigured came down out of heaven
Clad like a bride in splendor brave.
There, through the streets, with purling sound
Clear waters the clear agates lave,   20
Opal and pearl in pebbles strown;
The palaces with palms were crowned—
The water-palaces each one;
And from the fount of rivers shone
Soft rays as of Saint Martin's sun;   25
Last, dearer than ere Jason found,
A fleece—the Fleece upon a throne!
And a great voice he hears which saith,
Pain is no more, no more is death;
I wipe away all tears: Come, ye,   30
Enter, it is eternity.
And happy souls, the saved and blest,
Welcomed by angels and caressed,
Hand linked in hand like lovers sweet,
Festoons of tenderness complete—   35
Roamed up and on, by orchards fair
To bright ascents and mellower air;
Thence, highest, toward the throne were led,
And kissed, amid the sobbings shed
Of faith fulfilled.—In magic play   40
So to the meek one in the dream
Appeared the New Jerusalem:
Haven for which how many a day—
In bed, afoot, or on the knee—
He yearned: Would God I were in thee!   45

    The visions changed and counterchanged—
Blended and parted—distant ranged,
And beckoned, beckoned him away.
In sleep he rose; and none did wist
When vanished this somnambulist.   50

39. Obsequies

The camel's skull upon the beach
No more the sluggish waters reach—
No more the languid waters lave;
Not now they wander in and out
Of those void chambers walled about—   5
So dull the calm, so dead the wave.
Above thick mist how pallid looms,
While the slurred day doth wanly break,
Ammon's long ridge beyond the lake.

Down to the shrouded margin comes   10
Lone Vine—and starts: not at the skull,
The camel's, for that bides the same
As when overnight 'twas Mortmain's stool.
But, nigh it—how *that* object name?
Slant on the shore, ground-curls of mist   15
Enfold it, as in amethyst
Subdued, small flames in dead of night
Lick the dumb back-log ashy white.
What is it?—paler than the pale
Pervading vapors, which so veil,   20
That some peak-tops are islanded
Baseless above the dull, dull bed
Of waters, which not e'en transmit
One ripple 'gainst the cheek of It.

The start which the discoverer gave   25
Was physical—scarce shocked the soul,
Since many a prior revery grave
Forearmed against alarm's control.
To him, indeed, each lapse and end
Meet—in harmonious method blend.   30
Lowly he murmured, "Here is balm:
Repose is snowed upon repose—
Sleep upon sleep; it is the calm
And incantation of the close."
The others, summoned to the spot,   35

Were staggered: Nehemiah? no!
The innocent and sinless—what!—
Pale lying like the Assyrian low?

    The Swede stood by; nor after-taste
Extinct was of the liquid waste   40
Nor influence of that Wormwood Star
Whereof he spake. All overcast—
His genial spirits meeting jar—
Derwent on no unfeeling plea
Held back. Mortmain, relentless: "See: 45
To view death on the bed—at ease—
A dream, and draped; to minister
To inheriting kin; to comfort *these*
In chamber comfortable;—*here*
The elements all that unsay!   50
The first man dies. Thus Abel lay."
    The sad priest, rightly to be read
Scarce hoping,—pained, dispirited—
Was dumb. And Mortmain went aside
In thrill by only Vine espied: 55
Alas (thought Vine) thou bitter Swede,
Into thine armor dost thou bleed?

    Intent but poised, the Druze looked on:
"The sheath: the sword?"
                   "Ah, whither gone?"
Clarel, and bowed him there and kneeled: 60
"Whither art gone? thou friendliest mind
Unfriended—what friend now shalt find?
Robin or raven, hath God a bird
To come and strew thee, lone interred,
With leaves, when here left far behind?"   65
    "He's gone," the Jew; "czars, stars must go
Or change! All's chymestry. Aye so."—
"*Resurget*"—faintly Derwent there.
"*In pace*"—Vine, nor more would dare.

    Rolfe in his reaching heart did win   70
Prelude remote, yet gathering in:

"Moist, moist with sobs and balsam shed—
Warm tears, cold odors from the urn—
They hearsed in heathen Rome their dead
Nor hopeful of the soul's return.   75
Embracing them, in marble set,
The mimic gates of Orcus met—
The Pluto-bolt, the fatal one
Wreathed over by the hung festoon.
How fare we *now?* But were it clear   80
In nature or in lore devout
That parted souls live on in cheer,
Gladness would be—shut pathos out.
His poor thin life: the end? no more?
The end here by the Dead Sea shore?"   85
      He turned him, as awaiting nod
Or answer from earth, air, or skies;
But be it ether or the clod,
The elements yield no replies.
      Cross-legged on a cindery hight,   90
Belex, the fatalist, smoked on.
Slow whiffs; and then, "It needs be done:
Come, beach the loins there, Bethlehemite."—

      Inside a hollow free from stone
With camel-ribs they scooped a trench;   95
And Derwent, rallying from blench
Of Mortmain's brow, and nothing loth
Tacit to vindicate the cloth,
Craved they would bring to him the Book,
Now ownerless. The same he took,   100
And thence had culled brief service meet,
But closed, reminded of the psalm
Heard when the salt fog shrunk the palm—
They wending toward these waters' seat—
Raised by the saint, as e'en it lent   105
A voice to low presentiment:
Naught better might one here repeat:

      "Though through the valley of the shade
            I pass, no evil do I fear;

His candle shineth on my head: 110
     Lo, he is with me, even here."

That o'er, they kneeled—with foreheads bare
Bowed as he made the burial prayer.
Even Margoth bent him; but 'twas so
As some hard salt at sea will do   115
Holding the narrow plank that bears
The shotted hammock, while brief prayers
Are by the master read mid war
Relentless of wild elements—
The sleet congealing on the spar: 120
It was a sulking reverence.
     The body now the Arabs placed
Within the grave, and then with haste
Had covered, but for Rolfe's restraint:
"The Book!"—The Bible of the saint—   125
With that the relics there he graced,
Yea, put it in the hand: "Since now
The last long journey thou dost go,
Why part thee from thy friend and guide!
And better guide who knoweth? Bide."   130

They closed. And came a rush, a roar—
Aloof, but growing more and more,
Nearer and nearer. They invoke
The long Judaic range, the hight
Of nearer mountains hid from sight   135
By the blind mist. Nor spark nor smoke
Of that plunged wake their eyes might see;
But, hoarse in hubbub, horribly,
With all its retinue around—
Flints, dust, and showers of splintered stone,   140
An avalanche of rock down tore,
In somerset from each rebound—
Thud upon thump—down, down and down—
And landed. Lull. Then shore to shore
Rolled the deep echo, fold on fold,   145

Which, so reverberated, bowled
And bowled far down the long El Ghor.

    They turn; and, in that silence sealed,
What works there from behind the veil?
A counter object is revealed—   150
A thing of heaven, and yet how frail:
Up in thin mist above the sea
Humid is formed, and noiselessly,
The fog-bow: segment of an oval
Set in a colorless removal   155
Against a vertical shaft, or slight
Slim pencil of an aqueous light.
Suspended there, the segment hung
Like to the May-wreath that is swung
Against the pole. It showed half spent—   160
Hovered and trembled, paled away, and—went.

END OF PART 2

Part 3

Mar Saba

1. In the Mountain

WHAT REVERIES be in yonder heaven
Whither, if yet faith rule it so,
The tried and ransomed natures flow?
If there peace after strife be given
Shall hearts remember yet and know? 5
Thy vista, Lord, of havens dear,
May that in such entrancement bind
That never starts a wandering tear
For wail and willow left behind?
Then wherefore, chaplet, quivering throw 10
A dusk e'en on the martyr's brow
You crown? Do seraphim shed balm
At last on all of earnest mind,
Unworldly yearners, nor the palm
Awarded St. Teresa, ban 15
To Leopardi, Obermann?
Translated where the anthem's sung
Beyond the thunder, in a strain
Whose harmony unwinds and solves
Each mystery that life involves; 20

There shall the Tree whereon He hung,
The olive wood, leaf out again—
Again leaf out, and endless reign,
Type of the peace that buds from sinless pain?

Exhalings! Tending toward the skies   25
By natural law, from heart they rise
Of one there by the moundless bed
Where stones they roll to feet and head;
Then mount, and fall behind the guard
And so away.
                       But whitherward?   30
'Tis the high desert, sultry Alp
Which suns decay, which lightnings scalp.
For now, to round the waste in large,
Christ's Tomb re-win by Saba's marge
Of grots and ossuary cells,   35
And Bethlehem where remembrance dwells—
From Sodom in her pit dismayed
Westward they wheel, and there invade
Judah's main ridge, which horrors deaden—
Where Chaos holds the wilds in pawn,   40
As here had happed an Armageddon,
Betwixt the good and ill a fray,
But ending in a battle drawn,
Victory undetermined. Nay,
For how an indecisive day   45
When one side camps upon the ground
Contested.
              Ere, enlocked in bound
They enter where the ridge is riven,
A look, one natural look is given
Toward Margoth and his henchmen twain,   50
Dwindling to ants far off upon the plain.

"So fade men from each other!—Jew,
We do forgive thee now thy scoff,
Now that thou dim recedest off
Forever. Fair hap to thee, Jew: 55
Consolator whom thou disownest

Attend thee in last hour lonest!"
    Rolfe, gazing, could not all repress
That utterance; and more or less,
Albeit they left it undeclared, 60
The others in the feeling shared.

    They turn, and enter now the pass
Wherein, all unredeemed by weeds,
Trees, moss, the winding cornice leads
For road along the calcined mass 65
Of aged mountain. Slow they urge
Sidelong their way betwixt the wall
And flanked abyss. They hark the fall
Of stones, hoof-loosened, down the crags:
The crumblings note they of the verge. 70
In rear one strange steed timid lags:
On foot an Arab goes before
And coaxes him to steepy shore
Of scooped-out gulfs, would halt him there:
Back shrinks the foal with snort and glare. 75
Then downward from the giddy brim
They peep; but hardly may they tell
If the black gulf affrighted him
Or lingering scent he caught in air
From relics in mid lodgment placed, 80
Now first perceived within the dell—
Two human skeletons inlaced
In grapple as alive they fell,
Or so disposed in overthrow,
As to suggest encounter so. 85
A ticklish rim, an imminent pass
For quarrel; and blood-feud, alas,
The Arab keeps, and where or when,
Cain meeting Abel, closes then.
    That desert's age the gorge may prove, 90
Piercing profound the mountain bare;
Yet hardly churned out in the groove
By a perennial wear and tear
Of floods; nay, dry it shows within;
But twice a year the waters flow, 95

Nor then in tide, but dribbling thin:
Avers Mar Saba's abbot so.
Nor less perchance before the day
When Joshua met the tribes in fray,
What wave here ran through leafy scene   100
Like uplands in Vermont the green;
What sylvan folk by mountain-base
Descrying showers about the crown
Of woods, foreknew the freshet's race
Quick to descend in torrent down;   105
And watched for it, and hailed in glee,
Then rode the comb of freshet wild,
As peaked upon the roller free
With gulls for mates, the Maldives' merry child?
Or, earlier yet, could be a day,   110
In time's first youth and pristine May
When here the hunter stood alone—
Moccasined Nimrod, belted Boone;
And down the tube of fringed ravine
Siddim descried, a lilied scene?   115
But crime and earthquake, throes and war;
And heaven remands the flower and star.
    Aside they turn, and leave that gorge,
And slant upon the mountain long,
And toward a ledge they toilsome urge   120
High over Siddim, and overhung
By loftier crags. In spirals curled
And pearly nothings buoyant whirled,
Eddies of exhalations light,
As over lime-kilns, swim in sight.   125
The fog dispersed, those vapors show
Diurnal from the waters won
By the athirst demanding sun—
Recalling text of Scripture so;
For on the morn which followed rain   130
Of fire, when Abraham looked again,
The smoke went up from all the plain.
Their mount of vision, voiceless, bare,
It is that ridge, the desert's own,
Which by its dead Medusa stare,   135

Petrific o'er the valley thrown,
Congeals Arabia into stone.
With dull metallic glint, the sea
Slumbers beneath the silent lee
Of sulphurous hills. These stretch away 140
Toward wilds of Kadesh Barnea,
And Zin the waste.
           In pale regard
Intent the Swede turned thitherward:
"God came from Teman; in His hour
The Holy One from Paran came; 145
They knew Him not; He hid His power
Within the forking of the flame,
Within the thunder and the roll.
Imperious in its swift control,
The lion's instantaneous lick 150
Not more effaces to the quick
Than His fierce indignation then.
Look! for His wake is here. O men,
Since Science can so much explode,
Evaporated is this God?— 155
Recall the red year Forty-eight:
He storms in Paris; thence divides;
The menace scarce outspeeds the fate:
He's over the Rhine—He's at Berlin—
At Munich—Dresden—fires Vien; 160
He's over the Alps—the whirlwind rides
In Rome; London's alert—the Czar:
The portent and the fact of war,
And terror that into hate subsides.
There, through His instruments made known, 165
Including Atheist and his tribes,
Behold the prophet's marching One,
He at whose coming Midian shook—
The God, the striding God of Habakkuk."

    Distempered! Nor might passion tire, 170
Nor pale reaction from it quell
The craze of grief's intolerant fire
Unwearied and unweariable.

2. The Carpenter

From vehemence too mad to stem
Fain would they turn and solace them.
Turn where they may they find a dart.
For while recumbent here they view,
Beneath them spread, the seats malign,   5
Nehemiah recurs—in last recline
A hermit there. And some renew
Their wonderment at such a heart,
Single in life—in death, how far apart!
That life they question, seek a clew: 10
Those virtues which his meekness knew,
Marked these indeed but wreckful wane
Of strength, or the organic man?
The hardy hemlock, if subdued,
Decays to violets in the wood,   15
Which put forth from the sodden stem:
His virtues, might they breed like them?
    Nor less that tale by Rolfe narrated
(Thrown out some theory to achieve),
Erewhile upon Mount Olivet,   20
That sea-tale of the master fated;
Not wholly might it here receive
An application such as met
The case. It needed something more
Or else, to penetrate the core.   25
    But Clarel—made remindful so
Of by-gone things which death can show
In kindled meaning—here revealed
That once Nehemiah his lips unsealed
(How prompted he could not recall)   30
In story which seemed rambling all,
And yet, in him, not quite amiss.
In pointed version it was this:
    A gentle wight of Jesu's trade,
A carpenter, for years had made   35
His living in a quiet dell,
And toiled and ate and slept alone,

Esteemed a harmless witless one.
Had I a friend thought he, 'twere well.
A friend he made, and through device   40
Of jobbing for him without price.
But on a day there came a word—
A word unblest, a blow abhorred.
Thereafter, in the mid of night,
When from the rafter and the joist   45
The insect ticked; and he, lone sprite,
How wakeful lay, what word was voiced?
Me love; fear only man. And he—
He willed what seemed too strange to be:
The hamlet marveled and the glade: 50
Interring him within his house,
He there his monastery made,
And grew familiar with the mouse.
Down to the beggar who might sing,
Alms, silent alms, unseen he'd fling,   55
And cakes to children. But no more
Abroad he went, till spent and gray,
Feet foremost he was borne away.

      As when upon a misty shore
The watchful seaman marks a light   60
Blurred by the fog, uncertain quite;
And thereto instant turns the glass
And studies it, and thinks it o'er
By compass: Is't the cape we pass?
So Rolfe from Clarel's mention caught   65
Food for an eagerness of thought:
"It bears, it bears; such things may be:
Shut from the busy world's pell-mell
And man's aggressive energy—
In cloistral Palestine to dwell   70
And pace the stone!"
                  And Mortmain heard,
Attesting; more his look did tell
Than comment of a bitter word.
Meantime the ass, high o'er the bed

Late scooped by Siddim's borders there—   75
As stupefied by brute despair,
Motionless hung the earthward head.

3. Of the Many Mansions

"The Elysium of the Greek was given
By haughty bards, a hero-heaven;
No victim looked for solace there:
The marble gate disowned the plea—
Ye heavy laden, come to me.   5
Nor Fortune's Isles, nor Tempe's dale
Nor Araby the Blest did bear
A saving balm—might not avail
To lull one pang, one lot repair.
Dreams, narrow dreams; nor of a kind   10
Showing inventiveness of mind
Beyond our earth. But oh! 'twas rare,
In world like this, the world we know
(Sole know, and reason from) to dare
To pledge indemnifying good   15
In worlds not known; boldly avow,
Against experience, the brood
Of Christian hopes."
                    So Rolfe, and sat
Clouded. But, changing, up he gat:
"Whence sprang the vision? They who freeze,   20
On earth here, under want or wrong;
The Sermon on the Mount shall these
Find verified? is love so strong?
Or bounds are hers, that Python mars
Your gentler influence, ye stars?   25
If so, how seem they given o'er
To worse than Circe's fooling spell;
Enslaved, degraded, tractable
To each mean atheist's crafty power.
So winning in enthusiast plea,   30
Here may the Gospel but the more

Operate like a perfidy?"
   "So worldlings deem," the Swede in glow;
"Much so they deem; or, if not so,
Hereon they act. But what said he,   35
The Jew whose feet the blisters know,
To Christ as sore He trailed the Tree
Toward Golgotha: 'Ha, is it *Thou,*
The king, the god? Well then, be strong:
No royal steed with galls is wrung: 40
That's for the hack.' There he but hurled
The scoff of Nature and the World,
Those monstrous twins." It jarred the nerve
Of Derwent, but he masked the thrill.
For Vine, he kindled, sitting still;   45
Respected he the Swede's wild will
As did the Swede Vine's ruled reserve.
   Mortmain went on: "We've touched a theme
From which the club and lyceum swerve,
Nor Herr von Goethe would esteem;   50
And yet of such compulsive worth,
It dragged a god here down to earth,
As some account. And, truth to say,
Religion ofttimes, one may deem,
Is man's appeal from fellow-clay: 55
Thibetan faith implies the extreme—
That death emancipates the good,
Absorbs them into deity,
Dropping the wicked into bestialhood."

   With that for text to revery due,   60
In lifted waste, on ashy ground
Like Job's pale group, without a sound
They sat. But hark! what strains ensue
Voiced from the crags above their view?

4. The Cypriote

"Noble gods at the board
　　Where lord unto lord
Light pushes the care-killing wine:
　　　Urbane in their pleasure,
　　　Superb in their leisure—   5
　　　　Lax ease—
Lax ease after labor divine!

"Golden ages eternal,
　　Autumnal, supernal,
Deep mellow their temper serene: 10
　　　The rose by their gate
　　　Shall it yield unto fate?
　　　　They are gods—
They are gods and their garlands keep green.

"Ever blandly adore them;   15
　　But spare to implore them:
They rest, they discharge them from time;
　　　Yet believe, light believe
　　　They would succor, reprieve—
　　　　Nay, retrieve—   20
Might but revelers pause in the prime!"

"Who sings?" cried Rolfe; "dare say no Quaker:
Fine song o'er funeral Siddim here:
So, mindless of the undertaker,
In cage above her mistress' bier   25
The gold canary chirps. What cheer?
Who comes?"
　　　　　　　"Ay, welcome as the drums
Of marching allies unto men
Beleaguered—comes, who hymning comes—
What rescuer, what Delian?"   30
　　So Derwent, and with quick remove
Scaling the rock which hemmed their cove
He thence descried where higher yet

A traveler came, by cliffs beset,
Descending, and where terrors met.   35
　　Nor Orpheus of heavenly seed
Adown thrilled Hades' gorges singing,
About him personally flinging
The bloom transmitted from the mead;
In listening ghost such thoughts could breed   40
As did the vocal stranger here
In Mortmain, where relaxed he lay
Under that voice from other sphere
And carol laughing at the clay.
　　Nearer the minstrel drew. How fair   45
And light he leaned with easeful air
Backward in saddle, so to frame
A counterpoise as down he came.
Against the dolorous mountain side
His Phrygian cap in scarlet pride   50
Burned like a cardinal-flower in glen.
And after him, in trappings paced
His escort armed, three goodly men.
　　Observing now the other train,
He halted. Young he was, and graced   55
With fortunate aspect, such as draws
Hearts to good-will by natural laws.
No furtive scrutiny he made,
But frankly flung salute, and said:
"Well met in desert! Hear my song?"   60
"Indeed we did," cried Derwent boon.
"And wondered where you got that tune,"
Rolfe added there. "Oh, brought along
From Cyprus; I'm a Cypriote,
You see; one catches many a note   65
Wafted from only heaven knows where."
"And, pray, how name you it?" "The air?
Why, hymn of Aristippus." "Ah:
And whither wends your train?" "Not far;"
And sidelong in the saddle free   70
A thigh he lolled: "'Tis thus, you see:
My dame beneath Our Lady's star

Vowed in her need, to Saba's shrine
Three flagons good for holy wine:
Vowed, and through me performed. Even now   75
I come from Saba, having done
Her will, accomplishing the vow.
But late I made a private one—
Meant to surprise her with a present
She'll value more than juicy pheasant,   80
Good mother mine. Yes, here I go
To Jordan, in desert there below,
To dip this shroud for her." "Shroud, *shroud?*"
Cried Derwent, following the hand
In startled wonderment unfeigned,   85
Which here a little tap bestowed
In designation on a roll
Strapped to the pommel; "Azrael's scroll!
You do not mean you carry there
A—a—" "The same; 'tis woven fair: 90

    "My shroud is saintly linen,
        In lavender 'tis laid;
      I have chosen a bed by the marigold
        And supplied me a silver spade!"

    The priest gazed at the singer; then   95
Turned his perplexed entreating ken
Upon Djalea. But Rolfe explained:
"I chance to know. Last year I gained
The Jordan at the Easter tide,
And saw the Greeks in numbers there,   100
Men, women, blithe on every side,
Dipping their winding-sheets. With care
They bleach and fold and put away
And take home to await the day:
A custom of old precedent,   105
And curious too in mode 'tis kept,
Showing how under Christian sway
Greeks still retain their primal bent,

Nor let grave doctrine intercept
That gay Hellene lightheartedness 110
Which in the pagan years did twine
The funeral urn with fair caress
Of vintage holiday divine."
He turned him toward the Cypriote:
"Your courier, the forerunning note 115
Which ere we sighted you, we heard—
You're bold to trill it so, my bird."
"And why? It is a fluent song.
Though who they be I cannot say,
I trust their lordships think no wrong; 120
I do but trill it for the air;
'Tis anything as down we fare."
    Enough; Rolfe let him have his way;
Yes, there he let the matter stay.
And so, with mutual good-will shown, 125
They parted.
          For *l'envoy* anon
They heard his lilting voice impel
Among the crags this versicle:

  "With a rose in thy mouth
    Through the world lightly veer: 130
  Rose in the mouth
    Makes a rose of the year!"

    Then, after interval again,
But fainter, further in the strain:

  "With the Prince of the South 135
    O'er the Styx bravely steer:
  Rose in the mouth
    And a wreath on the bier!"

    Chord deeper now that touched within.
Listening, they at each other look; 140
Some charitable hope they brook,

Yes, vague belief they fondly win
That heaven would brim his happy years
Nor time mature him into tears.

    And Vine in heart of revery saith: 145
Like any flute inspired with breath
Pervasive, and which duly renders
Unconscious in melodious play,
Whate'er the light musician tenders;
So warblest thou lay after lay   150
Scarce self-derived; and (shroud before)
Down goest singing toward Death's Sea,
Where lies aloof our pilgrim hoar
In pit thou'lt pass. Ah, young to be!

5. THE HIGH DESERT

Where silence and the legend dwell,
A cleft in Horeb is, they tell,
Through which upon one happy day
(The sun on his heraldic track
Due sign having gained in Zodiac)   5
A sunbeam darts, which slants away
Through ancient carven oriel
Or window in the Convent there,
Illuming so with annual flush
The somber vaulted chamber spare   10
Of Catherine's Chapel of the Bush—
The Burning Bush. Brief visitant,
It makes no lasting covenant;
It brings, but cannot leave, the ray.
    To hearts which here the desert smote   15
So came, so went the Cypriote.
    Derwent deep felt it; and, as fain
His prior spirits to regain;
Impatient too of scenes which led
To converse such as late was bred,   20
Moved to go on. But some declined.

So, for relief to heart which pined,
Belex he sought, by him sat down
In cordial ease upon a stone
Apart, and heard his stories free   25
Of Ibrahim's wild infantry.

    The rest abide. To these there comes,
As down on Siddim's scene they peer,
The contrast of their vernal homes—
Field, orchard, and the harvest cheer.   30
At variance in their revery move
The spleen of nature and her love:
At variance, yet entangled too—
Like wrestlers. Here in apt review
They call to mind Abel and Cain—   35
Ormuzd involved with Ahriman
In deadly lock. Were those gods gone?
Or under other names lived on?
The theme they started. 'Twas averred
That, in old Gnostic pages blurred,   40
Jehovah was construed to be
Author of evil, yea, its god;
And Christ divine his contrary:
A god was held against a god,
But Christ revered alone. Herefrom,   45
If inference availeth aught
(For still the topic pressed they home)
The two-fold Testaments become
Transmitters of Chaldaic thought
By implication. If no more   50
Those Gnostic heretics prevail
Which shook the East from shore to shore,
Their strife forgotten now and pale;
Yet, with the sects, that old revolt
Now reappears, if in assault   55
Less frank: none say Jehovah's evil,
None gainsay that he bears the rod;
Scarce that; but there's dismission civil,
And Jesus is the indulgent God.

This change, this dusking change that slips   60
(Like the penumbra o'er the sun),
Over the faith transmitted down;
Foreshadows it complete eclipse?
    Science and Faith, can these unite?
Or is that priestly instinct right   65
(Right as regards conserving still
The Church's reign) whose strenuous will
Made Galileo pale recite
The Penitential Psalms in vest
Of sackcloth; which to-day would blight   70
Those potent solvents late expressed
In laboratories of the West?
    But in her Protestant repose
Snores faith toward her mortal close?
Nay, like a sachem petrified,   75
Encaved found in the mountain-side,
Perfect in feature, true in limb,
Life's full similitude in him,
Yet all mere stone—is faith dead *now,*
A petrifaction? Grant it so,   80
Then what's in store? what shapeless birth?
Reveal the doom reserved for earth?
How far may seas retiring go?
    But, to redeem us, shall we say
That faith, undying, does but range,   85
Casting the skin—the creed. In change
Dead always does some creed delay—
Dead, not interred, though hard upon
Interment's brink? At Saint Denis
Where slept the Capets, sire and son,   90
Eight centuries of lineal clay,
On steps that led down into vault
The prince inurned last made a halt,
The coffin left they there, 'tis said,
Till the inheritor was dead;   95
Then, not till then 'twas laid away.
But if no more the creeds be linked,
If the long line's at last extinct,

If time both creed and faith betray,
Vesture and vested—yet again 100
What interregnum or what reign
Ensues? Or does a period come?
The Sibyl's books lodged in the tomb?
Shall endless time no more unfold
Of truth at core? Some things discerned 105
By the far Noahs of India old—
Earth's first spectators, the clear-eyed,
Unvitiated, unfalsified
Seers at first hand—shall these be learned
Though late, even by the New World, say, 110
Which now contemns?
              But what shall stay
The fever of advance? London immense
Still wax for aye? A check: but whence?
How of the teeming Prairie-Land?
There shall the plenitude expand 115
Unthinned, unawed? Or does it need
Only that men should breed and breed
To enrich those forces into play
Which in past times could oversway
Pride at his proudest? Do they come, 120
The locusts, only to the bloom?
Prosperity sire them?
              Thus they swept,
Nor sequence held, consistent tone—
Imagination wildering on
Through vacant halls which faith once kept 125
With ushers good.
              Themselves thus lost,
At settled hearts they wonder most.
For those (they asked) who still adhere
In homely habit's dull delay,
To dreams dreamed out or passed away; 130
Do these, our pagans, all appear
Much like each poor and busy one
Who when the Tartar took Pekin,
(If credence hearsay old may win)

Knew not the fact—so vast the town,   135
The multitude, the maze, the din?
   Still laggeth in deferred adieu
The A. D. (Anno Domini)
Overlapping into era new
Even as the Roman A. U. C.   140
Yet ran for time, regardless all
That Christ was born, and after fall
Of Rome itself?
           But now our age,
So infidel in equipage,
While carrying still the Christian name—   145
For all its self-asserted claim,
How fares it, tell? Can the age stem
Its own conclusions? is't a king
Awed by his conquests which enring
With menaces his diadem?   150
Bright visions of the times to be—
Must these recoil, ere long be cowed
Before the march in league avowed
Of Mammon and Democracy?
   In one result whereto we tend   155
Shall Science disappoint the hope,
Yea, to confound us in the end,
New doors to superstition ope?
   As years, as years and annals grow,
And action and reaction vie,   160
And never men attain, but know
How waves on waves forever die;
Does all more enigmatic show?

   So they; and in the vain appeal
Persisted yet, as ever still   165
Blown back in sleet that blinds the eyes,
Not less the fervid Geysers rise.

   Clarel meantime ungladdened bent
Regardful, and the more intent
For silence held. At whiles his eye   170

Lit on the Druze, reclined half prone,
The long pipe resting on the stone
And wreaths of vapor floating by—
The man and pipe in peace as one.
How clear the profile, clear and true; 175
And he so tawny. Bust ye view,
Antique, in alabaster brown,
Might show like that. There, all aside,
How passionless he took for bride
The calm—the calm, but not the dearth— 180
The dearth or waste; nor would he fall
In waste of words, that waste of all.

    For Vine, from that unchristened earth
Bits he picked up of porous stone,
And crushed in fist: or one by one, 185
Through the dull void of desert air,
He tossed them into valley down;
Or pelted his own shadow there;
Nor sided he with anything:
By fits, indeed, he wakeful looked; 190
But, in the main, how ill he brooked
That weary length of arguing—
Like tale interminable told
In Hades by some gossip old
To while the never-ending night. 195
Apart he went. Meantime, like kite
On Sidon perched, which doth enfold,
Slowly exact, the noiseless wing:
Each wrinkled Arab Bethlehemite,
Or trooper of the Arab ring, 200
With look of Endor's withered sprite
Slant peered on them from lateral hight;
While unperturbed over deserts riven,
Stretched the clear vault of hollow heaven.

6. DERWENT

At night upon the darkling main
To ship return with muffled sound
The rowers without comment vain—
The messmate overboard not found:
So, baffled in deep quest but late,   5
These on the mountain.
                But from chat
With Belex in campaigning mood,
Derwent drew nigh. The sight of him
Ruffled the Swede—evoked a whim
Which took these words: "O, well bestowed!   10
Hither and help us, man of God:
Doctor of consolation, here!
Be warned though: truth won't docile be
To codes of good society."
    Allowing for pain's bitter jeer,   15
Or hearing but in part perchance,
The comely cleric pilgrim came
With what he might of suiting frame,
And air approaching nonchalance;
And "How to serve you, friends?" he said.   20
    "Ah, that!" cried Rolfe; "for we, misled,
We peer from brinks of all we know;
Our eyes are blurred against the haze:
Canst help us track in snow on snow
The footprint of the Ancient of Days?"   25
    "Scarce without snow-shoes;" Derwent mild
In gravity; "But come; we've whiled
The time; up then, and let us go."
    "Delay," said Mortmain; "stay, roseace:
What word is thine for sinking heart,   30
What is thy wont in such a case,
Who sends for thee to act thy part
Consoling—not in life's last hour
Indeed—but when some deprivation sore
Unnerves, and every hope lies flat?"   35
    That troubled Derwent, for the tone

Brake into tremble unbeknown
E'en to the speaker. Down he sat
Beside them: "Well, if such one—nay!
But never yet such sent for me—   40
I mean, none in that last degree;
Assume it though: to him I'd say—
'The less in hand the more in store,
Dear friend.' No formula I'd trace,
But honest comfort face to face;   45
And, yes, with tonic strong I'd brace,
Closing with cheerful Paul in lore
Of text—*Rejoice ye evermore.*"
        The Swede here of a sudden drooped,
A hump dropped on him, one would say;   50
He reached and some burnt gravel scooped,
Then stared down on the plain away.
The priest in fidget moved to part.
        "Abide," said Mortmain with a start;
"Abide, for more I yet would know: 55
Is God an omnipresent God?
Is He in Siddim yonder? No?
If anywhere He's disavowed
How think to shun the final schism—
Blind elements, flat atheism?"   60
        Whereto the priest: "Far let it be
That ground where Durham's prelate stood
Who saw no proof that God was good
But only righteous.—Woe is me!
These controversies. Oft I've said   65
That never, never would I be led
Into their maze of vanity.
Behead me—rid me of pride's part
And let me live but by the heart!"
        "Hast proved thy heart? first prove it. Stay: 70
The Bible, tell me, is it true,
And thence deriv'st thy flattering view?"
        But Derwent glanced aside, as vexed;
Inly assured, nor less perplexed
How to impart; and grieved too late   75

At being drawn within the strait
Of vexed discussion: nor quite free
From ill conjecture, that the Swede,
Though no dissembler, yet indeed
Part played on him: "Why question me?   80
Why pound the text? Ah, modern be,
And share the truth's munificence.
Look now, one reasons thus: Immense
Is tropic India; hence she breeds
Brahma tremendous, gods like seeds.   85
The genial clime of Hellas gay
Begat Apollo. Take that way;
Nor query—Ramayana true?
The Iliad?"
       Mortmain nothing said,
But lumped his limbs and sunk his head.   90
   Then Rolfe to Derwent: "But the Jew:
Since clime and country, as you own,
So much effect, how with the Jew
Herein?"
      There Derwent sat him down
Afresh, well pleased and leisurely,   95
As one in favorite theory
Invoked: "That bondman from his doom
By Nile, and subsequent distress,
With punishment in wilderness,
Methinks he brought an added gloom   100
To nature here. Here church and state
He founded—would perpetuate
Exclusive and withdrawn. But no:
Advancing years prohibit rest;
All turns or alters for the best.   105
Time ran; and that expansive light
Of Greeks about the bordering sea,
Their happy genial spirits bright,
Wit, grace urbane, amenity
Contagious, and so hard to ban   110
By bigot law, or any plan;
These influences stole their way,
Affecting here and there a Jew;

Likewise the Magi tincture too
Derived from the Captivity: 115
Hence Hillel's fair reforming school,
Liberal gloss and leavening rule.
How then? could other issue be
At last but ferment and a change?
True, none recanted or dared range: 120
To Moses' law they yet did cling,
But some would fain have tempering—
In the bare place a bit of green.
And lo, an advent—the Essene,
Gentle and holy, meek, retired,   125
With virgin charity inspired:
Precursor, nay, a pledge, agree,
Of light to break from Galilee.
And, ay, He comes: the lilies blow!
In hamlet, field, and on the road,   130
To every man, in every mode
How did the crowning Teacher show
His broad and blessed comity.
I do avow He still doth seem
Pontiff of optimists supreme!"   135
    The Swede sat stone-like. Suddenly:
"Leave thy carmine! From thorns the streak
Ruddies enough that tortured cheek.
'Twas Shaftesbury first assumed your tone,
Trying to cheerfulize Christ's moan."   140
     "Nay now," plead Derwent, earnest here,
And in his eyes the forming tear;
"But hear me, hear!"
              "No more of it!"
And rose. It was his passion-fit.
The other changed; his pleasant cheer,   145
Confronted by that aspect wild,
Dropped like the flower from Ceres' child
In Enna, seeing the pale brow
Of Pluto dank from scud below.

    Though by Gethsemane, where first   150
Derwent encountered Mortmain's mien,

Christian forbearance well he nursed,
Allowing for distempered spleen;
Now all was altered, quite reversed—
'Twas now as at the burial scene   155
By Siddim's marge. And yet—and yet
Was here a proof that priest had met
His confutation? Hardly so
(Mused Clarel) but he longed to know
How it could be, that while the rest   160
Contented scarce the splenetic Swede,
They hardly so provoked the man
To biting outburst unrepressed
As did the cleric's gentle fan.

    But had the student paid more heed   165
To Derwent's look, he might have caught
Hints of reserves within the thought.
Nor failed the priest ere all too late
His patience here to vindicate.

7. Bell and Cairn

"ELOI LAMA SABACHTHANI!"
And, swooning, strove no more.

                    Nor gone
For every heart, whate'er they say,
The eclipse that cry of cries brought down,
And clamors through the darkness blown.   5
More wide for some it spreads in sway,
Involves the lily of the Easter Day.

    A chance word of the Swede in place—
Allusion to the anguished face,
Recalled to Clarel now the cry,   10
The ghost's reproachful litany.
Disturbed then, he apart would go;
And passed among the crags; and there,
Like David in Adullam's lair—
Could it be Vine, and quivering so?   15

'Twas Vine. He wore that nameless look
About the mouth—so hard to brook—
Which in the Cenci portrait shows,
Lost in each copy, oil or print;
Lost, or else slurred, as 'twere a hint   20
Which if received, few might sustain:
A trembling over of small throes
In weak swoll'n lips, which to restrain
Desire is none, nor any rein.

  Clarel recalled the garden's shade,   25
And Vine therein, with all that made
The estrangement in Gethsemane.
Reserves laid bare? and can it be?
The dock-yard forge's silent mound,
Played over by small nimble flame—   30
Raked open, lo, the anchor's found
In white-heat's alb.
     With shrinking frame,
Grateful that he was unespied,
Clarel quite noiseless slipped aside:
Ill hour (thought he), an evil sign: 35
No more need dream of winning Vine
Or coming at his mystery.
O, lives which languish in the shade,
Puzzle and tease us, or upbraid;
What noteless confidant, may be,   40
Withholds the talisman, the key!
Or if indeed it run not so,
And he's above me where I cling;
Then how these higher natures know
Except in shadow from the wing?—   45

  Hark! as in benison to all,
Borne on waste air in wasteful clime,
What swell on swell of mellowing chime,
Which every drooping pilgrim rallies;
How much unlike that ominous call   50
Pealed in the blast from Roncesvalles!
Was more than silver in this shell

By distance toned. What festival?
What feast? of Adam's kind, or fay?
Hark—no, not yet it dies away.   55
    Where the sexton of the vaulted seas
Buries the drowned in weedy grave,
While tolls the buoy-bell down the breeze;
There, off the shoals of rainy wave
Outside the channel which they crave,   60
The sailors lost in shrouding mist,
Unto that muffled knelling list,
The more because for fogged remove
The floating belfry none may prove;
So, yet with difference, do these   65
Attend.
      "Chimes, chimes? but whence? thou breeze;"
Here Derwent; "convent none is near."
    "Ay," said the Druze, "but quick's the ear
In deep hush of the desert wide."
    "'Tis Saba calling; yea," Rolfe cried,   70
"Saba, Mar Saba summons us:
O, hither, pilgrims, turn to me,
Escape the desert perilous;
Here's refuge, hither unto me!"

    A lateral lodgment won, they wheeled,   75
And toward the abandoned ledge they glanced:
Near, in the high void waste advanced,
They saw, in turn abrupt revealed,
An object reared aloof by Vine
In whim of silence, when debate   80
Was held upon the cliff but late
And ended where all words decline:
A heap of stones in arid state.

    The cairn (thought Clarel), meant he—yes,
A monument to barrenness?   85

8. Tents of Kedar

They climb. In Indian file they gain
A sheeted blank white lifted plain—
A moor of chalk, or slimy clay,
With gluey track and streaky trail
Of some small slug or torpid snail.   5
With hooded brows against the sun,
Man after man they labor on.
    Corrupt and mortally intense,
What fumes ere long pollute the sense?
But, hark the flap and lumbering rise   10
Of launching wing; see the gaunt size
Of the ground-shadow thereby thrown.
Behind a great and sheltering stone
A camel, worn out, down had laid—
Never to rise. 'Tis thence the kite   15
Ascends, sails off in Tyreward flight.
As 'twere Apollyon, angel bad,
They watch him as he speeds away.
    But Vine, in mere caprice of clay,
Or else because a pride had birth   20
Slighting high claims which vaunted be
And favoring things of low degree—
From heaven he turned him down to earth,
Eagle to ass. She now, ahead
Went riderless, with even tread   25
And in official manner, sooth,
For bell and cord she'd known in youth;
Through mart and wild, bazaar and waste
Preceding camels strung in train,
Full often had the dwarf thing paced,   30
Conductress of the caravan
Of creatures tall. What meant Vine's glance
Ironic here which impish ran
In thievish way? O, world's advance:
We wise limp after!
              The cavalcade   35
Anon file by a pit-like glade

Clean scooped of last lean dregs of soil;
Attesting in rude terraced stones
The ancient husbandmen's hard toil,—
All now a valley of dry bones—   40
In shape a hopper. 'Twas a sight
So marked with dead, dead undelight,
That Derwent half unconscious here
Stole a quick glance at Mortmain's face
To note how it received the cheer.   45
Whereat the moody man, with sting
Returned the imprudent glance apace—
Wayward retort all withering
Though wordless. Clarel looking on,
Saw there repeated the wild tone   50
Of that discountenancing late
In sequel to prolonged debate
Upon the mountain. And again
Puzzled, and earnest, less to know
What rasped the Swede in such a man   55
Than how indeed the priest could show
Such strange forbearance; ventured now
To put a question to him fair.
"Oh, oh," he answered, all his air
Recovered from the disarray;   60
"The shadow flung by Ebal's hill
On Gerizim, it cannot stay,
But passes. Ay, and ever still—
But don't you see the man is mad?
His fits he has; sad, sad, how sad!   65
Besides; but let me tell you now;
Do you read Greek? Well, long ago,
In stage when goslings try the wing,
And peacock-chicks would softly sing,
And roosters small essay to crow;   70
Reading Theocritus divine,
Envious I grew of all that charm
Where sweet and simple so entwine;
But I plucked up and won a balm:
Thought I, I'll beat him in his place: 75

If, in my verses, and what not,
If I can't have this pagan grace,
Still—nor alone in page I blot,
But all encounters that may be—
I'll make it up with Christian charity."   80

    Another brink they win, and view
Adown in faintly greenish hollow
An oval camp of sable hue
Pitched full across the track they follow—
Twelve tents of shaggy goat's wool dun.   85
    "Ah, tents of Kedar may these be,"
Cried Derwent; "named by Solomon
In song? Black, but scarce comely, see.
Whom have we here? The brood of Lot?"
    "The oval seems his burial-plot,"   90
Said Rolfe; "and, for his brood, these men—
They rove perchance from Moab's den
Or Ammon's. Belex here seems well
To know them, and no doubt will tell."
    The Spahi, not at all remiss   95
In airing his Turk prejudice,
Exclaimed: "Ay, sirs; and ill betide
These Moabites and Ammonites
Ferrying Jordan either side—
Robbers and starvelings, mangy wights.   100
Sirs, I will vouch one thing they do:
Each year they harry Jericho
In harvest; yet thereby they gain
But meager, rusty spears of grain.
What right have such black thieves to live?   105
Much more to think here to receive
Our toll? Just Allah! say the word,
And——" here he signified with sword
The rest, impatient of delay
While yet on hight at brink they stay,   110
So bidden by Djalea, who slow
Descends into the hopper low,
Riding. "To parley with the knaves!"

Cried Belex; "spur them down; that saves
All trouble, sirs; 'twas Ibrahim's way;   115
When, in the Lebanon one day
We came upon a——"
                    "Pardon me,"
The priest; "but look how leisurely
He enters; yes, and straight he goes
To meet our friend with scowling brows,   120
The warder in yon outlet, see,
Holding his desert spear transverse,
Bar-like, from sable hearse to hearse
Of toll-gate tents. Foreboding ill,
The woman calls there to her brood.   125
But what's to fear! Ah, with good-will
They bustle in the war-like mood;
Save us from those long fish-pole lances!
Look, menacingly one advances;
But he, our Druze, he mindeth none,   130
But paces. So! they soften down.
'Tis Zar, it is that dainty steed,
High-bred fine equine lady brave,
Of stock derived from long ago;
'Tis she they now admiring heed,   135
Picking her mincing way so grave,
None jostling, grazing scarce a toe
Of all the press. The sulky clan,
Yes, make way for the mare—and man!
There's homage!"
                    "Ay, ay," Belex said,   140
"They'd like to steal her and retire:
Her beauty is their heart's desire—
Base jackals with their jades!"
                    Well sped
The Druze. The champion he nears
Posted in outlet, keeping ward,   145
Who, altering at that aspect, peers,
And him needs own for natural lord.
Though claiming kingship of the land
He hesitates to make demand:

Salute he yields. The Druze returns 150
The salutation; nor he spurns
To smoke with Ammon, but in way
Not derogating—brief delay.
They part. The unmolested train
Are beckoned, and come down. Amain 155
The camp they enter and pass through;
No conflict here, no weak ado
Of words or blows.
    This policy
(Djalea's) bred now a pleasing thought
In Derwent: "Wars might ended be, 160
Yes, Japhet, Shem, and Ham be brought
To confluence of amity,
Were leaders but discreet and wise
Like this our chief."
    The armed man's eyes
Turned toward him tolerantly there 165
As 'twere a prattling child.
    They fare
Further, and win a nook of stone,
And there a fountain making moan.
The shade invites, though not of trees:
They tarry in this chapel-of-ease; 170
Then up, and journey on and on,
Nor tent they see—not even a lonely one.

9. OF MONASTERIES

The lake ink-black mid slopes of snow—
The dead-house for the frozen, barred—
And the stone hospice; chill they show
Monastic in thy pass, Bernard.
Apostle of the Alps storm-riven, 5
How lone didst build so near the heaven!
  Anchored in seas of Nitria's sand,
The desert convent of the Copt—
No aerolite can more command

The sense of dead detachment, dropped   10
All solitary from the sky.
    The herdsmen of Olympus lie
In summer when the eve is won
Viewing white Spermos lower down,
The mountain-convent; and winds bear   15
The chimes that bid the monks to prayer;
Nor man-of-war-hawk sole in sky
O'er lonely ship sends lonelier cry.
    The Grand Chartreuse with crystal peaks
Mid pines—the wintry Paradise   20
Of soul which but a Saviour seeks—
The mountains round all slabbed with ice;
May well recall the founder true,
St. Bruno, who to heaven has gone
And proved his motto—that whereto   25
Each locked Carthusian yet adheres:
Troubled I was, but spake I none;
I kept in mind the eternal years.
    And Vallambrosa—in, shut in;
And Montserrat—enisled aloft;   30
With many more the verse might win,
Solitudes all, austere or soft.

    But Saba! Of retreats where heart
Longing for more than downy rest,
Fit place would find from world apart,   35
Saba abides the loneliest:
Saba, that with an eagle's theft
Seizeth and dwelleth in the cleft.
    Aloof the monks their aerie keep,
Down from their hanging cells they peep   40
Like samphire-gatherers o'er the bay
Faint hearing there the hammering deep
Of surf that smites the ledges gray.

    But up and down, from grot to shrine,
Along the gorge, hard by the brink   45
File the gowned monks in even line,

And never shrink!
With litany or dirge they wend
Where nature as in travail dwells;
And the worn grots and pensive dells   50
In wail for wail responses send—
Echoes in plaintive syllables.
    With mystic silvery brede divine,
Saint Basil's banner of Our Lord
(In lieu of crucifix adored   55
By Greeks which images decline)
Stained with the five small wounds and red,
Down through the darkling gulf is led—
By night ofttimes, while tapers glow
Small in the depths, as stars may show   60
Reflected far in well profound.

    Full fifteen hundred years have wound
Since cenobite first harbored here;
The bones of men, deemed martyrs crowned,
To fossils turn in mountain near;   65
Nor less while now lone scribe may write,
Even now, in living dead of night,
In Saba's lamps the flames aspire—
The votaries tend the far-transmitted fire.

10. BEFORE THE GATE

'Tis Kedron, that profound ravine
Whence Saba soars. And all between
Zion and Saba one may stray,
Sunk from the sun, through Kedron's way.
By road more menacingly dead   5
Than that which wins the convent's base
No ghost to Tartarus is led.
    Through scuttle small, that keepeth place
In floor of cellars which impend—
Cellars or cloisters—men ascend   10
By ladder which the monks let down

And quick withdraw; and thence yet on
Higher and higher, flight by flight,
They mount from Erebus to light,
And off look, world-wide, much in tone   15
Of Uriel, warder in the sun,
Who serious views this earthly scene
Since Satan passed his guard and entered in.
    But not by Kedron these now come
Who ride from Siddim; no, they roam   20
The roof of mountains—win the tall
Towers of Saba, and huge wall
Builded along the steep, and there
A postern with a door, full spare
Yet strong, a clamped and bucklered mass   25
Bolted. In waste whose king is Fear,
Sole port of refuge, it is here.
Strange (and it might repel, alas)
Fair haven's won by such a pass.
In London Tower the Traitors' Gate   30
Through which the guilty waters flow,
Looks not more grim. Yet shalt thou know,
If once thou enter, good estate.
    Beneath these walls what frays have been,
What clash and outcry, sabers crossed   35
Pilgrim and Perizzite between;
And some have here given up the ghost
Before the gate in last despair.
Nor, for the most part, lacking fair
Sign-manual from a mitered lord,   40
Admission shall that arch afford
To any.
       Weary now the train
At eve halt by the gate and knock.
No answer. Belex shouts amain:
As well invoke the Pico Rock.   45
"Bide," breathes the Druze, and dropping rein,
He points. A wallet's lowered down
From under where a hood projects
High up the tower, a cowl of stone,

Wherefrom alert an eye inspects 50
All applicants, and unbeknown.
Djalea promptly from his vest
A missive draws, which duly placed
In budget, rises from the ground
And vanishes. So, without sound 55
Monks fish up to their donjon dark
The voucher from their Patriarch,
Even him who dwells in damask state
On Zion throned. Not long they wait:
The postern swings. Dismounting nigh, 60
The horses through the needle's eye,
That small and narrow gate, they lead.
But while low ducks each lofty steed,
Behold how through the crucial pass
Slips unabased the humble ass. 65
And so they all with clattering din
The stony fortress court-yard win.
There see them served, and bidden rest;
Horse, ass too, treated as a guest.
Friars tend as grooms. Yet others call 70
And lead them to the frater-hall
Cliff-hung. By monks the board is spread;
They break the monastery bread,
Moist'ning the same with Saba's wine,
Product of painful toil mid stones 75
In terraces, whose Bacchic zones
That desert gird. Olive and vine
To flinty places well incline,
Once crush the flint. Even so they fared,
So well for them the brethren cared. 80
Refection done, for grateful bed
Cool mats of dye sedate, were spread:
The lamps were looked to, freshly trimmed;
And last (at hint from mellow man
Who seemed to know how all things ran, 85
And who in place shall soon be hymned)
A young monk-servant, slender-limbed,
And of a comely countenance,

Set out one flask of stature tall,
Against men's needs medicinal,   90
Travelers, subject to mischance;
Devout then, and with aspect bright
Invoked Mar Saba's blessing—bade good night.

He goes. But now in change of tune,
Shall friar be followed by buffoon?   95
Saba supply a Pantaloon?
Wise largess of true license yield.
Howe'er the river, winding round,
May win an unexpected bound;
The aim and destiny, unsealed   100
In the first fount, hold unrepealed.

11. The Beaker

"Life is not by square and line:
    Wisdom's stupid without folly:
Sherbet to-day, to-morrow wine—
    Feather in cap and the world is jolly!"

So he, the aforesaid mellow man,   5
Thrumming upon the table's span.
Scarce audible except in air
Mirth's modest overture seemed there.
Nor less the pilgrims, folding wing,
Weary, would now in slumber fall—   10
Sleep, held for a superfluous thing
By that free heart at home in hall.
    And who was *he* so jovial?
Purveyor, he some needful stores
Supplied from Syrian towns and shores;   15
And on his trips, dismissing care,—
His stores delivered all and told,
Would rest awhile in Saba's fold.
    Not broken he with fast and prayer:

The leg did well plump out the sock; 20
Nor young, nor old, but did enlock
In reconcilement a bright cheek
And fleecy beard; that cheek, in show,
Arbutus flaked about with snow,
Running-arbutus in Spring's freak 25
Overtaken so. In Mytilene,
Sappho and Phaon's Lesbos green,
His home was, his lax Paradise,
An island yet luxurious seen,
Fruitful in all that can entice. 30
    For chum he had a mountaineer,
A giant man, beneath whose lee
Lightly he bloomed, like pinks that cheer
The base of tower where cannon be.
That mountaineer the battle tans, 35
An Arnaut of no mean degree,
A lion of war, and drew descent
Through dames heroic, from the tent
Of Pyrrhus and those Epirot clans
Which routed Rome. And, furthermore, 40
In after-line enlinked he stood
To Scanderbeg's Albanian brood,
And Arslan, famous heretofore,
The horse-tail pennon dyed in gore.
    An Islamite he was by creed— 45
In act, what fortune's chances breed:
Attest the medal, vouch the scar—
Had bled for Sultan, won for Czar;
His psalter bugle was and drum,
Any scorched rag his *Labarum*. 50
For time adherent of the Turk,
In Saba's hold he sheathed his dirk,
Waiting arrival of a troop
Destined for some dragooning swoop
On the wild tribes beyond the wave 55
Of Jordan. Unconstrained though grave,
Stalwart but agile, nobly tall,

Complexion a burnt red, and all
His carriage charged with courage high
And devil-dare. A hawk's his eye.   60
While, for the garb: a snow-white kilt
Was background to his great sword-hilt:
The waistcoat blue, with plates and chains
Tarnished a bit with grapy stains;
Oaches in silver rows: stout greaves   65
Of leather: buskins thonged; light cloak
Of broidered stuff Damascus weaves;
And, scorched one side with powder smoke,
A crimson Fez, bald as a skull
Save for long tassel prodigal.   70
Last, add hereto a blood-red sash,
With dagger and pistol's silvery charms,
And there you have this Arnaut rash,
In zone of war—a trophy of arms.

    While yet the monks stood by serene,   75
He as to kill time, his moustache
Adjusted in his scimeter's sheen;
But when they made their mild adieu,
Response he nodded, seemly too.
And now, the last gowned friar gone,   80
His heart of onslaught he toned down
Into a solemn sort of grace,
Each pilgrim looking full in face,
As he should say: Why now, let's be
Good comrades here to-night.
                              Grave plea   85
For brotherly love and jollity
From such an arsenal of man,
A little strange seemed and remote.
To bring it nearer—spice—promote—
Nor mindless of some aspects wan,   90
Lesbos, with fair engaging tone,
Threw in some moral cinnamon:
"Sir pilgrims, look; 'tis early yet;
In evening arbor here forget

The heat, the burden of the day. 95
Life has its trials, sorrows—yes,
I know—I feel; but blessedness
Makes up. Ye've grieved the tender clay:
Solace should now all that requite;
'Tis duty, sirs. And—by the way— 100
Not vainly Anselm bade *good* night,
For see!" and cheery on the board
The flask he set.
    "I and the sword"
The Arnaut said (and in a tone
Of natural bass which startled one— 105
Profound as the profound trombone)
"I and the sword stand by the red.
But this will pass, this molten ore
Of yellow gold. Is there no more?"
  "Trust wit for that," the other said: 110
"Purveyor, shall he not purvey?"
And slid a panel, showing store
Of cups and bottles in array.
  "Then arms at ease, and ho, the bench!"
It made the slender student blench 115
To hark the jangling of the steel,
Vibration of the floor to feel,
Tremor through beams and bones which ran
As that ripe masterpiece of man
Plumped solid down upon the deal. 120
  Derwent a little hung behind—
Censorious not, nor disinclined,
But with self-querying countenance,
As if one of the cloth, perchance
Due bound should set, observe degree 125
In liberal play of social glee.
  Through instinct of good fellow bright
His poise, as seemed, the Lesbian wight
Divined: and justly deeming here
The stage required a riper cheer 130
Than that before—solicitous,

With bubbling cup in either hand,
Toward Derwent drew he, archly bland;
Then posed; and tunefully e'en thus:

"A shady rock, and trickling too,   135
    Is good to meet in desert drear:
    Prithee now, the beading here—
Beads of Saba, saintly dew:
Quaff it, sweetheart, I and you:
    Quaff it, for thereby ye bless   140
    Beadsmen here in wilderness.
Spite of sorrow, maugre sin,
Bless their larder and laud their bin:
    Nor deem that here they vainly pine
    Who toil for heaven and till the vine!"   145

    He sings; and in the act of singing,
Near and more near one cup he's bringing,
Till by his genial sleight of hand
'Tis lodged in Derwent's, and—retained.
    As lit by vintage sunset's hue   150
Which mellow warms the grapes that bleed,
In amber light the good man view;
Nor text of sanction lacked at need;
"At Cana, who renewed the wine?
Sourly did I this cup decline   155
(Which lo, I quaff, and not for food),
'Twould by an implication rude
Asperse that festival benign.—
We're brethren, ay!"
                    The lamps disclose
The Spahi, Arnaut, and the priest,   160
With Rolfe and the not-of-Sharon Rose,
Ranged at the board for family feast.
    "But where's Djalea?" the cleric cried;
"'Tis royalty should here preside:"
And looked about him. Truth to own,   165
The Druze, his office having done
And brought them into haven there,

Discharged himself of further care
Till the next start: the interim
Accounting rightfully his own;   170
And may be, heedful not to dim
The escutcheon of an Emir's son
By any needless letting down.

   The Lesbian who had Derwent served,
Officiated for them all;   175
And, as from man to man he swerved,
Grotesque a bit of song let fall:

    "The Mufti in park suburban
      Lies under a stone
     Surmounted serene by a turban   180
      Magnific—a marble one!"

So, man by man, with twinkling air,
And cup and text of stanza fair:

    "A Rabbi in Prague they muster
      In mound evermore   185
     Looking up at his monument's cluster—
      A cluster of grapes of Noah!"

   When all were served with wine and rhyme
"Ho, comrade," cried armed Og sublime,
"Your singing makes the filling scant;   190
The flask to me, let *me* decant."
With that, the host he played—brimmed up
And off-hand pushed the frequent cup;
Flung out his thigh, and quaffed apace,
Barbaric in his hardy grace;   195
The while his haughty port did say,
Who 's here uncivilized, I pray?
I know good customs: stint I ye?
   Indeed (thought Rolfe), a man of mark,
And makes a rare symposiarch;   200
I like him; I'll e'en feel his grip.

With that, in vinous fellowship
Frank he put out his hand. In mood
Of questionable brotherhood
The slayer stared—anon construed   205
The overture aright, and yet
Not unreservedly he met
The palm. Came it in sort too close?
Was it embraces were for foes?

    Rolfe, noting a fine color stir   210
Flushing each happy reveler,
Now leaned back, with this ditty wee:

       "The Mountain-Ash
         And Sumach fine,
           Tipplers of summer,   215
            Betray the wine
       In autumn leaf
         Of vermil flame:
       Bramble and Thorn
         Cry—Fie, for shame!"   220

    Mortmain aloof and single sat—
In range with Rolfe, as viewed from mat
Where Vine reposed, observing there
That these in contour of the head
And goodly profile made a pair,   225
Though one looked like a statue dead.
Methinks (mused Vine), 'tis Ahab's court
And yon the Tishbite; he'll consort
Not long, but Kedron seek. It proved
Even so: the desert-heart removed.   230
    But he of bins, whose wakeful eye
On him had fixed, and followed sly
Until the shadow left the door,
Turned short, and tristful visage wore
In quaint appeal. A shrug; and then   235
"Beseech ye now, ye friendly men,
Who's *he*—a cup, pray;—O, my faith!

That funeral cap of his means death
To all good fellowship in feast.
Mad, say he's mad!"
     Awhile the priest   240
And Rolfe, reminded here in heart
Of more than well they might impart,
Uneasy sat. But this went by:
Ill sort some truths with revelry.—
  The giant plied the flask. For Vine,   245
Relaxed he viewed nor spurned the wine,
But humorously moralized
On those five souls imparadised
For term how brief; well pleased to scan
The Mytilene, the juicy man.   250
Earth—of the earth (thought Vine) well, well,
So's a fresh turf, but good the smell,
Yes, deemed by some medicinal—
Most too if damped with wine of Xeres
And snuffed at when the spirit wearies.   255
I have it under strong advising
'Tis good at whiles this sensualizing;
Would I could joy in it myself;
But no!—
    For Derwent, he, light elf,
Not vainly stifling recent fret,   260
Under the table his two knees
Pushed deeper, so as e'en to get
Closer in comradeship at ease.
Arnaut and Spahi, in respect
Of all adventures they had known,   265
These chiefly did the priest affect:
Adventures, such as duly shown
Printed in books, seem passing strange
To clerks which read them by the fire,
Yet be the wonted common-place   270
Of some who in the Orient range,
Free-lances, spendthrifts of their hire,
And who in end, when they retrace
Their lives, see little to admire

Or wonder at, so dull they be   275
(Like fish mid marvels of the sea)
To every thing that is not pent
In self, or thereto ministrant.

12. THE TIMONEER'S STORY

But ere those Sinbads had begun
Their Orient Decameron,
Rolfe rose, to view the further hall.
Here showed, set up against the wall,
Heroic traditionary arms,   5
Protecting tutelary charms
(Like Godfrey's sword and Baldwin's spur
In treasury of the Sepulcher,
Wherewith they knighthood yet confer,
The monks or their Superior)   10
Sanctified heirlooms of old time;
With trophies of the Paynim clime;
These last with tarnish on the gilt,
And jewels vanished from the hilt.
　　Upon one serpent-curving blade   15
Love-motto beamed from Antar's rhyme
In Arabic. A second said
(A scimiter the Turk had made,
And likely, it had clove a skull)
IN NAME OF GOD THE MERCIFUL!   20
A third was given suspended place,
And as in salutation waved,
And in old Greek was finely graved
With this: HAIL, MARY, FULL OF GRACE!

　　'Tis a rare sheaf of arms be here,   25
Thought Rolfe: "Who's this?" and turned to peer
At one who had but late come in,
(A stranger) and, avoiding din
Made by each distant reveler,
Anchored beside him. His sea-gear   30

Announced a pilgrim-timoneer.
The weird and weather-beaten face,
Bearded and pitted, and fine vexed
With wrinkles of cabala text,
Did yet reveal a twinge-like trace   35
Of some late trial undergone:
Nor less a beauty grave pertained
To him, part such as is ordained
To Eld, for each age hath its own,
And even scars may share the tone.   40
Bald was his head as any bell—
Quite bald, except a silvery round
Of small curled bud-like locks which bound
His temples as with asphodel.
    Such he, who in nigh nook disturbed   45
Upon his mat by late uncurbed
Light revel, came with air subdued,
And by the clustered arms here stood
Regarding them with dullish eye
Of some old reminiscence sad.   50
    On him Rolfe gazed: "And do ye sigh?
Hardly they seem to cheer ye: why?"
    He pursed the mouth and shook the head.
"But speak!" "'Tis but an old bewailing."
"No matter, tell." "'Twere unavailing."   55
"Come, now."
              "Since you entreat of me—
'Tis long ago—I'm aged, see:
From Egypt sailing—hurrying too—
For spite the sky there, always blue,
And blue daubed seas so bland, the pest   60
Was breaking out—the people quailing
In houses hushed; from Egypt sailing,
In ship, I say, which shunned the pest,
Cargo half-stored, and—and—alack!
One passenger of visage black,   65
But whom a white robe did invest
And linen turban, like the rest—
A Moor he was, with but a chest;—

A fugitive poor Wahabee—
So ran his story—who by me   70
Was smuggled aboard; and ah, a crew
That did their wrangles still renew,
Jabbing the poignard in the fray,
And mutinous withal;—I say,
From Egypt bound for Venice sailing—   75
On Friday—well might heart forebode!
In this same craft from Cadiz hailing,
Christened by friar 'The Peace of God,'
(She laden now with rusted cannon
Which long beneath the Crescent's pennon   80
On beach had laid, condemned and dead,
Beneath a rampart, and from bed
Were shipped off to be sold and smelted
And into new artillery melted)
I say that to The Peace of God   85
(Your iron the salt seas corrode)
I say there fell to her unblest
A hap more baleful than the pest.
Yea, from the first I knew a fear,
So strangely did the needle veer.   90
A gale came up, with frequent din
Of cracking thunder out and in:
Corposants on yard-arms did burn,
Red lightning forked upon the stern:
The needle like an imp did spin.   95
Three gulls continual plied in wake,
Which wriggled like a wounded snake,
For I, the wretched timoneer,
By fitful stars yet tried to steer
'Neath shortened sail. The needle flew   100
(The glass thick blurred with damp and dew),
And flew the ship we knew not where.
Meantime the mutinous bad crew
Got at the casks and drowned despair,
Carousing, fighting. What to do?   105
To all the saints I put up prayer,
Seeing against the gloomy shades

Breakers in ghastly palisades.
Nevertheless she took the rocks;
And dinning through the grinds and shocks,   110
(Attend the solving of the riddle)
I heard the clattering of blades
Shaken within the Moor's strong box
In cabin underneath the needle.
How screamed those three birds round the mast   115
Slant going over. The keel was broken
And heaved aboard us for death-token.
To quit the wreck I was the last,
Yet I sole wight that 'scaped the sea."
   "But he, the Moor?"
                  "O, sorcery!   120
For him no heaven is, no atoner.
He proved an armorer, the Jonah!
And dealt in blades that poisoned were,
A black lieutenant of Lucifer.
I heard in Algiers, as befell   125
Afterward, his crimes of hell.
I'm far from superstitious, see;
But arms in sheaf, somehow they trouble me."

   "Ha, *trouble, trouble?* what's that, pray?
I've heard of it; bad thing, they say;   130

   "Bug there, lady bug, plumped in your wine?
    Only rose-leaves flutter by mine!"

The gracioso man, 'twas he,
Flagon in hand, held tiltingly.
   How peered at him that timoneer,   135
With what a changed, still, merman-cheer,
As much he could, but would not say:
So murmuring naught, he moved away.
   "Old, old," the Lesbian dropped; "old—dry:
Remainder biscuit; and alas,   140
But recent 'scaped from luckless pass."
   "Indeed? relate."—"O, by-and-by."

But Rolfe would have it then. And so
The incident narrated was
Forthwith.
                   Re-cast, it thus may flow: 145
The shipmen of the Cyclades
Being Greeks, even of St. Saba's creed,
Are frequent pilgrims. From the seas
Greek convents welcome them, and feed.
Agath, with hardy messmates ten,   150
To Saba, and on foot, had fared
From Joppa. Duly in the Glen
His prayers he said; but rashly dared
Afar to range without the wall.
Upon him fell a robber-brood,   155
Some Ammonites. Choking his call,
They beat and stripped him, drawing blood,
And left him prone. His mates made search
With friars, and ere night found him so,
And bore him moaning back to porch   160
Of Saba's refuge. Cure proved slow;
The end his messmates might not wait;
Therefore they left him unto love
And charity—within that gate
Not lacking. Mended now in main,   165
Or convalescent, he would fain
Back unto Joppa make remove
With the first charitable train.
     His story told, the teller turned
And seemed like one who instant yearned   170
To rid him of intrusive sigh:
"Yon happier pilgrim, by-the-by—
I like him: his vocation, pray?
Purveyor he? like me, purvey?"
     "Ay—for the conscience: he's our priest."   175
"Priest? he's a grape, judicious one—
Keeps on the right side of the sun.
But here's a song I heard at feast."

13. SONG AND RECITATIVE

"The chalice tall of beaten gold
 Is hung with bells about:
The flamen serves in temple old,
And weirdly are the tinklings rolled
 When he pours libation out.   5
O Cybele, dread Cybele,
Thy turrets nod, thy terrors be!

"But service done, and vestment doffed,
 With cronies in a row
Behind night's violet velvet soft,   10
The chalice drained he rings aloft
 To another tune, I trow.
O Cybele, fine Cybele,
Jolly thy bins and belfries be!"

With action timing well the song,   15
His flagon flourished up in air,
The varlet of the isle so flung
His mad-cap intimation—there
Comic on Rolfe his eye retaining
In mirth how full of roguish feigning.   20
 Ought I protest? (thought Rolfe) the man
Nor malice has, nor faith: why ban
This heart though of religion scant,
A true child of the lax Levant,
That polyglot and loose-laced mother?   25
In such variety he's lived
Where creeds dovetail into each other;
Such influences he's received:
Thrown among all—Medes, Elamites,
Egyptians, Jews and proselytes,   30
Strangers from Rome, and men of Crete—
And parts of Lybia round Cyrene—
Arabians, and the throngs ye meet
On Smyrna's quays, and all between
Stamboul and Fez:—thrown among these,   35

A caterer to revelries,
He's caught the tints of many a scene,
And so become a harlequin
Gay patchwork of all levities.
Holding to *now,* swearing by *here,*   40
His course conducting by no keen
Observance of the stellar sphere—
He coasteth under sail latteen:
Then let him laugh, enjoy his dinner,
He's an excusable poor sinner.   45
  'Twas Rolfe. But Clarel, what thought he?
For he too heard the Lesbian's song
There by the casement where he hung:
In heart of Saba's mystery
This mocker light!—
     But now in waltz   50
The Pantaloon here Rolfe assaults;
Then, keeping arm around his waist,
Sees Rolfe's reciprocally placed;
'Tis side-by-side entwined in ease
Of Chang and Eng the Siamese   55
When leaning mutually embraced;
And so these improvised twin brothers
Dance forward and salute the others,
The Lesbian flourishing for sign
His wine-cup, though it lacked the wine.   60
  They sit. With random scraps of song
He whips the tandem hours along,
Or moments, rather; in the end
Calling on Derwent to unbend
In lyric.
    "I?" said Derwent, "I?   65
Well, if you like, I'll even give
A trifle in recitative—
A something—nothing—anything—
Since little does it signify
In festive free contributing: 70

  "To Hafiz in grape-arbor comes
Didymus, with book he thumbs:

My lord Hafiz, priest of bowers—
Flowers in such a world as ours?
Who is the god of all these flowers?—   75
    "Signior Didymus, who knows?
None the less I take repose—
Believe, and worship here with wine
In vaulted chapel of the vine
Before the altar of the rose.   80

"Ah, who sits here? a sailor meek?"
It was that sea-appareled Greek.
"Gray brother, here, partake our wine."
    He shook his head, yes, did decline.
"Or quaff or sing," cried Derwent then,   85
"For learn, we be hilarious men.
Pray, now, you seamen know to sing."
"I'm old," he breathed.—"So's many a tree,
Yet green the leaves and dance in glee."
    The Arnaut made the scabbard ring: 90
"Sing, man, and here's the chorus—sing!"
    "Sing, sing!" the Islesman, "bear the bell;
Sing, and the other songs excel."
    "Ay, sing," cried Rolfe, "here now's a sample;
'Tis virtue teaches by example: 95

        "Jars of honey,
    Wine-skin, dates, and macaroni:
    Falling back upon the senses—
        O, the wrong—
    Need take up with recompenses: 100
        Song, a song!"

    They sang about him till he said:
"Sing, sirs, I cannot: this I'll do,
Repeat a thing Methodius made,
Good chaplain of The Apostles' crew: 105

    "Priest in ship with saintly bow,
War-ship named from Paul and Peter
Grandly carved on castled prow;

Gliding by the grouped Canaries
Under liquid light of Mary's   110
Mellow star of eventide;
Lulled by tinklings at the side,
I, along the taffrail leaning,
Yielding to the ship's careening,
　　Shared that peace the upland owns   115
Where the palm—the palm and pine
Meeting on the frontier line
　　Seal a truce between the zones.
This be ever! (mused I lowly)
Dear repose is this and holy;   120
Like the Gospel it is gracious
And prevailing.—There, audacious—
Boom! the signal-gun it jarred me,
Flash and boom together marred me,
　　And I thought of horrid war;   125
But never moved grand Paul and Peter,
　　Never blenched Our Lady's star!"

14. The Revel Closed

"Bless that good chaplain," Derwent here;
"All doves and halcyons round the sphere
Defend him from war's rude alarms!"
Then (Oh, sweet impudence of wine)
Then rising and approaching Vine   5
In suppliant way: "I crave an alms:
Since this gray guest, this serious one,
Our wrinkled old Euroclydon,
Since even he, with genial breath
His quota here contributeth,   10
Helping our gladness to prolong—
Thou too! Nay, nay; as everywhere
Water is found if one not spare
To delve—tale, prithee now, or song!"
　　Vine's brow shot up with crimson lights   15
As may the North on frosty nights

Over Dilston Hall and his low state—
The fair young Earl whose bloody end
Those red rays do commemorate,
And take his name.
               Now all did bend   20
In chorus, crying, "Tale or song!"
Investing him. Was no escape
Beset by such a Bacchic throng.
"Ambushed in leaves we spy your grape,"
Cried Derwent; "black but juicy one—   25
A song!"
          No way for Vine to shun:
"Well, if you'll let me here recline
At ease the while, I'll hum a word
Which in his Florence loft I heard
An artist trill one morning fine:—   30

   "What is beauty? 'tis a dream
      Dispensing still with gladness:
     The dolphin haunteth not the shoal,
      And deeps there be in sadness.

   "The rose-leaves, see, disbanded be—   35
      Blowing, about me blowing;
     But on the death-bed of the rose
      My amaranths are growing.

    "*His amaranths:* a fond conceit,
Yes, last illusion of retreat!   40
Short measure 'tis." "And yet enough,"
Said Derwent; "'tis a hopeful song;
Or, if part sad, not less adorning,
Like purple in a royal mourning.
We debtors be. Now come along   45
To table, we'll take no rebuff."
So Vine sat down among them then—
Adept—shy prying into men.
      Derwent here wheeled him: "But for sake
Of conscience, noble Arnaut, tell;   50

When now I as from dream awake
It just dawns on me: how is this?
Wine-bibbing? No! that kind of bliss
Your Koran bars. And Belex, man,
Thou'st smoked before the sun low fell;   55
And this month's what? your Ramadan?
May true believers thus rebel?"
     Good sooth, did neither know to tell,
Or care to know, what time did fall
The Islam fast; yet took it so   60
As Derwent roguish prompted, though
It was no Ramadan at all;
'Twas far ahead, a movable fast
Of lunar month, which to forecast
Needs reckoning.
           Ponderous pause   65
The Anak made: "Mahone has laws,
And Allah's great—of course:—forefend!
Ho, rouse a stave, and so an end:

"The Bey, the Emir, and Mamalook lords
   Charged down on the field in a grove of swords: 70
     Hurrah! hurrah and hurrah
     For the grove of swords in the wind of war!

"And the Bey to the Emir exclaimed, Who knows?
   In the shade of the scimiters Paradise shows!
     Hurrah! hurrah and hurrah   75
     For the grove of swords in the wind of war!"

     He sang; then settled down, a mate
For Mars' high pontiff—solemn sate,
And on his long broad Bazra blade
Deep ruminated. Less sedate,   80
The Spahi now in escapade
Vented some Turkish guard-room joke,
But scarce thereby the other woke
To laughter, for he never laughed,
Into whatever mood he broke,   85

Nor verbal levity vouchsafed,
So leonine the man. But here
The Spahi, with another cheer
Into a vein of mockery ran,
Toasting the feast of Ramadan,   90
Laughing thereat, removed from fear.
    It was a deep-mouthed mastiff burst,
Nor less, for all the jovial tone
The echo startling import won—
At least for Clarel, little versed   95
In men, their levities and tides
Unequal, and of much besides.
There by a lattice open swung
Over the Kedron's gulf he hung,
And pored and pondered: With what sweep   100
Doubt plunges, and from maw to maw;
Traditions none the nations keep—
Old ties dissolve in one wide thaw;
The Frank, the Turk, and e'en the Jew
Share it; perchance the Brahmin too.   105
Returns each thing that may withdraw?
The schools of blue-fish years desert
Our sounds and shores—but they revert;
The ship returns on her long tack:
The bones of Theseus are brought back: 110
A comet shall resume its path
Though three millenniums go. But faith?
Ah, Nehemiah—and, Derwent, thou!
'Twas dust to dust: what is it now
And here? Is life indeed a dream?   115
Are these the pilgrims late that heard
The wheeling desert vultures scream
Above the Man and Book interred—
Scream like the haglet and the gull
Off Chiloe o'er the foundered hull?   120

    But hark: while here light fell the clink
The five cups made touched brink to brink
In fair bouquet of fellowship,

And just as the gay Lesbian's lip
Was parted—jetting came a wail   125
In litany from Kedron's jail
Profound, and belly of the whale:

> "Lord, have mercy.
>   Christ, have mercy.
>   Intercede for me,   130
>   Angel of the Agony.
>   Spare me, spare me!
>   Merciful be—
>   Lord, spare me—
>   Spare and deliver me!"   135

    Arrested, those five revelers there,
Fixed in light postures of their glee,
Seemed problematic shapes ye see
In linked caprice of festal air
Graved round the Greek sarcophagi.   140

15. In Moonlight

The roller upon Borneo's strand
Halts not, but in recoiling throe
Drags back the shells involved with sand,
Shuffled and muffled in the flow
And hollow of the wallowing undertow.   5

    In night Rolfe waked, and whelming felt
That refluence of disquiet dealt
In sequel to redundant joy.
Around he gazed in vague annoy
Upon his mates. The lamp-light dim   10
Obscurely showed them, strangely thrown
In sleep, nor heeding eye of him;
Flung every way, with random limb—
Like corses, when the battle's done
And stars come up. No sound but slight   15

Calm breathing, or low elfin shriek
In dream. But Mortmain, coiled in plight,
Lay with one arm wedged under cheek,
Mumbling by starts the other hand,
As the wolf-hound the bone. Rolfe rose   20
And shook him. Whereat, from his throes
He started, glaring; then lapsed down:
"Soft, soft and tender; feels so bland—
Grind it! 'tis hers, Brinvilliers' hand,
My nurse." From which mad dream anon   25
He seemed his frame to re-command;
And yet would give an animal moan.
    "God help thee, and may such ice make
Except against some solid? nay—
But thou who mark'st, get thee away,   30
Nor in such coals of Tartarus rake."
    So Rolfe; and wide a casement threw.
Aroma! and is this Judæa?
Down the long gorge of Kedron blew
A balm beyond the sweet Sabæa—   35
An air as from Elysian grass;
Such freshening redolence divine
As mariners upon the brine
Inhale, when barren beach they pass
By night; a musk of wafted spoil   40
From Nature's scent-bags in the soil,
Not in her flowers; nor seems it known
Even on the shores wherefrom 'tis blown.
    Clarel, he likewise wakeful grew,
And rose, joined Rolfe, and both repaired   45
Out to a railed-in ledge. In view
Across the gulf a fox was scared
Even by their quiet coming so,
And noiseless fled along a line
Of giddy cornice, till more slow   50
He skulked out of the clear moonshine;
For great part of that wall did show,
To these beneath the shadowed hight,
With arras hung of fair moon-light.

The lime-stone mountain cloven asunder,   55
With scars of many a plunge and shock
Tremendous of the rifted rock;
So hushed now after all the thunder,
Begat a pain of troubled wonder.
The student felt it; for redress   60
He turned him—anywhere—to find
Some simple thing to ease the mind
Dejected in her littleness.
　　　Rolfe read him; and in quiet way
Would interpose, lead off, allay.   65
"Look," whispered he, "yon object white—
This side here, on the crag at brink—
'Tis touched, just touched by paler light;
Stood we in Finland, one might think
An ermine there lay coiled. But no,   70
A turban 'tis, Djalea's, aloof
Reclining, as he used to do
In Lebanon upon proud roof—
His sire's. And, see, long pipe in state,
He inhales the friendly fume sedate.   75
Yon turban with the snowy folds
Announces that my lord there holds
The rank of Druze initiate—
Not versed in portion mere, but total—
Advanced in secrets sacerdotal;   80
Though what these be, or high or low,
Who dreams? Might Lady Esther learn?"
　　　"Who?"
　　　　　　　"Lady Esther. Don't you know?
Pitt's sibyl-niece, who made sojourn
In Libanus, and read the stars;   85
Self-exiled lady, long ago
She prophesied of wizard wars,
And kept a saddled steed in stall
Awaiting some Messiah's call
Who came not.—But yon Druze's veil   90
Of Sais may one lift, nor quail?
We'll try."

         To courteous challenge sent,
The Druze responded, not by word
Indeed, but act: he came; content
He leaned beside them in accord,   95
Resting the pipe-bowl. His assent
In joining them, nay, all his air
Mute testimony seemed to bear
That now night's siren element,
Stealing upon his inner frame,   100
Pliant had made it and more tame.
    With welcome having greeted him,
Rolfe led along by easy skim
And won the topic: "Tell us here—
Your Druze faith: are there not degrees,   105
Orders, ascents of mysteries
Therein? One would not pry and peer:
Of course there's no disclosing these;
But what's that *working* thought you win?
The prelate-princes of your kin,   110
They—they—doubtless they take their ease."
    No ripple stirred the Emir's son,
He whiffed the vapor, kept him staid,
Then from the lip the amber won:
"No God there is but God," he said,   115
And tapped the ashes from the bowl,
And stood. 'Twas passive self-control
Of Pallas' statue in sacked Rome
Which bode till pushed from off the plinth;
Then through the rocky labyrinth   120
Betook him where cool sleep might come;
But not before farewell sedate:—
"Allah preserve ye, Allah great!"

16. THE EASTER FIRE

"There's politesse! we're left behind.
And yet I like this Prince of Pith;
Too pithy almost. Where'll ye find

Nobleman to keep silence with
Better than Lord Djalea?—But you—   5
It can not be this interview
Has somehow——" "No," said Clarel; "no,"
And sighed; then, "How irreverent
Was Belex in the wassail-flow:
His Ramadan he links with Lent."   10
    "No marvel: what else to infer?
Toll-taker at the Sepulcher.
To me he gave his history late,
The which I sought.—You've marked the state
Of warders shawled, on old divan,   15
Sword, pipe, and coffee-cup at knee,
Cross-legg'd within that portal's span
Which wins the Holy Tomb? Ay me,
With what a bored dead apathy
Faith's eager pilgrims they let in!"   20
    "Guard of the Urn has Belex been?"
Said Clarel, starting; "why then,—yes—"
He checked himself.—
                    "Nay, but confess,"
Cried Rolfe; "I know the revery lurks:
Frankly admit that for these Turks   25
There's nothing that can so entice
To disbelieve, nay, Atheize—
Nothing so baneful unto them
As shrined El Cods, Jerusalem.
For look now how it operates: 30
To Christ the Turk as much as Frank
Concedes a supernatural rank;
Our Holy Places too he mates
All but with Mecca's own. But then
If chance he mark the Cross profaned   35
By violence of Christian men
So called—*his* faith then needs be strained;
The more, if he himself have done
(Enforced thereto by harsh command)
Irreverence unto Mary's Son."   40

"How mean you?" and the speaker scanned.
"Why not alone has Belex been
An idling guard about The Tomb:
Nay, but he knows another scene
In fray beneath the self-same dome   45
At festivals. What backs he's scored
When on the day by Greeks adored,
St. Basil's Easter, all the friars
Schismatic, with the pilgrim tribes,
Levantine, Russian, heave their tides   50
Of uproar in among the shrines,
Waiting the burst of fraudful fires
From vent there in the Holy Tomb
Which closeteth the mongers. Room!
It jets! To quell the rush, the lines   55
Of soldiers sway: crack falls the thong;
And mid the press, some there, though strong,
Are trampled, trodden, till they die.
In transfer swift, igniting fly
The magic flames, which, caught along   60
By countless candles, multiply.
Like seas phosphoric on calm nights,
Blue shows the fane in fog of lights;
But here 'tis hurricane and high:
Zeal, furious zeal, and frenzying faith   65
And ecstasy of Atys' scath
When up the Phrygian mount he rushed
Bleeding, yet heeding not his shame,
While round him frantic timbrels pushed
In rites delirious to name.   70
No: Dindymus' nor Brahma's crew
Dream what these Christian fakirs do:
Wrecked banners, crosses, ragged palms—
Red wounds thro' vestments white ye view;
And priests who shout ferocious psalms   75
And hoarse hosannas to their king,
Even Christ; and naught may work a lull,
Nor timely truce of reason bring;

Not cutting lash, nor smiting sword,
Nor yet—Oh! more than wonderful—   80
The tomb, the pleading tomb where lay Our Lord."
        "But who ordains the imposture? speak."
"The vivid, ever-inventive Greek."
        "The Greek? But that is hard to think.
Seemly the port, gentle the cheer   85
Of friars which lodge upon this brink
Of Kedron, and do worship here
With rites august, and keep the creed."—
        "Ah, *rites august;*—this ancient sect,
Stately upholstered and bedecked,   90
Is but a catafalque, concede—
Prolongs in sacerdotal way
The Lower Empire's bastard sway;
It does not grow, it does but bide—
An orthodoxy petrified.   95
Or, if it grow, it grows but with
Russia, and thence derives its pith.
The Czar is its armed bishop. See,
The Czar's purse, so it comes to me,
Contributes to this convent's pride.   100
But what's that twinkling through the gloom
Far down? the lights in chantry? Yes!
Whence came the flame that lit? Confess,
E'en from Jerusalem—the Tomb,
Last Easter. Horseman from the porch   105
Hither each Easter spurs with torch
To re-ignite the flames extinct
Upon Good-Friday. Thus, you see,
Contagious is this cheatery;
Nay, that's unhandsome; guests we are;   110
And hosts are sacred—house and all;
And one may think, and scarcely mar
The truth, that it may so befall
That, as yon docile lamps receive
The fraudful flame, yet honest burn,   115
So, no collusive guile may cleave
Unto these simple friars, who turn

And take whate'er the forms dispense,
Nor question, *Wherefore?* ask not, *Whence?"*

    Clarel, as if in search of aught   120
To mitigate unwelcome thought,
Appealed to turret, crag and star;
But all was strange, withdrawn and far.

    "Yet need we grant," Rolfe here resumed,
"This trick its source had in a dream   125
Artless, which few will disesteem—
That angels verily illumed
Those lamps at Easter, long ago;
Though now indeed all come from prayer
(As Greeks believe—at least avow)   130
Of bishops in the Sepulcher.
Be rumor just, which small birds sing,
Greek churchmen would let drop this thing
Of fraud, e'en let it cease. But no:
'Tis ancient, 'tis entangled so   135
With vital things of needful sway,
Scarce dare they deviate that way.
The Latin in this spurious rite
Joined with the Greek: but long ago,
Long years since, he abjured it quite.   140
Still, few Rome's pilgrims here, and they
Less credulous than Greeks to-day.
Now worldlings in their worldliness
Enjoin upon us, *Never retract:*
With ignorant folk, think you, no less   145
Of policy priestcraft may exact?
But Luther's clergy: though their deeds
Take not imposture, yet 'tis seen
That, in some matters more abstract,
These, too, may be impeached herein.   150
While, as each plain observer heeds,
Some doctrines fall away from creeds,
And therewith, hopes, which scarce again,
In those same forms, shall solace men—

Perchance, suspended and inert   155
May hang, with few to controvert,
For ages; does the Lutheran,
To such disciples as may sit
Receptive of his sanctioned wit,
In candor own the dubious weather   160
And lengthen out the cable's tether?—
You catch my drift?"
                    "I do. But, nay,
Some ease the cable."
                    "Derwent, pray?
Ah, he—he is a generous wight,
And lets it slip, yes, run out quite.   165
Whether now in his priestly state
He seek indeed to mediate
'Tween faith and science (which still slight
Each truce deceptive) or discreet
Would kindly cover faith's retreat,   170
Alike he labors vainly. Nay,
And, since I think it, why not say—
Things all diverse he would unite:
His idol's an hermaphrodite."
        The student shrank. Again he knew   175
Return for Rolfe of quick distaste;
But mastered it; for still the hue
Rolfe kept of candor undefaced,
Quoting pure nature at his need,
As 'twere the Venerable Bede: 180
An Adam in his natural ways.
        But scrupulous lest any phrase
Through inference might seem unjust
Unto the friend they here discussed;
Rolfe supplements: "Derwent but errs—   185
No, buoyantly but overstates
In much his genial heart avers:
I cannot dream he simulates.
For pulpiteers which make their mart—
Who, in the Truth not for a day,   190
Debarred from growth as from decay,

Truth one forever, Scriptures say,
Do yet the fine progressive part
So jauntily maintain; these find
(For sciolists abound) a kind 195
And favoring audience. But none
Exceed in flushed repute the one
Who bold can harmonize for all
Moses and Comte, Renan and Paul:
'Tis the robustious circus-man: 200
With legs astride the dappled span
Elate he drives white, black, before:
The small apprentices adore.
Astute ones be though, staid and grave
Who in the wars of Faith and Science 205
Remind one of old tactics brave—
Imposing front of false defiance:
The King a corpse in armor led
On a live horse.—You turn your head:
You hardly like that. Woe is me: 210
What would you have? For one to hold
That he must still trim down, and cold
Dissemble—this were coxcombry!
Indulgence should with frankness mate:
Fraternal be: Ah, tolerate!" 215
  The modulated voice here won
Ingress where scarce the plea alone
Had entrance gained. But—to forget
Allusions which no welcome met
In him who heard—Rolfe thus went on: 220
"Never I've seen it; but they claim
That the Greek prelate's artifice
Comes as a tragic after-piece
To farce, or rather prank and game;
Racers and tumblers round the Tomb: 225
Sports such as might the mound confront,
The funeral mound, by Hellespont,
Of slain Patroclus. Linger still
Such games beneath some groves of bloom
In mid Pacific, where life's thrill 230

Is primal—Pagan; and fauns deck
Green theatres for that tattooed Greek
The Polynesian.—Who will say
These Syrians are more wise than they,
Or more humane? not those, believe,   235
Who may the narrative receive
Of Ibrahim the conqueror, borne
Dead-faint, by soldiers red with gore
Over slippery corses heaped forlorn
Out from splashed Calvary through the door   240
Into heaven's light. Urged to ordain
That nevermore the frenzying ray
Should issue—'That would but sustain
The cry of persecution; nay,
Let Allah, if he will, remand   245
These sects to reason. Let it stand.'—
Cynical Moslem! but didst err,
Arch-Captain of the Sepulcher?"—

          He stayed: and Clarel knew decline
Of all his spirits, as may one   250
Who hears some story of his line
Which shows him half his house undone.
Revulsion came: with lifted brows
He gazed on Rolfe: Is this the man
Whom Jordan heard in part espouse   255
The appeal of that Dominican
And Rome? and here, all sects, behold,
All creeds involving in one fold
Of doubt? Better a partisan!
Earnest he seems: can union be   260
'Twixt earnestness and levity?
Or need at last in Rolfe confess
Thy hollow, Manysidedness!

          But, timely, here diversion fell.
Dawn broke; and from each cliff-hung cell   265
'Twas hailed with hymns—confusion sweet
As of some aviary's seat:

Commemorative matin din:
'Tis Saba's festival they usher in.

17. A Chant

That day, though to the convent brood
A holiday, was kept in mood
Of serious sort, yet took the tone
And livery of legend grown
Poetical if grave. The fane   5
Was garnished, and it heard a strain
Reserved for festa. And befell
That now and then at interval
Some, gathered on the cliffs around,
Would sing Saint Cosmas' canticle;   10
Some read aloud from book embrowned
While others listened; some prefer
A chant in Scripture character,
Or monkish sort of melodrame.

    Upon one group the pilgrims came   15
In gallery of slender space,
Locked in the echoing embrace
Of crags: a choir of seemly men
Reposed in cirque, nor wanting grace,
Whose tones went eddying down the glen: 20

First Voice

No more the princes flout the word—
    Jeremiah's in dungeon cast:
The siege is up, the walls give way:
    This desolation is the last.
The Chaldee army, pouring in,   25
    Fiercer grown for disarray,
Hunt Zedekiah that fleeth out:
    Baal and Assyria win:
Israel's last king is shamed in rout,

Taken and blinded, chains put on,   30
And captive dragged to Babylon.

Second Voice

O daughter of Jerusalem,
    Cast up the ashes on the brow!
Nergal and Samgar, Sarsechim
    Break down thy towers, abase thee now.   35

Third Voice

Oh, now each lover leaveth!

Fourth Voice

None comfort me, she saith:

First Voice

Abroad the sword bereaveth:

Second Voice

At home there is as death.

The Four

Behold, behold! the days foretold begin: 40
A sword without—the pestilence within.

First and Second Voices

But thou that pull'st the city down,
    Ah, vauntest thou thy glory so?

Second and Third Voices

God is against thee, haughty one;

His archers roundabout thee go: 45

The Four

Earth shall be moved, the nations groan
At the jar of Bel and Babylon
  In din of overthrow.

First Voice

But Zion shall be built again!

Third and Fourth Voices

Nor shepherd from the flock shall sever;   50
For lo, his mercy doth remain,
  His tender mercy—

Second Voice

And forever!

The Four

Forever and forever!

Choral

Forever and forever   55
  His mercy shall remain:
In rivers flow forever,
  Forever fall in rain!

18. THE MINSTER

Huge be the buttresses enmassed
Which shoulder up, like Titan men,
Against the precipices vast
The ancient minster of the glen.

One holds the library four-square,   5
A study, but with students few:
Books, manuscripts, and—cobwebs too.
Within, the church were rich and rare
But for the time-stain which ye see:
Gilded with venerable gold,   10
It shows in magnified degree
Much like some tarnished casket old
Which in the dusty place ye view
Through window of the broker Jew.
    But Asiatic pomp adheres   15
To ministry and ministers
Of Basil's Church; that night 'twas seen
In all that festival confers:
Plate of Byzantium, stones and spars,
Urim and Thummim, gold and green;   20
Music like cymbals clashed in wars
Of great Semiramis the queen.
And texts sonorous they intone
From parchment, not plebeian print;
From old and golden parchment brown   25
They voice the old Septuagint,
And Gospels, and Epistles, all
In the same tongue employed by Paul.
Flags, beatific flags they view:
Ascetics which the hair-cloth knew   30
And wooden pillow, here were seen
Pictured on satin soft—serene
In fair translation. But advanced
Above the others, and enhanced
About the staff with ring and boss,   35
They mark the standard of the Cross.
That emblem, here, in Eastern form,
For Derwent seemed to have a charm.
"I like this Greek cross, it has grace;"
He whispered Rolfe: "the Greeks eschew   40
The long limb; beauty must have place—
Attic! I like it. And do you?"
    "Better I'd like it, were it true."
"What mean you there?"

"I do but mean
'Tis not the cross of Calvary's scene.
The Latin cross (by that name known) 45
Holds the true semblance; that's the one
Was lifted up and knew the nail;
'Tis realistic—can avail!"
    Breathed Derwent then, "These arches quite 50
Set off and aggrandize the rite:
A goodly fane. The incense, though,
Somehow it drugs, makes sleepy so.
They purpose down there in ravine
Having an *auto,* act, or scene, 55
Or something. Come, pray, let us go."

19. THE MASQUE

'Tis night, with silence, save low moan
Of winds. By torches red in glen
A muffled man upon a stone
Sits desolate sole denizen.
Pilgrims and friars on ledge above 5
Repose. A figure in remove
This prologue renders: "He in view
Is that Cartaphilus, the Jew
Who wanders ever; in low state,
Behold him in Jehoshaphat 10
The valley, underneath the hem
And towers of gray Jerusalem:
This must ye feign. With quick conceit
Ingenuous, attuned in heart,
Help out the actor in his part, 15
And gracious be;" and made retreat.
    Then slouching rose the muffled man;
Gazed toward the turrets, and began:
    "O city yonder,
Exposed in penalty and wonder, 20
Again thou seest me! Hither I
Still drawn am by the guilty tie
Between us; all the load I bear

Only thou know'st, for thou dost share.
As round my heart the phantoms throng   25
Of tribe and era perished long,
So *thou* art haunted, sister in wrong!
While ghosts from mounds of recent date
Invest and knock at every gate—
Specters of thirty sieges old   30
Your outer line of trenches hold:
Egyptian, Mede, Greek, Arab, Turk,
Roman, and Frank, beleaguering lurk.—
    "Jerusalem!
Not solely for that bond of doom   35
Between us, do I frequent come
Hither, and make profound resort
In Shaveh's dale, in Joel's court;
But hungering also for the day
Whose dawn these weary feet shall stay,   40
When Michael's trump the call shall spread
Through all your warrens of the dead.
    "Time, never may I know the calm
Till then? my lull the world's alarm?
But many mortal fears and feelings   45
In me, in me here stand reversed:
The unappeased judicial pealings
Wrench me, not wither me, accursed.
'Just let him live, just let him rove,'
(Pronounced the voice estranged from love)   50
'Live—live and rove the sea and land;
Long live, rove far, and understand
And sum all knowledge for his dower;
For he forbid is, he is banned;
His brain shall tingle, but his hand   55
Shall palsied be in power:
Ruthless, he meriteth no ruth,
On him I imprecate the truth.' "

    He quailed; then, after little truce,
Moaned querulous:
             "My fate!   60
Cut off I am, made separate;

For man's embrace I strive no more;
For, would I be
Friendly with one, the mystery
He guesses of that dreadful lore   65
Which Eld accumulates in me:
He fleeth me.
My face begetteth superstition:
In dungeons of Spain's Inquisition
Thrice languished I for sorcery,   70
An Elymas. In Venice, long
Immured beneath the wave I lay
For a conspirator. Some wrong
On me is heaped, go where I may,
Among mankind. Hence solitude   75
Elect I; in waste places brood
More lonely than an only god;
For, human still, I yearn, I yearn,
Yea, after a millennium, turn
Back to my wife, my wife and boy;   80
Yet ever I shun the dear abode
Or site thereof, of homely joy.
I fold ye in the watch of night,
Esther! then start. And hast thou been?
And I for ages in this plight?   85
Caitiff I am; but there's no sin
Conjecturable, possible,
No crime they expiate in hell
Justly whereto such pangs belong:
The wrongdoer he endureth wrong.   90
Yea, now the Jew, inhuman erst,
With penal sympathy is cursed—
The burden shares of every crime,
And throttled miseries undirged,
Unchronicled, and guilt submerged   95
Each moment in the flood of time.
Go mad I can not: I maintain
The perilous outpost of the sane.
Memory could I mitigate,
Or would the long years vary any!   100
But no, 'tis fate repeating fate:

Banquet and war, bridal and hate,
And tumults of the people many;
And wind, and dust soon laid again:
Vanity, vanity's endless reign!—   105
What's there?"

        He paused, and all was hush
Save a wild screech, and hurtling rush
Of wings. An owl—the hermit true
Of grot the eremite once knew
Up in the cleft—alarmed by ray   110
Of shifted flambeau, burst from cave
On bushy wing, and brushed away
Down the long Kedron gorge and grave.

    "It flees, but it will be at rest
Anon! But I—" and hung oppressed—   115
"Years, three-score years, seem much to men;
Three hundred—five—eight hundred, then;
And add a thousand; these I know!
That eighth dim cycle of my woe,
The which, ahead, did so delay,   120
To me now seems but yesterday:
To Rome I wandered out of Spain,
And saw thy crowning, Charlemagne,
On Christmas eve. Is all but dream?
Or is this Shaveh, and on high,   125
Is that, even *that,* Jerusalem?—
How long, how long? Compute hereby:
The years, the penal years to be,
Reckon by years, years, years, and years
Whose calendar thou here mayst see   130
On grave-slabs which the blister sears—
Of ancient Jews which sought this clime,
Inscriptions nigh extinct,
Or blent or interlinked
With dotard scrawl of idiot Time.   135
Transported felon on the seas
Pacing the deck while spray-clouds freeze;
Pacing and pacing, night and morn,
Until he staggers overworn;

Through time, so I, Christ's convict grim,   140
Deathless and sleepless lurching fare—
Deathless and sleepless through remorse for Him;
Deathless, when sleepless were enough to bear."

Rising he slouched along the glen,
Halting at base of crag—detached   145
Erect, as from the barrier snatched,
And upright lodged below; and then:
"Absalom's Pillar! See the shoal
Before it—pebble, flint, and stone,
With malediction, jeer or groan   150
Cast through long ages. Ah, what soul
That was but human, without sin,
Did hither the first just missile spin!
Culprit am I—this hand flings none;
Rather through yon dark-yawning gap,   155
Missed by the rabble in mishap
Of peltings vain—abject I'd go,
And, contrite, coil down there within,
Lie still, and try to ease the throe.
        "But nay—away!   160
Not long the feet unblest may stay.
They come: the vengeful vixens strive—
The harpies, lo—hag, gorgon, drive!"

There caught along, as swept by sand
In fierce Sahara hurricaned,   165
He fled, and vanished down the glen.

The Spahi, who absorbed had been
By the true acting, turned amain,
And letting go the mental strain,
Vented a resonant, *"Bismillah!"*   170
Strange answering which pealed from on high—
"Dies iræ, dies illa!"
        They looked, and through the lurid fume
Profuse of torches that but die,
And ghastly there the cliffs illume;   175
The skull-capped man they mark on high—

Fitful revealed, as when, through rift
Of clouds which dyed by sunset drift,
The Matterhorn shows its cragged austerity.

20. AFTERWARD

"Seedsmen of old Saturn's land,
  Love and peace went hand in hand,
    And sowed the Era Golden!

"Golden time for man and mead:
  Title none, nor title-deed,   5
    Nor any slave, nor Soldan.

"Venus burned both large and bright,
  Honey-moon from night to night,
    Nor bride, nor groom waxed olden.

"Big the tears, but ruddy ones,   10
  Crushed from grapes in vats and tuns
    Of vineyards green and golden!

"Sweet to sour did never sue,
  None repented ardor true—
    Those years did so embolden.   15

"Glum Don Graveairs slunk in den:
  Frankly roved the gods with men
    In gracious talk and golden.

"Thrill it, cymbals of my rhyme,
  Power was love, and love in prime,   20
    Nor revel to toil beholden.

"Back, come back, good age, and reign,
  Goodly age, and long remain—
    Saturnian Age, the Golden!"

The masquer gone, by stairs that climb,   25

In seemly sort, the friars withdrew;
And, waiting that, the Islesman threw
His couplets of the Arcadian time,
Then turning on the pilgrims: "Hoo!

    "The bird of Paradise don't like owls: 30
      A handful of acorns after the cowls!"

    But Clarel, bantered by the song,
Sad questioned, if in frames of thought
And feeling, there be right and wrong;
Whether the lesson Joel taught   35
Confute what from the marble's caught
In sylvan sculpture—Bacchant, Faun,
Or shapes more lax by Titian drawn.
Such counter natures in mankind—
Mole, bird, not more unlike we find: 40
Instincts adverse, nor less how true
Each to itself. What clew, what clew?

21. IN CONFIDENCE

Towers twain crown Saba's mountain hight;
And one, with larger outlook bold,
Monks frequent climb or day or night
To peer for Arabs. In the breeze
So the ship's lifted topmen hold   5
Watch on the blue and silver seas,
To guard against the slim Malay,
That perilous imp whose slender proa
Great hulls have rued—as in ill hour
The whale the sword-fish' lank assay.   10

    Upon that pile, to catch the dawn,
Alert next day see Derwent stand
With Clarel. All the mountain-land
Disclosed through Kedron far withdrawn,
Cloven and shattered, hushed and banned,   15

Seemed poised as in a chaos true,
Or throe-lock of transitional earth
When old forms are annulled, and new
Rebel, and pangs suspend the birth.
    That aspect influenced Clarel. Fair   20
Derwent's regard played otherwhere—
Expectant. Twilight gray took on
Suffusion faint of cherry tone.
The student marked it; but the priest
Marked whence it came: "Turn, turn—the East!   25
Oh, look! how like an ember red
The seed of fire, by early hand
Raked forth from out the ashy bed,
Shows yon tinged flake of dawn. See, fanned
As 'twere, by this spice-air that blows,   30
The live coal kindles—the fire grows!"
And mute, he watched till all the East
Was flame: "Ah, who would not here come,
And from dull drowsiness released,
Behold morn's rosy martyrdom!"   35
    It was an unaffected joy,
And showed him free from all annoy
Within—such, say, as mutiny
Of non-content in random touch
That he perchance had overmuch   40
Favored the first night's revelry.
    For Clarel—though at call indeed
He might not else than turn and feed
On florid dawn—not less, anon,
When wonted light of day was won,   45
Sober and common light, with that
Returned to him his unelate
And unalleviated tone;
And thoughts, strange thoughts, derived overnight,
Touching the Swede's dark undelight,   50
Recurred; with sequence how profuse
Concerning all the company—
The Arnaut, and the man of glee—
The Lesbian, and calm grave Druze,

And Belex; yes, and in degree   55
Even Rolfe; Vine too. Less he who trim
Beside him stood, eludes his doubt—
Derwent himself, whose easy skim
Never had satisfied throughout.
He now, if not deemed less devout   60
Through wassail and late hint of him,
Was keenlier scanned. Yet part might be
Effect of long society,
Which still detracts. But in review
Of one who could such doubt renew,   65
Clarel inveighs: Parhelion orb
Of faith autumnal, may the dew
Of earth's sad tears thy rays absorb?
Truth bitter: Derwent bred distrust
Heavier than came from Mortmain's thrust   70
Into the cloud—profounder far
Than Achor's glen with ominous scar.
　　All aliens now being quite aloof,
Fain would he put that soul to proof.
Yet, fearful lest he might displease,   75
His topics broached he by degrees.
Needless. For Derwent never shrunk:
　　"Lad, lad, this diffidence forget;
Believe, you talk here to no monk:
Who's old Duns Scotus? We're well met.   80
Glad that at last your mind you set
In frank communion here with me.
Better had this been earlier, though;
There lacked not times of privacy
Had such been sought. But yes, I know;   85
You're young, you're off the poise; and so
A link have felt with hearts the same
Though more advanced. I scarce can blame.
And yet perhaps one here might plead
These rather stimulate than feed.   90
Nor less let each tongue say its say;
Therefrom we truth elicit. Nay,
And with the worst, 'tis understood

We broader clergy think it good
No more to use censorious tone: 95
License to all.—We are alone;
Speak out, that's right."
                              The student first
Cited the din of clashed belief
So loud in Palestine, and chief
By Calvary, where are rehearsed   100
Within the Sepulcher's one fane
All rituals which, ere Luther's reign,
Shared the assent of Christendom.
Besides: how was it even at home?
Behind the mellow chancel's rail   105
Lurked strife intestine. What avail
The parlor-chapels liberal?
The hearers their own minds elect;
The very pews are each a sect;
No one opinion's steadfast sway: 110
A wide, an elemental fray.
As with ships moored in road unsafe,
When gales augment and billows chafe,
Hull drives 'gainst hull, endangering all
In crossing cables; while from thrall   115
Of anchor, others, dragged amain,
Drift seaward: so the churches strain,
Much so the fleets sectarian meet
Doubt's equinox. Yes, all was dim;
He saw no one secure retreat;   120
Of late so much had shaken him.
        Derwent in grave concern inclined.
"Part true, alas!" Nor less he claimed
Reserves of solace, and of kind
Beyond that in the desert named,   125
When the debate was scarce with men
Who owned with him a common ground—
True center where they might convene.
And yet this solace when unbound
At best proved vague (so Clarel deemed).   130
He thought, too, that the priest here seemed

Embarrassed on the sudden, nay,
He faltered. What could so betray?
In single contact, heart to heart,
With young, fresh, fervid earnestness,   135
Was he surprised into distress—
An honest quandary, a smart
More trying e'en than Mortmain's dart,
Grieving and graveling, could deal?
    But Derwent rallied, and with zeal: 140
"Shall everything then plain be made?
Not that there's any ambuscade:
In youth's first heat to think to know!
For time 'tis well to bear a cross:
Yet on some waters here below   145
Pilots there be, if one's at loss."
    The pupil colored; then restrained
An apt retort too personal,
Content with this: "Pilots retained?
But in debates which I recall   150
Such proved but naught. This side—that side,
They crossing hail through fogs that dwell
Upon a limitless deep tide,
While their own cutters toll the bell
Of groping."   155
        Derwent bit the lip;
Altered again, had fain let slip
"Throw all this burden upon HIM;"
But hesitated. Changing trim,
Considerate then he turned a look
Which seemed to weigh as in a book   160
Just how far youth might well be let
Into maturity's cabinet.
He, as in trial, took this tone:
"Not but there's here and there a heart
Which shares at whiles strange throbs alone.   165
Such at the freakish sting will start:
No umpirage! they cry—we dote
To dream heaven drops a casting vote,
In these perplexities takes part!"

Clarel, uncertain, stood at gaze,   170
But Derwent, riving that amaze,
Advanced impulsively: "Your hand!
No longer will I be restrained.
Yours is a sect—but never mind:
By function we are intertwined,   175
Our common function. Weigh it thus:
Clerics we are—clerics, my son;
Nay, shrink not so incredulous;
Paternally my sympathies run—
Toward you I yearn. Well, now: what joy,   180
What saving calm, what but annoy
In all this hunt without one clew?
What lack ye, pray? what would ye do?
Have Faith, which, even from the myth,
Draws something to be useful with: 185
In any form some truths will hold;
Employ the present-sanctioned mold.
Nay, hear me out; clean breast I make,
Quite unreserved—and for whose sake?
Suppose an instituted creed   190
(Or truth or fable) should indeed
To ashes fall; the spirit exhales,
But reinfunds in active forms:
Verse, popular verse, it charms or warms—
Bellies Philosophy's flattened sails—   195
Tinctures the very book, perchance,
Which claims arrest of its advance.
Why, the true import, deeper use
Shows first when Reason quite slips noose,
And Faith's long dead. Attest that gold   200
Which Bacon counted down and told
In one ripe tract, by time unshamed,
Wherein from riddle he reclaimed
The myths of Greece. But go back—well,
Reach to the years of first decay   205
Or totter: prithee, lad, but tell
How with the flamens of that day?
When brake the sun from morning's tents

And walked the hills, and gilded thence
The fane in porch; the priest in view 210
Bowed—hailed Apollo, as before,
Ere change set in; what else to do?
Or whither turn, or what adore?
What but to temporize for him,
Stranded upon an interim 215
Between the ebb and flood? He knew.—
You see? Transfer—apply it, you."
    "Ill know I what you there advise.—
Ah, heaven!" and for a moment stood;
Then turned: "A rite they solemnize— 220
An awful rite, and yet how sweet
To humble hearts which sorrows beat.
Tell, is that mystic flesh and blood—
I shrink to utter it!—Of old
For medicine they mummy sold— 225
Conjurer's balsam.—God, my God,
Sorely Thou triest me the clod!"

    Upon the impassioned novice here
Discreet the kind proficient throws
The glance of one who still would peer 230
Where best to take the hedge or close.
Ere long: "You'd do the world some good?
Well, then: no good man will gainsay
That good is good, done any way,
In any name, by any brotherhood. 235
How think you there?"
                From Clarel naught.
Derwent went on: "For lamp you yearn—
A lantern to benighted thought.
Obtain it—whither will you turn?
Still lost you'd be in blanks of snow. 240
My fellow-creature, do you know
That what most satisfies the head
Least solaces the heart? Less light
Than warmth needs earthly wight.
Christ built a hearth: the flame is dead 245

We'll say, extinct; but lingers yet,
Enlodged in stone, the hoarded heat.
Why not nurse that? Would rive the door
And let the sleet in? But, once o'er,
This tarrying glow, never to man,   250
Methinks, shall come the like again.
What if some camp on crags austere
The Stoic held ere Gospel cheer?
There may the common herd abide,
Having dreamed of heaven? Nay, and can you?   255
You shun that; what shall needier do?
Think, think!"
    The student, sorely tried,
The appeal and implication felt,
But comfort none.
    And Derwent dealt
Heaped measure still: "All your ado   260
In youth was mine; your swarm I knew
Of buzzing doubts. But is it good
Such gnats to fight? or well to brood
In selfish introverted search,
Leaving the poor world in the lurch?   265
Not so did Christ. Nor less he knew
And shared a troubled era too;
And shared besides that problem gray
Which is forever and alway:
His person our own shadow threw.   270
Then heed him, heed his eldership:
In all respects did Christ indeed
Credit the Jews' crab-apple creed
Whereto he yet conformed? or so
But use it, graft it with his slip   275
From Paradise? No, no—no, no!
Spare fervid speech! But, for the rest,
Be not extreme. Midway is best.
Herein 'tis never as by Nile—
From waste to garden but a stile.   280
Betwixt rejection and belief,
Shadings there are—degrees, in brief.
But ween you, gentle friend, your way

Of giving to yourself the goad
Is obsolete, no more the mode?   285
Our comrades—frankly let me say—
That Rolfe, good fellow though he be,
And Vine, methinks, would you but see,
Are much like prints from plates but old.
Interpretations so unfold—   290
New finding, happy gloss or key,
A decade's now a century.
Byron's storm-cloud away has rolled—
Joined Werter's; Shelley's drowned; and—why,
Perverse were now e'en Hamlet's sigh: 295
Perverse?—indecorous indeed!"
    "E'en so? e'en sadly is it so?"
"Not sad, but veritable, know.
But what—how's this!" For here, with speed
Of passion, Clarel turned: "Forbear!   300
Ah, wherefore not at once name Job,
In whom these Hamlets all conglobe.
Own, own with me, and spare to feign,
Doubt bleeds, nor Faith is free from pain!"
    Derwent averted here his face—   305
With his own heart he seemed to strive;
Then said: "Alas, too deep you dive.
But hear me yet for little space:
This shaft you sink shall strike no bloom:
The surface, ah, heaven keeps *that* green;   310
Green, sunny: nature's active scene,
For man appointed, man's true home."

    He ended. Saba's desert lay—
Glare rived by gloom. That comment's sway
He felt: "Our privacy is gone;   315
Here trips young Anselm to espy
Arab or pilgrim drawing nigh.
Dost hear him? come then, we'll go down.
Precede."
        At every step and steep,
While higher came the youthful monk,   320
Lower and lower in Clarel sunk

The freighted heart. It touched this deep:
Ah, Nehemiah, alone art true?
Secure in reason's wane or loss?
Thy folly that folly of the cross   325
Contemned by reason, yet how dear to you?

22. THE MEDALLION

In Saba, as by one consent,
Frequent the pilgrims single went;
So, parting with his young compeer,
And breaking fast without delay,
For more restorative and cheer,   5
Good Derwent lightly strolled away
Within this monkish capital.
Chapels and oratories all,
And shrines in coves of gilded gloom;
The kitchen, too, and pantler's room—   10
Naught came amiss.
                    Anear the church
He drew unto a kind of porch
Such as next some old minsters be,
An inner porch (named *Galilee*
In parlance of the times gone by),   15
A place for discipline and grief.
And here his tarry had been brief
But for a shield of marble nigh,
Set in the living rock: a stone
In low relief, where well was shown,   20
Before an altar under sky,
A man in armor, visor down,
Enlocked complete in panoply,
Uplifting reverent a crown
In invocation.
                    This armed man   25
In corselet showed the dinted plate,
And dread streaks down the thigh-piece ran;

But the bright helm inviolate
Seemed raised above the battle-zone—
Cherubic with a rare device;   30
Perch for the Bird-of-Paradise.
A victor seemed he, without pride
Of victory, or joy in fame:
'Twas reverence, and naught beside,
Unless it might that shadow claim   35
Which comes of trial. Yes, the art
So cunning was, that it in part
By fair expressiveness of grace
Atoned even for the visored face.

    Long time becharmed here Derwent stood,   40
Charmed by the marble's quiet mood
Of beauty, more than by its tone
Of earnestness, though these were one
In that good piece. Yes, long he fed
Ere yet the eye was lower led   45
To trace the inscription underrun:

    O fair and friendly manifested Spirit!
        Before thine altar dear
    Let me recount the marvel of the story
        Fulfilled in tribute here.   50

    In battle waged where all was fraudful silence,
        Foul battle against odds,
    Disarmed, I, fall'n and trampled, prayed: Death, succor!
        Come, Death: thy hand is God's!

    A pale hand noiseless from the turf responded,   55
        Riving the turf and stone:
    It raised, re-armed me, sword and golden armor,
        And waved me warring on.

    O fairest, friendliest, and ever holy—
        O Love, dissuading fate—   60

To thee, to thee the rescuer, thee sainted,
   The crown I dedicate:

To thee I dedicate the crown, a guerdon
   The winner may not wear;
His wound re-opens, and he goes to haven: 65
   Spirit! befriend him there.

"A hero, and shall he repine?
'Tis not Achilles;" and straightway
He felt the charm in sort decline;
And, turning, saw a votary gray: 70
"Good brother, tell: make this thing clear:
Who set this up?" "'Twas long ago,
Yes, long before I harbored here,
Long centuries, they say." "Why, no!
So bright it looks, 'tis recent, sure.   75
Who set it up?" "A count turned monk."
"What count?" "His name he did abjure
For Lazarus, and ever shrunk
From aught of his life's history:
Yon slab tells all or nothing, see.   80
But this I've heard; that when the stone
Hither was brought from Cyprus fair
(Some happy sculptors flourished there
When Venice ruled), he said to one:
'They've made the knight too rich appear—   85
Too rich in helm.' He set it here
In Saba as securest place,
For a memorial of grace
To outlast him, and many a year."

23. DERWENT WITH THE ABBOT

'Tis travel teaches much that's strange,
Mused Derwent in his further range;
Then fell into uneasy frame:
The visored man, relinquished name,
And touch of unglad mystery.   5

He rallied: I will go and see
The archimandrite in his court:
And thither straight he made resort
And met with much benignity.

The abbot's days were near the span,   10
A holy and right reverend man,
By name Christodulus, which means
Servant of Christ. Behind the screens
He kept, but issued the decree:
Unseen he ruled, and sightlessly: 15
Yes, blind he was, stone-blind and old;
But, in his silken vestment rolled,
At mid-day on his Persian rug,
Showed cosy as the puss Maltese
Demure, in rosy fire-light snug,   20
Upon the velvet hem at ease
Of seated lady's luxuries
Of robe. For all his days, and nights,
Which Eld finds wakeful, and the slights
Of churlish Time, life still could please.   25
And chief what made the charm to be,
Was his retention of that toy,
Dear to the old—authority.
And blent herewith was soothing balm,
Senior complacency of calm—   30
A settledness without alloy,
In tried belief how orthodox
And venerable; which the shocks
Of schism had stood, ere yet the state
Of Peter claimed earth's pastorate.   35
So far back his Greek Church did plant,
Rome's Pope he deemed but Protestant—
A Rationalist, a bigger Paine—
Heretic, worse than Arian;
He lumped him with that compound mass   40
Of sectaries of the West, alas!

Breathed Derwent: "This is a lone life;
Removed thou art from din and strife,

But from all news as well."

                        "Even so,
My son. But what's news here below?   45
For hearts that do Christ's promise claim,
No hap's important since He came.
Besides: in Saba here remain
Ten years; then back, the world regain—
Five minutes' talk with any one   50
Would put thee even with him, son.
Pretentious are events, but vain."

    "But new books, authors of the time?"
"Books have we ever new—sublime:
The Scriptures—drama, precept fine,   55
Verse and philosophy divine,
All best. Believe again, O son,
God's revelation, Holy Writ,
Quite supersedes and makes unfit
All text save comment thereupon.   60
The Fathers have we, these discuss:
Sweet Chrysostom, Basilius,
Great Athanase, and—but all's known
To you, no question."

               In the mien
Of Derwent, as this dropped in ear,   65
A junior's deference was seen.
Nothing he controverted. Here
He won the old man's heart, he knew,
And readier brought to pass the thing
That he designed: which was, to view   70
The treasures of this hermit-king.
At hint urbane, the abbot called
An acolyth, a blue-robed boy,
So used to service, he forestalled
His lighter wishes, and took joy   75
In serving. Keys were given. He took
From out a coffer's deeper nook
Small shrines and reliquaries old:
Beryl and Indian seed-pearl set
In little folding-doors of gold   80

And ivory, of tryptych form,
With starred Byzantine pictures warm,
And opening into cabinet
Where lay secured in precious zone
The honeycombed gray-greenish bone   85
Of storied saint. But prized supreme
Were some he dwelt upon, detained,
Felt of them lovingly in hand;
Making of such a text or theme
For grave particulars; far back   90
Tracing them in monastic dream:
While fondling them (in way, alack,
Of Jew his coins) with just esteem
For rich encasings. Here anew
Derwent's attention was not slack;   95
Yet underneath a reverence due,
Slyly he kept his pleasant state:
The dowager—her family plate.
    The abbot, with a blind man's way
Of meek divining, guessed the play   100
Of inkept comment: "Son," said he,
"These dry bones cannot live: what then?
In times ere Christianity
By worldlings was professed, true men
And brave, which sealed their faith in blood   105
Or flame, the Christian brotherhood
Revered—attended them in death;
Caught the last parting of the breath:
Happy were they could they but own
Some true memento, but a bone   110
Purchased from executioner,
Or begged: hence relics. Trust me, son,
'Twas love began, and pious care
Prolongs this homage." Derwent bowed;
And, bland: "Have miracles been wrought   115
From these?" "No, none by me avowed
From knowledge personal. But then
Such things may be, for they have been."
"Have been?" "'Tis in the Scripture taught

That contact with Elisha's bones   120
Restored the dead to life." "Most true,"
Eyeing the bits of skeletons
As in enlightened reverence new,
Forgetting that his host was blind,
Nor might the flattery receive.   125

    Erelong, observing the old man
Waxed weary, and to doze began,
Strange settling sidelong, half reclined,
His blessing craved he, and took leave.

24. VAULT AND GROTTO

But Clarel, bides he still by tower?
His was no sprightly frame; nor mate
He sought: it was his inner hour.
Yes, keeping to himself his state,
Nor thinking to break fast till late,   5
He moved along the gulf's built flank
Within the inclosures rank o'er rank.
Accost was none, for none he saw,
Until the Druze he chanced to meet,
Smoking, nor did the Emir draw   10
The amber from the mouth, to greet,
Not caring so to break the spell
Of that Elysian interval;
But lay, his pipe at lengthy lean,
Reclined along the crag serene,   15
As under Spain's San Pedro dome
The long-sword Cid upon his tomb;
And with an unobtrusive eye
Yet apprehending, and mild mien,
Regarded him as he went by   20
Tossed in his trouble. 'Twas a glance
Clarel did many a time recall,
Though its unmeant significance—
That was the last thing learned of all.

But passing on by ways that wind,   25
A place he gained secluded there
In ledge. A cenobite inclined
Busy at scuttle-hole in floor
Of rock, like smith who may repair
A bolt of Mammon's vault. The door   30
Or stony slab lay pushed aside.
Deeming that here the monks might store,
In times of menace which they bide,
Their altar plate, Clarel drew near,
But faltered at the friar's sad tone   35
Ascetical. He looked like one
Whose life is but a patience mere,
Or worse, a fretting doubt of cheer
Beyond; he toiled as in employ
Imposed, a bondman far from joy.   40
No answer made he to salute,
Yet deaf might be. And now, while mute
The student lingered, lo, down slipped
Through cleft of crags, the sun did win
Aloft in Kedron's citadel,   45
A fiery shaft into that crypt
(Like well-pole slant in farm-house well)
And lighted it: and he looked in.
On stony benches, head by head,
In court where no recorders be,   50
Preserved by nature's chemistry
Sat the dim conclave of the dead,
Encircled where the shadow rules,
By sloping theatres of skulls.
      He rose—retreated by the line   55
Of cliff, but paused at tones which sent:
"So pale? the end's nor imminent
Nor far. Stand, thou; the countersign!"—
It came from over Kedron's rent.
Thitherward then his glance he bent,   60
And saw, by mouth of grot or mine,
Rustic with wicket's rude design,
A sheeted apparition wait,

Like Lazarus at the charnel gate
In Bethany.
        "The countersign!"   65
  "Reply, say something; yea, say *Death*,"
Prompted the monk, erewhile so mute.
Clarel obeyed; and, in a breath,
"Advance!" the shroud cried, turning foot,
And so retired there into gloom   70
Within, and all again was dumb.
    "And who that man—or ghost?" he yearned
Unto the toiler; who returned:
"Cyril. 'Tis long since that he craved
Over against to dwell encaved.   75
In youth he was a soldier. Go."
But Clarel might not end it so:
"I pray thee, friend, what grief or zeal
Could so unhinge him? *that* reveal."
"Go—ask your world:" and grim toiled on,   80
Fitting his clamp as if alone,
Dismissing him austerely thus.
   And Clarel, sooth, felt timorous.
Conscious of seeds within his frame
Transmitted from the early gone,   85
Scarce in his heart might he disclaim
That challenge from the shrouded one.
He walked in vision—saw in fright
Where through the limitless of night
The spirits innumerable lie,   90
Strewn like snared miners in vain flight
From the dull black-damp. Die—to die!
To be, then not to be! to end,
And yet time never, never suspend
His going.—This is cowardice   95
To brood on this!—Ah, Ruth, thine eyes
Abash these base mortalities!
   But slid the change, anew it slid
As by the Dead Sea marge forbid:
The vision took another guise: 100
From 'neath the closing, lingering lid

Ruth's glance of love is glazing met,
Reproaching him: *Dost tarry, tarry yet?*

25. DERWENT AND THE LESBIAN

If where, in blocks unbeautified,
But lath and plaster may divide
The cot of dole from bed of bride;
Here, then, a page's slender shell
Is thick enough to set between   5
The graver moral, lighter mien—
The student and the cap-and-bell.
'Tis nature.
          Pastime to achieve,
After he reverent did leave
The dozer in the gallery,   10
Derwent, good man of pleasantry,
He sauntered by the stables old,
And there the ass spied through a door,
Lodged in a darksome stall or hold,
The head communing with the floor.   15
   Taking some barley, near at hand,
He entered, but was brought to stand,
Hearing a voice: "Don't bother her;
She cares not, she, for provender;
Respect her nunnery, her cell: 20
She's pondering, see, the asses' hell."
He turned; it was the Lesbian wag,
Who offered straight to be his guide
Even anywhere, be it vault or crag.
   "Well, thanks; but first to feed your nun,   25
She fasts overmuch.—There, it is done.
Come show me, do, that famous tide
Evoked up from the waste, they tell,
The canonized abbot's miracle,
St. Saba's fount: where foams it, pray?"   30
"Near where the damned ones den." "What say?"

"Down, plummets down. But come along;"
And leading, whiled the way with song:

> "Saintly lily, credit me,
>   Sweet is the thigh of the honey-bee!   35
>   Ruddy ever and oleose,
>   Ho for the balm of the red, red rose!"

    Stair after stair, and stair again,
And ladder after ladder free,
Lower and steeper, till the strain   40
Of cord irked Derwent: "Verily,
E'en as but now you lightly said,
'Tis to Avernus we are bending;
And how much further this descending?"
    At last they dropped down on the bed   45
Of Kedron, sought a cavern dead
And there the fount.
              "'Tis cool to sip,
I'm told; my cup, here 'tis; wilt dip?"
And proffered it: "With me, with me,
Alas, this natural dilution   50
Of water never did agree;
Mine is a touchy constitution;
'Tis a respectable fluid though.
Ah, you don't care. Well, come out, do.
The thing to mark here's not the well,   55
But Saba in her crescent swell,
Terrace on terrace piled. And see,
Up there by yon small balcony
Our famous palm stands sentinel.
Are you a good believer?" "Why?"   60
"Because that blessed tree (not I,
But all our monks avouch it so)
Was set a thousand years ago
By dibble in St. Saba's hand."
"Indeed? Heaven crown him for it. Palm!   65
Thou benediction in the land,
A new millennium may'st thou stand:

So fair, no fate would do thee harm."
    Much he admired the impressive view;
Then facing round and gazing up   70
Where soared the crags: "Yon grottoes few
Which make the most ambitious group
Of all the *laura* row on row,
Can one attain?" "Forward!" And so
Up by a cloven rift they plied—   75
Saffron and black—branded beside,
Like to some felon's wall of cell
Smoked with his name. Up they impel
Till Derwent, overwearied, cried:
"Dear Virgil mine, you are so strong,   80
But I, thy Dante, am nigh dead."
"Who *daunts* ye, friend? don't catch the thread."
"The ascending path was ever long."
"Ah yes; well, cheer it with a song:

    "My love but she has little feet   85
        And slippers of the rose,
     From under—Oh, the lavender sweet—
    Just peeping out, demurely neat;
        But she, she never knows—
        No, no, she never knows!   90

    "A dimpled hand is hers, and e'en
        As dainty as her toes;
     In mine confiding it she'll lean
    Till heaven knows what my tinglings mean;
        But she, she never knows—   95
        Oh no, she never knows!

"No, never!—Hist!"
                "Nay, revelers, stay.
Lachryma Christi makes ye glad!
Where joys he now shall next go mad?
His snare the spider weaves in sun: 100
But ye, your lease has yet to run;
Go, go: from ye no countersign."

Such incoherence! where lurks he,
The ghoul, the riddler? in what mine?
It came from an impending crag   105
Or cleft therein, or cavity.
The man of bins a bit did drag;
But quick to Derwent, "Never lag:
A crazy friar; but prithee, haste:
I know him,—Cyril; there, we've passed."   110
      "Well, that is queer—the queerest thing,"
Said Derwent, breathing nervously.
      "He's ever ready with his sting,
Though dozing in his grotto dull."
      "Demented—pity! let him be."   115
"Ay, if he like that kind of hull,
Let the poor wasp den in the skull."
      "What's that?" here Derwent; "that shrill cry?"
And glanced aloft; "for mercy, look!"
A great bird crossed high up in sky   120
Over the gulf; and, under him,
Its downward flight a black thing took,
And, eddying by the path's sheer rim,
Still spun below: "'Tis Mortmain's cap,
The skull-cap!" "Skull is't? say ye skull   125
From heaven flung into Kedron's lap?
The gods were ever bountiful!
No—there: I see. Small as a wren—
That death's head of all mortal men—
Look where he's perched on topmost crag,   130
Bareheaded brooding. Oh, the hag,
That from the very brow could pluck
The cap of a philosopher
So near the sky, then, with a mock,
Disdain and drop it." "Queer, 'tis queer   135
Indeed!" "One did the same to me,
Yes, much the same—pecked at my hat,
I mountain-riding, dozingly,
Upon a dromedary drear.
The devil's in these eagles-gier.   140
She ones they are, be sure of that,

That be so saucy.—Ahoy there, thou!"
Shooting the voice in sudden freak
Athwart the chasm, where wended slow
The timoneer, that pilgrim Greek,   145
The graybeard in the mariner trim,
The same that told the story o'er
Of crazy compass and the Moor.
But he, indeed, not hearing him,
Pursued his way.
     "That salted one,   150
That pickled old sea-Solomon,
Tempests have deafened him, I think.
He has a tale can make ye wink;
And pat it comes in too. But dwell!
Here, sit we down here while I tell."   155

26. Vine and the Palm

Along those ledges, up and down—
Through terce, sext, nones, in ritual flight
To vespers and mild evening brown;
On errand best to angels known,
A shadow creepeth, brushed by light.   5
Behold it stealing now over one
Reclined aloof upon a stone
High up. 'Tis Vine.
     And is it I
(He muses), I that leave the others,
Or do they leave me? One could sigh   10
For Achmed with his hundred brothers:
How share the gushing amity
With all? Divine philanthropy!
For my part, I but love the past—
The further back the better; yes,   15
In the past is the true blessedness;
The future's ever overcast—
The present aye plebeian. So,
Mar Saba, thou fine long-ago

Lithographed here, thee do I love;   20
And yet to-morrow I'll remove
With right good will; a fickle lover
Is only constant as a rover.
Here I lie, poor solitaire;
But see the brave one over there—   25
The Palm! Come now, to pass the time
I'll try an invocation free—
Invoke it in a style sublime,
Yet sad as sad sincerity:—

    "Witness to a watered land,   30
Voucher of a vernal year—
St. Saba's Palm, why there dost stand?
Would'st thou win the desert here
To dreams of Eden? Thy device
Intimates a Paradise!   35
Nay, thy plume would give us proof
That thou thyself art prince thereof,
Fair lord of that domain.
    "But, lonely dwelling in thy reign,
Kinship claimest with the tree   40
Worshipped on Delos in the sea—
Apollo's Palm? It ended;
Nor dear divinities befriended.—
    "Thou that pledgest heaven to me,
Stem of beauty, shaft of light,   45
Behold, thou hang'st suspended
Over Kedron and the night!
Shall come the fall? shall time disarm
The grace, the glory of the Palm?
    "Tropic seraph! thou once gone,   50
Who then shall take thy office on—
Redeem the waste, and high appear,
Apostle of Talassa's year
And climes where rivers of waters run?
    "But braid thy tresses—yet thou'rt fair: 55
Every age for itself must care:
Braid thy green tresses; let the grim
Awaiter find thee never dim!

Serenely still thy glance be sent
Plumb down from horror's battlement: 60
Though the deep Fates be concerting
A reversion, a subverting,
Still bear thee like the Seraphim."

　　He loitered, lounging on the stair:
Howbeit, the sunlight still is fair. 65
　　Next meetly here behooves narrate
How fared they, seated left but late—
Viewless to Vine above their dell,
Viewless and quite inaudible:
Derwent, and his good gossip cosy, 70
The man of Lesbos, light and rosy,
His anecdote about to tell.

27. MAN AND BIRD

"Yes, pat it comes in here for me:
He says, that one fine day at sea—
'Twas when he younger was and spry—
Being at mast-head all alone,
While he his business there did ply, 5
Strapping a block where halyards run,
He felt a fanning overhead—
Looked up, and so into the eye
Of a big bird, red-billed and black
In plume. It startled him, he said, 10
It seemed a thing demoniac.
From poise, it went to wheeling round him;
Then, when in daze it well had bound him,
It pounced upon him with a buffet;
He, enraged, essayed to cuff it, 15
But only had one hand, the other
Still holding on the spar. And so,
While yet they shouted from below,
And yet the wings did whirr and smother,
The bird tore at his old wool cap, 20

And chanced upon the brain to tap.
Up went both hands; he lost his stay,
And down he fell—he, and the bird
Maintaining still the airy fray—
And, souse, plumped into sea; and heard,   25
While sinking there, the piercing gird
Of the grim fowl, that bore away
The prize at last."
     "And did he drown?"
 "Why, there he goes!" and pointed him
Where still the mariner wended on: 30
"'Twas in smooth water; he could swim.
They luffed and flung the rope, and fired
The harpoon at the shark untired
Astern, and dragged him—not the shark,
But man—they dragged him 'board the barque;   35
And down he dropped there with a thump,
Being water-logged with spongy lump
Of quilted patches on the shirt
Of wool, and trowsers. All inert
He lay. He says, and true's the word,   40
That bitterer than the brine he drank
Was that shrill gird the while he sank."
 "A curious story, who e'er heard
Of such a fray 'twixt man and bird!"—
"Bird? but he deemed it was the devil,   45
And that he carried off his soul
In the old cap, nor was made whole
'Till some good vicar did unravel
The snarled illusion in the skein,
And he got back his soul again."   50
 "But lost his cap. A curious story—
A bit of Nature's allegory.
And—well, what now? You seem perplexed."
 "And so I am.—Your friend there, see,
Up on yon peak, he puzzles me.   55
Wonder where I shall find him next?
Last time 'twas where the corn-cribs be—
Bone-cribs, I mean; in church, you know;

The blessed martyrs' holy bones,
Hard by the porch as in you go—   60
Sabaïtes' bones, the thousand ones
Of slaughtered monks—so faith avers.
Dumb, peering in there through the bars
He stood. Then, in the spiders' room,
I saw him there, yes, quite at home   65
In long-abandoned library old,
Conning a venerable tome,
While dust of ages round him rolled;
Nor heeded he the big fly's buzz,
But mid heaped parchment leaves that mold   70
Sat like the bankrupt man of Uz
Among the ashes, and read and read.
Much learning, has it made him mad?
Kedron well suits him, 'twould appear:
Why don't he stay, yes, anchor here,   75
Turn anchorite?"
                    And do ye pun,
And he, he such an austere one?
(Thought Derwent then.) Well, run your rig—
Hard to be comic and revere;
And once 'twas tittered in mine ear   80
St. Paul himself was but a prig.
Who's safe from the derision?—Here
Aloud: "Why, yes; our friend is queer,
And yet, as some esteem him, not
Without some wisdom to his lot."   85
    "Wisdom? our Cyril is deemed wise.
In the East here, one who's lost his wits
For saint or sage they canonize:
That's pretty good for perquisites.
I'll tell you: Cyril (some do own)   90
Has gained such prescience as to man
(Through seldom seeing any one),
To him's revealed the mortal span
Of any wight he peers upon.
And that's his hobby—as we proved   95
But late."

"Then not in vain we've roved,
Winning the oracle whose caprice
Avers *we've* yet to run our lease."
    "Length to that lease! But let's return,
Give over climbing, and adjourn."   100
    "Just as you will."
                        "But first to show
A curious caverned place hard by.
Another crazed monk—start not so—
He's gone, clean vanished from the eye!
Another crazed one, deemed inspired,   105
Long dwelt in it. He never tired—
Ah, here it is, the vestibule."

    They reach an inner grotto cool,
Lighted by fissure up in dome;
Fixed was each thing, each fixture stone: 110
Stone bed, bench, cross, and altar—stone.
    "How like you it—Habbibi's home?
You see these writings on the wall?
His craze was this: he heard a call
Ever from heaven: O scribe, write, write!   115
Write this—that write—to these indite—
To them! Forever it was—write!
Well, write he did, as here you see.
What is it all?"
                "Dim, dim to me,"
Said Derwent; "ay, obscurely traced;   120
And much is rubbed off or defaced.
But here now, this is pretty clear:
'I, Self, I am the enemy
Of all. From me deliver me,
O Lord.'—Poor man!—But here, dim here: 125
'There is a hell over which mere hell
Serves—for—a—heaven.'—Oh, terrible!
Profound pit that must be!—What's here
Half faded: '. . . teen . . six,
The hundred summers run,   130
Except it be in cicatrix

The aloe—flowers—none.'—
Ah, Nostradamus; prophecy
Is so explicit.—But this, see.
Much blurred again: '. . . *testimony,*   135
. . . . . *grown fat and gray,*
The lion down, and—full of honey,
The bears shall rummage—him—in—May.'—
Yes, bears like honey.—Yon gap there
Well lights the grotto; and this air   140
Is dry and sweet; nice citadel
For study."
        "Or dessert-room. So,
Hast seen enough? then let us go.
Write, write—indite!—what peer you at?"
Emerging, Derwent, turning round,   145
Small text spied which the door-way crowned.
"Ha, new to me; and what is that?"
The Islesman asked; "pray read it o'er."
    " '*Ye here who enter Habbi's den,*
Beware what hence ye take!' " "Amen!   150
Why didn't he say that before?
But what's to take? all's fixture here."
"Occult, occult," said Derwent, "queer."
Returning now, they made descent,
The pilot trilling as they went: 155

    "King Cole sang as he clinked the can,
        Sol goes round, and the mill-horse too:
    A thousand pound for a fire-proof man!
        The devil vows he's the sole true-blue;
          And the prick-louse sings,   160
          See the humbug of kings—
    'Tis I take their measure, ninth part of a man!"

    Lightly he sheds it off (mused then
The priest), a man for Daniel's den.

    In by-place now they join the twain,   165
Belex, and Og in red Fez bald;

And Derwent, in his easy vein
Ear gives to chat, with wine and gladness,
Pleased to elude the Siddim madness,
And, yes, even that in grotto scrawled;   170
Nor grieving that each pilgrim friend
For time now leave him to unbend.
Yet, intervening even there,
A touch he knew of gliding care:
We loiterers whom life can please   175
(Thought he) could we but find our mates
Ever! but no; before the gates
Of joy, lie some who carp and tease:
Collisions of men's destinies!—
But quick, to nullify that tone   180
He turned to mark the jovial one
Telling the twain, the martial pair,
Of Cairo and his tarry there;
And how, his humorous soul to please,
He visited the dervishes,   185
The dancing ones: "But what think ye?
The captain-dervish vowed to me
That those same cheeses, whirl-round-rings
He made, were David's—yes, the king's
Who danced before the Ark. But, look: 190
This was the step King David took;"
And cut fantastic pigeon-wings.

28. MORTMAIN AND THE PALM

"See him!—How all your threat he braves,
Saba! your ominous architraves
Impending, stir him not a jot.
Scarce *he* would change with me in lot:
Wiser am I?—Curse on this store   5
Of knowledge! Nay, 'twas cursed of yore.
Knowledge is power: tell that to knaves;
'Tis knavish knowledge: the true lore
Is impotent for earth: '*Thyself*

Thou can'st not save; come down from cross!' 10
They cast it in His teeth; trim Pelf
Stood by, and jeered, *Is gold then dross?*—
Cling to His tree, and there find hope:
Me it but makes a misanthrope.
Makes? nay, but 'twould, did not the hate 15
Dissolve in pity of the fate.—
This legend, dream, and *fact* of life!
The drooping hands, the dancing feet
Which in the endless series meet;
And rumors of *No God* so rife!" 20

  The Swede, the brotherless—who else?
'Twas he, upon the brink opposed,
To whom the Lesbian was disclosed
In antic: hence those syllables.

  Ere long (at distance from that scene) 25
A voice dropped on him from a screen
Above: "Ho, halt!" It chanced to be
The challenged here no start incurred,
Forewarned of near vicinity
Of Cyril and his freak. He heard, 30
Looked up, and answered, "Well?" "The word!"
"Hope," in derision. "Stand, delay:
That was pass-word for yesterday."
"Despair." "Advance."
      He, going, scanned
The testimony of the hand 35
Gnawed in the dream: "Yea, but 'tis here.
Despair? nay, death; and what's death's cheer?
Death means—the sea-beat gains the shore;
He's home; his watch is called no more.
So looks it. Not *I* tax thee, Death, 40
With that, which might make Strength a trembler,—
While yet for me it scants no breath—
That, quiet under sleepiest mound,
Thou art a dangerous dissembler;

That he whose evil is profound   45
In multiform of life's disguises,
Whom none dare check, and naught chastises,
And in his license thinks no bound—
For him thou hoardest strange surprises!—
But what—the Tree? O holy Palm,   50
If 'tis a world where hearts wax warm
Oftener through hate than love, and chief
The bland thing be the adder's charm,
And the true thing virtue's ancient grief—
Thee yet it nourishes—even thee!   55
     "Envoy, whose looks the pang assuage,
Disclose thy heavenly embassage!
That lily-rod which Gabriel bore
To Mary, kneeling her before,
Announcing a God, the mother she;   60
That budded stalk from Paradise—
Like that thou shin'st in thy device:
And sway'st thou over here toward me—
Toward *me* can such a symbol sway!"

     In rounded turn of craggy way,   65
Across the interposed abyss,
He had encountered it. Submiss,
He dropped upon the under stone,
And soon in such a dream was thrown
He felt as floated up in cheer   70
Of saint borne heavenward from the bier.
Indeed, each wakeful night, and fast
(That feeds and keeps what clay would clutch)
With thrills which he did still outlast,
His fibres made so fine in end   75
That though in trials fate can lend
Firm to withstand, strong to contend;
Sensitive he to a spirit's touch.

     A wind awakened him—a breath.
He lay like light upon the heath,   80
Alive though still. And all came back,

The years outlived, with all their black;
While bright he saw the angel-tree
Across the gulf alluring sway:
Come over! be—forever be 85
As in the trance.—"Wilt not delay?
Yet hear me in appeal to thee:
When the last light shall fade from me,
If, groping round, no hand I meet;
Thee I'll recall—invoke thee, Palm: 90
Comfort me then, thou Paraclete!
The lull late mine beneath thy lee,
Then, then renew, and seal the calm."

    Upon the ledge of hanging stair,
And under Vine, invisible there, 95
With eyes still feeding on the Tree,
Relapsed he lingered as in Lethe's snare.

29. ROLFE AND THE PALM

Pursued, the mounted robber flies
Unawed through Kedron's plunged demesne:
The clink, and clinking echo dies:
He vanishes: a long ravine.
And stealthy there, in little chinks 5
Betwixt or under slab-rocks, slinks
The dwindled amber current lean.

    Far down see Rolfe there, hidden low
By ledges slant. Small does he show
(If eagles eye), small and far off 10
As Mother-Cary's bird in den
Of Cape Horn's hollowing billow-trough,
When from the rail where lashed they bide
The sweep of overcurling tide,—
Down, down, in bonds the seamen gaze 15
Upon that flutterer in glen
Of waters where it sheltered plays,

While, over it, each briny hight
Is torn with bubbling torrents white
In slant foam tumbling from the snow   20
Upon the crest; and far as eye
Can range through mist and scud which fly,
Peak behind peak the liquid summits grow.

    By chance Rolfe won the rocky stair
At base, and queried if it were   25
Man's work or nature's, or the twain
Had wrought together in that lane
Of high ascent, so crooked with turns
And flanked by coignes, that one discerns
But links thereof in flights encaved,   30
Whate'er the point of view. Up, slow
He climbed for little space; then craved
A respite, turned and sat; and, lo,
The Tree in salutation waved
Across the chasm. Remindings swell;   35
Sweet troubles of emotion mount—
Sylvan reveries, and they well
From memory's Bandusia fount;
Yet scarce the memory alone,
But that and question merged in one: 40

    "Whom weave ye in,
Ye vines, ye palms? whom now, Soolee?
Lives yet your Indian Arcady?
His sunburnt face what Saxon shows—
His limbs all white as lilies be—   45
Where Eden, isled, impurpled glows
In old Mendanna's sea?
Takes who the venture after me?
    "Who now adown the mountain dell
(Till mine, by human foot untrod—   50
Nor easy, like the steps to hell)
In panic leaps the appalling crag,
Alighting on the cloistral sod
Where strange Hesperian orchards drag,

Walled round by cliff and cascatelle—   55
Arcades of Iris; and though lorn,
A truant ship-boy overworn,
Is hailed for a descended god?
　　"Who sips the vernal cocoa's cream—
The nereids dimpling in the darkling stream?   60
For whom the gambol of the tricksy dream—
Even Puck's substantiated scene,
Yea, much as man might hope and more than heaven may mean?
　　"And whom do priest and people sue,
In terms which pathos yet shall tone   65
When memory comes unto her own,
To dwell with them and ever find them true:
'Abide, for peace is here:
Behold, nor heat nor cold we fear,
Nor any dearth: one happy tide—   70
A dance, a garland of the year:
Abide!'
　　　"But who so feels the stars annoy,
Upbraiding him,—how far astray!—
That he abjures the simple joy,
And hurries over the briny world away?   75
　　"Renouncer! is it Adam's flight
Without compulsion or the sin?
And shall the vale avenge the slight
By haunting thee in hours thou yet shalt win?"

He tarried. And each swaying fan   80
Sighed to his mood in threnodies of Pan.

30. THE CELIBATE

All distant through that afternoon
The student kept, nor might attune
His heart to any steadfast thought
But Ruth—still Ruth, yet strange involved
With every mystery unresolved   5
In time and fate. In cloud thus caught,

Her image labored like a star
Fitful revealed in midnight heaven
When inland from the sea-coast far
The storm-rack and dark scud are driven.   10
Words scarce might tell his frame, in sooth:
'Twas Ruth, and oh, much more than Ruth.

   That flank of Kedron still he held
Which is built up; and, passing on—
While now sweet peal of chimings swelled   15
From belfry old, withdrawn in zone—
A way through cloisters deep he won
And winding vaults that slope to hight;
And heard a voice, espied a light
In twinkle through far passage dim,   20
And aimed for it, a friendly gleam;
And so came out upon the Tree
Mid-poised, and ledge-built balcony
Inrailed, and one who, leaning o'er,
Beneath the Palm—from shore to shore   25
Of Kedron's overwhelming walls
And up and down her gap and grave,
A golden cry sent, such as calls
To creatures which the summons know.
And, launching from crag, tower, and cave   30
Beatified in flight they go:
St. Saba's doves, in Saba bred.
For wonted bounty they repair,
These convent-pensioners of air;
Fly to their friend; from hand outspread   35
Or fluttering at his feet are fed.
Some, iridescent round his brow,
Wheel, and with nimbus him endow.
   Not fortune's darling here was seen,
But heaven's elect. The robe of blue   40
So sorted with the doves in hue
Prevailing, and clear skies serene
Without a cloud; so pure he showed—
Of stature tall, in aspect bright—

He looked an almoner of God,   45
Dispenser of the bread of light.
'Twas not the intellectual air—
Not solely that, though that be fair:
Another order, and more rare—
As high above the Plato mind   50
As this above the Mammon kind.
In beauty of his port unsealed,
To Clarel part he stood revealed
At first encounter; but the sweet
Small pecking bills and hopping feet   55
Had previous won; the host urbane,
In courtesy that could not feign,
Mute welcome yielding, and a seat.
It charmed away half Clarel's care,
And charmed the picture that he saw,   60
To think how like that turtle pair
Which Mary, to fulfill the law,
From Bethlehem to temple brought
For offering; these Saba doves
Seemed natives—not of Venus' court   65
Voluptuous with wanton wreath—
But colonnades where Enoch roves,
Or walks with God, as Scripture saith.
    Nor myrtle here, but sole the Palm
Whose vernal fans take rich release   70
From crowns of foot-stalks golden warm.
O martyr's scepter, type of peace,
And trouble glorified to calm!
    What stillness in the almoner's face:
Nor Fomalhaut more mild may reign   75
Mellow above the purple main
Of autumn hills. It was a grace
Beyond medallions ye recall.
    The student murmured, filial—
"Father," and tremulously gleamed,   80
"Here, sure, is peace." The father beamed;
The nature of the peace was such
It shunned to venture any touch

Of word. "And yet," went Clarel on;
But faltered there. The saint but glanced.   85
"Father, if Good, 'tis unenhanced:
No life domestic do ye own
Within these walls: woman I miss.
Like cranes, what years from time's abyss
Their flight have taken, one by one,   90
Since Saba founded this retreat:
In cells here many a stifled moan
Of lonely generations gone;
And more shall pine as more shall fleet."

    With dove on wrist, he, robed, stood hushed,   95
Mused on the bird, and softly brushed.
Scarce reassured by air so mute,
Anxiously Clarel urged his suit.
The celibate let go the dove;
Cooing, it won the shoulder—lit   100
Even at his ear, as whispering it.
But he one pace made in remove,
And from a little alcove took
A silver-clasped and vellum book;
And turned a leaf, and gave that page   105
For answer.—
        Rhyme, old hermit-rhyme
Composed in Decius' cruel age
By Christian of Thebæan clime:
    'Twas David's son, and he of Dan,
With him misloved that fled the bride,   110
And Job whose wife but mocked his ban;
Then rose, or in redemption ran—
The rib restored to Adam's side,
And man made whole, as man began.
    And lustral hymns and prayers were here: 115
Renouncings, yearnings, charges dread
Against our human nature dear:
Worship and wail, which, if misled,
Not less might fervor high instill
In hearts which, striving in their fear   120
Of clay, to bridle, curb or kill;

In the pure desert of the will
Chastised, live the vowed life austere.

   The given page the student scanned:
Started—reviewed, nor might withstand.   125
He turned; the celibate was gone;
Over the gulf he hung alone:
Alone, but for the comment caught
Or dreamed, in face seen far below,
Upturned toward the Palm in thought,   130
Or else on him—he scarce might know.
Fixed seemed it in assent indeed
Which indexed all? It was the Swede.
Over the Swede, upon the stair—
Long Bethel-stair of ledges brown   135
Sloping as from the heaven let down—
Apart lay Vine; lowermost there,
Rolfe he discerned; nor less the three,
While of each other unaware,
In one consent of frame might be.   140
     How vaguely, while yet influenced so
By late encounter, and his glance
Rested on Vine, his reveries flow
Recalling that repulsed advance
He knew by Jordan in the wood,   145
And the enigma unsubdued—
Possessing Ruth, nor less his heart
Aye hungering still, in deeper part
Unsatisfied. Can be a bond
(Thought he) as David sings in strain   150
That dirges beauteous Jonathan,
Passing the love of woman fond?
And may experience but dull
The longing for it? Can time teach?
Shall all these billows win the lull   155
And shallow on life's hardened beach?—

   He lingered. The last dove had fled,
And nothing breathed—breathed, waved, or fed,
Along the uppermost sublime

Blank ridge. He wandered as in sleep;   160
A saffron sun's last rays were shed;
More still, more solemn waxed the time,
Till Apathy upon the steep
Sat one with Silence and the Dead.

31. THE RECOIL

"But who was SHE (if Luke attest)
Whom generations hail for blest—
Immaculate though human one;
What diademed and starry Nun—
Bearing in English old the name   5
And hallowed style of HOLIDAME;
She, She, the Mater of the Rood—
Sprang she from Ruth's young sisterhood?"

    On cliff in moonlight roaming out,
So Clarel, thrilled by deep dissent,   10
Revulsion from injected doubt
And many a strange presentiment.
    But came ere long profound relapse:
The Rhyme recurred, made voids or gaps
In dear relations; while anew,   15
From chambers of his mind's review,
Emerged the saint, who with the Palm
Shared heaven on earth in gracious calm,
Even as his robe partook the hue.
    And needs from that high mentor part?   20
Is strength too strong to teach the weak?
Though tame the life seem, turn the cheek,
Does the call elect the hero-heart?—
The thunder smites our tropic bloom:
If live the abodes unvexed and balmy—   25
No equinox with annual doom;
If Eden's wafted from the plume
Of shining Raphael, Michael palmy;
If these in more than fable be,

With natures variously divine— 30
Through all their ranks they are masculine;
Else how the power with purity?
Or in yon worlds of light is known
The clear intelligence alone?
Express the Founder's words declare, 35
Marrying none is in the heaven;
Yet love in heaven itself to spare—
Love feminine! Can Eve be riven
From sex, and disengaged retain
Its charm? Think this—then may ye feign 40
The perfumed rose shall keep its bloom,
Cut off from sustenance of loam.
But if Eve's charm be not supernal,
Enduring not divine transplanting—
Love kindled thence, is that eternal? 45
Here, here's the hollow—here the haunting!
Ah, love, ah wherefore thus unsure?
Linked art thou—locked, with Self impure?
Yearnings benign the angels know,
Saint Francis and Saint John have felt: 50
Good-will—desires that overflow,
And reaching far as life is dealt.
That *other* love!—Oh heavy load—
Is naught then trustworthy but God?

On more hereof, derived in frame 55
From the eremite's Thebæan flame,
Mused Clarel, taking self to task,
Nor might determined thought reclaim:
But, the waste invoking, this did ask:
"Truth, truth cherubic! claim'st thou worth 60
Foreign to time and hearts which dwell
Helots of habit old as earth
Suspended 'twixt the heaven and hell?"
    But turn thee, rest the burden there;
To-morrow new deserts must thou share. 65

32. Empty Stirrups

The gray of dawn. A tremor slight:
The trouble of imperfect light
Anew begins. In floating cloud
Midway suspended down the gorge,
A long mist trails white shreds of shroud   5
How languorous toward the Dead Sea's verge.
Riders in seat halt by the gate:
Why not set forth? For one they wait
Whose stirrups empty be—the Swede.
Still absent from the frater-hall   10
Since afternoon and vesper-call,
He, they imagined, had but sought
Some cave in keeping with his thought,
And reappear would with the light
Suddenly as the Gileadite   15
In Obadiah's way. But—no,
He cometh not when they would go.
Dismounting, they make search in vain;
Till Clarel—minding him again
Of something settled in his air—   20
A quietude beyond mere calm—
When seen from ledge beside the Palm
Reclined in nook of Bethel stair,
Thitherward led them in a thrill
Of nervous apprehension, till   25
Startled he stops, with eyes avert
And indicating hand.—
                    'Tis *he*—
So undisturbed, supine, inert—
The filmed orbs fixed upon the Tree—
Night's dews upon his eyelids be.   30
To test if breath remain, none tries:
On those thin lips a feather lies—
An eagle's, wafted from the skies.
The vow: and had the genius heard,
Benignant? nor had made delay,   35
But, more than taking him at word,

Quick wafted where the palm-boughs sway
In Saint John's heaven? Some divined
That long had he been undermined
In frame; the brain a tocsin-bell   40
Overburdensome for citadel
Whose base was shattered. They refrain
From aught but that dumb look that fell
Identifying; feeling pain
That such a heart could beat, and will—   45
Aspire, yearn, suffer, baffled still,
And end. With monks which round them stood
Concerned, not discomposed in mood,
Interment they provided for—
Heaved a last sigh, nor tarried more.   50

    Nay; one a little lingered there;
'Twas Rolfe. And as the rising sun,
Though viewless yet from Bethel stair,
More lit the mountains, he was won
To invocation, scarce to prayer: 55

    "Holy Morning,
What blessed lore reservest thou,
Withheld from man, that evermore
Without surprise,
But, rather, with a hurtless scorning   60
In thy placid eyes,
Thou viewest all events alike?
Oh, tell me, do thy bright beams strike
The healing hills of Gilead now?"

And glanced toward the pale one near   65
In shadow of the crag's dark brow.—
    Did Charity follow that poor bier?
It did; but Bigotry did steer:
Friars buried him without the walls
(Nor in a consecrated bed)   70
Where vulture unto vulture calls,
And only ill things find a friend:

There let the beak and claw contend,
There the hyena's cub be fed:
Heaven that disclaims, and him beweeps   75
In annual showers; and the tried spirit sleeps.

END OF PART 3

Part 4

Bethlehem

1. In Saddle

O F OLD, if legend truth aver,
     With hearts that did in aim concur,
     Three mitered kings—Amerrian,
Apelius, and Damazon—
By miracle in Cassak met   5
(An Indian city, bards infer);
Thence, prompted by the vision yet
To find the new-born Lord nor err,
Westward their pious feet they set—
With gold and frankincense and myrrh.   10
Nor failed they, though by deserts vast
And voids and menaces they passed:
They failed not, for a light was given—
The light and pilotage of heaven:
A light, a lead, no longer won   15
By any, now, who seekers are:
Or fable is it? but if none,
Let man lament the foundered Star.

    And Kedron's pilgrims: In review
The wilds receive those guests anew.   20

Yet ere, the MANGER now to win,
Their desert march they re-begin,
Belated leaving Saba's tower;
Reverted glance they grateful throw,
Nor slight the abbot's parting dower   25
Whose benedictions with them go.
      Nor did the sinner of the isle
From friendly cheer refrain, though lax:
"Our Lady of the Vines beguile
Your travel and bedew your tracks!"   30
Blithe wishes, which slim mirth bestow;
For, ah, with chill at heart they mind
Two now forever left behind.
But as men drop, replacements rule:
Though fleeting be each part assigned,   35
The eternal ranks of life keep full:
So here—if but in small degree—
Recruits for fallen ones atone;
The Arnaut and pilgrim from the sea
The muster joining; also one   40
In military undress dun—
A stranger quite.
                    The Arnaut rode
For escort mere. His martial stud
A brother seemed—as strong as he,
As brave in trappings, and with blood   45
As proud, and equal gravity,
Reserving latent mettle. Good
To mark the rider in his seat—
Tall, shapely, powerful and complete;
A'lean, too, in an easy way,   50
Like Pisa's Tower confirmed in place,
Nor lacking in subordinate grace
Of lighter beauty. Truth to say,
This horseman seemed to waive command:
Abeyance of the bridle-hand.   55
But winning space more wide and clear,
He showed in ostentation here
How but a pulse conveyed through rein

Could thrill and fire, or prompt detain.
On dappled steed, in kilt snow-white,   60
With burnished arms refracting light,
He orbits round the plodding train.
    Djalea in quiet seat observes;
'Tis little from his poise he swerves;
Sedate he nods, as he should say: 65
"Rough road may tame this holiday
Of thine; but pleasant to look on:
Come, that's polite!" for on the wing,
Or in suspense of curveting
Chiron salutes the Emir's son.   70

    Meantime, remiss, with dangling sword,
Upon a cloistral beast but sad,
A Saba friar's befitting pad
(His own steed, having sprained a cord,
Left now behind in convent ward)   75
The plain-clad soldier, heeding none
Though marked himself, in neutral tone
Maintained his place. His shoulders lithe
Were long-sloped and yet ample, too,
In keeping with each limb and thew: 80
Waist flexile as a willow withe;
Withal, a slouched reserve of strength,
As in the pard's luxurious length;
The cheek, high-boned, of copperish show
Enhanced by sun on land and seas;   85
Long hair, much like a Cherokee's,
Curving behind the ear in flow
And veiling part a saber-scar
Slant on the neck, a livid bar;
Nor might the felt hat hide from view   90
One temple pitted with strange blue
Of powder-burn. Of him you'd say—
A veteran, no more. But nay:
Brown eyes, what reveries they keep—
Sad woods they be, where wild things sleep.   95
    Hereby, and by yet other sign,

To Rolfe, and Clarel part, and Vine,
The stranger stood revealed, confessed
A native of the fair South-West—
Their countryman, though of a zone   100
Varied in nature from their own:
A countryman—but how estranged!
Nor any word as yet exchanged
With them. But yester-evening's hour
Then first he came to Saba's tower,   105
And saw the Epirot aside
In conference, and word supplied
Touching detention of the troop
Destined to join him for the swoop
Over Jordan. But the pilgrims few   110
Knew not hereof, not yet they knew,
But deemed him one who took his way
Eccentric in an armed survey
Of Judah.
            On the pearl-gray ass
(From Siddim riderless, alas!)   115
Rode now the timoneer sedate,
Jogging beneath the Druze's lee,
As well he might, instructed late
What perils in lack of convoy be.
    A frater-feeling of the sea   120
Influenced Rolfe, and made him take
Solace with him of salt romance,
Albeit Agath scarce did wake
To full requital—chill, perchance
Derived from years or diffidence;   125
Howe'er, in friendly way Rolfe plied
One-sided chat.
                As on they ride
And o'er the ridge begin to go,
A parting glance they turn; and lo!
The convent's twin towers disappear—   130
Engulfed like a brig's masts below
Submerging waters. Thence they steer
Upward anew, in lane of steeps—

Ravine hewn-out, as 'twere by sledges;
Inwalled, from ledges unto ledges, 135
And stepwise still, each rider creeps,
Until, at top, their eyes behold
Judæa in highlands far unrolled.
A horseman so, in easier play
Wheeling aloft (so travelers say) 140
Up the Moor's Tower, may outlook gain
From saddle over Seville's plain.
        But here, 'twixt tent-lapped hills, they see,
Northward, a land immovably
Haggard and haggish, specked gray-green— 145
Pale tint of those frilled lichens lean,
Which on a prostrate pine ye view,
When fallen from the banks of grace
Down to the sand-pit's sterile place,
Blisters supplant the beads of dew. 150
Canker and palmer-worm both must
Famished have left those fields of rust:
The rain is powder—land of dust:
There few do tarry, none may live—
Save mad, possessed, or fugitive. 155
        Exalted in accursed estate,
Like Naaman in his leprous plight
Haughty before Elisha's gate,
Show the blanched hills.
                        All now alight
Upon the Promethean ledge. 160
The Druze stands by the imminent edge
Peering, and rein in hand. With head
Over her master's shoulder laid,
The mare, too, gazed, nor feared a check,
Though leaning half her lovesome neck, 165
Yet lightly, as a swan might do.
An arm Djalea enfolding stretched,
While sighs the sensitive creature fetched,
As e'en that waste to sorrow moved
Instinctive. So, to take the view 170
See man and mare, lover and loved.

Slant palm to brow against the haze,
Meantime the salt one sent his gaze
As from the mast-head o'er the pale
Expanse. But what may eyes avail?   175
Land lone as seas without a sail.
"Wreck, ho—the wreck!" Not unamazed
They hear his sudden outcry. Crazed?
Or subject yet by starts dismayed
To flighty turns, for friars said   180
Much wandered he in mind when low.
But never Agath heeded them:
Forth did his leveled finger go
And, fixing, pointed: "See ye, see?
'Way over where the gray hills be;   185
Yonder—no, there—that upland dim:
Wreck, ho! the wreck—Jerusalem!"
    "Keen-sighted art thou!" said Djalea
Confirming him; "ay, it is there."
    Then Agath, that excitement gone,   190
Relapsed into his quiet tone.

2. THE ENSIGN

Needs well to know the distant site
(Like Agath, who late on the way
From Joppa here had made delay)
Ere, if unprompted, thou aright
Mayst single Zion's mountain out   5
From kindred summits roundabout.
Abandoned quarry mid the hills
Remote, as well one's dream fulfills
Of what Jerusalem should be,
As that vague heap, whose neutral tones   10
Blend in with Nature's, helplessly:
Stony metropolis of stones.
    But much as distant shows the town
Erst glorious under Solomon,
Appears now, in these latter days,   15

To languid eyes, through dwelling haze,
The city St. John saw so bright
With sardonyx and ruby? Gleam
No more, like Monte Rosa's hight,
Thy towers, O New Jerusalem? 20
To Patmos now may visions steal?
Lone crag where lone the ospreys wheel!

Such thought, or something near akin,
Touched Clarel, and perchance might win
(To judge them by their absent air) 25
Others at hand. But not of these
The Illyrian bold: impatient stare
He random flung; then, like a breeze
Which fitful rushes through the glen
Over clansmen low—Prince Charlie's men— 30
Shot down the ledges, while the clang
Of saber 'gainst the stirrup rang,
And clinked the steel shoe on the stone.
His freak of gallantry in cheer
Of barbarous escort ending here, 35
Back for the stronghold dashed he lone.
When died the din, it left them more
Becalmed upon that hollow shore.

Not slack was ocean's wrinkled son
In study of the mountain town— 40
Much like himself, indeed, so gray
Left in life's waste to slow decay.
For index now as he stretched forth
His loose-sleeved arm in sailor way
Pointing the bearings south and north, 45
Derwent, arrested, cried, "Dost bleed?"
Touching the naked skin: "Look here—
A living fresco!" And indeed,
Upon the fore-arm did appear
A thing of art, vermil and blue, 50
A crucifixion in tattoo,
With trickling blood-drops strange to see.

Above that emblem of the loss,
Twin curving palm-boughs draping met
In manner of a canopy   55
Over an equi-limbed small cross
And three tri-spiked and sister crowns:
And under these a star was set:
And all was tanned and toned in browns.
    In chapel erst which knew the mass,   60
A mullioned window's umber glass
Dyed with some saintly legend old,
Obscured by cobwebs; this might hold
Some likeness to the picture rare
On arm here webbed with straggling hair.   65
    "Leave out the crucifixion's hint,"
Said Rolfe, "the rest will show in tint
The *Ensign:* palms, cross, diadems,
And star—the *Sign!*—Jerusalem's,
Coeval with King Baldwin's sway.—   70
Skilled monk in sooth ye need have sought
In Saba."
        Quoth the sea-sage: "Nay;
Sketched out it was one Christmas day
Off Java-Head. Little I thought
(A heedless lad, scarce through youth's straits—   75
How hopeful on the wreckful way)
What meant this thing which here ye see,
The bleeding man upon the tree;
Since then I've felt it, and the fates."
    "Ah—yes," sighed Derwent; "yes, indeed!   80
But 'tis the *Ensign* now we heed."
    The stranger here his dusk eye ran
In reading sort from man to man,
Cleric to sailor—back again.
    "But, shipmate," Derwent cried; "tell me: 85
How came you by this blazonry?"
    "We seamen, when there's naught to do
In calms, the straw for hats we plait,
Or one another we tattoo
With marks we copy from a mate,   90

Which he has from his elders ta'en,
And those from prior ones again;
And few, if any, think or reck
But so with pains their skin to deck.
This crucifixion, though, by some   95
A charm is held 'gainst watery doom."

    "Comrades," said Rolfe, "'tis here we note
Downhanded in a way blind-fold,
A pious use of times remote.
Ah, but it dim grows, and more dim,   100
The gold of legend, that fine gold!
Washed in with wine of Bethlehem,
This *Ensign* in the ages old
Was stamped on every pilgrim's arm
By grave practitioners elect   105
Whose calling lacked not for respect
In Zion. Like the sprig of palm,
Token it was at home, that he
Which bore, had kneeled at Calvary.
Nay, those monk-soldiers helmet-crowned,   110
Whose effigies in armed sleep, lie—
Stone, in the stony Temple round
In London; and (to verify
Them more) with carved greaves crossed, for sign
Of duty done in Palestine;   115
Exceeds it, pray, conjecture fair,
These may have borne this blazon rare,
And not alone on standard fine,
But pricked on chest or sinewy arm,
Pledged to defend against alarm   120
His tomb for whom they warred? But see,
From these mailed Templars now the sign,
Losing the import and true key,
Descends to boatswains of the brine."

    Clarel, reposing there aside,   125
By secret thought preoccupied,
Now, as he inward chafe would shun,

A feigned quick interest put on:
"The import of these marks? Tell me."
        "Come, come," cried Derwent; "dull ye bide!   130
By palm-leaves here are signified
Judæa, as on the Roman gem;
The cross scarce needs a word, agree;
The crowns are for the magi three;
This star—the star of Bethlehem."   135
        "One might have known;" and fell anew
In void relapse.
                "Why, why so blue?"
Derwent again; and rallying ran:
"While now for Bethlehem we aim,
Our stellar friend the post should claim   140
Of guide. We'll put him in the van—
Follow the star on the tattooed man,
We wise men here.—What's that?"
                        A gun,
At distance fired, startles the group.
Around they gaze, and down and up;   145
But in the wilds they seem alone.
Long time the echo sent its din,
Hurled roundabout, and out and in—
A foot-ball tossed from crag to crag;
Then died away in ether thin—   150
Died, as they deemed, yet did but lag,
For all abrupt one far rebound
Gave pause; that o'er, the hush was crowned.
        "We loiter," Derwent said, in tone
Uneasy; "come, shall we go on?"   155
        "Wherefore?" the saturnine demands.
Toward him they look, for his eclipse
There gave way for the first; and stands
The adage old, that one's own lips
Proclaim the character: "A gun: 160
A gun's man's voice—sincerest one.
Blench we to have assurance here,
Here in the waste, that kind is near?"
        Eyes settle on his scars in view,

Both warp and burn, the which evince   165
Experience of the thing he hints.
    "Nay—hark!" and all turn round anew:
Remoter shot came duller there:
"The Arnaut—and but fires in air,"
Djalea averred: "his last adieu."   170

    By chance directed here in thought,
Clarel upon that warrior haught
Low mused: The rowel of thy spur
The robe rips of philosopher!
Naught reckest thou of wisest book: 175
The creeds thou star'st down with a look.
And how the worse for such wild sense?
And where is wisdom's recompense?
And as for heaven—Oh, heavens enlarge
Beyond each designated marge: 180
Valhalla's hall would hardly bar
Welcome to one whose end need be
In grace and grief of harnessed war,
To sink mid swords and minstrelsy.

    So willful! but 'tis loss and smart,   185
Clarel, in thy dissolving heart.
Will't form anew?
                    Vine's watchful eye,
While none perceived where bent his view,
Had fed on Agath sitting by;
He seemed to like him, one whose print   190
The impress bore of Nature's mint
Authentic; man of nature true,
If simple; naught that slid between
Him and the elemental scene—
Unless it were that thing indeed   195
Uplooming from his ancient creed;
Yet that but deepen might the sense
Of awe, and serve dumb reverence
And resignation.—"Anywhere,"
Asked Vine—here now to converse led—   200

"In those far regions, strange or rare,
Where thou hast been, may aught compare
With Judah here?"
                          "Sooth, sir," he said,
"Some chance comparison I've made
In mind, between this stricken land   205
And one far isle forever banned
I camped on in life's early days:
I view it now—but through a haze:
Our boats I view, reversed, turned down
For shelter by the midnight sea;   210
The very slag comes back to me
I raked for shells, but found not one;
That harpy sea-hawk—him I view
Which, pouncing, from the red coal drew
Our hissing meat—we lounging nigh—   215
An instant's dash—and with it flew
To his sea-rock detached, his cry
Thence sent, to mock the marl we threw:—
I hear, I see; return those days
Again—but 'tis through deepening haze: 220
How like a flash that life is gone—
So brief the youth by sailors known!"

        "But tell us, tell," now others cried,
And grouped them as by hearth-stone wide.
The timoneer, at hazard thrown   225
With men of order not his own,
Evinced abashment, yes, proved shy.
They urged; and he could but comply.
        But, more of clearness to confer—
Less dimly to express the thing   230
Rude outlined by this mariner,
License is claimed in rendering;
And tones he felt but scarce might give,
The verse essays to interweave.

3. The Island

"In waters where no charts avail,
Where only fin and spout ye see,
The lonely spout of hermit-whale,
God set that isle which haunteth me.
There clouds hang low, but yield no rain—   5
Forever hang, since wind is none
Or light; nor ship-boy's eye may gain
The smoke-wrapped peak, the inland one
Volcanic; this, within its shroud
Streaked black and red, burns unrevealed;   10
It burns by night—by day the cloud
Shows leaden all, and dull and sealed.
The beach is cinders. With the tide
Salt creek and ashy inlet bring
More loneness from the outer ring   15
Of ocean."
        Pause he made, and sighed.—
"But take the way across the marl,
A broken field of tumbled slabs
Like ice-cakes frozen in a snarl
After the break-up in a sound;   20
So win the thicket's upper ground
Where silence like a poniard stabs,
Since there the low throb of the sea
Not heard is, and the sea-fowl flee
Far off the shore, all the long day   25
Hunting the flying-fish their prey.
Haply in bush ye find a path:
Of man or beast it scarce may be;
And yet a wasted look it hath,
As it were traveled ceaselessly—   30
Century after century—
The rock in places much worn down
Like to some old, old kneeling-stone
Before a shrine. But naught's to see,
At least naught there was seen by me,   35
Of any moving, creeping one.

No berry do those thickets bear,
Nor many leaves. Yet even there,
Some sailor from the steerage den
Put sick ashore—alas, by men   40
Who, weary of him, thus abjure—
The way may follow, in pursuit
Of apples red—the homestead-fruit
He dreams of in his calenture.
He drops, lost soul; but we go on—   45
Advance, until in end be won
The terraced orchard's mysteries,
Which well do that imp-isle beseem;
Paved with jet blocks those terraces,
The surface rubbed to unctuous gleam   50
By something which has life, you feel:
And yet, the shades but death reveal;
For under cobwebbed cactus trees,
White by their trunks—what hulks be these
Which, like old skulls of Anaks, are   55
Set round as in a Golgotha?
But, list,—a sound! Dull, dull it booms—
Dull as the jar in vaulted tombs
When urns are shifted. With amaze
Into the dim retreats ye gaze.   60
Lo, 'tis the monstrous tortoise drear!
Of huge humped arch, the ancient shell
Is trenched with seams where lichens dwell,
Or some adhesive growth and sere:
A lumpish languor marks the pace—   65
A hideous, harmless look, with trace
Of hopelessness; the eyes are dull
As in the bog the dead black pool:
Penal his aspect; all is dragged,
As he for more than years had lagged—   70
A convict doomed to bide the place;
A soul transformed—for earned disgrace
Degraded, and from higher race.
Ye watch him—him so woe-begone:
Searching, he creeps with laboring neck,   75

Each crevice tries, and long may seek:
Water he craves, where rain is none—
Water within the parching zone,
Where only dews of midnight fall
And dribbling lodge in chinks of stone.   80
For meat the bitter tree is all—
The cactus, whose nipped fruit is shed
On those bleached skull-like hulks below,
Which, when by life inhabited,
Crept hither in last journey slow   85
After a hundred years of pain
And pilgrimage here to and fro,
For other hundred years to reign
In hollow of white armor so—
Then perish piecemeal. You advance: 90
Instant, more rapid than a glance,
Long neck and four legs are drawn in,
Letting the shell down with report
Upon the stone; so falls in court
The clattering buckler with a din.   95
There leave him, since for hours he'll keep
That feint of death.—But for the isle——
Much seems it like this barren steep:
As here, few there would think to smile."

So, paraphrased in lines sincere   100
Which still similitude would win,
The sketch ran of that timoneer.
He ended, and how passive sate:
Nature's own look, which might recall
Dumb patience of mere animal,   105
Which better may abide life's fate
Than comprehend.
                    What may man know?
(Here pondered Clarel;) let him rule—
Pull down, build up, creed, system, school,
And reason's endless battle wage,   110
Make and remake his verbiage—
But solve the world! Scarce that he'll do:

Too wild it is, too wonderful.
Since *this* world, then, can baffle so—
Our natural harbor—it were strange   115
If *that* alleged, which is afar,
Should not confound us when we range
In revery where its problems are.—
Such thoughts! and can they e'en be mine
In fount? Did Derwent true divine   120
Upon the tower of Saba—yes,
Hinting I too much felt the stress
Of Rolfe—or whom? Green and unsure,
And in attendance on a mind
Poised at self-center and mature,   125
Do I but lacquey it behind?
Yea, here in frame of thought and word
But wear the cast clothes of my lord?

4. AN INTRUDER

Quiet Agath, with a start, just then
Shrieked out, abhorrent or in fright.
Disturbed in its pernicious den
Amid dry flints and shards of blight,
A crabbed scorpion, dingy brown,   5
With nervous tail slant upward thrown
(Like to a snake's wroth neck and head
Dilating when the coil's unmade
Before the poor affrighted clown
Whose foot offends it unbeknown)   10
Writhing, faint crackling, like wire spring,
With anguish of the poisonous bile
Inflaming the slim duct, the while
In act of shooting toward the sting;
This, the unblest, small, evil thing,   15
'Tis this they mark, wriggling in range,
Fearless, and with ill menace, strange
In such a minim.

Derwent rose,
And Clarel; Vine and Rolfe remained
At gaze; the soldier too and Druze.   20
Cried Rolfe, while thus they stood enchained:
"O small epitome of devil,
Wert thou an ox couldst thou thus sway?
No, disproportionate is evil
In influence. *Evil* do I say?   25
But speak not evil of the evil:
Evil and good they braided play
Into one cord."
                        While they delay,
The object vanished. Turning head
Toward the salt one, Derwent said: 30
"The thing's not sweet; but why start so,
My good man, you that frequent know
The wonders of the deep?" He flushed,
And in embarrassment kept dumb.
But Rolfe here to the rescue pushed: 35
"Men not deemed craven will succumb
To such an apparition. Why,
Soldiers, that into battle marching
Elastic pace with instep arching—
Sailors (and *he's* a sailor nigh)   40
Who out upon the jib-boom hie,
At world's end, in the midnight gale,
And wrestle with the thrashing sail,
The while the speared spar like a javelin flies
Slant up from thundering seas to skies   45
Electric:—these—I've known one start
Seeing a spider run athwart!"

In common-place here lightly blew
Across them through the desert air
A whiff from pipe that Belex smoked: 50
The Druze his sleek mare smooth bestroked,
Then gave a sign. One parting view
At Zion blurred, and on they fare.

5. OF THE STRANGER

While Agath was his story telling
(Ere yet the ill thing worked surprise)
The officer with forest eyes
Still kept them dwelling, somber dwelling
On that mild merman gray. His mien   5
In part was that of one who tries
Something outside his own routine
Of memories, all too profuse
In personal pain monotonous.
And yet derived he little here,   10
As seemed, to soothe his mind—austere
With deep impressions uneffaced.
At chance allusion—at the hint
That the dragged tortoise bore the print
Of something mystic and debased,   15
How glowed the comment in his eyes:
No cynic fire sarcastic; nay,
But deeper in the startled sway
Of illustrations to surmise.
        Ever on him they turned the look,   20
While yet the hearing not forsook
The salt seer while narration ran.
The desert march resumed, in thought
They dwell, till Rolfe the Druze besought
If he before had met this man—   25
So distant, though a countryman
By birth. Why, yes—had met him: see,
Drilling some tawny infantry
In shadow of a Memphian wall,
White-robed young conscripts up the Nile;   30
And, afterward, on Jaffa beach,
With Turkish captains holding speech
Over some cannon in a pile
Late landed—with the conic ball.
No more? No more the Druze let fall,   35
If more he knew.
                Thought Rolfe: Ay me,
Ay me, poor Freedom, can it be

A countryman's a refugee?
What maketh him abroad to roam,
Sharing with infidels a home? 40
Is it the immense charred solitudes
Once farms? and chimney-stacks that reign
War-burnt upon the houseless plain
Of hearthstones without neighborhoods?
Is it the wilds whose memories own 45
More specters than the woods bestrown
With Varus' legions mossy grown?
Is't misrule after strife? and dust
From victor heels? Is it disgust
For times when honor's out of date 50
And serveth but to alienate?
The usurping altar doth he scout—
The Parsee of a sun gone out?
And this, may all this mar his state?
His very virtues, in the blench 55
And violence of fortune's wrench,
Alas, serve but to vitiate?
Strong natures have a strong recoil
Whose shock may wreck them or despoil.
Oh, but it yields a thought that smarts, 60
To note this man. Our New World bold
Had fain improved upon the Old;
But the hemispheres are counterparts.
    So inly Rolfe; and did incline
In briefer question there to Vine, 65
Who could but answer him with eyes
Opulent in withheld replies.
    And here—without a thought to chide—
Feeling the tremor of the ground—
Reluctant touching on the wound 70
Unhealed yet in our mother's side;
Behooveth it to hint in brief
The rankling thing in Ungar's grief;
For bravest grieve.—That evil day,
Black in the New World's calendar— 75
The dolorous winter ere the war;
True Bridge of Sighs—so yet 'twill be

Esteemed in riper history—
Sad arch between contrasted eras;
The span of fate; that evil day   80
When the cadets from rival zones,
Tradition's generous adherers,
Their country's pick and flower of sons,
Abrupt were called upon to act—
For life or death, nor brook delay—   85
Touching construction of a pact,
A paper pact, with points abstruse
As theologic ones—profuse
In matter for an honest doubt;
And which, in end, a stubborn knot   90
Some cut but with the sword; that day
With its decision, yet could sway
Ungar, and plunging thoughts excite.
Reading and revery imped his pain,
Confirmed, and made it take a flight   95
Beyond experience and the reign
Of self; till, in a sort, the man
Grew much like that Pamphylian
Who, dying (as the fable goes)
In walks of Hades met with those   100
Which, though he was a sage of worth,
Did such new pregnancies implant,
Hadean lore, he did recant
All science he had brought from earth.
Herewith in Ungar, though, ensued   105
A bias, bitterness—a strain
Much like an Indian's hopeless feud
Under the white's aggressive reign.
Indian's the word; nor it impeach
For over-pointedness of speech;   110
No, let the story rearward run
And its propriety be shown:

    Up Chesapeake in days of old,
By winding banks whose curves unfold
Cape after cape in bright remove,   115
Steered the ship *Ark* with her attendant *Dove.*

From the non-conformists' zeal or bile
Which urged, inflamed the civil check
Upon the dreaded Popish guile,
The New World's fairer flowers and dews 120
Welcomed the English Catholic:
Like sheltering arms the shores expand
To embrace and take to heart the crews.
Care-worn, sea-worn, and tempest-tanned,
Devout they hail that harbor green; 125
And, mindful of heaven's gracious Queen
And Britain's princess, name it Mary-Land.
It was from one of Calvert's friends
The exile of the verse descends;
And gifts, brave gifts, and martial fame 130
Won under Tilly's great command
That sire of after-sires might claim.
But heedless, in the Indian glade
He wedded with a wigwam maid,
Transmitting through his line, far down, 135
Along with touch in lineaments,
A latent nature, which events
Developed in this distant son,
And overrode the genial part—
An Anglo brain, but Indian heart. 140
And yet not so but Ungar knew
(In freak, his forest name alone
Retained he now) that instinct true
Which tempered him in years bygone,
When, spite the prejudice of kin 145
And custom, he with friends could be
Outspoken in his heart's belief
That holding slaves was aye a grief—
The system an iniquity
In those who plant it and begin; 150
While for inheritors—alas,
Who knows? and let the problem pass.
  But now all that was over—gone;
Now was he the self-exiled one.
Too steadfast! Wherefore should be lent 155
The profitless high sentiment?

Renounce conviction in defeat:
Pass over, share the spoiler's seat
And thrive. Behooves thee else turn cheek
To fate with wisdom of the meek.   160
Wilt not? Unblest then with the store
Of heaven, and spurning worldly lore
Astute, eat thou thy cake of pride,
And henceforth live on unallied.—
His passion, that—mused, never said;   165
And his own pride did him upbraid.

    The habit of his mind, and tone
Tenacious touching issues gone,
Expression found, nor all amiss,
In thing he'd murmur: it was this: 170

        "Who abideth by the dead
    Which ye hung before your Lord?
    Steadfast who, when all have fled
    Tree and corse abhorred?
    Who drives off the wolf, the kite—   175
    Bird by day, and beast by night,
    And keeps the hill through all?
    It is Rizpah: true is one
    Unto death; nor then will shun
    The Seven throttled and undone,   180
    To glut the foes of Saul."

    That for the past; and for the surge
Reactionary, which years urge:

    "Elating and elate,
    Do they mount them in their pride?   185
        Let them wait a little, wait,
    For the brimming of the flood
        Brings the turning of the tide."

    His lyric. Yet in heart of hearts
Perchance its vanity he knew,   190

At least suspected. What to do?
Time cares not to avenge your smarts,
But presses on, impatient of review.

6. BETHLEHEM

Over uplands now toward eve they pass
By higher uplands tinged with grass.
Lower it crept as they went on—
Grew in advance, and rugged the ground;
Yea, seemed before these pilgrims thrown   5
To carpet them to royal bound.
Each rider here in saddle-seat
Lounges relaxed, and glads his sight;
Solomon whinnies; those small feet
Of Zar tread lightly and more light: 10
Even Agath's ass the awakened head
Turns for a nibble. So they sped,
Till now Djalea turns short aside,
Ascends, and by a happy brink
Makes halt, and beckons them to ride   15
And there with him at pleasure drink
A prospect good.
          Below, serene
In oliveyards and vineyards fair,
They view a theater pale green
Of terraces, which stair by stair   20
Rise toward most venerable walls
On summits twin, and one squared heap
Of buttressed masonry based deep
Adown the crag on lasting pedestals.
    Though on that mount but towers convene,   25
And hamlet none nor cot they see,
They cannot choose but know the scene;
And Derwent's eyes show humidly:
"What other hill? We view it here:
Blessed in story, and heart-cheer,   30
Hail to thee, Bethlehem of Judæa!

Oh, look: as if with conscious sense
Here nature shows meet reverence:
See, at the sacred mountain's feet
How kneels she with her fragrance sweet,   35
And swathes them with her grasses fair:
So Mary with the spikenard shed
A lowly love, and bowed her head
And made a napkin of her trailing hair."

He turned, but met no answering eyes;   40
The animation of surprise
Had vanished; strange, but they were dumb:
What wayward afterthought had come?
Those dim recurrings in the mind,
Sad visitations ill defined,   45
Which led the trio erst that met
Upon the crown of Olivet
Nehemiah's proffer to decline
When he invited them away
To Bethany—might such things sway   50
Even these by Bethlehem? The sign
Derwent respected, and he said
No more. And so, with spirits shrunk
Over the placid hills they tread
And win the stronghold of the monk.   55

7. AT TABLE

As shipwrecked men adrift, whose boat
In war-time on the houseless seas
Draws nigh to some embattled hull
With pinnacles and traceries—
Grim abbey on the wave afloat;   5
And mark her bulwarks sorrowful
With briny stains, and answering mien
And cenobite dumb discipline,
And homely uniform of crew

Peering from ports where cannon lean, 10
Or pacing in deep galleries far,
Black cloisters of the god of war;
And hear a language which is new
Or foreign: so now with this band
Who, after desert rovings, win 15
The fort monastic, close at hand,
Survey it, meditate it—see,
Through vaultings, the girt Capuchin,
Or list his speech of Italy.

Up to the arch the graybeard train 20
Of Bethlehemites attend, salute,
And in expectancy remain
At stand; their escort ending here,
They wait the recompense and fruit;
'Tis given; and with friendly cheer 25
Parting, they bear a meed beyond
The dry price set down in the bond.
The bonus Derwent did suggest,
Saying: "They're old: of all sweet food
Naught they take in so cheers their blood 30
As ruddy coin; it pads the vest."
Belex abides—true as his steel
To noble pilgrims which such largess deal.
While these now at refection sit,
Rolfe speaks: "Provided for so well, 35
Much at our ease methinks we dwell.
Our merit's guerdon? far from it!
Unworthy, here we welcome win
Where Mary found no room at inn."
"True, true," the priest sighed, staying there 40
The cup of Bethlehem wine in hand;
Then sipped; yet by sad absent air
The flavor seeming to forswear;
Nor less the juice did glad the gland.
The abstemious Ungar noted all, 45
Grave silence keeping. Rolfe let fall:

"Strange! of the sacred places here,
And all through Palestine indeed,
Not one we Protestants hold dear
Enough to tend and care for."
                      "Pray,"   50
The priest, "and why now should that breed
Astonishment? but say your say."
      "Why, Shakespeare's house in Stratford town
Ye keep with loving tendance true,
Set it apart in reverence due: 55
A shrine to which the pilgrim's won
Across an ocean's stormy tide:
What zeal, what faith is there implied;
Pure worship localized in grace,
Tradition sole providing base."   60
      "Your drift I catch. And yet I think
That they who most and deepest drink
At Shakespeare's fountain, scarce incline
To idolize the local shrine:
What's in mere place that can bestead?"   65
      "Nay, 'tis the heart here, not the head.
You note some pilgrims hither bring
The rich or humble offering:
If that's irrational—what then?
In kindred way your Lutheran   70
Will rival it; yes, in sad hour
The Lutheran widow lays her flower
Before the picture of the dead:
Vital affections do not draw
Precepts from Reason's arid law."   75
      "Ah, clever! But we won't contend.
As for these *Places,* my dear friend,
Thus stands the matter—as you know:
Ere Luther yet made his demur,
These legend-precincts high and low   80
In custody already were
Of Greek and Latin, who retain.
So, even did we wish to be

Shrine-keepers here and share the fee—
No sites for Protestants remain."   85

    The compline service they attend;
Then bedward, travel-worn, they wend;
And, like a bland breeze out of heaven,
The gracious boon of sleep is given.

    But Ungar, islanded in thought   90
Which not from place a prompting caught,
Alone, upon the terrace stair
Lingered, in adoration there
Of Eastern skies: "Now night enthrones
Arcturus and his shining sons;   95
And lo, Job's chambers of the South:
How might his hand not go to mouth
In kiss adoring ye, bright zones?
Look up: the age, the age forget—
There's something to look up to yet!"   100

8. THE PILLOW

When rule and era passed away
With old Sylvanus (stories say),
The oracles adrift were hurled,
And ocean moaned about the world,
And wandering voices without name   5
At sea to sailors did proclaim,
Pan, Pan is dead!
            Such fables old—
From man's deep nature are they rolled,
Pained and perplexed—awed, overawed
By sense of change? But never word   10
Aërial by mortal heard,
Rumors that vast eclipse, if slow,
Whose passage yet we undergo,
Emerging on an age untried.

If not all oracles be dead,   15
The upstart ones the old deride:
Parrots replace the sibyls fled—
By rote repeat in lilting pride:

    Lodged in power, enlarged in all,
    Man achieves his last exemption—   20
    Hopes no heaven, but fears no fall,
    King in time, nor needs redemption.

    They hymn. But these who cloistral dwell
In Bethlehem here, and share faith's spell
Meekly, and keep her tenor mild—   25
What know they of a world beguiled?
Or, knowing, they but know too well.

    Buzzed thoughts! To Rolfe they came in doze
(His brain like ocean's murmuring shell)
Between the dream and slumber's light repose.   30

9. The Shepherds' Dale

"Up, up! Around morn's standard rally;
She makes a sortie—join the sally:
Up, slugabeds; up, up!"
               That call
Ere matins did each pilgrim hear
In cell, and knew the blithe voice clear.   5
    "Beshrew thee, thou'rt poetical,"
Rolfe murmured from his place withdrawn.
    "Ay, brother; but 'tis not surprising:
Apollo's the god of early rising.
Up, up! The negro-groom of Night   10
Leads forth the horses of the Dawn!
Up, up!" So Derwent, jocund sprite—
Although but two days now were passed
Since he had viewed a sunrise last—
Persuaded them to join him there   15

And unto convent roof repair.
Thought one: He's of no nature surly,
So cheerful in the morning early.
    Sun-worship over, they came down:
And Derwent lured them forth, and on. 20
    Behind the Convent lies a dale,
The Valley of the Shepherds named,
(And never may the title fail!)
By old tradition fondly claimed
To be in truth the very ground 25
About whose hollow, on the mound
Of hills, reclined in dozing way
That simple group ere break of day,
Which, startled by their flocks' dismay—
All bleating up to them in panic 30
And sparkling in scintillant ray—
Beheld a splendor diaphanic—
Effulgence never dawn hath shot,
Nor flying meteors of the night;
And trembling rose, shading the sight; 35
But heard the angel breathe—*Fear not.*
So (might one reverently dare
Terrene with heavenly to compare),
So, oft in mid-watch on that sea
Where the ridged Andes of Peru 40
Are far seen by the coasting crew—
Waves, sails and sailors in accord
Illumed are in a mystery,
Wonder and glory of the Lord,
Though manifest in aspect minor— 45
Phosphoric ocean in shekinah.

    And down now in that dale they go,
Meeting a little St. John boy
In sackcloth shirt and belt of tow,
Leading his sheep. Ever behind 50
He kept one hand, stained with a shrub,
The which an ewe licked, never coy;
And all the rest with docile mind

Followed; and fleece with fleece did rub.
   Beyond, hard by twin planted tents,   55
Paced as in friendly conference
Two shepherds on the pastoral hill,
Brown patriarchs in shaggy cloak;
Peaceful they went, as in a yoke
The oxen unto pasture oak   60
To lie in shade when noon is still.
Nibbling the herb, or far or near,
Advanced their flocks, and yet would veer,
For width of range makes wayward will.

   Ungar beheld: "What treat they of?   65
Halving the land?—This might reclaim
Old years of Lot and Abraham
Just ere they parted in remove:
A peaceful parting: 'Let there be
No strife, I pray thee, between me   70
And thee, my herdmen and thine own;
For we be brethren. See, the land
Is all before thee, fenced by none:
Then separate thyself from me,
I pray thee. If now the left hand   75
Thou, Lot, wilt take, then I will go
Unto the right; if thou depart
Unto the right, then I will go
Unto the left.'—They parted so,
And not unwisely: both were wise.   80
'Twas East and West; but *North* and *South!*"
   Rolfe marked the nip of quivering mouth,
Passion repressed within the eyes;
But ignorance feigned: "This calm," he said,
"How fitly hereabout is shed: 85
The site of Eden's placed not far;
In bond 'tween man and animal
Survives yet under Asia's star
A link with years before the Fall."
   "Indeed," cried Derwent, pleased thereat,   90
"Blest, blest is here the creature's state.

Those pigeons, now, in Saba's hold,
Their wings how winsome would they fold
Alighting at one's feet so soft.
Doves, too, in mosque, I've marked aloft,   95
At hour of prayer through window come
From trees adjacent, and a'thrill
Perch, coo, and nestle in the dome,
Or fly with green sprig in the bill.
How by the marble fount in court,   100
Where for ablution Turks resort
Ere going in to hear the Word,
These small apostles they regard
Which of sweet innocence report.
None stone the dog; caressed, the steed;   105
Only poor Dobbin (Jew indeed
Of brutes) seems slighted in the East."

    Ungar, who chafed in heart of him
At Rolfe's avoidance of his theme
(Although he felt he scarce could blame),   110
Here turned his vexed mood on the priest:
"As cruel as a Turk: Whence came
That proverb old as the crusades?
From Anglo-Saxons. What are they?
Let the horse answer, and blockades   115
Of medicine in civil fray!
The Anglo-Saxons—lacking grace
To win the love of any race;
Hated by myriads dispossessed
Of rights—the Indians East and West.   120
These pirates of the sphere! grave looters—
Grave, canting, Mammonite freebooters,
Who in the name of Christ and Trade
(Oh, bucklered forehead of the brass!)
Deflower the world's last sylvan glade!"   125
    "Alas, alas, ten times alas,
Poor Anglo-Saxons!" Derwent sighed.
    "Nay, but if there I lurched too wide,
Respond to this: Old ballads sing

Fair Christian children crucified   130
By impious Jews: you've heard the thing:
Yes, fable; but there's truth hard by:
How many Hughs of Lincoln, say,
Does Mammon in his mills, to-day,
Crook, if he do not crucify?"   135
   "Ah, come," said Derwent; "come, now, come;
Think you that we who build the home
For foundlings, and yield sums immense
To hospitals for indigence——"
   "Your alms-box, smaller than your till,   140
And poor-house won't absolve your mill.
But what ye are, a straw may tell—
Your dearth of phrases affable.
Italian, French—more tongues than these—
Addresses have of courtesies   145
In kindliness of man toward man,
By prince used and by artisan,
And not pervertible in sense
Of scorn or slight. Ye have the *Sir,*
That sole, employed in snub or slur,   150
Never in pure benevolence,
And at its best a formal term
Of cold regard."
         "Ah, why so warm
In mere philology, dear sir?"
Plead Derwent; "there, don't that confer   155
Sweet amity? I used the word."
   But Ungar heeded not—scarce heard;
And, earnest as the earnest tomb,
With added feeling, sting, and gloom
His strange impeachment urged. Reply   160
Came none; they let it go; for why
Argue with man of bitter blood?
But Rolfe he could but grieve within
For countryman in such a mood—
Knowing the cause, the origin.   165

10. A Monument

Wise Derwent, that discourse to end,
Pointed athwart the dale divine:
"What's yonder object—fountain? shrine?
Companions, let us thither go
And make inspection."
                    In consent   5
Silent they follow him in calm.
It proved an ancient monument—
Rude stone; but tablets lent a charm:
Three tablets on three sides. In one
The Tender Shepherd mild looked down   10
Upon the rescued weanling lost,
Snugged now in arms. In emblem crossed
By pastoral crook, Christ's monogram
(Wrought with a medieval grace)
Showed on the square opposed in face.   15
But chiefly did they feel the claim
Of the main tablet; there a lamb
On passive haunches upright sate
In patience which reproached not fate;
The two fine furry fore-legs drooping   20
Like tassels; while the shearer, stooping,
Embraced it with one arm; and all
The fleece rolled off in seamless shawl
Flecked here and there with hinted blood.
It did not shrink; no cry did come: 25
In still life of that stone subdued
Shearer and shorn alike were dumb.

As with a seventy-four, when lull
Lapses upon the storm, the hull
Rights for the instant, while a moan   30
Of winds succeeds the howl; so here
In poise of heart and altered tone
With Ungar. Respite brief though dear
It proved; for he: "This type's assigned
To One who sharing not man's mind   35

Partook man's frame; whose mystic birth
Wrecked him upon this reef of earth
Inclement and inhuman. Yet,
Through all the trials that beset,
He leaned on an upholding arm—   40
Foreknowing, too, reserves of balm.
But how of them whose souls may claim
Some link with Christ beyond the name,
Which share the fate, but never share
Aid or assurance, and nowhere   45
Look for requital? Such there be;
In by-lanes o'er the world ye see
The Calvary-faces." All averse
Turned Derwent, murmuring, "Forbear.
Such breakers do the heaven asperse!"   50
      But timely he alert espied,
Upon the mountain humbly kneeling,
Those shepherds twain, while morning-tide
Rolled o'er the hills with golden healing.
It was a rock they kneeled upon,   55
Convenient for their rite avowed—
Kneeled, and their turbaned foreheads bowed—
Bowed over, till they kissed the stone:
Each shaggy sur-coat heedful spread
For rug, such as in mosque is laid.   60
About the ledge's favored hem
Mild fed their sheep, enringing them;
While, facing as by second-sight,
Toward Mecca they direct the rite.
      "Look; and their backs on Bethlehem turned,"   65
Cried Rolfe. The priest then, who discerned
The drift, replied, "Yes, for they pray
To Allah. Well, and what of that?
Christ listens, standing in heaven's gate—
Benignant listens, nor doth stay   70
Upon a syllable in creed:
Vowels and consonants indeed!"
      And Rolfe: "But here were Margoth now,
Seeing yon shepherds praying so,

His gibe would run from man to man: 75
'Which is the humble publican?
Or do they but prostrate them there
To flout you Franks with Islam's prayer?' ''
        ''Doubtless: some shallow thing he'd say,
Poor fellow,'' Derwent then; ''but, nay,   80
Earnest they are; nor yet they'd part
(If pealed the hour) in street or mart,
From like observance.''
                        ''If 'tis so''
The refugee, ''let all avow
As openly faith's loyal heart.   85
By Christians too was God confessed
How frankly! in those days that come
No more to misnamed Christendom!
Religion then was the good guest,
First served, and last, in every gate: 90
What mottoes upon wall and plate!
She every human venture shared:
The ship in manifest declared
That not disclaiming heaven she thrust
Her bowsprit into fog and storm: 95
Some current silver bore the palm
Of Christ, token of saint, or bust;
In line devout the pikemen kneeled—
To battle by the rite were sealed.
Men were not lettered, but had sense   100
Beyond the mean intelligence
That knows to read, and but to read—
Not think. 'Twas harder to mislead
The people then, whose smattering now
Does but the more their ignorance show—   105
Nay, them to peril more expose—
Is as the ring in the bull's nose
Whereby a pert boy turns and winds
This monster of a million minds.
Men owned true masters; kings owned God—   110
Their master; Louis plied the rod
Upon himself. In high estate,

Not puffed up like a democrat
In office, how with Charlemagne?
Look up he did, look up in reign—   115
Humbly look up, who might look down:
His meekest thing was still his crown:
How meek on *him;* since, graven there,
Among the Apostles twelve—behold,
Stern Scriptural precepts were enrolled,   120
High admonitions, meet for kings.
The coronation was a prayer,
Which yet in ceremonial clings.
The church was like a bonfire warm:
All ranks were gathered round the charm."   125
  Derwent, who vainly had essayed
To impede the speaker, or blockade,
Snatched at the bridle here: "Ho, wait;
A word, impetuous laureate!
This *bric-a-brac-ish* style (outgrown   130
Almost, where first it gave the tone)
Of lauding the quaint ages old—
But nay, that's satire; I withhold.
Grant your side of the shield part true:
What then? why, turn the other: view   135
The buckler in reverse. Don't sages
Denominate those times Dark Ages?
Dark Middle Ages, time's midnight!"
  "If night, it was no starless one;
Art still admires what then was done: 140
A strength they showed which is of light.
Not more the Phidian marbles prove
The graces of the Grecian prime
And indicate what men they were,
Than the grand minsters in remove   145
Do intimate, if not declare
A magnanimity which our time
Would envy, were it great enough
To comprehend. Your counterbuff,
However, holds. Yes, frankly, yes,   150
Another side there is, admit.

Nor less the very worst of it
Reveals not such a shamelessness
Of evildoer and hypocrite,
And sordid mercenary sin   155
As these days vaunt and revel in."
    "No use, no use," the priest aside;
"Patience! it is the maddest tide;"
And seated him.
               And Ungar then:
"What's overtaken ye pale men?   160
Shrewd are ye, the main chance ye heed:
Has God quite lost his throne indeed
That lukewarm now ye grow? Wilt own,
Council ye take with fossil-stone?
Your sects do nowadays create   165
Churches as worldly as the state.
And, for your more established forms—
Ah, once in York I viewed through storms
The Minster's majesty of mien—
Towers, peaks, and pinnacles sublime—   170
Faith's iceberg, stranded on a scene
How alien, and an alien time;
But now"—he checked himself, and stood.

    Whence this strange bias of his mood
(Thought they) leaning to things corroded,   175
By many deemed for aye exploded?
But, truly, knowing not the man,
At fault they in conjecture ran.
But Ungar (as in fitter place
Set down) being sprung from Romish race,   180
Albeit himself had spared to feed
On any one elected creed
Or rite, though much he might recall
In annals bearing upon all;
And, in this land named of Behest,   185
A wandering Ishmael from the West;
Inherited the Latin mind,
Which late—blown by the adverse wind

Of harder fortunes that molest—
Kindled from ember into coal.   190

    The priest, as one who keeps him whole,
Anew turns toward the kneeling twain:
"Your error's slight, or, if a stain,
'Twill fade. Our Lord enjoins good deeds
Nor catechiseth in the creeds."   195
    A something in the voice or man,
Or in assumption of the turn
Which prior theme did so adjourn,
Pricked Ungar, and a look he ran
Toward Derwent—an electric light   200
Chastising in its fierce revolt;
Then settled into that still night
Of cloud which has discharged the bolt.

11. DISQUIET

At breakfast in refectory there
The priest—if Clarel not mistook—
The good priest wore the troubled air
Of honest heart striving to brook
Injury, which from words abstained,   5
And, hence, not readily arraigned;
Which to requite in its own sort
Is not allowed in heaven's high court,
Or self-respect's. Such would forget,
But for the teasing doubt or fret   10
Lest unto worldly witness mere
The injury none the less appear
To challenge notice at the least.

    Ungar withdrew, leaving the priest
Less ill at ease; who now a thought   15
Threw out, as 'twere in sad concern
For one whose nature, sour or stern,
Still dealt in all unhandsome flings

At happy times and happy things:
" 'The bramble sayeth it is naught:'   20
Poor man!" But that; and quite forbore
To vent his grievance. Nor less sore
He felt it—Clarel so inferred,
Recalling here too Mortmain's word
Of cutting censorship. How then?   25
While most who met him frank averred
That Derwent ranked with best of men,
The Swede and refugee unite
In one repugnance, yea, and slight.
How take, construe their ill-content?   30
A thing of vein and temperament?
Rolfe liked him; and if Vine said naught,
Yet even Vine seemed not uncheered
By fair address. Then stole the thought
Of how the priest had late appeared   35
In that one confidential hour,
Ambiguous on Saba's tower.
There he dismissed it, let it fall:
To probe overmuch seems finical.
Nor less (for still the point did tease,   40
Nor would away and leave at ease),
Nor less, I wonder, if ere long
He'll turn this off, not worth a song,
As lightly as of late he turned
Poor Mortmain's sally when he burned?   45

12. Of Pope and Turk

Marking the priest not all sedate,
Rolfe, that a friend might fret discard,
Turned his attention to debate
Between two strangers at the board.
In furtherance of his point or plea   5
One said:

        "Late it was told to me,
And by the man himself concerned,

A merchant Frank on Syria's coast,
That in a fire which traveled post,
His books and records being burned,   10
His Christian debtors held their peace;
The Islam ones disclaimed release,
And came with purses and accounts."
     "And duly rendered their amounts?
'Twas very kind. But oh, the greed,   15
Rapacity, and crime at need
In satraps which oppress the throng."
"True. But with these 'tis, after all,
Wrong-doing purely personal—
Not legislated—not a wrong   20
Law-sanctioned. No: the Turk, admit,
In scheme of state, the scheme of it,
Upon the civil arm confers
A sway above the scimeter's—
The civil power itself subjects   25
Unto that Koran which respects
Nor place nor person. Nay, adjourn
The jeer; for now aside we'll turn.
Dismembered Poland and her throe
In Ninety-Five, all unredressed: 30
Did France, did England then protest?"
     "England? I'm sure I do not know.
Come, I distrust your shifting so.
Pray, to what end now is this pressed?"
     "Why, here armed Christendom looking on,   35
In protest the Sultan stood alone."
     "Indeed? But all this, seems to me,
Savors of Urquhart's vanity."
     "The commentator on the East?"
     "The same: that very inexact   40
Eccentric ideologist
Now obsolete."
                    "And that's your view?
He stands for God."
                    "*I* stand by fact."
     "Well then, another fact or two;

When Poland's place in Thirty-One   45
Was blotted out, the Turk again
Protested, with one other man,
The Pope; these, and but these alone;
And in the protest both avowed
'Twas made for justice's sake and God.—   50
You smile."
        "Oh no: but very clear
The protest prompted was by fear
In Turk and Pope, that time might come
When spoliation should drive home
Upon themselves. Besides, you know   55
The Polish church was Catholic:
The Czar would wrest it to the Greek:
'Twas *that* touched Rome. But let it go.—
In pith, what is it you would show?
Are Turks our betters? Very strange   60
Heaven's favor does not choicely range
Upon these Islam people good:
Bed-rid they are, behindhand all,
While Europe flowers in plenitude
Of wealth and commerce."
          "I recall   65
Nothing in Testament which saith
That worldliness shall not succeed
In that wherein it laboreth.
Howbeit, the Sultan's coming on:
Fine lesson from ye has he won   70
Of late; apt pupil he indeed:
Ormus, that riches did confer,
Ormus is made a borrower:
Selim, who grandly turbaned sat,
Verges on bankruptcy and—hat.   75
But this don't touch the rank and file;
At least, as yet. But preach and work:
You'll civilize the barbarous Turk—
Nay, all the East may reconcile:
That done, let Mammon take the wings of even,   80
And mount and civilize the saints in heaven."

"I laugh—I like a brave caprice!
And, sir——"
            But here did Rolfe release
His ear, and Derwent too. A stir
In court was heard of man and steed—   85
Neighings and mountings, din indeed;
And Rolfe: "Come, come; our traveler."

13. THE CHURCH OF THE STAR

They rise, and for a little space
In farewell Agath they detain,
Transferred here to a timelier train
Than theirs. A work-day, passive face
He turns to Derwent's *Luck to thee!*   5
No slight he means—'tis far from that;
But, schooled by the inhuman sea,
He feels 'tis vain to wave the hat
In God-speed on this mortal strand;
Recalling all the sailing crews   10
Destined to sleep in ocean sand,
Cheered from the wharf with blithe adieus.
Nor less the heart's farewell they say,
And bless the old man on his way.

    Led by a slender monk and young,   15
With curls that ringed the shaven crown,
Courts now and shrines they trace. That thong
Ascetic which can life chastise
Down to her bleak necessities,
They mark in coarse serge of his gown,   20
And girdling rope, with cross of wood
For tag at end; and hut-like hood
Superfluous now behind him thrown;
And sandals which expose the skin
Transparent, and the blue vein thin   25
Meandering there: the feet, the face
Alike in lucid marble grace.

His simple manners self-possessed
Both saint and noble-born suggest;
Yet under quietude they mark   30
The slumbering of a vivid spark—
Excitable, if brought to test.
A Tuscan, he exchanged the charm
Val d'Arno yields, for this dull calm
Of desert. Was his youth self-given   35
In frank oblation unto heaven?
Or what inducement might disarm
This Isaac when too young to know?

    Hereon they, pacing, muse—till, lo,
The temple opens in dusk glades   40
Of long-drawn double colonnades:
Monoliths two-score and eight.
Rolfe looked about him, pleased in state:
"But this is goodly! Here we rove
As down the deep Dodona grove: 45
Years, years and years these boles have stood!—
Late by the spring in idle mood
My will I made (if ye recall),
Providing for the Inn of Trees:
But ah, to set out trunks like these   50
In harbor open unto all
For generations!" So in vein
Rolfe free descanted as through fane
They passed. But noting now the guide
In acquiescence by their side,   55
He checked himself: "Why prate I here?
This brother—I usurp his sphere."

    They came unto a silver star
In pavement set which none do mar
By treading. Here at pause remained   60
The monk; till, seeing Rolfe refrained,
And all, from words, he said: "The place,
Signori, where that shining grace
Which led the Magi, stood; below,

The Manger is." They comment none;   65
Not voicing everything they know,
In cirque about that silver star
They quietly gaze thereupon.
But, turning now, one glanced afar
Along the columned aisles, and thought   70
Of Baldwin whom the mailed knights brought,
While Godfrey's requiem did ring,
Hither to Bethlehem, and crowned
His temples helmet-worn, with round
Of gold and velvet—crowned him king—   75
King of Jerusalem, on floor
Of this same nave august, above
The Manger in its low remove
Where lay, a thousand years before,
The Child of awful worshiping,   80
Destined to prove all slights and scorns,
And a God's coronation—thorns.
    Not Derwent's was that revery;
Another thing his heart possessed,
The clashing of the East and West,   85
Odd sense of incongruity;
He felt a secret impulse move
To start a humorous comment slant
Upon the monk, and sly reprove.
But no: I'll curb the Protestant   90
And modern in me—at least here
For time I'll curb it. Perish truth
If it but act the boor, in sooth,
Requiting courtesy with jeer;
For courteous is our guide, with grace   95
Of a pure heart.
              Some little trace,
May be, of Derwent's passing thought
The Tuscan from his aspect caught;
And turned him: "Pardon! but the crypt:
This way, signori—follow me."   100
Down by a rock-hewn stair they slipped,
Turning by steps which winding be,

Winning a sparry chamber brave
Unsearched by that prose critic keen,
The daylight. Archimago's cave 105
Was here? or that more sorcerous scene
The Persian Sibyl kept within
For turbaned musings? Bowing o'er,
Crossing himself, and on the knee,
Straight did the guide that grot adore; 110
Then, rising, and as one set free:
"The place of the Nativity."
    Dim pendent lamps, in cluster small
Were Pleiads of the mystic hall;
Fair lamps of silver, lamps of gold— 115
Rich gifts devout of monarchs old,
Kings catholic. Rare objects beamed
All round, recalling things but dreamed:
Solomon's talismans garnered up,
His sword, his signet-ring and cup. 120
In further caverns, part revealed,
What silent shapes like statues kneeled;
What brown monks moved by twinkling shrines
Like Aztecs down in silver mines.

    This, this the Stable mean and poor? 125
Noting their looks, to ward surprise,
The Italian: "'Tis incrusted o'er
With marbles, so that now one's eyes
Meet not the natural wall. This floor——"
    "But how? within a cave we stand!" 130
"Yes, caves of old to use were put
For cattle, and with gates were shut.
One meets them still—with arms at hand,
The keepers nigh. Sure it need be
That if in Gihon ye have been, 135
Or hereabouts, yourselves have seen
The grots in question."
               They agree;
And silent in their hearts confess
The strangeness, but the truth no less.

Anew the guide: "Ere now we get   140
Further herein, indulge me yet;"
But paused awhile: "Though o'er this cave,
Where Christ" (and crossed himself) "had birth,
Constantine's mother reared the Nave
Whose Greek mosaics fade in bloom,   145
No older church in Christendom;
And generations, with the girth
Of domes and walls, have still enlarged
And built about; yet convents, shrines,
Cloisters and towers, take not for signs,   150
Entreat ye, of meek faith submerged
Under proud masses. Be it urged
As all began from these small bounds,
So, by all avenues and gates,
All here returns, hereto redounds: 155
In this one Cave all terminates:
In honor of the Manger sole
Saints, kings, knights, prelates reared the whole."
He warmed. Ah, fervor bought too dear:
The fingers clutching rope and cross;   160
Life too intense; the cheek austere
Deepening in hollow, waste and loss.
They marked him; and at heart some knew
Inklings they loved not to pursue.
But Rolfe recalled in fleeting gleam   165
The first Franciscan, richly born—
The youthful one who, night and morn,
In Umbria ranged the hills in dream,
And first devised the girdling cord
In type that rebel senses so   170
Should led be—led like beast abroad
By halter. Tuscan! in the glow
And white light of thy faith's illumings,
In vigils, fervent prayers and trances,
Agonies and self-consumings—   175
Renewest thou the young Saint Francis?
So inly Rolfe; when, in low tone
Considerate Derwent whispered near:

"'Tis doubtless the poor boy's first year
In Bethlehem; time will abate   180
This novice-ardor; yes, sedate
He'll grow, adapt him to the sphere."

    Close to the *Sanctum* now they drew,
A semicircular recess;
And there, in marble floor, they view   185
A silver sun which (friars profess)
Is set in plummet-line exact
Beneath the star in pavement-tract
Above; and raying from this sun
Shoot jasper-spikes, which so point out   190
Argent inscription roundabout
In Latin text; which thus may run:
THE VIRGIN HERE BROUGHT FORTH THE SON.
    The Tuscan bowed him; then with air
Friendly he turned; but something there   195
In Derwent's look—no matter what—
An open levity 'twas not—
Disturbed him; and in accents clear,
As challenged in his faith sincere:
"I trust tradition! Here He lay   200
Who shed on Mary's breasts the ray:
Salvator Mundi!"
            Turning now,
He noted, and he bade them see
Where, with a timid piety
A band of rustics bent them low   205
In worship mute: "Shepherds these are,
And come from pastoral hills not far
Whereon they keep the night-watch wild:
These, like their sires, adore the CHILD,
And in same spot. But, mixed with these,   210
Mark ye yon poor swart images
In other garb? But late they fled
From over Jordan hither; yes,
Escaping so the heinousness
Of one with price upon his head.   215

But look, and yet seem not to peer,
Lest pain ye give: an eye, an ear,
A hand, is mutilate or gone:
The mangler marked them for his own;
But Christ redeems them." Derwent here   220
His eyes withdrew, but Ungar not,
While visibly the red blood shot
Into his thin-skinned scar, and sent,
As seemed, a pulse of argument
Confirming so some angry sense   225
Of evil, and malevolence
In man toward man.
                    Now, lower down
The cave, the Manger they descry,
With marble lined; and, o'er it thrown,
A lustrous saint-cloth meets the eye.   230
And suits of saint-cloths here they have
Wherewith to deck the Manger brave:
Gifts of the Latin princes, these—
Fair Christmas gifts, these draperies.
A damask one of gold and white   235
Rich flowered with pinks embroidered bright,
Was for the present week in turn
The adornment of the sacred Urn.
Impressive was it here to note
Those herdsmen in the shaggy coat: 240
Impressive, yet partook of dream;
It touched the pilgrims, as might seem;
Which pleased the monk; but in disguise
Modest he dropped his damsel-eyes.

      Thought Derwent then: Demure in sooth!   245
'Tis like a maid in lily of youth
Who grieves not in her core of glee,
By spells of grave virginity
To cozen men to foolish looks;
While she—who reads such hearts' hid nooks?—   250
What now? "Signori, here, believe,
Where night and day, while ages run,
Faith in these lamps burns on and on,

'Tis good to spend one's Christmas Eve;
Yea, better rather than in land   255
Which may your holly tree command,
And greens profuse which ye inweave."

14. SOLDIER AND MONK

Fervid he spake. And Ungar there
Appeared (if looks allow surmise)
In latent way to sympathize,
Yet wonder at the votary's air;
And frequent too he turned his face   5
To note the grotto, and compare
These haunted precincts with the guide,
As so to realize the place,
Or fact from fable to divide;
At times his changeful aspect wore   10
Touch of the look the simple shepherds bore.
    The Tuscan marked; he pierced him through,
Yet gently, gifted with the clew—
Ascetic insight; and he caught
The lapse within the soldier's thought,   15
The favorable frame, nor missed
Appealing to it, to enlist
Or influence, or drop a seed
Which might some latter harvest breed.
Gently approaching him, he said: 20
"True sign you bear: your sword's a cross."
Ungar but started, as at loss
To take the meaning, and yet led
To marvel how that mannered word
Did somehow slip into accord   25
With visitings that scarce might cleave—
Shadows, but shadows fugitive.
He lifted up the steel: the blade
Was straight; the hilt, a bar: "'Tis true;
A cross, it is a cross," he said;   30
And touched seemed, though 'twas hardly new.

Then glowed the other; and, again:
"Ignatius was a soldier too,
And Martin. 'Tis the pure disdain
Of life, or, holding life the real,   35
Still subject to a brave ideal—
'Tis this that makes the tent a porch
Whereby the warrior wins the church:
The habit of renouncing, yes,
'Tis good, a good preparedness.—   40
Our founder"—here he raised his eyes
As unto all the sanctities—
"Footing it near Rieti town
Met a young knight on horseback, one
Named Angelo Tancredi: 'Lo,'   45
He said, 'Thy belt thou'lt change for cord,
Thy spurs for mire, good Angelo,
And be a true knight of the Lord.'
And he, the cavalier——" Aside
A brother of the cowl here drew   50
This ardent proselyting guide,
Detaining him in interview
About some matter. Ungar stood
Lost in his thoughts.
                     In neighborhood
Derwent by Rolfe here chanced to bide;   55
And said: "It just occurs to me
As interesting in its way,
That these Franciscans steadily
Have been custodians of the Tomb
And Manger, ever since the day   60
Of rescue under Godfrey's plume
Long centuries ago." Rolfe said:
"Ay; and appropriate seems it too
For the Franciscan retinue
To keep these places, since their head,   65
St. Francis, spite his scouted hood,
May claim more of similitude
To Christ, than any man we know.
Through clouds of myth investing him—

Obscuring, yet attesting him,   70
He burns with the seraphic glow
And perfume of a holy flower.
Sweetness, simplicity, with power!
By love's true miracle of charm
He instituted a reform   75
(Not insurrection) which restored
For time the spirit of his Lord
On earth. If sad perversion came
Unto his order—what of that?
All Christianity shares the same: 80
Pure things men need adulterate
And so adapt them to the kind."
    "Oh, oh! But I have grown resigned
To these vagaries.—And for him,
Assisi's saint—a good young man,   85
No doubt, and beautiful to limn;
Yes, something soft, Elysian;
Nay, rather, the transparent hue
Unearthly of a maiden tranced
In sleep somnambulic; no true   90
Color of health; beauty enhanced
To enervation. In a word,
For all his charity divine,
Love, self-devotion, ardor fine—
Unmanly seems he!"
               "Of our Lord   95
The same was said by Machiavel,
Or hinted, rather. Prithee, tell,
What is it to be *manly?*"
             "Why,
To be man-like"—and here the chest
Bold out he threw—"man at his best!"   100
    "But even at best, one might reply,
Man is that thing of sad renown
Which moved a deity to come down
And save him. Lay not too much stress
Upon the carnal manliness: 105
The Christliness is better—higher;

And Francis owned it, the first friar.
Too orthodox is that?"
                    "See, see,"
Said Derwent, with kind air of one
Who would a brother's weak spot shun: 110
"Mark this most delicate drapery;
If woven by some royal dame—
God bless her and her tambour frame!"

15. SYMPHONIES

Meanwhile with Vine there, Clarel stood
Aside in friendly neighborhood,
And felt a flattering pleasure stir
At words—nor in equivocal tone
Freakish, or leaving to infer,   5
Such as beforetime he had known—
Breathed now by that exceptional one
In unconstraint:
                    "'Tis very much
The cold fastidious heart to touch
This way; nor is it mere address   10
That so could move one's silver chord.
How he transfigured Ungar's sword!
Delusive is this earnestness
Which holds him in its passion pale—
Tenant of melancholy's dale   15
Of mirage? To interpret him,
Perhaps it needs a swallow-skim
Over distant time. Migrate with me
Across the years, across the sea.—
How like a Poor Clare in her cheer   20
(Grave Sister of his order sad)
Showed nature to that Cordelier
Who, roving in the Mexic glade,
Saw in a bud of happy dower
Whose stalk entwined the tropic tree,   25
Emblems of Christ's last agony:

In anthers, style, and fibers torn,
The five wounds, nails, and crown of thorn;
And named it so the passion-flower.
What beauty in that sad conceit!   30
Such charm, the title still we meet.
Our guide, methinks, where'er he turns
For him this passion-flower burns;
And all the world is elegy.
A green knoll is to you and me   35
But pastoral, and little more:
To him 'tis even Calvary
Where feeds the Lamb. This passion-flower—
But list!"
            Hid organ-pipes unclose
A timid rill of slender sound,   40
Which gains in volume—grows, and flows
Gladsome in amplitude of bound.
Low murmurs creep. From either side
Tenor and treble interpose,
And talk across the expanding tide: 45
Debate, which in confusion merges—
Din and clamor, discord's hight:
Countering surges—pæans—dirges—
Mocks, and laughter light.
      But rolled in long ground-swell persistent,   50
A tone, an under-tone assails
And overpowers all near and distant;
Earnest and sternest, it prevails.
      Then terror, horror—wind and rain—
Accents of undetermined fear,   55
And voices as in shipwreck drear:
A sea, a sea of spirits in pain!
      The suppliant cries decrease—
The voices in their ferment cease:
One wave rolls over all and whelms to peace.   60

      But hark—oh, hark!
Whence, whence this stir, this whirr of wings?
Numbers numberless convening—

Harps and child-like carolings
In happy holiday of meaning:　　　　　　　　　　65

　　To God be glory in the hight,
　　　　For tidings glad we bring;
　　Good will to men, and peace on earth
　　　　We children-cherubs sing!

　　To God be glory in the depth,　　　　　　　70
　　　　As in the hight be praise;
　　He who shall break the gates of death
　　　　A babe in manger rays.

　　Ye people all in every land,
　　　　Embrace, embrace, be kin:　　　　　　　75
　　Immanuel's born in Bethlehem,
　　　　And gracious years begin!

　　It dies; and, half around the heavenly sphere,
Like silvery lances lightly touched aloft—
Like Northern Lights appealing to the ear,　　　80
An elfin melody chimes low and soft.
That also dies, that last strange fairy-thrill:
Slowly it dies away, and all is sweetly still.

16. THE CONVENT ROOF

To branching grottoes next they fare,
Old caves of penitence and prayer,
Where Paula kneeled—her urn is there—
Paula the Widow, Scipio's heir
But Christ's adopted. Well her tomb　　　　　5
Adjoins her friend's, renowned Jerome.
　　Never the attending Druze resigned
His temperate poise, his moderate mind;
While Belex, in punctilious guard,
Relinquished not the martial ward:　　　　　10
"If by His tomb hot strife may be,

Trust ye His cradle shall be free?
Heed one experienced, sirs." His sword,
Held cavalier by jingling chain,
Dropping at whiles, would clank amain   15
Upon the pave.
         "I pray ye now,"
To him said Rolfe in accents low,
"Have care; for see ye not ye jar
These devotees? they turn—they cease
(Hearing your clanging scimeter)   20
Their suppliance to the Prince of Peace."

Like miners from the shaft, or tars
From forth the hold, up from those spars
And grottoes, by the stony stair
They climb, emerge, and seek the air   25
In open space.
        "Save me, what now?"
Cried Derwent, foremost of the group—
"The holy water!"
         Hanging low
Outside, was fixed a scalloped stoup
Or marble shell, to hold the wave   30
Of Jordan, for true ones to lave
The finger, and so make the sign,
The Cross's sign, ere in they slip
And bend the knee. In this divine
Recess, deliberately a lip   35
Was lapping slow, with long-drawn pains,
The liquid globules, last remains
Of the full stone. Astray, alas,
Athirst and lazed, it was—the ass;
The friars, withdrawn for time, having left   40
That court untended and bereft.
"Was ever Saracen so bold!"
   "Well, things have come to pretty pass—
The mysteries slobbered by an ass!"
   "Mere Nature do we here behold?"   45
So they. But he, the earnest guide,

Turning the truant there aside,
Said, and in unaffected tone:
"What should it know, this foolish one?
It is an infidel we see: 50
Ah, the poor brute's stupidity!"
   "I hardly think so," Derwent said;
"For, look, it hangs the conscious head."
The friar no relish had for wit,
No sense, perhaps, too rapt for it,   55
Pre-occupied. So, having seen
The ass led back, he bade adieu;
But first, and with the kindliest mien:
"Signori, would ye have fair view
Of Bethlehem of Judæa, pray   60
Ascend to roof: ye take yon stair.
And now, heaven have ye in its care—
Me save from sin, and all from error!
Farewell."—But Derwent: "Yet delay:
Fain would we cherish when away: 65
Thy name, then?" "Brother Salvaterra."
"'Tis a fair name. And, brother, we
Are not insensible, conceive,
To thy most Christian courtesy.—
He goes. Sweet echo does he leave   70
In *Salvaterra:* may it dwell!
Silver in every syllable!"
"And import too," said Rolfe.
                         They fare
And win the designated stair,
And climb; and, as they climb, in bell   75
Of Derwent's repetition, fell:
"Me save from sin, and all from error!
So prays good brother Salvaterra."

   In paved flat roof, how ample there,
They tread a goodly St. Mark's Square   80
Aloft. An elder brother lorn
They meet, with shrunken cheek, and worn
Like to a slab whereon may weep
The unceasing water-drops. And deep

Within his hollow gown-sleeves old   85
His viewless hands he did enfold.
He never spake, but moved away
With shuffling pace of dragged infirm delay.
    "Seaward he gazed," said Rolfe, "toward home:
An empty longing!"
                    "Cruel Rome!"   90
Sighed Derwent; "See, though, good to greet
The vale of eclogue, Boaz' seat.
Trips Ruth there, yonder?" thitherward
Down pointing where the vineyards meet.
At that dear name in Bethlehem heard,   95
How Clarel starts. Not Agar's child—
Naomi's! Then, unreconciled,
And in reaction falling low,
He saw the files Armenian go,
The tapers round the virgin's bier,   100
And heard the boys' light strophe free
Overborne by the men's antistrophe.
Illusion! yet he knew a fear:
"Fixed that this second night we bide
In Bethlehem?" he asked aside.   105
Yes, so 'twas planned. For moment there
He thought to leave them and repair
Alone forthwith to Salem. Nay,
Doubt had unhinged so, that her sway,
In minor things even, could retard   110
The will and purpose. And, beyond,
Prevailed the tacit pilgrim-bond—
Of no slight force in his regard;
Besides, a diffidence was sown:
None knew his heart, nor might he own;   115
And, last, feared he to prove the fear?
With outward things he sought to clear
His mind; and turned to list the tone
Of Derwent, who to Rolfe: "Here now
One stands emancipated."   120
                    "How?"
"The air—the air, the liberal air!
Those witcheries of the cave ill fare

Reviewed aloft. Ah, Salvaterra,
So winning in thy dulcet error—
How fervid thou! Nor less thy tone,   125
So heartfelt in sincere effusion,
Is hardly that more chastened one
We Protestants feel. But the illusion!
Those grottoes: yes, void now they seem
As phantoms which accost in dream—   130
Accost and fade. Hold you with me?"
    "Yes, partly: I in part agree.
In Kedron too, thou mayst recall,
The monkish night of festival,
And masque enacted—how it shrank   135
When, afterward, in nature frank,
Upon the terrace thrown at ease,
Like magi of the old Chaldæa,
Viewing Rigel and Betelguese,
We breathed the balm-wind from Sabæa.   140
All shows and forms in Kedron had—
Nor hymn nor banner made them glad
To me. And yet—why, who may know!
These things come down from long ago.
While so much else partakes decay,   145
While states, tongues, manners pass away,
How wonderful the Latin rite
Surviving still like oak austere
Over crops rotated year by year,
Or Cæsar's tower on London's site.   150
But, tell me: stands it true in fact
That robe and ritual—every kind
By Rome employed in ways exact—
However strange to modern mind,
Or even absurd (like cards Chinese   155
In ceremonial usages),
Not less of faith or need were born—
Survive untampered with, unshorn;
Date far back to a primal day,
Obscure and hard to trace indeed—   160

The springing of the planted seed
In the church's first organic sway?
Still for a type, a type or use,
Each decoration so profuse
Budding and flowering? Tell me here."   165
　　"If but one could! To be sincere,
Rome's wide campania of old lore
Ecclesiastic—that waste shore
I've shunned: an instinct makes one fear
Malarial places. But I'll tell   170
That at the mass this very morn
I marked the broidered maniple
Which by the ministrant was worn:
How like a napkin does it show,
Thought I, a napkin on the arm   175
Of servitor. And hence we know
Its origin. In the first days
(And who denies their simple charm!)
When the church's were like household ways,
Some served the flock in humble state—   180
At Eucharist, passed cup or plate.
The thing of simple use, you see,
Tricked out—embellished—has become
Theatric and a form. There's Rome!
Yet what of this, since happily   185
Each superflux men now disown."
　　"Perchance!—'Tis an ambiguous time;
And periods unforecast come on.
Recurs to me a Persian rhyme:
In Pera late an Asian man,   190
With stately cap of Astracan,
I knew in arbored coffee-house
On bluff above the Bosphorus.
Strange lore was his, and Saadi's wit:
Over pipe and Mocha long we'd sit   195
Discussing themes which thrive in shade.
In pause of talk a way he had
Of humming a low air of his:

I asked him once, What trills your bird?
And he recited it in word,   200
To pleasure me, and this it is:

    "Flamen, flamen, put away
  Robe and mitre glorious:
    Doubt undeifies the day!
  Look, in vapors odorous   205
    As the spice-king's funeral-pyre,
    Dies the Zoroastrian fire
    On your altars in decay:
  The rule, the Magian rule is run,
  And Mythra abdicates the sun!"   210

17. A TRANSITION

"Fine, very fine," said Derwent light;
"But, look, yon rustics there in sight
Crossing the slope; and are they not
Those Arabs that we saw in grot?"
    "Why, who they be their garb bespeaks: 5
Yes, 'tis those Arab Catholics."
    "Catholic Arabs? Say not that!
Some words don't chime together, see."
    "Oh, never mind the euphony:
We saw them worship, and but late.   10
Our Bethlehemites, the guard, they too
Are Catholics. I talked with one,
And much from his discourse I drew,
Which the conventicles would shun:
These be the children of the sun: 15
They like not prosing—turn the lip
From Luther's jug—prefer to sip
From that tall chalice brimmed with wine
Which Rome hath graved, and made to shine
For haughty West and barbarous East,   20
To win all people to her feast."
    "So, so! But, glamoured in that school

Of taking shows and charmful rites,
What ween they of Christ's genuine rule,
These credulous poor neophytes?   25
Alas for such disciples! No,
At mass before the altar, own,
The celebrant in mystic gown
To them is but a Prospero,
A prince of magic. I deplore   30
That zeal in such conversions seeks
Less Christians than good Catholics:
And here one might append much more.
But drop.—Yon vineyards they are fair.
For hill-side scenery—for curve   35
Of beauty in a meek reserve—
'Tis Bethlehem the bell may bear!"
Longer he gazed, then turned aside.

    Clarel was left with Rolfe. In view
Leaned Ungar, watching there the guide   40
Below, who passed on errand new.
"Your judgment of him let me crave—
Him there," here lowly Rolfe.
                    "I would
I were his mate," in earnest mood
Clarel rejoined; "such faith to have,   45
I'd take the rest, even Crib and Cave."
    "Ah, you mistake me; *him* I mean,
Our comrade, Ungar."
                "He? at loss
I am: at loss, for he's most strange;
Wild, too, adventurous in range;   50
And suffers; so that one might glean
An added import from the word
The Tuscan spake: *You bear a cross,*
Referring to the straight-hilt sword."
    "I know. And when the Arnaut ran,   55
But yesterday, with arms how bright
(Like wheeling Phœbus flashing light),
Superb about this sombrous man—

A soldier too with vouching tinge;
Methought, O War, thy bullion fringe   60
Never shall gladsome make thy pall.
Ungar is Mars in funeral
Of reminiscence—not in pledge
And glory of brave equipage
And manifesto. But some keen   65
Side-talk I had with him yestreen:
Brave soldier and stout thinker both;
In this regard, and in degree,
An Ethan Allen, by my troth,
Or Herbert lord of Cherbury,   70
Dusked over. 'Tis an iron glove,
An armed man in the Druid grove."

18. The Hill-Side

Pertaining unto nations three—
Or, rather, each unto its clan—
Greek, Latin, and Armenian,
About the fane three convents be.
Confederate on the mountain fair,   5
Blunt buttressed huge with masonry,
They mass an Ehrenbreitstein there.
     In these, and in the Empress' fane
Enough they gather to detain
Or occupy till afternoon;   10
When some of them the ridge went down
To view that legendary grot
Whose milky chalkiness of vest
Derived is (so the hinds allot)
From droppings of Madonna's breast: 15
A fairy tale: yet, grant it, due
To that creative love alone
Wherefrom the faun and cherub grew,
With genii good and Oberon.

     Returning, part way up the hight,   20
Ungar they met; and Vine in sight.

Here all repose them.
                "Look away,"
Cried Derwent, westward pointing; "see,
How glorified yon vapors be!
It is the dying of the day;   25
A hopeful death-bed: yes, need own
There is a morrow for the sun."

    So, mild they sat in pleased delay.
Vine turned—what seemed a random word
Shyly let fall; and they were stirred   30
Thereby to broach anew the theme—
How wrought the sites of Bethlehem
On Western natures. Here some speech
Was had; and then: "For me," Rolfe said,
"From Bethlehem here my musings reach   35
Yes—frankly—to Tahiti's beach."
    "Tahiti?" Derwent; "you have sped!"
"Ay, truant humor. But to me
That vine-wreathed urn of Ver, in sea
Of halcyons, where no tides do flow   40
Or ebb, but waves bide peacefully
At brim, by beach where palm trees grow
That sheltered Omai's olive race—
Tahiti should have been the place
For Christ in advent."
                "Deem ye so?   45
Or on the topic's budding bough
But lights your fancy's robin?"
                     "Nay,"
Said Ungar, "err one if he say
The God's design was, part, to broach
Rebuke of man's factitious life;   50
So, for his first point of approach,
Came thereunto where that was rife,
The land of Pharisees and scorn—
Judæa, with customs hard as horn."
This, chief, to Rolfe and Derwent twain.   55
But Derwent, if no grudge he knew,
Still felt some twinges of the pain

(Vibrations of the residue)
That morning in the dale incurred;
Wherefore, at present he abstained,   60
When Ungar spake, from any word
Receptive. Rolfe reply maintained;
And much here followed, though of kind
Scarce welcome to the priest. Resigned
He heard; till, at a hint, the Cave   65
He named:
              "If on the first review
Its shrines seemed each a gilded grave;
Yet, reconsidered, they renew
The spell of the transmitted story—
The grace, the innocence, the glory: 70
Shepherds, the Manger, and the CHILD:
What wonder that it has beguiled
So many generations! Ah,
Though much we knew in desert late,
Beneath no kind auspicious star,   75
Of lifted minds in poised debate—
'Twas of the brain. Consult the heart!
Spouse to the brain—can coax or thwart:
Does *she* renounce the trust divine?
Hide it she may, but scarce resign;   80
Like to a casket buried deep
Which, in a fine and fibrous throng,
The rootlets of the forest keep—
'Tis tangled in her meshes strong."
         "Yes, yes," cried Rolfe; "that tone delights;   85
But oh, these legends, relics, sites!
Of yore, you know, Greeks showed the place
Where Argo landed, and the stone
That served to anchor Argo; yes,
And Agamemnon's scepter, throne;   90
Mars' spear; and so on. More to please,
Where the goddess suckled Hercules—
Priests showed that spot, a sacred one."
         "Well then, Madonna's but a dream,
The Manger and the Crib. So deem;   95

So be it; but undo it! Nay,
Little avails what sages say:
Tell Romeo that Juliet's eyes
Are chemical; e'en analyze
The iris; show 'tis albumen—   100
Gluten—fish-jelly mere. What then?
To Romeo it is still love's sky:
He loves: enough! Though Faith no doubt
Seem insubstantial as a sigh,
Never ween that 'tis a water-spout   105
Dissolving, dropping into dew
At pistol-shot. Besides, review
That comprehensive Christian scheme:
It catches man at each extreme:
Simple—august; strange as a dream,   110
Yet practical as plodding life:
Not use and sentiment at strife."
    They hearken: none aver dissent,
Nor one confirms him; while his look
Unwitting an expression took,   115
Scarce insincere, yet so it lent
Provocative to Ungar's heart;
Who, bridling the embittered part,
Thus spake: "This yieldeth no content:
Your implication lacketh stay: 120
There is a callousness in clay.
Christ's pastoral parables divine,
Breathing the sweet breath of sweet kine,
As wholesome too; how many feel?
Feel! rather put it—comprehend?   125
Not unto all does nature lend
The gift; at hight such love's appeal
Is hard to know, as in her deep
Is hate; a prior love must steep
The spirit; head nor heart have marge   130
Commensurate in man at large."
    "Indulge me," Derwent; "Grant it so
As you present it; 'tis most strange
How Christ could work his powerful change:

The world turned Christian long ago."   135
"The world but joined the Creed Divine
With prosperous days and Constantine;
The world turned Christian, need confess,
But the world remained the world, no less:
The world turned Christian: where's the odds?   140
Hearts change not in the change of gods.
Despite professions, outward shows—
So far as working practice goes,
More minds with shrewd Voltaire have part
Than now own Jesus in the heart."   145
      "Not rashly judge," said Derwent grave;
"Prudence will here decision waive."
      "No: shift the test. How Buddha pined!
Pierced with the sense of all we bear,
Not only ills by fate assigned,   150
But misrule of our selfish mind,
Fain would the tender sage repair.
Well, Asia owns him. But the *lives:*
Buddha but in a name survives—
A name, a rite. Confucius, too: 155
Does China take his honest hue?
Some forms they keep, some forms of his;
But well we know them, the Chinese.
Ah, Moses, thy deterring dart!—
Etherial visitants of earth,   160
Foiled benefactors, proves your worth
But sundry texts, disowned in mart,
Light scratched, not graved on man's hard heart?
'Tis penalty makes sinners start."

19. A NEW-COMER

"Good echoes, echo it! Ho, chant,
'Tis penalty we sinners want:
By all means, penalty!"
                What man
Thus struck in here so consonant?

They turn them, and a stranger scan.   5
As through the rigging of some port
Where cheek by jowl the ships resort—
The sea-beat hulls of briny oak—
Peereth the May-day's jocund sun;
So through his inlaced wrinkles broke   10
A nature bright, a beaming one.

   "Hidalgos, pardon! Strolling here
These fine old villa-sites to see,
I caught that good word *penalty*,
And could not otherwise than cheer.   15
Pray now, here be—two, four, six, eight—
Ten legs; I'll add one more, by leave,
And eke an arm."
                  In hobbling state
He came among them, with one sleeve
Loose flying, and one wooden limb,   20
A leg. All eyes the cripple skim;
Each rises, and his seat would give:
But Derwent in advance: "Why, Don—
My good Don Hannibal, I mean;
Señor Don Hannibal Rohon   25
Del Aquaviva—a good e'en!"
   "Ha, thou, is't thou?" the other cried,
And peered and stared not unamazed;
Then flung his one arm round him wide:
Then at arm's length: "St. James be praised,   30
With all the calendar!"
                        "But, tell:
What wind wafts here Don Hannibal?
When last I left thee at *'The Cock'*
In Fleet Street, thou wert like a rock
For England—bent on anchoring there."   35
   "Oh, too much agitation; yes,
Too proletarian it proved.
I've stumped about since; no redress;
Norway's too cold; Egypt's all glare;
And everywhere that I removed   40

This cursed *Progress* still would greet.
Ah where (thought I) in Old World view
Some blest asylum from the New!
At last I steamed for Joppa's seat,
Resolved on Asia for retreat.   45
Asia for me, Asia will do.
But just where to pitch tent—invest—
Ah, that's the point; I'm still in quest,
Don Derwent.—Look, the sun falls low;
But lower the funds in Mexico   50
Whereto he's sinking."
                    "Gentlemen:"
Said Derwent, turning on them then;
"I introduce and do commend
To ye Don Hannibal Rohon;
He is my estimable friend   55
And well beloved. Great fame he's won
In war. Those limbs—"
                    "St. James defend!"
Here cried Don Hannibal; "stop! stop!
Pulled down is Montezuma's hall!—
Hidalgos, I am, as ye see,   60
Just a poor cripple—that is all;
A cripple, yet contrive to hop
Far off from Mexic liberty,
Thank God! I lost these limbs for that;
And would that they were mine again,   65
And all were back to former state—
I, Mexico, and poor Old Spain.
And for Don Derwent here, my friend—
You know his way. And so I end,
Poor penitent American: 70
Oh, 'tis the sorriest thing! In me
A *reformado* reformed ye see."

     Ungar, a very Indian here
Too serious far to take a jest,
Or rather, who no sense possessed   75
Of humor; he, for aye austere,

Took much in earnest; and a light
Of attestation over-bright
Shot from his eyes, though part suppressed.
　　"But penalties, these *penalties*,"   80
Here cried the crippled one again;
"Proceed, hidalgo; name you these
Same capital good penalties:
They're needed."
　　　　　"Hold, let me explain,"
Cried Derwent: "We, as meek as worms—   85
Oh, far from taking any pique
As if the kind but formed a clique—
Have late been hearing in round terms
The sore disparagement of man,
Don Hannibal." "You think I'll ban?   90
Disparage him with all my heart!
What villain takes the rascal's part?
Advance the argument."
　　　　　"But stay:
'Tis too much odds now; it won't do,
Such reinforcement come. Nay, nay,   95
I of the Old World, all alone
Maintaining hope and ground for cheer
'Gainst ye, the offspring of the New?
Ah, what reverses time can own!"
So Derwent light. But earnest here,   100
Ungar: "*Old* World? if age's test
Be this—advanced experience,
Then, in the truer moral sense,
Ours is the Old World. You, at best,
In dreams of your advanced Reform,   105
Adopt the cast skin of our worm."
　　"Hey, hey!" exclaimed Don Hannibal;
"Not *cast* yet quite; the snake is sick—
Would wriggle out. 'Tis pitiful!
But brave times for the empiric.—   110
You spake now of Reform. For me,
Among reformers in true way
There's one—the imp of Semele;

Ay, and brave Raleigh too, we'll say.
Wine and the weed! blest innovations,   115
How welcome to the weary nations!
But what's in this Democracy?
Eternal hacking! Woe is me,
She lopped these limbs, Democracy."
        "Ah, now, Don Hannibal Rohon   120
Del Aquaviva!" Derwent cried;
"I knew it: two upon a side!"
        But Ungar, earnest in his plea—
Intent, nor caring to have done;
And turning where suggestion led   125
At tangent: "Ay, Democracy
Lops, lops; but where's her planted bed?
The future, what is that to her
Who vaunts she's no inheritor?
'Tis in her mouth, not in her heart.   130
The Past she spurns, though 'tis the past
From which she gets her saving part—
That Good which lets her Evil last.
Behold her whom the panders crown,
Harlot on horseback, riding down   135
The very Ephesians who acclaim
This great Diana of ill fame!
Arch strumpet of an impious age,
Upstart from ranker villanage,
'Tis well she must restriction taste   140
Nor lay the world's broad manor waste:
Asia shall stop her at the least,
That old inertness of the East.
She's limited; lacking the free
And genial catholicity   145
Which in Christ's pristine scheme unfurled
Grace to the city and the world."
        "By Cotopaxi, a brave vent!"
(And here he took a pinch of snuff,
Flapping the spill off with loose cuff)   150
"Good, excellenza—excellent!
But, pardon me," in altered tone;

"I'm sorry, but I must away;"
And, setting crutch, he footing won;
"We're just arrived in cloister there, 155
Our little party; and they stay
My coming for the convent-fare.
Adieu: we'll meet anon—we'll meet,
Don Derwent. Nay, now, never stir;
Not I would such a group unseat; 160
But happy the good rein and spur
That brought thee where once more we greet.
Good e'en, Don Derwent—not good-by;
And, cavaliers, the evil eye
Keep far from ye!" He limped away, 165
Rolling a wild ranchero lay:
"House your cattle and stall your steed:
Stand by, stand by for the great stampede!"

20. DERWENT AND UNGAR

"Not thou com'st in the still small voice,"
Said Derwent, "thou queer Mexican!"
And followed him with eyes: "This man,"
And turned here, "he likes not grave talk,
The settled undiluted tone; 5
It does his humorous nature balk.
'Twas ever too his sly rebuff,
While yet obstreperous in praise,
Taking that dusty pinch of snuff.
An oddity, he has his ways; 10
Yet trust not, friends, the half he says:
Not he would do a weasel harm;
A secret agent of Reform;
At least, that is my theory."
    "The quicksilver is quick to skim," 15
Ungar remarked, with eye on him.
    "Yes, nature has her levity,"
Dropped Derwent.
                    Nothing might disarm

The other; he: "Your word *reform:*
What meaning's to that word assigned?   20
From Luther's great initial down,
Through all the series following on,
The impetus augments—the blind
Precipitation: blind, for tell
Whitherward does the surge impel?   25
The end, the aim? 'Tis mystery."
    "Oh, no. Through all methinks I see
The object clear: belief revised,
Men liberated—equalized
In happiness. No mystery,   30
Just none at all; plain sailing."
                           "Well,
Assume this: is it feasible?
Your methods? These are of the world:
Now the world cannot save the world;
And Christ renounces it. His faith,   35
Breaking with every mundane path,
Aims straight at heaven. To founded thrones
He says: Trust not to earthly stanchions;
And unto poor and houseless ones—
My Father's house has many mansions.   40
Warning and solace be but this;
No thought to mend a world amiss."
    "Ah now, ah now!" plead Derwent.
                              "Nay,
Test further; take another way:
Go ask Aurelius Antonine—   45
A Cæsar wise, grave, just, benign,
Lord of the world—why, in the calm
Which through his reign the empire graced—
Why he, that most considerate heart
Superior, and at vantage placed,   50
Contrived no secular reform,
Though other he knew not, nor balm."
    "Alas," cried Derwent (and, in part,
As vainly longing for retreat)
"Though good Aurelius was a man   55

Matchless in mind as sole in seat,
Yet pined he under numbing ban
Of virtue without Christian heat:
As much you intimated too,
Just saying that no balm he knew.   60
Howbeit, true reform goes on
By Nature; doing, never done.
Mark the advance: creeds drop the hate;
Events still liberalize the state."
    "But tell: do men now more cohere   65
In bonds of duty which sustain?
Cliffs crumble, and the parts regain
A liberal freedom, it is clear.
And for conventicles—I fear,
Much as a hard heart aged grown   70
Abates in rigor, losing tone;
So sects decrepit, at death's door,
Dote into peace through loss of power."
    "You put it so," said Derwent light:
"No more developments to cite?"   75
    "Ay, quench the true, the mock sun fails
Therewith. Much so, Hypocrisy,
The false thing, wanes just in degree
That Faith, the true thing, wanes: each pales.
There's *one* development; 'tis seen   80
In masters whom not low ye rate:
What lack, in some outgivings late,
Of the old Christian style toward men—
I do not mean the wicked ones,
But Pauperism's unhappy sons   85
In cloud so blackly ominous,
Grimy in Mammon's English pen—
Collaterals of his overplus:
How worse than them Immanuel fed
On hill-top—helped and comforted.   90
Thou, Poverty, erst free from shame,
Even sacred through the Savior's claim,
Professed by saints, by sages prized—
A pariah now, and bastardized!

Reactions from the Christian plan   95
Bear others further. Quite they shun
A god to name, or cite a man
Save Greek, heroical, a Don:
'Tis Plato's aristocratic tone.
All recognition they forego   100
Of Evil; supercilious skim
With spurious wing of seraphim
The last abyss. Freemen avow
Belief in right divine of Might,
Yet spurn at kings. This is the light—   105
Divine the darkness. Mark the way
The Revolution, whose first mode,
Ere yet the maniacs overrode,
Despite the passion of the dream
Evinced no disrespect for God;   110
Mark how, in our denuding day,
E'en with the masses, as would seem,
It tears the fig-leaf quite away.
Contrast these incidents: The mob,
The Paris mob of Eighty-nine,   115
Haggard and bleeding, with a throb
Burst the long Tuileries. In shrine
Of chapel there, they saw the Cross
And Him thereon. Ah, bleeding Man,
The people's friend, thou bled'st for us   120
Who here bleed, too! Ragged they ran—
They took the crucifix; in van
They put it, marched with drum and psalm
And throned it in their Notre Dame.
But yesterday—how did they then,   125
In new uprising of the Red,
The offspring of those Tuileries men?
They made a clothes-stand of the Cross
Before the church; and, on that head
Which bowed for them, could wanton toss   130
The sword-belt, while the gibing sped.
Transcended rebel angels! Woe
To us; without a God, 'tis woe!"

21. UNGAR AND ROLFE

"Such earnestness! such wear and tear,
And man but a thin gossamer!"
So here the priest aside; then turned,
And, starting: "List! the vesper-bell?
Nay, nay—the hour is passed. But, oh,   5
He must have supped, Don Hannibal,
Ere now. Come, friends, and shall we go?
This hot discussion, let it stand
And cool; to-morrow we'll remand."
          "Not yet, I pray," said Rolfe; "a word;"   10
And turned toward Ungar; "be adjured,
And tell us if for earth may be
In ripening arts, no guarantee
Of happy sequel."
                  "Arts are tools;
But tools, they say are to the strong: 15
Is Satan weak? weak is the Wrong?
No blessed augury overrules:
Your arts advance in faith's decay:
You are but drilling the new Hun
Whose growl even now can some dismay;   20
Vindictive in his heart of hearts,
He schools him in your mines and marts—
A skilled destroyer."
                    "But, need own
That portent does in no degree
Westward impend, across the sea."   25
    "Over there? And do ye not forebode?
Against pretenses void or weak
The impieties of 'Progress' speak.
What say *these,* in effect, to God?
'How profits it? And who art Thou   30
That we should serve Thee? Of Thy ways
No knowledge we desire; *new* ways
We have found out, and better. Go—
Depart from us; we do erase
Thy sinecure: behold, the sun   35

Stands still no more in Ajalon:
Depart from us!'—And if He do?
(And that He may, the Scripture says)
Is aught betwixt ye and the hells?
For He, nor in irreverent view,   40
'Tis He distills that savor true
Which keeps good essences from taint;
Where He is not, corruption dwells,
And man and chaos are without restraint."
      "Oh, oh, you do but generalize   45
In void abstractions."
                        "Hypothesize:
If be a people which began
Without impediment, or let
From any ruling which fore-ran;
Even striving all things to forget   50
But this—the excellence of man
Left to himself, his natural bent,
His own devices and intent;
And if, in satire of the heaven,
A world, a new world have been given   55
For stage whereon to deploy the event;
If such a people be——well, well,
One hears the kettle-drums of hell!
Exemplary act awaits its place
In drama of the human race."   60
      "Is such act certain?" Rolfe here ran;
"Not much is certain."
                        "God is—man.
The human nature, the divine—
Have both been proved by many a sign.
'Tis no astrologer and star.   65
The world has now so old become,
Historic memory goes so far
Backward through long defiles of doom;
Whoso consults it honestly
That mind grows prescient in degree;   70
For man, like God, abides the same
Always, through all variety

Of woven garments to the frame."
    "Yes, God is God, and men are men,
Forever and for aye. What then?   75
There's Circumstance—there's Time; and these
Are charged with store of latencies
Still working in to modify.
For mystic text that you recall,
Dilate upon, and e'en apply—   80
(Although I seek not to decry)
Theology's scarce practical.
But leave this: the New World's the theme.
Here, to oppose your dark extreme,
(Since an old friend is good at need)   85
To an old thought I'll fly. Pray, heed:
Those waste-weirs which the New World yields
To inland freshets—the free vents
Supplied to turbid elements;
The vast reserves—the untried fields;   90
These long shall keep off and delay
The class-war, rich-and-poor-man fray
Of history. From that alone
Can serious trouble spring. Even that
Itself, this good result may own—   95
The first firm founding of the state."
    Here ending, with a watchful air
Inquisitive, Rolfe waited him.
And Ungar:
            "True heart do ye bear
In this discussion? or but trim   100
To draw my monomania out,
For monomania, past doubt,
Some of ye deem it. Yet I'll on.
Yours seems a reasonable tone;
But in the New World things make haste: 105
Not only men, the *state* lives fast—
Fast breeds the pregnant eggs and shells,
The slumberous combustibles
Sure to explode. 'Twill come, 'twill come!
One demagogue can trouble much: 110

How of a hundred thousand such?
And universal suffrage lent
To back them with brute element
Overwhelming? What shall bind these seas
Of rival sharp communities   115
Unchristianized? Yea, but 'twill come!"
   "What come?"
            "Your Thirty Years (of) War."
  "Should fortune's favorable star
Avert it?"
        "Fortune? nay, 'tis doom."
"Then what comes after? spasms but tend   120
Ever, at last, to quiet."
          "Know,
Whatever happen in the end,
Be sure 'twill yield to one and all
New confirmation of the fall
Of Adam. Sequel may ensue,   125
Indeed, whose germs one now may view:
Myriads playing pygmy parts—
Debased into equality:
In glut of all material arts
A civic barbarism may be: 130
Man disennobled—brutalized
By popular science—Atheized
Into a smatterer——"
       "Oh, oh!"
  "Yet knowing all self need to know
In self's base little fallacy;   135
Dead level of rank commonplace:
An Anglo-Saxon China, see,
May on your vast plains shame the race
In the Dark Ages of Democracy."

  America!
       In stilled estate,   140
On him, half-brother and co-mate—
In silence, and with vision dim
Rolfe, Vine, and Clarel gazed on him;

They gazed, nor one of them found heart
To upbraid the crotchet of his smart,   145
Bethinking them whence sole it came,
Though birthright he renounced in hope,
Their sanguine country's wonted claim.
Nor dull they were in honest tone
To some misgivings of their own: 150
They felt how far beyond the scope
Of elder Europe's saddest thought
Might be the New World's sudden brought
In youth to share old age's pains—
To feel the arrest of hope's advance,   155
And squandered last inheritance;
And cry—"To Terminus build fanes!
Columbus ended earth's romance:
No New World to mankind remains!"

22. OF WICKEDNESS THE WORD

Since, for the charity they knew,
None cared the exile to upbraid
Or further breast—while yet he threw,
In silence that oppressive weighed,
The after-influence of his spell—   5
The priest in light disclaimer said
To Rolfe apart: "The icicle,
The dagger-icicle draws blood;
But give it sun!" "You mean his mood
Is accident—would melt away   10
In fortune's favorable ray.
But if 'tis happiness he lacks,
Why, let the gods warm all cold backs
With that good sun. But list!"
                              In vent
Of thought, abrupt the malcontent: 15
"What incantation shall make less
The ever-upbubbling wickedness!
Is this fount nature's?"

                    Under guard
Asked Vine: "Is wickedness the word?"
"The right word? Yes; but scarce the *thing*   20
Is there conveyed; for one need know
Wicked has been the tampering
With wickedness the word." "Even so?"
"Ay, ridicule's light sacrilege
Has taken off the honest edge—   25
Quite turned aside—perverted all
That Saxon term and Scriptural."
"Restored to the incisive wedge,
What means it then, this wickedness?"
Ungar regarded him with look   30
Of steady search: "And wilt thou brook?
Thee leaves it whole?—This wickedness
(Might it retake true import well)
Means not default, nor vulgar vice,
Nor Adam's lapse in Paradise;   35
But worse: 'twas this evoked the hell—
Gave in the conscious soul's recess
Credence to Calvin. What's implied
In that deep utterance decried
Which Christians labially confess—   40
Be born anew?"
                    "Ah, overstate
Thou dost!" the priest sighed; "but look there!
No jarring theme may violate
Yon tender evening sky! How fair
These olive-orchards: see, the sheep   45
Mild drift toward the folds of sleep.
The blessed Nature! still her glance
Returns the love she well receives
From hearts that with the stars advance,
Each heart that in the goal believes!"   50
    Ungar, though nettled, as might be,
At these bland substitutes in plea
(By him accounted so) yet sealed
His lips. In fine, all seemed to yield
With one consent a truce to talk.   55

But Clarel, who, since that one hour
Of unreserve on Saba's tower,
Less relished Derwent's pleasant walk
Of myrtles, hardly might remain
Uninfluenced by Ungar's vein: 60
If man in truth be what you say,
And such the prospects for the clay,
And outlook of the future—cease!
What's left us but the senses' sway?
Sinner, sin out life's petty lease: 65
We are not worth the saving. Nay,
For me, if thou speak true—but ah,
Yet, yet there gleams one beckoning star—
So near the horizon, judge I right
That 'tis of heaven?
                  But wanes the light—   70
The evening *Angelus* is rolled:
They rise, and seek the convent's fold.

23. DERWENT AND ROLFE

There as they wend, Derwent his arm,
Demure, and brotherly, and grave,
Slips into Rolfe's: "A bond we have;
We lock, we symbolize it, see;
Yes, you and I: but he, but *he!*"   5
And checked himself, as under warm
Emotion. Rolfe kept still. "Unlike,
Unlike! Don Hannibal through storm
Has passed; yet does his sunshine strike.
But Ungar, clouded man! No balm   10
He'll find in that unhappy vein;"
Pausing, awaiting Rolfe again.
Rolfe held his peace. "But grant indeed
His strictures just—how few will heed!
The hippopotamus is tough;   15
Well bucklered too behind. Enough:
Man has two sides: keep on the bright."

"Two sides imply that one's not right;
So that won't do."—"Wit, wit!"—"Nay, truth."
"Sententious are ye, pithy—sooth!"   20
Yet quickened now that Rolfe began
To find a tongue, he sprightlier ran:
"As for his Jeremiad spells,
Shall these the large hope countermand?
The world's outlived the oracles,   25
And the people never will disband!
Stroll by my hedge-rows in the June,
The chirruping quite spoils his tune."
     "Ay, birds," said Rolfe; nor more would own.
"But, look: to hold the censor-tone,   30
One need be qualified: is he?"
"He's wise." "Too vehemently wise!
His factious memories tyrannize
And wrest the judgment." "In degree,
Perchance." "But come: shall we accord   35
Credentials to that homely sword
He wears? Would it had more of grace!
But 'tis in serviceable case."
"Right! war's his business." "*Business,* say you?"
Resenting the unhandsome word;   40
"Unsay it quickly, friend, I pray you!
Fine business driving men through fires
To Hades, at the bidding blind
Of Heaven knows whom! but, now I mind,
In this case 'tis the Turk that hires   45
A Christian for that end."—"May be,"
Said Rolfe. "And pretty business too
Is war for one who did instill
So much concern for *Lincoln Hugh*
Ground up by Mammon in the mill.   50
Or was it rhetoric?" "May be,"
Said Rolfe. "And let me hint, *may be*
You're curt to-day. But, yes, I see:
Your countryman he is. Well, well,
That's right—you're right; no more I'll dwell: 55

Your countryman; and, yes, at heart
Rather you sidled toward his part
Though playing well the foil, pardee!
Oh, now you stare: no need: a trick
To deal your dullish mood a prick.   60
But mind you, though, some things you said
By Jordan lounging in the shade
When our discourse so freely ran?
But whatsoe'er reserves be yours
Touching your native clime and clan,   65
And whatsoe'er *his* thought abjures;
Still, when he's criticised by one
Not of the tribe, not of the zone—
Chivalric still, though doggedly,
You stand up for a countryman: 70
I like your magnanimity;"
And silent pressed the enfolded arm
As he would so transmit a charm
Along the nerve, which might insure,
However cynic challenge ran,   75
Faith genial in at least one man
Fraternal in love's overture.

24. TWILIGHT

    "Over the river
In gloaming, ah, still do ye plain?
    Dove—dove in the mangroves,
    How dear is thy pain!

    "Sorrow—but fondled;   5
Reproaches that never upbraid
    Spite the passion, the yearning
    Of love unrepaid.

    "Teach me, oh! teach me
Thy cadence, that Inez may thrill   10

With the bliss of the sadness,
And love have his will!"

Through twilight of mild evening pale,
As now returning slow they fare—
In dubious keeping with the dale   15
And legends, floating came that air
From one invisible in shade,
Singing and lightly sauntering on
Toward the cloisters. Pause they made;
But he a lateral way had won: 20
Viewless he passed, as might a wave
Rippling, which doth a frigate lave
At anchor in the midnight road.

Clarel a fleeting thought bestowed:
Unkenned! to thee what thoughts belong—   25
Announced by such a tropic song.

25. The Invitation

Returned to harbor, Derwent sought
His Mexic friend; and him he found
At home in by-place of a court
Of private kind—some tools around,
And planks and joiner's stuff, and more,   5
With little things, and odds and ends,
Conveniences which ease commends
Unto some plain old bachelor.
And here, indeed, one such a stay
At whiles did make; a placid friar,   10
A sexton gratis in his way,
When some poor brother did require
The last fraternal offices.
    This funeral monk, now much at ease,
Uncowled, upon a work-bench sat—   15
Lit by a greenish earthen lamp
(With cross-bones baked thereon for stamp)
Behind him placed upon a mat—

Engaged in gossip, old men's chat,
With the limb-lopped Eld of Mexico;   20
Who, better to sustain him so
On his one leg, had niched him all
In one of some strange coffins there,
A 'lean and open by the wall
Like sentry-boxes.—
                    "Take a chair,   25
Don Derwent; no, I mean—yes, take
A—coffin; come, be sociable."
     "Don Hannibal, Don Hannibal,
What see I? Well, for pity's sake!"
     "Eh? This is brother Placido,   30
And we are talking of old times,
For, learn thou, that in Mexico
First knew he matins and the chimes.
But, come, get in; there's nothing else;
'Tis easy; here one lazy dwells   35
Almost as in a barber's chair;
See now, I lean my head."
                    "Ah, yes;
But I—don't—feel the weariness:
Thanks, thanks; no, I the bench prefer.—
Good brother Placido, I'm glad   40
You find a countryman." And so
For little time discourse he made;
But presently—the monk away
Being called—proposed that they should go,
He and Don Hannibal the gray,   45
And in refectory sit down
That talk might more convenient run.
     The others through the courts diverge,
Till all to cots conducted fare
Where reveries in slumber merge,   50
While lulling steals from many a cell
A bee-like buzz of bed-side prayer—
Night in the hive monastical.

     And now—not wantonly designed
Like lays in grove of Daphne sung,   55

But helping to fulfill the piece
Which in these cantoes finds release,
Appealing to the museful mind—
A chord, the satyr's chord is strung.

26. THE PRODIGAL

In adolescence thrilled by hope
Which fain would verify the gleam
And find if destiny concur,
How dwells upon life's horoscope
Youth, always an astrologer,   5
Forecasting happiness the dream!

    Slumber interred them; but not all,
For so it chanced that Clarel's cell
Was shared by one who did repel
The poppy. 'Twas a prodigal,   10
Yet pilgrim too in casual way,
And seen within the grots that day,
But only seen, no more than that.
In years he might be Clarel's mate.
Not talkative, he half reclined   15
In revery of dreamful kind;
Or might the fable, the romance
Be tempered by experience?
For ruling under spell serene,
A light precocity is seen.   20
That mobile face, voluptuous air
No Northern origin declare,
But Southern—where the nations bright,
The costumed nations, circled be
In garland round a tideless sea   25
Eternal in its fresh delight.
Nor less he owned the common day;
His avocation naught, in sooth—
A toy of Mammon; but the ray
And fair aureola of youth   30

Deific makes the prosiest clay.
From revery now by Clarel won
He brief his story entered on:
A native of the banks of Rhone
He traveled for a Lyons house   35
Which dealt in bales luxurious;
Detained by chance at Jaffa gray,
Rather than let ripe hours decay,
He'd run o'er, in a freak of fun,
Green Sharon to Jerusalem,   40
And thence, not far, to Bethlehem.
    Thy silvery voice, irreverent one!
'Twas musical; and Clarel said:
"Greatly I err, or thou art he
Who singing along the hill-side sped   45
At fall of night."
          "And heard you me?
'Twas sentimental, to be sure:
A little Spanish overture,
A Tombez air, which months ago
A young Peruvian let flow.   50
Locked friends we were; he's gone home now."
    To Clarel 'twas a novel style
And novel nature; and awhile
Mutely he dwelt upon him here.
Earnest to know how the most drear   55
Solemnity of Judah's glade
Affect might such a mind, he said
Something to purpose; but he shied.
One essay more; whereat he cried:
"*Amigo!* favored lads there are,   60
Born under such a lucky star,
They weigh not things too curious, see,
Albeit conforming to their time
And usages thereof, and clime:
Well, mine's that happy family."   65
    The student faltered—felt annoy:
Absorbed in problems ill-defined,
Am *I* too curious in my mind;

And, baffled in the vain employ,
Foregoing many an easy joy?   70
That thought he hurried from; and so
Unmindful in perturbed estate
Of that light intimation late,
He said: "On hills of dead Judæa
Wherever one may faring go,   75
He dreams—Fit place to set the bier
Of Jacob, brought from Egypt's mead:
Here's Atad's threshing-floor."
                              "Indeed?"
Scarce audible was that in tone;
Nor Clarel heard it, but went on: 80
"'Tis Jephthah's daughter holds the hight;
She, she's the muse here.—But, I pray,
Confess to Judah's mournful sway."
He held his peace. "You grant the blight?"
"No Boulevards." "Do other lands   85
Show equal ravage you've beheld?"
"Oh, yes," and eyed his emerald
In ring. "But here a God commands,
A judgment dooms: you that gainsay?"
Up looked he quick, then turned away,   90
And with a shrug that gave mute sign
That here the theme he would decline.
But Clarel urged. As in despair
The other turned—invoked the air:
"Was it in such talk, Don Rovenna,   95
We dealt in Seville, I and you?
No! chat of love-wile and duenna
And *saya-manto* in Peru.
Ah, good Limeno, dear *amigo*,
What times were ours, the holidays flew;   100
Life, life a revel and clear *allegro*;
But home thou'rt gone; pity, but true!"
        At burst so lyrical, yet given
Not all without some mock in leaven,
Once more did Clarel puzzled sit;   105
But rallying in spite of it,

Continued: "Surely now, 'tis clear
That in the aspect of Judæa—"
    "My friend, it is just naught to me!
Why, why so pertinacious be? 110
Refrain!" Here, turning light away,
As quitting so the theme: "How gay
Damascus! orchard of a town:
Not yet she's heard the tidings though."
"Tidings?"
          "Tidings of long ago: 115
Isaiah's dark burden, malison:
Of course, to be perpetual fate:
Bat, serpent, screech-owl, and all that.
But truth is, grace and pleasure there,
In Abana and Pharpar's streams 120
(O shady haunts! O sherbert-air!)
So twine the place in odorous dreams,
How may she think to mope and moan,
The news not yet being got to town
That she's a ruin! Oh, 'tis pity, 125
For she, she is earth's senior city!—
Pray, who was he, that man of state
Whose footman at Elisha's gate
Loud rapped? The name has slipped. Howe'er,
That Damascene maintained it well: 130
'We've better streams than Israel,
Yea, fairer waters.' " Weetless here
Clarel betrayed half cleric tone:
"Naaman, you mean. Poor leper one,
'Twas Jordan healed him."
          "As you please." 135
And hereupon the Lyonese—
(Capricious, or inferring late
That he had yielded up his state
To priggish inroad) gave mute sign
'Twere well to end.
          "But Palestine," 140
Insisted Clarel, "do you not
Concede some strangeness to her lot?"

    "Amigo, how you persecute!
You all but tempt one to refute
These stale megrims. You of the West,   145
What devil has your hearts possessed,
You can't enjoy?—Ah, dear Rovenna,
With talk of donna and duenna,
You came too from that hemisphere,
But freighted with quite other cheer: 150
No pedant, no!" Then, changing free,
Laughed with a light audacity:
"Well, me for one, dame Judah here
Don't much depress: she's not austere—
Nature has lodged her in good zone—   155
The true wine-zone of Noah: the Cape
Yields no such bounty of the grape.
Hence took King Herod festal tone;
Else why the tavern-cluster gilt
Hang out before that fane he built,   160
The second temple?" Catching thus
A buoyant frolic impetus,
He bowled along: "Herewith agrees
The ducat of the Maccabees,
Graved with the vine. Methinks I see   165
The spies from Eshcol, full of glee
Trip back to camp with clusters swung
From jolting pole on shoulders hung:
'Cheer up, 'twill do; it needs befit;
Lo ye, behold the fruit of it!'   170
And, tell me, does not Solomon's harp
(Oh, that it should have taken warp
In end!) confirm the festa? Hear:
'Thy white neck is like ivory;
I feed among thy lilies, dear: 175
Stay me with flagons, comfort me
With apples; thee would I enclose!
Thy twin breasts are as two young roes.' "

    Clarel protested, yet as one
Part lamed in candor; and took tone   180

In formal wise: "Nay, pardon me,
But you misdeem it: Solomon's Song
Is allegoric—needs must be."
   "Proof, proof, pray, if 'tis not too long."
"Why, Saint Bernard——"
                        "Who? *Sir* Bernard?   185
Never that knight for me left card!"
   "No, *Saint* Bernard, 'twas he of old
The Song's hid import first unrolled—
Confirmed in every after age:
The chapter-headings on the page   190
Of modern Bibles (in that Song)
Attest his rendering, and prolong:
A mystic burden."
              "Eh? so too
The Bonzes Hafiz' rhyme construe
Which lauds the grape of Shiraz. See,   195
They cant that in his frolic fire
Some bed-rid fakir would aspire
In foggy symbols. Me, oh me!—
What stuff of Levite and Divine!
Come, look at straight things more in line,   200
Blue eyes or black, which like you best?
Your Bella Donna, how's she dressed?"
   'Twas very plain this sprightly youth
Little suspected the grave truth
That he, with whom he thus made free,   205
A student was, a student late
Of reverend theology:
Nor Clarel was displeased thereat.
   The other now: "There is no tress
Can thrall one like a Jewess's.   210
A Hebrew husband, Hebrew-wed,
Is wondrous faithful, it is said;
Which needs be true; for, I suppose,
As bees are loyal to the rose,
So men to beauty. Of his girls,   215
On which did the brown Indian king,
Ahasuerus, shower his pearls?

Why, Esther: Judah wore the ring.
And Nero, captain of the world,
His arm about a Jewess curled—   220
Bright spouse, Poppæa. And with good will
Some Christian monarchs share the thrill,
In palace kneeling low before
Crowned Judah, like those nobs of yore.
These Hebrew witches! well-a-day,   225
Of Jeremiah what reck they?"

        Clarel looked down: was he depressed?
The prodigal resumed: "Earth's best,
Earth's loveliest portrait, daintiest,
Reveals Judæan grace and form: 230
Urbino's ducal mistress fair—
Ay, Titian's Venus, golden-warm.
Her lineage languishes in air
Mysterious as the unfathomed sea:
That grave, deep Hebrew coquetry!   235
Thereby Bathsheba David won;
In bath a purposed bait!—Have done!—
Blushing? The cuticle's but thin!
Blushing? yet you my mind would win.
Priests make a goblin of the Jew: 240
Shares he not flesh with me—with you?"
        What wind was this? And yet it swayed
Even Clarel's cypress. He delayed
All comment, gazing at him there.
Then first he marked the clustering hair   245
Which on the bright and shapely brow
At middle part grew slantly low:
Rich, tumbled, chestnut hood of curls,
Like to a Polynesian girl's,
Who, inland eloping with her lover,   250
The deacon-magistrates recover—
With sermon and black bread reprove
Who fed on berries and on love.
        So young (thought Clarel) yet so knowing;

With much of dubious at the heart, 255
Yet winsome in the outward showing;
With whom, with what, hast thou thy part?
In flaw upon the student's dream
A wafture of suspicion stirred:
He spake: "The Hebrew, it would seem, 260
You study much; you have averred
More than most Gentiles well may glean
In voyaging mere from scene to scene
Of shifting traffic." Irksomeness
Here vexed the other's light address; 265
But, ease assuming, gay he said:
"Oh, in my wanderings, why, I've met,
Among all kinds, Hebrews well-read,
And some nor dull nor bigot-bred;
Yes, I pick up, nor all forget." 270
    So saying, and as to be rid
Of further prosing, he undid
His vesture, turned him, smoothed his cot:
"Late, late; needs sleep, though sleep's a sot."
    "A word," cried Clarel: "bear with me: 275
Just nothing strange at all you see
Touching the Hebrews and their lot?"
    Recumbent here: "Why, yes, they share
That oddity the Gypsies heir:
About *them* why not make ado? 280
The Parsees are an odd tribe too;
Dispersed, no country, and yet hold
By immemorial rites, we're told.
Amigo, do not scourge me on;
Put up, put up your monkish thong! 285
Pray, pardon now; by peep of sun
Take horse I must. Good night, with song:

    "Lights of Shushan, if your urn
        Mellow shed the opal ray,
    To delude one—damsels, turn, 290
        Wherefore tarry? why betray?

Drop your garlands and away!
Leave me, phantoms that but feign;
Sting me not with inklings vain!

"But, if magic none prevail,   295
    Mocking in untrue romance;
Let your Paradise exhale
    Odors; and enlink the dance;
    And, ye rosy feet, advance
Till ye meet morn's ruddy Hours   300
Unabashed in Shushan's bowers!"

No more: they slept. A spell came down;
And Clarel dreamed, and seemed to stand
Betwixt a Shushan and a sand;
The Lyonese was lord of one,   305
The desert did the Tuscan own,
The pale pure monk. A zephyr fanned;
It vanished, and he felt the strain
Of clasping arms which would detain
His heart from such ascetic range.   310
He woke; 'twas day; he was alone,
The Lyonese being up and gone:
Vital he knew organic change,
Or felt, at least, that change was working—
A subtle innovator lurking.   315
    He rose, arrayed himself, and won
The roof to take the dawn's fresh air,
And heard a ditty, and looked down.
Who singing rode so debonair?
His cell-mate, flexible young blade,   320
Mounted in rear of cavalcade
Just from the gate, in rythmic way
Switching a light malacca gay:

        "Rules, who rules?
Fools the wise, makes wise the fools—   325
    Every ruling overrules?
Who the dame that keeps the house,

Provides the diet, and oh, so quiet,
Brings all to pass, the slyest mouse?
    Tell, tell it me: 330
Signora Nature, who but she!"

27. BY PARAPET

"Well may ye gaze! What's good to see
Better than Adam's humanity
When genial lodged! Such spell is given,
It lured the staid grandees of heaven,
Though biased in their souls divine   5
Much to one side—the feminine.—
He is the pleasantest small fellow!"

    It was the early-rising priest,
Who up there in the morning mellow
Had followed Clarel: "Not the least   10
Of pleasures here which I have known
Is meeting with that laxer one.
We talked below; but all the while
My thoughts were wandering away,
Though never once mine eyes did stray,   15
He did so pleasingly beguile
To keep them fixed upon his form:
Such harmony pervades his warm
Soft outline.—Why now, what a stare
Of incredulity you speak   20
From eyes! But it was some such fair
Young sinner in the time antique
Suggested to the happy Greek
His form of Bacchus—the sweet shape!
Young Bacchus, mind ye, not the old: 25
The Egyptian ere he crushed the grape.—
But—how? and home-sick are you? Come,
What's in your thoughts, pray? Wherefore mum?"
    So Derwent; though but ill he sped,
Clarel declining to be led   30

Or cheered. Nor less in covert way
That talk might have an after-sway
Beyond the revery which ran
Half-heeded now or dim: This man—
May Christian true such temper wish?   35
His happiness seems paganish.

28. DAVID'S WELL

The Lyonese had joined a train
Whereof the man of scars was one
Whose office led him further on
And barring longer stay. Farewell
He overnight had said, ere cell   5
He sought for slumber. Brief the word;
No hand he grasped; yet was he stirred,
Despite his will, in heart at core:
'Twas countrymen he here forsook:
He felt it; and his aspect wore   10
In the last parting, that strange look
Of one enlisted for sad fight
Upon some desperate dark shore,
Who bids adieu to the civilian,
Returning to his club-house bright,   15
In city cheerful with the million.
    But Nature never heedeth this:
To Nature nothing is amiss.

    It was a morning full of vent
And bustle. Other pilgrims went.   20
Later, accoutered in array
Don Hannibal and party sate
In saddle at the convent gate,
For Hebron bound.—"Ah, well-a-day!
I'm bolstered up here, tucked away: 25
My spare spar lashed behind, ye see;
This crutch for scepter. Come to me,
Embrace me, my dear friend," and leant;

"I'm off for Mamre; under oak
Of Abraham I'll pitch my tent,   30
Perchance, far from the battle's smoke.
Good friars and friends, behold me here
A poor one-legged pioneer;
I go, I march, I am the man
In fore-front of the limping van   35
Of refluent emigration. So,
Farewell, Don Derwent; Placido,
Farewell; and God bless all and keep!—
Start, dragoman; come, take your sheep
To Hebron."
               One among the rest   40
Attending the departure there
Was Clarel. Unto him, oppressed—
In travail of transition rare,
Scarce timely in its unconstraint
Was the droll Mexican's quirkish air   45
And humorous turn of hintings quaint.
   The group dispersed.
                    Pleased by the hill
And vale, the minster, grot and vine,
Hardly the pilgrims found the will
To go and such fair scene decline.   50
But not less Bethlehem, avow,
Negative grew to him whose heart,
Swayed by love's nearer magnet now,
Would fain without delay depart;
Yet comradeship did still require   55
That some few hours need yet expire.
   Restive, he sallied out alone,
And, ere long, place secluded won,
And there a well. The spot he eyed;
For fountains in that land, being rare,   60
Attention fix. "And, yes," he sighed,
Weighing the thing; "though everywhere
This vicinage quite altered be,
The well of Jesse's son I see;
For this in parched Adullam's lair   65

How sore he yearned: *ah me, ah me,*
That one would now upon me wait
With that sweet water by the gate!—
He stood: But who will bring to *me*
That living water which who drinks   70
He thirsteth not again! Let be:
A thirst that long may anguish thee,
Too long ungratified will die.
But whither now, my heart? wouldst fly
Each thing that keepeth not the pace   75
Of common uninquiring life?
What! fall back on clay commonplace?
Yearnest for peace so? sick of strife?
Yet how content thee with routine
Worldly? how mix with tempers keen   80
And narrow like the knife? how live
At all, if once a fugitive
From thy own nobler part, though pain
Be portion inwrought with the grain?"

But here, in fair accosting word,   85
A stranger's happy hail he heard
Descending from a vineyard nigh.
He turned: a pilgrim pleased his eye
(A Muscovite, late seen by shrine)
Good to behold—fresh as a pine—   90
Elastic, tall; complexion clear
As dawn in frosty atmosphere
Rose-tinged.
              They greet. At once, to reach
Accord, the Russian said, "Sit here:
You sojourn with the Latin set,   95
I with the Greeks; but well we're met:
All's much the same: many waves, one beach.
I'm mateless now; one, and but one
I've taken to: and he's late gone.
You may have crossed him, for indeed   100
He tarried with your Latin breed
While here: a juicy little fellow—

A Seckel pear, so small and mellow."
"We shared a cell last night." "Ye did?
And, doubtless, into chat ye slid: 105
The theme, now; I am curious there."
"Judæa—the Jews." With hightened air
The Russ rejoined: "And tell me, pray:
Who broached the topic? he?" "No, I;
And chary he in grudged reply   110
At first, but afterward gave way."
"Indeed?" the Russ, with meaning smile;
"But (further) did he aught revile?"
"The Jews, he said, were misconceived;
Much too he dropped which quite bereaved   115
The Scripture of its Runic spell.
But *Runic* said I? That's not well!
I alter, sure."
    Not marking here
Clarel in his self-taxing cheer;
But full of his own thoughts in clew,   120
"Right, I was right!" the other cried:
"Evade he cannot, no, nor hide.
Learn, he who whiled the hour for you,
His race supplied the theme: a Jew!"
   Clarel leaped up; "And can it be?   125
Some vague suspicion peered in me;
I sought to test it—test: and he—
Nay now, I mind me of a stir
Of color quick; and might it touch?"
And paused; then, as in slight demur: 130
"His cast of Hebrew is not much."
  "Enough to badge him."
       "Very well:
But why should he the badge repel?"
  "Our Russian sheep still hate the mark;
They try to rub it off, nor cease   135
On hedge or briar to leave the fleece
In tell-tale tags. Well, much so he,
Averse to Aaron's cipher dark
And mystical. Society

Is not quite catholic, you know,   140
Retains some prejudices yet—
Likes not the singular; and so
He'd melt in, nor be separate—
Exclusive. And I see no blame.
Nor rare thing is it in French Jew,   145
Cast among strangers—traveling too—
To cut old grandsire Abraham
As out of mode. I talked, ere you
With this our friend. Let me avow
My late surmise is surety now."   150

    They strolled, and parted. And amain
Confirmed the student felt the reign
Of reveries vague, which yet could mar,
Crossed by a surging element—
Surging while aiming at content: 155
So combs the billow ere it breaks upon the bar.

29. THE NIGHT RIDE

It was the day preceding Lent,
Shrove Tuesday named in English old
(Forefathers' English), and content,
Some yet would tarry, to behold
The initiatory nocturn rite.   5
    'Twas the small hour, as once again,
And final now, in mounted plight
They curve about the Bethlehem urn
Or vine-clad hollow of the swain,
And Clarel felt in every vein—   10
At last, Jerusalem! 'Twas thence
They started—thither they return,
Rounding the waste circumference.
    Now Belex in his revery light
Rolls up and down those guineas bright   15
Whose minted recompense shall chink
In pouch of sash when travel's brink

Of end is won. Djalea in face
Wears an abstraction, lit by grace
Which governed hopes of rapture lend: 20
On coins *his* musings likewise bend—
The starry sequins woven fair
Into black tresses. But an air
Considerate and prudent reigns;
For his the love not vainly sure: 25
'Tis passion deep of man mature
For one who half a child remains:
Yes, underneath a look sedate,
What throbs are known!
                  But desolate
Upon the pilgrims strangely fall 30
Eclipses heavier far than come
To hinds, which, after carnival,
Return to toil and querulous home.
Revert did they? in mind recall
Their pilgrimage, yes, sum it all? 35
Could Siddim haunt them? Saba's bay?
Did the deep nature in them say—
Two, two are missing—laid away
In deserts twin? They let it be,
Nor spake; the candor of the heart 40
Shrank from suspected counterpart.
   But one there was (and Clarel he)
Who, in his aspect free from cloud,
Here caught a gleam from source unspied,
As cliff may take on mountain-side, 45
When there one small brown cirque ye see,
Lit up in mole, how mellowly,
Day going down in somber shroud—
October-pall.
              But tell the vein
Of new emotion, inly held, 50
That so the long contention quelled—
Languor, and indecision, pain.
Was it abrupt resolve? a strain
Wiser than wisdom's self might teach?

Yea, now his hand would boldly reach   55
And pluck the nodding fruit to him,
Fruit of the tree of life. If doubt
Spin spider-like her tissue out,
And make a snare in reason dim—
Why hang a fly in flimsy web?   60
One thing was clear, one thing in sooth:
Stays not the prime of June or youth:
At flood that tide makes haste to ebb.
Recurred one mute appeal of Ruth
(Now first aright construed, he thought),   65
She seemed to fear for him, and say:
"Ah, tread not, sweet, my father's way,
In whom this evil spirit wrought
And dragged us hither where we die!"
Yes, now would he forsake that road—   70
Alertly now and eager hie
To dame and daughter, where they trod
The Dolorosa—quick depart
With them and seek a happier sky.
Warblings he heard of hope in heart,   75
Responded to by duty's hymn;
He, late but weak, felt now each limb
In strength how buoyant. But, in truth,
Was part caprice, sally of youth?
What pulse was this with burning beat?   80
Whence, whence the passion that could give
Feathers to thought, yea, Mercury's feet?
The Lyonese, to sense so dear,
Nor less from faith a fugitive—
Had he infected Clarel here?   85
        But came relapse: What end may prove?
Ah, almoner to Saba's dove,
Ah, bodeful text of hermit-rhyme!
But what! distrust the trustful eyes?
Are the sphered breasts full of mysteries   90
Which not the maiden's self may know?
May love's nice balance, finely slight,
Take tremor from fulfilled delight?

Can nature such a doom dispense
As, after ardor's tender glow, 95
To make the rapture more than pall
With evil secrets in the sense,
And guile whose bud is innocence—
Sweet blossom of the flower of gall?
Nay, nay: Ah! God, keep far from me 100
Cursed Manes and the Manichee!
At large here life proclaims the law:
Unto embraces myriads draw
Through sacred impulse. Take thy wife;
Venture, and prove the soul of life, 105
And let fate drive.—So he the while,
In shadow from the ledges thrown,
As down the Bethlehem hill they file—
Abreast upon the plain anon
Advancing.
       Far, in upland spot 110
A light is seen in Rama paling;
But Clarel sped, and heeded not,
At least recalled not Rachel wailing.

Aside they win a fountain clear,
The Cistern of the Kings—so named 115
Because (as vouched) the Magi here
Watered their camels, and reclaimed
The Ray, brief hid. Ere this they passed
Clarel looked in and there saw glassed
Down in the wave, one mellow star; 120
Then, glancing up, beheld afar
Enisled serene, the orb itself:—
Apt auspice here for journeying elf.

And now those skirting slopes they tread
Which devious bar the sunken bed 125
Of Hinnom. Thence uplifted shone
In hauntedness the deicide town
Faint silvered. Gates, of course, were barred;
But at the further eastern one,

St. Stephen's—there the turbaned guard   130
(To Belex known) at whispered word
Would ope. Thither, the nearer way,
By Jeremy's grot—they shun that ground,
For there an Ottoman camp's array
Deters. Through Hinnom now they push   135
Their course round Zion by the glen
Toward Rogel—whither shadowy rush
And where, at last, in cloud convene
(Ere, one, they sweep to gloomier hush)
Those two black chasms which enfold   140
Jehovah's hight. Flanking the well,
Ophel they turn, and gain the dell
Of Shaveh. Here the city old,
Fast locked in torpor, fixed in blight,
No hum sent forth, revealed no light: 145
Though, facing it, cliff-hung Siloam—
Sepulchral hamlet—showed in tomb
A twinkling lamp. The valley slept—
Obscure, in monitory dream
Oppressive, roofed with awful skies   150
Whose stars like silver nail-heads gleam
Which stud some lid over lifeless eyes.

30. THE VALLEY OF DECISION

Delay!—Shall flute from forth the Gate
Issue, to warble welcome here—
Upon this safe returning wait
In gratulation? And, for cheer,
When inn they gain, there shall they see   5
The door-post wreathed?
                           Howe'er it be,
Through Clarel a revulsion ran,
Such as may seize debarking man
First hearing on Coquimbo's ground
That subterranean sullen sound   10
Which dull foreruns the shock. His heart,

In augury fair arrested here,
Upbraided him: Fool! and didst part
From Ruth? Strangely a novel fear
Obtruded—petty, and yet worse   15
And more from reason too averse,
Than that recurrent haunting bier
Molesting him erewhile. And yet
It was but irritation, fret—
Misgiving that the lines he writ   20
Upon the eve before the start
For Siddim, failed, or were unfit—
Came short of the occasion's tone:
To leave her, leave her in grief's smart:
To leave her—her, the stricken one: 25
Now first to feel full force of it!
Away! to be but there, but there!
Vain goadings: yet of love true part.
But then the pledge with letter sent,
Though but a trifle, still might bear   30
A token in dumb argument
Expressive more than words.
      With knee
Straining against the saddle-brace,
He urges on; till, near the place
Of Hebrew graves, a light they see   35
Moving, and figures dimly trace:
Some furtive strange society.
Yet nearer as they ride, the light
Shuts down. "Abide!" enjoined the Druze;
"Waylayers these are none, but Jews,   40
Or I mistake, who here by night
Have stolen to do grave-digger's work.
During late outbreak in the town
The bigot in the baser Turk
Was so inflamed, some Hebrews dread   45
Assault, even here among their dead.
Abide a space; let me ride on."
  Up pushed he, spake, allayed the fright
Of them who had shut down the light

At sound of comers.
                              Close they draw—   50
Advancing, lit by fan-shaped rays
Shot from a small dark-lantern's jaw
Presented pistol-like. They saw
Mattocks and men, in outline dim
On either ominous side of him   55
From whom went forth that point of blaze.
Resting from labor, each one stays
His implement on grave-stones old.
New-dug, between these, they behold
Two narrow pits: and (nor remote)   60
Twin figures on the ground they note
Folded in cloaks.
                        "And who rest there?"
Rolfe sidelong asked.
                        "Our friends; have care!"
Replied the one that held in view
The lantern, slanting it a'shift,   65
Plainer disclosing them, and, too,
A broidered scarf, love's first chance gift,
The student's (which how well he knew!)
Binding one mantle's slender span.
        With piercing cry, as one distraught,   70
Down from his horse leaped Clarel—ran,
And hold of that cloak instant caught,
And bared the face. Then (like a man
Shot through the heart, but who retains
His posture) rigid he remains—   75
The mantle's border in his hand,
His glazed eyes unremoved. The band
Of Jews—the pilgrims—all look on
Shocked or amazed.
                        But speech he won:
"No—yes: enchanted here!—her name?"   80
    "Ruth, Nathan's daughter," said a Jew
Who kenned him now—the youth that came
Oft to the close; "but, thou—forbear;
The dawn's at hand and haste is due:

See, by her side, 'tis Agar there."   85
    "Ruth? Agar?—*art* thou, God?—But ye—
All swims, and I but blackness see.—
How happed it? speak!"
              "The fever—grief:
'Twere hard to tell; was no relief."
    "And ye—your tribe—'twas *ye* denied   90
Me access to this virgin's side
In bitter trial: take my curse!—
O blind, blind, barren universe!
Now am I like a bough torn down,
And I must wither, cloud or sun!—   95
Had I been near, this had not been.
Do spirits look down upon this scene?—
The message? some last word was left?"
    "For thee? no, none; the life was reft
Sudden from Ruth; and Agar died   100
Babbling of gulls and ocean wide—
Out of her mind."
            "And here's the furl
Of Nathan's faith: then perish faith—
'Tis perjured!—Take me, take me, Death!
Where Ruth is gone, me thither whirl,   105
Where'er it be!"
          "Ye do outgo
Mad Korah. Boy, this is the Dale
Of Doom, God's last assizes; so,
Curb thee; even if sharp grief assail,
Respect these precincts lest thou know   110
An ill."
      "Give way, quit thou our dead!"
Menaced another, striding out;
"Art thou of us? turn thee about!"
    "Spurn—I'll endure; all spirit's fled
When one fears nothing.—Bear with me,   115
Yet bear!—Conviction is not gone
Though faith's gone: that which shall not be
It *ought* to be!"
      But here came on,

With heavy footing, hollow heard,
Hebrews, which bare rude slabs, to place 120
Athwart the bodies when interred,
That earth should weigh not on the face;
For coffin was there none; and all
Was make-shift in this funeral.

　　Uncouthly here a Jew began 125
To re-adjust Ruth's cloak. Amain
Did Clarel push him; and, in hiss:
"Not thou—for me!—Alone, alone
In such bride-chamber to lie down!
Nay, leave one hand out—like to this— 130
That so the bridegroom may not miss
To kiss it first, when soon he comes.—
But 'tis not she!" and hid his face.

　　They laid them in the under-glooms—
Each pale one in her portioned place. 135
The gravel, from the bank raked down,
Dull sounded on those slabs of stone,
Grave answering grave—dull and more dull,
Each mass growing more, till either pit was full.

　　As up from Kedron dumb they drew, 140
Then first the shivering Clarel knew
Night's damp. The Martyr's port is won—
Stephen's; harsh grates the bolt withdrawn;
And, over Olivet, comes on
Ash Wednesday in the gray of dawn. 145

31. Dirge

Stay, Death. Not mine the Christus-wand
Wherewith to charge thee and command:
I plead. Most gently hold the hand
Of her thou leadest far away;
Fear thou to let her naked feet 5
Tread ashes—but let mosses sweet

Her footing tempt, where'er ye stray.
Shun Orcus; win the moonlit land
Belulled—the silent meadows lone,
Where never any leaf is blown   10
From lily-stem in Azrael's hand.
There, till her love rejoin her lowly
(Pensive, a shade, but all her own)
On honey feed her, wild and holy;
Or trance her with thy choicest charm.   15
And if, ere yet the lover's free,
Some added dusk thy rule decree—
That shadow only let it be
Thrown in the moon-glade by the palm.

32. Passion Week

Day passed; and passed a second one,
A third—fourth—fifth; and bound he sate
In film of sorrow without moan—
Abandoned, in the stony strait
Of mutineer thrust on wild shore,   5
Hearing, beyond the roller's froth,
The last dip of the parting oar.
Alone, for all had left him so;
Though Rolfe, Vine, Derwent—each was loth,
How loth to leave him, or to go   10
Be first. From Vine he caught new sense
Developed through fate's pertinence.
Friendly they tarried—blameless went:
Life, avaricious, still demands
Her own, and more; the world is rent   15
With partings.
              But, since all are gone,
Why lingers he, the stricken one?
Why linger where no hope can be?
Ask grief, love ask—fidelity
In dog that by the corse abides   20
Of shepherd fallen—abides, abides

Though autumn into winter glides,
Till on the mountain all is chill
And snow-bound, and the twain lie still.

How oft through Lent the feet were led   25
Of this chastised and fasting one
To neutral silence of the dead
In Kedron's gulf. One morn he sate
Down poring toward it from the gate
Sealed and named Golden. There a tomb,   30
Erected in time's recent day,
In block along the threshold lay
Impassable. From Omar's bloom
Came birds which lit, nor dreamed of harm,
On neighboring stones. His visage calm   35
Seemed not the one which late showed play
Of passion's throe; but here divine
No peace; ignition in the mine
Announced is by the rush, the roar:
These end; yet may the coal burn on—   40
Still slumberous burn beneath the floor
Of pastures where the sheep lie down.
      Ere long a cheerful choral strain
He hears; 'tis an Armenian train
Embowered in palms they bear, which (green,   45
And shifting oft) reveal the mien
Of flamens tall and singers young
In festal robes: a rainbow throng,
Like dolphins off Madeira seen
Which quick the ship and shout dismay.   50
With the blest anthem, censers sway,
Whose opal vapor, spiral borne,
Blends with the heavens' own azure Morn
Of Palms; for 'twas Palm Sunday bright,
Though thereof he, oblivious quite,   55
Knew nothing, nor that here they came
In memory of the green acclaim
Triumphal, and hosanna-roll
Which hailed Him on the ass's foal.

But unto Clarel that bright view   60
Into a dusk reminder grew:
He saw the tapers—saw again
The censers, singers, and the wreath
And litter of the bride of death
Pass through the Broken Fountain's lane;   65
In treble shrill and bass how deep
The men and boys he heard again
The undetermined contest keep
About the bier—the bier Armenian.
Yet dull, in torpor dim, he knew   70
The futile omen in review.

Yet three more days, and leadenly
From over Mary's port and arch,
On Holy Thursday, he the march
Of friars beheld, with litany   75
Filing beneath his feet, and bent
With crosses craped to sacrament
Down in the glenned Gethsemane.
Yes, Passion Week; the altars cower—
Each shrine a dead dismantled bower.   80

But when Good Friday dirged her gloom
Ere brake the morning, and each light
Round Calvary faded and the TOMB,
What exhalations met his sight:—
Illusion of grief's wakeful doom: 85
The dead walked. There, amid the train,
Wan Nehemiah he saw again—
With charnel beard; and Celio passed
As in a dampened mirror glassed;
Gleamed Mortmain, pallid as wolf-bone   90
Which bleaches where no man hath gone;
And Nathan in his murdered guise—
Sullen, and Hades in his eyes;
Poor Agar, with such wandering mien
As in her last blank hour was seen.   95
And each and all kept lonely state,

Yea, man and wife passed separate.
But Ruth—ah, how estranged in face!
He knew her by no earthly grace:
Nor might he reach to her in place.　　　　　　100
And languid vapors from them go
Like thaw-fogs curled from dankish snow.

　　　Where, where now He who helpeth us,
The Comforter?—Tell, Erebus!

33. EASTER

BUT ON THE THIRD DAY CHRIST AROSE;
And, in the town He knew, the rite
Commemorative eager goes
Before the hour. Upon the night
Between the week's last day and first,　　　　5
No more the Stabat is dispersed
Or Tenebræ. And when the day,
The Easter, falls in calendar
The same to Latin and the array
Of all schismatics from afar—　　　　　　10
Armenians, Greeks from many a shore—
Syrians, Copts—profusely pour
The hymns: 'tis like the choric gush
Of torrents Alpine when they rush
To swell the anthem of the spring.　　　　15
　　　That year was now. Throughout the fane,
Floor, and arcades in double ring
About the gala of THE TOMB,
Blazing with lights, behung with bloom—
What child-like thousands roll the strain,　　20
The hallelujah after pain,
Which in all tongues of Christendom
Still through the ages has rehearsed
That Best, the outcome of the Worst.

Nor blame them who by lavish rite 25
Thus greet the pale victorious Son,
Since Nature times the same delight,
And rises with the Emerging One;
Her passion-week, her winter mood
She slips, with crape from off the Rood. 30
    In soft rich shadow under dome,
With gems and robes repletely fine,
The priests like birds Brazilian shine:
And moving tapers charm the sight,
Enkindling the curled incense-fume: 35
A dancing ray, Auroral light.

    Burn on the hours, and meet the day.
The morn invites; the suburbs call
The concourse to come forth—this way!
Out from the gate by Stephen's wall, 40
They issue, dot the hills, and stray
In bands, like sheep among the rocks;
And the Good Shepherd in the heaven,
To whom the charge of these is given,
The Christ, ah! counts He there His flocks? 45
    But they, at each suburban shrine,
Grateful adore that Friend benign;
Though chapel now and cross divine
Too frequent show neglected; nay,
For charities of early rains 50
Rim them about with vernal stains,
Forerunners of maturer May,
When those red flowers, which so can please,
(*Christ's-Blood-Drops* named—anemones),
Spot Ephraim and the mountain-way. 55
    But heart bereft is unrepaid
Though Thammuz' spring in Thammuz' glade
Invite; then how in Joel's glen?
What if dyed shawl and bodice gay
Make bright the black dell? what if they 60
In distance clear diminished be

To seeming cherries dropped on pall
Borne graveward under laden tree?
The cheer, so human, might not call
The maiden up; *Christ is arisen:*   65
But Ruth, may Ruth so burst the prison?

    The rite supreme being ended now,
Their confluence here the nations part:
Homeward the tides of pilgrims flow,
By contrast making the walled town   70
Like a depopulated mart;
More like some kirk on week-day lone,
On whose void benches broodeth still
The brown light from November hill.

    But though the freshet quite be gone—   75
Sluggish, life's wonted stream flows on.

34. VIA CRUCIS

Some leading thoroughfares of man
In wood-path, track, or trail began;
Though threading heart of proudest town,
They follow in controlling grade
A hint or dictate, nature's own,   5
By man, as by the brute, obeyed.

    Within Jerusalem a lane,
Narrow, nor less an artery main
(Though little knoweth it of din),
In part suggests such origin.   10
The restoration or repair,
Successive through long ages there,
Of city upon city tumbled,
Might scarce divert that thoroughfare,
Whose hill abideth yet unhumbled   15

Above the valley-side it meets.
Pronounce its name, this natural street's:
The *Via Crucis*—even the way
Tradition claims to be the one
Trod on that Friday far away   20
By Him our pure exemplar shown.

'Tis Whitsun-tide. From paths without,
Through Stephen's gate—by many a vein
Convergent brought within this lane,
Ere sun-down shut the loiterer out—   25
As 'twere a frieze, behold the train!
Bowed water-carriers; Jews with staves;
Infirm gray monks; over-loaded slaves;
Turk soldiers—young, with home-sick eyes;
A Bey, bereaved through luxuries;   30
Strangers and exiles; Moslem dames
Long-veiled in monumental white,
Dumb from the mounds which memory claims;
A half-starved vagrant Edomite;
Sore-footed Arab girls, which toil   35
Depressed under heap of garden-spoil;
The patient ass with panniered urn;
Sour camels humped by heaven and man,
Whose languid necks through habit turn
For ease—for ease they hardly gain.   40
In varied forms of fate they wend—
Or man or animal, 'tis one:
Cross-bearers all, alike they tend
And follow, slowly follow on.

But, lagging after, who is he   45
Called early every hope to test,
And now, at close of rarer quest,
Finds so much more the heavier tree?
From slopes whence even Echo's gone,
Wending, he murmurs in low tone: 50
"They wire the world—far under sea

They talk; but never comes to me
A message from beneath the stone."

Dusked Olivet he leaves behind,
And, taking now a slender wynd,   55
Vanishes in the obscurer town.

35. Epilogue

If Luther's day expand to Darwin's year,
Shall that exclude the hope—foreclose the fear?

Unmoved by all the claims our times avow,
The ancient Sphinx still keeps the porch of shade;
And comes Despair, whom not her calm may cow,   5
And coldly on that adamantine brow
Scrawls undeterred his bitter pasquinade.
But Faith (who from the scrawl indignant turns)
With blood warm oozing from her wounded trust,
Inscribes even on her shards of broken urns   10
The sign o' the cross—*the spirit above the dust!*

Yea, ape and angel, strife and old debate—
The harps of heaven and dreary gongs of hell;
Science the feud can only aggravate—
No umpire she betwixt the chimes and knell: 15
The running battle of the star and clod
Shall run forever—if there be no God.

Degrees we know, unknown in days before;
The light is greater, hence the shadow more;
And tantalized and apprehensive Man   20
Appealing—Wherefore ripen us to pain?
Seems there the spokesman of dumb Nature's train.
But through such strange illusions have they passed
Who in life's pilgrimage have baffled striven—

Even death may prove unreal at the last,   25
And stoics be astounded into heaven.

    Then keep thy heart, though yet but ill-resigned—
Clarel, thy heart, the issues there but mind;
That like the crocus budding through the snow—
That like a swimmer rising from the deep—   30
That like a burning secret which doth go
Even from the bosom that would hoard and keep;
Emerge thou mayst from the last whelming sea,
And prove that death but routs life into victory.

Editorial Appendix

HISTORICAL AND CRITICAL NOTE
By Walter E. Bezanson

HISTORICAL SUPPLEMENT
By Hershel Parker

TEXTUAL RECORD

RELATED DOCUMENTS

THE FIRST *of the four parts of this* APPENDIX *is a historical and critical essay by Walter E. Bezanson interpreting* Clarel *and sketching its background, composition, publication, reception, and later critical history (to 1960). This essay was first published as the introduction to Bezanson's Hendricks House edition of* Clarel *in 1960; it is reprinted here, by permission of the publisher, in Bezanson's slightly revised form.*

The second part is a historical supplement to Bezanson's essay by Hershel Parker, consisting of notes on important matters brought to light since 1960. As contributing scholar Mark Niemeyer worked with Parker on this supplement.

The third part of the APPENDIX *records textual information and offers explanatory discussions. It consists of (1) a note on the textual history of* Clarel *and on the editorial principles of this edition and (2) a list of emendations—both this list and the note prepared by G. Thomas Tanselle with Alma A. MacDougall; (3) discussions of proper names, allusions, and other points of interest in the text, prepared originally by Walter E. Bezanson for his 1960 edition, and now revised, augmented, and verified for this edition by Harrison Hayford and Alma A. MacDougall, with his approval; and discussions of certain problematical textual readings, prepared by G. Thomas Tanselle.*

The fourth part of the APPENDIX *presents five related documents, with analyses: (1) Melville's annotated copy of* Clarel, *used as a basis for emending the text; (2) Elizabeth Shaw Melville's two copies of* Clarel; *(3) the "Ditty of Aristippus" manuscript; (4) a table of parallel passages in* Clarel *and Melville's 1856–57 journal; and (5) Melville's surviving manuscript of "Monody." The first three of these documents were prepared by G. Thomas Tanselle, the fourth by Walter E. Bezanson with Alma A. MacDougall, and the fifth by Harrison Hayford.*

To insure uniform textual policy in all volumes of the edition the same three editors, Harrison Hayford, Hershel Parker, and G. Thomas Tanselle, participate in the planning and establishment of textual policy for all volumes, except as otherwise noted; even when other editors are specifically named (as in the case of certain writings edited from manuscript) the final decisions still rest with one or more of these editors, as noted in individual volumes. Final responsibility for all aspects of every volume is exercised by the general editor, Harrison Hayford.

Editorial work on the Northwestern-Newberry Clarel *was begun in 1965 under an initial grant from the U.S. Office of Education. Richard Harter Fogle, at this early stage, supplied a historical note, which was not ultimately used because of a change in editorial policy.*

Alma A. MacDougall, as a joint editor of this volume and as editorial coordinator of the Edition, contributed to every aspect of the volume. In addition to the contributions listed above, she supervised its production and provided copyediting and proofreading.

Lynn Horth, as executive editor of the Edition, under grants from the National Endowment for the Humanities, supervised the keyprocessing and proofreadings of the text, assisted in the additional research for the explanatory discussions, and helped with the final production of the book.

These members of the Melville Edition staff performed collations and proofreadings: Mary K. Bercaw, Harrison Hayford, Jennifer S. Johnson, Richard Colles Johnson, Kermit Moyer, Peter Roode, and Robert Sandberg.

The editors were given frequent aid and counsel by the bibliographical associate, Richard Colles Johnson. Robert C. Ryan, the manuscript associate, reexamined numerous difficult textual readings in the manuscripts used. R. D. Madison, editorial associate, proofread the initial printouts of the explanatory discussions. Staff members of the Newberry Library deserve thanks for indispensable assistance: Kenneth Cain for photographing illustrations and John Aubrey for finding numerous books. Further editorial assistance was given by Theresa Biancheri, Jo Ann Casey, Jill Fahlgren, Ann Larson, Carla Reiter, James A. Schulz, and Mary Valentine.

Authorization to edit manuscripts and permission to publish material from their collections has been granted by (1) the American Antiquarian Society, Worcester, Mass.; (2) the Berkshire Athenæum, Pittsfield, Mass.; (3) the Houghton Library, Harvard University; (4) The Newberry Library, Chicago (Melville Collection); (5) the New York Public Library, Astor, Lenox and Tilden Foundations (Duyckinck Collection and Melville Family Papers, Gansevoort-Lansing Collection, Rare Books and Manuscripts Division). The editors have also made use of materials in the collections of Indiana University Library, the Milwaukee Public Library, the New York Public Library, Northwestern University Library, the University of Chicago Library, and the Widener Library of Harvard University. They are indebted for information and assistance to Norwood Andrews, Jr., Leon Aufdemberge, Roger Carlson, Brendan Cassidy, Ruth T. Degenhardt, Shirley Dettlaff, Arthur Freeman, Daniel Garrison, Robert Jay Haber, Dr. Roslyn A. Haber, Charles W. Hayford, Josephine W. Hayford, Thomas F. Heffernan, Bernard McGinn, Robert Michaelson, Lewis Mudge, William Reese, Heddy-Ann Richter, Viola Sachs, Gary Scharnhorst, and Gary Elliott Yela. And they also wish to acknowledge the support of Martin Mueller, chairman of the Department of English, College of Arts and Sciences, Northwestern University, which provided an office and other services to the editorial staff.

Renewed acknowledgment is made here to those whose assistance was recorded by Walter E. Bezanson in his 1960 edition of Clarel and to Gail Coffler.

Tintype (original size four by three in.), New York, circa 1870.
Courtesy of the Berkshire Athenæum.

Historical and Critical Note

OF ALL Melville's major writings *Clarel* has suffered most from undeserved oblivion and casual plundering. Until midcentury even the most partisan of Melville's modern advocates hesitated to endure the rigors of a four-part poem of 150 cantos that runs to almost eighteen thousand lines. An age little given to the reading of narrative verse lived easily with the notion that

EDITORS' NOTE: The present essay by Walter E. Bezanson was published as the "Introduction" to his edition of *Clarel* (New York: Hendricks House, 1960). It is reprinted here by arrangement with Hendricks House, Inc. Unlike the essay uniformly titled HISTORICAL NOTE in the other volumes of the Northwestern-Newberry Edition, it is a critical as well as historical essay, presenting its author's interpretation of the work unmodified by the editors (apart from updating of its textual and bibliographical references) and with only his own minor changes. Bezanson's 1960 "The Characters: A Critical Index," also with only his own minor changes, appears as the final section of his essay (pp. 613–35). Although the essay represents an earlier stage of Melville studies, it is generally recognized as the still indispensable introduction to Melville's long, difficult, and highly allusive poem, which, more than his other works, continues to require such initial critical assistance to its readers. Subsequent biographical and scholarly, but not all critical, developments are covered and some topics further amplified in the HISTORICAL SUPPLEMENT by Hershel Parker, pp. 639–73 below. Bezanson's "Explanatory Notes" from his 1960 edition, revised and supplemented by Harrison Hayford and Alma A. MacDougall with his cooperation, are presented in the DISCUSSIONS, along with textual discussions by G. Thomas Tanselle.

Clarel neither invoked obligations nor promised rewards. On the basis of faint-hearted readings that let go after a hundred pages, the poem was assumed to be too complex and discursive, overly private in reference and symbol, and above all, interminably long. Under the consoling myths that *Clarel* was the late flickering of a waned imagination and that poetry was a left-handed venture for Melville, the poem lay until the 1940's where the critics had dropped it in the summer of 1876—among the cold ashes of a presumably superannuated talent.

The attractions of *Clarel* are several. Recent critics have assured us it is a much better poem than had been realized; the poem is labyrinthine, but it is no morass. Melville's poetic style, a curious mingling of modern and archaic idiom, has probably profited from changing tastes. Even the idea of a long narrative poem is more attractive now that we have fresh, contemporary translations of Homer, Virgil, Dante, and Goethe.

The poem will interest modern readers who have been captured by the image of the man who wrote it, for it abounds with revelations of his inner life. Melville did not soften up in his later years, as Whitman and Emerson did, but remained unsimple and hard to the end. The period of the late sixties and early seventies, when Melville was composing *Clarel*, lies almost midway between *Moby-Dick* (1851) and *Billy Budd, Sailor* (left unfinished in 1891), though it is probable Melville lived with the themes of his poem from the winter of his Mediterranean voyage (1856–57) to the summer of publication (1876). Thus a great chunk of his imaginative life is better examined here than anywhere else.

Again, there are few works of Anglo-American literature which rival *Clarel* as a rendering of the spiritual exigencies of the late Victorian era. The poem is an intricate documentation of a major crisis in Western civilization—the apparent smash-up of revealed religion in the age of Darwin. To the lyric despair of Tennyson, Arnold, and Clough, and to the softer distress of Longfellow and Lowell, Melville added not only a more sizable lamentation, but this in-close fictional study of what the crisis meant to various representative men. He did his utmost to project more than his own spiritual dilemma. His effort to cope with the major tensions of an age makes *Clarel* a historical document almost of the first order.

And finally, the reawakening of the religious sensibility after World War II and the emergence of depth psychology brought a new relevance to the matter and mode of Melville's poem.

There is still, of course, the problem of how good a poet Melville was. It may well be that his poetic stature has been unduly overshadowed by his eminence as a prose romancer. We have not lived long enough with the idea that he was a poet at all to decide justly how good a poet he was. Fearing that claims for his verse would seem a generous illusion stemming from love of his prose, we may have sold the poetry short. Or we may have been unwittingly baffled by finding in the poetry many of the conceptual values of the novels expressed without that rich copiousness which is the hallmark of his best-known prose. Once we face up to the idea that Melville's poetry is not an extension of the lyric vein of his famous novels but is a wholly new mode of contracted discourse we will be more ready to judge the poetry. Melville was capable of pretty lines now and then. Sometimes he indulged his marginal gift for songs of sentiment. But essentially he was drawn to a non-lyrical, even harsh, prosodic line. Center for him as poet was usually the weight and texture of a "situation." He was so convinced of the complexity of the human condition that he preferred to make his poems situational constructions, as if to say that personality and circumstance are always shaping belief, meaning, and sensibility. If this narrative impulse links him with Browning and Meredith, among his English contemporaries, his characteristic idiom binds him also to Emerson and Dickinson. Though Melville is too intellectual a poet ever to be popular, he is surely among any cluster of the half-dozen best poets of nineteenth-century America.

Clarel, his major effort in verse, shows almost the full range of his poetic powers and limitations, both of which are considerable. A poetic fiction about a naive American youth named Clarel,[1] on pilgrimage through the Palestinian ruins with a provocative cluster of companions, gave Melville his "situation." A great deal lay back of the choice.

---

1. Pronounced *Clăr′ ĕl* according to family tradition in referring to the title of the poem; the metrical demands of the poem generally support the first-syllable accent. Parenthetical references to the text of *Clarel* are to part, canto, and line. In the section on "Sources" at the end of this NOTE its documentation is explained and its short citations are given in full.

I

MEDITERRANEAN JOURNEY: 1856–57

IN THE BEGINNING the East was the dream of a child—according to one of Melville's early projections. "For I very well remembered," young Redburn confessed,

> staring at a man myself, who was pointed out to me by my aunt one Sunday in Church, as the person who had been in Stony Arabia, and passed through strange adventures there, all of which with my own eyes I had read in the book which he wrote, an arid-looking book in a pale yellow cover.
>
> "See what big eyes he has," whispered my aunt, "they got so big, because when he was almost dead with famishing in the desert, he all at once caught sight of a date tree, with the ripe fruit hanging on it."
>
> . . . When church was out, I wanted my aunt to take me along and follow the traveler home. But she said the constables would take us up, if we did; and so I never saw this wonderful Arabian traveler again. But he long haunted me; and several times I dreamt of him, and thought his great eyes were grown still larger and rounder; and once I had a vision of the date tree. (chap. 1, pp. 5–6)

By the time Melville wrote *Redburn* (1849) his own yearning for palm-tree lands had already taken him to the Pacific. Except for the short voyage to Liverpool in 1839, he had adventured westward, as was right for the young American in the times of Emerson and Greeley. But the "vision" of the date tree in an Eastern desert would not dissolve.

With the proof sheets of *White-Jacket* (1850) in his trunk, Melville, October 11, 1849, boarded the *Southampton* in the North River. At the age of thirty he had persuaded himself that as a practical young man with a glittering literary reputation he would do well to market his fifth book in person at the London publishing offices. That he was also in the mood for new adventures soon appeared. With two shipboard companions, a cousin of Bayard Taylor and George J. Adler, a German scholar, he plotted a romantic expedition: "This afternoon Dr Taylor & I sketched a plan for going down the Danube from Vienna to Constantinople; thence to Athens in the steamer; to Beyroot & Jerusalem—Alexandia and the Pyramids . . . I am full (just now) of this glorious *Eastern* jaunt. Think of it!— Jerusalem & the Pyramids—Constantinople, the Egean, & old

Athens" (*Journals*, p. 7). But the expenses were reckoned at four hundred dollars, and when, in London, Melville found he could not get for *White-Jacket* the terms he had hoped for, he and Adler said good-by to Dr. Taylor, who went off to the East without them, Melville consoling himself with chops and ale at the Edinburgh Castle tavern. He must have been reminded of his disappointment when he spent a fine evening with Albert Smith, the comic writer, just back from the East and full of stories, and again when he met Alexander William Kinglake at one of Samuel Rogers's famous breakfast parties; Kinglake was as famous for an Eastern romance, *Eöthen* (1844), as Melville was for two Polynesian idylls, *Typee* (1846) and *Omoo* (1847). Sailing back to New York in December, Melville carried with him a case of books acquired in London and Paris; among them were William Beckford's voluptuous Eastern fantasy, *Vathek* (1786), and Thomas Hope's Byronic romance, *Anastasius* (1819).[2] At least vicariously he would have his jaunt after all.

For Melville it was youth's last indulgence. The *Typee-Omoo* days were done. In both art and experience maturation and disquietude were at hand. With the move to Pittsfield in the fall of 1850 came the immense surrender to the Whale; then, with the willed disaster of *Pierre* (1852), he entered the whirlpool. By the fall of 1856, with two more novels and more than a dozen stories and sketches completed, he was exhausted and damaged. It was then that he went to the Levant.

Family records and his own writings make clear Melville's distress in the five years before his Mediterranean voyage. "We all felt anxious," his wife Elizabeth recorded in a memorandum,

> about the strain on his health in Spring of 1853. . . . In Feb 1855 he had his first attack of severe rheumatism in his back—so that he was helpless—and in the following June an attack of Sciatica—Our neighbor in Pittsfield Dr. O. W. Holmes attended & prescribed for him—. . . . In Fall of 1856 he went to Europe and travelled 6 or 7 months going to the Holy Land came home about the time the Confidence Man was published in 1857—and with much improved health.

2. Sealts 54, 282; for Melville's list of books acquired on his 1849–50 trip see *Journals*, pp. 144–45.

And in a later recollection she reemphasized the fact of "his health being impaired by too close application" just before he left.[3] Melville's writings of the period amply indicate the psychosomatic nature of much of this illness. From *Pierre* to *The Confidence-Man* (1857) they reflect a profound introversion, either explicit or masked by a sometimes worked-up robustiousness, and "I and My Chimney" seems to support the family tradition that relatives and neighbors questioned his sanity during these years. Yet through the discipline of his craft—the muted precision of a "Bartleby"—he held himself at what he was to define in *Clarel* as "The perilous outpost of the sane" (3.19.98).

There can be no question that the sturdy, bearded American who boarded the screw-steamer *Glasgow* on October 11, 1856, precisely seven years after the European voyage, was a changed man from the young romantic. To be sure, two nights before sailing he had joined heartily with a small party of friends in New York, "warming like an old sailor over the supper." But the mood was no longer characteristic. Hawthorne saw the difference at once when Melville sought him out at the consulate in Liverpool. "He said that he already felt much better than in America; but observed that he did not anticipate much pleasure in his rambles, for that the spirit of adventure is gone out of him. He certainly is much overshadowed since I saw him last. . . ." Hawthorne's famous account of Melville's brief visit[4] is of extreme interest in relation to *Clarel* since it gives a shrewd yet sympathetic analysis of Melville's temper just as he left for the experience out of which the poem was to come. Hawthorne found him

3. Quoted from her original notebook now in the Houghton Library of Harvard University; also in Sealts, *Early Lives*, pp. 169, 171.

4. See *Journals*, pp. 628–33, reprinted from *The English Notebooks by Nathaniel Hawthorne*, ed. Randall Stewart (New York: Modern Language Society of America, 1941), pp. 432–33, 437, with minor changes verified from the original notebook in the Morgan Library. Those portions italicized in the quotation below were not printed in Sophia Hawthorne's edition of *Passages from the English Note-Books of Nathaniel Hawthorne* (Boston: Fields, Osgood, 1870), II, 105–6, which Melville owned and no doubt read while composing *Clarel* (Sealts 251). Her edition used five sets of ellipses in this entry of November 30—surely an infinitely tantalizing fact to Melville. Mrs. Hawthorne said in her "Preface" that she had omitted some of her husband's remarks that were "too personal with regard to himself or others"—as indeed was the case here, by her terms.

looking much as he used to do *(a little paler, and perhaps a little sadder)*, *in a rough outside coat*, and with his characteristic gravity and reserve of manner. . . . *Melville has not been well, of late; he has been affected with neuralgic complaints in his head and limbs, and no doubt has suffered from too constant literary occupation, pursued without much success, latterly; and his writings, for a long while past, have indicated a morbid state of mind*. . . . I do not wonder that he found it necessary to take an airing through the world, after so many years of toilsome pen-labor *and domestic life*, following upon so wild and adventurous a youth as his was. . . . we took a pretty long walk together, and sat down in a hollow among the sand hills (sheltering ourselves from the high, cool wind) *and smoked a cigar*. Melville, as he always does, began to reason of Providence and futurity, and of everything that lies beyond human ken, *and informed me that he had "pretty much made up his mind to be annihilated"; but still he does not seem to rest in that anticipation; and, I think, will never rest until he gets hold of a definite belief. It is strange how he persists—and has persisted ever since I knew him, and probably long before—in wandering to-and fro over these deserts, as dismal and monotonous as the sand hills amid which we were sitting. He can neither believe, nor be comfortable in his unbelief; and he is too honest and courageous not to try to do one or the other. If he were a religious man, he would be one of the most truly religious and reverential*; he has a very high and noble nature, and better worth immortality than most of us.

Hawthorne made out Melville's visa for him and signed it, took care of his trunk at the consulate when he left, and completed the publication contract for *The Confidence-Man* "on behalf of Herman Melville" with Messrs. Longman and Company. Such helpful, kindly acts quieted, without dissolving, whatever ambiguities still followed in the wake of the intensive fifteen-month friendship of 1850–51. This man Hawthorne was still of special importance to Melville, as *Clarel* was to testify.

Melville's journey of five months and fifteen thousand miles that winter took him to three continents and nine countries. He traveled alone, for the most part, confiding to three small notebooks whatever he had time or need to save from the welter of his impressions. The 1856–57 journal—prime source for *Clarel*—is an extraordinary document, different in kind from the essentially matter-of-fact record he had kept on his previous European tour of 1849–50. To be sure, he entered the names of scores of places and people, and recorded random tourist reactions; but he also made deeper explorations into the geography and events of his inner life than in his other journals. For readers of *Clarel* interest in the 1856–57 journal divides between the account of Melville's three weeks in the Holy Land and the larger aura of significant moods in which his whole Mediterranean experience was bathed. Melville was well aware that he had reached a turning point in his life. Here in the ancient world, long dreamed of for its fabulous resources, he might or might not be able to renew the rhythms of existence.

Going through the Straits of Gibraltar that sunset evening in November of 1856 was a dreamlike return to the womb of history. He noted in his journal the great Rock lit up, throwing the rest in shadow; then: "Calm within Straits. Long swell took us. The Meditterranean." The next day was rejuvenating: "Beautiful morning. Blue sea & sky. Warm as May. . . . Threw open my coat.—Such weather as one might have in Paridise. Pacific" (p. 52). But the Paradise-Pacific mood of expectation in which, momentarily, he had entered the Mediterranean could not be sustained as he sailed by the Greek Islands: "Among others, Delos, of a most barren aspect, however flowery in fable. I heard it was peculiarly sterile. Patmos, too, not remote; another disenchanting isle" (p. 71). The equation gave way: "The former [Greek islands] have lost their virginity. The latter [Pacific islands] are fresh as at their first creation. The former look worn, and are meagre, like life after enthusiasm is gone. The aspect of all of them is sterile & dry" (p. 72). These fundamental antonyms of the 1856–57 journal—Paradise and earthly existence, innocence and experience, creativeness and sterility, fable and fact—were to become metaphoric polarities of the poem. The split was a haunting one to Melville, a symptom of the double vision that had become and would remain his painful gift, as Hawthorne had noted. At Cyprus he wrote: "From these waters rose Venus from the foam. Found it as hard to realize such a thing as to realize on Mt Olivet that from there Christ rose" (p. 95). At times he was able to be ruefully calm: "One finds that, after all, the most noted localities are made up of common elements of earth, air, & water" (p. 96). But again he was almost savagely angry that it should be so:

> Was here again afflicted with the great curse of modern travel—skepticism. Could no more realize that St: John had ever had revelations here [Patmos], than when off Juan Fernandez, could beleive in Robinson Crusoe according to De Foe. When my eye rested on arid heigh, spirit partook of the barreness.—Heartily wish Niebuhr & Strauss to the

dogs.—The deuce take their penetration & acumen. They have robbed us of the bloom. If they have undeceived any one—no thanks to them. (p. 97)

The position was philosophically naive, but it remains a penetrating historical commentary on two basic tensions of the nineteenth-century artist: the war within the imagination (romantic vision versus the realistic eye) and the conflict over soul (supernaturalism against naturalism). Yet Melville's divided sensibility reached beyond the critical spirit of the age and matched some profound disunion which he cherished in himself. Though at intervals he was able to enjoy many sights that were "picturesque"—a favorite word—and to respond to Eastern pageantry and pomp at times, loneliness and introversion overcame him regularly, and drove him to suffer restless nights, eye pains, and the familiar symptoms of deep anxiety.

Three ancient sites stirred an enervating clash of moods. The first, in December of 1856, was Constantinople (pp. 57–68). The very sight of Asia oppressed him as "sort of used up—superannuated" (p. 57), yet he recorded in his journal the approach to the city in the fog in the romantic idiom of the day, likening its gradual appearance through the mist to the coquettings of a veiled woman (p. 58). He found his "picturesqueness" in the bridges and loved the "scene" of the Bosporus: "Magnificent! The whole scene one pomp of art & Nature" (p. 64). The prospect from Scutari was a "Noble view," and so on (p. 68). Counterpointed against these effusive enjoyments beyond the city was the psychic terror he felt within the city. He got lost several times within its warrens and alleys, becoming almost panic-stricken to find some tower from which he could see where he was. He hired guides but found they could not be trusted. He was sure that thieves and assassins pursued him through the streets (e.g., pp. 58–59, 60–61, 64). Once he called the city a maze, and several times, a labyrinth (pp. 58, 60, 64). So he alternated—from enthusiastic romanticism to a lonely mood of nightmare exhaustion and introversion. At the roots of his intellectual disillusion lay a profound distress. The island paradise was irrecoverable.

At the pyramids on New Year's Eve Melville endured the second traumatic experience of the journey (pp. 73–78). Already excited by Cairo, "a grand masquerade of mortality," he began reiterating in his journal (p. 73) symbolic images from his recent writings: the "sometimes high blank walls" ("Bartleby") and the "mysterious passages"

("I and My Chimney"). The pyramids themselves nearly over-whelmed him: "Never shall forget this day" (p. 73). The pyramids for Melville were a primal image of the unknown self—immense, mysterious, penetrable only here and there by dark shafts.[5] He described the ascent of an old man exhausted by climbing: "Tried to go into the interior—fainted—brought out—leaned against the pyramid by the entrance—pale as death. Nothing so pathetic. Too much for him; oppressed by the massiveness & mystery of the pyramids." And then: "I myself too. A feeling of awe & terror came over me" (p. 75). Self-penetration carried the risk of madness; total descent into the self could scarcely lead elsewhere.[6] Beyond self, Melville went on to say, lay the more terrifying concept of the primitive Hebrew God: "I shudder at idea of ancient Egyptians. It was in these pyramids that was conceived the idea of Jehovah. Terrible mixture of the cunning and awful. Moses learned in all the lore of the Egyptians. The idea of Jehovah born here" (p. 75). Was it really the concept of Jehovah that made Melville shudder, or was it the remembered Calvin-God, known to a child chiefly through the image of his own father? That father had died raving when Melville was twelve. In "The Great Pyramid" he later wrote:

> Slant from your inmost lead the caves
> And labyrinths rumored. These who braves
> And penetrates (old palmers said)
> Comes out afar on deserts dead
> And, dying, raves.

Six weeks out of Liverpool, and here he was at it again, re-exploring the self-father-God symbols that had ravaged him for five years. The old plan of a "glorious *Eastern* jaunt" was bearing strange fruit. And this was the mood in which he made the dangerous small-boat landing through the breakers at Jaffa, and on January 6, 1857, first set foot on Holy Land, the third and most memorable site.

5. One recalls the image of the mining into the pyramid in *Pierre* (bk. 21, pp. 285, 288–89); the chimney-pyramid images of "I and My Chimney" (in the Northwestern-Newberry *Piazza Tales* volume, pp. 352–77); and the problem of sanity in his short poem "The Great Pyramid"—quoted below (*Timoleon*; in the Northwestern-Newberry *Published Poems* volume, pp. 315–16).

6. This theme of annihilation through introversion is the context in which Mortmain, a major character of the poem, is best understood.

In Jaffa, Melville at once hired a dragoman and started on horse-back across the Plain of Sharon toward Jerusalem, forty-five miles distant. He put up at Ramleh for the night, but the poor accommodations and fleas drove him out by two o'clock in the morning. Twelve hours later he ascended the arid, mountainous steeps which lead up to the Holy City. Jerusalem! The enraptured comments of most travelers upon their first sight of Jerusalem were a commonplace. Melville's acquaintance Bayard Taylor, sentimentalist with an eye for the great tradition, had written: "I know not how it was—my sight grew weak, and all objects trembled and wavered in watery film."[7] What Melville felt at this moment he did not record. He put up at the dampest of the three shabby "hotels," the Mediterranean, overlooking the Pool of Hezekiah, and from here at once began eight days of wandering about Jerusalem (January 7–17, 1857, with three days out for the Dead Sea and Mar Saba expedition).

Melville's Jerusalem experiences, brilliantly though chaotically recalled in his journal, afterwards, while awaiting the steamer at Jaffa, were to provide the milieu for Part 1, "Jerusalem," of Clarel. "In pursuance of my object," he wrote, "the saturation of my mind with the atmosphere of Jerusalem, offering myself up a passive subject, and no unwilling one, to its weird impressions, I always rose at dawn & walked without the walls."[8] There was little within the city itself for the non-archaeological visitor, with the notable exception of the Church of the Holy Sepulcher. The city walls were points of advantage, and Melville followed the common practice of lingering by the city gates, watching the motley flow of travelers during the day or the recreations of the natives in the cool of the evening. Beyond the walls lay countless broken monuments of sacred history, best seen by circling the city along rock-strewn paths (see Map A, p. 707). North of the Damascus Gate lay the Vale of Ashes and the Sepulcher of Kings. Coming down through the dry gully of the Kedron one had the sloping ridges of Olivet above him to the east and the city walls looming to the west. Here in the Valley of Jehoshaphat, across from St. Stephen's Gate, was Mary's Tomb and the small fenced-in garden of ancient olives—Gethsemane. Continuing south one looked up at

7. Bayard Taylor, *The Lands of the Saracen* (New York: Putnam, 1855), p. 58.
8. P. 86, in the Jerusalem section (pp. 82–94). Only a few weeks before, while waiting for his ship to Jaffa, he had sat all day in the Victoria Hotel in Alexandria reading "a book on Palestine" (*Journals*, p. 73).

the long-sealed Golden Gate of the triumphal entry, passed by the tombs of Absalom, St. James, and Zechariah, and wandered among innumerable graves of Jews come home to die in Joel's "valley of decision." Beyond the southeast shoulder of the city lay the cliff-side huts of Siloam "village" and, down below, the miracle-haunted Pool of Siloam. At En-Rogel the dry valleys of Kedron and Hinnom merged and the Kedron Valley cleft its way southeastward into the black wilderness toward Mar Saba and the Dead Sea. Judas's Hill of Evil Counsel and the road to Bethlehem lay to the south. Swinging around the Hill of Zion, the southwest shoulder of the city, one came up the shallow part of Hinnom, passed the pool at Lower Gihon, and so came to David's Tower by Jaffa Gate on the west wall.

The most famous view of Jerusalem and its environs was from the Mount of Olives, east of the city (see *Journals*, p. 427). From one of its three or four ridges one looked half a mile across the Hinnom to Jerusalem, some two hundred feet below. Nineteenth-century artists invariably drew the city from here; they saw it as a line drawing— walls, square towers, and flat rooftops falling away like broken steps, scattered domes and minarets above. Here tourists were advised to come first, map and Bible in hand. From here non-Moslems had their only view of Moriah—the great tabletop in southeastern Jerusalem, once the site of Solomon's Temple and now of the beautiful garden-encircled Mosque of Omar, traditional site of Mohammed's ascension. From a ridge further north on Olivet, near the Christian Church of the Ascension, one looked south to Bethlehem, two hours on horseback, and east to the once-pleasant village of Bethany, an hour's walk. Away beyond Bethany lay the wild, rough country of the Judaean wilderness descending to Jericho and the lower Jordan Valley; from there came the leaden glint of the Dead Sea. Beyond reared the great blue wall of the Moab Mountains in trans-Jordan. In the wilderness between the Dead Sea and Bethlehem, out of sight among the cliffs of the Kedron ravine, lay the ancient Greek monastery of Mar Saba.

Hours at a time Melville wandered in the glaring sunlight over rocky wastes and sprawling terraces beyond the city, following his dragoman along worn paths that went everywhere and no-where. The hillsides were honeycombed with caves and cisterns half-full of rubbish or inhabited now by squalid natives as once they had been by penitent anchorites. *"Wandering among the tombs*—till I began to think myself one of the possessed with devels" (p. 84). Jerusalem was in the bleak and hard land of Judaea: "Stony mountains & stony plains; stony torrents & stony roads; stony walls & stony feilds, stony houses & stony tombs; stony eyes & stony hearts" (p. 90). It was the landscape of exhaustion: "The color of the whole city is grey & looks at you like a cold grey eye in a cold old man" (p. 90). Everywhere, remnants of ancient death: "The city besieged by army of the dead" (p. 86).

Melville's dismay at Jerusalem was a historically valid observation as well as a response of his destructive mood. In the nineteenth century, Palestine, as every traveler remarked, was a stripped and denuded land. Some attributed this to fulfillment of prophecy, others to the falling off of terrace cultivation; but whether a traveler chose divine or human explanation, the fact was inescapable. "So complete is the desolation of Palestine at this day," wrote the Reverend James Aitken Wylie, "that when the traveller enters it he is almost overpowered. Here nothing is to be seen but barren mountains, from whose rocky sides the sun's rays are flung back with intolerable fierceness. . . . His heart sinks as he surveys the desolation which surrounds him; and he needs to rouse himself by the remembrance, that the land in which he journeys was in ancient times the theatre of wonders."[9] It was Melville's own theme: "No country will more quickly dissipate romantic expectations than Palestine—particularly Jerusalem. To some the disappointment is heart sickening. &c" (p. 91). On the one hand his response was naturalistic, aware of "the indifference of Nature & Man to all that makes the spot sacred to the Christian," and noting how "on Olivet every morning the sun indifferently ascends over the Chapel of the Ascension" (p. 85). In a more startling response he blended the supernatural and the psychological: "Is the desolation of the land the result of the fatal embrace of the Deity? Hapless are the favorites of heaven" (p. 91). The comment is Hebraic-Calvinistic, yet romantic in tone. Question and answer alike were drawn from the catechism of Melville's own symbolic mythology.

Near Melville's hotel stood the most important shrine in Christendom, the Church of the Holy Sepulcher, whose battered dome he could see from his chamber window. Here in tawdry splendor were

9. *The Modern Judea* (Glasgow: Collins, 1841), p. 57.

crowded under one roof all the sacred sites connected with the death of Christ, particularly the supposed place of the Crucifixion and the original tomb. During the fifteen hundred years since Constantine (or his mother Helena) had claimed to have found here the sepulcher and the true cross, successive buildings had housed the chapels of warring churches and sects from all parts of Christendom. Undisturbed by contemporary archaeological skepticism that even a single site was valid, contentious monks still showed nineteenth-century travelers not only the tomb and place of the cross, but some twenty or more sites within the church—where Christ was imprisoned, bound, whipped, crucified, and buried, where he appeared to Mary, and so on. Here Melville came almost daily. The dingy light, the mouldy smell, and the "plague-stricken splendor" (p. 88) of the place disgusted him, as did the peddlers and hawkers of relics before the doors, the vile excrement at the outside back-wall of the church, and the insolent Turkish police who sat cross-legged and smoking at their duty of keeping order. Melville went into the tomb (in a small chapel within the church) as all travelers did: "Wedged & half-dazzled, you stare for a moment on the ineloquence of the bedizened slab, and glad to come out, wipe your brow glad to escape as from the heat & jam of a show-box. All is glitter & nothing is gold. A sickening cheat" (p. 88). Yet unquestionably he was fascinated by the collision of values here—the tawdry rituals of a decadent Christendom, the impassioned devotion or bewilderment of pilgrims seeking out the tangible symbols, the contempt of nonbelievers. There was an upper gallery that overlooked the tomb, "and here almost every day I would hang, looking down upon the spectacle of the scornful Turks on the divan, & the scorned pilgrims kissing the stone of the anointing" (p. 87). It was a spectacle that held a peculiar fascination for Melville, encompassing many of the complex elements of his position as an objective, yet entangled, observer of Christianity.

Almost no traveler ever visited Jerusalem without making a brief caravan trip of a day or two down to the Jordan and the Dead Sea. Among the numerous variations on this excursion the most popular was the one Melville chose (see Map B, p. 709)—a roughly rectangular route which led from Jerusalem northeast to Jericho (6 hours); from Jericho east to the Jordan (2 hours); from the Jordan south to the edge of the Dead Sea (1 hour); from the Siddim Plain southwest up the long ridge to the monastery of Mar Saba (4½ hours); from Mar Saba west to Bethlehem (3 hours); and from Bethlehem north back to Jerusalem (2 hours). By the middle of the nineteenth century this three-day trip on horseback had become one of the staples of Eastern travel. Notable contemporary travelers who left accounts of making this trip included such Americans as the explorer John Lloyd Stephens, the popular traveler and writer J. Ross Browne (whose whaling book Melville had reviewed), Melville's literary friends George William Curtis and Bayard Taylor, and the more notable William Cullen Bryant, J. W. De Forest, and Mark Twain. English pilgrims included the successful Eliot Warburton (whose dragoman Melville met at Beirut) and the indefatigable Harriet Martineau, who had to sleep outside the walls of Mar Saba; both Kinglake (with whom it will be recalled Melville had breakfasted at Rogers's) and Thackeray also wrote of travels in Palestine, though neither visited Mar Saba. Three famous French travelers who made the round trip were Chateaubriand and Lamartine (both mentioned in *Clarel*), and Flaubert, who was in the Middle East during 1849–50.[10] Add to these the nameless tourists who spared the public a published account, a distinguished group of forgotten archaeologists and scholars in sacred geography, and a small but earnest army of

10. Stephens, *Incidents of Travel in Egypt, Arabia Petræa, and the Holy Land* (New York: Harper, 1837; rpt. 1838, etc.), II, 197–218. Browne, *Yusef; or, The Journey of the Frangi* (New York: Harper, 1853), pp. 359–90 (for Melville's 1847 review of his *Etchings of a Whaling Cruise* see the Northwestern-Newberry *Piazza Tales* volume, pp. 205–11). Curtis, *The Howadji in Syria* (New York: Harper, 1852), pp. 192–203. Taylor, *Lands of the Saracen*, pp. 60–71. Bryant, *Letters from the East* (New York: Putnam, 1869), p. 185. De Forest, *Oriental Acquaintance: or, Letters from Syria* (New York: Dix, Edwards, 1856), pp. 91–107. Mark Twain, *The Innocents Abroad* (Hartford: American Publishing Co., 1869), chap. 55, pp. 586–603. Kinglake, *Eöthen; or, Traces of Travel Brought Home from the East* (New York: Wiley & Putnam, 1845), pp. 104–9, 129–32. Warburton, *The Crescent and the Cross; or, Romance and Realities of Eastern Travel* (New York: Wiley & Putnam, 1845), II, 103–13. Martineau, *Eastern Life, Present and Past* (London: Moxon, 1848), pp. 415–29. M. A. Titmarsh [Thackeray], *Notes of a Journey from Cornhill to Grand Cairo* (London: Chapman & Hall, 1846), pp. 184–236. F. A. de Chateaubriand, *Itinéraire de Paris à Jérusalem* ... (1811), translated as *Travels in Greece, Palestine, Egypt, and Barbary*, trans. F. Shoberl (London: Colburn, 1811–12; New York: Van Winkle & Wiley, 1814), pp. 249–76. Alphonse de Lamartine, *Voyage en Orient* (1835), translated as *A Pilgrimage to the Holy Land* (London: Bentley, 1835, etc.; Philadelphia: Carey, Lea, & Blanchard, 1835, etc.), I, 285–301. Gustave Flaubert, *Correspondance* (Paris: Gallimard, 1973), I, 523–733.

clerics on sabbatical. The trail from Jerusalem to the Dead Sea, returning by Mar Saba and Bethlehem, was well hoof-marked.

However, the trip involved some hardships: the route was rough and wild, extremes of temperature could be expected, and attacks from marauding Bedouins were still common. Unless one made the trip at Easter, when thousands of pilgrims from the Greek Church swarmed down to the Jordan to dip their shrouds in holy water, it was necessary to hire a dragoman as guide and pay armed natives as guards. Melville's journal gives us no direct evidence of what other travelers were included in his party, but it is likely that Frederick Cunningham, a young Harvard graduate and merchant who became a companion during part of his Jerusalem stay, went with him.[11]

The journey from Jerusalem to the Dead Sea provided the milieu for Part 2, "The Wilderness," of *Clarel*. Melville's party left Jerusalem by St. Stephen's Gate, wound over Olivet, dropped down to the little village of Bethany, and began the long descent of nearly thirty-seven hundred feet toward Jericho and the Jordan Valley. Just beyond Quarantania, traditionally the mountain where Christ was tempted, they came to a halt and pitched their tents near Jericho. Melville reported a "fine dinner—jolly time—sitting at door of tent looking at mountains of Moab" (p. 83). It is the one cheerful note in his three-day trip, and when taken in context with the phrase he added to it—"tent the charmed circle, keeping off the curse" (p. 83)—suggests a nervous exuberance. The Dead Sea, for the imaginative mind, was still a powerful symbol. The biblical account of the destruction of Sodom and Gomorrah by fire and ashes rained down upon a corrupt people had for thousands of years invested the area with a violent sense of evil. The natural desolation of the surrounding mountains, the slimy shores of the sea, and especially the acrid, vile-tasting waters in which no life could survive, had in turn fostered a lively uprising of evil lore. Credulous and awed travelers easily verified old legends and seldom departed without adding new ones. Sir John Mandeville, for instance, whose "monstrosities" Melville had half-seriously defended in *Mardi* (chap. 98, p. 298), told about the famed Sodom apples that turned to ashes in the mouth, and believed that the Dead Sea made barren

11. *Journals*, pp. 79–80, 422.

whatever it touched.[12] There were tales still current of vapors coming from the sea that would kill a bird flying over it. Although contemporary scientific expeditions were rapidly putting an end to such legends, there was no denying the ominous cast of the landscape. Mark Twain, who thought his famous tour of 1867 only "a picnic on a gigantic scale," found the Siddim Plain "a scorching, arid, repulsive solitude. A silence broods over the scene that is depressing to the spirits. It makes one think of funerals and death."[13] Even the easygoing, sentimental Curtis argued that "it is not the desolation of pure desert which girds the Dead Sea, and *that* is its awfulness. . . . It is not the spell of Death, but of Insanity."[14] The weird sense that at the Dead Sea one was thirteen hundred feet below the level of the Mediterranean, the unforgettable story of the corrupt cities, the stripped and miasmic landforms, the intense heat—few travelers escaped the spell.

For Melville history, geology, and myth combined their strange tales into a singular enchantment, long anticipated in the tropes of his own imaginative writing.[15] That night a storm broke. Thunder ricocheted from the mountains, lightning flashed, and after brief torrential rains came the howl of wolves and jackals. In the morning the cavalcade crossed muddy plains to find the Jordan yellow and turbid from the storm. Bedouins threatened from across the river. And then the sea: "foam on beach & pebbles like slaver of mad dog—smarting bitter of the water,—carried the bitter in my mouth all day—bitterness of life—thought of all bit-

12. Mandeville's account is collected in *Early Travels in Palestine*, ed. Thomas Wright (London: Bohn, 1848), pp. 127–252; this description occurs on p. 179. See also p. 534 and footnote 34 below.

13. *The Innocents Abroad*, chap. 1, p. 19, and chap. 55, p. 595. Mark Twain went on: "I can not describe the hideous afternoon's ride from the Dead Sea to Mars Saba. It oppresses me yet, to think of it. . . . The ghastly, treeless, grassless, breathless canons smothered us as if we had been in an oven" (p. 597).

14. *The Howadji in Syria*, p. 199; italics added.

15. Melville had evoked Dead Sea images several times as the root metaphor of the first sketch in "The Encantadas," transferring Hebraic attributes of penalty, curse, and barrenness to the unmythical Galápagos. He summoned the sea itself, apples of Sodom, "Lords of Asphaltum," and "split Syrian gourds"; and as his theme culminated, asserted that "in my time I have indeed slept upon evilly enchanted ground" (Northwestern-Newberry *Piazza Tales* volume, pp. 125–29). This was written about three years before the Palestinian adventure.

ter things—Bitter is it to be poor & bitter, to be reviled, & Oh bitter are these waters of Death, thought I" (p. 83).

Part 3 of *Clarel*, "Mar Saba," developed out of the second night's experience. About eight miles west of the northern part of the sea and some eighteen hundred feet above its sunken valley rose the twin towers of Mar Saba. "In the wild grandeur of its situation," reported the standard guidebook of the day, "Mâr Saba is the most extraordinary building in Palestine."[16] Built in the fifth century by the Greek Church in honor of St. Saba (*Mâr* is Arabic for *Christian Saint*), it had long been Palestine's most solitary outpost of Christianity. Great buttresses upheld the monastery over a ravine six hundred feet deep, yet over the centuries Mar Saba had often been ravaged by wild tribes. Even in the nineteenth century its narrow gate was unbarred only to male travelers bearing a letter from the patriarch at Jerusalem, though once within they were welcome to purchase the frugal and somewhat dirty hospitality of the sixty-five Greek monks then dwelling there. Within, staircases led from grotto to grotto, by which it was possible to descend far down into the ravine or mount to the towers. Climbing up the tortuous route from the Dead Sea, Melville still tasted bitterness: "Whitish mildew pervading whole tracts of landscape—bleached—leprosy—encrustation of curses" (p. 83). Then the ramparts of Mar Saba loomed above the Judaean wilderness and we have his cryptic record of the second night's stay:

> *St. Saba*—zig-zag along Kedron, sepulchral ravine, smoked as by fire, caves & cells—immense depth—all rock—enigma of the depth—rain only two or 3 days a year—wall of stone on ravine edge—Monastery (Greek) rode on with letter—hauled up in basket into hole—small door of massive iron in high wall—knocking—opened—salaam of monks—Place for pilgrims—divans—St Saba wine—"*racka*"—comfortable.—At dusk went down by many stone steps & through mysterious passages to cave & trap doors & hole in wall—ladder—ledge after ledge—winding—to bottom of Brook Kedron—sides of ravine all caves of recluses—Monastery a congregation of stone eyries, enclosed with wall—Good bed & night's rest—Went into chapel &c—little hermitages in rock—balustrade of iron—lonely monks. black-birds—feeding with bread—

16. John Murray's *A Handbook for Travellers in Syria and Palestine*, 2 vols. (London, 1858), I, 204.

numerous terraces, balconies—solitary Date Palm mid-way in precipice——Good bye. (p. 84)[17]

Part 4 of *Clarel*, "Bethlehem," is an imaginative extension of the last stage of the journey. On the third morning the party left Mar Saba and rode up the hills to the lovely mountain town where the idyll of Ruth had been enacted and where Christ had been born. Its only major monument was the Church of the Nativity, a sprawling pile of buildings with Latin, Greek, and Armenian convents massed about it. Beneath the church lay the Chapel of the Nativity, where amidst marble-covered walls and the gift accumulations of centuries—gold, silk, and silver—a silver star was embedded in the floor: HIC DE VIRGINE MARIA JESUS CHRISTUS NATUS EST. Nearby was the manger, and among innumerable grottos were the cell and study of St. Jerome, Father of the Church. Melville was shown through the chapel by a Latin monk and afterwards went up on the roof to see the famous view looking over the fields of Ruth, David, and the shepherds who watched by night. It was a rapid visit. The party was soon in the saddle for the two-hour ride back to Jerusalem, "pressing forward to save the rain" (p. 84).

Melville left Jerusalem for Jaffa, January 18, with Cunningham and his dragoman. Cunningham and the others took ship for Alexandria; Melville waited out impatiently and alone the arrival almost a week later of the Austrian steamer to Beirut. Here where Jonah had set out on the fateful voyage that Father Mapple took as text in *Moby-Dick*, Melville had full chance to experience, as he variously reiterated, "the old—genuine, old Jonah feeling" (p. 81). It was a fitting enough climax to his Palestine experience that he should find himself marooned here in the city that tradition proclaimed the oldest in the world. He felt acutely how "antidiluvian—a port before the Flood" (p. 81), Jaffa was: too ancient even to have antiquities. Such was the end point of his journey back through time.

In days and miles the Holy Land adventure had not been much—three weeks of small travels along conventional tourist routes. Outwardly Melville had been just another American enacting one of the rituals of Anglo-American civilization in his time. But the buried

17. Melville subsequently made numerous penciled underlinings in this passage, probably during composition of *Clarel*. See RELATED DOCUMENTS, pp. 871–81 below.

experience had been massive. Though he could not have known it then, it would be nearly twenty years before it would surface in a completed verse fiction.

II
COMPOSITION AND PUBLICATION

M ELVILLE WAS thirty-seven when he went to the Levant, nearly fifty-seven when *Clarel* was published. The circumstances of these two decades explain to some extent why *Clarel* was so long delayed. They also contributed to the poem, winding themselves in around past experience. The poem, when at last it was finished, embodied the moods and meditations of twenty years quite as much as the "events" of January, 1857.

The overriding difficulty of the first decade was the need for Melville to face the harsh fact that he had pretty well lost his reputation and his energy in the past five years. The ten books he had published in twelve years had fallen so far from public notice as to offer a mere driblet of income. Family insistence that he not begin again the killing pace that had produced them matched his own rueful instinct; he must choose between an altered way of life and disaster. It was not a new question for him, but at this point he really must act out the answer. For the moment he decided not to write at all but to try for a place in the New York Customs. Not succeeding, he gave three rather unsatisfying winters to the lyceum circuit, put together a sheaf of poems which Scribner refused to publish, made a voyage to San Francisco on the clipper *Meteor* captained by his beloved brother Tom, and came home in November of 1860 to find his country at the edge of war. Failing in a reawakened effort to win appointment as a government consul, he began a series of shifts which in 1863 brought his family back to New York City and marked the end of the Pittsfield era. Growing concern with the daily triumphs and disasters of the war, made vivid by a quick visit to the front lines in April of 1864, finally gave him a coordinating theme for his efforts in verse. *Battle-Pieces* came out in the summer of 1866, his only book between the Eastern journey and *Clarel*. As the year ended he found himself steady employment at last, entering the New York Customs as a waterfront inspector, a job that was to last for nineteen years. Thus pragmatically Melville slowly withdrew down the slopes of his fame as a writer.

It was family feeling that he had come back from the Levant improved in health but not recovered, and the same verdict was pronounced on the effects of the *Meteor* voyage. The tangible injury to his back when he was thrown from a wagon just before leaving Pittsfield became part of a deeper malady. Though he was often sparklingly alive at family or social occasions, he was more often mildly grim and moody, and at times ill. Chronic depressions became necessary to him. There were moments when he was unable to keep from exacting anxiety about his condition from family and friends. The need for recognition—and he was not getting it as a writer—was not easily stilled. His family—that massive pyramid of Melvilles, Gansevoorts, and Shaws, based at New York City, Albany, and Boston—stood firmly in support of his ordinary human needs, but cast a warning shadow over any sphinx-like purposes his unpredictable genius might be contemplating.

Though he had been forced to make compromises, he did not propose to let them include the life of the mind. The record shows at least seventy-five book titles, many of them in several volumes, which Melville bought or borrowed during these two decades, and there were certainly more beyond the records.[18] His reading included the Elizabethans (Chapman, Dekker, Webster, and his beloved Shakespeare), seventeenth-century writers (Herrick, Herbert, Marvell, Taylor, Milton), romantics (Shelley, Byron, Burns, Schiller, Madame de Staël), contemporary essayists (Hazlitt, Arnold, Emerson), and epic writers (Homer, Dante, Camões). His interest in art, stimulated by his Mediterranean trip and the preparation of a lyceum lecture on "Statues in Rome," drew him into half a dozen ponderous studies (including Vasari, Reynolds, and Ruskin); in the meantime he was accumulating a good amateur's collection of prints and engravings. He read many minor writers on whom he chanced simply

18. Sealts, *Melville's Reading*, and Bercaw, *Melville's Sources*, are indispensable for any study of Melville's intellectual development. Further data on volumes cited may be found there. See especially sect. 8 of Sealts's introductory essay, "Melville as Reader" (pp. 111–23). For Melville's marginalia see Leyda's *Log* and Cowen, *Melville's Marginalia*. Melville's own copies have been consulted for the present HISTORICAL AND CRITICAL NOTE.

because he found them compatible with his own moods. Sometimes he reveled openly in antiquarianism. For the most part, however, he read exactingly in the great writers, often with pencil in hand. When he went aboard the *Meteor*, for example, his portable library included Béranger, the New Testament and the Psalms, Alexander Campbell, Dante, Hawthorne, Milton, Wordsworth, Chapman's Homer in five volumes, and Schiller.

The markings and annotations which he made in many of his books provide a rich index to his complexity of mind and temperament in these years. They show an alert sensibility, quick to respond to aesthetic delights and happy phrasings; a mind ready to absorb information, commend an insight, or argue a point; a spirit at times easily moved to bitterness or compassion. He was interested most in problems of self, civilization, art, and God, and his pencil was quick at noting even parenthetical commitments on such matters when he was in a tracking mood. He was given to comparing other times and places with his own, cherishing particularly all honest confessions of defeat, perplexity, and alienation. Clearly he read in part for companionship. He sat down among his books as among friends, with the air of a man who has earned the right to compare experiences. Books gave him room in which to live.

The rejection of his first manuscript of verse in 1860 led Melville to increase his study of poets and poetry. His reading of Homer, Child's *English and Scottish Ballads*, and Mackay's *Songs of England* suggests he wanted to cast his net to bring in the primary resources of poetic tradition—epic, ballad, and song. His reading of at least nine secondary poets in a single year—Collins, Churchill, Shenstone, Fergusson, Hood, Moore, Heine, Henry Kirke White, James Clarence Mangan—plus Arnold, suggests also that in 1862 he was studying recent verse as models of craftsmanship. Many of these volumes Melville marked and annotated in ways that confirm this. For example, in the poems of Mangan—for the most part translations from the darker ballads of Schiller, Uhlan, Tieck, Richter, Goethe, and Herder—he noted on the back flyleaves some poetic archaisms that interested him, such as "at whiles" and "aneath," and jotted rhyme-words such as "e'ening—meaning," "sternest—earnest," and "lonely—only." In the editor's introduction to Hood's poems he marked passages that described Hood's habit of printing out poems for better critical examination, and that suggested that Hood could have benefited from the practice of some artists in writing with the left hand "in the hope of checking the fatal facility which practice had conferred on the right." In the same volume he checked, lined, and underlined a phrase (italicized here) on "that poetical vigour which seemed to advance *just in proportion as his physical health declined.*" In his well-marked copy of Arnold's *Poems*, Melville lined a passage in the preface on "the indispensable mechanical part" of poetry-writing. He took Arnold to be his most serious poetic contemporary, and his reading of the *Poems* in 1862, and of *New Poems* in 1871, turned out to be a major resource for *Clarel*. In Madame de Staël's *Germany* (also purchased in 1862), he triple-lined, checked, and underlined four words (italicized here) in the comment that "the effects of poetry depend still more on the *melody of words* than on the *ideas* which they serve to express," adding the pertinent annotation: "This is measureably true of all but dramatic poetry, and, perhaps, narrative verse." Melville's marginalia in this period reveal him in the double role of critic and apprentice to the craft of poetry.[19]

His apprenticeship led him to demonstrate that now he could write publishable verse. As the war drew on to its bloody close, he began to put together a series of occasional poems on its heroisms and tragedies, from the portentous moment when the gaunt shadow of John Brown darkened the Shenandoah until the people's passion was consummated in the death of Lincoln. The seventy-two poems of *Battle-Pieces and Aspects of the War* (1866), many of them developed from newspaper accounts published in the twelve-volume *Rebellion Record*, reflected "moods of involuntary meditation," as he said in a preface. The war had given him a coordinating theme—perhaps the very thing his earlier, unsuccessful collection of verse had lacked— and he seems to have written with relative speed and self-confidence. The poems explored a wide variety of forms ranging from the conventional quatrains of "In the Prison Pen" to the experimental narrative form of "Donelson," with its reliance on popular idiomatic

19. Mangan, *Poems* (New York: Haverty, 1859; Sealts 347). Thomas Hood, *The Poetical Works* (Boston: Little, Brown, 1860; Sealts 279). Matthew Arnold, *Poems* (Boston: Ticknor & Fields, 1856; Sealts 21); *New Poems* (Boston: Ticknor & Fields, 1867; Sealts 20); for a detailed study, see my "Melville's Reading of Arnold's Poetry," in which I draw the contours of Melville's poetic sensibility and concern for craft during the apprenticeship for *Clarel* and suggest numerous specific debts to Arnold. Staël, *Germany* (New York: Derby & Jackson, 1859; Sealts 487).

speech and use of newspaper bulletins. In merit the range was wide; tightly structured poetic statements mingled with hasty effusions in a singsong manner. The book received chiefly abrupt dismissals from reviewers upset by its unevenness, experimental prosody, and complexity of view. No one seemed to care that next to Whitman's *Drum-Taps* this was probably the best verse to come out of the war. As for Melville, he grimly acknowledged the book's failure to sell more than a few hundred copies and went on about his new duties as Inspector of Customs. After ten years of disconcerting silence he had at last spoken out in his role as poet. But he had not yet solved the problem of getting a book out of the Mediterranean journey.

The problem of form for his Eastern materials seems to have been a bedevilment to Melville from the beginning. In the absence of any documentation as to when he first chose the form of a long narrative poem it seems wise to assume that he came to it only in the second decade, after the publication of *Battle-Pieces*. In any case the problem from the first was a choice among several different conventions of the Anglo-American literary scene.

Three popular media of the day were letters to newspapers, magazine articles, and lyceum lectures. When Bryant in 1853 traveled by donkey from Cairo to Jerusalem and visited the Dead Sea he wrote letters back to his own *Evening Post* which later became a book, and George William Curtis had comparable letters published in the *Tribune*. *Harper's New Monthly Magazine* presented a two-year sequence, "Memoirs of the Holy Land," in 1852–53, written by the irrepressible Jacob Abbott (author of the twenty-eight-volume Rollo Series), and in 1858 printed a sixteen-page story with woodcuts, "From Sinai to Wady Mousa." Though Melville rejected both newspapers and magazines as a paying market for travel accounts, he did drain off some of his journal materials into two of his three lyceum lectures.[20] The successive annual topics he chose—"Statues in Rome," "The South Seas," and "Traveling: Its Pleasures, Pains, and Profits"— reflected his moods and problems. The first was an effort to popularize a series of analogies between the modern world and the ancient world which he had just visited. The second was a half-hearted at-

20.   Melville's use of his Mediterranean journal for ideas and particulars in his lectures and writings is summarized in the HISTORICAL NOTE to the Northwestern-Newberry *Journals* volume, pp. 189–94. The lectures are reconstructed by Merton M. Sealts, Jr., in the Northwestern-Newberry *Piazza Tales* volume, pp. 398–423.

tempt to recoup the Pacific story which had made him famous; yet even here his ethnographic bookishness disappointed audiences who wanted a dramatic recital of personal adventures. In the third lecture he tried unsuccessfully to find generalizations that might please the public and yet not overwhelm himself with a sense of banality. So ended his only foray into popular culture.

"I am surprised," wrote Melville's uncle Peter Gansevoort from Albany (December 17, 1857), "that he has not made his travels the subject of a Lecture, to be hereafter woven into a Book." The kind of book he had in mind, Uncle Peter went on to say, was one that "would not make a requisition on his imagination," an ironically accurate description of the mass of prose travel accounts then on the Anglo-American market. "The East is exhaustless!" commented a reviewer for *Putnam's Monthly Magazine* just as Melville headed East,[21] and there was ample proof in the newspapers, magazines, and popular books of the day. The core of Anglo-American interest was the evangelical Protestant fascination with the Holy Land as the sacred theater where the Christian drama had been played, enlivened by discreet overtones retained from the oriental romance. The crest of the wave came in the fifties, just as Melville landed in Jaffa. His being there was the clear expression of a literary-religious pattern of contemporary culture, and the natural outcome of the trip, he was well aware, was a prose travel account.

A more amusing alternative was the English tradition of the oriental romance, which had originally stirred his hunger to see the Middle East. The older classics such as *Vathek* (1786) and *Anastasius* (1819) had been imitated by Kinglake's *Eöthen* (1844) and Disraeli's more serious *Tancred* (1847).[22] But Melville's unwillingness to return to the South Sea idyll as a means of recouping his reputation set the terms for refusing an exotic exploitation of the Levant. In the oriental romance the East was perfumes and incense and strange customs, a veiled and beautiful woman living indiscreetly through Arabian nights. Disseminated though American culture, the myth bloomed softly in the pages of gift books and annuals, or shot lurid accents of color into the decor of Poe's arabesque chambers. By 1857 the

21. VIII (November, 1856), 544. The book under review was De Forest's *Oriental Acquaintance* (see footnote 10 above).

22. Disraeli drew on the Eastern phase of his grand tour of 1828–31 for the setting of *Tancred*.

tradition had reached its late afternoon, but there was still time for sunset effects had Melville wanted to dramatize the picturesque-romantic mood that wandered in and out of his Mediterranean journal. For his own reasons he did not. Nor was he up to the exhausting implications of sustained fiction, at least in prose.

Short stories and poems were further alternatives. While traveling he had been thinking about sketches or stories, how "something comical," or "good," or "ironical" could be made out of situations he was encountering.[23] A newly projected magazine, the *Atlantic Monthly*, was after him as a contributor in the summer he returned, and it is a mark of the finality of his abdication from prose that he did not go ahead and try something in the manner of "The Encantadas" with a Palestinian setting. As late as 1868 he apparently replied to the editors of the revived *Putnam's* that he would probably be a contributor, but nothing came of it. Probably a theory that poetry demanded less energy was at the root of his otherwise willful abandonment of prose. The decision may have been encouraged by the lively market for Eastern poetry since the forties. Current successes included translations, poems in the Eastern manner, and poems about the East by travelers.[24] A cluster of traveler's poems almost certainly formed part of his rejected manuscript of 1860 (versions of those eventually published privately as "Fruit of Travel Long Ago" in *Timoleon* [1891]). These short poems of 1858–60 seem to be mainly explorations of art and psychology against the background of Mediterranean settings; the germ of most of them can be found in the 1856–57 journal.

His dilemma was at least clear. He was unwilling to write newspaper letters or magazine articles. He had rejected the idea of a popular travel narrative or an oriental romance. For whatever reason he had abandoned the short story form after mastering it. The lyceum

23. *Journals*, pp. 82, 115, 126; note also the manner, as if plotting a story, at p. 105; for others see p. 187 in the *Journals* HISTORICAL NOTE.

24. For example: John Pierpont's repeatedly revised book of 1816, *Airs of Palestine and Other Poems* (e.g., Boston: Munroe, 1840); Richard Monckton Milnes, *Palm Leaves* (London: Moxon, 1844); Bayard Taylor, *Poems of the Orient* (Boston: Ticknor & Fields, 1855); William Rounseville Alger, *The Poetry of the East* (Boston: Whittemore, Niles, & Hall, 1856). After the war there was still time for the Reverend Edward Payson Hammond's *Sketches of Palestine* (London: Morgan & Chase, 1869)—very popular in America—and Richard Henry Stoddard's *The Book of the East and Other Poems* (Boston: Osgood, 1871). Melville knew most of these people, possibly all of these books, and certainly some similar books.

had been a frustration, and the book of short poems including Eastern verses had failed to win a publisher. Would he ever find his form?

Within a few months after the publication of *Battle-Pieces*, Melville began his nineteen years of service as Inspector Number 75 in the New York Customs. It was a menial job at best, but it provided a minimum of economic security and put him at last in the guiltless role of steady wage earner. At least whatever time he could salvage from evenings and weekends would be his own to do with as he might choose. Under these circumstances he was now ready for his Holy Land project, taken in his own way and done at his own speed.

At some definite point between the end of the war and 1870, when he began to purchase books for his work, he made the crucial decisions which enabled him to go ahead with *Clarel*. It is possible, since we have no documents on the matter, that this was merely the moment when he found circumstances right for beginning a project which had been maturing in his mind for a decade, and for which he had been grooming himself by the study and practice of verse. This would imply a surer sense of pattern than seems to emerge from this period in Melville's life. In either case, there is speculative evidence that Melville had written something like a quarter or third of his poem by 1870.[25] The best hypothesis would seem to be that Melville began his poem about 1867.[26]

His decisions involved both themes and structure. Passing up any direct treatment of the weeks he had spent in Greece, Turkey, Egypt, and Italy, he began shaping his memorable nineteen days in Palestine into a fiction, using the ancient pattern of a pilgrimage. Out of his own three-day trip to the Dead Sea, Mar Saba, and Bethlehem, he projected a more leisurely journey by a young American in the company of a group of Representative Men of the contemporary Western world. The fictional journey (it turned out to be ten days) provided the simple narrative line he had long preferred and gave him freedom

25.   Of the twenty-five or more passages in *Clarel* which are either probably or certainly based on Arthur Penrhyn Stanley's *Sinai and Palestine in Connection with Their History* (New York: Widdleton, 1863), acquired by Melville in April, 1870 (Sealts 488; Bercaw 668), almost all occur in the last two-thirds of the poem. See my unpublished dissertation (Yale, 1943), pp. 354–55.

26.   Fragments of his poetic writings before and during the war probably went into *Clarel*. However, I see no evidence for Jean Simon's speculation that the general plan and much of the first volume were worked out before *Battle-Pieces* (see p. 548 below).

for the episodic enrichment of theme which he had always cherished. Unlike his previous fictions the present one was in verse—a long narrative poem that gave him a sustained opportunity to cope with the prosodic problems which had now moved to the center of his interests. Working slowly and deliberately, with time for reading and meditation as he pondered the predicament of modern man, he filled in the margins of his daily life with the steady act of creation. If in the end his poem should be published, then well; and if not, then what would be would be.

Since all working drafts and the final manuscript of *Clarel* have been lost or destroyed,[27] and since correspondence and other documents are scanty, structural analysis and source study tell us what we know of Melville's process of composition. For the first time in his writing career he drew extensively from a personal journal the hard particulars which give imaginative writing its sense of validity. Although less than a quarter of his notes related directly to the Holy Land, he made more than a hundred borrowings from them, transposing facts, images, and attitudes—activating moods, scenes, and events of more than ten years earlier.[28] These he blended constantly with biblical events and citations. The Bible, as Nathalia Wright has skillfully demonstrated, had long been Melville's primary literary resource, and its uses for the present narrative were unique. In the most literal sense the Bible was *the* basic historical guide to Palestine, as all travelers' handbooks were quick to acknowledge. The several hundred scriptural allusions in *Clarel* were not always drawn directly from the Bible, however. Melville worked also with commentary or concordance at hand.[29] Or again, if he was using John Murray's excellent *A Handbook for Travellers in Syria and Palestine*, as is probable,

27. The only known fragment of the poem in Melville's own hand is a later copy of one of its songs (see RELATED DOCUMENTS, pp. 867–70 below).

28. All borrowings from the journals are cited in the list of parallel passages (pp. 871–81 below); further information appears in the DISCUSSIONS. For general discussions of these borrowings see *Journals*, pp. 193–94, and Bezanson in "Herman Melville's *Clarel*," pp. 108–13.

29. Howard P. Vincent suggested in *The Trying-Out of MOBY-DICK*, pp. 271–72, that Melville was a user of John Kitto's *A Cyclopædia of Biblical Literature*, 2 vols. (Edinburgh: Black, 1845; successive reprintings from plates of the New York 1845 edition; Bercaw 421). Nathalia Wright's study, pp. 13–14, suggests further possibilities. In the course of annotating *Clarel*, I found no single biblical commentary adequate, though Kitto is often useful.

he found biblical allusions cited there. So too with most travel books he was plundering: apt quotation from Scripture was a standard convention of Holy Land literature. If in one sense Melville's travel experience lay back of the demands he now made on the Bible as a source, in another sense the Bible lay back of his experience and that of all other travelers he read.

As Melville had once acquired books on whaling he now gathered volumes on Palestine, especially in the early seventies.[30] In his reading he was less a systematic scholar than a writer out for pillage.[31] The most solid account with which we know he worked, and the one from which he borrowed most heavily, was Stanley's *Sinai and Palestine*. Stanley's judicial temperament, breadth of learning, and incisive style admirably suited Melville's needs.[32] The two annotations Melville made in *Sinai and Palestine* commended Stanley for remarks that

30.   As early as 1859 Melville ordered on his Harper account, to be delivered to his brother Allan probably for redelivery to himself, a full-morocco copy of William Thomson's *The Land and the Book* (New York: Harper, 1858; Sealts 523). In January, 1870, he bought William Bartlett's *Forty Days in the Desert* (New York: Scribner, [186–?]; Sealts 48); and at some unknown time his *The Nile Boat* (New York: Scribner, [186–?]; Sealts 49); both volumes he marked, the first in more detail. April, 1870, he bought Stanley's *Sinai and Palestine* and marked it heavily. November, 1870, he ordered John Macgregor's *The Rob Roy on the Jordan, Nile, Red Sea, and Gennesareth* (New York: Harper, 1870; Sealts 340); Melville's copy has been lost, but examination of other copies shows the book was not a source. For Christmas, 1870, he gave his wife Bartlett's popular table-book, *Walks about the City and Environs of Jerusalem* (London: Virtue, [186–?]; Sealts 50); to his credit the pages are unmarked, but for considerable evidence that both the text and illustrations affected *Clarel*, see the DISCUSSIONS. June, 1872, he purchased Edward Henry Palmer's *The Desert of the Exodus* (New York: Harper, 1872; Sealts 396; Bercaw 538); the copy is lost, and the book was not a source. Location of these books, when known, is given in Sealts.

31.   However he checked in *Sinai and Palestine*, p. ix, a reference to a thirty-page bibliographical article on the Holy Land previously published by Stanley in the *Quarterly Review* (March, 1854), and may have used it for guidance. I find no evidence that he used either of the two most formidable triumphs of contemporary scholarship in historical geography—Edward Robinson's *Biblical Researches in Palestine*, 3 vols. (1841; see the discussion at 1.28.96), or the English abridgment to 4 vols. of Carl Ritter's massive *Erdkunde von Asien* (trans. 1866).

32.   Arthur Penrhyn Stanley (1815–81), famous Rugby boy and the biographer of Arnold's father, became Regius Professor of Ecclesiastical History at Oxford in the year his book on Palestine came out (1856). To his own graphic narrative of a trip from Egypt through the wilderness and up into Palestine he added critical commentaries based on the entire available literature of the Levant, documenting and sifting evidence with a master's hand.

he found "very suggestive" and "just." Some sixty markings and
many subsequent borrowings for *Clarel* show the constant utility of
this work to Melville as he wrote.[33]

As the poem grew Melville moved in and out of many other
classics and popular works on the Holy Land. Probably he scanned
the writings of Josephus, a standard item of the nineteenth-century
home library in either the Whiston or the Traill translation. He read
with special delight the medieval pilgrimages in the Bohn Antiquari-
an Library collection, building one canto of *Clarel* from a saint's
legend there, and pored over an edition of at least one ripe old
seventeenth-century folio of wonders, George Sandys's *A Relation of
a Journey Begun An: Dom: 1610.*[34] He was familiar with the lives and
writings of such eighteenth- and early nineteenth-century travelers as
Volney, Chateaubriand, Lamartine, and Burckhardt. Recollections
of earlier readings in *Vathek, Anastasius,* and *The Talisman* gave him
moods to re-create or criticize, and a relative ease with the vocabulary
of Eastern romance.[35] He made at least minor appropriations from
Kinglake's *Eöthen,* Warburton's *The Crescent and the Cross,* and Cur-
zon's *A Visit to Monasteries in the Levant.*[36] We cannot always tell

33. Wright (1947). A more extensive study of Melville's use of Stanley may be
found in my "Herman Melville's *Clarel,*" pp. 114–33.

34. The Bohn volume was *Early Travels in Palestine,* cited in footnote 12 above;
for the legend see *Clarel,* 1.35. Sandys's *Relation* (London, 1615 and later editions),
has an account, p. 124 (but no picture), of the Jerusalem cross; Melville at some later
time jotted a reference to this account in the Jerusalem section of his 1856–57 journal
(see *Journals,* p. 432, the inaccurate discussion at 84.28; superseded by the discussion
at 4.2.68–69 below).

35. C. F. Volney, *Voyage en Égypt et en Syrie* (1787), translated as *Travels
through Syria and Egypt, in the Years 1783, 1784, and 1785* (London: G. G. J. Robinson,
1787; second ed. 1788); Chateaubriand and Lamartine are cited above; all three are
mentioned in *Clarel* (2.16), as is the Knight of the Leopard—"Scott's dreamed
knight"—from *The Talisman* (1825). Examples of Eastern words that appear in Wil-
liam Beckford's *Vathek: An Arabian Tale* (London: Bentley, 1849; Sealts 54) include:
Giaour, Mani, Muezins, Koran, Bismallah, Santons, Brahmins, Eblis; in Thomas Hope's
Anastasius; or, Memoirs of a Greek: Written at the Close of the Eighteenth Century
(London: Murray, 1836; Sealts 282; Bercaw 372): *Arnaoot, Spahee, Osmanlee,
Mamluke, Emir, Ramadan, Bedawee, Simoom, Santon, Franks, Bey;* all these words
occur in *Clarel,* though spellings may vary. Whether or not Melville read Johann
Ludwig Burckhardt's badly written but informed *Travels in Syria and the Holy Land*
(London: Murray, 1822), he knew something of his death and life (*Clarel,* 1.40; 2.30).

36. Hon. Robert Curzon, *A Visit to Monasteries in the Levant* (New York: Put-
nam, 1849).

precisely from which book Melville was drawing, for most of the works he used were themselves composites of other books, but many examples of how he used borrowed materials will be found in the DISCUSSIONS of the present volume. They range from the merest fragments—a quick metaphor on the look of Jerusalem from Mt. Olivet (1.36.31), the name of a wayside plant (4.33.54)—on to substantial pillagings for whole cantos (2.30). Sometimes he apparently blended more than one source, as in the story of the Easter Fire (3.16). Always, as much as he could, he exercised his own gifts, lyricizing the prosaic or, more characteristically, bringing in data at an angle of original meaning, giving it his own situational context. At times he must have been desolate with his inability to master these materials, or touch them with magic. As he had written of that would-be novelist-hero of *Pierre* (bk. 21), "the heavy unmalleable element of mere book-knowledge would not congenially weld the wide fluidness and ethereal airiness of spontaneous creative thought. He would climb Parnassus with a pile of folios on his back" (p. 283). He had committed himself, however, in a way that the callow Pierre could not have dreamed. He composed, we may assume, by the light of mature convictions set down in his short poem "Art":

> In placid hours well-pleased we dream
> Of many a brave unbodied scheme.
> But form to lend, pulsed life create,
> What unlike things must meet and mate:
> A flame to melt—a wind to freeze;
> Sad patience—joyous energies;
> Humility—yet pride and scorn;
> Instinct and study; love and hate;
> Audacity—reverence. These must mate,
> And fuse with Jacob's mystic heart,
> To wrestle with the angel—Art.
>   (*Timoleon;* in *Published Poems,* p. 280)

It was an aesthetic theory rooted in what Melville called "Primal Philosophy."

"Herman is pretty well and very busy," wrote Melville's wife, Elizabeth, to her mother in the spring of 1875; "pray do not mention to *any one* that he is writing poetry—you know how such things spread and he would be very angry if he knew I had spoken of it—and of course I have not, except in confidence to you and the family." He

New York, Aug. 26, '75

My dear Uncle Peter:

Last evening I received through a note from Mr. Lansing a check for $1200, which he says you requested him to send me. — I shall at once deposite the money in a Savings Bank, there to remain till needed for the purpose designed.

And now, my dear uncle, in receiving this

Melville's note of thanks (August 26, 1875) to his uncle Peter Gansevoort.

Generous gift from you, so much
enhanced by the circumstances, I feel
the same sentiments which I
expressed to you in person at
Albany when you so kindly
made known your intention.
I will not repeat them here; but
only pray God to bless you, and
have you in His keeping.

With respect and true affection,
Your nephew
Herman Melville

Courtesy of the New York Public Library, Gansevoort-Lansing Collection.

had been alternately well and ill as the years passed, carrying on his customs duties, enduring family losses and enjoying family parties, celebrating his silver wedding anniversary, watching the flights and returns of his only remaining son ("possessed with a demon of *restlessness*," as Elizabeth remarked).[37] The heavy toll of death had sounded insistently through the sixties. Chief Justice Shaw, Melville's father-in-law, the substantial head of the Boston family who had financed his Mediterranean tour, died in 1861. Harder to take was the loss in 1863 of two younger friends associated with happier days in New York and Pittsfield—George Duyckinck and the merry, party-loving Sarah Morewood. Hawthorne died the next year, a major shock not minimized by the fact that Melville had not seen him for seven years. The closest personal tragedy was the self-inflicted death, possibly accidental, of eighteen-year-old Malcolm, Melville's oldest son, in 1867; it left permanent scars of grief and guilt. The next year Melville went with Evert Duyckinck to the funeral of George Adler, old friend of the proposed jaunt to the East in 1849, who had been in an asylum (under protest) for fifteen years. A cluster of family deaths opened the seventies. He lost a favorite cousin, the dashing young Colonel Henry Gansevoort whom he had so admired as a heroic type in the war; his younger brother Allan, the New York lawyer who had guided Herman's literary affairs so patiently; and his mother, Maria Gansevoort Melville. These events threw massive shadows around Melville as he pondered and then set to work on *Clarel*; even the act of publication was darkened by the death of his uncle Peter Gansevoort, its sponsor, and Melville's sister Augusta, early in 1876.

Meanwhile reading, study, and writing had gone on and his poem was nearing completion. The well-kept secret of this major effort was soon to be known. In a defensively jocular mood Melville set out for his usual two-week vacation, August, 1875, writing to the Albany relatives: "But as for meeting me on the wharf—dont mention it. When the Shah of Persia or the Great Khan of Tartary come to Albany by the night-boat—*him* meet on the wharf and with salvoes of artillery—but not a Custom House Inspector." On that visit his uncle Peter, a sick old man of eighty-six, long a civic pillar in the city which knew him as the Honorable Peter Gansevoort, concluded an agreement with Melville to pay the entire cost of publishing this

37. In a letter of May 26, 1873 (*Log*, II, 733).

poem someone had reported to him. Perhaps he thought this was the book he had been urging Melville to write fifteen years ago when he had called for something "that would not make a requisition on his [Melville's] imagination." In any case, Uncle Peter's order that a draft for twelve hundred dollars be sent to Melville, one in a long series of benefactions to his favorite nephew, was a warmly generous move. Without it very likely the poem would have remained unpublished in Melville's lifetime. (See his note of thanks, pp. 536–37.)

That fall Melville set furiously to work completing and revising his manuscript; early in January, 1876, he made arrangements for publication with G. P. Putnam's Sons. In February, Elizabeth had to refuse guests: "The book is going through the press, and every minute of Herman's time and mine is devoted to it—the mere mechanical work of reading proof &c is so great and absorbing." But the situation was more acute than this letter to Melville's cousin Kate Lansing stated; in a separate enclosure Elizabeth summed up the hints of distress which had been accumulating for several years:

> I have written you a note that Herman could see, as he wished, but want you to know how painful it is for me to write it, and also to have to give the real cause—The fact is, that Herman, poor fellow, is in such a frightfully nervous state, & particularly now with such an added strain on his mind, that I am actually *afraid* to have any one here for fear that he will be upset entirely, & not be able to go on with the printing—He was not willing to have even his own sisters here. . . . If ever this dreadful *incubus* of a *book* (I call it so because it has undermined all our happiness) gets off Herman's shoulders I do hope he may be in better mental health—but at present I have reason to feel the gravest concern & anxiety about it—to put it in mild phrase—please do not speak of it. . . . Rather pity & pray for your ever affectionate cousin—Lizzie.

The psychic cost of *Clarel* had been high.

For the second time—*Pierre* was the first—Melville wanted a book of his published anonymously. He had come to feel what Guérin called "a secret absurdity" in the whole literary career, as compared with the "well-kept secret of one's self and one's thoughts."[38] But on April 22 Lizzie was able to write Kate that "Herman has

---

38. Heavily marked in Melville's copy of Arnold's *Essays in Criticism* (Boston: Ticknor & Fields, 1865; Sealts 17; Bercaw 25), p. 102, and annotated: "This is the first verbal statement of a truth which every one who thinks in these days must have felt." Acquired in 1869, but probably marked in 1871.

consented on the *very strong* representations of the publishers, to put his name on the title-page, for which I am very glad—and *therefore* he has changed his mind about having a dedication—"; that decided, appropriately, Melville inscribed *Clarel* to Uncle Peter, who had died in January. By this time, Lizzie told Kate, the entire manuscript was in type, and on June 3, 1876, after "a series of the most vexatious delays," *Clarel* was published.[39] The two-volume octavo sets were published at three dollars and bound in cloth of various colors; a variation of the "ensign" of Jerusalem described in 4.2 was stamped in gilt on the front covers—a Jerusalem cross, over palm leaves and under three crowns and a star.[40] The title pages carried no reference to Melville's other books, and the volumes contained no illustrations or advertisements. There was no English edition, but the Putnam edition was distributed in England.[41] Since Melville had paid for the entire publication, including review copies and advertising, these circumstances doubtless expressed his wishes.

Melville offered his poem to a generally unconcerned public with the hope that it had "enough of original life to redeem it at least from vapidity," as he phrased it in his heavy-handed author's note to the first volume: "Be that as it may, I here dismiss the book—content beforehand with whatever future awaits it." His sense of relief that it was done also comes through the inscription in the copy he gave to Elizabeth.[42] Eight years after publication Melville reiterated his

39. As Mrs. Melville said in a letter the following day to Kate. Precisely what caused the delays is not known, but physical evidence in the published volumes indicates that the original production plan was for single-volume duodecimos instead of two-volume octavos and confirms that the dedication was a late addition; see the NOTE ON THE TEXT, pp. 678–79. The inscription in the copy Melville presented to his wife was dated June 6 (see RELATED DOCUMENTS, pp. 864–66); the date of copyright deposit was June 9.

40. See the illustration on p. 674 below and the discussion at 4.2.68–69.

41. The distributor was Sampson Low, Marston, Low & Searle. Putnam's had printed only "a small edition," according to Mrs. Melville's reply in the *New York Times Saturday Review of Books and Art* (October 5, 1901, pp. 706–7) to a request for information about Melville's books. She commented that *Clarel* "was withdrawn from circulation by Mr. Melville on finding that it commanded but a very limited sale, being in strong contrast to his previous popular works." See p. 659 below.

42. "This copy is specially presented to my wife, without whose assistance in manifold ways I hardly know how I could have got the book (under the circumstances) into shape, and finally through the press." The inscription is reproduced below, p. 864.

new York by Harper & Brothers.

"Clarel", published by George P. Putnam's Sons, New York. — a metrical affair, a pilgrimage or what not, of several thousand lines, eminently adapted for unpopularity. — The notification to you here is ambidexter, as it were: it may intimidate or allure.

Again thanking you for your friendly note, and with best wishes to yourself and your circle, I am

Very truly yours

Herman Melville

Excerpt from Melville's letter of October 10, 1884, describing *Clarel* to James Billson. Courtesy of Sotheby's.

original resignation, with a paradoxical twist, when he wrote his young English correspondent, James Billson, in October of 1884 that *Clarel* was "a metrical affair, a pilgrimage or what not, of several thousand lines, eminently adapted for unpopularity.—The notification to you here is ambidexter, as it were: it may intimidate or allure." Three months later he again wrote Billson (and this exhausts his own commentary on the poem): "In a former note you mentioned that altho' you had unearthed several of my buried books, yet there was one—'Clarel'—that your spade had not succeeded in getting at. Fearing that you never will get at it by yourself, I have disinterred a copy for you." Melville had wryly cast himself in the role of sexton to his own verse. Other than small private printings of two slim volumes of poetry, *John Marr and Other Sailors* (1888), and *Timoleon* (1891), he was through with publishing.

III
CRITICAL RESPONSES TO *CLAREL*:
1876–1951

T HE STATE of American poetry in the 1870's partly explains the poor reception of *Clarel*. All three best American poets of the century were alive, but Emerson was failing and not even up to editing alone his *Selected Poems* (1876); Whitman was able to get out a Centennial (Sixth) Edition of *Leaves of Grass* (1876) but had been gravely ill for three years, and still was not being read; and Emily Dickinson, in the long run the best of the three, was simply unheard of, though by 1876 she had but ten more years to live. The reins of poetry thus fell to minor hands. The "coming" group were the second-rate apostles of ideality and refinement, verse-makers like Taylor, Stedman, Stoddard, and Aldrich. Public esteem still stood with the New England worthies—Bryant, Whittier, and the Cambridge group of Longfellow, Lowell, and Holmes—all men of real but gentle gifts. They appeared now in Little Classics and Vest Pocket series, or in such special editions as the Household, Centennial, or Blue and Gold. By the end of the decade Longfellow was available in some eight different editions. Thus there was an established rule of elderly gentlemen-poets, flanked by a middle-aged coterie of gentility that held power and set editorial tone. The older group had run out of themes, the younger were never to find any. Under these circumstances the accumulated skills of Victorian verse-making drifted naturally into translations.[43] Poetically the decade after the Civil War was an era of canonization, at loss for contemporary themes, devoid of intellectuality except in scholarship, and unaccustomed to prosodic experiment.

The reviewer in the June 16 *New-York Daily Tribune* (it may have been E. C. Stedman) found *Clarel* "something of a puzzle, both in design and execution." He was bothered by the lack of "distinct conclusions" and the shadowiness of the characters. In line with the conventions of the day he liked the "fragments of fresh, musical lyrics" but was baffled by the "rough, distorted" prosody of the rest. The *New-York Times* (July 10) found "signs of power" in *Clarel*, but except for its "descriptions" and "Oriental atmosphere" felt it was a failure and "should have been written in prose." The reviewer in the June 26 *World* (it may have been Stoddard) was impatiently merciless, seeing only chance virtues "lost in the overwhelming tide of mediocrity." Slight solace to Melville that his brother-in-law John Hoadley, a wealthy engineer and good amateur poet, thought the *World* review "very flippant and foolish in the extreme." Hoadley insisted that *Clarel* was very difficult, "will grow on thoughtful reading," and might well mark a new high in Melville's achievement.[44]

American magazines were scarcely more flattering. Of the three major weeklies of the day, *Harper's Weekly* ignored it, the *Nation* merely listed the title on two occasions, and the *Independent*, the preeminent American religious weekly, contented itself with a statement of having received Melville's "vast work," which it briskly characterized as "destitute of interest or metrical skill," no doubt thereby saving the need of reading it.[45] Not one of the four leading monthlies of the 1870's—*Harper's, Scribner's,* the *Atlantic,* and the *North American Review*—even so much as

43. Between 1867 and 1872 there appeared, among others, a complete *Divina Commedia* by Longfellow, an *Inferno* by Thomas W. Parsons, a *New Life* by Charles Eliot Norton; Bryant's *Iliad* and *Odyssey*; and Taylor's complete *Faust*.

44. Letter of July 8, 1876 (*Log*, II, 751); see also pp. 662–65 below.

45. *Nation*, XXII (June 15, 1876), and "Register of Books Received During the Half-Year Ending June 30, 1876." *Independent*, XXVIII (July 6, 1876).

noticed the poem. That Palestine was still good subject matter, however, if not taken too seriously, *Harper's* made clear in the issue most likely to have reviewed *Clarel* (August, 1876); it printed a six-page sentimental "romance" about a disguised lover, blacked up as a courier, who follows the family of his American sweetheart down to the Jordan and up to Mar Saba, handily rewinning her favor by saving her from drowning in the Jordan. And in the half year after *Clarel's* publication the *Atlantic* serialized a gay and debonair account of Charles Dudley Warner's adventures in the Holy Land.[46] The *Library Table* (August, 1876) gave *Clarel* a few lines which said flatly that the poem was too long, and then added sagely that there might be readers who would think it was not too long! The August number of *Galaxy*, New York's rival to Boston's *Atlantic*, quibbled over the grammar of the subtitle and concluded weightily, "It is not given even to the gods to be dull; and Mr. Melville is not one of the gods." The one sizable review in a major American periodical was in *Lippincott's Magazine* (September, 1876). After recalling Melville's early books as "among the joys of adolescence," the reviewer went sadly on to *Clarel's* problem-world; there he found "no new light," strength of characterization but "no story," and "not six lines of genuine poetry in it." Somehow he got the impression that the poem was "full of prettiness" and the author "bright and genial." The pattern of American reception was to ignore *Clarel* completely, or dispense with it brusquely; no review indicates anything more than a hasty skimming of the poem. The poem simply did not speak to Melville's American contemporaries.

English reception was divided. The piece in the October *Westminster and Foreign Quarterly Review* is worth quoting:

> "Clarel" is a long poem of about twenty-seven thousand lines, of which we can only say that we do not understand a single word. Here is a specimen:—
> > Although he nought confessed,
> > In Derwent, marking there the scene,
> > What interference was expressed

46. *Atlantic,* XXXVIII (July–November, 1876). A further episode, "Saunterings about Constantinople," appeared in *Scribner's,* o.s. XIII (December, 1876). And as soon as Warner's book, *In the Levant* (2 vols.), came out it was enthusiastically reviewed in *Harper's,* LIV (March, 1877).

> As of harsh grit in oiled machine—
> Disrelish grating interest.
>
> [2.14.72–76]

Talleyrand used to say that he always found nonsense singularly refreshing. He would certainly have set a high value on "Clarel."

Replying to an old review is indeed a gratuitous task, but the problem of intelligibility was so recurrent a theme with Melville's contemporaries that one weakens. The lines quoted are not first-rate poetry, but can there be any question of "nonsense" here, or not understanding? The "scene" referred to is clear from the preceding lines: as the pilgrims come through Achor on the way down to the Dead Sea the vale of Jordan opens up before them suddenly; over it passing clouds throw down shadows—

> The Swede, intent: "Lo, how they trail,
> The mortcloths in the funeral
> Of gods!"
>
> (2.14.70–72)

It is an immense image, elaborately relevant to the central theme of the poem, asserting simultaneously the spell of death over Jordan, and the deadness of faith. But to Derwent, the scene itself—so contrary to his pastoral expectations—and the mordant image created by Mortmain, is an "interference" like "harsh grit in oiled machine." The counterimage is a long, long leap from Jordan, but it is a vivid and precise simile, though not a pretty one. It is also thematically relevant and not merely bizarre; in the poem the grinding force of nineteenth-century technology is held partly accountable for the fall from faith. The last line extends the simile, undramatically, but conscientiously: Derwent's "interest" is suddenly worn down by "disrelish," by the grit in the machine. One is forced to conclude that commentators like the gentleman in the *Westminster and Foreign Quarterly Review* simply did not know how to read poetry.

Perhaps the only contemporary reviewer, in America or England, who moved into the area where it now seems the poem exists, was the man for the London *Academy* (August 19), who found it

> a book of very great interest, and poetry of no mean order. The form is subordinate to the matter, and a rugged inattention to niceties of rhyme and metre here and there seems rather deliberate than careless. In this, in the musical verse where the writer chooses to be musical, in

the subtle blending of old and new thought, in the unexpected turns of argument, and in the hidden connexion between things outwardly separate, Mr. Melville reminds us of A. H. Clough. He probably represents one phase of American thought as truly as Clough did one side of the Oxford of his day. . . . We advise our readers to study this interesting poem, which deserves more attention than we fear it is likely to gain in an age which craves for smooth, short, lyric song, and is impatient for the most part of what is philosophic or didactic.[47]

Modern criticism of *Clarel* began with the rediscovery of Melville as a major American writer. Its gradually lengthening lines of inquiry point toward numerous possibilities for today's reader.

When Frank Jewett Mather, Jr., in 1919 wrote a brief estimate of Melville's literary achievement for a weekly magazine, he was talking about a man most Americans had never heard of. Astonishingly enough Mather had collected and read almost everything of Melville's; of those who had actually read the two volumes of *Clarel* he reported himself as "presumably the only survivor." Admitting "*longueurs* and lapses," Mather insisted that the poem's "vividness, humor, irony, and mind-stuff" made it America's best example of the Victorian faith-doubt literature. Raymond Weaver dramatized who this man Melville was when in 1921 he published the first biography. Reserving only a final hasty chapter for the last thirty-five years of Melville's life, and significantly titling it "The Long Quietus," Weaver commented that now *Clarel* had *two* readers, but predicted that "it would be over-optimistic to presume that there will soon be a third." Though he too found "more irony, vividness, and intellect" (he seems to have missed the humor) than in almost all the contemporary poets put together, Weaver thought "the poem never quite fulfils itself." He liked parts of it well enough, however, offering three pages of quotations that stressed the social criticism from Part 4.[48] A passing judgment of Weaver's set the tone for much subsequent criticism: "*Clarel* is by all odds the most important record we have of what was the temper of Melville's deeper thoughts during his

47. The Springfield (Mass.) *Republican* of September 8 reprinted part of this review noting that Melville's poem "receives kindlier countenance in England than it has in his own land." The *Republican*'s own brief notice of July 18 had not been flattering. I am indebted to Jay Leyda for both *Republican* notices.

48. Evidently it was here that V. L. Parrington picked up the page and a half of quotations (pp. 266–67) which he threw in at the end of his account of Melville in the second volume (1927) of his widely read *Main Currents in American Thought*.

long metaphysical period." In 1924 the poem, which had now be-
come almost unobtainable, was published in Constable's Standard
Edition.[49] Reviewing this English edition, John Middleton Murry
thought Melville a rather "clumsy" poet working with "tremen-
dous" materials. He warned that *Clarel* lacked conventional verbal
beauties, being "obscure, compressed, craggy"; to be enjoyed it must
be read as a whole. Its theme, he maintained rather largely, was noth-
ing less than "the essential mystery of the Christian religion, which is
the mystery of the universe." Such claims John Freeman, in his En-
glish Men of Letters volume, contradicted brusquely. In both matter
and manner Freeman named *Clarel* the worst of Melville's generally
interesting poetry, written without imagination and retaining the
power only to bore—as if done by "a pious Byron or a travelled and
garrulous Wordsworth." Freeman's peremptory decree on *Clarel* is
the only unqualified dismissal in Melville criticism up to that time.

Lewis Mumford in 1929 struck an old tone and two new ones. He
granted *Clarel*'s "failure as poetry," and began the particularization:
the misconceived choice of rhyming iambic tetrameter led Melville
into archaic language and ugly rhymes and rhythms in order to fill
out his lines, in effect creating "a long, weary poem." But Mum-
ford's broad social humanism was so deeply stirred by this same bad
verse that he explicated in some detail the mordant social realism of
Clarel, commenting eloquently on its perceptive view of nineteenth-
century institutions—the Church, the new science, revolutionary
movements, technology, and the overriding powers of industrialism.
On a biographical level Mumford saw the poem as the record of a
new "animal faith" in Melville, an undogmatic acknowledgment that
life is "not good or bad, malicious or forbearing, true or false," but
simply "livable." These two themes—Melville's personal reorienta-
tion, and the poem's vigorous social commentary—were to become
staples of subsequent criticism.

Two foreign critics took the lead in the thirties. K. H. Sun-
dermann cited *Clarel* constantly in his heavily categorical analysis of
Melville's religious, philosophical, and historical thought. The mer-
its of this kind of abstraction of an artist's "ideas" are indeed doubt-
ful, but in a general way, perhaps, Sundermann demonstrated the
ideological density of the poem. His *Gestaltenanalyse* in a section on

49. Vols. XIV–XV of *The Works of Herman Melville* (London, 1922–24).

Glaubens- und Konfessionsproblem was the first fairly intensive study of the individual characters. His thesis here was that each of the major figures projected some aspect of Melville's complex attitudes on belief, minor characters serving as contrast figures. Sundermann saw a consolatory glimmer of light in the Epilogue, but no signs of an acquired belief. Without a knowledge of sacred geography, Sundermann noted in passing, a reader would have difficulties with *Clarel*. The French critic Jean Simon put the hazards more forcefully: unless the reader took notes as he read he would be pretty sure to get lost in the labyrinth! For Simon, a romantic critic of some scope, the perils of the labyrinth were worth risking. He found there an extraordinary revelation of a tormented soul, valuable commentary on the major religions, a fine picture of a complex age, and, occasionally, astonishing poetic flashes. "Par rang de huit, les syllabes défilent, régiment après régiment," Simon lamented, noting that *Clarel* is longer than the epics of Homer, Virgil, Tasso, or Milton. Yet Simon was clearly taken by the poem, and had to work hard to keep from overrating it. After a long précis of the narrative (in spite of minor errors the best to that time) Simon took a speculative plunge. The poem breaks roughly in half, he argued, the second volume being marked by a shift in purpose, a reshuffling of the characters, less reliance on the journal, and a notably improved skill in prosody. The break he attributed to Melville's having written most of one volume before *Battle-Pieces* (1866), most of the other, after. Hence two distinct spiritual crises were projected into the poem. The first half reflects Melville's desperate need before 1866 to find a specific religious faith (dreaming even of Rome, of mosques, of synagogues!); then the quest was abandoned. The crisis of the second half was whether to join the social world of men, or accept an isolated life of silent meditation; Melville chose the latter, says Simon. Meanwhile an American scholar, Willard Thorp, was warning that "the casual reader is sure to be hopelessly bewildered" by the poem's difficulties, for it calls for saturation in the primary images, themes, and allusions of Melville's other writings. He reemphasized its relevance to central Victorian issues and pronounced it the key to Melville's thought in the later years.

The criticism of the war years opened up some of the difficulties. William Braswell, in a study of Melville's religious thought which made use not only of the published works but of manuscripts, letters, and books read by Melville, and Melville marginalia when available, sharpened considerably the changing and complex patterns of Melville's doubts and beliefs. In his brief comments on *Clarel*, Braswell called attention to doubts of God's benevolence, elements of the Gnostic heresy, increased appreciation of Catholicism, and the continuing influence of Christ's doctrine of love; he concluded, "While Melville yearned for the peace that Catholicism and Protestantism gave to many, his critical nature . . . prevented him from attaining it." Henry Wells came in from a different angle, devoting one chapter to *Clarel* in his study of native elements in the mode and matter of sixteen American poets. In style, symbolism, and intellectual temper, Wells located *Clarel* in a definably native tradition rooted in Emerson, Thoreau, and some of Whittier, and flowering in Dickinson and Robinson. He praised the "economy of expression," the intentional harshness, the "mass, vigor, thought" of the lines. He saw the typical force and restlessness of an American temperament in the prosody and themes, and in certain characters. Though Melville ended without finding a faith, Wells suggested, he came to the view that "only in terms of a religion of some sort is life properly fulfilled." For Wells the massive allusiveness of Melville's poem led "to a fresh and definite purpose and with the most enlivening consequences for his art. He never staggers beneath his burden." Also in 1943, the present writer completed a doctoral dissertation on *Clarel*. This study made an analysis of Melville's Eastern trip and the cultural patterns that lay back of it, examined the years leading to composition, and offered a detailed study of the poem's sources. The major section was an interpretation of the poem and Melville's spiritual history through close analysis of the characters. The following year William Ellery Sedgwick brought a sensitive moral concern and a theological urgency to his chapter on *Clarel*. Sedgwick's version of Melville's dilemma was that he found the nineteenth century "invertebrate, amorphous," as a result of the "process of disfiguration" which began with the Reformation. Melville was "drawn to Catholicism and repelled by Protestantism." Emotionally reoriented by the Civil War, Sedgwick's argument ran, "Melville has recanted his mind's Promethean role"; the tight rhetoric of the poem, compared to Melville's earlier prose in the high style, expressed Melville's shift away from his radical Protestantism.

The burgeoning of Melville interest after the war brought five general criticisms of his works all of which include sections on *Clarel*. Geoffrey Stone, writing from an announced Catholic viewpoint, makes it clear that Melville's general sympathy toward the Roman Church is historical only and not based on acquaintance with Catholic apologetics. Melville's rationalization of Rome is on "natural" grounds, and hence, says Stone, "soon open to perversion." His position in the poem, like that of his major characters, is marked by "reluctance to make the full surrender asked by faith," for reasons beyond examination; yet Stone admires his "resolute grappling" with doubt. Stone judges the poem "a second-rate piece of work, in the kindest judgment. Yet . . . almost every page shows the evidences of a first-rate mind." Stone's concern is with the matter of the dialogues; the "description" he would willingly forgo, for the most part, and his opinion of the verse is that the poem means most "if we close our ears as we read it"! Richard Chase's approach also bypasses aesthetic problems, but makes numerous provocative movements in and out of the poem. Taking the sterility of modern life as the central symbolic idea of the poem, he sees the outward theme as "the developing thoughts and emotions of a young American divinity student"; as such the poem is an "education." Internally the major achievement is Rolfe—"Melville's ultimate humanist, the representative figure he had been working toward since he had purged the extremities of his titanism in *Pierre*—the figure, indeed, toward whom the strongest current of Melville's thought had always been flowing. . . . He is the human core of the high Promethean hero." Thus Chase, whose approach to Melville is through the mythical and symbolical sequences of his psychology, finds the poem a kind of culmination from which *Billy Budd* is in some senses a falling off. In his 1950 study of Melville, Newton Arvin made the strongest case of any critic thus far for the poem as a poem. Having established in an earlier article the distinctive mode of Melville's verse as being non-lyrical (his view parallels that of Wells), Arvin sees the blemishes as "far from fatal." *Clarel* is "a novel of ideas in verse," in which Melville was aiming at "a middle tone between poetry and prose." Arvin finds "the feeling for scene . . . masterly," and the characters "a remarkable assemblage of distinct and freshly noticed people" who anticipate more literary conventions than they follow. The problem was to dramatize "the spiritual ordeal of an age in which, for many men, religious faith had ceased to be possible on the old grounds without ceasing to be desperately necessary." Melville in the course of the poem reaches a kind of "Middle Way" which is full of paradoxes, involves considerable rejection of the intellect, and can best be described as "a New Manicheanism." Ronald Mason, whose book *The Spirit above the Dust* studies all the works but takes its title from the Epilogue to *Clarel*, digs up English criticism where Freeman had buried it and has another look. Freeman was right, he says, that the poem fails as art. But Mason "insists" that *Clarel* cannot be so easily dismissed. The poem is "a contemplative recapitulation of all Melville's imaginative life; an impressive intellectual attempt to impose order upon the distresses into which hitherto his incompletely controlled imagination had led him." Mason virtually reverses Arvin's position; his main argument is that in *Clarel* Melville for the first time makes his center of attention not characters but ideas, substituting for the dramatic mode "the historical, even dialectical, approach." The characters, though credible and sufficiently well differentiated, are intentionally "static," designed as "animated heads of discussion. . . . The main action of the poem is not the journey at all, but . . . the analysis of conflicting principles." Somewhat in the exuberant tone of Mumford and Sedgwick, Mason too finds "a new faith." He sees a repudiation of "landlessness" for "the principle of discipline" (this accounts for the sympathy to Rome). His somewhat rapt conclusion is that *Clarel* is "a poem of acceptance, not of rejection," and is the "return journey" from Taji's outward quest in *Mardi*: "The triumph [in the Epilogue] is in fact not Clarel's but Melville's." In the same year Leon Howard put the outcome quite differently: "His [Melville's] scepticism became, in *Clarel*, the dominant quality of his mind." Coming at Melville's problem of belief in the perspective of the data assembled by Jay Leyda in *The Melville Log*, Howard finds in the poem "a detached interest in the human problem of belief." The "sum of the wisdom Melville acquired" was that "there was no absolute certainty anywhere for a whole man. He could only be what he was made to be." Melville had learned to "face uncertainty without despair." Howard's reading of the characters leaves a good deal to be desired, but his grasp of the biographical context pretty well disposes of the need for erratic speculation as to Melville's motives.

In spite of confusing divergences in the first generation of serious criticism, significant agreements and disagreements emerge.

Most seem agreed that *Clarel* is a major biographical document for the years between *The Confidence-Man* and *Billy Budd*. Melville was trying to make up his mind about many basic religious and historical questions while he was writing *Clarel*, though what he decided seems to vary with the critic. This is a poem in which "ideas" count, though whether or not this is the center of the poem is in dispute. Is the stress on people or propositions? on characters or conceptions? And—this brings us fully into the circle of combat—how good a work of art is it, if indeed it is one at all?

Perhaps the area of greatest agreement is that the poem, though difficult, demanding, and not to be drained off in the course of a summer's afternoon, is very much better than had been supposed. In some corners there is even enthusiasm. No doubt some of this enthusiasm can be attributed to Melville's generally ascending reputation; also biographical and historical study have helped place the poem, and perhaps changing tastes continue to work favorably toward its themes and the manner of the verse. The heart of the matter, however, is simpler: by midcentury its critics had begun to read the poem.

IV

CLAREL: A READING OF THE POEM

IT IS CONFUSING indeed to encounter, as we have at times, the notion that *Clarel* is full of "bad poetry" but somehow is a "good poem." Of course one section can be good, another bad. But I take it that something else is meant—that somehow *Clarel* is an effective revelation of Melville's spiritual and psychological history, and of the contemporary crisis in general, though unfortunately the "poetry" is bad. In what follows I shall assume that it is not possible for bad poetry to communicate a significant, ordered world of imaginative values. Whatever limitations the poem has are inherent in the poetry; what is not well said never gets into the poem. Whatever is genuinely there is there because of, indeed through, the verse, however often it may be endangered by ineptitudes. The question, then, is what the poem is about.

Any summary of plot will surely convince us at once that *Clarel* is dull going if by plot we mean only the outward narrative. "Clarel himself," one such recital runs,

a young divinity student tormented by doubts, a "pilgrim-infidel," has arrived at Jerusalem on his travels. In the midst of the holy places he strikes up a variety of casual acquaintanceships, and falls in love with a young Jewish girl, Ruth, whose father, an immigrant to Palestine from America, is killed by hostile Arab raiders. In the period of mourning that follows, Clarel is forbidden by Jewish custom to see anything of the girl, and in his grief and restlessness he sets out with a group of companions on horseback on a pilgrimage that takes them to the Jordan, the Dead Sea, the Greek monastery of Mar Saba in the mountains, then Bethlehem, and at length Jerusalem again. On his return to the city Clarel finds that Ruth has died of grief in his absence, and his own future seems more uncertain than ever.

The passage is from Arvin (1950, p. 270); although it could be from almost any other of the criticisms, I have chosen this one because it is a plain, easily agreed-on statement of the "plot," and also because Arvin's further commentary on the poem is so generally rich and cogent that no thought of invidiousness need occur. As Arvin would be among the first to insist, such a summary simply gets us started.

The love theme is too intermittent to sustain any large architectural purpose. Is it necessary, then, to dismiss the poem as not pretending to significant structure by classifying it simply as a travel narrative, a random sequence of events incurred along a time-space line? The apparent failure of either the love plot or the travel line to provide a sufficient architecture lies at the root of one's initial discomfort before the poem. The poem lacks availability. Only a deeper reading opens an interior order beneath the loose outer form. Clarel's falling out of faith and into love, his particular kind of subsequent journey, the layered context of situation and personality in which the pilgrimage occurs, and the predictable return to tragedy, provide a series of large and powerful movements. It is time to try for a reading that defines these movements.

Symbolic site and situation unlock the poem's resources. We first see young Clarel, an American theological student, alone in his chamber on his first evening in Jerusalem; it is the Feast of the Epiphany, but as he looks out over the Pool of Hezekiah to the dome of the Church of the Holy Sepulcher and Mt. Olivet beyond, no manifestation comes.

We last see him in his martyrdom and passion, following a procession through St. Stephen's Gate and along the Via Crucis; it is Whitsuntide, but he is visited by no cloven tongues of flame. Between the two scenes lie the long weeks, leading up to an unfulfilled Easter, during which Clarel enacts his symbolic search, making the round of a Night Journey with a pilgrim cavalcade. The tone and quality of that search, the intricate cross-exchanges of talk, action, and subtle gesture among the ten major pilgrims, and the imposing, symbolic monuments and landforms through which they roam, fill out the structure of the poem. There are four primary locations: Jerusalem (at the beginning and the end); the road to Jericho and the Dead Sea area; the Judaean wilderness and the monastery of Mar Saba; and Bethlehem. Through them emerges the wide context of history, theology, and psychology which sustains the four parts of the poem.

In Part 1, "Jerusalem," the narrator presents the microcosm of a threatened world. The reader must presuppose the centuries-old, golden image of Jerusalem, fabulous and mythically divine: "sacred and glorious," wrote a seventeenth-century pilgrim, "elected by God for his seat . . . like a Diadem crowning the head of the mountains; the theatre of mysteries and miracles."[50] But *that* Jerusalem, as well as the Jerusalem of euphoric nineteenth-century evangelists, exists here only as counterimage. The City of the poem—

> Like the ice-bastions round the Pole,
> Thy blank, blank towers, Jerusalem!
>
> (1.1.60–61)

—is an image from one of Poe's world's-end fantasies. The City is locked up from within—"blind arches," "sealed windows," "portals masoned fast" (lines 163–64). The City is a labyrinth of narrow, uninhabited byplaces, of haunts that hide stowaways, criminals, penitents, anchorites, and kinless ones. There is the story of Emim Bey the Mameluke, who fled from Cairo, then to the desert,

> but, fox-like, on,
> And ran to earth in Zion's town;
> Here maimed, disfigured, crouched in den,
> And crouching died—securest then.
>
> (1.21.36–39)

50. Sandys, *Relation* (1652, 1658, 1670, 1673), p. 120.

The City is a place of mutilation also for the lepers. Living in "a reptile lane" where "stone huts face the stony wall," these humans whose faces are defacements live on in "voiceless visagelessness" (1.25.3, 1; 1.26.8). Beneath the City, in a world of "ducts and chambered wells and walls" (1.16.8), lies history's rubble, the disintegrated achievements of men; and even though there be some mild domestic scenes—a mother holding her child—

> Under such scenes abysses be—
> Dark quarries where few care to pry.
>
> (1.16.33–34)

Jerusalem is a town of "Dismantled, torn, / Disastrous houses" which "Yawn . . . like plundered tombs" (1.21.12, 13, 19). No wonder Clarel is haunted by the night silences, by the cracking and crumbling of walls. He goes to the city walls—for air, for breath, to watch people. Yet beyond the City lies the Desert,

> Where baskets of the white-ribbed dead
> Sift the fine sand.
>
> (1.5.168–69)

And the Desert is moving in:

> 'Twas yellow waste within as out,
> The student mused: The desert, see,
> It parts not here, but silently,
> Even like a leopard by our side,
> It seems to enter in with us—
> At home amid men's homes would glide.
>
> (1.24.80–85)

The Zion of *Clarel* is no theater of miracles and mysteries. This Holy City is not the City of God, not even the City of Man. Neither promise nor refuge is here. This is a Fallen City. It is *Città Dolente*, the City of Dis (1.36.29).

The qualities of the City simultaneously characterize young Clarel. Surrounded by the Desert of the contemporary world, he is lost within the labyrinth of his own doubts. Like Roderick Usher he fears that he and his house are doomed. Like the Ancient Mariner he is becalmed in a world of nightmare. He is Eliot's wastelander confronted with the Unreal City. Like Kafka's K he cannot get to the Castle, or rather he is there and finds no one. In the old legends

Jerusalem was the navel of the world's body, the center of the earth, the place where the sun cast no shadow. But for Clarel there is no medieval magic or miracle, no voice, no sign. He cannot pray. His visit to the Church of the Holy Sepulcher plunges him into a "gulf of dizzying fable" (1.5.219). Reared in the provincialism of American sectarian faith, Clarel is bewildered by the traffic of tribes and sects at this crossroad of world religions. The wild rites of Georgian, Maronite, Armenian, and Greek seem to him a malediction; it prefigures the journey he will take:

> O heart profane,
> O pilgrim-infidel, begone!
> Nor here the sites of Faith pollute,
> Thou who misgivest we enthrone
> A God untrue, in myth absurd.
>
> . . . .
>
> We know thee, thou there standing mute.
> Out, out—begone! try Nature's reign
> Who deem'st the super-nature vain:
> To Lot's Wave by black Kedron rove;
> On, by Mount Seir, through Edom move;
> There crouch thee with the jackall down—
> Crave solace of the scorpion!
>
> (1.6.18–22, 25–31)

In Part 1, Clarel makes two responses to his desolate plight. One is to find some person who can solve his spiritual crisis. So begins a major pattern of the poem: the lost hero in search of a guide. Outside the Jaffa Gate, wandering alone, he suddenly discovers he is on the way to Emmaus (a representative example of the significance of site: Luke 24.13–48): would that *he* could meet some stranger who would expound the mysteries to him. So Nehemiah, a sweet old man with the sacred Book, enters the poem (1.7). A millenarian and irrepressible dispenser of tracts, Nehemiah has left America to be on hand for the Second Coming. Through him Clarel fitfully recaptures the pastoral dream of the Holy City of the Gospels, with apocalyptic colors from Revelation. But he is even more deeply stirred by a second potential guide, the young renegade Catholic, Celio, whom he meets near the demoniac tombs of Lower Gihon (1.11). Celio is a hunchback; his twisted body is the sign of his inner torments. From him, in two brief wordless encounters with "the Unknown" (1.11.51),

Clarel wins a flashing insight into the cost of rebellious defiance. One night there is a "piercing cry from out the dark" and Celio, the alienated Christ-defier (1.13), is dead (1.18.90–91). Days pass, and Clarel meets two more-formidable guides: by the "rifled *Sepulcher of Kings*" (line 24), Vine (1.28); wandering on the hills above Gethsemane, Rolfe (1.31). Both are Americans, of middle years, mature and sensitive; both are men of genius. In the course of the poem we are given enough covert hints about their backgrounds and temperaments to make clear that Vine is the narrator's fictionalized portrayal of Nathaniel Hawthorne, and Rolfe a partial projection of Herman Melville (see sect. 8). Rolfe and Vine are thus of peculiar biographical interest, but their first function in the poem is simply that of two anonymous men of genius whose merits fascinate and bewilder young Clarel. Rolfe, a sun-browned adventurer who has roamed the world and lived on Pacific isles, read widely and become unafraid of heresy, proves a sturdy good-companion who assumes the role of master of discourse. Vine is "Admetus' shepherd," a man of "gifts unique" (1.29.20, 6); a shy, quiet man of rich sensibilities, he remains untouched by argument. This is Clarel's first contact with "Exceptional natures," the narrator tells us (1.31.45), and they are to cause him much perplexity.

If Clarel's first response to his dilemma is to search for guides, his second is to fall in love. The beautiful young Jewess Ruth wakes him from passiveness and stirs in him dreams of the American landscape—green orchards, birds, and woodlands which rise in contrast to the Judaean wasteland. Though Clarel feels that love can override his distress, the narrator hints that such innocent dreams are not to be (1.39.49). Events cut in. The murder of Ruth's father temporarily separates the lovers. His friends propose a pilgrimage on horseback to the Dead Sea. Obsessed by fear that something may happen to Ruth in his absence, yet anxious to explore the resources of his three guides—Nehemiah, Rolfe, and Vine—the young seeker finally agrees to enter the symbolic round of descent and return. It will be "Brief term of days," the narrator warns as Part 1 concludes, "but a profound remove" (1.44.50).

The three remaining parts of the poem describe the journey of the hero and his guides, of whom several more join the pilgrimage (2.1). One is Derwent, a Broad-Church Anglican clergyman of rosy temperament untroubled by the modern dilemma—his motto: "All turns or alters for the best" (3.6.105). His warmth and affability toward the disturbed young theological student, for whom he feels some professional responsibility, make him a special problem that will test Clarel's acuteness. Open antagonist to Derwent, and perhaps the most memorable character of the poem, is Mortmain, the bitter Swede. Misanthropic and introverted, Mortmain is consumed by the intense perception of the world's evil which finally drove him from revolutionary politics in France. His name and the black skullcap he wears are ominous enough signs of his future. Mortmain is an Empedocles figure (Melville annotated Arnold's poem in 1871) on whom the hand of death is set. Part 2, which culminates at the Dead Sea, belongs increasingly to him.

Part 2 is the Night Journey. From the top of Olivet the pilgrims had looked far down on "the mystic sea" and felt the loops of Laocoön's serpent coil about them (1.37.114–17). Now they begin the descent, after pausing symbolically by Gethsemane (2.3) and passing the lyric town of Bethany (2.6). "Down going, down, to Jericho" (2.7.11), the narrator chants as the cavalcade descends through arid ravines and ugly turns of ground where "A certain man went down from Jerusalem to Jericho, and fell among thieves" (Luke 10.30). Alarmed at the prospect, a Greek banker and his rakish son-in-law to be turn about, and the narrator offers the reader a chance to join them:

> They fled. And thou? The way is dun;
> Why further follow . . . ?
> .   .   .   .
> Part here, then, would ye win release
> From ampler dearth; part, and in peace.
>
> (2.13.112–13, 118–19)

Down they go, until Quarantania, the Mount of Christ's temptation, looms above them like a great slag-pile. Here Mortmain in a dangerous gesture leaves the party to spend the night alone under Quarantania. The next morning they watch a Syrian monk ascend Quarantania to undergo the Passion, as Margoth, a Jewish geologist, descends with his hammer and specimens of Jura limestone (2.19). At the Jordan the unpredictable Rolfe leads the pilgrims in the traditional river rite, singing *Ave Maris Stella* (2.24)—and from here on star images hover over the poem. In a representative touch of characterization, Nehemiah drinks the muddy Jordan water pronouncing it sweet as sugar; Margoth, sworn enemy of all myths, tries it too and spews it out (2.24). As the pilgrims cross the slimy Siddim Plain, fog and rack set in, withering the branches plucked by Jordan (2.28). By the Dead Sea Mortmain returns out of the shadows, his veined face like ice streaked with volcanic ash. An Arab guard sings a monitory song:

> "Would ye know what bitter drink
>   They gave to Christ upon the Tree?
> Sip the wave that laps the brink
>   Of Siddim: taste, and God keep ye!
> It drains the hills where alum's hid—
> Drains the rock-salt's ancient bed;
>   Hither unto basin fall
>   The torrents from the steeps of gall—
> Here is Hades' water-shed.
>   Sinner, would ye that your soul
>   Bitter were and like the pool?
> Sip the Sodom waters dead;
>   But never from thy heart shall haste
>   The Marah—yea, the after-taste."
>
> (2.34.50–63)

Mortmain has moved to the edge of the sea:

>   Arrested as he stooped,
> Did Mortmain his pale hand recall?
> No; undeterred the wave he scooped,
> And tried it—madly tried the gall.
>
> (2.34.64–67)

It is the taste of the Dead Sea, rather than of Jordan, that lingers acridly through the poem.

The two cantos that follow, "Prelusive" and "Sodom," bring Part 2 to climax. Tension flows from the narrator's preliminary exploitation of the subconscious in an intricate image of the labyrinthian world of Piranesi's prints, concluding:

> The thing implied is one with man,
> His penetralia of retreat—
> The heart, with labyrinths replete . . . .
>
> (2.35.20–22)

Again the reader is given a choice: either reflect on St. Paul's "mystery of iniquity" (line 24), or, if he would preserve "Childhood's illusion" (line 39), pass by what follows. It is night; thirteen hundred feet below the Mediterranean the pilgrims crouch at the edge of the Sea of Death and Wickedness. The legendary poisonous haze hangs over the water. Relentlessly Mortmain takes possession; seated on a salt-slagged camel's skull he has a premonition of his coming death as he looks up through the murk:

> "It is the star
> Called Wormwood. Some hearts die in thrall
> Of waters which yon star makes gall."
>
> (2.36.22–24)

He leads the pilgrims on to consider the subtle nature of the sins of the Five Cities whose drowned ruins lie, as they feel, at their feet. They sit enchanted by the mephitic bubblings of the water and the divine madness of Mortmain. That night the saintly, deluded Nehemiah, in a final somnambulistic act, walks toward an ecstatic vision of the New Jerusalem. In the morning his corpse floats at the water's edge, near the camel's skull on which Mortmain had sat the night before and pointed at "the star / Called Wormwood."

The Dead Sea embodies variously the risk of annihilation, absolute evil, and the unbearable limits of introspection. Melvillean sea-images reinforce the meanings of the site, stressing that the Siddim Plain is beneath ocean level—"a lead-line's long reach down" (2.14.3)—and that "the sunken slimy plain" is like "the quaking sea-bed bared" :

> All was still:
> So much the more their bosoms thrill
> With dream of some withdrawn vast surge
> Its timed return about to urge
> And whelm them.
>
> (2.23.30, 32, 33–37)

But the overriding emphasis, a major implication of the poem, is implied by references to Acheron, Hades, Orpheus, and Eblis. Though relieved from utter blackness by rainbows which on two occasions hover tantalizingly for a moment over the dread scene (2.29, 2.39), the Siddim Plain is a Dante-world of the soul's eternal torment.

Part 3, "Mar Saba," is a Purgatorio to the Inferno of Part 2. As the pilgrims ascend the wild Judah ridge, some eighteen hundred feet above the valley, they move from a site of absolute evil; though chaos reigns along the ridge, it is the chaos of oppositions. The bleak, riven landforms stress this dual world, apparent scene of some ancient Armageddon. The pilgrims pass "Two human skeletons inlaced / In grapple as alive they fell" (3.1.82–83). In a memorable scene on the High Desert, under "the clear vault of hollow heaven," they sit and argue over the Gnostic heresy, and Zoroastrian themes of "Ormuzd involved with Ahriman / In deadly lock" (3.5.204, 36–37).

Meanwhile mellow chimes entice the pilgrims on to Mar Saba, a fifth-century Greek monastery whose twin towers rise over the Judah wilderness. That night in temporary release they revel until dawn, with songs and stories and ample flasks of St. Saba wine. It is a ceremonial assertion of manly brotherhood and good-fellowship, a "forgetting" of death and debate in which only the innocent Clarel and the exhausted Mortmain do not participate (3.11–14). Though Mar Saba's towers rise triumphantly over the wilderness, their base lies six hundred feet down in the bed of the Black Brook, Kedron, which we are reminded flows into the Dead Sea. At Saba, once the revels are over, there is a balance of effects. A palm tree, the one Melville had seen growing on an upper ledge of the monastery, emerges as a central symbol of the hope of immortality, or grace, or at least peace (3.26–29); there is also an inner cell where a mad monk guards heaps of bones, and demands from visitors such a password as "*Death*" (3.24.66). A choir of monks on a crag renders a long chant about the fall of Jerusalem that turns into a hymn to God's mercy (3.17), but other monks present a masque of the unforgiven Wandering Jew which is acted deep in the ravine by the light of red torches (3.19). So in complex strophe and antistrophe the poem moves on. Part 3 concludes when Mortmain's psychic exhaustion merges into death; he is found, eyes fixed upon the Palm, an eagle feather at his lips (3.32).

What meanwhile of the reluctant hero? Since leaving Jerusalem, Clarel has moved in the shadows, a brooding observer of the life-ways of his associates: "Learning, unlearning, word by word" (2.14.52). Even in life, Nehemiah's goodness was perhaps too simple, Mortmain's passion too complex, to be usable patterns for Clarel; in any case both men are now dead. Derwent's campaign at last overextends itself, and Clarel turns savagely in attack (3.21). Clarel's emotional overtures toward Vine have been firmly rebuked (2.27); the discovery of Vine in a moment of lonely weakness of his own brings Clarel to a troubled perception:

> Ill hour (thought he), an evil sign:
> No more need dream of winning Vine
> Or coming at his mystery.
> O, lives which languish in the shade,
> Puzzle and tease us, or upbraid;
> What noteless confidant, may be,
> Withholds the talisman, the key!
> Or if indeed it run not so,
> And he's above me where I cling;
> Then how these higher natures know
> Except in shadow from the wing?—
>
> (3.7.35–45)

Perhaps Rolfe is the one who has retained most stature during the journey. Yet

> How reconcile Rolfe's wizard chord
> And forks of esoteric fire
> With common-place of laxer mien?
> May truth be such a spendthrift lord?
>
> (2.32.97–100)

Though baffled by Rolfe's "Manysidedness" (3.16.263), Clarel finds himself increasingly imitating his views and language (4.3.119–23). Young Clarel's spiritual state while he is at Mar Saba is accurately reflected back to him by the wilderness:

> All the mountain-land
> Disclosed through Kedron far withdrawn,
> Cloven and shattered, hushed and banned,
> Seemed poised as in a chaos true,
> Or throe-lock of transitional earth
> When old forms are annulled, and new
> Rebel, and pangs suspend the birth.
>
> (3.21.13–19)

Clarel aches for a rebirth that is denied him. On the last evening at the monastery he feels "Suspended 'twixt the heaven and hell" (3.31.63)—and this is the key to Part 3.

Part 4 brings the pilgrims on to Bethlehem for their last three days before returning to Jerusalem. Bethlehem of Judaea, with its lovely vineyards, olive groves, green terraces—surely the lyric mountain town will offer some hint of Paradise to these weary travelers? But they are no mitered kings led on by a miracle. "Let man lament the foundered Star" (4.1.18), the narrator says, and later Rolfe echoes:

> "The rule, the Magian rule is run,
> And Mythra abdicates the sun!"
>
> (4.16.209–10)

In due time they stand inside the Church of the Nativity: at their feet, set in the pavement, a silver star, directly over the Manger. An ardent Franciscan monk, Salvaterra, tells them of its "shining grace"; standing silently in a circle—

> They comment none;
> Not voicing everything they know.
>
> (4.13.63, 65–66)

The sense of what the pilgrims "know"—their long predicament, the grim happenings of their journey thus far—has been heightened by two new pilgrims who joined their ranks at Mar Saba. One, who leaves them soon after they reach Bethlehem, is Agath, an old Greek pilot "schooled by the inhuman sea" (4.13.7) and beaten by men. Illiterate and by preference uncommunicative about his private tragedies, Agath survives in a brutal world by animal tenacity. He is succeeded by Ungar, "A wandering Ishmael from the West" (4.10.186). Ungar is an American refugee from the defeated South who has become a wandering professional soldier. Ungar's memories of "personal pain monotonous" (4.5.9) have made him a bitter judge of man and society, the most articulate social critic of the poem. His monomania marks him as kin to Mortmain, though with the hardness to survive, and his brief but impassioned formulations in "Of Wickedness the Word" (4.22) take us from the Bethlehem hillsides back to Mortmain's theme in "Sodom" (2.36). Even in the town of the nativity, Ungar's discourse points to "The ever-upbubbling wickedness!" (4.22.17). Before so "wild" a nature, Clarel is "at loss" (4.17.48–50).

In these final days of the pilgrimage Clarel is tempted toward two new extremes: the ascetic ideal of a Celibate (3.30) and the apostasy of a Prodigal (4.26). Confused, he finally decides to confront whatever awaits him at journey's end, and on the tenth night of the pilgrimage begins his ride back to Jerusalem, the "deicide town" (4.29.127). So at last he enters "The Valley of Decision" (4.30). Clarel's many premonitions of this moment are now fulfilled; as the horsemen round the southern city wall:

> The valley slept—
> Obscure, in monitory dream
> Oppressive, roofed with awful skies
> Whose stars like silver nail-heads gleam
> Which stud some lid over lifeless eyes.
>
> (4.29.148–52)

There by lantern light he sees the men at work with mattocks, burying the bodies of Ruth and her mother. The discovery is the enactment of a ritual. It is not a plot disclosure so much as a recognition scene. Ruth—as somehow he has constantly feared—is dead. So after the "profound remove" of the Night Journey, Clarel is back to the "complex passion." And now his guides depart, leaving him alone in Jerusalem.

We may use the phrase "complex passion" to signify the total historical, theological, and psychological dilemma which permeates the poem. So Clarel had phrased it that day at the Holy Sepulcher when he supposed the rites were a malediction toward himself (1.5.217). The complexity he had then felt as a generalized emotion he now knows through experience. With "gods declined to heraldries," as Mortmain once memorably phrased it (2.31.56), new problems of infinite complexity are at hand; the thesis of the poem is that they can neither be solved nor escaped. It had been Clarel's hope, in the early days, that by winning Ruth he could enter an Eden where

> tales abstruse
> Of Christ, the crucified, Pain's Lord,
> Seem foreign—forged—incongruous.
>
> (1.28.9–11)

The essence of his journey is that these tales are not abstruse; whether the world is of nature or super-nature the Cross is the one unmistakable reality. The Cross as a tragic symbol dominates the imaginations of the four monomaniacs. Celio faced its paralyzing power at the Arch of Ecce Homo (1.13). Mortmain scrawled his bitter lament to the Slanted Cross on a great rock overlooking the Dead Sea (2.31).

Agath wore a sailor's "crucifixion in tattoo" on his forearm (4.2.51). Ungar's sword, his primary symbol, becomes a double emblem: " 'Tis true; / A cross, it is a cross,' he said" (4.14.29–30). Even Vine, in one of his few moments of verbal "unconstraint," stresses the "beauty in that sad conceit" of passion-flowers as "Emblems of Christ's last agony" (4.15.8, 30, 26). For Rolfe the grace of the Greek cross, which Derwent prefers, cannot match "the true semblance" of the Latin cross:

> "that's the one
> Was lifted up and knew the nail;
> 'Tis realistic—can avail!"
>
> (3.18.47–49)

Each of these pilgrims is outside the Church, and for all of them the Cross is a symbol of pain, not hope. Just before he returned to Jerusalem, Clarel had been able to phrase his problem:

> "What! fall back on clay commonplace?
> Yearnest for peace so? sick of strife?
> . . . .
>   . . . how live
> At all, if once a fugitive
> From thy own nobler part, though pain
> Be portion inwrought with the grain?"
>
> (4.28.77–78, 81–84)

The recognition at last of the tragic view is Clarel's major insight. He too must endure the Passion.

The poem concludes ritualistically. After the Ash Wednesday of Ruth's death, Clarel endures the Passion Week of his own despair (4.32). Easter dawns with no jubilation for him (4.33). We see him last at Whitsuntide, unspoken to by tongues of flame. He is following a train of pilgrims:

> Cross-bearers all, alike they tend
> And follow, slowly follow on.
>
> (4.34.43–44)

Entering the Gate of St. Stephen the martyr, Clarel moves up the Via Crucis and vanishes in the City. The dream of Eden has been transformed to Gethsemane. The rites of initiation are over.

Like a compassionate father talking to his hurt son, the narrator speaks in the Epilogue (4.35), reminding Clarel to keep his courage "though yet but ill-resigned" (line 27). In a baffling world—who knows?—even Stoics may at the last "be astounded into heaven" (line 26).[51]

V
POETICS

N O READING can give the whole poem. The one above omits the multiplicity of incidents which both particularize and obscure the main effects. It skips lightly over the winding flow of discussion and debate, bypassing conceptualized argument and skirting dense thickets of historical allusion. It neglects that tone of the "picturesque" by which some of the lighter passages are colored. It merely types major characters whose intricacies of temperament are constantly unfolding. It ignores the parade of minor characters. And except through citations, it only hints at the language, images, and verse movements by which the poem exists. Yet perhaps the reading does give us what has proved so hard to come by—a sense of the primary design.

The characters and major images are so central to meaning that we shall soon want to look closely at them, but first we might ask how language, prosody, and formal structure relate to this primary design.

The language of the poem is in part genteel and weakly traditional. Where it is, it vitiates the sense of real crisis. In the first canto, for example, we encounter a series of dusty old words, the secondhand stock of a long run of English poets, at about the rate of one every ten lines: *anon, fro, boon, oft, lorn, paynims, Afric's, needs be, opes, lo, visage, thereat, e'en, flaw* (sudden gust of wind), *o'er, main* (sea), *portals* (ordinary doors), *wends*. Too often we meet with "Ah!"—that tedious Romantic-Victorian syllable from which Arnold drained all the poignancy. Again, words or phrases are abused to meet the tight line-and-rhyme pattern. We find *pard, wildered*, and *bide*, chopped-off substitutes for *leopard, bewildered*, and *abide*. We are often aware that an article (*a, an,* or *the*) has been

---

51.   But see the discussion at 4.35.25–26.

expunged to make the beat work—aware because both practices
occur. On the other hand, to fatten lines, we find unfelt repeti-
tions, unnecessary particles, or spread-out words like *bewrinkled,*
ungladsome, arborous, chanceful, and *cascatelle.* One notes the archaic
sate (for *sat*) in order to get rhymes with *gate, state, eight, late, fate,*
and *mate.* These loppings and stretchings, this dredging up of
what is needed, may be skillful or crude. One feels a poet who
sensed the violence with which at times language must be ripped
and cut and jammed into place, but who was not always able, like
the good poet, to make one feel the rightness of the result. If one
margin of the verse is softened by the worn-out language of the
contemporary genteel tradition, the opposite margin is hardened
by crudeness.

At the successful center there is a curious mixture of the archaic
and the contemporary both in language and materials. Melville may
well have had some notion that his ancient setting justified, even
called for, a measure of antiquarianism. Thus we find forms of *kern,*
scrip, carl, tilth, caitiff, dizzard, wynd, cruze, ken, wight, boon, gat, hap,
fane, ingle, and scores more like them. Clearly he relished the sound
and weight of such words. One suspects, too, a good cut of willful
pedantry, as if to say the light-minded *could* not, rather than would
not, read on: the problems of the poem were to be denied those for
whom the past was nonexistent. Yet the poem also speaks for the
contemporary crisis, the abrasive present: and so we find modern
words, modern idiom, and modern referents for metaphor. Arvin's
excellent analysis of the "powerfully prosaic vocabulary" of Mel-
ville's shorter poems, particularly *Battle-Pieces,* notes how they re-
flect the terminology of a new age, an age of business, technology,
and professional services.[52] In *Clarel* we find words from shop and
factory, from the laboratory, from trading, seafaring, and war.
We encounter wires, tools, chemicals, business and law terms, an
elaborate vocabulary of seamanship, Civil War language, etc. For
example, the Elder, a fierce Scottish churchman turned even
fiercer positivist,

52. In the present section I am indebted to Arvin's highly original analysis of
Melville's language, both in his *Herman Melville,* pp. 262–69, and in the somewhat
ampler version, "Melville's Shorter Poems." Another excellent piece on the manner
of the short poems is Robert Penn Warren's "Melville the Poet." Laurence W. Bar-
rett has commented more generally in "The Differences in Melville's Poetry."

                                             bore
A pruning-knife in belt; in vest
A measuring-tape wound round a core;
And field-glass slung athwart the chest;
While peeped from holsters old and brown,
Horse-pistols.

                                        (2.1.95–100)

Or we get a colloquial image of Mortmain in his conspiratorial, pam-
phleteering days:

              Wear and tear and jar
        He met with coffee and cigar.

                                        (2.4.46)

Such passages are meant to collide with the archaic world of
sepulchers and flamens through which the pilgrims move. The same
effect comes from words like *balloon, trombone, iron plated, football*; or
from half-slang words such as *pippin, Hog-Latin, riff-raff, hullabaloo,*
and *hee-haw*, often enough occurring in the midst of passages of bibli-
cal tone. A good example of this wide variety of language, stepped up
by a nervous dialogue of fast give-and-take, may be examined in
"The Fog" (2.28). Though Melville was unable to realize fully a style
based on the interplay of harmony and dissonance, he made a strong
try for it. As Robert Penn Warren suggests, even his failures are often
interesting and instructive.

    The choice of an iambic tetrameter line, rhyming at irregular
intervals, was odd for a poem of such length. What models influ-
enced Melville—Butler's *Hudibras*, Byron's oriental *The Giaour*,
or Arnold's short poem on faith-doubt, "Stanzas from the Grande
Chartreuse"—is less important than how the chosen form oper-
ates in *Clarel*.[53] One can dislike the cramping effect of endless
octosyllabic lines inevitably linked one to the other, as a good
share of the critics do. But there can be no question of appropri-
ateness. It is an essential part of the poem that the verse form is
constricting and bounded, that the basic movements are tight,
hard, constrained. This is an unbannered verse, without proces-
sional possibilities. Only under high emotion (Celio at the Arch,

    53.   See my "Melville's Reading of Arnold's Poetry," pp. 388–90, for pos-
sible specific indebtedness to the "Stanzas" in general theme, kinds of events,
actual vocabulary, technical devices, and rhythmic patterns.

Mortmain by Sodom, the narrator's Epilogue) do the lines flow forward with a sustained sense of destination. Typically the verse movements are short, exploratory, sometimes jerky. To wish that *Clarel* had been written in blank verse, for example, is simply to wish for a completely different poem. In earlier years Melville had often set Shakespearean rhythms echoing through his high-keyed prose with extraordinary effect. But now the bravura mood was gone. Melville did not propose a broad heroic drama in the Elizabethan manner. Pentameter—especially blank verse—was too ample and flowing for his present mood and theme. The tragedy of modern man, as Melville now viewed it, was one of constriction.

The tight rhyme-scheme of the poem hooks every line to one or more other lines. They may be bound in couplets, held in quatrain, or set in looser patterns; but the rhyme inevitably comes. No one could possibly have kept so tight a scheme interesting through thousands of lines, writing in English. Whenever the poetic metabolism sinks, the reader becomes overconscious of rhymes and meter and gets bored. But a quite different matter is the calculated effect, when poetic energies are high, whereby the reader gets uneasy and restless under the confining bonds of the short, rhymed lines. In one variety of successful passage there is a kind of internal ricochet along the hard walls of the end-rhymes. It is an attribute of the prosody as well as the psychology of the poem that all possibilities are locked in, that there is no broad release for either poetry or self. Variations from the basic prosodic pattern are so infrequent as to keep the movement along an insistently narrow corridor.[54]

Language, prosodic effects, and poetic imagination come together with startling force at regular intervals in this poem. Take, for example, the opening fifteen lines of "Night in Jericho" (2.16). They divide exactly in half to give two images: the bandit crow and the lawless sheik; though the first is meant to serve the second, in fact each makes the other memorable. The "fires autumnal" are literal, and not a poeticism for fall foliage; the "luckless land" has been the site of a forest fire, say in New England. The analogy is part of an

---

54. The only notable and effective divergences occur in the varied forms of the short lyrics and in the expanded five-beat line of the Epilogue. For the rest, one encounters an occasional five-beat line at the end of a section of a canto (as in 3.1.24 and 4.12.80–81), or simply when the line gets out of hand (2.21.95). Such special effects as two-beat lines in the middle of a section, for example, are rare (3.19.63, 67).

insistent metaphor (cf. the opening of 2.29) about the Siddim Plain as a burnt-over region, a part of hell, and the mythic scene of the divine "blastment" (a beautifully archaic yet also technological word). From top of tower and pine, in ominous, lawless power, sheik and crow cry out. Repeated *l* sounds of the first line start a flow of liquid, incantatory tone that carries through to the weird climax of "Lord" and "wild hullabaloo." Against this plays a concatenation of *k* sounds, some thirteen in all. They begin with the peremptory opening word ("Look"); rise to the haunting, mutinous "killed, not overthrown" (the *c* of "gigantic" doubling the *k* sound); are reasserted in "captain-crow," which sets up the full onomatopoeia for "caws." Continuing, "scar" (placed for emphasis) echoes in "Crusaders' " and "sheik" and comes to the climax of the strophe—"Kings it"—a bold, cawing, homemade verb that summarizes all. This is one of several kinds of exciting poetry one encounters in *Clarel*.

The four-part structure of *Clarel* provides a firm, even rigid, base for the prosodic pattern. The 150 cantos are divided with sufficient evenness. Individual cantos vary somewhat in length but average out at three to four pages each.[55] Each canto ordinarily divides into several sections (they are not formal enough to be called stanzas) which mark slight shifts of subject matter, space the dialogue, or simply break the visual monotony. When one section ends in a part-line of less than four beats, the next starts by making up the rest of the line. Usually the form of one canto is like that of another; with each turn of the kaleidoscope, one more symmetrical pattern falls into view. Thus meter, rhyme, canto, and part restrict the flow of experience, keeping it not only ordered, as all art does, but limited. Typically the cantos cluster in units of from two to five, giving a series of nine or ten movements to each part. This internal rhythm of action is evident only after considerable familiarity with the poem, as some rhythms overlay others or are interrupted by diversions.

Several devices slightly relieve the prosodic and structural rigidity. The most notable divergence is the sizable number of short poems, or fragments of poems, which are sung, spoken, or read by one of the characters or the narrator in the course of events. If the count includes mere snatches of song, there are some forty-

55. The shortest canto is but nineteen lines ("Dirge": 4.31); the longest is one of three that exceed three hundred lines ("Nathan": 1.17). The term *canto*, by the way, is used by the narrator (4.25.57).

five such pieces in a variety of forms. Nineteen are lighthearted songs sung by the gay blades—Glaucon, the Cypriote, the Mytilene, the Lyonese; these are love lyrics, drinking songs, fragments after the Persian manner, mimic songs-from-the-dramatists. Yet their genuine levity never threatens the poem's center of gravity. Another group—about a third—are religious pieces, ranging from short hymns, invocations, or a bit of doggerel, to a four-voiced chant on the fall of Jerusalem (3.17) and a long masque on the Wandering Jew (3.19).[56] In addition to the short poems there are a scattering of elaborate Homeric similes, which at intervals offer quick looks out the window at other times and places.[57] Thus the songs and similes give prosodic and thematic relief, or pictorial refreshment. Yet they are but pellets which scarcely dent the armor of rhyming tetrameters. Even the Epilogue, whose opened five-beat lines are a most welcome and effective coda, restates in close rhyme the fundamental complexity, the agnostic pro and con. This final counterpoint of major themes, rather than the concluding image of possible rebirth, is the final "summary."

To a meaningful degree, then, the language, prosody, and formal structure reflect the central tensions of the poem between what was and what is, between what might and what must be.

VI
CHARACTERS

SOON AFTER leaving Jerusalem, where he phrased his "problem" as a series of questions about faith, dogma, and creeds, Clarel's concern shifts toward the study of personalities. Put bluntly, he goes increasingly from asking whose beliefs are right to asking who is the right kind of man. Though he clings to his original hope of finding an Answer, the search becomes in effect an effort to judge why the others believe as they do, and what their beliefs or doubts do

---

56. Four of these religious "complaints" are especially effective: Hymn to the Slanted Cross (Mortmain), 2.31; Salt-Song (Beltha), 2.34; Invocation (Rolfe), 3.32; Persian Rhyme (Rolfe), 4.16.

57. The window is usually a porthole. Some examples of these brilliant sea-similes begin at 1.41.69; 3.2.59; 3.7.56; 3.29.11; 4.4.40. Similes (or songs) often open cantos; they fracture reader complacency (as with 2.16, analyzed above, or 4.7).

to them. Although questions of belief continue throughout the poem, even reaching a tone of insistence in the final cantos, the inner movement, as defined by Clarel's experience, is away from theology toward a kind of pragmatic humanism, or speculative psychology. Thus character analysis becomes itself a theme of the narrative.

The narrator is the presiding intelligence in this quest for character evaluation. Since the poem is not pure drama, he makes the transpositions between speeches, gets the pilgrims to horse or to bed, as the case may be, and keeps things going. Usually he opens the canto with some allusion or extended metaphor, sometimes coming on stage from unexpected angles; and as the canto ends he often remains behind for a private word with the reader. During the "scenes" he not only manipulates the movement but often gives the sense of sitting invisibly among his characters, carefully noting the give and take, recording the gestures, speculating on their dynamics. For his ability to read and voice unspoken thoughts of the characters does not extend to an assured sense of what is meant by them. He is watching the cards as they are played, and no one ponders more deeply than he how the game will go. His powers extend to taking over cantos completely for himself, inserting a "Dirge" (4.31), presenting little essays-in-verse on stones (2.10), on deserts (2.11), on monasteries (3.9). Nor does he hesitate to preempt a pilgrim's story in order to tell it more effectively (4.2–3). The narrator lacks interest in keeping himself consistently in, or consistently out of, the narrative, but he is, in general, arbiter of the point of view. He is often more tangible as a sensibility than the nominal hero, for Clarel's passivity, inarticulateness, and baffling tendency to "disappear" (as if captured by Bedouins), make for a vaporous rather than real presence; Clarel is more problem than person.

The major characters other than Clarel are vigorously and subtly drawn, however, and in terms of their attitude toward the complex passion may be thought of as falling into three clusters.[58] First are Rolfe and Vine, who, along with the narrator, are rational and imaginative observers of the common plight. Rolfe, as a more visible master of discourse than the narrator, not only broaches the subject matter for many of the discussions but sees that the exchange keeps going. Sometimes he takes sides for the purpose of argument—to the

58. Summary descriptions and analyses of major and minor characters will be found in the "Critical Index" (pp. 613–35 below).

annoyance of Mortmain and Ungar, and to the bafflement of Clarel. His intermediary role includes arbitration between the benign Derwent, whom he dislikes as a mind but likes as a person, and the bitter monomaniacs, with whom he has important affinities. Vine, in contrast, seems hardly to participate at all in the group; yet his status is very high, and his presence is deeply felt by the pilgrims in spite of his reticence. Abstract ideas and theorizings interest him but little, so that he seems to have no personal stake in the arguments over faith and doubt. People do interest him, however, and a keen sense for moral psychology makes him a shrewd judge of motivations. Lurking quietly at the edge of the group, Vine registers his usually unspoken evaluations obliquely, through gesture, glance, or symbolic act (as at the end of 3.5). The sense of his approval or disapproval bears considerable weight with pilgrims and narrator.

To the left of this central cluster lies the ominous sequence of monomaniacs: Celio-Mortmain-Agath-Ungar. Rolfe and Vine are harmoniously balanced men compared to these passionately distraught figures, who successively cast their shadows over the pilgrim train. The ultimate motivation of these monomaniacs, the first two of whom court and win annihilation, is necessarily masked, but bitter outpourings at intervals reveal their inner rage. They are beyond compromise or peace. Their best hope is not adjustment to the complex passion (as with Rolfe, Vine, and someday, perhaps Clarel) but sheer survival beneath the weight of it. Overwhelmed, or nearly so, by an intense recognition of evil, they are not themselves evil men. Their function is to state the condition of things, seen from the dark side. To Clarel they constitute a warning of what he must cope with, rather than any hint of a way out of his dilemma.

To the right of the central cluster stand the major figures of Nehemiah and Derwent. Both characters are strongly conceived and have high individuality. From several points of view they seem contrasting rather than comparable; how could the fanatic old beggar man, dispensing his millennial tracts, be less like the urbane English cleric with his suave and conciliatory gifts? They may be paired, however, as far as the key question of the pilgrims is concerned: there is no theological crisis for either of them. For Nehemiah this is because his evangelical orthodoxy, as a sectarian, Bible-Christian, is inviolate; he cannot conceive that his faith might be illusion. For Derwent there is no crisis simply because he refuses to see any; a rainbow-watcher from way back, he does not propose to have either his digestion or his professional equilibrium upset. At times Clarel cherishes both men, responding genuinely to their different kinds of humanity. But to share either kind of serenity he would have to be able to ignore the monomaniacs, and temperament and events remind him that he cannot do that. Clarel belongs increasingly in the middle group with those skeptical humanists, Rolfe, Vine, and the narrator.

Grouping the major characters this way helps keep first things first, thematically. It helps too with the minor characters, many of whom are variants on the left, center, or right groups. For example, the mad monk Cyril of Mar Saba exaggerates the monomaniac position; so do the cell inscriptions left by the long-dead Habbibi; and Don Hannibal, the jolly-bilious Mexican cripple, is a sport of the same species. To the right belongs an interesting sequence of antagonists to the passion—the dour Scottish Elder, the craven mammonist Banker, and the materialist and geologist, Margoth—all of whom the narrator limns with a touch of savage glee. To this group belong also such gay blades as Glaucon and the Lyonese, as well as that older epicurean, the Lesbian—extensions in a way of Derwent's essentially glandular optimism. A variety of unquestioning believers also extend Nehemiah's narrowly sectarian position into Hebraic, Mohammedan, and various Christian dogmas; many of these religious figures are so intense that extreme right joins with extreme left, and the line becomes a circle.

Such groupings of course are purely diagrammatic, and need to be erased as soon as they have been drawn. Only minor characters of the poem are clear types. It is in fact a major premise of the narrative that the individual life is invariably complex and buried. To see what a sizable proportion of the verse consists in delicate or bold probings toward the inner world of some character is to come close indeed to a major value of the poem. How does one or another of the pilgrims respond to the physical danger of Bedouins, the symbolic threat of the Dead Sea, or the joys of wine and song after travail? What motivates a Mortmain when he announces he will spend the night alone by Quarantania, the bleak Mount of Temptation? Where *is* Vine when brooding in his bemused silences? How can Rolfe lead the attack on the Church one moment and defend the Church another? Why should the quiet

Agath, who has endured many violences, suddenly shriek out at the sight of a tiny scorpion on the rocky trail? Such talismans are seized on avidly in an effort to come at the "mystery."

This esoteric concept of personality is worth exploration, for one of the relevances of *Clarel* to a later time is the narrator's concern with the kind of threshold materials out of which modern depth psychology has been constructed. Even minor acts relate meaningfully to fundamental commitments and tensions within the self. There is close attention to the symbolic role of gesture: the meaning of a glance, a pause in speech, a facial flush, a turning toward or away from, absence as well as presence. And always, an effort to capture the special tone of the gesture.

Out of the narrator's attitude toward individual psychology grows the almost awkward force of the group interchanges. At regular intervals throughout the poem the pilgrims square off against, or circle round, one another for "talk." Now the subject of the argument that usually ensues is often bookish, even quaintly archaic, to the modern ear. But the manner is something again. The real interest in these discussions (if one feels any) lies in the exchange of private tensions. A good test for the reader might be, for example, the first exchange among the pilgrims when, with the journey just begun, they pause at Gethsemane (2.3). Such "events"—and the poem is a long, rhythmic chain of them—resemble modern experiments in group dynamics. By more literary terms, Eliot's proposition that Hawthorne was "the one English-writing predecessor of James whose characters are *aware* of each other" helps establish the lineage of this particular aspect of *Clarel*.[59]

To the narrator's sense of the pressure of personality on personality, and to his acute feeling for individual gesture, we may add a third psychological resource. At intervals within the poem there are moments of sudden, unconscious self-revelation. There is, for example, the moment when Clarel comes upon the well-controlled Vine with "reserves laid bare"; the Vine who seemed to scorn the recent desperate debate ("The High Desert") now sits alone, quivering:

59. T. S. Eliot, "Henry James," *The Little Review* (August, 1918), uncollected, reprinted in *The Shock of Recognition*, ed. Edmund Wilson (New York: Doubleday, Doran, 1943), p. 863.

He wore that nameless look
About the mouth—so hard to brook—
Which in the Cenci portrait shows,

. . . .

A trembling over of small throes
In weak swoll'n lips, which to restrain
Desire is none, nor any rein.

. . . .

Reserves laid bare? and can it be?
The dock-yard forge's silent mound,
Played over by small nimble flame—
Raked open, lo, the anchor's found
In white-heat's alb.

                    (3.7.16–18, 22–24, 28–32)

A comparable exposure of Nehemiah occurs when he falls asleep in his Jerusalem hermitage (1.22), and his "tranced" face reveals him for a moment unmasked: "Death freezes, but sleep thaws" (lines 102, 106). Whatever the meaning of his sleep-naked face—"Be it sealed," says the narrator (line 109)—Clarel leaves quickly and in terror. Or we have the vivid night-scene (3.15) of Mortmain locked in some "mad dream," and gnawing away at one of his own hands "As the wolf-hound the bone" (lines 25, 20). Rolfe shakes him, turning to throw open a casement:

"God help thee, and may such ice make
Except against some solid? nay—
But thou who mark'st, get thee away,
Nor in such coals of Tartarus rake."

                                   (lines 28–31)

Such tropes and situations stress the latent aspects of personality. We note banked fires (twice), the apocalyptic word "sealed," and the intensity of the fire-ice polarity.

The chief characters, including of course the disturbed Clarel who is undergoing a series of self-confrontations, live in a world of subliminal tensions. As the young hero puts it in the opening canto:

                              Ah!
These under-formings in the mind,
Banked corals which ascend from far,
But little heed men that they wind

> Unseen, unheard—till lo, the reef—
> The reef and breaker, wreck and grief.

(1.1.74–79)

The starkly symbolic landforms through which they move serve as magnets on their buried lives. Between the routine acts of horseback travel, the staged exchanges of rational discourse, a dreamworld of psychic reality swirls about them.

Shadowy figures they are on first acquaintance, some of these pilgrims, drifting about like phantoms at a seance. With some the lighting is kept purposely low. Vine, for instance, is a twilight figure. In the end, however, almost all have hard, clean contours, and in part it is possible to see the means by which this is accomplished.

Most characters enter the poem at a significant site. We have already noted Nehemiah discovered on the way to Emmaus, Celio by the demoniac caves at Gihon, and Vine in the porch of the Sepulcher of Kings. Rolfe first appears wandering on Olivet, above Gethsemane, a hint of his role as the restless explorer of the Passion. Margoth, with gross pertinence, is first seen down amidst the filth by the Dung Gate. Shortly after such first appearances there comes, usually, a canto of personal ecology—earnest fragments of fact and speculation about the kind of man he may be in terms of the kind of experience he may have had.

Strong hints often lie in the names; they may be allegorical or allusive. Celio (possibly a wordplay on *cielo*: heaven) and Mortmain (dead hand) seem to have linguistic equivalents. Nehemiah (the rebuilder of Jerusalem) is biblical—here in a pathetic-ironical sense. Derwent's name is fittingly traditional and literary (the pastoral English river, the name of Coleridge's son). More heavily allegorical is Margoth (to mar like a Goth), and deeply symbolic is Vine (at once wine-source, the true vine, the Way).

Some characters also have simple equivalents in body, costume, or possession. Celio has a humped back but a fair head; Mortmain wears a black cap; Ungar carries his sword (Cross). Or there is Nehemiah's Bible, open in his hand, inseparable from him, buried with him. The considerable attention given to the mounts of the pilgrims and other travelers goes beyond routine description. The humble, stubborn ass is ridden by the meek-militant Nehemiah, afterwards by the enduring, penalty-ridden Agath. The magnificent mare, Zar, is the mount of the Druze, Djalea, head guide and one of the top figures in the spiritual hierarchy of the poem. More subtly the rider's seat may suggest the inner life: the vigorous Rolfe sits his high saddle like an Osage scout or South American Gaucho, and Vine, even when absorbed in reveries, exhibits his "lurking will" (2.1.245) in the way he reins his mount.

Such indirections of delineation never cease during the pilgrimage. Site, sign, and symbol forecast configurations that are filled in as the narrative develops. The characteristic responses accumulate, the individual idiom gets heard. Bodily appearance merges with meaningful presence: Rolfe's bronzed face and intense blue eyes, Vine's waving Lydian hair, the pale features of young Clarel, Mortmain's burning eyes.

Certain conditions shared by the pilgrims establish their group attributes. These are rootless men. Of the five Americans (Clarel, Rolfe, Vine, Nehemiah, Ungar) the last two are emigrés; Vine seems to be an American artist or writer who has spent time in Italy, but his "kin, tribe, estate" are expressly denied the reader (1.29.3); Rolfe is a traveler and adventurer; and whether or not Clarel will return home after his tragedy we do not know. Ruth's family are American Zionists, and mother and daughter yearn for home. Of the five other major figures only the plump Englishman, Derwent, is tied to country; Margoth's nationality we never learn; Agath is a wandering Greek sailor; Celio is an Italian expatriate; and Mortmain, the wild Swede, is in flight from all civilization. Overwhelmingly these are *hommes déracinés*. They have, or had, their trades or professions, but if a single one of the major figures has wife, children, or relatives, or in any nameable sense belongs to a specific community, we do not know it; the absence of surnames expresses this. The sense of being "cut off"—a key phrase of the poem (e.g., 1.14.24, 2.7.21)—is an arranged condition of the narrative. In turn this is supplemented by an aura of apostasy hovering about the group as a whole, and specifically, through canto titles, enwrapping two marginal characters (Margoth—"An Apostate"; the Lyonese—"The Prodigal").

Again, almost all have experienced disaster. For the monomaniacs life has been crippling (Celio—his hump), overwhelming (Mortmain—his intolerable sense of evil), brutal (Agath—shipwrecked, and beaten by robbers), devastating (Ungar—defeated in war). Nehemiah's terrorizing "secret" is partially explained through analogies of shipwreck (later retracted) and betrayal in friendship. Rolfe and Vine have been sensitized to tragic experience in undefined ways. And the whole "point" of the love plot is that Clarel may enter the community of men only after loss. Thus Derwent, with his temperamental optimism, and Margoth, with his denial of nonmaterial values, are antagonists to the central condition. The decisive weight of past experience lies within the world of pain and penalty. The six deaths that occur within the brief time-span of the narrative keep it there.

If abdication from family, community, country, and creed has set most of the pilgrims loose from the institutions which ordinarily give men definable social roles, what is left? Personality, character, self, soul—these suggest the remnant. The preferred term of the poem is "self," and the profusion of compound words built on "self" defines one of the energy centers of the poem.[60] At odds with the societies to which they belonged, they have variously mutinied or been shipwrecked. We have here an assortment of Western men, cast away, as it were, on the Palestinian beach, jointly engaged in the struggle for moral and psychic survival.

VII
IMAGES

T HIS SEA METAPHOR brings us into position to examine selected images of the poem. We have already seen that the Palestinian landforms serve as both stimulus and equivalent to the pilgrims' dilemma. The image of the Fallen City (thrown against memories of the Holy City) expresses the condition that *is* the complex passion. The dangerous road going down to Jericho is the Descent into Darkness. The Dead Sea area, a nightmare world of loss and evil, is that Darkness. The toiling effort to return by the Judah mountains marks an Ascent, for Mar Saba is a temporary Refuge; the great stone hive, large enough to encompass revelry and remorse, a layered citadel of ascending and descending stairs, is a place for

60. Here are twenty-one examples: *self-asserted, self-center, self-consumings, self-control, self-derived, self-devotion, self-exiled, self-given, self-hood, self-knowledge, self-love, self-possessed, self-querying, self-rebukeful, self-respect, self-restraint, self-satisfied, self-sufficing, self-surprised, self-sustained, self-taxings*.

reassessment. The lyric mountain-town of Bethlehem proffers Beati-
tude, but in reaction the pilgrims enter renewed complexity. And so
the Return to the wrecked city, now more deeply known through
experience and articulation.

In a more general sense the entire landscape of the poem, except
for Bethlehem, is to be taken as wilderness. This wilderness is an
actual world of rocks and sand. As the root metaphor of the poem, it
is also the radical equivalent of that wasteland of the spirit which the
protagonists have entered; the pilgrimage is simultaneously a journey
in inner and outer worlds. So large a metaphor necessarily exfoliates
in many different ways in the course of the narrative. The archetype is
of course the Old Testament story of the forty years in the wilder-
ness, whose setting is just to the south of where the pilgrims travel.
Rimming the immediate wilderness of the narrative (Melville uses
the term to designate the area between Jerusalem and the Dead Sea,
and later the Judah wilderness about Mar Saba) are a series of famous
biblical wilderness-deserts which cast their spell across the pilgrim-
age—among them Zin, Paran, the Libyan waste, and "El Tih, the
great, the terrible" (1.5.177).

Nathalia Wright, exploring recurrent images of the wilderness in
Melville's writings, finds it "the symbolic scene of mature experience
throughout Melville," the place of truth, revelation, and vision, as in
the Bible. Thus in *Clarel* it becomes not only an image of the faithless
contemporary world but once again the place that "must be visited if
the riddle of existence is at all to be solved." Wright also shows how
the wilderness-figure of Ishmael is the prototype of most of Mel-
ville's heroes, and suggests that in *Clarel* "all the characters are
Ishmaels of a sort, for all have forsaken society to dwell temporarily
in the desert."[61]

It is to this redeeming aspect of the wilderness that Mortmain in
his agony turns; as Rolfe says,

> "Man sprang from deserts: at the touch
> Of grief or trial overmuch,
> On deserts he falls back at need;

---

61.   *Melville's Use of the Bible*, pp. 47–60. W. H. Auden has a very provocative
discussion of the Sea and the Desert in the first essay of his *The Enchafèd Flood: or,
The Romantic Iconography of the Sea*.

> Yes, 'tis the bare abandoned home
> Recalleth then."
>
> (2.16.106–10)

Mortmain's "wild plunge" (line 114) beyond civilization the night he spends alone at Quarantania is clearly his Passion. "Mad John," Rolfe sympathetically calls him (2.34.39); and elsewhere the narrator says of desert and wilderness:

> But to pure hearts it yields no fear;
> And John, he found wild honey here.
>
> (2.11.90–91)

And at Mar Saba we learn of celibates who

> In the pure desert of the will
> Chastised, live the vowed life austere.
>
> (3.30.122–23)

The paradox of the desert is that it may bring either beatitude or annihilation; to Mortmain it brings, at last, both.

Counterimage to the wilderness is the garden. Through Part 1, clustering chiefly about Ruth and her mother Agar, rise memories and metaphors of rural America—"June in some far clover land" (1.16.186); morning-glories by the kitchen door (1.27.56); serenely rolling prairies, golden with tawny lilies (1.17.16–23). Sifting through the hot sands come memories of "green uplands" and "gala orchards" (1.28.2–3), of summer evening showers with robins singing at sunset (1.39.1–5). During the stony descent the narrator remembers coming down a (New England) mountain, where open pastures lead to orchards and on to little villages (2.7.1–9). Down on the sterile Siddim Plain the momentary bow suddenly recalls to Nehemiah his past world of scythes, orchards, haycocks, and mossed roofs under the homestead trees at evening (2.29.132–37). On the Judah ridge the pilgrims, broken by the recent loss of Nehemiah, sit down on the High Desert (here, a desert of nerveless weariness):

> To these there comes,
> As down on Siddim's scene they peer,
> The contrast of their vernal homes—
> Field, orchard, and the harvest cheer.
>
> (3.5.27–30)

The garden of these passages suggests not only longing for nature's health and beauty, but envy of the warm, communal life of man which the pilgrims have abandoned.

In Part 4 the American-countryside images fall off, partly in keeping with the mounting theme that "No New World to mankind remains!" (4.21.159), and partly because the lush fields and flocks of Bethlehem are now at hand. Only Derwent fully gives himself to the pastoral beauty of Bethlehem; the rest, "In dubious keeping with the dale" (4.24.15), find themselves caught up in the most sustained dawn-to-dusk debate of the poem. Bethlehem reminds Rolfe of Eden (4.9.86) and of Tahiti (4.18.36)—two extensions of the garden image, and a reappearance (here and elsewhere in the poem) of the Paradise-Pacific theme of Melville's 1856–57 journal. A remembered America across the seas, Pacific isles, far-off Asiatic oases, the ancient palmy days of Palestine—of all such lost gardens the prototype is Eden. In the far background of the poem, as in Rolfe's memory, lies the haunting dream of a garden of original innocence.[62]

In the close foreground stands Gethsemane, site of the Passion.

> Yes, memory
> Links Eden and Gethsemane,
>
> (1.30.10–11)

says the narrator. It is here among the gnarled olives that Clarel feels the leopard-spring of the Passion's narrative, though Nehemiah falls asleep (1.30). It is here, just as the pilgrimage gets under way, while the Banker and Glaucon look for olive-wood trinkets, that Mortmain, beginning his long feud with Derwent, names man's viciousness as the lesson of Gethsemane and recalls Christ's suffering:

> "This day, with some of earthly race,
> May passion similar go on?"
>
> (2.3.150)

The ever-cheerful Derwent, man of "sound digestion" and "good spirits" (2.3.74–75), ignores the site; he turns his back on Gethsemane, as the aroused Mortmain pointedly remarks, and talks about a canter across English sod (his kind of garden), as later he luxuriates in the pastoral beauty of the Bethlehem countryside. But for the

---

62. R. W. B. Lewis's *The American Adam* brilliantly draws the contours of this important image of the American imagination.

agonizers the only garden left is Gethsemane. Eden may be the hope; Gethsemane is the reality.

The sea is persistently used as an analogy for the wilderness throughout the poem. As openly stated in the canto "Of Deserts":

> Sands immense
> Impart the oceanic sense:
> The flying grit like scud is made:
> Pillars of sand which whirl about
> Or arc along in colonnade,
> True kin be to the water-spout.

(2.11.36–41)

The constancy with which this analogy unrolls throughout the narrative is astonishing, and at first, grotesque. From direct allusions, similes, and buried metaphors can be compiled a considerable list of nautical words—kinds of craft, parts of a ship and ship's gear, personnel, navigation aids, harbor and customs terms, sea terms, phenomena and weather, ship handling, etc.[63] In the opening canto, for example, occur a dozen or more sea references of typical variety: direct allusion to landing at Jaffa, and to gazing seaward from a tower; Ramleh as a "sail-white town," a piece of wasteland as a "stony strait," Jerusalem as "ice-bastions round the Pole"; the view down on Hezekiah's pool as if from the stern-lights of a three-decker, and a convent as lighthouse; a full metaphor of the unconscious mind in terms of coral reefs; a metaphoric aphorism: "To avoid the deep saves not from storm"; and half-buried figures on the moon's light at low tide, evening at full tide, "time's vast sea," and a hum "half

---

63.   *Ship, frigate, brig, barque, ship-of-the-line, seventy-four, three-decker, battleship, ship of steel, boat, proa, cutter, raft, sailboat, fleet; hull, keel, kelson, hold, porthole, cabin, stern-light, taffrail, bulwarks, rigging, sail, mast, mast-head, spar, jib-boom, prow, rope, anchor, cable, tackle, ballast; watch, mid-watch, crew, tars, sailor, stowaway, messmate, topman, rower, ship-boy, boatswain, pilot, captain, mate, mariner, mutineer, castaway; glass, compass, chart, rocket, signal-gun, bell, bell-buoy, buoy, light-ship, light-house; port, harbor, haven, wharf, ship's manifest, channel, road, dock-yard forge, quay, night-patrolman; wave, surge, billow, wake, flood, current, drift, calm, swell, tide, ebb, flow, foam, spray, roller, surf, spray-cloud, sea, ocean, main, sea-bed, ocean-bed, island, strait, isthmus, cape, cove, shallow, deep, shoal, reef, rock, bar, sandbar, coral, iceberg, beach, strand, sand, undertow, shell, kelp, weed, coast, coastline, lee; waterspout, corposant, phosphorus, fog, mist, scud, rack, wind, storm, tempest, trade-wind; to anchor, to steer, to moor, to sail, to speak, to hail, to wreck, to founder, etc. Also references to a variety of fish and seabirds; and to whales* (1.37.82; 2.10.217; 3.14.127; 3.21.10; 4.3.3).

drowned." After this introduction the sea allusions fall off in concentration but continue to appear.

There are only two mariners among the characters. Rolfe has been round the Horn, and Agath, who does not appear until late, is a timoneer (pilot) in Mediterranean waters. One gets the illusion, however, that most of the pilgrims have sailed before the mast because of the way the narrator weaves sea images about the group as a whole. For an omniscient narrator so to personalize himself by this special vocabulary is disconcerting; it almost throws him over into a first-person role. One gets used to it, though it is an egregious example of the difficulties that flow from Melville's loose practice in point of view. There is no alternative except to grant that the narrator is an ex-sailor.

In spite of some technical ineptness the sea symbolism is a genuine force in the poem. There are conventional enough traveler's analogies—the coming and going of a person is like a ship sighted, spoken, and passed; caravans are fleets; a stopping place becomes an island or a huge ship. The blind muezzin calls to prayer from "the marble mast-head" of his minaret (1.15.38), and Clarel watching the stars from his Jerusalem terrace is a "ship-boy at mast-head alone" (1.18.41). But the narrator's images are restless, and usually move beyond primness to larger meanings. Jerusalem's "Wild solitudes" are "like shoals in seas / Unsailed" (1.16.26–27): an extension of the City-as-Wilderness to the City-as-Sea. The Mar Saba monks ascend the twin towers to look for marauding Bedouins as sailors set watches against the canoes of Malay pirates (3.21.1–9): a double view of the dangers of Wilderness-Sea. As the pilgrims leave the monastery the towers go down like a brig's masts, and a few minutes later, Agath, the "pickled old sea-Solomon" (3.25.151), with "Slant palm to brow against the haze," cries out dramatically, "Wreck, ho—the wreck!"; far across the mountains he has sighted Jerusalem (4.1.172–77): an epitome of the central theme. The straggling cavalcade comes up to the massive convent at Bethlehem like "shipwrecked men adrift" coming alongside the stained hull of a great armed, foreign ship of battle—"Black cloisters of the god of war" (4.7.1–12): a metaphoric cannonade against the garden symbol. Such passages are not mere grace notes; they do thematic work.

The most emotionally concentrated section of the poem, the Descent (Part 2), toys with two sea analogues. One, about an ominous-haggard-horrible crag by the Dead Sea (2.30), is undeveloped, but sufficiently hints of Cape Horn to blend one kind of ordeal—rounding the Horn—with the pilgrims' crisis by the Dead Sea.[64] The other, a haunting sense of the Siddim Plain as the sea-bed of withdrawn oceans, is a really furious trope in terms of the brimming waters of Melville's sea tales; conscious and unconscious elements mingle in the imagery. The theme is foreshadowed by Clarel's meditation in Jerusalem:

> see, day and night
> The sands subsiding from the height;
> In time, absorbed, these grains may help
> To form new sea-bed, slug and kelp.
>
> (1.24.73–76)

After the descent—at lead-line depth on the sunken slimy plain and bared sea-bed—comes the "dream" that the sea might roll back (2.23.35–37). Panic is implied by the sudden breaking and running of one of the horses—Mortmain's: "Horse too run mad?" cries the ever-sane Derwent (2.23.38–40). In the climactic canto "Sodom" the Dead Sea becomes a sort of giant stagnant pool, the brine-thick remnant of ocean, from which

> bubbling air-beads mount and break
> As charged with breath of things alive.
>
> (2.36.8–9)

If one may risk an extension of the conscious imagery here, under the water lie not only the victims of the wicked cities (who after all were destroyed by *fire*) but all the drowned of ocean. These only half-dead "sinners" (sailors?) are

> whirled in shoals
> Of gurgles which your gasps send up.
>
> (2.36.66–68)

The canto concludes with a metaphor of the *innocent* heart that

> Moves as along the ocean's bed
> Amid the dragon's staring crew.
>
> (lines 127–28)

This is the place, as it were (drawing on a later image),

64. See the discussion at 2.30.68.

> Where the sexton of the vaulted seas
> Buries the drowned in weedy grave,
> While tolls the buoy-bell down the breeze.
>
> (3.7.56–58)

This whole situation on the Siddim Plain is very complex indeed; one source of its psychic power is the sub-rational sensation of being dead at the bottom of the sea.

Four sea tales of varying length incorporated in the poem all have the theme of disaster. Rolfe's sketch (1.37) of the twice-wrecked ship's master, who after going aground on a hidden rock that broke his ship went back to sea only to be stove by a whale, is the parable of a man made meek by grim disaster. Of the three tales associated with Agath, one (3.12) recounts his betrayal by a man whom he smuggled aboard; a spinning compass, gales, corposants, pursuing birds, and a mutinous crew put the ship on the rocks, the timoneer alone escaping. A second (3.27) tells how a great devil-bird once attacked him at the masthead with such violence as to hurl him into the sea, where, pursued by a shark, he nearly drowned before being dragged aboard. And a third sketch (4.2–3) recalls "that isle which haunteth me" (4.3.4), a drear, cindered isle, godforsaken and vacant of all but giant tortoises who drag themselves endlessly about like lost souls (the "Encantadas" theme); and this isle, says Agath, is the only place on earth that rivals Palestine— "this stricken land" (4.2.205). All four episodes echo earlier sea tales by Melville.

The effect of such abundant sea references is to create the fragments at least of a second voyage—by sea, to parallel the one by land. The "fit" is not close or overt but loose and buried. Its effect is to complement and extend the meanings of the wilderness image. By treating the Wilderness as Sea, Melville was able to bring an immense amount of precise details into the poem from that profession he knew best (next to writing)—to draw on its gear, and events, and mythology. Many of the Homeric similes are nautical. And rippling in and out of the verses are hundreds of half-images of the sea, some tritely conventional (the "heaving sea / Of heads," 1.12.74–75), some awkwardly exact (the "trade-wind" of his thoughts, 1.41.111), some powerfully mythic ("the foundered Star," 4.1.18). Overwhelmingly the images limn a savage sea, a massive crippling force to be endured by men if possible. The sea here is not a place of adventure but of misadventure. Successive images create a rhythm of disaster. Ships are dismasted, they toil under gales, they roll helplessly in fog amid tolling bells, they send up rockets, they drag anchor, they run in shoal water, they crack on submerged reefs. Captains are wrecked, crews are cast away, sailors mutiny or drown. Whereas the fresh-water images—fountains, streams, wells, rivers, and lakes—speak of an unrealizable Garden where there is life, bloom, and growth, the Sea-Wilderness is pitiless. These pilgrim-mariners are "wrecked" men to whom the port would not be pitiful if an adequate one could be found.

VIII
ASPECTS OF SELF

C LAREL is a personal poem. The filaments of self spread through it everywhere, so much so that one feels Melville welcomed it as a chance for sorting out some old entanglements in his own history. Three of the larger configurations concern us here: Rolfe as a self-projection, the relation of the Mortmain-Agath-Ungar sequence to Rolfe and to Melville, and Vine as Hawthorne.

There are tangible though scattered hints that Rolfe is a partial self-portrait. He looks like an adventurer, the narrator tells us early, who might have plied his business "On waters under tropic sky" (1.31.7). Toward the briny old mariner, Agath, he has "A frater-feeling of the sea" which leads him to exchange sea stories with him (4.1.120). Rolfe knows a tale of a mariner wrecked once and later stove in by a whale, so that he was forced to take to the land and resign himself to a customs job as night inspector (1.37). In telling Clarel the story of the Easter Fire, Rolfe turns for an analogy to the Polynesians and "some groves of bloom / In mid Pacific" (3.16.229–30); another time he recalls guarded altars deep in the woods of "far island-chains" (2.10.67–68). The mild loveliness of early evening on a hillside near Bethlehem also takes Rolfe back, in his musings, "to Tahiti's beach" (4.18.36). The nearest thing we have to a life-history of Rolfe is his reverie by the Palm at Mar Saba (3.29): he remembers how he jumped ship in the Pacific, and on an island let himself down by dangerous climbing into a lovely valley where priest and people, hailing him as a descended god, begged him to remain with them forever; but abjuring "the simple joy" (line 74), Rolfe returned to civilization, only to be haunted by the memory ever after. Rolfe has experienced Pacific adventures such as young Melville experienced and then translated into *Typee* and *Omoo*; yet it is interesting that Rolfe paints them with the hues of the older Melville's Mediterranean journal. The general contours of Rolfe's appearance, manner, speech, and mind bear surprising resemblance to the outward image of Melville that letters and biographical data of the period 1845–51 suggest. Rolfe's relation to the world is hearty and vigorous. There is about him an implied physical power. In the pilgrim train he rides "Indian-like" in his high-pommeled saddle, like an Osage scout or Gaucho (2.1.225–29).[65] Something of a *bon vivant*, he is as fond of fellowship, song, and revelry as was the Melville who sparkled so at the Duyck-inck parties in New York, or at the early Pittsfield picnics. In spite of the sober context of the pilgrimage, Rolfe's expansive humanity and occasional facetiousness are in the early Melville vein, as are his general flow of speech, intellectual curiosity, critical boldness, and wide range of allusion. Entering the poem as both student and "messmate of the elements," a man of "genial heart" and "brain austere" (1.31.21, 14), Rolfe is a not unreasonable idealization of the vigorous young Melville.

The tendency to self-romanticization in the portrait—the bronzed face, the "marble brow," the air of a fine gentleman—is amusing and validating (1.31.11, 22). The self-image here has the overtones of an Elizabethan or Renaissance figure of modestly heroic proportions. Bearing in mind that the portrait is a secret one (the hints are carefully fragmentary), the reader will find special interest in the narrator's canto "Of Rama" (1.32), a cryptic self-fantasy on a major scale in which Rolfe is likened to one of the incarnations of Vishnu, who was born a god though he knew it not. The analogy is excessive, for the Rolfe of the poem is fortunately quite un-divine, but the idea does recur in Rolfe's soliloquy to the Palm when he recalls being "hailed

---

65. *The American Notebooks by Nathaniel Hawthorne*, ed. Claude M. Simpson (Columbus: Ohio State University Press, 1972), pp. 447–48, reports an interesting parallel: "a cavalier on horseback came along the road, and saluted me in Spanish; to which I replied by touching my hat, and went on with the newspaper. But the cavalier renewing his salutation, I regarded him more attentively, and saw that it was Herman Melville!" The passage was not included in Mrs. Hawthorne's abridged edition, *Passages from the American Note-Books of Nathaniel Hawthorne* (Boston: Ticknor & Fields, 1868), which Melville acquired in 1870 (Sealts 250).

for a descended god" by island natives (3.29.58). On the other side of
the coin from the Rama image is an equally interesting design of self-
criticism. Rolfe's major weakness by the narrator's terms is a tenden-
cy to be too outspoken:

> Too frank, too unreserved, may be,
> And indiscreet in honesty.

(1.31.24–25)

For example, the symbolic Dead Sea crag strikes Derwent as merely
"queer"; to Rolfe it "Looks horrible—and I *say* so" (2.30.70–74). But
Rolfe frequently himself regrets his determination to "*say* so," as
when he insists on "that truth no type shall set" and then chides
himself with "Earnest again!—well, let it go" (2.32.63–65). Or again,
finding his dark talk about desert places interrupted by Derwent's
placid comments on the rising moon, Rolfe refuses to continue:

> "No matter," Rolfe said; "let it go.
> My earnestness myself decry;
> But as heaven made me, so am I."

(2.16.129–31)

So hypersensitive is Rolfe to his own earnestness that on one occa-
sion, after insisting on the grounds for religious doubt, he makes a
self-conscious renouncement of his fundamental impulse to probe:

> "Nay,"
> Starting abrupt, "this earnest way
> I hate. Let doubt alone; best skim,
> Not dive."[66]

(2.21.100–103)

Rolfe's embarrassment at overextending himself—"You let me
prate" (1.31.129) or "Why prate I here?" (4.13.56)—is a problem for
him, and the key word is *earnest*. When we see that Melville in a letter
of February 17, 1863, wrote a flowing criticism of "this dishonorable
epoch" only to break in with "But dont let us become too earnest. A
very bad habit,"[67] we get not only some confirmation of the general

---

66. A momentary rejection by Rolfe of Melville's famous "I love all men who
dive" (letter to Evert Duyckinck, March 3, 1849).

67. Or see in his letter to Hawthorne of June 29, 1851, the sudden apology:
"But I am falling into my old foible—preaching."

Rolfe-Melville parallel but recognize that the recurrent focus on this problem of Rolfe's throws light into Melville's own self-doubts.

Though Rolfe is plagued by his own "earnestness," it is precisely this element of temperament which is too mild to round out Melville's self-projection. The vigorous sallies and withdrawals of Rolfe, though tempered by fear of overextension, are those of a thoroughly sociable being, an intellectual man-of-the-world well in command of his psychic energies. Biographical data on the younger Melville generally parallels this image, and there is evidence that even in his middle years he still occasionally flowered in social interchange. We have seen, however, that in the two decades after *Moby-Dick* his descent into self had made him acquainted with an underworld of recalcitrant shades: the sense of defeat, willful isolation, unmanageable moods, fear of death, and anxiety over his own physical and mental health. Rolfe knows of such things, but he does not exhibit them. These darker elements of Melville's sensibility are channeled into the striking series of monomaniacs who follow one another so ominously through the poem: Celio, Mortmain, Agath, and Ungar.

The case of Celio is separate and prelusive; appearing and disappearing early, he is an alter ego for the young Clarel, just awakening to "under-formings in the mind" (1.1.75). Celio's rage, though eloquent, is pure and childlike; condemned from birth to a misshapen body, he vents his anguish and dies. As the poem moves into the pilgrimage Mortmain appears and opens the complex and unified cycle of monomania embodied in Mortmain-Agath-Ungar. It is worth noting at once that none of this group in any way belong to Clarel. From first to last he looks on them as characters from another world, attending their commentary with painful determination, but unable to comprehend. He turns rather to the relative stability of the other pilgrims, and what little he ever understands about the monomaniacs comes by way of them, especially Rolfe. For Rolfe is their chief interlocutor and apologist. Not distraught himself, Rolfe is the prime link between their distress and the world; no pariah, Rolfe imagines himself "host to all that stray / In desert" (2.15.35–36). It is Rolfe who knows Mortmain's history (though the narrator tells it: 2.4.6ff.), who movingly justifies his "wild plunge" into the desert (2.16.106–20), who sees him asleep in the moonlight torn with nightmare (3.15.6ff.), and who lingers behind after Mortmain's death to raise an invocation (3.32.51ff.). As Celio was "A second self" to

Clarel (1.19.26), so Mortmain is to Rolfe. Sitting by Elisha's Fountain near Jericho, Rolfe, in a genial fantasy about himself, says:

> "Perchance set down it is in fate
> That fail I must ere we fulfill
> Our travel. Should it happen true—
>
> .   .   .   .
>
> Bury me by the road, somewhere
> Near spring or brook."
>
> (2.15.25–27, 30–31)

To this oblique jest add the pointed observation of Vine during the revels at Mar Saba:

> Mortmain aloof and single sat—
> In range with Rolfe, as viewed from mat
> Where Vine reposed, observing there
> That these in contour of the head
> And goodly profile made a pair,
> Though one looked like a statue dead.
>
> (3.11.221–26)

Mortmain dies that Rolfe may live. It is Mortmain, not Rolfe, who madly tries the gall of the Dead Sea water as Melville had when he "carried the bitter in my mouth all day" (*Journals*, p. 83). Mortmain bears the role of "madness" and self-annihilation vicariously for both; he is the night side of Rolfe.

Agath is a transitional figure. He marks the beginnings of a way back from Mortmain's self-destruction, first appearing at Mar Saba when Mortmain is far down the steeps to oblivion. Mortmain "died" by the Dead Sea; only the shade of him hovers about Mar Saba, to which he has ascended for a hero's transfiguration by the Palm. It is interesting that for a type to withstand extinction Melville turned back to the sea. Bearded, wrinkled, and deafened by tempests, this "pickled old sea-Solomon" (3.25.151) is a briny ancient from the bottom of the sea. His penalty-ridden body has been beaten by man and nature until he survives as do the giant island-tortoises of which he tells, by drawing into his shell—not dead, but in a "feint of death" (4.3.97).[68] Inarticulate and uncomprehending, Agath wears

68.   Agath's anonymous "island" is clearly in the Galápagos, the site of Melville's "The Encantadas." It is quite as desperate a world as that of the Chola widow, Hunilla, in Sketch Eighth of that piece.

> Nature's own look, which might recall
> Dumb patience of mere animal,
> Which better may abide life's fate
> Than comprehend.
>
> (4.3.104–7)

Like Mortmain's, his cap has been stolen by a giant bird (3.25.120ff.; 3.27.20–28). The mere sight of a scorpion brings a shriek from him, so raw is he before the touch of evil (4.4.1–5). But "schooled by the inhuman sea" (4.13.7), preserved as it were in brine, Agath lives on.[69]

    Ungar completes the cycle with a human rather than animal endurance: Ungar's strength is both physical and intellectual. After standing quietly aside during the opening cantos of Part 4, when Agath dominates the scene, he moves in and carries the final version of monomania. His rancor at the Southern defeat spurs him to fierce attacks on modern civilization. His quarrel is with history, and back of that with the nature of man. For him the fall of the South, and all the cruel deprivations attending it, is a reenactment of the fall of man; historically it marks for him an end to man's last great free chance to build a New World:

>   "Know,
> Whatever happen in the end,
> Be sure 'twill yield to one and all
> New confirmation of the fall
> Of Adam."
>
> (4.21.121–25)

Rolfe is the one who understands the roots of Ungar's bitterness (4.5.36ff.), who conjures up arguments, as Ungar realizes, "To draw my monomania out" (4.21.101). If Rolfe is embarrassed by his own earnestness, he is willing father to the impeachments of this man, "earnest as the earnest tomb" (4.9.158). Rolfe's satisfaction with Ungar as "Brave soldier and stout thinker both," includes the subtle characterization of him as "An armed man in the Druid grove" (4.17.67, 72). His meaning lies, as the narrator says, in his "slouched reserve of strength" (4.1.82). Rolfe's final judgment is precise: "He's wise" (4.23.32).

---

69. Cf. Melville's cluster-poem entitled "Pebbles" (*John Marr;* in *Published Poems*, pp. 243–49): "Healed of my hurt, I laud the inhuman Sea" (VII, p. 249).

The cycle of monomaniacs gave Melville his opportunity to review some of his own private tensions of the past twenty-five years, and in part, as the calculated sequence suggests, make some resolution of them. He had long been plagued by images of self-destroying types—the purely evil Jackson of *Redburn*; the "grand, ungodly, godlike man, Captain Ahab" (*Moby-Dick*, chap. 16, p. 79); Pierre, the fool of virtue; the gentle man of preferences, Bartleby; and the self-exhausting Benito Cereno. The distance between Mortmain and Ungar is crucial. Mortmain's descent becomes unmanageable; he is seized by what divers call the rapture of the depths. Ungar's mania is not toward self-extinction, but the eradication of evil. War is his business; he is a professional. Ungar is Mortmain with a resuscitated will, Agath with a mind. Quietly, between days of toil as an inspector of customs, Melville made his reappraisal.

We are not to have Vine's "history" from the narrator or his own reticent lips. Introducing him (1.29), the narrator refuses to tell anything about his home, kin, tribe, or estate, on the grounds that "gifts unique" are not thus explainable. Other than his being a middle-aged American, we know only one biographical particular—he has spent some time in an artist's studio in Florence.[70] Djalea's instinctive deference toward Vine is explained by Rolfe: he may well have a notion that Vine is "some lord" who is traveling "For delicate cause, incognito" (2.10.102–3). The sense of genius is matched by an air of cover-up. We get shadows from the flame, with Melville in his right as commentator playing the moth. We get also the almost prurient curiosity of young Clarel about both Vine and Rolfe. From such dartings and peerings there slowly emerges a character that strikingly resembles Hawthorne's personality and the fictional world he created.[71]

70.   3.14.29. Hawthorne's experiences among the artists in Italy are fictionalized in *The Marble Faun* (Boston: Ticknor & Fields, 1860; Sealts 247); abridged accounts of his many visits to Hiram Powers's studio in Florence are in his *Passages from the French and Italian Note-Books* (Boston: Osgood, 1872; Sealts 252, acquired in 1872).

71.   Sealts lists nineteen different works by or about Hawthorne which Melville or members of his family owned (244–61, 367). Many of them are marked; at least six of these were acquired during 1868–72 when Melville was well into *Clarel* and buying books for it. Some general identification of Vine as Hawthorne has been accepted by many critics. I discussed it with F. O. Matthiessen just before his book appeared; he did not feel he knew *Clarel* well enough at that time to be sure of it, but in *American Renaissance*, p. 490, he noted it in passing as

Even at the first meeting, Vine withdraws as "one who would keep separate" (1.28.51), and the descriptive canto allotted him (1.29) is named "The Recluse." At Gethsemane (1.30) he sits swallowed up in meaningful reverie while the others talk. Typically he is mute, passive, reserved. Of this aloofness Vine is himself aware, and as he begins his soliloquy to the Palm the narrator has him think of his separateness and his addiction to the past as a kind of problem (3.26). If this line in the portrait at first seems excessive, one does well to recall that all who knew Hawthorne well, including himself, have testified to his almost fierce shyness.[72] Its leavening counterpart in Vine is an "Ambiguous elfishness" as of "an Ariel unknown" (1.29.50–51). The sight of a brisk tourist in Gethsemane awakens him to "freakish mockery, elfin light" (1.30.109). There is a Puckish twist of unpredictability in him, a "tropic eye / Freakishly impish" (2.33.72–73).[73] Vine's humor is not genuinely gay but, as in Hawthorne's fictions, ironic. For beneath Vine's shyness and elfish humor is a deep-grained moral force. Austere self-control underlies his "opulent softness" (1.29.31–33), and he reins his mount with a "lurking will," even though

---

"possible." Bezanson, "Herman Melville's *Clarel*," pp. 175–214, is an earlier version of the present discussion. Sedgwick, p. 206, is "convinced" of the parallel. Stone, pp. 156–58, generally accepts it. Chase, p. 247, thinks it "very probable." Mason, p. 235, considers it "possible" but prefers Vine as an attribute of Melville. Howard, p. 300, sees "a good deal of Hawthorne in the character of Vine," but specifically denies the relevance of the Vine-Clarel scene. See RELATED DOCUMENTS, pp. 883–93.

72.   Elizabeth Peabody, in Julian Hawthorne, *Nathaniel Hawthorne and His Wife* (Boston: Osgood, 1884), I, 178–79, said "he looked, at first, almost fierce with his determination not to betray his sensitive shyness, which he always recognized as a weakness." Julian himself put it directly: "if he chatted with a group of rude sea-captains . . . or talked metaphysics with Herman Melville on the hills of Berkshire, he would aim to appear in each instance a man like as they were; he would have the air of being interested in their interests and viewing life by their standards. Of course, this was only apparent; the real man stood aloof and observant" (I, 88–89). Introducing *The Scarlet Letter* (1850) in "The Custom House," Hawthorne speaks of keeping "the inmost Me behind its veil," and even his letters to Sophia, though warm, admit reticences.

73.   The cluster of phrases that catch this attribute of Vine are similar to many applied to little Pearl in *The Scarlet Letter*; their mood also appears often in Hawthorne's children's stories.

> He seemed to be
> In reminiscence folded ever,
> Or some deep moral fantasy.[74]

(2.1.245, 234–36)

The signs and symbols of evil do not antagonize (as with Mortmain-Ungar) so much as entrance him. At his first sight of the Dead Sea, from Olivet,

> With wordless look intent,
> As if the scene confirmed some thought
> Which in heart's lonelier hour was lent,
> Vine stood at gaze.

(1.36.46–49)

To Nehemiah's reverential account of the Good Samaritan's deed Vine whispers an aside: "There was a Levite and a priest" (2.9.85). It is he who first catches sight of the tormented ascetic on Quarantania (2.14.103), and he who imagines the Jordan willows saying to the merrily bubbling river:

> "Ah, tarry, for at hand's a sea
> Whence ye shall never issue out
> Once in."[75]

(2.27.30–32)

Vine sits entranced by a palm tree cast up by the Dead Sea, "free from decay / But dead" (2.33.12–20). The one who discovers the drowned body of Nehemiah, he remains internally calm,

> Since many a prior revery grave
> Forearmed against alarm's control.

(2.39.27–28)

Vine eagerly prompts Ungar to his diatribe, "Of Wickedness the Word" (4.22). Derwent is acute in judging Vine a "black but juicy one" (3.14.25)—and that word *black* throws us back at once to Melville's impassioned essay on Hawthorne in which he reiterates

---

74. In his preface to *The Marble Faun* Hawthorne explained that he "proposed to himself merely to write a fanciful story, evolving a thoughtful moral." His short stories can be accurately called "moral fantasies."

75. Compare with Hawthorne's favorite theme of the absorptive power of sin.

that it is "that blackness in Hawthorne . . . that so fixes and fascinates me."[76]

Vine's interest in character study makes him an observer rather than a participator—another persistent problem-theme of Hawthorne's fiction. He has "the zest / Of a deep human interest," for example, in a story told to explain Nehemiah (1.37.15–16). Even more he is aroused by the suicidal Mortmain, eager to know for example what Rolfe thinks of him (2.16.132). Ungar's bitterness also fascinates him, and for Vine it is so exciting a moment when Ungar's sword is called, by a fanatic monk, a cross, that he breaks his reserve and cries: "How he transfigured Ungar's sword!" (4.15.12); still under this excitement Vine himself develops the passion-flower as a symbol of the monk's burning zeal. When Vine is not absorbed in "some deep moral fantasy" of his own he is observing motivations; he is a student of sin and morality; his imagination works in symbols. Though we are not told Vine is a writer, it is quite clear that he is some kind of artist absorbed in moral-aesthetic values and deeply committed to the past.

It seems likely that Melville used the composition of *Clarel* as an opportunity to brood privately and at length over the man who had meant most in his own life. Their six-year friendship, especially the neighborly fifteen months from August, 1850, to November, 1851, when Arrowhead and the little red house at Lenox held them only six miles apart, had been psychologically intense. Meeting at a time when both men were at the height of their powers, Melville had formed a reckless emotional attachment for Hawthorne, fifteen years his senior and an authoritative craftsman. Hawthorne's *The American Notebooks* and hints from their correspondence graph the outlines—the magic of endless words, the rituals of drinking and smoking far into the night, the exchange of life images. The older man—handsome, passive, outwardly reserved but passionate within—elicited deep emotional vibrations from Melville. In all of Melville's writings there are few chapter sequences that rival in emotional eloquence his letters to Hawthorne, with "Hawthorne and His Mosses" as magnificent

76. "Hawthorne and His Mosses," written for the New York *Literary World* probably just after Melville met Hawthorne in August of 1850. The essay is included in the Northwestern-Newberry *Piazza Tales* volume, pp. 239–53; this quotation appears on p. 244 (subsequent page references appear in the text).

prelude and the brief poem "Monody" as afterword. When Melville wrote "In Token of My Admiration for His Genius, This Book Is Inscribed to Nathaniel Hawthorne" and made it part of the manuscript of *Moby-Dick*, he did the most that could be done. Before all this Hawthorne responded, for a shy man, with remarkable warmth. Yet what response could be adequate to insatiable hunger?

In the *Mosses* essay Melville, having written of Hawthorne's "depth of tenderness," "boundless sympathy," and "omnipresent love" (p. 242), went on to confess: "But already I feel that this Hawthorne has dropped germinous seeds into my soul. He expands and deepens down, the more I contemplate him; and further, and further, shoots his strong New-England roots into the hot soil of my Southern soul" (p. 250). In his letters to Hawthorne the same impassioned tone alternates with embarrassed jocularity, culminating in the breathless on-running letter of November 17?, 1851, acknowledging Hawthorne's appreciation of *Moby-Dick*: "your heart beat in my ribs and mine in yours, and both in God's"; he talked of their drinking from the same "flagon of life," and concluded the first of two postscripts with: "The divine magnet is on you, and my magnet responds. Which is the biggest? A foolish question—they are *One*." Melville's "foolish question" was not to be rid of so quickly, as we shall see in a moment; but first to the business of being "*One*."

In the poem the hunger for full reciprocation from Vine is turned over to Clarel. The young student has become so enamored of Vine's personal attributes that by the time the pilgrims reach the Jordan (2.27) he wants a lover's affection.[77] In a moment of wine-warmed intimacy they lie in a bower on the riverbank, separated by a screen of leaves "As were Venetian slats between" (line 11). The scene is a Sybaritic one, Vine luxuriating in the shadows, "Light sprays above his temples blown" (line 14). As Vine goes murmuring on in conversation—a rare moment of release for him—young Clarel is suddenly overwhelmed by Vine's presence:

> O, now but for communion true
> And close; let go each alien theme;
> Give me thyself!

> (lines 68–70)

77. Arvin, pp. 206–8, also sees this scene as a Melville-Hawthorne projection.

But Vine, with no suspicion of "Clarel's thrill / Of personal long-ing" (lines 72–73), keeps on talking while the younger man yearns for "confidings that should wed / Our souls in one" (lines 106–7). As Clarel lets fall "inklings" of his mood (line 111), a shadow passes over Vine. The youth has gone too far; Vine rejects him. At this moment the narrator moves in and imagines Vine's thoughts: Clarel will have to make his own resolution of doubts, and not count on Vine for help; "The negatives of flesh" (line 126) prevent ultimate reciprocation between man and man, as Hawthorne had always known, and as Melville found out.[78] The canto remains, however, a confession of the personal attractiveness of Vine to the narrator. The shift of role here—with Clarel rather than Rolfe being protagonist—is a transference of the onus of guilt from Rolfe to the innocent young man.

Clarel is a poem in which no absolutes of heart or head go unscrutinized. If Rolfe's strength is endangered by earnestness, Vine's is compromised by anti-intellectualism. Sometimes after the pilgrims' debates Vine openly expresses his ennui, pulling a weed and carefully picking it apart (1.34.68–69), plaiting a wreath of thorns (2.18–19), or flinging dead driftwood back into the Dead Sea at the close of discussion (2.33.106–8). One such instance is not only Hawthornesque; it is Hawthorne's. From a cliff's edge on the High Desert, when grave issues are being pondered, Vine responds to the "weary length of arguing" by crushing porous stones,

> or one by one,
> Through the dull void of desert air,
> He tossed them into valley down;
> Or pelted his own shadow there.

(3.5.192, 185–88)

In Hawthorne's *Passages from the American Note-Books* we read: "An idle man's pleasures and occupations and thoughts during a day spent by the sea-shore; among them, that of sitting on the top of a

---

78. Kenyon says, in *The Marble Faun*, chap. 31: "I am a man, and between man and man there is always an insuperable gulf. They can never quite grasp each other's hands; and therefore man never derives any intimate help, any heart suste-nance, from his brother man, but from woman,—his mother, his sister, or his wife."

cliff, and throwing stones at his own shadow, far below."⁷⁹ The image is too precise to be coincidental. When the pilgrims move on, a heap of stones is left by Vine—"A monument to barrenness" (3.7.83–85).

In a poem that makes much of personal interactions, none are more intricate than those involving Vine. Vine's judgments of Rolfe and the narrator's own response to them, for example, are intricately documented. Just after they meet, Rolfe launches into an impassioned analysis of man's need for God:

> Intense he spake, his eyes of blue
> Altering, and to eerie hue,
> Like Tyrrhene seas when overcast;
> The which Vine noted, nor in joy,
> Inferring thence an ocean-waste
> Of earnestness without a buoy:
> An inference which afterward
> Acquaintance led him to discard
> Or modify, or not employ.
>
> (1.31.197–205)

Here Vine is the one critical of Rolfe's earnestness, but it is the narrator's subtle gradations of concern—the uncertain *decrescendo* of the last three lines—that betray the real stakes. If this blue-eyed Rolfe is surrogate for the blue-eyed Melville who so often poured out his speculations to an ultimately diffident Hawthorne, then this passage and similar ones give us Melville's anxious guesses, though now somewhat bemused, as to what Hawthorne had actually felt about him.⁸⁰ And well Melville might have wondered! Hawthorne's published account of their last long talk together on the sand hills at Southport probably lay within arm's reach as Melville composed. What could be more tantalizing than to read about oneself: "Melville, as he always does, began to reason of

79. I, 87; ed. Simpson, p. 154 (see footnote 65 above). A similar image occurs in "Foot-Prints on the Sea-Shore" in *Twice-Told Tales* (vol. II, 1837), a copy of which Hawthorne had given to Melville in 1851 (Boston: Munroe, 1842; Sealts 260). Melville marked the passage (p. 324) and used the image again in his poem "Shelley's Vision" in *Timoleon* (*Published Poems*, p. 283).

80. 1.31.267–70; 2.15.41–47. Melville wrote to Hawthorne (April? 16?, 1851) regarding *The House of the Seven Gables*: "finally, in one corner, there is a dark little black-letter volume in golden clasps, entitled 'Hawthorne: A Problem.' "

Providence and futurity, and of everything that lies beyond human ken"—and then to run into Sophia Hawthorne's prudent ellipses? Melville's suspicions were well founded, as the restored text shows; to Hawthorne these questions were "dismal and monotonous as the sand hills amid which we were sitting."[81] Though Hawthorne seems genuinely to have loved and respected Melville, the younger man's special brand of "ontological heroics"[82] simply were not his style.

The narrator is not content to let Vine go as an anti-intellectual. Vine's "settled neutral frame," he suggests, may be "assumed" (1.30.86–87), and back of this "coyness" may there not be "fear— / Fear or an apprehensive sense?" (1.29.46–47). Could there be some design in his neutrality, his retreats into his "dumb castle" (1.31.59)? These questions are put just after Rolfe and Vine meet, before the reader quite knows what is afoot; they indicate that the narrator has pretty well decided Vine bars the gate from fear of invasion. Shortly after Vine rejects Clarel by the Jordan comes a dramatic sequel— amusingly transparent in its psychology—in which Clarel discovers a hidden weakness in Vine (3.7.12–45). The narrator's ambiguous description of what Clarel sees in Vine's face, there among the crags when Vine thinks he is alone, is explosive. For the Cenci theme had long been dynamite to both Hawthorne and Melville.[83] Taken severely it would support Julian Hawthorne's notion that Melville really believed there was "some secret"—presumably a sin—in Hawthorne's past;[84] short of that it suggests unnameable private terrors and sufferings (not a casual surmise, considering the complexity of Hawthorne's final crack-up). In either case young Clarel has found some ambiguous and discrediting weakness in the noble Vine. If one accepts the Hawthorne identification, then here is Melville's secret conviction: beneath his shy and opulent serenity Hawthorne was scared.

81. See sect. 1 above and footnote 4. Reasoning "of Providence and futurity" of course echoes the derogation of the hell scene in *Paradise Lost*, 2.555ff.; Hawthorne and Melville both knew the passage.

82. See Melville's letter to Hawthorne of June 29, 1851.

83. See the discussion at 3.7.18.

84. *Hawthorne and His Circle* (New York: Harper, 1903), p. 33. For Julian Hawthorne's varying "memories" of Hawthorne, see Harrison Hayford's 1945 dissertation, pp. 303–7, 324–34.

A recurrent theme of the poem, explicable in terms of the Melville and Hawthorne identifications and not easily otherwise, is the tournament of merits which from the beginning is set up between Rolfe and Vine. Clarel's first judgment that they are "peers" gives way before Rolfe's opening barrage of speculations, and he decides the reserved Vine is "choicer treasure" (1.31.42, 283). After Rolfe contends that Nehemiah's belief in the Second Coming of Christ is either "craze" or "simplicity," Clarel wonders if there can be truth in such "bluntness" and if this man Rolfe is going to be helpful or harmful (2.10.230–31, 234–45). Then one night when he can't sleep Clarel suddenly begins to realize that Rolfe's frankness may be important for him, and that Vine, though attractive, is so far "a fountain sealed"; suddenly he has a quick intuition: there is in Rolfe "A gleam of oneness more than Vine's" (2.17.13–34). Shortly afterward Clarel again decides (this time without reference to Vine) that Rolfe is "sterling" in spite of his "illogical wild range," and that he, Clarel, simply must learn to endure this kind of strength (2.21.125–34). Meanwhile, however, he has been so overwhelmed by the personal attractiveness of Vine that he tries to "wed . . . souls" with Vine by the Jordan (2.27), resulting, as we have seen, in Vine's rebuke and Clarel's subsequent discovery of Vine in a state of trembling weakness. With Vine unmasked, there now seems no use of expecting either of "winning" him or "coming at his mystery" (3.7.36–37). The whole force of the contest now seems drained off. Rolfe's long talk with Clarel on the night following the revels again bewilders Clarel:

> Earnest he seems: can union be
> 'Twixt earnestness and levity?
> Or need at last in Rolfe confess
> Thy hollow, Manysidedness!
>
>   (3.16.260–63)

Yet by the time they are on the way to Bethlehem, Clarel recognizes he is now using Rolfe's agnostic idiom (4.3.119–28). Thus Rolfe's victory is quietly completed, as is Melville's act of self-justification.

Significantly Vine retains his original prestige during the rest of the journey. He continues to communicate his special sense of power and grace almost as if the unmasking had not occurred. When the pilgrimage is over the narrator dismisses the travelers abruptly; only Vine receives a passing tribute—through him Clarel, in the light of his recent tragedy, catches some kind of "new sense" (4.32.11). As to the relations of Rolfe and Vine, they have been satisfactory enough, though not at all what Clarel had hoped that first time he saw the two together and predicted such great things from "contact true— / Frank, cordial contact of the twain." For "Clarel was young," the narrator wryly notes (1.31.39–53). The dominant psychological thesis of *Clarel* is that individual lives are infinitely complex, men do and think as they must, self-knowledge is hard won and limited, and full understanding between man and man is more than can be expected. By these terms Clarel got all that was due from his two mentors; Rolfe and Vine leave, after friendship, intact.

Some four years after Nathaniel Hawthorne at the age of sixty died quietly in his sleep in a hotel room in Plymouth, New Hampshire, Melville wrote on the title page of his own copy of *Our Old Home*: "(May 19, 1864)," the date of death. At some unrecorded time he wrote the lyric "Monody":[85]

> To have known him, to have loved him,
>   After loneness long;
> And then to be estranged in life,
>   And neither in the wrong;
> And now for death to set his seal—
>   Ease me, a little ease, my song!
>
> By wintry hills his hermit-mound
>   The sheeted snow-drifts drape,
> And houseless there the snow-bird flits
>   Beneath the fir-tree's crape:
> Glazed now with ice the cloistral vine
>   That hid the shyest grape.
>
> (*Timoleon;* in *Published Poems*, p. 276)

The tribute was to the man who had excited and sustained him at his own ripest time, to whom he had written in November, 1851: "A sense of unspeakable security is in me this moment, on account of your having understood the book. . . . Knowing you persuades me more than the Bible of our immortality." The

85. See "Melville's 'Monody': For Hawthorne?" pp. 883–93 below.

letters to Hawthorne had always had such apocalyptic touches laced in between bits of literary and barnyard gossip. His fundamental vision of the two of them was somehow sacramental. Writing to Duyckinck in the early days of the relationship (February 12, 1851) he spoke of one of Hawthorne's works as "an earlier vintage from his vine." In his eloquent fantasy of the two of them in a champagne heaven (June, 1851), he concluded with a symbolic allusion to "the vine which is to bear the grapes that are to give us the champagne hereafter." Then when Hawthorne was gone, he put it down again: ice glazed "the cloistral vine / That hid the shyest grape." He could not forget this man who had so twined himself about him. As Melville turned inward for the reenactment of the Palestine experience, there he saw him again:

> But who is he uncovered seen,
> Profound in shadow of the tomb
> Reclined, with meditative mien
> Intent upon the tracery?
> A low wind waves his Lydian hair:
> A funeral man, yet richly fair—
> Fair as the sabled violets be.[86]
>
> (1.28.37–43)

Evoked literally from the tomb, this "funeral man" is resurrected out of the "rifled *Sepulcher of Kings*" for one more journey; he sits "where beauty clings, / Vining a grot how doubly dead" (1.28.22–24), in meditation over an ancient frieze. "Name him—Vine" (1.29.2). During the weary months and years of composition Melville could not resist subjecting Vine to analysis, as he did the others. As the narrator says when Clarel is at Celio's grave:

> Whom life held apart—
> Life, whose cross-purposes make shy—
> Death yields without reserve of heart
> To meditation.
>
> (1.40.31–34)

86.   This violet turns up again even more pointedly at the end of 2.22, where Vine's "heart's shadow" is called "the Violet of the Dead." Ardent symbolists may wish to extend this death theme to Vine's second quatrain sung at Mar Saba (3.14.35–38); here the rose-leaves (life) blow down about him; but on their "death-bed" grow amaranths (an immortality symbol in *Pierre*); sad but hopeful, says Derwent, "Like purple in a royal mourning" (3.14.44).

If Vine's motives are at times ruthlessly linked with passive ennui, overt anti-intellectualism, pride, and some ambiguous hidden fear, on the whole the criticisms are secondary. Vine retains to the end a sovereignty, not by present act or word, but as if by decree given years ago.

IX
CONTEXTS OF HISTORY

C LAREL is a historical poem. The only *visualized* history of the poem is a documentary view of two cities, one monastery, and the countryside between them, in Palestine. This is not without interest in its own right as the report of a sensitive Western observer of the polyglot world of the Middle East in the mid-nineteenth century. The poem provides a close-up of a fragmented social world of subcultures, variously defined by an intricate criss-cross of national, racial, and religious affiliations. Our concern here, however, is with that historical phase of the poem which is not visual but verbal: the projection in debate of the ethos of the contemporary Western world as Melville saw it. In particular we shall note his version of what was happening to postbellum America, and his view of the science-versus-religion controversy.

The culture in which Melville had matured as man and artist before the Civil War was marked by unlimited enthusiasm for the possibilities of democracy. The primary configuration of Young America was a widely shared faith in which political and religious ideals merged in predicting the unique role assigned America. This faith, especially as phrased by an Emerson or Whitman, transcended common experience, and yet it seemed generally valid in terms of the newly discovered bounty of the land and the energies and ingenuity of an ambitious people drawn here by its promise. America was building itself at a phenomenal rate. Settlers followed the frontiersmen west so rapidly that the continent was spanned almost within a generation; simultaneously merchantmen and whalers boldly opened a second frontier on the seas of the world. At home mechanics and farmers worked in an open-ended economy where land and materials were plentiful and manpower was at a premium. The young clerk bent over his Blackstone at night and dreamed of the city of Washington. The lyceum speaker with his "philosophical apparatus" (air pumps) or his cabinet of geological specimens demonstrated that the new science was handmaiden to the arts and the solid base for useful knowledge. The reformer moved about from one community to another, the draft of a third hanging from his coat pocket. The preacher taught the everyday virtues, pointed out an uncomplicated road to personal salvation, and hazarded a prophecy on the fullness of time that was just ahead. Labor struggles, the economic crisis that began in 1837, worries about foreigners, deepening sectional conflicts, the war with Mexico, the rising menace of the slavery issue—somehow these were borne along on a general wave of euphoria and patriotism that most shared. In the America in which Melville spent his youth, invention, success, and prophecy ran riot; social faith was unbounded.

In the middle of the fifth decade of the century, just at the moment when the democratic faith was nearing the crest of the wave, Melville returned from his global wanderings and began the self-development which he himself placed at his twenty-fifth year (1844–45). His reactions to what he now saw were divided: he experienced the emotional power of the age, yet at the same time he felt a temperamental opposition to its buoyant optimism. In his writings through *Moby-Dick* one sees the chiaroscuro of his own social faith and doubt. In *Mardi* (chaps. 158–62) the section on Vivenza (the United States) offers both satiric oratory and serious invocations to the lusty and independent young America—"the foremost and goodliest stripling of the Present," a land which "brims with the future" (p. 520). The major event in the visit to Vivenza is the reading by a fiery youth of an anonymous scroll in which America is reminded of its great good fortune in land and space and warned of the "recoil" that may come with its exhaustion, is admonished that "Each age thinks its own is eternal," and is advised that "freedom is only good as a means; is no end in itself" (pp. 526, 528). The lessons of the past are urged on a nation concerned only with the present and its own future: "And though all evils may be assuaged; all evils can not be done away. For evil is the chronic malady of the universe; and checked in one place, breaks forth in another" (p. 529). In particular Melville cites the anomaly of slavery in a free country and takes the South bitterly to task. Yet in *Redburn* (chap. 33) his young narrator eloquently speaks the American dream: "We are the heirs of all time, and with all nations we divide our inheritance. . . . The other world beyond this, which was longed for by the devout before Columbus' time, was found in the New. . . . Not a Paradise then, or now; but to be made so, at God's good pleasure, and in the fullness and mellowness of time" (p. 169). In *White-Jacket* (chap. 36) he picked up again the analogy that the New England settlers had cherished: "And we Americans are the peculiar, chosen people—the Israel of our time; we bear the ark of the liberties of the world" (p. 151). This sense of a divine destiny for America runs in and out of his writing; among the complexities of *Moby-Dick* one of young Ishmael's assurances (chap. 26) is of "that democratic dignity which, on all hands, radiates without end from God; Himself! The great God absolute! The centre and circumference of all democracy! His omnipresence, our divine equality!" (p. 117). Melville in his early writings was as much an enraptured advocate of the democratic dream as he was shrewd critic of particular American institutions. Thus in "Hawthorne and His Mosses" he called on American writers to assert themselves through "that unshackled, democratic spirit of Christianity in all things" (p. 248). It was not by chance that Melville's greatest writing coincided with the highest wave of democratic faith. In later years he marked a famous passage in Arnold which exactly explained what had happened: "for the creation of a master-work of literature two powers must concur, *the power of the man and the power of the moment*, and the man is not enough without the moment" (Melville's underlining italicized).[87] Romantic democracy had been midwife to *Moby-Dick*.

During the twenty-five years that elapsed between the publications of *Moby-Dick* and *Clarel* profound changes took place in the American democratic process. Qualifying that "democratic spirit of Christianity in all things," the nation plunged into civil war, forsook its humanitarian traditions in a brutal Reconstruction, and entered an orgy of economic self-exploitation. For the first time the acquisitive spirit and its vocabulary became the dominant one in American life. In the center of things was a visible island of brazenly corrupt practices. The spiritual exhortations of Emerson were pinned on rolltop desks to sanction aggrandizement. American democracy as reported by Lord Bryce in 1888 was scarcely recognizable as the same

87. *Essays in Criticism* (cited in footnote 38 above), p. 5.

philosophy De Tocqueville had so generously described in 1835; and in practice it was not the same. An unregulated capitalism which preserved the ideal of a Christian democracy chiefly in its philanthropic concessions was transforming the nation into a mighty machine for production and, at worst, exploitation.

During the same period Melville had gone through psychic exhaustion and a subsequent long period of depression. Thus in some measure, and mostly by chance, his own disillusionment corresponded with an American historical cycle. By the time he went to the Holy Land his essentially romantic apprehension of the world had crumbled at the foundations; and within four years after his return the guns at Fort Sumter were pounding at the base of romantic democracy. The sense of a "Sad arch between contrasted eras" which the narrator defines in *Clarel* (4.5.79) is everywhere apparent in his later writings. Whereas in *Mardi* he had warned of dangers confronting a democracy in which he felt a stake, in *Clarel* he stood hostile to the whole spirit of the age. He was not alone. The formerly buoyant Whitman in *Democratic Vistas* (1871) turned savagely on the business classes, the government, the People: "society, in these States, is canker'd, crude, superstitious, and rotten." Mark Twain made his indictment in *The Gilded Age* (1873) sufficiently graphic to brand it permanently. Henry Adams's retrospective account in *The Education* (1907) was scathingly ironic. Though recent scholarship has somewhat modified criticism of the quarter century before 1900, partly in support of the current conservatism, no case has been made for the decade after the Civil War, nor does one seem possible; and that is the decade out of which *Clarel* grew. The publicists of 1876, the centennial year, of course did their job undaunted, conveniently taking the long view backwards and forwards. But to men of sensibility the era was a rotten time unsweetened by the encomiums amid the flimsy architecture of the Philadelphia Exposition.

Two direct contacts with realistic democracy had influenced Melville. One was the lyceum. Up to about 1850 the lyceum movement had genuinely meant something by its motto, "Knowledge is power," but by the time Melville came to its platform it had lost much of its early seriousness of purpose to the star system which was already beginning to predominate. At the time of his lectures, especially in "Statues in Rome," Melville was full of the Mediterranean, and seems to have wanted more than anything else to convey to his audiences some sense of the enormous reaches of history and his own newest sense of the human immediacy of classical civilization. Looking out over the gas-lighted auditoriums of the nation, he felt little response to the things he had to say; there was such a thing, he learned, as "a theme / From which the club and lyceum swerve" (3.3.49–50). His second and severer experience was through the customs job which he held at four dollars a day all during the writing of *Clarel*. Had he been in search of the particular experience most likely to reveal the corruption, intrigue, and materialism of America after the Civil War he could not have chosen a better vantage point than the New York Customs. A dozen years before Melville began his duties there in 1866, Stoddard, an acquaintance of Melville's, had found its employees "incapable 'fogies' of all ages,—the mentally lame, halt, and blind,—for the Custom-House was an asylum for nonentities."[88] The fact that New York handled five-sixths of the total imports of the United States made the post of collector the most famous political plum in America. Nowhere else did the spoils system and political racketeering flourish with such unchecked gusto. When the president of the United States found it necessary to suspend from the customs two nationally known figures, C. A. Arthur and A. B. Cornell, he did so because for several years they had made the customs a center of dirty political manipulations. At the customs— though he was mainly assigned to wharf duties—Melville surely learned first hand the penalties of unchecked democratic license.

Rolfe, Mortmain, and Ungar lead in the critical attack on the modern age; as the pilgrims note more than once, two of them are Americans. Mortmain's bitter version of the successive failures of revolutionary politics in France may also be taken as Melville's; the evidence of the poem is that Melville was thoroughly disillusioned with radical political action, that the adventures of the Paris Commune in 1871 increased the disenchantment, and that as he grew older experience seemed to support the essentially republican-aristocratic philosophy which his family had stood for. All three critics accuse the age of being content with superficial knowledge, shrewdly concerned with the main chance only, arrogantly humanistic, worshipful of

88. R. H. Stoddard, *Recollections Personal and Literary* (New York: Barnes, 1903), p. 137. For a cautious description of customs procedures five years after Melville began work there see T. B. Thorpe, "The New York Custom-House," *Harper's New Monthly Magazine*, XLIII (June, 1871), 11–26.

Mammon, and indifferent toward art, philosophy, and religion. That these charges had come to represent Melville's primary response to contemporary society, particularly American society, is corroborated by hints from his letters of the period,[89] by his marginalia in the books he was reading,[90] and by the miscellaneous verse he was writing.[91] The scattered attacks of the poem culminate toward the end of *Clarel* in Ungar's tirade against democracy (4.19–21). He denounces democracy as the "Arch strumpet of an impious age" (4.19.138), and in the heated argument with Derwent which this provokes chastises contemporary society for its collapse of spiritual power. Led on by Rolfe, Ungar lashes the New World for its capitulation to speed and demagogism, predicting a "Thirty Years (of) War." His forecast for democracy is bleak:

> "Myriads playing pygmy parts—
> Debased into equality:
> In glut of all material arts
> A civic barbarism may be:
> Man disennobled—brutalized
> By popular science—Atheized
> Into a smatterer——"
>   "Oh, oh!"
>   "Yet knowing all self need to know
> In self's base little fallacy;
> Dead level of rank commonplace:
> An Anglo-Saxon China, see,
> May on your vast plains shame the race
> In the Dark Ages of Democracy."
>   (4.21.117, 127–39)

89. As in his comment of 1863 on "this dishonorable epoch" (February 17); his brusque characterization of the Centennial of 1876 after visiting it, as "a sort of tremendous Vanity Fair" (October 12); his remarks in 1876 about "these 'degenerate days'" (December 25); and his evident disgust with the Hayes fiasco of 1876–77 (March 6, 1877).

90. For example, his extensive markings in Arnold's *Essays in Criticism* include some twenty passages on mediocrity in England and America.

91. Among the short poems, "The Ravaged Villa," "The Enthusiast," and "The Age of the Antonines," all in *Timoleon (Published Poems,* pp. 266, 279, 286–87), and, unpublished by Melville, "The American Aloe on Exhibition," "In the Hall of Marbles," "Angel o' the Age!" and "Gold in the Mountain" (in the Northwestern-Newberry volume *BILLY BUDD, SAILOR and Other Late Manuscripts*).

It was not a page of *Clarel* to be left open in the case of Putnam exhibits at Philadelphia, "a pretty and modest case, in which Washington Irving is the star."[92] The whole theory of America's divine origins—that a continent was preserved on purpose for the American millennial Eden—strikes Ungar as having come down to a humanistic riot "in satire of the heaven" (4.21.54). The myth has come full circle, Rolfe thinks:

> Our New World bold
> Had fain improved upon the Old;
> But the hemispheres are counterparts.

> (4.5.61–63)

In her fratricidal war and her "misrule after strife" (4.5.48) and particularly in her surrender to "King Common-Place" (1.34.23) America had forfeited her claims to divine origin and destiny. Only a deep sense of irony could have prompted Melville's introduction of the character Don Hannibal into the last section of the poem: this boisterous Mexican, having lost an arm and a leg in his fight for democracy, has now fled the curses of progress and reform and has come seeking asylum from the New World in the Old! Melville was bitter about the loss of the social myth which he had often criticized but which had nourished his life and art.

Related to the changes in American social philosophy after the war was the crisis in religious thought. The upheaval generally followed the pattern of controversy being enacted abroad. Inherited beliefs were struggling especially with three successive developments in science: geology, with its implicit attack on Genesis and hence revelation; higher criticism, advocate of a new approach to Sacred History in keeping with scientific methods; and evolution, exponent of biological process as the explanation of man's history. As the century developed, the Church was increasingly hard pressed to square its dogma and traditions with the new knowledge provided by Lyell, the English disciples of Continental scholars, and Darwin. The American churches felt the blow at second hand but none the less severely soon after the country emerged from the war. During the seventies and eighties there was much internal conflict. Huxley and Tyndall crossed the water to confront vast audiences of bewildered Americans with the new theories. In defense of the churches an army

---

92. *The Independent*, XXVIII (July 20, 1876), 11.

of great evangelical preachers rose to meet the challenge—Beecher, Talmadge, Moody, Chapin, Bellows, and Brooks. Within a twenty-year period the religious magazines of the country doubled in number, many of them created especially to defend the faith. Leading secular magazines carried symposiums on such subjects as immortality, evolution, God, hell, Sabbatarianism. Theological liberals like John Fiske, John W. Draper, James Freeman Clarke, and Andrew Dickson White were popularizing comparative religion and minimizing dogma, while all over the country local clergymen dug in and defended or modified their commitments. The intellectuals were discussing *Essays and Reviews*, Renan, Strauss, and Darwin; for the educated it was hard to be indifferent.

It is in terms of such controversy that much of the foreground of *Clarel* is to be understood. Apparently an avid skimmer of current journals and newspapers, Melville became saturated with the vocabulary of the debate. He dramatized the Victorian suspicion that science was the confirmed enemy of revealed religion and the prime antagonist in the struggle. Beneath Mortmain's Slanted Cross, scrawled on the sea-face of a giant rock that faces the Dead Sea, Margoth, the geologist, triumphantly chalks:

> I, Science, I whose gain's thy loss,
> I slanted thee, thou Slanting Cross.

(2.31.99–100)

But both Rolfe and the narrator take a more complex view of science. Spurred by Margoth's presence, Rolfe argues that modern science is merely a supplement to the great conceptions of early thinkers, that Newton did not once and for all solve the world's riddle, and that the lapse of the Christian dream leaves man islanded:

> "Where stretched an isthmus, rolls a strait:
> Cut off, cut off! Can'st feel elate
> While all the depths of Being moan,
> Though luminous on every hand,
> The breadths of shallow knowledge more expand?
> Much as a light-ship keeper pines
> Mid shoals immense, where dreary shines
> His lamp, we toss beneath the ray
> Of Science' beacon. This to trim
> Is now man's barren office."

(2.21.91–100)

It is a memorable image of science as an aid to navigation but not a port. Science elucidates man's ignorance, Rolfe says, but also deepens and enlarges it (1.31.191–93). So with the narrator, who takes the position that since "truth requires strong retinue," poetry, science, and instinct should all be brought to bear (2.11.17–19). The theme of his Epilogue is that science is a party of the feud and not an umpire; we know more, but the more light, the more shadow.

Melville was a religious type. Long since he had rebelled against the stern Calvinism in which he had been reared, but he needed a myth of comparable force to take its place. His prose writings are those of a fabulist whose need for mythmaking was almost a matter of survival. Perhaps this is why he turned from short poems to the writing of *Clarel*, where he could have scope for his drama of paradise lost. Over and again there runs through it the double vision: the world of miracle and divine event on the one hand, the world of broken monuments and scattered stone on the other. Scarcely a canto fails to make the point, outrightly or through buried image or allusion, that the gods of Christendom parallel the gods of Greece and Rome, and *both* are gone. Whether or not the first will return is not answered, though Rolfe's instinct is that time and God are inexhaustible:

> "Though some be hurled
> From anchor, nor a haven find;
> Not less religion's ancient port,
> Till the crack of doom, shall be resort
> In stress of weather for mankind.
> Yea, long as children feel affright
> In darkness, men shall fear a God;
> And long as daisies yield delight
> Shall see His footprints in the sod."
>
> (1.31.182–90)

Melville was like one of William James's case histories for *The Varieties of Religious Experience* (1902); the need to be twice-born was in his bloodstream. The kinds of questions to which the great religions addressed themselves were precisely those Melville's temperament and training would not let him do without. It was the same problem that Clough, Arnold, and Tennyson wrote into many of their poems, that underlay Lowell's lament in "The Cathedral" (1869), and that motivated scores of Dickinson's brilliant, fractured inquiries. Hawthorne hit it almost right about Melville: "He can neither believe, nor be comfortable in his unbelief; and he is too honest and courageous not to try to do one or the other." The loss of faith is the basic assumed fact of the poem, and its largest problem is how to endure the overwhelming sense of a shattered vision.

A CRITICAL INDEX OF THE CHARACTERS

T HE INDEX provides critical analyses of thirty-two characters of the poem, listed alphabetically. Of these, ten may be considered major characters and are marked with an asterisk (*); further commentary on the major characters will be found in sections 4, 6, and 8 above. Each analysis provides in general:

Identification: first and last appearance, by cantos, followed by simple data on race, creed, background, occupation, etc.

Interpretation: primary symbols, ideological roles, meanings.

Status: for most major figures an evaluation of the character's relative standing in the moral-psychological hierarchy of the poem, by the terms of the narrator and selected major characters.

Source: when known, possible origins in Melville's experience or reading.

ABDON. 1.2–44

Host at the inn in Jerusalem where Clarel stays. He is a "Black Jew," presumably of the lost tribes dwelling in Cochin. From India he went to Amsterdam as a trader and now has come to Jerusalem to die and be buried with his fathers in Jehoshaphat.

His symbols are those of the Judaic faith: mezuzah, phylactery, fringed robe, scroll, and tallith. As well as representing ANCIENT ORTHODOXY, Abdon stands for EXPERIENCE THROUGH AGE. He is stoically resigned to disillusionment but is not cynical or given to self-pity.

Prototypes for Abdon may have been either of the keepers of two hotels where Melville stayed on his 1856–57 trip: the English "hotel" at Jaffa—M. Blattner, a German Jew (see *Journals*, pp. 80–81, 426), for Melville transfers some details of this hotel to Clarel's room in Jerusalem; or the keeper of the Mediterranean Hotel in Jerusalem where Clarel is evidently staying, "a German converted Jew, by name, *Hauser*" (*Journals*, p. 79). But Abdon's history clearly came from Warburton's *The Crescent and the Cross* (cited in footnote 10 above), II, 125: "The place where the ten tribes have lain concealed for 2,500 years is still a mere matter of conjecture. Now we hear of them along the shores of the Caspian Sea; then among the American Indians; now among the warriors of Cochin, and the fierce tribes of Affghanistan." A footnote to "Cochin" explains: "There are two races of Jews settled along the coast of Malabar: the *black*, and the *white*, as they are called. The former is the oldest, and is supposed to have wandered thus far East long before the destruction of Jerusalem." Cochin is a seaport town in the Malabar district, southwest coast of India.

AGAR.   1.17–42; 4.30
The mother of Ruth. An American Jewess who unwillingly left the New World to come to Jerusalem with her Gentile-Zionist husband (Nathan) and two children. After the murder of Nathan she dies of grief, as does Ruth.

A madonna-like representation of DOMESTIC WOMAN, she is gifted in sentiment and virtue. Lacking powers of reason, she remains subordinate to her husband. Agar is best understood in terms of Victorian ideals of womanhood, Milton's Eve, and possibly some traits of Elizabeth Shaw Melville.

The name Agar is a New Testament variation of Hagar, mother of Ishmael (Gal. 4.22–25), "in bondage with her children."

*AGATH.   3.12–4.13
An old Greek timoneer (pilot) whom the pilgrims meet at Mar Saba and who accompanies them as far as Bethlehem. He is the third figure in the monomaniac sequence (Celio-Mortmain-Agath-Ungar).

Visiting Mar Saba, where Greek sailors were always welcome, Agath wasassaulted in the glen below it by Ammonite robbers, stripped and beaten; he has been convalescing since. The incident is typical for this "pickled old sea-Solomon" (3.25.151)—bearded, wrinkled, weather-beaten, half deaf, and "schooled by the inhuman sea" (4.13.7). He is exclusively A MAN OF DISASTERS, and it is fitting he ride Nehemiah's ass. His "story" begins with a long-ago misadventure (told in 3.12) on his unblest ship, *The Peace of God*: fleeing the

Egyptian plague with a cargo of salvaged cannons, he struck a gale, the compass spun, corposants danced on the yardarms, three gulls pursued, the crew mutinied, the ship went on the rocks; only Agath survived, with the too-late knowledge that a Moor whom he had smuggled aboard to save him from the plague had stowed a chest-full of swords beneath the cabin compass and so turned the compass. In Agath's simple mythology, the Moor was "A black lieutenant of Lucifer" (3.12.124). Again (3.27), a great devil-bird had attacked him at the masthead, stealing his cap (cf. Mortmain in 3.25 and Ahab in *Moby-Dick*, chap. 130, p. 539) and tapping his brain, driving him into the sea where a shark followed him. Thus it is no wonder that he shrieks out at the mere sight of a scorpion (4.4), for this Job-like old man has been much tried and tested. The "crucifixion in tattoo" on his arm is sign that he too is a "bleeding man upon the tree" (4.2.51, 78). The Holy City, sighted from the mountains near Mar Saba, leads him to cry out as if from the masthead: "Wreck, ho! the wreck—Jerusalem!" (4.1.187), and his analogy for Palestine is a long account of a bleak volcanic island, where the only life that survives is the giant, languorous tortoise, encased against all danger. Agath is A STUDY IN SURVIVAL.

Agath wins from the narrator the deepest compassion; though he is inarticulate and broken, and past hope of comprehending life, he somehow withstands it with an animal-like patience (4.3.105). His story of the island leads Clarel to decide that man will never *solve* the world; in saying this Clarel realizes suddenly that he is taking Rolfe's point of view (4.3.122–23). Vine watches Agath closely, likes him, finds him "authentic," and respects his "dumb reverence / And resignation" (4.2.192, 198–99). His crucial role in the monomaniac cycle is suggested in section 8 above.

Agath is in a major fictional line of Melville's writing. He relates especially to the world of "The Encantadas" and an important character sequence that includes Jarl (*Mardi*), the Dansker (*Billy Budd, Sailor*), and Daniel Orme (in the late sketch "Daniel Orme"). Agath's blue and vermillion tattoo of the Crucifixion and his mystically "pitted" face (3.12.33) are both links: Jarl has a similar tattoo on his arm; the Dansker's face has been "peppered" with cartridge burns; and the almost purely symbolic Orme both has his face "peppered" and has a "cross of the Passion" tattooed on his chest. All are weird, oracular old sea-dogs.

ARNAUT, The.   3.11–4.2

A huge Albanian warrior temporarily resident at Mar Saba, evidently as a military escort for pilgrims. He is descended from ancient nobility, and has fought for the czar and the sultan. He is a Mohammedan.

He wears the brilliant national military costume of the Albanians—red, white, and blue; his symbols are weapons, a medal, and a scar. His enormous body and deep bass voice emphasize his role as a NOBLE BARBARIAN, a "ripe masterpiece of man" (3.11.119), vain, but leonine. Rolfe is intuitively drawn to him as a kind of VALHALLA HERO, but later stresses Christliness over "carnal manliness" (4.14.105). The Arnaut stands in low relation to the moral warrior, Ungar.

Melville probably saw Arnauts in the East, as many of these rough, wild, picturesque Albanians were in the service of the Turks. However, he took from Warburton's *The Crescent and the Cross* details for his dress (see the discussion at 3.11.61). (See also the HISTORICAL SUPPLEMENT, p. 669.)

ASS, The.   1.44–4.16

Nehemiah's mount until his death; afterwards ridden by Agath.

The ass is a symbol of PATIENCE, HUMILITY, AND RESIGNATION. In its patience and humility it is an extension of Nehemiah's own temperament, and in its resignation to the blows of fate, of Agath's. For pointed comparison with "each lofty steed" see 3.10.63. In its animal realism the ass becomes also A CARICATURE OF NATURALISTIC PHILOSOPHY: it twitches the Jordan palm from its ears (2.27.172–73), or matter-of-factly drinks the holy water at Bethlehem—"The mysteries slobbered by an ass!" (4.16.44).

Melville's keen interest in the Cairo donkeys—"Tipe of honesty. &c."—is the amusing prototype in the *Journals*, p. 77; but his serious treatment of the animal of the poem bespeaks the chastened mood of his own later years. See also the discussion at 2.1.203.

BANKER, The.   2.1–13

One of the original members of the pilgrimage who turns back with his future son-in-law, Glaucon, when he reaches the Wilderness. Of Greek-English background, he has come from his great estate in Thessalonica to make a business deal in Beirut; while awaiting the conclusion of transactions he has joined the pilgrimage to kill time.

The Banker is a bitter caricature of MAMMONISM, betrayed by his Parisian garb, Angora rug, expensive cigarettes, and obesity. A second element is his almost pathological FEAR OF DEATH. It is from terror of the Dead Sea that he turns back.

The mammonism theme is an old one with Melville, perhaps in part because of his father's axiom that "money is the only solid substance on which men can safely build in this world" (William H. Gilman, *Melville's Early Life*, p. 16). Allan Melvill was an importer of French luxuries; he died in bankruptcy and great mental distress. Melville's own visit to the Abbott family's wealthy country estate in Thessalonica, *Journals*, pp. 55–56, gave him the Banker's background, and perhaps more (see also the discussion at 2.1.104).

BELEX. 2.1–4.29

Leader of the six Arab Bethlehemites who are the guards of the pilgrimage. He is an Osmanli (European Turk), and so of course a Mohammedan. Formerly one of the Spahi (Turkish cavalry) who served under the sultan, he escaped Mahmoud's treacherous slaughter of the troops and became one of the cynical toll-takers at the Church of the Holy Sepulcher in Jerusalem.

Belex is a tough old WARRIOR, always ready to fight. A strict FATALIST, he accepts calmly his past misfortunes and present degradation. A good minor character, he suffers in comparison with Djalea, who is equally fearless but has a nobler serenity.

CELIBATE, The. 3.30–31

This Greek monk is a celibate almoner living in Mar Saba, where he is seen by Clarel and stirs a temporary ascetic ideal to live in "the pure desert of the will" (3.30.122).

He represents A SUPERIOR TYPE OF INNOCENCE. His symbols are his robe of blue (like the sky), the Saba doves which he feeds daily, and a vellum book containing hymns of heavenly love. The narrator places him, as ONE OF HEAVEN'S ELECT, above Plato.

The mood and setting of this figure are Pre-Raphaelite in tone.

*CELIO. 1.11–20

A handsome Italian youth with a humped back, ward of the Franciscan monks in Jerusalem's Terra Santa monastery. Clarel meets him twice. Celio is the first figure of the monomaniac sequence (Celio-Mortmain-Agath-Ungar).

The well-born Celio, embittered by his deformity and in revolt against the Roman Church, came to Palestine in the hope of extracting some new talisman from Judah's ancient secret. But here he is only the more ravished by doubt. One of the better dramatic sequences of the poem is his eloquent defiance of Christ at the Arch of Ecce Homo along the Via Crucis, his flight out the Gate of St. Stephen, his night hours alone in the tomb of St. James after he finds the city gate locked against him, and his rebellious challenge to the Terra Santa monks whom he follows that night to Lazarus's Tomb in Bethany (1.13–14). Soon after, he withdraws from the monastery and dies deep within the city. Clarel's two encounters with Celio, by the cave of the demoniacs and at dawn by the Martyr's Gate, are brief and wordless, but establish an intuitive sympathy which is filled out when he later reads Celio's journal and there finds "A second self" (1.19.26). Thus Celio stands throughout the poem as a model for THE COST OF REBELLION: the killing pain and loneliness of dissent. His theme at the arch, that if Christianity is not true then Christ's death merely "enlarged the margin for despair" (1.13.46), is the same theme confronting Clarel at the end (4.32–34), after which he too enters the Martyr's Gate and follows the "cross-bearers" (4.34.43) into the city.

In spite of his twisted body and spirit, Celio ranks high in the poem. The narrator openly compares him to Savonarola and Leopardi, martyrs of faith and of doubt (1.14). If the name Celio is a wordplay on "cielo" ("heaven" in Italian) it could be at once ironic and an accolade.

CHRISTODULUS.   3.23

The abbot of Mar Saba.

A type of UNQUESTIONING BELIEVER, blind Christodulus ("Servant of Christ") sits behind a screen in the midst of the relics and bones of his ancient faith.

*CLAREL.   1.1–4.34

The central character of the poem, discussed at length in section 4 above. See also the discussion at 4.26.0.

CYPRIOTE, The. 3.4–5

A handsome youth who passes the pilgrims as they ascend toward Mar Saba from the Dead Sea. Having taken flagons of wine to Saba for his mother, he is on his way down to the Jordan, to dip her shroud in its holy water.

A gay singer of light love songs, the Cypriote is the essence of UNTROUBLED YOUTH, epitomized in his scarlet cap (cf. Mortmain's black skullcap). Like Glaucon, the Lyonese, and the Lesbian he is in dramatic contrast with the wearily thoughtful pilgrims who have just known death. Cap and shroud point the opposition.

Melville's knowledge of the Greek ritual of the shrouds came from Stanley's *Sinai and Palestine* (cited in footnote 25 above), pp. 308–10.

CYRIL. 3.24–27

Once a soldier, now a "mad" monk living alone in a grotto at Mar Saba.

Dressed in a shroud, Cyril emerges from his cave to demand from passersby such a countersign as "*Death*" (3.24.66). He moves Clarel deeply, annoys the Lesbian, stirs pity in Derwent. One of the more violent manifestations of MONOMANIA in the poem.

Melville doubtless took the name from an actual monk, Cyril of Jerusalem, who lived at Mar Saba in the early centuries, noted in Murray's *Handbook for Travellers in Syria and Palestine* (cited in footnote 16 above), I, 205.

*DERWENT. 2.1–4.32

A priest of the Anglican Church whose English inheritance is lightened by a strain of Creole temperament. He is one of only four among the original nine pilgrims who complete the pilgrimage (with Clarel, Rolfe, and Vine).

Mature in years and gracious in personal relations, Derwent is a friendly good-fellow and traveling companion who does his unsuccessful best to make the pilgrimage a holiday. Among all the major characters he alone speaks for a MELIORIST VIEW OF MAN AND SOCIETY, and a BENIGN VIEW OF GOD AND NATURE. Essentially an institutional type, Derwent is committed to a relaxed Broad-Church view of experience that postulates man's goodness and social progress. His persistent optimism is rooted in good health, natural sociability, and a comfortable sense of status. A cleric, he is yet the most secular of the major pilgrims. Not unaware of man's sometimes-disastrous history, he prefers a generous version of events, past or present. Thus he brings a determinedly cheerful mood to the pilgrimage, riding easily and with light rein, trying to minimize debate, and warding off the ominous landscape with light reading (cf. Nehemiah's Book). A religious aesthete, he prefers gracefulness to grace. The pilgrims' uncompromising sense of theological crisis makes Derwent uncomfortable, and he does his best to provide a professional gloss that will keep him from being entangled. Derwent is an APOSTLE OF MODERNITY; his temperamental buoyancy and addiction to whatever is new and progressive thus throw him into ironic contrast with his disillusioned New World companions. Convinced of "the truth's munificence" (3.6.82), Derwent sees the recent findings of higher criticism, comparative religion, and physical science as in some general way lending support to his religion of the heart. The age has its difficulties, to be sure, but good works, a liberal view, and compromise as necessary guarantee a hopeful future. In nature as in religion and society Derwent is partial to the pleasant. A ritualistic watcher of sunrises, sunsets, and rainbows, he is a gentle apostle of PASTORAL NATURE in the midst of a blasted landscape. As K. H. Sundermann suggests (p. 199), it is probable that he is named after Wordsworth's "fairest of all rivers," the Derwent (*Prelude*, 1.270, 275; not in Melville's edition of the *Complete Poetical Works*, ed. Henry Reed [Philadelphia: Kay, 1839; Sealts 563a]; see Howard, p. 158).

The narrator's view of Derwent at times wavers between enjoyment of him as a good fellow (though open to Chaucerian caricature as a worldly priest) and severe indictment of his facile optimism. Rolfe enjoys intellectual debate with Derwent, but the burden of attack lies with the monomaniacs, to whom he is a charlatan as they, to him, are madmen. Through an opposition of temperaments that emerges before the journey is fairly under way (2.3), Derwent and Mortmain antagonize one another increasingly (3.6). After Mortmain's death Ungar takes up the running battle so vehemently that Derwent is all but demolished (4.20); in the showdown of allegiances that follows, Rolfe stands by Ungar against Derwent (4.21–23). The crucial evaluation of Derwent, however, comes from Clarel. As the two stand on Saba's tower watching the sun rise, the desperate student bares his theological difficulties (3.21). Derwent's refusal, or inability, to deal with doubt, his slick glossing over of difficulties, and his warning to beware of the influences of Rolfe and Vine ("giving to yourself the goad"—line 284) make Clarel turn savagely on him; Derwent's acknowledgment to Clarel—"Alas, too deep you dive" (line 307)—puts him low in the hierarchy of the poem, recalling, as it does, Melville's memorable comment in a letter to Evert Duyckinck (March 3, 1849): "I love all men who *dive*."

If Melville encountered someone like Derwent in the Holy Land, he left no record of it. Derwent is possibly related to his friends the Duyckincks, or to one or more of the many clerics he knew or heard at home and abroad. Jay Leyda's perceptive short sketch of Evert Duyckinck in the *Log* (I, xxv) includes Poe's remark that Duyckinck's character was "distinguished for the *bonhommie* of his manner," among other attributes. In any case Derwent is part of a series of Melville characters who practice their law, medicine, or theology so professionally as to endanger their response to experience (cf. the lawyer in "Bartleby," Surgeon Cuticle in *White-Jacket*, and the Reverend Mr. Falsgrave in *Pierre*).

DJALEA.   2.1–4.29

Guide and head guard of the pilgrimage. The son of an Emir, he is in exile. Djalea is a Druze of Lebanon, that curious Eastern religion which so fascinated the Western mind of the nineteenth century because of its secret rituals and beliefs.

Djalea stands very high in the poem's hierarchy of value. His garb as a Druze initiate—vertically striped cloak and especially the white turban and white sash—symbolizes his HIGH SOCIAL AND SPIRITUAL RANK. Although he carries arms, ready instantly for war or peace, he rides his magnificent mare (Zar) without spurs: his CONTROL is more than physical. Even the wild Bedouin robbers fear and respect him. Djalea keeps apart and maintains almost perpetual silence. The long pipe he smokes at the end of each day's journey expresses his SECRET OF SERENITY—before God, man, and himself. Asked once by Rolfe what belief sustains him, the Druze replies: "No God there is but God" (3.15.115), for which Rolfe names him "Lord Djalea" (3.16.5). He has POISE and MODERATION, though he is passionately in love. When young Clarel attempts to penetrate one of Djalea's serene glances, the narrator comments: "That was the last thing learned of all" (3.24.24). He may be taken as one of the ideals which Melville set himself in his middle years.

Melville's conception of Djalea probably began with Cunning-ham's dragoman, "the Druse, Abdallah," in Jerusalem (*Journals*, p. 80), who may well have led the pilgrimage to the Dead Sea. Most travelers commented briefly on the sect (e.g., Murray, I, xli). He may also have read Browning's play "The Return of the Druses" (published in 1843 as No. IV of *Bells and Pomegranates*). The Druze were an eleventh-century offshoot of Mohammedanism who respected the Koran and the Bible but had their own scriptures. The initiated group to which Djalea belongs (3.15.78) were a privileged fifteen percent called *Akils*; they were characterized by extreme devo-tion, strict moral code, and infinite capacity for secrecy. Of several doctrines the central one was the incomprehensible, indefinable, and passionless nature of one God, whose only sure attribute was exis-tence. No converts were allowed.

DOMINICAN, The. 2.25–26

A French Catholic priest who overtakes the pilgrims by the Jor-dan while they are singing *Ave Maris Stella*, describes his own faith, and departs leaving them to discuss Catholicism.

The Dominican, who wears the white robe of his order, has sat in the French legislature. As a Catholic and a democrat, he suggests both THE PERMANENCE AND THE ADAPTABILITY OF THE CHURCH. The pilgrims grant the great human appeal of Catholicism, especially the concept of Abba, Father. Rolfe suggests its coming historical role as an answer to the chaos of rampant democracy and materialism, and plays with the idea that in the modern world Rome is the truly "prot-estant" Church.

The priest is doubtless a fiction; his significance is best under-stood in terms of Cardinal John Henry Newman's *Apologia pro Vita Sua* (1864), Arnold's later essays, and the spiritual history of such diverse Americans as Orestes Brownson and Henry Adams.

DON HANNIBAL. 4.19–28

An old friend of Derwent's whom the pilgrims meet in Bethle-hem, a Mexican with the amusing name of Señor Don Hannibal Rohon Del Aquaviva (we learn the full name of no other character of the poem). See the discussion at 4.19.26.

Don Hannibal (military overtone) fought for Mexican liberty, losing an arm and a leg in battle; but now, loudly skeptical of democracy and its uses, he is in flight from the proletarian movement and "cursed *Progress*" (4.19.41). "A *reformado* reformed" (4.19.72), he is convinced that man is a rascal whose only salvation lies in PENAL-TIES. Jovial and hearty (punned on in Aquaviva; cf. aqua vitae), Don Hannibal nevertheless has ideological links with Mortmain through his POLITICAL DISILLUSIONMENT. He is an interesting experiment by Melville in attempting a JOLLY MONOMANIAC.

Don Hannibal's lost limbs give him some physical identity with Ahab, but his spiritual allegiance is more with that curious series of cripples in *The Confidence-Man*: the Negro cripple, the first guise of the confidence man; the misanthropist, a bitter customs officer; and the cripple of the Tombs, who is at first taken for a hero of the Mexican War.

DRUZE, The. See DJALEA

ELDER, The.   2.1–10
A Scottish Presbyterian, one of the original pilgrims, who turns back after his harsh moods make him unwelcome.

The Elder is a dour, argumentative, fire-eating Scottish literalist, representative of SECTARIAN INTOLERANCE. In Rome he had belligerently kept his hat on when the Host went by, and now he is in the Holy Land carrying horse-pistols and wearing a ring of blackthorn (the tree which bears the bitter sloe). At the same time the Elder represents THE MODERN CRITICAL SPIRIT in that he has come to "disenchant" the Holy Land with the field glasses, surveyor's tape, and pruning knife which he carries. This second element is developed more fully in Margoth, a thorough materialist, after the Elder leaves. For a relevant contemporary description of the archaeological "invader" of the Holy Land see the surveyor in Lyman Abbot's "The Recovery of Jerusalem," *Harper's New Monthly Magazine*, XLIII (July, 1871), 195–206.

The Elder may also parody Melville's own Scottish ancestry and family.

GLAUCON.   2.1–13
Rides with the Greek Banker, whose son-in-law he is shortly to become, and returns with him when the pilgrims reach the Wilderness. He is of a wealthy family of Smyrna.

The Smyrniote symbolizes IRRESPONSIBLE AND HAPPY YOUTH, atheistic in attitude if not in belief. His deliberately rakish manner is emphasized by his light songs and his flippant remarks about the Holy Land.

Glaucon could have only an ironical relation to Socrates' friend in *The Republic*, where Melville probably first saw the name. Perhaps he is in part based on "Henry," the "singular young man" in Florence who presented Melville "with a flower, and talked like one to whom the world was delightful. May it prove so." Melville thought "Something good might be written" about "that 'Henry' & the flower-girls" (*Journals*, pp. 115, 495). So came about Glaucon's song to "This flower-girl of Florence" (2.5.54–69). See also the discussion at 2.5.46 for the similarity between Glaucon and another man Melville met on his trip.

[HABBIBI]. 3.27

A Greek monk, long since dead, who once inhabited a bare grotto in Mar Saba. His cell is visited by Derwent and the Lesbian.

The inscriptions on the cell walls indicate that he was a MONOMA-NIAC, obsessed by the terrors of life, the preying of man on man, and of man on himself.

Several of the inscriptions suggest the influence of Dante.

LESBIAN, The. 3.10–4.1

From Mytilene on Lesbos, a purveyor of supplies to Mar Saba, where he mingles with the pilgrims during their stay.

Middle-aged but carefree and happy-go-lucky, the "Islesman's" philosophy is one of "Holding to *now*, swearing by *here*" (3.13.40). His fleecy beard and pink cheeks characterize him as a mellow, "gracioso man" (3.12.133). A "not-of-Sharon Rose" (3.11.161), he is aware of sorrow but finds joy and revelry more than adequate compensation. His MIDDLE-AGED EPICUREANISM and physical friendliness are moderately attractive to Rolfe. He stands midway between the young pleasure-seekers (the Cypriote, Glaucon, the Lyonese) and the meliorist Derwent.

Two passages in the 1856–57 journal (pp. 68–69, 71) suggest his background: a rich description of Mytilene, and a comment on the Greek as a natural dandy.

LYONESE, The.   4.24–28

A gay young French Jew traveling for a Lyons house as a sales-
man of French luxuries. Having been detained at Jaffa, he has run
over to Bethlehem to see its traditionally pretty girls. He occupies a
room with Clarel for one night.

Outwardly the Lyonese represents CARELESS YOUTH, marked by
his gay love songs, and WEALTH, indicated by his emerald ring and
malacca cane. But the point of this character is that he is A PRODIGAL
who not only ignores his Jewish heritage (like the apostate Margoth)
but hides it. Thus he is a temptation to Clarel to deny his own spiritu-
al conflicts, an opposite force to the fiercely ascetic pull of Salvaterra
during the Bethlehem stay. The Lyonese also represents SENSUALITY:
he is introduced by the narrator with a "satyr's chord" (4.25.59) and
stirs Derwent to a rhapsody (4.27) on "the sweet shape" (line 24) of
this beguiling young Bacchus. Clarel is deeply disturbed by his femi-
nine beauty, which the narrator likens to "a Polynesian girl's"
(4.26.249).

*MARGOTH.   1.24; 2.19–3.1

A Jewish geologist whom Clarel sees briefly in Jerusalem and
whom the pilgrims meet, and then discuss, near Quarantania.

Margoth is a savage caricature of SCIENTIFIC MATERIALISM in the
nineteenth century. Short, round-shouldered, and powerfully built,
Margoth's person is not unlike the brutal hammer always in his hand.
For him all is mere geology; there are no mysteries beyond the reach
of the physical senses. He speaks also for the driving COMMERCIALISM
of the age, recommending a telegraph on Olivet and a railroad station
at Gethsemane. He is an announced antagonist not only to "theologic
myth" (2.20.49) but to the whole realm of values that concern the
major pilgrims. Seen first by the Dung Gate in Jerusalem, he reap-
pears descending from the Mount of Temptation with limestone
specimens. He spits out the Jordan water which Nehemiah finds
sweet, refuses to carry a palm leaf but picks a Sodom apple, delights
in refuting biblical prophecy, scrawls notice on a rock that Science
has slanted the Slanted Cross, sees the Dead Sea as merely a geologi-
cal fact. The narrator's impatience with him is once expressed by
three carefully timed brays from the ass (2.33.66–74). Rolfe bears the
burden of the attack on his materialist position, but at parting wryly
wishes him well. Though considerable point is made of his being a

Jew, the narrator states outright that no general criticism of Jews is implied (2.20.16–18); the criticism leveled here is that he is AN APOSTATE (cf. the Lyonese, a "prodigal," or the contrast with Abdon). Margoth's name sums up in a pun his destructive impulses, by the poem's terms.

The character seems a pure fiction based on Melville's long-standing quarrel with dogmatic materialism, positivism, and atheism. Historically Margoth exemplifies the crucial role of geology in the pre-Darwinian assault on supernaturalism, and culminates a long series of such references in Melville's writings.

*MORTMAIN.   2.1–3.32

The dominant dark figure of Parts 2 and 3. A Swede who has served as a revolutionary leader in Paris, Mortmain is now a self-exiled wanderer over "the gray places of the earth" (2.4.130). Arriving in Palestine in time to join the pilgrimage, he makes a ritual descent to the Dead Sea, submits to its spell, and dies of psychic exhaustion at Mar Saba. Mortmain is the second figure of the monomaniac sequence (Celio-Mortmain-Agath-Ungar).

From his first appearance Mortmain is committed by name ("Dead Hand": "so in whim / Some moral wit had christened him," 2.1.188–89) and by symbol (his black skullcap) to SELF-ANNIHILATION. The roots of his personal malaise, running subtle and deep, have flowered into political, philosophical, and religious despair. His youthful commitment to revolutionary goals in 1848 had brought precocious success and the dream of achieving an ideal social Good. But "Experience with her sharper touch / Stung Mortmain" (2.4.60–61): he found his cohorts false, his own theories impractical, the use of force an evil means, and victories so tainted as to need new revolt. By such harsh social insights he has been driven back to a Hobbesian view of human nature: "Man's vicious: snaffle him with kings" (2.3.180). Aware of brutal wrongs and a whole catalogue of refined sins and moral inversions that the law can never reach (2.36), Mortmain has uncovered AN IMPOSSIBLY EVIL WORLD in which the good have but a patch and the rest is divided between malice and ignorance (2.4). In flight from "the cut-throat town" (2.15.77), he is taking "the wild plunge" (2.16.114) back into the deserts from which man sprung (2.15–16). Hence his night vigil at Quarantania, his hymn to the Slanted Cross (2.31), the drinking of the Dead Sea water (2.34), his apostrophe to Sodom and the star called Wormwood (2.36), and the loss of his cap to a gier-eagle (3.25), among other dramatic events. Mortmain had been born out of wedlock to a mother who hated him and a father who gave him money but no love. Yet it is not these primary deprivations, nor the thwarting of his social dreams, the narrator tells us, that have seized him (2.4.131ff.), but something "deeper—deep as nature's mine" (line 136: see the discussion at line 142). The marks of it are fierce outbursts, hissing, burning eyes, nightmares during which he gnaws his hand. Consumed by psychic fury, driven to INTOLERABLE INTROVERSION, Mortmain has no strength left to hold back his own will to self-destruction. Mortmain bewails the loss of faith; though he sees little hope of immortality, at the end he turns to the Palm of Mar Saba and invokes the Holy Spirit (3.28), perhaps "in assent" (3.30.132). His most persistent theological perception has been that Christ's life confirms THE TRAGIC ROLE OF GOODNESS in an evil world.

Mortmain's intense recognition of evil in no way, the narrator makes clear, imputes an evil in him (2.36.116ff.). Only Derwent fails to sense Mortmain's heroic elements, readily wishing to dispose of him as "mad" or "queer" (the last phrase recalling Stubb's favorite word of dismissal, in *Moby-Dick*, for whatever is beyond his grasp). Rolfe and Vine, major sensibilities, are fascinated by Mortmain, and Rolfe especially takes his part. Clarel, faced with such opposite models as Mortmain and Derwent (3.21.49–72), comes to distrust Derwent's "easy skim" far more than "Mortmain's thrust / Into the cloud" (lines 58, 70–71). At the end the narrator gives him a hero's death, with an eagle feather at his lips. Melville's own psychic involvement with Mortmain is suggested in section 8 above.

It would be silly indeed to try to explain Mortmain by citing sources. He belongs with the satanic-heroic figures of Melville's writing that reach from Jackson (*Redburn*) through Ahab to Claggart, though his guiltlessness is unique; he is especially related to Bartleby. He has a prophetic tone which relates him to Elijah (2.34.20; 3.11.228; 3.32.15) and to John the Baptist (2.34.39), and his bastardy and exile make him another of Melville's Ishmael figures, though not so named directly. Mortmain is also an Empedocles figure, and Melville's reading of Arnold's "Empedocles on Etna" in *New Poems* during the composition of *Clarel* must be taken into account (see Bezanson, "Arnold's Poetry," pp. 379–84; and the discussion below at

1.19.29). Mortmain is also comparable to Alphonse de Lamartine, the idealistic French revolutionary of 1848, whom Rolfe once recalls as having had "his fine social dream" smashed by grim Fate (2.16.50–53); if we think of Mortmain as a kind of Swedish Lamartine, then Melville's meeting, on board ship in 1849, with a Swede who one evening got into a "curious discussion" with a Frenchman about Lamartine gives us perhaps the earliest specific of character construction (*Journals*, p. 9). The word *mortmain* is also a law term, indicating perpetual ownership, as by ecclesiastics or corporations; Melville perhaps heard it first from his lawyer-brother Allan.

MYTILENE, The. See The LESBIAN

NATHAN. 1.16–42

An American Gentile Zionist farmer, the father of Ruth, murdered by Arabs beyond the walls of Jerusalem.

Nathan is primarily a case history in AMERICAN DOUBT AND BELIEF (see 1.17, the longest canto of the poem), and only secondarily a representative of ZIONISM. Born in Puritan New Hampshire, Nathan grew to manhood on the plains of Illinois. He passed from his inherited belief in Christian orthodoxy to precocious doubt; found savage nature (his uncle had been buried by the Willey slide in New Hampshire) a confirmation of his disillusionment; was led on further by reading the deists (Paine); reached complete rejection of all orthodoxy; fell into pantheism; was repelled by local sectarianism; and so at last, with his marriage to an American Jewess, Agar, came to the Hebrew faith. As a solution to all his doubts he plunged passionately into Zionism, taking his family back to Jerusalem to reclaim the soil and reestablish Zion's ancient glory. Nathan's "solution" is erratic to the narrator, but his honest early efforts to grapple with doubt evoke three of the most "Melvillean" lines of the poem (1.17.193–95).

Nathan's tortuous history is an epitome of American experience, but the Zionist phase Melville drew from the numerous zealots he met or heard of in the East, as recorded in his 1856–57 journal. He noted, for example, "Warder Crisson of Philadelphia—An American turned Jew—divorced from former wife—married a Jewess &c—Sad" (*Journals*, p. 85; see p. 442 for Abigail Ruth, their daughter). The account of Deacon Dickson of Massachusetts (pp. 93–94) shows Melville's mixed curiosity and pity; Dickson was wounded, and his son-in-law killed, in an Arab uprising of 1858 (see *Journals*, p. 442). For an account of the early Zionist movement by a contemporary see Wylie's *The Modern Judea* (cited in footnote 9 above), pp. 533–45. Melville thought the nineteenth-century Zionist movement "preposterous" and "half melancholy, half farcical" (*Journals*, p. 94).

*NEHEMIAH.   1.7–2.39

The aged American millennialist who befriends Clarel in Jerusalem, introduces him to Ruth, joins the pilgrimage at Clarel's expense, and drowns in the Dead Sea.

Nehemiah is the only major pilgrim committed to that NARROW SECTARIAN ORTHODOXY of which Clarel has recently been dispossessed. AN EVANGELICAL and MILLENARIAN, his prime symbol is the open Bible he always carries and which is buried with him, and the tracts on the Second Coming and the New Jerusalem which he dispenses at random. A series of incidents portray his imperviousness to doubt: clearing away stones in the rock-strewn wilderness, drinking the muddy waters of the Jordan and pronouncing them sweet as sugar, chanting the Twenty-third Psalm as the pilgrims ride through vile Dead Sea fogs, falling gently asleep beneath an ominous crag, and finally sleepwalking to his death in the Dead Sea in pursuit of a vision of the New Jerusalem. In his charity, good will, cheer, and meekness (symbolized by the Ass he rides) he is an epitome of cardinal NEW TESTAMENT VIRTUES. His childlike innocence and erratic ways mark him as a SANTON or Holy Man to the Mohammedans (1.8.71).

The narrator at first seems tempted to develop Nehemiah toward monomania, stressing his individualism, his hidden woe (1.22), and his recognition of himself as "The chief of sinners" (2.24.84). Rolfe's early analogy between Nehemiah and the heroic, ill-fated mariner (1.37), however, is replaced by Clarel's later account of a story Nehemiah told him of a harmless, witless solitary and carpenter (3.2). In the interim the poem has unfolded the more powerful characters of Rolfe, Vine, and Mortmain, in deference to whom Nehemiah's potentialities have dwindled. In the end Clarel, who began the pilgrimage riding beside Nehemiah, joins the narrator in seeing him as a sweet and good old man, given over to illusion, a figure of pathos rather than tragedy. His world of visions is a fairyland. His history evokes mainly compassion, his death is that of a friend but not a mentor.

The general historical background for Nehemiah is the millennial movement which culminated in America in the 1840's, discussed in Ralph H. Gabriel's *The Course of American Democratic Thought* (New York: Ronald Press, 1940), pp. 34–37, and in Ernest Tuveson, *Redeemer Nation: The Idea of America's Millennial Role* (Chicago: University of Chicago Press, 1968). An example of those who went to the Holy Land "so as to be on the spot" for the Second Coming was the American consul-general of Syria and Palestine whom Thackeray reported in *Notes of a Journey from Cornhill to Grand Cairo* (cited in footnote 10 above), pp. 184–236. Melville mentions in his 1856–57 journal the actual prototype for Nehemiah, seen in Jerusalem: "The old Connecticut man wandering about with tracts &c—knew not the language—hopelessness of it—his lonely batchelor rooms—he maintained that the expression 'Oh Jerusalem!' was an argument proving that Jerusalem was a byeword &c" (*Journals*, p. 85). From another American traveler, William C. Prime, in his *Tent Life in the Holy Land* (New York: Harper, 1857), p. 317, we learn that Melville's "old Connecticut man" was a Mr. Roberts: "An old gentleman, Mr. Roberts, an American, who has taken up his residence in Jerusalem. . . . He is a New Englander . . . distributing the Bible, in the languages of the countries he visits, of which he knows nothing himself. It may seem a sort of monomania. Perhaps it is. But I commend him to all travelers as a good, noble old man, who is content to die at Jerusalem in this work to which he has sacrificed himself." And finally, the Mr. Dickson who may have contributed to Nathan's Zionism is perhaps relevant here: "Mr Wood saw Mr Dickson going about Jerusalem with open Bible, looking for the opening asunder of Mount Olivet and the preparing of the highway for the Jews. &c" (*Journals*, p. 94; cf. *Clarel*, 1.11.89); Dickson was "a thorough Yankee, about 60, with long oriental beard, blue Yankee coat, & Shaker waistcoat" (*Journals*, p. 93; cf. the coat Nehemiah had brought from home, "Ashen in shade, by rustics wrought," 1.8.62ff.). The biblical Nehemiah, rebuilder of the walls of Jerusalem, is perhaps an ironic prototype.

*ROLFE. 1.31–4.32

A roving American adventurer whom Clarel and Nehemiah meet on the slopes of Olivet soon after encountering Vine. The central figure among Clarel's companions on the pilgrimage.

Rolfe is an experienced world-traveler, mariner, and intellectual who quickly assumes leadership among the pilgrims. The best-rounded temperament of the group, he represents an ideal UNION OF HEAD AND HEART. His ranging mind, general literacy, and speculative gifts are balanced by a personal warmth that ranges from jocularity to compassion. Rolfe is an ardent DEFENDER OF HUMANISTIC AND RELIGIOUS VALUES. As a social critic and moral philosopher he is as unafraid of attacking convention as he is anxious to establish fundamental values. His religious views are tolerant and nonsectarian, but he feels deeply the acute spiritual and institutional crisis of his time. More than any other pilgrim he brings to bear on the events and problems of the pilgrimage A KNOWLEDGE OF THE PAST, an intense but not uncritical respect for the ancient world. Exponent of the two great heritages of Western civilization, the Hellenic and Hebraic worlds of value, he is especially fascinated by analogies and distinctions between them. Rolfe is SEEKER AND SKEPTIC COMBINED; willing enough to consider new experience, earnest in pursuit of understanding, he has a jaundiced eye for all claims that any one person, creed, or society has final answers. He leans toward the monomaniacs (Mortmain, Agath, and Ungar) and away from the varied assurances of a Nehemiah, a Margoth, or a Derwent. In the long run Rolfe is sure only that God exists, that good and evil are tightly braided together, that the world is undecipherable and will remain so, and that the tragic view is the only tenable one. Believing that people are as they are made, and do what they have to do, his final standard for judging men is not creed but serious "selfhood" (2.22.103).

Rolfe is admired and respected equally by pilgrims and guides. His versatile probings alternately bewilder and extend Clarel; in the last analysis it is Rolfe who is his prime mentor and goad. Rolfe's "wizard chord / And forks of esoteric fire" (2.32.97–98), his Adam-like naturalness and candor (3.16.181), and his display of "a mind / Poised at self-center and mature" (4.3.124–25)—such traits finally bring Clarel to acknowledge Rolfe as "my lord" (4.3.128). The narrator goes boldly beyond this: in a cryptic interlude (1.32) he gives gnomic hints that Rolfe is like the Indian hero-god, Rama, who without knowing it was one of the incarnations of Vishnu. For Rolfe's autobiographical implications see section 8 above.

RUTH.   1.16–39; 4.30; and *passim*

Clarel's sweetheart, the daughter of Nathan and Agar, whom he meets in Jerusalem through Nehemiah. After the murder of Nathan the house is closed to Clarel; while he is on pilgrimage, Ruth dies of grief.

Less a person than a symbol of VESTAL LOVE, Ruth wears a snowy robe, keeps her tresses veiled. To Clarel she is all innocence and beauty, a dream of Eden before the Fall, and an illusory hope of release from the complex passion.

Ruth is best understood in terms of Yillah (*Mardi*) and Lucy (*Pierre*), both of whom she resembles. She provides another instance of Melville's failure to write about heterosexual love, except allegorically.

SALVATERRA.   4.13–16

Franciscan guide at the Latin Church of the Star in Bethlehem, who came from the Arno Valley in Tuscany to be near Christ's birthplace.

The coarse gown, hood, and rope-and-cross about the waist are the symbols of his order. They also express the INTENSE FERVOR of his devotion, which has so wasted his body that the narrator suggests it has been "bought too dear" (4.13.159). He is given to proselytizing, as his name suggests, and his ardent asceticism (less serene than that of the Celibate) creates such tension in Clarel that in a dream Salvaterra and the Lyonese appear in opposition (4.26.305–7).

Perhaps he is a projection of the Latin monk, *Journals*, p. 84, whom Melville merely mentions as guide at the church. (See also the HISTORICAL SUPPLEMENT, pp. 669–70, for another source.)

SMYRNIOTE, The. See GLAUCON

SPAHI, The. See BELEX

SYRIAN MONK, The.   2.18–19

An anonymous young anchorite whom the pilgrims meet on a slope near Quarantania, where he is undergoing a forty-day reenactment of Christ's temptation.

His ASCETICISM is symbolized by his thin and wasted body, his ragged robe pinned with a thorn, and the hair girdle tightly drawn about his hollow waist. The VIOLENCE OF SPIRITUAL CONFLICT is indicated by his squeezing a stone until blood oozed from his nails, during his lonely vision of Christ and the Devil on the Mount. The dramatic opposition of the Syrian reascending Quarantania to endure his temptation, while Margoth comes down with specimens of Jura limestone, is not lost on Clarel (2.19.92–94).

For Melville's comments in his 1856–57 journal on Quarantania, the germ of this fictional character, see the discussion at 2.14.56.

TIMONEER, The. See AGATH

*UNGAR.   4.1–28
The dominant dark figure of Part 4. An ex-officer of the Southern Confederacy, self-exiled after defeat, this part-Indian American has come to the Middle East to perform miscellaneous military services for the Egyptians and Turks, and so turns up at Mar Saba. He rides with the pilgrims to Bethlehem, then leaves. Ungar is the final phase of the monomaniac sequence (Celio-Mortmain-Agath-Ungar).

The sign of this VETERAN OF PAIN AND DEFEAT is a livid sabre-scar on his neck and a blue powder-burn (which links him to Agath) on his temple. Memories of fratricidal strife, of unhoused chimneys among ruins, of the rottenness of Reconstruction, still make him smart and bring blood to his thin-skinned scar. Ungar is also a merciless critic of democratic America, lamenting its spiritual collapse, its capitulation to speed and demagogy, materialism and ignorance. Thus democracy, "Arch strumpet of an impious age" and "Harlot on horseback" (4.19.138, 135), will glut and barbarize the people until a new Thirty Years War brings the Dark Ages of democracy (4.19–21). Ungar's Mortmain-like conviction of the fact of the fall of man (4.22) has in him a new dimension: THE FALL OF THE NEW WORLD itself, the debasement of the last Eden. Descended partly from an Anglo-Catholic family of early Maryland, Ungar is no longer committed to any one church or creed (4.10.179–83), holding simply to God's sure existence, man's evil, and the need for religion. He is unable to sustain his flickering vision of Christ's efficacy, feeling the tragedy (scarce hope) of Christ's death (4.10.34–48). His sensibility is profoundly religious, however, as the ascetic monk Salvaterra points out: "True sign you bear: your sword's a cross" (4.14.21), and the narrator has him ride a "cloistral beast" (4.1.72). The other part of

Ungar's heritage and temperament is Indian. His ancestor's marriage to an Indian girl accounts for his "forest name," his lithe body, copper-hued skin, high cheekbones, long black hair, and "forest eyes" (4.5.142, 3). This wild strain in Ungar gives special quality to him as a symbol of STOIC ENDURANCE IN DEFEAT. A professional soldier and moral warrior, he takes his leave of the pilgrims with the look of a man "enlisted for sad fight / Upon some desperate dark shore" (4.28.12–13).

Ungar ranks very high. Rolfe clearly sees the contrast between his somber, veteran strength and the martial splendor of the giant Arnaut (4.17.55–72). Derwent of course is in constant opposition to Ungar, as he had been to Mortmain. Clarel finds Ungar difficult—so "strange" and "wild" in his suffering that he cannot yet cope with his meaning (4.17.48–51). But the narrator has utmost respect for his "slouched reserve of strength" and the world of muted reveries that lurk in his brown eyes (4.1.82, 94). For his autobiographical implications, see section 8 above.

Ungar, a significant projection from the contemporary American scene, is very close to Melville's own sensibility. "A wandering Ishmael from the West" (4.10.186), he is Melville's last important portrait of his central fictional type.

*VINE.   1.28–4.32

A middle-aged American of high but anonymous talents whom Clarel and Nehemiah meet at the Sepulcher of Kings in Jerusalem. He becomes a major figure of the pilgrimage.

Vine is a powerful but ambiguous influence in the poem. His past history is curiously denied the reader (1.29.3–4). Perhaps more than anything else he symbolizes THE POWER AND MYSTERY OF GENIUS. For a special aura surrounds this man of undefined "gifts unique" (1.29.6) from the moment of his discovery meditating on the friezes of the Sepulcher of Kings (1.28) until the end of the journey when Clarel parts from him with an undefined "new sense" of his meaning (4.32.11). His aesthetic sensibility—he is apparently some kind of painter or writer—is rich and devious. A devotee of the beautiful, but with a keen moral sense, he is little given to intellectual argument or abstract discussion. Vine's self-isolation is surpassed only by the Druze's; it flowers into a personal grace that marks him a natural (not social) aristocrat. Absorbed with the past and watchfully brooding over the other pilgrims, Vine is from the first "The Recluse" (1.29), and to the end remains "a fountain sealed" (2.17.22). The shadowy temper of the man is lightened from time to time by rays of caprice, but he is not genuinely communicative and his motives remain hidden. Vine is a model of THE INWARDNESS OF THE MORAL-AESTHETIC WORLD.

Rolfe is the only other pilgrim of comparable stature by the poem's terms, and Clarel sees at once that they are "peers" (1.31.42). Yet the Rolfe-Vine relationship is most intricate, and Clarel's attempt to possess Vine ends in rebuff (2.27) and an astonishing discovery of hidden weakness in him (3.7). The complexities of Vine's character, and their possible relation to the Melville-Hawthorne friendship, are suggested in section 8 above. See also the discussion at 1.30.112.

The biblical connotations roused by Vine's name are rich. One main line is the idea of self-sufficiency suggested in the Old Testament: "But they shall sit every man under his vine and under his fig tree; and none shall make them afraid . . ." (Micah 4.4, also 1 Kings 4.25); the second is the more mystical concept of salvation in the New Testament: "I am the true vine . . ." (John 15.1 and *passim*).

SOURCES

R EFERENCES TO DATES, events, and documents that are not otherwise documented in this NOTE have been drawn mainly from original manuscripts but may be located conveniently in the following printed sources: *The Letters of Herman Melville*, ed. Merrell R. Davis and William H. Gilman (New Haven: Yale University Press, 1960), of which a revised and augmented edition will appear as *Correspondence*, Volume 14 of the Northwestern-Newberry Edition of *The Writings of Herman Melville;* Jay Leyda, *The Melville Log* (New York: Harcourt Brace, 1951; enl. ed., New York: Gordian Press, 1969), a revised edition of which, titled *The New Melville Log,* edited by Jay Leyda and Hershel Parker, is forthcoming from Gordian Press; Merton M. Sealts, Jr., *Melville's Reading: A Check-List of Books Owned and Borrowed* (Madison: University of Wisconsin Press, 1966; rev. and enl. ed., Columbia: University of South Carolina Press, 1988)— cited as "Sealts" and followed by a reference number; Mary K. Bercaw, *Melville's Sources* (Evanston: Northwestern University Press, 1987)—cited as "Bercaw" and followed by a reference number; Wilson Walker Cowen, *Melville's Marginalia* (Ph.D. dissertation, Harvard, 1965; New York: Garland, 1988); Brian Higgins, *Herman Melville: An Annotated Bibliography, . . . 1846–1930* and *Herman Melville: A Reference Guide, 1931–1960* (New York: G. K. Hall, 1979, 1987). All documents are quoted *literatim;* any variation between a document as transcribed in these sources and as printed in this NOTE is based on an examination of the original. Quotations from Melville's works (and page references cited) follow the already published or forthcoming Northwestern-Newberry texts. In this NOTE all quotations from reviews are drawn from the original magazine and newspaper printings.

The following twentieth-century books and articles are cited in the NOTE without full bibliographical information: Newton Arvin, "Melville's Shorter Poems," *Partisan Review*, XVI (October, 1949), 1034–46; Arvin, *Herman Melville* (New York: William Sloane Associates, 1950), pp. 269–78, 283–87; W. H. Auden, *The Enchafèd Flood: or, The Romantic Iconography of the Sea* (New York: Random House, 1950); Laurence W. Barrett, "The Differences in Melville's Poetry," *PMLA*, LXX (September, 1955), 606–23; Walter E. Bezanson, "Herman Melville's *Clarel*" (Ph.D. dissertation, Yale University, 1943); Bezanson, "Melville's Reading of Arnold's Poetry," *PMLA*, LXIX (June, 1954), 365–91; William Braswell, *Melville's Religious Thought: An Essay in Interpretation* (Durham, N.C.: Duke University Press, 1943), pp. 109–22; Richard Chase, *Herman Melville: A Critical Study* (New York: Macmillan, 1949); John Freeman, *Herman Melville* (New York: Macmillan, 1926), pp. 166–69; William H. Gilman, *Melville's Early Life and REDBURN* (New York: New York University Press, 1951); Harrison Hayford, "Melville and Hawthorne: A Biographical and Critical Study" (Ph.D. dissertation, Yale University, 1945); Leon Howard, *Herman Melville: A Biography* (Berkeley and Los Angeles: University of California Press, 1951), pp. 297–309; R. W. B. Lewis, *The American Adam* (Chicago: University of Chicago Press, 1955); Ronald Mason, *The Spirit above the Dust: A Study of Herman Melville* (London: John Lehmann, 1951); Frank Jewett Mather, Jr., "Herman Melville," *The Review*, I (August, 1919), 276–78, 298–301; F. O. Matthiessen, *American Renaissance* (New York: Oxford University Press, 1941); Lewis Mumford, *Herman Melville* (New York:

Harcourt, Brace, 1929), pp. 307–25; John Middleton Murry, review of the Constable edition of *Clarel,* in the *New York Times Book Review* (August 10, 1924), p. 7; V. L. Parrington, *Main Currents in American Thought* (New York: Harcourt, Brace, 1927), II, 266–67; Merton M. Sealts, Jr., *The Early Lives of Melville* (Madison: University of Wisconsin Press, 1974); William Ellery Sedgwick, *Herman Melville: The Tragedy of Mind* (Cambridge: Harvard University Press, 1944), pp. 198–230; Jean Simon, *Herman Melville: Marin, Métaphysicien, et Poète* (Paris: Boivin, 1939), pp. 467–90; K. H. Sundermann, *Herman Melvilles Gedankengut: Eine kritische Untersuchung seiner weltanschaulichen Grundideen* (Berlin: Collignon, 1937), pp. 37–57; Willard Thorp, *Herman Melville: Representative Selections, with Introduction, Bibliography, and Notes* (New York: American Book Co., 1938), pp. lxxxviii–xciii; Howard P. Vincent, *The Trying-Out of MOBY-DICK* (Boston: Houghton Mifflin, 1949); Robert Penn Warren, "Melville the Poet," *Kenyon Review,* VIII (1946), 208–23; Raymond M. Weaver, *Herman Melville: Mariner and Mystic* (New York: Doran, 1921), pp. 357–65; Henry W. Wells, *The American Way of Poetry* (New York: Columbia University Press, 1943), pp. 78–88; Nathalia Wright, "A Source for Melville's *Clarel*: Dean Stanley's *Sinai and Palestine,*" *MLN,* LXII (February, 1947), 110–16; Wright, *Melville's Use of the Bible* (Durham, N.C.: Duke University Press, 1949).

Melville's March 27, 1879, authorization to pulp 220 sets (of probably about 350 printed) of *Clarel* (see p. 659 below). Courtesy of Bernard Quaritch, Ltd.

Historical Supplement

THE FOLLOWING HISTORICAL SUPPLEMENT, by Hershel Parker, is a series of entries which update the historical aspects of Bezanson's HISTORICAL AND CRITICAL NOTE and amplify certain topics; they are keyed to it by page and a quoted sentence or phrase; their full documentation is supplied on pp. 670–73 below.

p. 505   *Clarel* has suffered . . . from undeserved oblivion.

Until the publication of the present edition, recognition of *Clarel* was still being retarded by the difficulty of laying hands on a copy of it outside a library. Two-thirds (it seems) of its first printing was pulped (see facing page), and at the time of the Melville revival it was "practically impossible to come by" (Weaver 1921, p. 360). Its first reprinting was in 1924 in the sixteen-volume Constable Edition, but by midcentury that set rarely came up for sale in the United States (a few copies of the poem, in two volumes, were remaindered separately in the mid 1940's). Inclusion in the Hendricks House Edition in 1960 did not guarantee that *Clarel* was readily available in the following decades, and the only other edition published in this period was available only as part of a set, the 1963 Russell & Russell or the 1983 Japanese reprint of the Constable Edition. In the 1960's the original

639

1876 two-volume edition could still be purchased as a costly rare book, but since then it has become virtually unobtainable (a 1970 census reports only thirty-four copies of the first edition in libraries [Johnson 1970]). Appearance of selections from *Clarel* in a few anthologies did little to increase the number of its readers. In the first edition of the widely used classroom *Norton Anthology of American Literature* (1979) Hershel Parker offered thirty-six pages of annotated excerpts, but teachers who answered the publisher's questionnaires overwhelmingly recommended dropping the section, and nothing from *Clarel* has appeared in later editions (see also Cohen 1964 and Warren 1970).

Like other readers, poets have been slow to devote attention to *Clarel*. A notable exception is Robert Penn Warren, whose judgment became increasingly sympathetic in the course of two articles on Melville's poetry (1946—cited on p. 637 above; 1967) and of his introduction and notes to the seventy pages of excerpts from *Clarel* in his *Selected Poems of Herman Melville: A Reader's Edition* (1970). Another poet's recognition of Melville's achievement is dramatically attested by Richard L. Blevins (1989): "I was an undergraduate at Kent State in 1972, the night that Ed Dorn declared from his instructor's seat that the great unread *Clarel* will prove, in this century, to be The Great American Poem. . . . In [Dorn's 1968–69] *Gunslinger*, Clarel's frustrated search across the Holy Land for significant form, for confirmation of the miracle of personal faith in the nineteenth century, is recast for a postmodern audience as the Slinger's eyes-wide-open (even dilated by hallucinogens) New World *trip* (pun intended) to Las Vegas. We note that the desert outside of Jerusalem has become Four Corners, USA."

p. 508   the East was the dream of a child . . . Redburn.

Melville's older brother Gansevoort around 1839 took careful notes on an anonymous two-volume work published by Harper & Brothers in 1837 (with a new edition the same year and numerous reprintings), *Incidents of Travel in Egypt, Arabia Petræa, and the Holy Land*; its author was John Lloyd Stephens, who became one of the most popular American travel writers. Stephens was—or suggested—the unidentified big-eyed "person who had been in Stony Arabia," whom as a child Melville's Redburn saw in church, whose book he had read, and who haunted Redburn's memory and dreams

(*Redburn*, chap. 1, pp. 5–6; Stephens [1838 ff.], chap. 15, I, 199–200). The real Stephens was not famished for food but exceedingly thirsty. He and his companions rushed toward "a single palm-tree" not because it bore dates but because they knew it shaded a fountain. In *Redburn* the boy takes his aunt's tall tale literally.

p. 509 Family records . . . make clear Melville's distress in the five years before his Mediterranean voyage.

Deeper knowledge of the 1850–56 period in Melville's life (both the maturation and the disquietude, in Bezanson's phrasing) has emerged from study of documents discovered since 1960 (see the accounts in the HISTORICAL NOTES to *Moby-Dick*, *The Piazza Tales*, and *The Confidence-Man*). In July of 1850 Melville broke off work on his whaling manuscript to vacation in a memory-fraught region, the Berkshires, where he stayed at what a cousin called his "first love," the farm where he had visited his uncle Thomas Melvill in his youth (Parker in *Moby-Dick*, pp. 610–11). After meeting Nathaniel Hawthorne (who was renting a cottage a few miles away, outside Lenox), he wrote an essay for the New York *Literary World*, "Hawthorne and His Mosses," which contained an oblique but rapturous exposition of his secret thought that he might in his whaling book approach the greatness of the unapproachable Shakespeare. Both men were strongly drawn to each other, and the shy Hawthorne took the extraordinary measure of inviting the younger writer to visit him and his family for a few days before returning to New York. As the weeks of late summer passed, Melville surrendered to the idea that he could make his book as great as he hoped if he could remain there, inspired by the splendor of the Berkshires and the proximity of the only American writer he could count as his equal. His father-in-law, Lemuel Shaw (Chief Justice of the Massachusetts Supreme Court), advanced him the money to purchase a farm adjoining the old Melvill place, to which in early October he moved with his wife and year-and-a-half-old son Malcolm, his mother, and three of his sisters.

With the move to Pittsfield came, as Bezanson says, the immense surrender to the Whale—a surrender made at the cost of unforeseen tensions in the new household, where Melville, the only man, imperfectly met the diverse social and emotional needs of the women (NYPL-GL); into his manuscript he worked at some time during the next year his conviction that a happy domestic life ("the wife, the heart, the bed, the table, the saddle, the fire-side, the country" [chap. 94, p. 416]) was incompatible with the highest life of the intellect and the imagination. During the last months of the writing, confident that the greatness of his achievement would be matched by its popularity, Melville borrowed $2,050 from his old friend T. D. Stewart, binding himself to pay $92.25 in interest each November and May then to repay the principal in five years. His second son, Stanwix, was born in October, 1851, the month *The Whale* was published in London, the month before it appeared in New York as *Moby-Dick*. But the book proved less than the great success he had expected it to be, and the Harpers offered him a much less profitable contract for his new book, *Pierre*. Melville recklessly began to write his frustrations with his career into the already contracted-for manuscript (after his additions it ran some 160 pages longer than the original estimate) and failed to sell the engorged book in England (Parker in *Moby-Dick*, pp. 660, 689ff.). In May he missed an interest payment on his loan; thereafter until 1856 he defaulted every time an interest payment was due.

In the summer and fall of 1852 the Melvilles, Shaws, and Gansevoorts endured the public denunciations of *Pierre* in reviews and news items for its depiction of unnatural domestic relationships in an equally unnatural style (see *Pierre*, pp. 300ff.). It may be that some members of the family endured private shame as well, for a recently published family letter has been taken to mean that Melville himself, like Pierre, had an illegitimate half-sister—that Melville, like Pierre, had dropped his angle into the well of childhood and drawn up uncatalogued fishes (Emmers 1978; Murray, Myerson, and Taylor 1985; Young 1987). In any case, with the disastrous reception of *Pierre* Melville entered, as Bezanson says, the whirlpool. By Thanksgiving, when the reviews had run their course, Melville was a man who had brought shame upon his family rather than the fame they had at first rejoiced in.

Just before *Pierre* was published Melville heard the story of a long-suffering Nantucket woman, Agatha Hatch (Parker, "*The Isle of the Cross*," 1990). Shortly thereafter he offered the details of her story to Hawthorne, who had by then moved to Concord. The notes Hawthorne took during a vacation at the Isles of Shoals suggest that he was thinking about the project, but his attention was diverted by the election of his classmate Franklin Pierce as president of the United States and the certainty that he would receive a lucrative foreign appointment. In December of 1852 Melville discussed the story with Hawthorne at Concord, and afterwards resolved to write it himself. By early 1853 Melville's mother was determined to gain for him a foreign consulship such as Hawthorne had been awarded, and when Melville's brother Allan and his father-in-law coordinated a wire-pulling campaign, the older romancer did his best to assist their efforts (Hayford and Davis 1949; NYPL-GL). In June Melville faced a double shame—the failure to gain a political appointment and the failure to get into print *The Isle of the Cross*, the book he had completed in late May, about the day his first daughter, Bessie, was born. Somehow "prevented" from publishing it, that summer Melville resolutely turned to the composition of short pieces for *Harper's New Monthly Magazine* and *Putnam's Monthly Magazine*, surer markets than he could gain for his books.

When his earnings still proved insufficient for the needs of the family, his mother early in 1854 urged him to go the rounds of the lecture halls (see pp. 644–45 below). Instead, he persisted in writing and farming (although his body soon began to manifest the emotional sufferings he was enduring), and the money he earned from his magazine pieces and the serialized *Israel Potter* (published as a book in March, 1855, just after the birth of his fourth child, Fanny) staved off the utter collapse of his career until 1856, when (about the time of the appearance in book form of his *Putnam's* pieces as *The Piazza Tales*) he had to confess to his father-in-law his desperate straits (Barber 1977). He was an exhausted man, damaged in physique and psyche, now with a wife and four children, pressed hard by a creditor who was about to force the sale of the farm, and worried about being a year late with an interest payment to John M. Brewster, the previous owner of the farm. In a complicated benefaction, Shaw helped rescue Melville from his financial crisis in 1856. It was also Shaw's money that paid for Melville's trip to the Levant in 1856–57. Melville's *The Confidence-Man*, finished before he sailed and published in New York and London in April, 1857, earned him not a penny in either country.

p. 511   [Melville informed Hawthorne] that he had "pretty much made up his mind to be annihilated."

That Melville was telling Hawthorne of his loss of faith in immortality (not his foreseeing secular destruction) is suggested by Hawthorne's word "futurity" and his final comment that Melville's noble nature makes him "better worth immortality than most of us." But beyond that, Hawthorne, steeped like Melville in Milton, may have heard a Miltonic echo in Melville's remark; in his recently discovered copy of Milton's *Poetical Works* (see p. 646n. below) Melville checked the passage in Book VI of *Paradise Lost* where Milton explains that spirits like Satan cannot be killed piecemeal—"Vital in every part," they "Cannot but by annihilating die." There was still a defiant edge to Melville's resignation.

p. 524   He decided not to write at all but to try for a place in the New York Customs.

Soon after Melville's return to the United States in late May of 1857 his young brother-in-law Lemuel Shaw, Jr., quoted him as saying that he wished "to get a place in the N. Y. Custom House" and that he was "not going to write any more at present" (*Log*, II, 580). Melville seems to have involved himself in the office-seeking even less than in 1853, and the campaign fizzled out in late June, about the time he began advertising the farm for sale. Yet Melville seems to have had some reason for high hopes in July, still, while the farm remained unsold, for in that month he signed a contract to purchase a house in Brooklyn, and he waited until August before canceling the agreement (Barber 1973).

One alternative to writing had been on Melville's mother's mind for years. In February of 1854 she investigated the lyceum scene in Lawrence and then wrote Melville's sister Augusta at Arrowhead, with "this message to Herman":

> That *one Lecture* prepared by himself can be repeated seventy times with success. That Mr Saxe has done so, that all the lecturers *now* prepare one lecture & travel the rounds with this one for the whole season, are feasted made much of, & seldom less than fifty dollars are given to the lecturer. Many places double that, at Lawrence $25. are given[.] Robert Winthrop, Oliver W. Holmes, Mr Giles are not too big to receive even this comparatively small sum. Josiah Quincey lectured last week, & Mr Giles this week at Lawrence. This is the present style of enlightening the many who have no time to devote to reading & research—
>
> & now my dear darling Herman all your friends, relatives & admirers, say that you are the very man to carry an audience, to create a sensation, to do wonders, to close this subject I will only request you to think over this *not* new subject, when in a happy hopeful state of

mind, and there is a chance of your coming to the wise conclusion, to do that thing, which at once, and by the same agreeable act, will bring us fame & fortune. (NYPL-GL)

Whether or not sharing in his mother's early optimism, Melville decided during the summer of 1857 to go on the lecture circuit (see pp. 528–29 above). But public performance was frustrating, for the man who had been called incomparable in dramatic storytelling proved now to be incapable, at times, of making himself heard throughout a hall, and incapable, all too often, of holding the attention of his auditors (Sealts in *Piazza Tales*, pp. 516ff.).

p. 524 Failing . . . to win appointment . . . , he began a series of shifts which . . . marked the end of the Pittsfield era.

After Lincoln's inauguration Melville hoped to obtain the consulship at Florence. He was in Washington, pulling the few political strings he could grasp, when news came that his father-in-law was dying. In the aftermath of Judge Shaw's death the Melvilles spent the winter of 1861–62 in New York City and the winter of 1862–63 in a rented house in the village of Pittsfield, then late in 1863 went back to New York City.

p. 525 The record shows at least seventy-five book titles . . . Melville bought or borrowed during these two decades.

By 1990 the record shows almost two hundred book titles which Melville bought or borrowed in the 1860's and 1870's (see Sealts 1988 and 1990). In the present printing of his essay Bezanson adds Dante and Milton to the list of writers he named in 1960; copies of their works owned and marked by Melville have recently surfaced (see p. 646 below). (For Camões, listed by Bezanson, see also Monteiro 1978 and Andrews 1989; Bercaw 111, 112.) Melville also knew the poems of Ossian long before he wrote *Clarel* (Sealts 343, Bercaw 467).

As Bezanson says (p. 526), Melville read in part for companionship, and he was rewarded by finding allies, such as William Hazlitt. In the recently discovered copy (see below) of *Lectures on the English Comic Writers and Lectures on the English Poets* that he purchased in March, 1862, Melville wrote the comment:

I am rejoiced to see Hazlitt speak for Ossian. There is nothing more contemptable in that contemptable man (tho' good poet, in his department) Wordsworth, than his contempt for Ossian. And nothing that more raises my idea of Napoleon than his great admiration of him.—The loneliness of the spirit of Ossian harmonized with the loneliness of the greatness of Napoleon.

Melville had read Ossian attentively enough to underline Hazlitt's "he is even without God in the world" and write: "True: no gods, I think, are mentioned in Ossian."

Bezanson also says acutely that Melville sat down among his books as among friends; but sometimes, as when he read Wordsworth, he sat down as with an acquaintance to be kept at arm's length.

p. 527   Melville's marginalia . . . reveal him in the double role of critic and apprentice to the craft of poetry.

The discovery since 1960 of Melville's copies of Milton, Vasari, Dante, Wordsworth, and Hazlitt* reminds us that our sense of Melville's reading is greatly contingent on the books he owned which happen to have been preserved and studied (see Sealts 1988, pp. 111–23). Melville's marginalia in these books show that the relation between subject and style in narrative verse was high among his aesthetic concerns. In an undated marginal comment in his copy of Milton which he acquired in 1849 and carried on the *Meteor* in 1860 Melville argued with the poet over Jesus' dismissal of Greek learning in Book IV of *Paradise Regained*:

> This comes rather unhandsomely from Milton, disparaging the Greeks thus in compliment to the Jews:—especially as he himself was so Greek in spirit & so much indebted to the Greek genius. Milton got nothing from the Jews but a subject; but from the Greeks he got *style*—sublimity—inspiration—melody.

*Milton: *Poetical Works* (Boston: Hilliard & Gray, 1836); Sealts 358b; Sotheby's Auction Catalogue No. 5927, November 9–10, 1989, Lot 182; Hayford and Horth in *Moby-Dick* pp. 957–59. Vasari: *Lives* (London: Bohn, 1849–52); Sealts 534a; Whitburn 1988; Sotheby's Auction Catalogue No. 5729, June 7, 1988, Lot 158. Dante: *The Vision: or, Hell, Purgatory, and Paradise*, trans. Cary (London: Bohn, 1847); Sealts 174; *Melville Society Extracts*, No. 63 (September, 1985), 10–12, and No. 64 (November, 1985), 10; Sotheby's Auction Catalogue No. 5927, November 9–10, 1989, Lot 181. Wordsworth: *Complete Poetical Works*, ed. Reed (Philadelphia: James Kay, Jun. and Brother; Boston: Munroe; Pittsburgh: Kay, 1839); Sealts 563a; Heffernan 1977. Hazlitt: *Lectures on the English Comic Writers . . . Lectures on the English Poets* (New York: Derby & Jackson, 1859); Sealts 263b (see also Sealts 1990); Sotheby's Auction Catalogue No. 5880, June 27, 1989, Lot 67.

In his five-volume set of Vasari's *Lives of the Most Eminent Painters, Sculptors, and Architects*, purchased in March, 1862, he jotted down guiding principles for the artist who would achieve greatness:

> Attain the highest result.—
>   A quality of Grasp.—
> The habitual choice of noble subjects.—
>   The Expression.—
> Get in as much as you can.—
>   Finish is completeness, fulness,
> not polish.—
> Greatness is a matter of scale.—
>   Clearness & firmness.—
> The greatest number of the greatest ideas.—

Among contemporary poets, Bezanson shows, Matthew Arnold was important to Melville during the composition of *Clarel* (see p. 527 above), and Melville may have encountered various writings by Arnold in periodicals, such as the New York *Every Saturday*, which in 1867–68 printed essays later collected in *Culture and Anarchy* (Dettlaff 1978; see also Cannon 1976). But others may have been equally important. He may already have known Whitman's poetry well (as he certainly did later on—see p. 656 below), and he may have known more of Robert Browning's work than has yet been established (see p. 622 above, Shurr 1972, pp. 71–73, and Baker 1980). He would have seen "The Duke's Interview with the Envoy" (i.e., "My Last Duchess") in the September 8, 1849, *Literary World;* the heavy-handed introduction (by Thomas Powell) commented: "The genius of Browning is as peculiar and *provoking*, as it is *undoubted*: he enjoys the singular merit of being the most wilful and impracticable poet of the present time. He delights in putting the reader into the difficult position of either believing himself or the poet to be at fault." The phrase "A quality of Grasp" in Melville's marginalia in his Vasari seems to be an echo of Browning's "Andrea del Sarto," the main source of which was Vasari's *Lives*. Browning's subtitle ("Called 'The Faultless Painter' ") sets up the contrast between high professional competence and the higher grandeur attainable by great but less tidy genius. Like many of his contemporaries, Melville seems to have been struck by the poem's most challenging lines (already passing into proverbial status), Andrea's honest admission that the perfection of his own work dooms it to less than greatness: "Ah, but a man's reach should exceed his grasp, / Or what's a heaven for?" As he wrote *Clarel* Melville was at a stage of life when his reach did not, anymore, much exceed his grasp, and when he did not necessarily want it to, but he now could posit the opinions of aestheticians as well as his own instincts against his century's overvaluation of superficial perfection in art.

p. 528   The book received chiefly abrupt dismissals.

The reviews of *Battle-Pieces* should have given Melville ample warning that he would not regain his lost fame by writing more volumes of poetry. They set the tone that reviewers were to take toward *Clarel* and made some of the same specific criticisms. The known reviews of *Battle-Pieces* are surveyed in the Northwestern-Newberry *Published Poems* volume (see also Hayes, Mailloux, and Parker, forthcoming).

p. 531   Melville began his . . . service in the New York Customs.

At different locations and with different badge numbers on wharves on the Hudson and the North (i.e., East) River Melville served for nineteen years (Garner 1978, 1986). He was plunged at once into a stew of political corruption where a customs officer not on the take was suspect; anyone learning where he worked might simply assume that he was corrupt. During these years cash political contributions to the Republican Party were expected, not to say extorted, from all employees who wanted to keep their jobs, especially vulnerable during shifts in administrations and wavelets of reform. Melville's plight is best revealed in a letter (*Log*, II, 730–31) his brother-in-law John C. Hoadley on January 9, 1873, wrote to George Boutwell, Secretary of the Treasury, at the beginning of Grant's second and monumentally corrupt term:

> There is one person in the employment of the Revenue Service, in whom I take so deep an interest, that I venture a second time to write you about him;—not to solicit promotion, a favor, or indulgence of any sort,—but to ask you, if you can, to do or say anything in the proper quarter to secure him permanently, or at present, the undisturbed enjoyment of his modest, hard-earned salary, as deputy inspector of the Customs in the City of New York—Herman Melville.— Proud, shy, sensitively honorable,—he had much to overcome, and has much to endure; but he strives earnestly to so perform his duties as to make the slightest censure, reprimand, or even reminder,—

impossible from any superior—Surrounded by low venality, he puts it all quietly aside,—quietly declining offers of money for special services,—quietly returning money which has been thrust into his pockets behind his back, avoiding offence alike to the corrupting merchants and their clerks and runners, who think that all men can be bought, and to the corrupt swarms who shamelessly seek their price;—quietly, steadfastly doing his duty, and happy in retaining his own self-respect—

Hoadley's tribute, plainly founded on intimate knowledge of what Melville's working days were like, reveals just how much self-restraint was required to keep so precariously subservient a job—the sort of alert, self-effacing control his White Jacket had exercised in order to avoid flogging.

p. 531   It was a menial job at best, but it . . . put him at last in the guiltless role of steady wage earner.

Melville had never supported his wife and family by his earnings. Loans and legacies from her family had paid for the three houses he was ever to own, and from the mid 1850's through the end of 1866 her money paid for almost all his clothing, his food and that other necessity of life, tobacco, and the books which he extravagantly bought, even in a year like 1862, when he had no income at all (Metcalf 1953, pp. 146–206). Through the 1850's his wife received a little money every year from a trust fund, and after her father's death in 1861 she received additional income from property in Boston—some of it destroyed by fire in November, 1872. Getting out of the house during the day and earning money did not erase the tensions which had been building in Melville's home life for many years. During 1867, the first year after Melville became a wage-earner, emotions at 104 East Twenty-sixth Street were so turbulent that serious writing after his day's work may have been impossible. What happened between Melville and his wife and between him and his children must be inferred from the few facts (and some family legends—see Metcalf 1953, pp. 159, 207–15) now known. Those facts mostly derive from a letter that Elizabeth Melville's half-brother, Samuel Shaw, on May 6, 1867, wrote from Boston to the Melvilles' New York minister, Henry W. Bellows (Kring and Carey 1975; reprinted in Yannella and Parker 1981). Shaw specified that his "sisters case" had been "a cause of anxiety to all of us for years past." Melville had so "ill treated" his wife that she was at last forced to consider very seriously a separation from him. Samuel during these years "over and over again" had discussed the situation with her and had assured her that he and his brother Lemuel would assist her to the best of their ability. At last, "quite recently," probably early in 1867, "the Melvilles" had "expressed a willingness to lend their assistance." By "the Melvilles" Samuel presumably meant the Massachusetts brothers-in-law at nearby Brookline (George Griggs) and Lawrence (John C. Hoadley) but beyond doubt he meant also Melville's brother Allan in New York, who had handled Melville's legal affairs, including his financial relationships with his father-in-law and (after Judge Shaw's death) with Samuel and Lemuel. The Melvilles who agreed "to lend their assistance" may or may not have included Melville's mother and his sisters, but Samuel emphasized to the minister the new united front against Melville: "The whole family understands the case and the thing has resolved itself into the mere question of my sisters willingness to say the word."

Bellows had proposed a scheme by which Samuel and Lemuel would stage a kidnapping—that is, carry Lizzie off apparently against her will. Samuel, a lawyer and a cautious man, rejected that plan out of hand. Of the various painful alternatives by which his sister could take refuge with her brothers, Samuel had settled on the simplest and most straightforward: "I think that the safest course is to let her real position become apparent from the first, namely that of a wife, who, being convinced that her husband is insane *acts* as if she were so convinced and applies for aid and assistance to her friends and acts *with* them." In his opinion, she would have done this long ago "if not for imaginary and groundless apprehensions of the censure of the world upon her conduct." But once again that month, May of 1867, Lizzie declined to separate from her husband and the summer passed in outward calm, except for problems that developed with the Melvilles' oldest son, Malcolm. At eighteen he was of an age to see himself as his mother's best protector, after his uncles had failed. No surviving evidence, only such an observed pattern in family psychology, links the marital crisis of the spring with the tragedy of the late summer, but the conflict between Malcolm and his father culminated on September 11, when Malcolm did not get up to go to work in the insurance office of Richard Lathers (his uncle Allan's brother-in-law by his first marriage), and did not answer his mother's knocks during the day. When Melville came home from work he broke in and found Malcolm "in his night clothes in bed with a pistol shot in his head and apparently several hours dead" (Metcalf 1953, pp. 207–15; see also Shneidman 1976).

The grief Malcolm's death imposed on both parents may have helped in time to resolve the "lamentable state of things" which had darkened the previous years. As time passed Melville, it seems, was not only, as Bezanson suggests, free to work on the Holy Land materials but perhaps also urgently needed to submerge himself once more in writing an all-absorbing book—and for the first time a book which did not take him away from his responsibility to support his family (but exactly when he did so is uncertain—see the next entry).

p. 531   At some definite point between the end of the war and 1870 . . . he made the crucial decisions which enabled him to go ahead with *Clarel*.

Bezanson's hypothesis that *Clarel* was most likely begun around 1867 has not been verified, and it is still not known when and under what circumstances *Clarel* was conceived, designed, developed, and completed. For other suggestions as to the date of composition see Simon (discussed on p. 548 above), Warren (1967, p. 72), and Cannon (1976); for the possible dating of various passages, see the discussions below at 1.1.10, 1.5.131, 1.31.138, 1.32.56, 1.33.32, 1.37.0, 1.40.0, 1.41.109, 2.30.0, 2.34.33, 3.13.55, and 4.16.190. On the one hand, no evidence has been discovered that absolutely rules out Melville's beginning the poem at any time after his 1856–57 journey, although all the known evidence points to his writing only three lectures and enough short poems to make up a book by the spring of 1860. After his return from his 1860 trip to San Francisco, in particular, he was not engaged in any other literary work that we know of besides the poems that went into *Battle-Pieces* (1866), and it is possible that he worked intermittently on *Clarel* during some or all of the 1860's. On the other hand, no evidence has been discovered that absolutely proves he began the poem before the 1870's (the first surviving letter which may refer to it is dated 1875).

For others of Melville's late works, manuscript pages survive, often because he reused them in inscribing later prose or poetry, but oddly no such scraps of manuscript for *Clarel* survive to provide any basis for conjecture about the dating and sequence of composition. In the absence of such documentary evidence, the study of internal characteristics (passages in relation to other parts of the poem) or of known sources in relation to parts of the poem may provide some clues (no complete reexamination of Melville's sources has yet been made). The firmest evidence yet discovered is that in 1870 Melville was buying books about the Holy Land which were used as sources for *Clarel* (see p. 533, footnote 30 above); but he may have bought or borrowed such books both earlier and later of which we have no record. Bezanson may be correct in his assumption that Melville had written roughly a third of the poem before April, 1870, when he acquired Stanley's *Sinai and Palestine* (a frequent source for passages in the last two-thirds of the poem), but it is possible that Melville wrote "Jerusalem" and part of "The Wilderness" after acquiring this book but before making use of it. Stanley devotes some two dozen pages to Jerusalem, but Melville may have used other sources for that part of the poem, such as guidebooks to supplement his own journal, even if he already owned a copy of *Sinai and Palestine*. (See Finkelstein 1961 for his Eastern source materials.)

Bezanson did not put his identification of Vine as a portrait of Hawthorne in the context of a hypothesis about Melville's planning of the poem. For all we know, a decision to dramatize (and fantasize) a "tournament of merits" between a character like himself and one like Hawthorne could have been a factor (perhaps even a precipitating one) in his ability to begin at last to make use of his experiences in the Holy Land. Therefore the portrayal of Vine needs to be seen in relation to the attention paid by the press to Hawthorne's posthumous writings (see the next entry) and to Melville's known reading and rereading of Hawthorne in the late 1860's and early 1870's and his acquisition of Hawthorne books (see pp. 593–94, footnote 71 above). It might be possible, for instance, to correlate early and late portions of the depiction of Vine with Melville's purchase of *Passages from the American Note-Books* (on June 8, 1870) and of *Passages from the French and Italian Note-Books* (on March 23, 1872), but so far no one has attempted to do so.

The date Melville finished the poem is not known. Elizabeth Melville wrote to her stepmother on March 9, 1875, that Melville was writing poetry (see p. 535 above), but there is at present no way of being sure that she was referring to *Clarel*. Jay Leyda *(Log,* II, 741) implied by his placement of Melville's draft title-page for *Parthenope* that the poetry being written was some of the Burgundy Club material, but Robert C. Ryan (in the Northwestern-Newberry edition) regards Leyda's reasoning and evidence (which involves the paper and ink) as inconclusive. Unless new evidence is found, the draft title-page will not be placed in "Spring? 1875" in the *New Melville Log*, so that the reader will not be directed to take her letter as referring to something other than *Clarel*. We do know that during his vacation in August of 1875 Melville talked with his uncle Peter in Albany about *Clarel* (perhaps not for the first time), that on the eighth or ninth of that month his uncle "made known" his intention to subsidize the publication of the poem, and that Melville on that occasion expressed his "sentiments" of gratitude and affection (letter to Peter Gansevoort, August 26, 1875 [pp. 536–37 above]; *Log*, II, 744).

A troublesome point remains, the phrasing of M's prefatory note to the poem, presumably written in late spring, 1876:

> If during the period in which this work has remained unpublished, though not undivulged, any of its properties have by a natural process exhaled; it yet retains, I trust, enough of original life to redeem it at least from vapidity. Be that as it may, I here dismiss the book—content beforehand with whatever future awaits it.

First of all, how the poem had been divulged before publication is uncertain. From someone Peter Gansevoort heard a "report" that it existed in manuscript, as stated in the dedication. By this comment in the prefatory note was Melville reproaching his wife for gossiping about the poem? (See also her letter quoted on p. 535 above.) Had he for years entrusted John C. Hoadley, the other poet in the family, and others with the knowledge that he was writing a long poem? However much or little the members of the family had heard, they had difficulty getting the title right. On May 25, 1876, Catherine Gansevoort Lansing wrote to Hoadley at Lawrence, "*The Book* comes out early in June & Cousin Lizzie wishes me to send you G. P. Putnam's Sons, address . . . . I hope the Boston Papers will notice the Book it is called I believe 'Clara or the New Jerusalem.' " Not until June 6 did Elizabeth Melville "enclose" the "name of the book" in a letter to Catherine, and the title remained vague to at least one more member of the family, Melville's sister Fanny, who on June 18 from the Hoadley house wrote to Catherine, "Are you reading 'Charel & a Pilgrimage to the Holy Land' I have not yet seen it, Mr. Hoadley having got a copy the day he left Boston. From Helen, I heard of the beautiful inscription to Uncle" (NYPL-GL). Or was Melville merely referring to a newspaper notice, such as the one in the *New-York Daily Tribune* on January 12 (see p. 658 below)? Then another question is how long the poem had remained completed but unpublished: ten months, at least, and possibly many more, or even two or three years or more. We have no way of knowing.

Bezanson reminds us that Melville lived with the poem for years. What governed Melville's sense that the poem remained long unpublished may simply have been the literal fact that any parts written, say, in 1870 had indeed remained long unpublished, by any measure. It would have been only natural if he felt he had experienced many changes in his attitudes toward parts of the poem. Although the time-scheme of the poem is only ten days, arguably too short for realistic depiction of dramatic shifts and revelations of character in the pilgrims, the real time that elapsed allowed Melville to arrive at new stages in his understanding of the pilgrims: to believe that Vine is based on Hawthorne is not necessarily to believe that Melville knew when he started the poem just how Vine would stand at the end and just how that standing would reflect his own attitude toward Hawthorne's strengths and weaknesses. Robert C. Ryan thinks it would be possible to make the case that there is some development in the character of Derwent; and it is even more likely that Vine might be portrayed differently at the end than toward the beginning (assuming something like a sequential composition). Therefore Melville might well have felt that the early parts of the poem were quite remote from the last parts he had written.

Furthermore, we need to remember that Melville typically had experienced little delay between writing a book and seeing it in print, at least in page proofs. He had worked his thoughts about the European revolutions of 1848 into his supposedly completed manuscript of *Mardi*, and less than a year later was in print as a commentator on still-current history. If in *Clarel* he wrote (previously unanticipated) passages on the Commune of Paris, the revolutionary government of March 18 to May 28, 1871, at or soon after that time, then he may well have felt that the lapse of three or four or five years had rendered his commentary less than current, however far it remained from vapidity. Similarly, he may have felt that some of the other topics of the poem, particular theological or political issues for example, had been current as he wrote but might seem less so by the middle of 1876. In view of these considerations, it is not necessary to read the prefatory note as Melville's assertion that the poem had remained completed and unpublished for years.

p. 531 he projected a . . . journey by a young American in the company of a group of Representative Men.

If Bezanson's identification of Vine (first advanced in his 1943 dissertation) is correct (see pp. 593–604 above), one of these Representative Men was Hawthorne. In the years after the romancer's death in 1864 he had been exalted beyond even Washington Irving as America's greatest fiction writer (Tompkins 1985; Brodhead 1986). With the reception of *Passages from the American Note-Books* (1868) and *Passages from the English Note-Books* (1870) a pattern had begun to emerge: the new generation of Hawthorne lovers began to think of Melville as the sea-writer who had enlivened Hawthorne's brief stay in the Berkshires. This hypothetical identification of Vine would suggest that, with his own reputation first besmirched then forgotten, Melville began to reflect (jealously, skeptically, judiciously, and still lovingly) on the mental and aesthetic qualities of the man who had so bewitched him and, in a decision which hardly complicated his subject and may have simplified his plot, brought Hawthorne along on the pilgrimage as one of two pilgrims between whose values and attitudes the young hero feels he must choose. Bezanson in 1960 withheld his identification of Vine until late in his essay, where its obvious significance and potential for controversy would not overwhelm his essay as a whole. The identification has been widely accepted, even though the bases upon which it rests have not been critically examined (see pp. 593–94, footnote 71, above and RELATED DOCUMENTS, pp. 883–93 below). The broader notion of portraying a group of Representative Men may have developed from an idea jotted at some unknown time after his trip in one of Melville's 1856–57 journal notebooks, as Howard C. Horsford suggests in *Journals*, p. 193: "the speculative title 'Frescoes of Travel by Three Brothers / Poet, Painter, and Idler' [p. 154] . . . was a contributing idea to the structure of *Clarel*, the idea of observation and meditation from multiple perspectives."

p. 532   Unlike his previous fictions the present one was in verse—a long narrative poem.

Melville in his decision to cast his book about the Holy Land as a long narrative poem was looking far back to the most popular verse forms of his childhood, the long narrative poems of Sir Walter Scott (his brother Gansevoort could recite "The Lady of the Lake" *in extenso* [Murray 1984]) and Byron, many of which were in iambic tetrameter. As Shirley Dettlaff (1989 letter to Parker on Byron and *Clarel*) has pointed out, the verse form of Byron's *The Giaour*, *The Siege of Corinth*, and *Mazeppa* was iambic tetrameter—variously in rhymed couplets, in quatrains rhymed *abab* or *abba*, occasionally in triplets or other variations. During his early career Melville must have perceived that long narrative poems tended to receive longer reviews than novels, including his own. Longfellow's *Evangeline* (a copy of which Melville was given by his mother-in-law in 1848; Sealts 332) was a great success, for instance; and in 1851 Longfellow's *The Golden Legend* was lavishly reviewed (in early 1854 John C. Hoadley read it aloud to his wife Catherine Melville Hoadley, his mother-in-law, and his sister-in-law Fanny [NYPL-GL]). Martin Farquhar Tupper's long pop-philosophic poems had been wildly successful during Melville's early career (when his mother had idolized the Englishman as the Christian writer her son was not)(NYPL-GL). Walt Whitman had taken something of his poetic form from Tupper, and Melville may have known something of the long poems by his contemporary New Yorker. John C. Hoadley's copy of *Leaves of Grass* (now in the Kent State University Library) was purchased in 1855, the year it was first published, and later he owned *Drum-Taps* (1865) (location unknown). In 1888 Melville "said so much of Whitman" to E. C. Stedman that Stedman sent him his chapter on the poet (*Log*, II, 806; Sealts 1974, pp. 242–43 and *passim*), but there is no evidence that Whitman had yet entered Melville's consciousness at the time he wrote *Clarel*. In the 1860's Robert Browning, George Eliot, and Alfred Tennyson all published long poems. Despite the reviews of *Battle-Pieces*, Melville was not repudiating all chances of popularity in choosing the form for *Clarel*.

Indeed, the fact that John Greenleaf Whittier's *Snow-Bound* was a literary sensation in 1866 and immensely popular afterwards may have encouraged Melville to think the form he chose for *Clarel* might prove appealing. He had praised Whittier in his essay on "Hawthorne and His Mosses" (*Piazza Tales*, p. 247), and members of the family cherished some of Whittier's poems (during the composition of *Moby-Dick* Augusta Melville copied some of them into her commonplace book [BA]). *Snow-Bound* dealt with a situation Melville would have been especially sensitive to: family chores and amusements during a New England snowstorm that isolates a farmhouse from the outside world. Incidental details would have intrigued him—a passage adapted from the sea-going Quaker Thomas Chalkley's *Journal* (1747) on cannibalism providentially averted; a passage on the Isles of Shoals, associated in his mind with Hawthorne and the story of Agatha (see pp. 642–43 above); the character of an idealistic young country-school teacher, better educated than he had been as a schoolteacher in 1837; the "crazy Queen of Lebanon," Lady Hester (or Esther) Lucy Stanhope, who "under Eastern skies" awaited the Second Coming of Jesus; the war for Greek independence against the Turks; and an intensely felt passage on the direction Reconstruction should take. Furthermore, it also was written in the then-unpopular iambic tetrameter once favored by Byron, most often couplets but also irregularly rhymed, as *Clarel* was to be.

p. 532   prosodic problems . . . had now moved to the center of his interests.

Some of Melville's recently discovered annotations deal with the sort of preparation required for writing a great narrative poem. In the "Life of Milton" in his *Poetical Works* of Milton (see p. 646n. above), Melville marked this passage:

> Milton's immense reading extended over the whole field of literature, and in every direction; and it required all his learning, collected by painful study during the best years of his life, long deposited in his memory, and remoulded by his genius, to build up his immortal poem. Where is there an extensive work of established reputation to be found, that is not evidently the result of long study, and assiduous labours?

Such labor Melville had committed himself to.

p. 534   He made at least minor appropriations from . . . .

It seems very likely that Melville also made minor use of Stephens's *Incidents of Travel in Egypt, Arabia Petræa, and the Holy Land* (see pp. 669–70 below).

p. 535   "Herman . . . is writing poetry."

Melville's granddaughter, Eleanor Melville Metcalf, recorded what her mother, Frances Melville Thomas, told her of Melville's way of sharing his creation with his family: "My mother used . . . to deride the rhythm with which her father would recite, while pacing the floor, certain verses he had written, looking for approbation, she thought, from his wife and daughters. These must have been lines from *Clarel* . . ." (Metcalf 1953, pp. 76–77).

pp. 538–39   an agreement . . . to pay the entire cost of publishing this poem.

On learning that her father's $1200 had not covered all the "supplementary charges," such as those for advertising and review copies, Catherine (Kate) Gansevoort Lansing in August sent Melville a check for $100. What followed was a long exchange in which Melville and Mrs. Lansing proved themselves to be cousins indeed, each outdoing the other in pride, punctiliousness, and courtesy. The matter seemed to have ended in September, when Melville wrote her that he had donated the money to the New York Society for the Relief of the Ruptured & Crippled, and on September 17 she accepted Melville's gesture as a gift he had bestowed on her in giving her the credit for his "own 'sweet charity' to the destitute & suffering." But four months later she apparently had the last word by sending another check, and at this point Melville graciously gave up—until March 7, when he revoked his "assent" (*Log*, II, 754, 755, 758, 759).

p. 539   in January . . . he made arrangements for publication.

The publishing agreement was made January 4, according to Melville's letter of this date to Abraham Lansing, and on January 12 the *New-York Daily Tribune* announced: "A narrative and descriptive poem on the Holy Land, by Herman Melville, is in press by G. P. Putnam's Sons" (*Log*, II, 746). This delay between the arrangement with his uncle and the publishing agreement suggests that Melville needed some months to get the manuscript of *Clarel* into a form he could submit to a publisher. The subsequent proofreading, which began in a matter of weeks, Melville took with utmost seriousness, impressing his wife to his service and treating his daughters much as Milton had treated his, as adjuncts to his literary needs. His daughter Frances (according to her own daughter Eleanor Melville Metcalf) recalled being "roused from sleep at two in the morning to read proof with her father of a long, obscure poem on the Holy Land" (Metcalf 1953, p. 215).

p. 540 n. 41   *Clarel* "was withdrawn . . . by Mr. Melville on finding that it commanded but a very limited sale."

The "limited sale" is borne out by a recently discovered document (reproduced on p. 638) showing that almost three years after publication 220 sets were pulped. On March 27, 1879, evidently at the Putnam office, Melville wrote this authorization: "Please dispose of cases 2 & 3 ('Clarel') containing two hundred and twenty four copies, on my account, to paper-mill." Someone at Putnam's noted on his letter, "Sent to Paper Mill April 18 / 79 . . . 220 Sets 110 Pounds of Covers 305 . . . of Clarel." Conjecturally, if case 1, like 2 and 3, contained about 110 copies, some of which had been sent out for review, the total number printed would have been around 330, or perhaps a run of some 350. This authorization to pulp the remaining copies must have been the withdrawal Mrs. Melville was referring to in her 1901 comment quoted above. (Melville's letter was quoted in Bernard Quaritch Catalogue 1066 [London, 1986], item 116, and quoted and reproduced in Catalogue 1083 [London, 1989], pp. 30–31, item 30, and in *Melville Society Extracts*, No. 66 [May, 1986], 14.)

p. 542   Other than small private printings . . . he was through with publishing.

When Melville died he was actively preparing the *Weeds and Wildings* poems for publication (Ryan 1967), and there are signs in the manuscript of *Billy Budd* that Elizabeth had begun, at some mid-stage of the composition, to help him prepare that manuscript for the printer (Hayford and Sealts 1962, p. 7). The Burgundy Club pieces were in preparation and likewise might have been printed had he lived (see Sandberg's three 1990 items). But in any of these last works he would probably have controlled not only the printing but the distribution, as he did with *John Marr* and *Timoleon*.

p. 542   the poor reception of *Clarel*

Judging from the handful of known reviews, it appears that Putnam distributed review copies mainly in the Northeast, apart from those in London, and Bezanson discusses almost all of them (see pp.

542–46 above). Four more have since been found. On June 10 the reviewer for the Boston *Daily Evening Transcript* had looked over the "two handsomely printed and bound volumes" of *Clarel* and commented that so many pages of rhymed verse were "rather apt to create a disgust for poetry if one is obliged to read them conscientiously and crucially." He was spared that disgust, for the "heat of the season" allowed him to "forego" the pleasure of attacking the volumes. He concluded laconically: Melville's "chances for writing a readable poem of the above length are as good as those of any one else we know of." The reviewer in the *Chicago Tribune* (July 1) professed to be favorably disposed toward "any new literary effort" by the author of what the paper called " 'Amoo' and 'Typee,' " but he was put off first by the length and the subject then by the dedication, which he took as revealing that *Clarel* was merely a vanity press poem. After claiming to have examined it faithfully "from end to end," he offered this grudging tribute: "The manufacture of the poem must have been a work of love. It bears internal evidence of having been labored over as a blacksmith hammers at his forge, and only a mastering passion for the severest task-work could have sustained the author through it all." In London the *Saturday Review* (August 26) gave a one-sentence dismissal: "We have to note the unusual phenomenon of a poem in two volumes—*Clarel*, a versified account of a pilgrimage in Palestine, not remarkable either for elevation of sentiment or for poetic excellence."

In January, 1877, the New York *International Review* gave the poem its most thoughtful American review in two long paragraphs. The reviewer was astounded that "the hero of whaling and Polynesian adventures, whose model seemed to be Defoe, should become a theological mystic in his ripened years." He arrived at an opinion not unwarranted by Melville's prefatory note:

> It is one of those works which the author writes for himself, and not for the reader, wherein he simply follows the bent of his own interests and fancies, and relies either upon his personal value or assumed height of achievement for his popular success. This is an experiment which Browning has lately tried, compelling the sentence of failure from unwilling critics. We doubt whether the very greatest of poets could practice it successfully for any length of time unless the principles of his art had entered into and become an integral part of his imagination. How then should Herman Mel-

ville, who has not yet achieved a recognized place as a poet, hope to succeed with a public which has, first of all, to be taught faith in his powers?

The reviewer looked at the plot and characters for a clue to guide him "through a chaos of description, incident, conversation, and conflict of ideas and beliefs, wherein there is no single governing and harmonizing conception." He was hoping to find some sign of "coherent spiritual development to his chief character," but whatever "modifications of belief" he could perceive in Clarel he saw arising from "the intimate personal intercourse of the parties rather than from the arguments they use." Expecting that in such a poem religious discussions would lead the character toward a particular theological standpoint, he was disappointed:

> Throughout the whole work we trace, under many masks, the wanderings of a questioning and unsatisfied soul: yet at the close we do not feel clearly that peace has been attained, or, if it has been, upon what basis. The literary character of the poem corresponds to the intellectual. It is astonishingly unequal. After a couplet, quatrain or brief passage which bears a high poetical stamp, we stumble upon one which is awkward, feeble and immetrical. Reading the best parts, we can not understand why the whole poem is not greatly better: reading the worst, we are surprised to find it so good.

Thus even this lengthy review did no more than dispense with *Clarel* rather brusquely, after a hasty skimming. As Bezanson says (p. 544), the poem "simply did not speak to Melville's American contemporaries."

Some further quotations from the reviews which Bezanson discusses may be useful in assessing Melville's reputation as a poet. Knowing Melville's interest in Hafiz (Sealts 176; Sealts 1988, p. 30; Bercaw 312; Finkelstein 1961, pp. 91ff.) and Blake (Sealts 224, 520; Bercaw 66; letter to Billson, April 2, 1886; Stanton 1987), the reader may want to know that the reviewer (possibly E. C. Stedman) in the *New-York Daily Tribune* found the "fragments of fresh, musical lyrics" in *Clarel* "suggestive" of both these poets. The reviewer in the *World* was sure any reader would find the style especially provoking:

> After a lot of jog-trot versifying—Mr. Melville rhymes "hand" and "sustained," "day" and "Epiphany" in the first ten lines—and just as he is prepared to abandon the book as a hopeless case, he stumbles on a

passage of striking original thought, or possessing the true lyrical ring and straightway is lured over another thousand lines or so, the process being repeated till the book ends just where it began.

He disliked both the "philosophizing" and the "analyzations of character," and judged the descriptive passages best, "notwithstanding frequent turgidity and affectation." "On the whole," he concluded, "it is hardly a book to be commended, for a work of art it is not in any sense of measure, and if it is an attempt to grapple with any particular problem of the universe, the indecision as to its object and processes is sufficient to appal or worry the average reader." The reviewer in the *New-York Times* recognized that the octosyllabic meter was one "which Scott used in his narrative poems," and recalled that Byron had confessed that a " 'fatal facility' " was inherent in this particular meter; Melville, he commented wryly, did not "appear to have suffered" from that facility. The reviewer for the Springfield *Republican* (July 18) recalled *Typee*, *Omoo*, and *Moby-Dick* and observed that Melville still "lives in his novels,—a sort of posthumous life, it is true, yet they are worth reading, particularly the last, with those preposterous heroes, the White Whale and Capt Ahab." (This is the first known use of a phrase like "posthumous life" for Melville's survival of his fame; a decade later such terms became commonplace.) The reviewer in *Lippincott's Magazine* commented sadly on the problem-world of the poem:

> The personages are used, like figures in landscape-painting, to animate the scenes through which we follow the author: their conversation turns chiefly on the religious doubt and disbelief which beset many— Mr. Melville seems to think all—thoughtful men in our times, and the social, political and scientific questions interwoven with them.

As Bezanson notes (p. 544), his response was that "no new light is thrown upon these questions." He found "a few striking descriptions, such as that of the monk of Saba feeding the doves, which is like a picture of Mr. Holman Hunt's, and some good images and metaphors, especially those drawn from Mr. Melville's old sea-life."

p. 543   his brother-in-law John Hoadley, a . . . good amateur poet, thought . . .

Melville's family, so far as we know, had never demonstrated special acuteness as readers of his books, and *Clarel* was far less open to casual reading than any book he had yet published. Nevertheless, Edward Sanford (Uncle Peter's brother-in-law by his first marriage) was reading it carefully in March, 1877, when he wrote about it to his niece, Catherine Gansevoort Lansing (*Log*, II, 760). Hoadley read the entire poem with great attentiveness soon after it was published. Bezanson refers to the July 8 letter to Abraham Lansing, son-in-law of Melville's Uncle Peter, in which Hoadley scoffed at "the criticism" in the *World*, "if such it can be called even by courtesy." Hoadley also said:

> "Clarel" is not easy reading. It requires determined study, and my attention must be at its freshest, to relish it until after several perusals.
> . . .
> But it will . . . give Mr. Melville a firm footing on a higher plane than anything he has before written.
> I wish it might make him at once rich, famous and happy!—Noble Fellow! He deserves to be all three!— (NYPL-GL)

Hoadley's annotations in his surviving copy (now in the collection of William Reese, who kindly allowed examination of the volumes and helped decipher some difficult words) show that he may have kept the volumes at hand through the fall, repondering the lines, and they demonstrate how alertly he read the entire poem. They show him as a man with a practicing poet's notions of what is proper in matters of punctuation, grammar, syntax, and rhyme. He watched for typographical errors and what he saw as nonstandard punctuation. He clarified the sense by putting commas around "a fly" at 4.29.60 ("Why hang a fly in flimsy web?"), impatiently changed "which" to "who" over half a dozen times when the referent was a human being, changed "laid" to the proper "lain" once, and worried about substituting "Whom" for "Who" at 4.26.250. At 3.21.193 he queried changing "reinfunds" to "reinvests." At the end of 1.32.45–46 he changed "disclose" to "discloses" to agree with "page." At 3.8.88 he worried about Melville's use of the Song of Solomon 1.5: black like a woman or black like the tents of Kedar? At 3.11.255 he changed the syntax to personify "spirit": "And snuffed at by the spirit weary." At 1.38.50 ("Who? Small was Clarel's wondering.") he noted (debatably) that the pause after "Who?" "is equivalent to a syllable." Like several of the reviewers of *Battle-Pieces* who had deplored "such technical blemishes" as the rhyming of either "law" or "war" with "Shenandoah" or of "more" with "Keneshaw," Hoadley was offended by—and misdiagnosed—"a frequent blemish," the "strange addition of the sound of r to broad a" (he noted at 2.1.110 that "Thessalonica" had to rhyme with "cigar"). Upsettingly "Bad!" was the usage at 4.3.56, where, Hoadley noted, Golgotha had to be pronounced "Golgothur!" (For this kind of "r" in Melville's spelling and presumed pronunciation, see Hayford 1969, pp. 343–47.)

Hoadley also identified people and things Melville was referring to, including a literary source, and noted some scientific errors. Because Margoth is not named on his first appearance, Hoadley wrote down his name and the page number of his next entrance; he wrote down the full name of Lady Esther Stanhope; he noted that Melville was referring to "St. Francis de Assisi," who was "Son of a Merchant." At 3.30.75 Hoadley identified "Fomalhaut" as being in the constellation Piscis Austrinus. The identification of a source is at 1.34.27 ("Affirming it [the moon] a clinkered blot"), where he noted: "M. F. Tuppers word applied to the moon. 'Art thou the blot?' " (Hoadley, like the Melvilles, knew Tupper's poetry—even the obscure "The Moon," not in the famous *Proverbial Philosophy*—see p. 751 below, the discussion at 1.34.26.) At 1.35.50 ("The mica in the marble knew") Hoadley remarked succinctly, "There is no mica in marble." At 4.1.61 ("With burnished arms refracting light") he changed "refracting" to "reflecting," noting that "refraction requires transmission through the refracting body."

In the fervor of an election year, Hoadley fussed about political (or political-religious) matters as he went through *Clarel*, perhaps more than once before the year ended. At 2.21.84–86 he marked the lines on the world's becoming "a den / Worse for Christ's coming, since his love / (Perverted) did but venom prove," and in the margin identified the perverter: "Rome!—even if the author didn't mean it!" At 4.5.36–63, along Rolfe's bitter meditation which moves from the suffering of the South in war and Reconstruction to the loss of belief in the Adamic American, Hoadley wrote: "Strong: but sympathy ill-bestowed." On the Sunday before the November election, Hoadley interpreted according to his own fears the lyric in which Ungar apparently foresees retribution to the Radical Republicans for their harshness toward the South (4.5.184–88): "Tilden? No. 5/ '76" (he feared that a victory for the Democrat Tilden would exalt the South to its pre-war power). At 4.9.108–25, Ungar's denunciation of Anglo-Saxon materialistic imperialism and Northern cruelty in wartime, Hoadley burst out in an impassioned protest (imperfectly transcribed here from his difficult scrawl) against Northern kindness to the South after the war: "No grace—So faith [fable?]-foolish, So stupidly prizing the unrepentant, was ever accorded under heaven or among men, by men, or gods, as by North to [?] South!" At 4.19.126–47, Ungar's diatribe against democracy as the "Arch strumpet of an impious age," Hoadley wrote woefully in the margin: "Truer, in literal sense, than the Author meant: O *Democracy!*"

Toward the end of the first volume, along the margins of 2.38.4–27, Hoadley offered his first tribute to the poem: "very beautiful." In the margins of "Before the Gate" (3.10) he wrote "all this is fine" then "Fine, very fine description." At 4.3.1–16 he wrote "Fine." At 4.21.121–39, Ungar's passionate denunciation of the debasement of values in democratic America, he wrote "Powerful!" It is altogether fitting that Melville's devoted and generous brother-in-law should emerge as the best nineteenth-century critic of *Clarel*.

p. 552   by midcentury its critics had begun to read the poem.

Bezanson's own reading of the poem, developed in the early 1950's from his 1943 dissertation and published in 1960 (see p. 505n.) in the first scholarly edition, has been acknowledged as the starting point of later criticism of the poem. Unlike Bezanson's full account of criticism to 1951, the following survey of subsequent criticism can only highlight several salient examples. Representative is William H. Shurr's *The Mystery of Iniquity* (1972), which expatiates on major symbols of the poem and on the topography and the major and minor characters in ways unparalleled in any study before Bezanson's. One persistent focus of post-1960 criticism has been on Clarel's sexual confusion, already sketched by Bezanson (see the discussion at 4.26.0 below). Nina Baym, for example, in 1974 took *Clarel* as one of Melville's works which set out "with a combined erotic and philosophical situation" but held that unlike either *Mardi* or *Pierre* it "carries the erotic theme all the way through to the conclusion." She argued that "Melville has dramatized the way in which his [Clarel's] understanding of Christianity makes it impossible for Clarel to accept his own sexuality, and incapacitates him for relationships with the opposite sex"; Melville "has shown, conversely, how the protagonist's heterosexual drives make him incapable of living up to his Christian ideals." Although Clarel is strongly drawn to women, he "feels that sexual love is inherently impure and that his erotic feelings must therefore necessarily separate him from God." The fullest commentary on Baym's argument is by Shirley Dettlaff in her 1978 dissertation:

> Nina Baym concludes that the erotic "motif" is not just one thread in the complexly woven tapestry of Clarel but the framework for the entire design. Seeing the action of the story as Melville's sophisticated rendering of the conventional nineteenth-century conflict between intellect and nature, Baym asserts that Clarel's flight from feminine love into skeptical intellectualizing is ultimately sterile and that salvation lies only in a return to Ruth, a return which Clarel's neurotic fear of sex makes difficult. But one must consider the way that women in general are seen in the poem. And that is the traditional biblical or Hebraic one, which while sometimes appearing to admire, still really sees woman as a trap, a snare that will lure man to his doom by personifying those very qualities in himself which he would like to yield to but must transcend if he is to achieve salvation. Thus woman is associated with youth, beauty, charm, pleasure—unthinking physical or emotional comfort in this world—those very joys which the Hellenes celebrated. Baym, in following and over-emphasizing a suggestion of Bezanson's, has pushed her naturalistic and psychological interpretation too far with the result that it contradicts the major thrust of the poem's theme: the need for the person with the deep-diving Imagination to eschew the commonplace and become the heroic quester.

In 1986 Hershel Parker offered a reading of "Vine and Clarel" (2.27) as a "comic passage in which Vine and Clarel proceed on parallel tracks with few inklings as to each other's states of mind" (see also pp. 668–69 below). Both these arguments suggest just how provocatively Baym had pursued the "erotic motif" in Clarel beyond the point where Bezanson stopped. Other critics in growing numbers have enlisted Melville among homosexual American writers and interpreted his life and works, especially his relationship with Hawthorne, Ishmael's with Queequeg, and Clarel's with Vine, in this erotic vein (e.g., Miller 1975 and Martin 1986; see the background discussion by Parker in Moby-Dick, pp. 732ff.). Without seeing Melville as homosexual or his relationship with Hawthorne as primarily erotic, Parker (1986) nevertheless recognizes that Melville consciously portrayed some of Clarel's feelings toward Vine as homosexual.

Dettlaff in her 1978 dissertation and her 1982 article on "Ionian Form and Esau's Waste: Melville's View of Art in *Clarel*" analyzed the aesthetic implications of Melville's distinction between the Hebraic and Hellenic visions of life; his "definition of art" is one "which unifies a Greek sense of beauty with a Judaic sense of the sublime." In a later essay (1986), Dettlaff summed up the argument of her article:

> [A]lthough during the period in which Melville was writing *Clarel* he clearly developed a strong interest in form, he defined art in the poem as a synthesis of both "Nature's Terror" and "ordered form," giving form a somewhat subordinate role. Melville's reading in such modern Hellenes as Goethe, Schiller, and Arnold may have partially influenced him to value more highly than he had before a classical notion of form and beauty, yet in *Clarel* he still advocated that art reveals the characteristics of the Burkean sublime—an indeterminacy and inconclusiveness that seem incompatible with clarity and form. Nor did Melville follow the Hellenes in believing that art should elevate the reader to an ideal realm or produce joy in him.

What Dettlaff says here is to some extent provisional, awaiting the availability of the fuller evidence of Melville's poetics in the forthcoming Northwestern-Newberry texts and genetic reports of his published and unpublished poems.

Critics have begun to acknowledge that a second phase of assimilation and analysis of *Clarel* is upon us. Thomas F. Heffernan in his 1977 survey of the marginalia in Melville's newly recovered copy of Wordsworth's poetry (see p. 646n. above) concluded that *Clarel* needs to be read in the light of Melville's markings in *The Excursion*: "The similarity of moral and religious concerns, the patience with characters' long and thorough definitions of themselves, the awareness of immensity around the central drama, and even the diction and meter (though *Clarel*'s lines are tetrameter) argue that the long Wordsworth poem stayed in Melville's mind." In her 1986 essay Dettlaff emphasized that scholars have not yet provided a comprehensive study of Melville's later ideas about art as presented in *Clarel* and the other poetry:

> His letters, readings, and marginalia should be scrutinized in order to explore the full range of his thoughts about art while he was writing poetry. The question of just how important a role form played in his later theory requires fuller treatment. To be researched also is the pos-

sibility that a theory of poetry that he espoused influenced Melville's switch to this genre during most of his later writings.

For Melville's whole career, in fact, new letters, new evidence of his reading, and new samples of his marginalia have come to light surprisingly often in the 1980's and 1990's (see Horth 1990 and Sealts 1990, p. 5). Among his newly discovered letters there is only one possibly belonging to the period of *Clarel*. It is an undated note (before August, 1878) to Evert Duyckinck; with it Melville returns a work which he identifies only as "D.D." and characterizes as "the last leaf out of the *Omnium Gatherum* of miscellaneous opinion touching the indeterminate Ethics of our time" (Parker 1990). Here the vigor of expression confirms Bezanson's 1960 analysis of Melville as a reader. Through discovery of actual books or of letters which mention books, the record of Melville's reading is being reconstituted book by book, and some of the retrievements promise to be of crucial significance, most notably his copy of Milton's poems. Merton M. Sealts's revised and enlarged *Melville's Reading* (1988), with an extended new introduction, has already been followed up by a supplement (1990), and it is complemented by Mary K. Bercaw's *Melville's Sources* (1987), which lists all the printed sources ever attributed for his works, whether or not the copies of them he used are known (as listed by Sealts). As Heffernan and Dettlaff suggest, in the next decades the best essays on *Clarel* will incorporate new biographical discoveries and will assimilate the implications of any new Melville letters, books he made use of, and his markings and marginalia.

p. 601 Vine retains his original prestige during the rest of the journey.

In "The Character of Vine in Melville's *Clarel*" (see p. 666 above) Parker suggested that Vine loses some of that prestige in the course of the poem: "The implications of the longer speeches and thoughts of Vine are that Melville had decided Hawthorne was not merely burnt-out as an artist at an early age—he had also decided that in later life Hawthorne was coasting on an unmerited reputation for mental force, not to say profound intelligence." Emphasizing the "discrepancy between the way Vine is introduced and his ultimate status in the poem, between, on the one hand, the admiring response Vine evokes from several characters, and, on the other hand, his deeds and words," Parker concluded that "Vine's deeds often reveal an erratic

staginess and contempt for himself and others, and his words, how-
ever prettily melancholy they are, reflect the shallowness and discon-
tinuity of his mind—the mind of a man 'Whose race of thought long
since was run— / For whom the spots enlarge that blot the golden
sun' [2.33.110–11]."

p. 616   ARNAUT, The.

Since Warburton (the principal source for the Arnaut) does not
say anything about the Koran's prohibition of alcohol, Melville may
have taken his Arnaut's winebibbing from John Lloyd Stephens's
description in *Incidents of Travel* (see pp. 640–41 above) of his own
"wild Arnaout" (II, 133):

> I soon succeeded, however, in establishing myself on a good footing
> with my kervash [the Arnaout], and learned that his reading of the
> Koran did not forbid the winecup to the followers of the Prophet. He
> admitted that the sultan, as being of the blood of the Prophet, and the
> viceregent of God upon earth, ought not to taste it; but as to the Pacha
> of Egypt, he drank good wine whenever he could get it, and this gave
> *his* subjects a right to drink as often as they pleased.

On II, 142, the Arnaout is asleep upon a divan, "as drunk as a lord."

p. 632   SALVATERRA.

Salvaterra may also owe something to John Lloyd Stephens's de-
piction in *Incidents of Travel* (see pp. 640–41 above) of a young Italian
monk, a Franciscan, at Bethlehem (II, 139):

> The superior was a young man, not more than thirty, with a face
> and figure of uncommon beauty; though not unhealthy, his face was
> thin and pale, and his high, projecting forehead indicated more than
> talent. Genius flashed from his eyes, though, so far as I could judge
> from his conversation, he did not sustain the character his features and
> expression promised. He was not insensible to the advantages of his
> personal appearance. The rope around his waist, with the cross dan-
> gling at the end, was laid as neatly as a soldier's sword-belt; the top of
> his head was shaved, his beard combed, and the folds of his long coarse
> dress, his cowl, and the sandals on his feet, all were arranged with a
> precision that, under other circumstances, would have made him a
> Brummel. There was something, too, in the display of a small hand
> and long taper fingers that savoured more of the exquisite than of the
> recluse; but I ought not to have noted him too critically, for he was

young, handsome, and gentlemanly, and fit for better things than the
dronish life of a convent. . . .

SOURCES

N EW INFORMATION presented without source citations in this
HISTORICAL SUPPLEMENT is based mainly on documents that will
be included in the forthcoming *New Melville Log*, edited by Jay Leyda
and Hershel Parker, and reported in Parker's forthcoming biography
(citations of the *Log* refer to the 1951 edition and its 1969 supple-
ment—see p. 635 above); those now in the Gansevoort-Lansing Col-
lection of the New York Public Library are cited as NYPL-GL and in
the Berkshire Athenæum as BA. The same principles of quotation
stated on p. 636 above also apply here. New letters by Melville,
with the surviving letters to him, are included in the forthcoming
Northwestern-Newberry *Correspondence* volume, edited by Lynn
Horth; see her article cited below. Melville's marginalia reported here
are transcriptions made by Hershel Parker from the original volumes.
All known reviews of *Clarel* are listed in Kevin J. Hayes, Steven J.
Mailloux, and Hershel Parker's revised edition of *Checklist of Melville
Reviews,* forthcoming from the Melville Society. Vincent Kenny's
bibliography in John Bryant's *A Companion to Melville Studies*
(Westport, Conn.: Greenwood Press, 1986), pp. 375–406, lists signif-
icant *Clarel* studies to 1986. Abstracts of the *Clarel* dissertations to
1987 are reprinted in Tetsumaro Hayashi, *Herman Melville: Research
Opportunities and Dissertation Abstracts* (Jefferson, N.C., and London:
McFarland, 1987).

The following books and articles are referred to in this SUPPLE-
MENT without full bibliographical information, contribute to topics
discussed there, or amplify the report of post-1960 criticism: Nor-
wood Andrews, Jr., *Melville's Camões* (Bonn: Bouvier, 1989); S. C.
Baker, "Two Notes on Browning Echoes in *Clarel,*" *Melville Society
Extracts*, No. 44 (November, 1980), 14–15; Patricia Barber, "Herman
Melville's House in Brooklyn," *American Literature*, XLV (Novem-
ber, 1973), 433–34; Barber, "Two New Melville Letters," *American
Literature*, XLIX (November, 1977), 418–21; Nina Baym, "The
Erotic Motif in Melville's *Clarel*," *Texas Studies in Literature and Lan-
guage*, XVI (Summer, 1974), 315–28; Mary K. Bercaw, *Melville's
Sources* (Evanston: Northwestern University Press, 1987); Richard L.

Blevins, "Recasting Melville: *The Confidence-Man* and *Clarel* in Ed Dorn's *Gunslinger*," *Melville Society Extracts*, No. 77 (May, 1989), 15–16; Richard H. Brodhead, *The School of Hawthorne* (New York: Oxford University Press, 1986); Agnes Dicken Cannon, "On Translating *Clarel*," *Essays in Arts and Sciences*, V (July, 1976), 160–80; Hennig Cohen, ed., *Selected Poems of Herman Melville* (Carbondale: Southern Illinois University Press, 1964), pp. 60–94, 198–210; Shirley M. Dettlaff, "Hebraism and Hellenism in Melville's *Clarel*: The Influence of Arnold, Goethe, and Schiller" (Ph.D. dissertation, University of Southern California, 1978); Dettlaff, "Ionian Form and Esau's Waste: Melville's View of Art in *Clarel*," *American Literature*, LIV (May, 1982), 212–28; Dettlaff, "Melville's Aesthetics," in *Companion*, pp. 625–65; Amy Puett Emmers, "Melville's Closet Skeleton: A New Letter about the Illegitimacy Incident in *Pierre*," *Studies in the American Renaissance 1977*, ed. Joel Myerson (Boston: Twayne, 1978), pp. 339–43; Dorothee Metlitsky Finkelstein, *Melville's Orienda* (New Haven and London: Yale University Press, 1961); Stanton Garner, "Melville in the Customhouse, 1881–82: A Rustic Beauty among the Highborn Dames of Court," *Melville Society Extracts*, No. 34 (May, 1978), 13–14; Garner, "Surviving the Gilded Age: Herman Melville in the Customs Service," *Essays in Arts and Sciences*, XV (June, 1986), 1–13; Harrison Hayford and Merrell Davis, "Herman Melville as Office-Seeker," *Modern Language Quarterly*, X (June, 1949), 168–83, and (September, 1949), 377–88; Hayford and Merton M. Sealts, Jr., eds., *Billy Budd, Sailor* (Chicago: University of Chicago Press, 1962); Hayford, ed., in *Omoo* (New York: Hendricks House, 1969), pp. 343–47; Thomas F. Heffernan, "Melville and Wordsworth," *American Literature*, XLIX (November, 1977), 338–51; Lynn Horth, "Letters Lost/Letters Found: A Progress Report on Melville's *Correspondence*," *Melville Society Extracts*, No. 81 (May, 1990), 1–8; Richard Colles Johnson, "An Attempt at a Union List of Editions of Melville, 1846–1891," *Book Collector*, XIX (Autumn, 1970), 333–47; Vincent Kenny, *Herman Melville's "Clarel": A Spiritual Autobiography* (Hamden, Conn.: Shoe String Press, 1973); Walter D. Kring and Jonathan S. Carey, "Two Discoveries Concerning Herman Melville," *Proceedings of the Massachusetts Historical Society*, LXXXVII (1975), 137–41 (reprinted in Yannella-Parker); Robert K. Martin, *Hero, Captain, and Stranger: Male Friendship, Social Critique, and Literary Form in the Sea*

Novels of Herman Melville (Chapel Hill and London: University of North Carolina Press, 1986), pp. 95–99; Eleanor Melville Metcalf, *Herman Melville: Cycle and Epicycle* (Cambridge: Harvard University Press, 1953); Edwin Haviland Miller, *Melville: A Biography* (New York: Braziller, 1975); George Monteiro, "Poetry and Madness: Melville's Rediscovery of Camões in 1867," *New England Quarterly*, LI (December, 1978), 561–65; Henry A. Murray, "Another Triumph for Maria's Firstborn," *Melville Society Extracts*, No. 58 (May, 1984), 1–3; Murray, Harvey Myerson, and Eugene Taylor, "Allan Melvill's By-Blow," *Melville Society Extracts*, No. 61 (February, 1985), 1–6; Hershel Parker, ed., "Melville," in *Norton Anthology of American Literature*, vol. I (New York: Norton, 1979); Parker, "The Character of Vine in Melville's *Clarel*," *Essays in Arts and Sciences*, XV (June, 1986), 91–113; Parker, "Herman Melville's *The Isle of the Cross*: A Survey and a Chronology," *American Literature*, LXII (March, 1990), 1–16; Parker, "Melville to Duyckinck: A New Letter," *Melville Society Extracts*, No. 81 (May, 1990), 9; Helene Rozenberg (Sacks), "A Phenomenological Study of Melville's *Clarel*" (Ph.D. dissertation, University of Paris, 1974); Robert C. Ryan, "*Weeds and Wildings Chiefly: With a Rose or Two*, by Herman Melville; Reading Text and Genetic Text, Edited from the Manuscripts, with Introduction and Notes" (Ph.D. dissertation, Northwestern University, 1967); Ryan, "The Aesthetic of Melville's Poems," *Melville Society Extracts*, No. 41 (February, 1980), 1–2; Robert A. Sandberg, "Melville's Unfinished *Burgundy Club* Book: A Reading Edition Edited from the Manuscripts with Introduction and Notes" (Ph.D. dissertation, Northwestern University, 1989); Sandberg, " 'The Adjustment of Screens': Putative Narrators, Authors, and Editors in Melville's Unfinished *Burgundy Club* Book," *Texas Studies in Literature and Language*, XXXI (Fall, 1989), 426–50; Sandberg, " 'House of the Tragic Poet': Melville's Draft of a Preface to His Unfinished Burgundy Club Book," *Melville Society Extracts*, No. 79 (November, 1989), 1, 4–7; Merton M. Sealts, Jr., *The Early Lives of Melville: Nineteenth-Century Biographical Sketches and Their Authors* (Madison: University of Wisconsin Press, 1974); Sealts, *Pursuing Melville* (Madison: University of Wisconsin Press, 1982); Sealts, *Melville's Reading* (Columbia: University of South Carolina Press, 1988); Sealts, "A Supplementary Note to *Melville's Reading* (1988)," *Melville Society Extracts*, No. 89 (February, 1990), 5–10; Edwin S. Shneidman, "Some Psychological Reflections on the Death of Malcolm Melville," *Suicide and Life Threatening Behavior*, VI (1976), 231–42; Bryan C. Short, "Form as Vision in Herman Melville's *Clarel*," *American Literature*, L (January, 1979), 553–69; William H. Shurr, *The Mystery of Iniquity: Melville as Poet, 1857–1891* (Lexington: University of Kentucky Press, 1972); Michael N. Stanton, "Blake, 'B. V.,' and *Billy Budd*," *Melville Society Extracts*, No. 71 (November, 1987), 12–16; Jane Tompkins, *Sensational Designs: The Cultural Work of American Fiction, 1790–1860* (New York: Oxford University Press, 1985), pp. 28–29; Robert Penn Warren, "Melville's Poems," *Southern Review*, N.S. III (Autumn, 1967), 799–831; Warren, ed., *Selected Poems of Herman Melville: A Reader's Edition* (New York: Random House, 1970), pp. 35–48, 203–73, 385–410; Raymond Weaver, *Herman Melville: Mariner and Mystic* (New York: Doran, 1921); Larry Wegener, *A Concordance to Herman Melville's "Clarel,"* 2 vols. (Glassboro: Melville Society, 1979); Diane and Merrill Whitburn, "Melville's Vasari," *Melville Society Extracts*, No. 75 (November, 1988), 9; Donald Yannella and Hershel Parker, *The Endless, Winding Way in Melville: New Charts by Kring and Carey* (Glassboro: Melville Society, 1981); Philip Young, "Small World: Emerson, Longfellow, and Melville's Secret Sister," *New England Quarterly*, LX (September, 1987), 382–402.

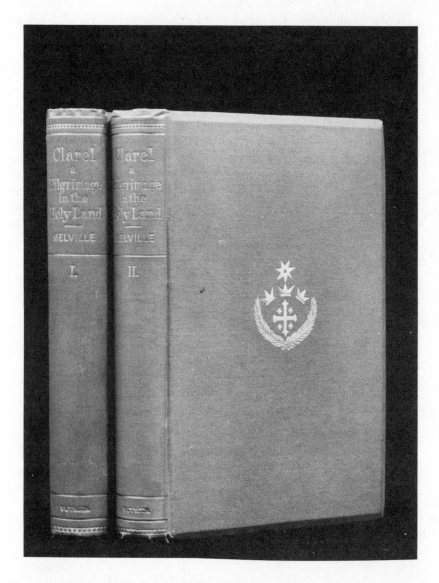

The two-volume first edition of *Clarel* (Putnam, 1876), with the "ensign of Jerusalem" stamped in gilt on the front cover (of each volume). Pictured is the copy Melville inscribed to his wife (see pp. 864–66 below); courtesy of the Houghton Library of Harvard University.

Note on the Text

THIS EDITION of *Clarel* presents an unmodernized critical text, prepared according to the theory of copy-text formulated by Sir Walter Greg.[1] Central to that theory is the distinction between substantives (the words of a text) and accidentals (spelling and punctuation). Persons involved in the printing and publishing of texts have often taken it upon themselves to alter accidentals; and authors, when examining or revising printed forms of their work, have often been relatively unconcerned with accidentals.[2] An author's failure to change certain accidentals altered by a copyist,

This NOTE was prepared by G. Thomas Tanselle with Alma A. MacDougall.

1. "The Rationale of Copy-Text," *Studies in Bibliography*, III (1950–51), 19–36, reprinted in his *Collected Papers*, ed. J. C. Maxwell (Oxford: Clarendon Press, 1966), pp. 374–91. For an application of this method to the period of Melville, see the Center for Editions of American Authors, *Statement of Editorial Principles and Procedures* (rev. ed.; New York: Modern Language Association of America, 1972) and the various discussions recorded in *The Center for Scholarly Editions: An Introductory Statement* (New York: Modern Language Association of America, 1977; also printed in *PMLA*, XCII [1977], 586–97).

2. Accidentals can affect the meaning (or substance) of a text, and Greg's distinction is not meant to suggest otherwise; rather, its purpose is to emphasize the fact that persons involved in the transmission of texts have habitually behaved differently in regard to the two categories.

publisher, or compositor does not amount to an endorsement of those accidentals. When the aim of a critical edition, as here, is to establish a text that represents as nearly as possible the author's intentions, it follows that—in the absence of contrary evidence—the formal texture of the work will be most accurately reproduced by adopting as copy-text[3] either the fair-copy manuscript or the first printing based on it. The printed form is chosen if the manuscript does not survive or if the author worked in such a way that corrected proof became in effect the final form of the manuscript. This basic text may then be emended with any later authorial alterations (whether substantive or accidental) and with other obvious corrections. Following this procedure maximizes the probability of keeping authorial readings when evidence is inconclusive as to the source of an alteration in a later authorized edition. The resulting text is the product of critical judgment and does not correspond exactly to any single authorized edition; but its aim is to come closer to the author's intentions— insofar as they are recoverable—than any such edition.

The Putnam edition of *Clarel* in two volumes, the only edition of the work published during Melville's lifetime, was set directly from the manuscript Melville furnished the printer, and, in the absence of that manuscript, the text of the Putnam edition becomes the copy-text for the present edition.[4] To test for variants among copies of this edition, three machine collations[5] have been made, involving four sets, one of them the copy (possibly containing some early sheets) in

3. "Copy-text" is the text accepted as the basis for an edition.

4. The particular copy of the Putnam edition that served (in the form of a marked Xerox reproduction) as the copy for computer keyboarding was designated as set 1 (see footnote 6).

5. These collations were performed on a Hinman Collator, which, by superimposing page images, enables the human collator's eye to see differences, including minute changes not otherwise easily detected, such as resettings and type damage. The number of collations that must be performed in order to detect all significant variations in a given text can never be prescribed with certainty, since chance determines, at least to some extent, the particular copies available for collation. Whether or not variant states of a first printing are detected, for example, depends largely upon whether or not at least one copy of an earlier state is present in the collection of copies assembled for collation; regardless of the size of the collection, there is always the chance that an unknown earlier state is missing. To reduce the element of chance somewhat, the present editors have checked many points in the four sets of *Clarel* in the Melville Collection of The Newberry Library and have examined copies in other collections. The term *edition*, as used here, refers to all copies printed from a single setting of type; *printing* refers to copies of an edition printed at one time.

which Melville wrote a number of corrections and revisions.[6] In addition, routine procedures in the process of compiling, checking, and preparing the textual information for publication have resulted in a larger total number of collations.[7]

Although these collations called attention to a few readings in need of emendation, the principal sources for emendations were Melville's annotated copy and the editors' close reading of the text. The present edition incorporates 193 emendations into the Putnam copy-text, 39 of them drawn from Melville's marked copy. In order to make clear the evidence and rationale on which these decisions rest, a brief account of the textual history of the work is given below, followed by a discussion of the treatment in this text of substantives and accidentals and an explanation of the editorial apparatus through which the evidence is presented.

THE TEXTS

N O MANUSCRIPT of *Clarel* is known to survive (except a folded sheet on which Melville in 1888 copied out from *Clarel* a twenty-one-line lyric, titling it "Ditty of Aristippus" [3.4.1–21]).[8] Therefore the only authoritative text is that of the first edition, published by G. P. Putnam's Sons in early June, 1876—on June 3,

6. The four sets used for these three machine collations were designated sets 1, 2, 3, and 4; they are here recorded by identification number (for those sets in the Melville Collection of The Newberry Library) or by library name and call number (for any set not in the Melville Collection): set 1 = M67–1394–2; set 2 = Copyflo reproduction of Harvard *AC85M4977.876c(B); set 3 = M67–1060–3 (Volume I) and M67–722–155 (Volume II); set 4 = Gift M69–32 (Raymond Weaver/Leon Howard set). The collations were: set 1 *vs.* set 2; set 2 *vs.* set 3; and set 3 *vs.* set 4.

7. Proofreading provided the chief opportunity for making these additional collations. Two proofreadings were made of the computer printout (based on set 1—see footnotes 4 and 6 above) against photocopies of set 1; two were made of the first page proofs against photocopies of sets 1 and 2; and two were made of the final page proofs against set 5 (M68–1396–1 [Volume I] and M67–1060–3 [Volume II]) and set 6 (Northwestern 811.3M531cl).

8. For discussion of this manuscript, see RELATED DOCUMENTS, pp. 867–70. References to the text of *Clarel* are to part, canto, and line(s), separated by periods. When "0" appears as the line number, the reference is to the title line of a canto. (Line numbers in these references are those marginally assigned in the present edition; they do not always match those marginally assigned in the Hendricks House edition [see p. 680 below] because two consecutive part-lines are here counted as one line, whereas in the Hendricks House edition they are counted as two.)

according to a letter Melville's wife wrote to Catherine Gansevoort Lansing the next day.[9] Although copies of this edition contain a few instances of broken type or defective inking that affect one's reading of the text,[10] no variations in the text (at these points or at others) have been discovered among copies of the 1876 edition.

The Putnam edition as published does, however, preserve some clues to the production history of the book. Evidently the original plan was for a single-volume duodecimo: most of the printed signatures correspond to a plan for twelve-leaf gatherings;[11] in such a duodecimo scheme, the beginning of Part 3 of the poem would have fallen in the middle of a regular gathering, but there is no deviation in the signatures after that point to suggest that two half-sheet gatherings had been contemplated; and the pagination at the beginning—with the table of contents ending on "iii" and the verso of the next leaf (the first leaf of text) numbered "8"—suggests that two more

9.   "Congratulate us, for the *book* was published yesterday. . . ." See also the HISTORICAL AND CRITICAL NOTE, p. 540 and footnote 39 above.

10.   In a few cases a punctuation mark is missing completely, such as the end punctuation at 1.42.82, 2.1.221, 3.3.64, 4.26.257, and 4.29.113; in a few other instances a mark is damaged so as to be ambiguous, such as the punctuation at the end of 2.22.41, 2.23.162, and 3.16.134, which appears in each case as the upper dot of a colon or semicolon, or the quotation mark at 4.1.177, which appears to be a single (not a double) superscript comma. The present discussion is not concerned with bibliographical details discovered in the process of collation unless they bear on textual questions, and it therefore does not mention instances of damaged type or defective inking (like the first "l" in "thrill" at 1.3.175, the "m" in "grim" at 2.28.33, or the colons—which, as the spacing shows, can only be colons, not periods—at 2.18.139 and 3.16.220) in which letters or marks of punctuation are partly visible and are recognizable (except those few noted by Melville in Copy B at Harvard—see RELATED DOCUMENTS, pp. 849–63).

11.   Those on the following twenty pages would have fallen—if duodecimo gathering had actually been carried out—on the rectos of the first or fifth leaves of gatherings (a conventional duodecimo signing scheme): pp. 33 (signature 2*), 49 (3), 57 (3*), 73 (4), 105 (5*), 145 (7), 177 (8*), 193 (9), 217 (10), 265 (12), 289 (13), 393 (17*), 409 (18), 417 (18*), 457 (20), 465 (20*), 481 (21), 513 (22*), 529 (23), 537 (23*). Twenty-eight other scattered pages which, according to this scheme, should have signatures are in fact unsigned, suggesting that perhaps some effort was made to remove the duodecimo signatures after the switch to octavo format was made. There are six other printed signatures (on pp. 65 [2*], 255 [8*], 359 [13], 549 [20], 557 [18], 568 [8]) that are anomalous—five of them not corresponding to either duodecimo or octavo gathering and one (on p. 65) happening to coincide with the opening page of an octavo gathering (but not representing the correct signature for that page).

pages may originally have been allowed for the table of contents, to accommodate the listing for Parts 3 and 4.[12]

Even after the decision to shift the format to octavo, there is some question whether allowance for binding in two volumes was made in planning imposition of the type pages. The nineteenth gathering, which would have contained the first two leaves of Part 3 as its last two leaves, was apparently printed in the usual way, for in the published copies of the book those two leaves are disjunct leaves (and thus stuck in, rather than sewn), having been cut from the rest of the gathering to be placed in the second volume (and making disjunct as well the first two leaves of the gathering, pp. 289–92, with which they had once been conjugate). On the other hand, the first gathering of the first volume (containing text of the poem as well as preliminaries) was imposed for octavo with the table of contents for only Parts 1 and 2 included. In any case, it seems clear that the dedication to Peter Gansevoort came at a still later stage, for the dedication leaf is not one of the eight conjugate leaves of the first gathering but instead is a disjunct leaf that has been stuck in following the title leaf. This inference is confirmed by Melville's wife's letter of April 22 to Catherine Lansing, stating that since Melville "has consented on the *very strong* representations of the publishers, to put his name on the title-page . . . *therefore* he has changed his mind about having a dedication."[13]

One custom-bound copy of the Putnam edition (Copy B at Harvard), in which Melville made notes for corrections and revisions, may contain some sheets that antedate the regular press run (see RELATED DOCUMENTS, pp. 849–63); but this copy matches other copies in the observed places where broken type and defective inking show up in the text. No later printings of the Putnam edition, after the original one,

---

12. It is also conceivable that the two pages were meant to provide a divisional title leaf for Part 1, corresponding to such divisional leaves preceding the other three parts; but there is no apparent reason, other than sheer oversight, for the omission of such a leaf, as there is for the omission of the table of contents for Parts 3 and 4. The fact that the pagination of Volume II continues the numbering from Volume I is of course consistent with the idea of single-volume presentation; but it is not in itself proof of such presentation, for nineteenth-century (like twentieth-century) practice was mixed regarding whether the volumes of multivolume works should be separately paginated.

13. In the same letter she reported that "the *plate-printing*" would be finished in a few days. On February 2 she had written that "The book is going through the press, and every minute of Herman's time is devoted to it—the mere mechanical work of reading proof &c is so great and absorbing."

were called for; and the copy-text for the present edition can therefore be defined simply as the text of the 1876 Putnam edition.[14]

That edition was distributed in England by Sampson Low, Marston, Low & Searle, with this firm's name stamped on the original Putnam title page. No other editions appeared during Melville's lifetime, and only two have been published since then, before the present edition. The Constable edition of *Clarel* (1924)—Volumes XIV and XV of the collected *Works*—is significant because it was the first edition after Melville's death and because it is part of the only complete set of Melville's works that has been available to scholars in the past and has therefore often been cited as standard. Its text departs from the Putnam edition occasionally in punctuation and spelling (especially through the substitution of British forms), and it offers no explanation of its editorial policy. In contrast to the Constable edition, Walter E. Bezanson's 1960 edition, the sixth volume to appear in the Hendricks House edition of Melville, contains a careful statement of editorial procedures and a list of 283 emendations. Bezanson incorporates Melville's revisions and corrections from Harvard Copy B; his other emendations are largely aimed at reducing inconsistencies in spelling and punctuation.[15]

TREATMENT OF SUBSTANTIVES

T HE TEXTUAL HISTORY of *Clarel* is simple: there was only one authorized printing, and the only known revisions, or possible revisions, that Melville made are the few he noted in Copy B at Harvard (one of which he also entered in the copy he presented to his wife—see RELATED DOCUMENTS, pp. 865–66). Therefore an editor's

14. Some facts about the publishing history of *Clarel* are given in the HISTORICAL AND CRITICAL NOTE, p. 540, and the HISTORICAL SUPPLEMENT, pp. 638–40 and 658–59. The volumes were bound in diagonal fine-ribbed cloth with beveled edges and brown endpapers; copies have been noted in dark yellowish green, dark reddish orange, light grayish reddish brown, and brownish gray (see the illustration on p. 674 above). A precise physical description will appear in the full-scale bibliography to be published in conjunction with the Northwestern-Newberry Edition.

15. Fuller details about the Constable and Hendricks House editions will be included in the forthcoming descriptive bibliography. The generalization about the text of the Constable edition is based on a partial collation of a copy of the Putnam edition (M67-1394-2) with a copy of the Constable *Clarel* (Newberry Y255M5). For some background relating to the Constable texts, see Philip Durham, "Prelude to the Constable Edition of Melville," *Huntington Library Quarterly*, XXI (1957–58), 285–89.

task is, first, to decide on the status of those revisions and, second, to locate and correct any errors in the 1876 copy-text—readings that cannot be the ones Melville intended, either obvious mistakes such as typographical errors or less obvious mistakes of whatever origin that are recognized when the sense of a passage is carefully considered.[16]

On a leaf that is preserved in Harvard Copy B between the front binder's leaf and the title leaf for Volume I, Melville listed twenty-three page references to Volume I (some out of numerical order, perhaps indicating the order in which he noted them). One of them (86)[17] he lined through; the remaining nineteen of the first twenty have check marks after them and in one instance (160) a phrase as well; the last three (298, 282, 262, in that order) have no check marks, and two of them (282, 262) have annotations. He also entered sixteen page references to Volume II (again out of numerical order) and in each case annotated them; and he wrote one further phrase from Volume II but did not indicate its page number (actually 461). In the text of Volume I he made notes or marks on all the pages listed except the one he deleted (86), in four instances making two alterations on the same page (29, 47, 161, 252); and he also marked on four pages (176, 193, 209, 240) that are not on his list. In the text of Volume II he made no markings whatever, although on the divisional title page for Part 3 (p. [301]) he made one pencil annotation, now erased but legible, relating to a line in Part 4. Nine of his markings can be eliminated from consideration as possible sources of emendation. In five of these instances the purpose of the markings is not clear: one consists of a check mark only (10), one of a deleted page number with no additional annotation (86), and one of a phrase that is identical to the printed text (461), and two consist only of check marks and underlinings (both on 252). In the other four instances, the purpose of his markings was apparently to call attention to damaged or improperly inked type (193, 209) and to wrong-font type (176, 240).

16. A third small task is to examine the manuscript of "Ditty of Aristippus" for variants; the only two (other than one of spacing) are in accidentals and will be taken up below.

17. The parenthetical numbers, in this and the next two paragraphs, refer to page numbers of the first edition listed by Melville or pages of the first edition on which he made marks or notes. Readers wishing to see what alterations are involved in each case should turn to RELATED DOCUMENTS, pp. 854–63, where a full list of Melville's alterations (accompanied by photographs) is provided, keyed to page numbers of the first edition and to line numbers of the present edition.

An editor is left, then, with forty annotations that can be considered as bases for emendations; of them sixteen involve changes in substantives. Just when Melville made these notes is undetermined, but it is possible that the set of Volume I sheets on which he marked was at that time bound in the regular publisher's binding (though perhaps the copy was an early or special one—see RELATED DOCUMENTS, pp. 849–53). If so, the reason these alterations are not incorporated into the printed text is not that Melville rejected them but that the sheets were already printed and bound. Even so, one might still argue that these substantive alterations, or some of them at any rate, were proposed tentatively by Melville and do not reflect a firm decision on his part, since those in Volume I, entered in the margins, are not accompanied by any cancellations in the text. Of the eight annotations involving substantives in Volume I, three (160, 199, 222) are accompanied by underlining in the text, making clear what word or words in the text are at issue; the other five (48, 116, 172, 268, 298) are not accompanied by any marking in the text, leaving the location of the proposed substitution unclear in at least one instance (172), and of course less explicit in all of them. One of those unaccompanied by marking within the text, however, is a necessary correction about which Melville could not have been undecided—the substitution of "inference" for "influence" (116), the latter word doubtless having resulted from a misreading of Melville's hand. Yet this alteration is entered in the margin no differently from the other four; nor does there seem to be any distinction in the kinds of alterations being proposed between that group of four and the group of three that do have accompanying underlinings. This situation is mirrored in the fifteen annotations involving accidentals in Volume I. In eight instances the location of the proposed alteration is made explicit—through a caret in the text (30, 31, 214, and the first alteration on 29), a canceling slash in the text (the second alteration on 29), a comma inserted in the text (the first alteration on 47), or a phrase copied out in the list at the front to show the place of the accompanying punctuation (262, 282)—and in the other seven instances there is only a marginal annotation (50, 145, 161 twice, 163, 233, and the second alteration on 47). Yet at least eleven of the fifteen annotations make necessary corrections (all but 262, the two on 29, and possibly 145), six of them being annotations that occur only in the margin, without markings in the text (50, 161 twice, 163, 233, and the second alteration on 47). This evidence suggests that the presence of a mark in the text is not a necessary condition for judging the alterations to have been regarded by Melville as settled. Thus there seems no clear basis for adopting some, but not all, of the alterations in Volume I as reflecting Melville's final intention.

In Volume II the situation is somewhat different, since there are no marginal annotations at all on those pages, all but one of the proposed alterations being entered solely in the list at the front, with the remaining one (now erased) appearing on the divisional title page for Part 3. But in every case the location of the proposed alteration is clear because Melville always wrote down (in the case of substantives) at least one word in addition to the substituted one or (in the case of accidentals) at least one word in addition to the revised punctuation.[18] Of the seven entries in Melville's list involving substantives in Volume II, one is a necessary correction ("become" for "became" on 357); and at least three others (395, 399, 568) correct readings that can be seen, in the light of Melville's annotations, to be definite compositorial errors. Similarly, of the eight entries involving punctuation in Volume II (343, 352, 363, 372, 397, 400, 450, 542), all but perhaps two (352, 397) are necessary corrections. Yet there is nothing in the way that the necessary corrections of either substantives or accidentals are listed to suggest that they are being differentiated from the proposed alterations that do not seem absolutely required. The one remaining annotation indicating a substantive alteration—the one on the divisional title page for Part 3 (p. [301]), proposing a change from "excellence" to "rectitude" at 4.21.51—falls into a class by itself, not only because of its location but also because it is now erased (though legible). The fact that this annotation was not gathered into the list of other alterations for Volume II may suggest that it was rejected by Melville, particularly in light of its having been erased. Who erased it is of course not known; but it seems unlikely that Melville's wife would have done so, since she allowed other annotations to stand and was particularly concerned that the binder retain Melville's list of revisions, and it is possible that Melville himself made the erasure. For these reasons, the present edition adopts all the alterations indicated by Melville in Copy B except for the erased one on p. [301].[19]

18. The one alteration of spelling ("Bandusia" on 425) is of course clear with only the one word entered in the list.

19. In some cases the precise form the emendation should take is debatable, and those instances are commented on in the DISCUSSIONS. (See the entries with asterisks in the list in RELATED DOCUMENTS, pp. 854–57.)

In addition, the present editors have located fifteen points, not among those noted by Melville, where they believe emendations of substantives are warranted. A few, like the change from "In" to "By" (2.9.70), "though" to "through" (3.1.100), "Sibyls" to "Sibyl's" (3.5.103), and "no" to "not" (3.28.86), correct simple slips (authorial or compositorial). Most of them, however, correct errors that most likely arose from a misreading of Melville's hand: for instance, the change from "rear-wall" to "rear-ward" (1.17.215), "Then" to "Than" (1.25.15), "need" to "needs" (1.25.95), "dearth" to "death" (1.28.29), "each" to "such" (4.26.310), and "scare" to "stare" (4.27.19). There are other problematical substantive readings in the text that are not emended, either because they are not certainly incorrect or because no plausible emendations have suggested themselves; see, for example, the entries in the Discussions for 1.1.44; 1.15.12; 1.17.224; 2.19.85; 2.29.67; and 4.1.99. Factual errors are corrected only when they are clearly slips that Melville did not intend; when it seems possible that Melville may have altered facts for poetic effect the errors are of course not emended. Thus at 1.24.60 there is no reason for the citation of Lamentations to give the incorrect verse number, and "fourteenth" is emended to "fifteenth", a correction that does not affect the meter and scarcely alters the sound pattern. But the statement at 3.5.91 that the Capets ruled for eight centuries (rather than the correct four) may be a figurative expression (and is not likely to have resulted from a misreading of handwriting), and it is therefore allowed to stand. Some errors, unquestionably Melville's, may not have been intended but nevertheless cannot be altered: at 1.8.22, for example, one gate of the heavenly Jerusalem is said to be of beryl, when all the gates were envisioned as pearl by St. John; "pearl," however, would change the meter and sound pattern, and no emendation can be undertaken. Some readings that do not reflect Melville's intention must inevitably have gone undetected by the present editors, but there is reason to believe that they are more likely to have originated as errors than as the publisher's intentional alterations: since Melville was paying Putnam's to print and distribute the book, it may well have been subjected to a minimum of publishing-house editing.

TREATMENT OF ACCIDENTALS

IN THE ABSENCE of a final manuscript, the degree to which the author was responsible for the accidentals—the spelling and punctuation—of a printed text is a matter impossible to settle conclusively. Even though some of the spelling and punctuation of the first edition of *Clarel* undoubtedly reflects the habits of the compositors who set it (and possibly the preferences of editors at Putnam's as well), the Putnam edition is nevertheless the only source of the text, and its accidentals, even when they may not be Melville's own, at least represent contemporary practice. Accordingly, the accidentals of the 1876 Putnam edition of *Clarel* have been retained in the present edition, except in the instances outlined below, even when the spelling and punctuation may appear incorrect or inconsistent by late-twentieth-century standards. Certainly the Putnam edition was full of inconsistencies. However many resulted from the compositors, many others were no doubt present in the manuscript; and, although Melville may not have been aware of them, they constitute a suggestive part of his total expression, since patterns of accidentals do affect the texture of a literary work. If Melville asked his wife and others to copy his manuscript of *Clarel*, omitting the punctuation as they had been instructed to do for earlier works, some of the places where necessary punctuation is missing in the first edition of *Clarel* may be evidence of Melville's oversights in inserting punctuation in the copied manuscript. But most of the inconsistencies probably reflect an indifference to consistency on Melville's part. Still others may of course have resulted from changes (either intentional or inadvertent) introduced in the printing shop. Because Melville was paying for the production of *Clarel* and Putnam's was not assuming any risk, it is unclear how much styling the Putnam editors would have engaged in; it is possible that they paid less attention to the details of the manuscript than they would have done if the work were being published at Putnam's risk, and the characteristics of the manuscript supplied by Melville may therefore be more faithfully represented in the printed book than would otherwise be the case. In any event, to regularize the spelling and punctuation would mean taking the risk of choosing nonauthorial forms[20] and imposing on the text a consistency alien to Melville. Completely to regularize the accidentals would involve making thousands of changes, inevitably taking the text

20. Melville's habits in the extant manuscripts and letters are not definite enough to offer grounds for emendation (and in any case the letters, not intended for publication, do not provide a parallel situation). Neither is enough known about Putnam house styling to be helpful in determining precisely what elements of the spelling and punctuation of *Clarel* resulted from it.

farther away from the manuscript and, in fact, producing a modernization. Therefore, no attempt has been made in this edition to impose general consistency on either spelling or punctuation,[21] and changes have been made sparingly, according to the following guidelines:

21.   For example, no emendations are made to secure consistency in the use of capital letters; the insertion of hyphens in compounds; the use of apostrophes in inflected second-person forms of verbs and in adjectives prefixed with "a"; the use and placement of punctuation in association with quotation marks and parentheses; the length of dashes; the punctuation of penultimate items in series; and the use of italics or of quotation marks (or both at once) for such items as biblical quotations and paraphrases, foreign words, mottoes, titles of books, words cited as words, and the like (the use of quotation marks is discussed more fully below on pp. 691–92).

Thus both "book" (e.g., 1.7.80) and "Book" (1.7.70) appear, as do "fane" (1.3.14) and "Fane" (1.3.76), "nature" (3.16.179) and "Nature" (4.28.17, 18), "passion" (1.3.185) and "Passion" (1.3.83), and "urn" (1.3.180) and "Urn" (1.5.2). The first word following a question mark is uncapitalized at dozens of places, even when the statement or question it introduces is syntactically complete (e.g., 1.5.217; 2.4.100; 3.12.129; 4.17.48); but at other places such a word is capitalized, even when it introduces only a phrase (e.g., 1.17.212; 3.8.89) and even when a similar word is uncapitalized in the same passage (e.g., cf. 1.15.53 with 1.15.56; 4.27.27 with 4.27.28). The same mixture of capitalized and uncapitalized words occurs after exclamation points (e.g., lower case at 1.2.129 and 2.25.1; upper case at 3.9.33 and 4.17.26). Although the opening word of direct discourse is usually capitalized, sometimes it is not (e.g., 2.29.145; 2.34.41); sometimes a capital follows a colon (e.g., 2.25.128) and sometimes not (e.g., 1.9.24); sometimes the second element of a hyphenated word is capitalized (e.g., "Ninety-Five" at 4.12.30 and "Thirty-One" at 4.12.45) and sometimes not (e.g., "Forty-eight" at 2.4.99 and 3.1.156 and "Eighty-nine" at 4.20.115). There is a hyphen at 1.37.36 in "over-rulings" but not at 4.26.326 in "overrules", at 4.2.131 in "palm-leaves" but not at 1.16.110 in "palm leaves". Apostrophes are generally used in second-person verb forms to mark an omitted "e", as in "com'st" (4.20.1), "fann'st" (2.36.50), "hold'st" (2.18.93), "mad'st" (1.13.71), "mark'st" (3.15.30), "need'st" (1.37.71), "rank'st" (2.27.180), and "speak'st" (2.18.100), but sometimes they are not, as in "servedst" (2.36.74); and those forms—like "didst" and "couldst"—that conventionally do not require apostrophes sometimes have them here, as in "Can'st" (2.21.92), "may'st" (3.25.67), and "Would'st" (3.26.33). Apostrophes are also present in certain adjectives beginning with "a", sometimes without a space (as in "A'lean" at 4.1.50, "a'thrill" at 4.9.97, and "a'shift" at 4.30.65) and sometimes with a space (as in "A 'lean" at 4.25.24)— and, by analogy, in "a'Becket" (1.3.108).

Punctuation associated with quotation marks and parentheses varies in several ways, as it does in Melville's other works: sometimes there is no punctuation separating an introductory clause or phrase from the direct quotation that follows (e.g., 1.3.195; 2.19.51; 2.27.19, 38; 3.11.188, 235), and sometimes there is no punctuation separating a quotation from the words that follow it (e.g., 2.25.124); sometimes a dash, marking an interrupted quotation, is placed outside the closing quotation mark (e.g., 2.10.48; 4.10.173) and sometimes within (e.g., 2.26.42); sometimes a comma

SPELLING. The general rule adopted here is to retain any spellings (even when inconsistent) that were acceptable by the standards of 1876, as well as any obsolete variants that may have been intended by Melville or reflect his reading in earlier material; spellings are corrected only when they do not fall into these categories. One available guide for decisions about spelling is the 1847 revision of Webster's *American Dictionary of the English Language* (Springfield, Mass., 1848). Webster's was the dictionary used by Harper & Brothers, publishers of most of Melville's earlier books, for Melville remarked, in his letter to John Murray, his first English publisher, on January 28, 1849, that "my printers here 'go for' Webster." The Harper accounts

---

precedes an opening parenthesis, with no punctuation after the closing one (e.g., 2.26.87; 4.9.22), and sometimes a comma (e.g., 2.22.67) or semicolon (e.g., 4.3.108) appears just before a closing parenthesis. Dashes are usually one em in length, but occasionally longer ones appear (e.g., 1.24.48; 1.28.20; 1.31.38; 3.8.117; 4.3.97; 4.9.139; 4.12.83; 4.13.129; 4.14.49; 4.21.57, 133)—presumably as subjective indications of longer pauses or more abrupt interruptions of direct discourse than one-em dashes would signify. Variation in the practice of punctuating the penultimate item in a series is illustrated, within a single passage, by the contrast between 2.39.143 and 2.39.161.

Among the inconsistent but acceptable spellings retained here are "Ay" (e.g., 2.8.18; 3.11.159; 4.23.29) and "Aye" (3.30.148); "by-" (1.21.11) and "bye-" (1.23.10); "bazaar" (3.8.28) and "bazar" (1.3.131); "can not" (3.16.6) and "cannot" (3.16.188); "chemistry" (2.21.34; 3.24.51) and "chymestry" (2.39.67); "æther" (2.11.23) and "ether" (2.27.64; 2.39.88); "height" (1.3.37; 1.26.31) and "hight" (2.28.36; 4.15.66, 71); "jackals" (3.8.143) and "jackall" (1.6.30); "loath" (1.27.97; 2.4.56) and "loth" (1.37.2; 2.39.97; 4.32.9, 10); "May be" (2.22.62; 4.23.51) and "Maybe" (2.16.71); "mold" (2.10.97) and "mould" (1.17.20); "Natheless" (1.25.88) and "nathless" (2.10.191); "O" (2.26.149) and "Oh" (3.16.80); "oftimes" (1.27.96) and "ofttimes" (2.32.46); "over night" (1.5.97) and "overnight" (2.25.29); "poignard" (3.12.73) and "poniard" (4.3.22); "sepulcher" (1.14.70; 1.41.117; 3.12.8; 3.16.12, 131, 248) and "sepulchre" (1.3.0, 15); "siren" (3.15.99) and "syrens" (2.26.71); and "subtile" (1.2.86) and "subtle" (1.1.67). In some instances a final consonant is doubled before a suffix (as in "shrivelled" at 2.28.7), and in other instances it is not (as in "traveler" at 1.41.101, "worshipers" at 1.35.71, and "worshiping" at 4.13.80). Melville had earlier preferred the "-or" ending to "-our", but the two are almost evenly mixed in the first edition of *Clarel* and may have been similarly inconsistent in the printer's-copy manuscript. The present edition retains both forms, both "Savior" (4.20.92) and "Saviour" (1.4.3; 2.18.79; 3.9.21), and such "-or" forms as "neighboring" (2.18.161) and "savor" (4.21.41) and such "-our" forms as "glamour" (1.17.220; 4.17.22). Finally, some acceptable variations in canto titles occur between the first-edition table of contents and at canto heads and in running titles: "Afterwards" *vs.* "Afterward" (3.20.0); "Fulfillment" *vs.* "Fulfilment" (1.19.0); "Hillside" *vs.* "Hill-Side" (4.18.0); and "Skull Cap" *vs.* "Skull-Cap" (2.2.0). (For a comment on diacritical marks, see the discussion at 1.37.115.)

show that Melville ordered at least three copies of Webster's (on April 10 and November 15, 1847, and on November 16, 1848), the third of which could have been the 1848 edition. Recourse to it and to other nineteenth-century dictionaries, such as Worcester's *A Universal and Critical Dictionary of the English Language* (Boston, 1847), to editions of American poetry and other works published in the 1860's and 1870's, as well as to such sources for the historical study of spelling as the *Oxford English Dictionary* and the *Dictionary of American English*, has provided the editors with sufficient contexts to justify the retention of some anomalous-appearing copy-text forms, such as "acolyth" (3.23.73), "campania" (4.16.167), "cantoes" (4.25.57), "cirque" (3.17.19), "coignes" (3.29.29), "Council" (for "Counsel," 1.26.35), "cruze" (2.18.6), "doated" (1.27.9), "fagot" (1.14.2), "festa" (3.17.7), "gairish" (1.34.42), "grandam" (2.14.119), "hight" (1.35.13 and many other places), "indue" (1.44.28), "lacquey" (4.3.126), "latteen" (3.13.43), "nathless" (2.10.191), "oftimes" (1.27.96), "roseace" (3.6.29), "scath" (1.26.19), "scimeter" (2.9.14 and elsewhere), "Septemberists" (2.16.47), "smooths" (2.6.40), "sojurning" (1.41.101), "suit" (for "suite," 2.35.40), "'Till" (3.27.48), "tryptych" (3.23.81), "vermil" (4.2.50), and "villanage" (4.19.139).

A few other forms, not found in reliable parallels in such contemporary sources, have been corrected; but any changes to bring spelling into conformity with an 1876 standard have been made cautiously so as to preserve the wide latitude allowed in contemporary usage, especially for proper names. First-edition forms of ordinary words that have been corrected are "archimandrate" (3.23.7), "optomists" (3.6.135), and "sign-manuel" (3.10.40). Some proper names, too, have been corrected, where the first-edition forms seem to be compositorial errors (such as "Hela" for "Hecla" at 2.13.25 and "Malbrino's" for "Mambrino's" at 2.20.99) or likely misreadings of Melville's hand (such as "Adullum's" for "Adullam's" at 3.7.14, "Ashtaroth" for "Ashtoreth" at 2.16.139, "Athanese" for "Athanase" at 3.23.63, "Cosmos'" for "Cosmas'" at 3.17.10, "Houran" for "Hauran" at 2.13.98, "Sargossa's" for "Sargasso's" at 2.17.33, "Shaddei" for "Shaddai" at 1.16.122, and "Thummin" for "Thummim" at 3.18.20); Melville himself corrected "Bandusa" to "Bandusia" (3.29.38) in Copy B at Harvard. Proper names in languages that use the Roman alphabet are corrected when no tradition (including Melville's own habitual practice) supports the first-edition form (e.g., "Frederic" at 2.26.130, "Nostrodamus" at 3.27.133, "Piranezi's" at 2.35.1 and "Sylvio" at 1.37.105), but seemingly anomalous forms are allowed to stand when there is such a tradition (e.g., "Bastile" at 1.7.11 and 2.35.6, "Betelguese" at 4.16.139, "De Gama's" at 2.18.21, "Haytian" at 2.10.126, "Melancthon" at 2.25.100, "Mendanna's" at 3.29.47, "Narraganset's" at 1.8.5, "Pekin" at 3.5.133, "Spinosa" at 2.22.110, 125, "Sydney's" at 2.27.85, "Sybella" at 1.25.79, "Thibetan" at 3.3.56, "Tombez" at 4.26.49, "Vallambrosa" at 3.9.29, and "Werter's" at 3.21.294). No alterations, however, are made in the first-edition spellings of Middle Eastern proper names (except in those few instances that seem clearly to be misreadings of Melville's hand), so long as they are attempts to represent the pronunciation of the intended words, because standardized English transliterations were not then (indeed, in many cases are not now) established and because many variant forms had been used in earlier books that Melville consulted (cf. the discussion of "Tamura" at 1.14.37). Some of the perhaps anomalous forms thus retained are "Adommin" (2.9.0, 18; 2.10.117; see the discussion at 2.9.0), "Aldemah" (2.37.5), "Astracan" (4.16.191), "Bazra" (3.14.79), "Cherith" (2.34.20), "Esdraleon" (1.17.18), "Karek's" (2.29.37), both "Mamaluke" (1.21.30) and "Mamalook" (3.14.69), "Mythra" (4.16.210), "Rama" (1.17.208; 4.29.111), and both "Siloh" (1.1.24) and "Siloa" (1.15.30).

PUNCTUATION. Emendations in punctuation are made only to correct obvious typographical errors and evidently incorrect pointing; but when punctuation is not manifestly wrong no alterations are made to bring it into conformity with some presumed standard, except when consistency is clearly intended. Melville's punctuation generally conforms to the rhetorical style of punctuation common in the nineteenth century, rather than to the syntactical style that has been more common in the twentieth century. Some of Melville's punctuation that appears strange to twentieth-century readers, particularly his use of semicolons, may seem more intrusive in *Clarel* than in the prose works; but any alteration of the punctuation to make it more syntactical would conflict with the aim in volumes of the Northwestern-Newberry Edition to present an unmodernized text. Neither is it normally feasible to consider questioning the choice of rhetorical punctuation at particular places, because the basis for rhetorical punctuation is too subjective to allow one to determine conclusively that the copy-text punctuation could not have been intended by Melville. Of course, when a period falls within a sentence, when a comma or semicolon appears at the end of a sentence, or when end punctuation is entirely missing, correction is obviously called for, and seventeen emendations of such typographical errors are made in this edition.[22]

There are, as it turns out, a few other places where emendation of punctuation can confidently be undertaken. In some thirty-four instances, punctuation is lacking at the ends of verse lines in situations where even the rhetorical system calls for some mark (whether comma, semicolon, colon, or dash) to complete the setting off of a phrase from the rest of the sentence. That the end of the verse line itself was not regarded as a sufficient break, rendering punctuation superfluous, is indicated not only by the thousands of other similar lines that end with punctuation but also by Melville's own correction of some of these defective spots; in Copy B at Harvard, he supplied punctuation at the ends of ten lines, three times inserting a comma (1.7.15; 1.12.113; 2.16.107), four times a colon (1.6.1; 1.12.114; 2.1.218; 2.33.64), twice a dash (3.21.290; 3.22.59), and once a colon and dash together (1.41.116).[23] Under these circumstances, the present editors have felt it necessary to insert commas at the ends of twenty-four additional lines in the belief that Melville would have inserted punctuation at those places if he had noticed its absence when marking this copy;[24] in the rhetorical system, semicolons, colons, or dashes could have been used at some of these places, but instead of trying to guess which mark Melville would have used the present editors have supplied a comma in each instance, as the least intrusive mark that nevertheless indicates a required pause. There are in addition just eight places where, for the same reason, the insertion of punctuation within

22. Periods within sentences are deleted at 1.16.8 and 4.2.191 (the latter marked by Melville in Copy B at Harvard) and are changed to commas at 1.1.75, 2.29.52, 4.16.2, and 4.21.84. Commas are emended to periods at 2.24.96, 3.25.112, 4.21.83, and 4.23.19, and a semicolon is emended to a period at 2.9.31. Of the six instances of missing end punctuation, Melville corrected three in Copy B, inserting a period once (2.1.221), an exclamation mark once (3.14.113), and a question mark once (4.26.257); the present editors have inserted periods at two of the other places (1.42.82 and 4.29.113) and a question mark at one of them (3.3.64).

23. The reasons for adopting all of Melville's alterations in accidentals in Copy B as definite (not tentative) revisions are explained above in the discussion of substantives (pp. 681–83).

24. The twenty-four lines are 1.3.168; 1.8.15; 1.12.23, 27; 1.15.15; 1.16.136; 1.31.157, 175; 2.5.47; 2.14.70; 2.21.64; 2.26.9; 3.1.23, 135; 3.2.8; 3.3.30; 3.5.107, 135; 3.11.245; 3.19.132, 144; 4.1.3; 4.11.41; 4.19.1.

a line seems absolutely necessary; at one of those places Melville's annotation in Copy B suggests the insertion of a hyphen (at 1.5.218 in "tempest-tossed"), at another place he inserted a comma (3.11.38), and the present editors have inserted six more such commas (1.16.50; 3.1.47; 4.3.41 twice, 4.19.151, 4.30.86). Melville also found, when marking Copy B, three places where he wished to revise punctuation already present (altering a dash—presumably to a comma—at 1.5.218, adding a dash after the question mark in 2.27.138, and shifting a dash to a colon at 3.12.57); and the present editors have made eight more similar changes (deleting the hyphen in "shrinking-frame" at 3.7.32 and altering a colon to a period at 1.5.63, 1.37.17, 3.6.53, and 3.13.82, a period to a question mark at 3.1.109,[25] a question mark to an exclamation point at 4.19.107, and a comma to a semicolon at 4.34.27).[26]

The only other category of punctuation that calls for particular discussion is quotation marks. The poem contains, within its regular metrical scheme, a great deal of direct discourse and many supposed quotations from literary and religious works (which often occur within direct discourse); it also incorporates some forty lyrics (generally spoken by characters) that often have their own stanzaic forms.[27] These passages are not marked as units of text in any consistent way. The problem this situation poses for an editor is not the inconsistency itself but the question whether there are any categories of inconsistency that represent an unfulfilled attempt at consistency. The present editors have concluded that the compositors of *Clarel*, and pre-

25. It should be noted that there are interrogative sentences elsewhere in the poem that do not end with question marks (e.g., exclamation points at 4.16.143, 178, and 4.27.3; periods at 3.6.133 and 4.24.26); the reason for providing a question mark here is that this sentence is one of a pair of linked questions, the second of which ends with a question mark in the first edition.

26. Five other emendations of punctuation are corrections of faulty typography (at places where the correction requires an editorial decision—cf. footnote 10 for comment on the places where a decision is not involved). Three times (at 2.22.41, 2.23.162, and 3.16.134) only the upper dot of a colon or semicolon is present in the first edition. In the first and third instances Melville indicated in Copy B that the intended mark is a colon; in the second instance the present editors have concluded that a colon is the mark probably intended, by analogy with similar constructions in this passage. The first edition prints at 2.13.124 a one-en dash where a one-em dash was presumably intended and at 4.1.177 half of a quotation mark.

27. The precise number depends on how one classifies biblical paraphrases, both spaced (as at 2.28.44–47) and unspaced (as at 2.38.29–31), and whether one counts interrupted lyrics (as at 4.5.171–88) as one or two.

sumably Melville himself, intended to employ consistently three con-
ventions in the use of quotation marks: (1) that quotation marks, if
they are used at all, must mark both the beginning and the ending of
the quoted matter; (2) that each paragraph opening within a quotation
should be provided with an opening quotation mark to signal the
continuation of the quotation (which does not end until a
closing quotation mark appears); and (3) that quotation marks should
regularly take the form of double superscript commas (or "inverted
commas," as they are often called, though only the opening set is
inverted), with the exception that those used to indicate a quotation
within a quotation should take the form of single superscript commas
(the next level of quotation reverting to double superscript commas,
and so on). The present text incorporates the few emendations re-
quired to produce consistency in these practices, on the ground that
such consistency was intended. Thus beginning quotation marks are
inserted at 2.26.23 and 3.4.129 (the ends of these two quotations
being already marked), and ending quotation marks are inserted at
1.13.74, 2.2.31 (both of these entered by Melville in Copy B at Har-
vard), 2.34.27, 3.6.25, 3.18.56, 4.16.26, 4.26.178 (a single superscript
comma), and 4.28.84 (the beginnings of these eight quotations being
already marked); quotation marks are inserted nineteen times at the
beginnings of verse paragraphs or stanzas within quotations (1.2.116;
1.15.6; 1.31.161; 2.13.129; 3.13.76; 3.19.34, 160; 3.20.4, 7, 10, 13, 16,
19, 22; 3.26.39, 44, 50, 55; 3.28.56), and once a quotation mark at the
end of a paragraph is deleted because the quotation continues in the
next paragraph (2.31.70); and three times a set of single superscript
commas is substituted for a set of double ones because the quoted
matter is within quotations (1.31.94, 95; 2.21.79; 4.19.33).[28] Alto-
gether forty emendations involving quotation marks have been made
in the present edition.[29]

28.   Three further emendations correct (1) an erroneous set of double super-
script commas at the end of a quotation within a quotation that properly begins with
a single superscript comma (2.10.155); (2) an erroneous set of double superscript
commas at the beginning of a quotation within a quotation that properly ends with a
single superscript comma (3.27.126); and (3) an erroneous single superscript comma
(the spacing of which suggests that another such comma may have failed to print
properly) at the beginning of a quotation that ends with double superscript commas
(4.1.177). And the placing of one quotation mark (3.27.135) is altered so that ellipsis
dots come within the quotation, as they do in the parallel instance six lines earlier.

29.   Counting pairs of quotation marks as two.

No other inconsistencies, or seeming inconsistencies, in the treatment of quoted matter are regularized here, since they may reflect nuances of meaning and since, even if they do not, they point to no single standard and reflect no concern for consistency. The text is therefore left with instances where unspoken thoughts or reveries or musings are placed in quotation marks (e.g., 1.5.33–43; 1.7.33–36; 1.27.83; 3.31.60–63), though in general they are not (e.g., 1.7.46–52; 2.27.64; 3.6.156–58; 4.3.107–28). The same is true of imagined speeches or statements of what a look or a glance "said" (e.g., in quotation marks at 2.27.26–34 and 4.21.30–37, but not in quotation marks at 2.20.109–11 and 3.11.197–98). Sometimes biblical quotations or paraphrases are placed in quotation marks (e.g., 1.13.74; 2.12.52–53; 4.9.69–79), sometimes in quotation marks and between line-spaces (e.g., 2.28.44–47), sometimes in italics (e.g., 1.13.36, 47; 2.38.29–31; 3.3.5; 4.33.65), sometimes in italics within quotation marks (e.g., 1.14.107–8; 1.24.61–63; 1.35.47–48; and between line-spaces, 2.39.108–11), sometimes in large and small capitals (e.g., in quotation marks at 1.40.48, and without quotation marks at 4.33.1) or large capitals only (e.g., in quotation marks at 3.7.1), and sometimes without any of these devices (e.g., 2.10.22; 4.20.37, 40). A similar mixture occurs in the handling of other quotations (spoken statements are generally enclosed in quotation marks, but sometimes not, as at 2.1.165–66 and 3.27.1–2, and sometimes they are in italics, as at 1.17.269 and 4.13.5, or italics plus quotation marks, as at 1.25.41–43); of mottoes, proverbs, and allusive sayings (in italics, as at 1.18.76 and 3.28.7; in italics and quotation marks, as at 3.12.78 [cf. 3.12.85] and 3.19.172; in large and small capitals, as at 3.12.20 and 4.13.193; with no marking, as at 2.20.60 and 3.9.27–28); and of words cited as words (generally in italics, as at 2.27.107 and 4.19.14; but also in italics and quotation marks, as at 2.3.60 and 2.21.79, and in capitals, as at 1.2.101 and 3.31.6—or even without any distinguishing marking at all, most noticeably throughout 4.22, which is entitled "Of Wickedness the Word"). Quotations within quotations are sometimes enclosed, as one would expect, in single superscript commas (e.g., 1.37.71–73; 2.22.89–91); but many times italics (with no superscript commas) are used (e.g., 1.18.100; 2.3.68; 2.31.43–44; 3.28.12; 4.16.77; 4.28.66–68), and occasionally italics plus superscript commas (e.g., 3.27.123–25, 149–50), or no special marking at all (e.g., 2.18.133–36 [cf. 2.18.140–43]; 3.7.72–74; 3.21.167–69; 3.27.157–59, 161–62; 4.16.199; 4.19.2–3), or no marking except a paragraph break (e.g., 1.1.92–99).

Similarly, the lyrics that are set off with line-spaces before and after are sometimes provided with quotation marks in the first edition and sometimes not. When they are not parts of larger quotations, they generally have quotation marks (1.41.106–15; 2.13.122–35; 2.25.193–204; 2.28.44–47; 2.34.50–63; 3.4.1–21,[30] 135–38; 3.11.1–4, 135–45, 178–81, 184–87, 213–20; 3.13.1–14, 96–101; 3.25.34–37; 3.27.156–62; 3.29.41–79; 3.32.56–64; 4.5.171–81, 184–88; 4.24.1–12; 4.26.324–31) and twice quotation marks and italics (2.39.108–11; 3.14.128–35); but a few times there are no quotation marks, leaving the spacing itself to mark the sung or spoken unit (3.22.47–66; 4.8.19–22; 4.15.66–77)—or speech headings, as in a play (3.17.21–58). When, however, such spaced lyrics do fall within larger quotations, the stanza openings are treated like paragraph openings and are provided with quotation marks for that reason; but generally no additional quotation marks are present to mark the lyrics themselves (2.2.24–26; 2.5.54–69; 2.10.41–48; 3.4.91–94; 3.12.131–32; 3.13.106–27; 3.14.31–38, 69–76; 3.20.30–31; 3.25.85–96; 4.16.202–10; 4.26.288–301), the only exception being the lyric at 2.31.50–70.

The presence of spaced lyrics calls attention to the fact that spacing is often a textual matter in poetry, not just a matter of graphic design. Indentation and line-spacing must be regarded among the accidentals, as a kind of punctuation. In *Clarel* two indentation practices seem intended to be consistent: the indentation of the opening lines of verse paragraphs (including those that follow a line-space) and the placement of part-lines so that each successive part-line begins near the point where in the line above the previous part-line ended.[31] Twenty emendations are required by this observation, falling into two categories: paragraph indentations that follow line-spaces and those that do not. The latter category consists of only four emendations: at 1.1.35 a paragraph indentation is inserted in the present text because in the original edition a quotation mark in a continuing quotation shows that a new paragraph opening was intended; at

30.   The lyrics that fall at the beginnings of cantos are listed here if they have closing quotation marks (and, if more than one stanza, opening quotation marks for stanzas after the first). The design of the first edition does not allow opening quotation marks at the beginnings of cantos; see footnote 40.

31.   The exact amount of indentation and the exact placement of part-lines are not in themselves textual matters, however. There are a few instances in the first edition, apparently unintended, where the paragraph indentations and the positions of part-lines vary from the norm. In the present edition the amount of paragraph indentation and the placement of part-lines are made consistent as a matter of design.

1.1.101 a slight indentation is removed from the second line of a paragraph, and at 3.13.16–17 a similar indentation is removed from the second and third lines of a paragraph (obviously compositorial errors). The other category entails the consideration of twenty places where the verse lines immediately following line-spaces are not indented. It is clear from thousands of other instances that line-spaces, except for those following spaced lyrics, are considered to produce paragraph breaks (but do not render paragraph indentations superfluous); lines immediately following spaced lyrics presumably may or may not begin new paragraphs and thus do not always require indentation. This edition supplies the necessary paragraph indentations in lines that do not follow spaced lyrics at twelve places (1.34.63; 2.1.14, 182; 2.16.89; 2.30.69; 3.12.129; 3.19.144; 4.33.37, 67, 75; 4.34.7, 22); of the eight nonindented lines that follow spaced lyrics, the present editors consider that four certainly (in light of the practice throughout) begin new paragraphs (3.13.15; 3.14.77; 4.8.23; 4.26.302) and that the status of the other four (3.11.182; 3.12.133; 3.25.97; 3.32.65) is not certain enough to justify emendation, even though somewhat similar lines are indented elsewhere (cf. 3.11.182 with 3.4.133; 3.12.133 with 2.2.27).[32]

In other respects spacing practices vary in such a way that one cannot conclude the variations are unintended. Indeed, line-spaces seem to be an expressive feature, marking more pronounced breaks than those indicated by paragraphing; thus many paragraph openings are not preceded by line-spaces, but many others are. Given this situation, one cannot convincingly argue for inserting line-spaces to set off speeches that seem to be lyrics of the kind frequently set off (e.g., 4.26.95–102); Melville may have thought of them as different from the spaced lyrics and regarded them simply as direct discourse. The present edition therefore does not emend the first-edition text by inserting any pairs of line-spaces to set off speeches or lyrics; but in two instances a single line-space is inserted at the end of a lyric (after 1.2.122 and 3.26.63) because a space is present preceding the lyric. Whether single line-spaces (and, indeed, paragraph indentations as well) need to be inserted or deleted elsewhere is a difficult question.

32. In the former group, one instance, 3.13.15, is actually indented slightly, but no more so than the two following lines and thus is counted here as unindented— that is, unindented in such a way as to mark a paragraph opening (see the discussion at 3.13.15–17). In the latter group, one instance, 3.32.65, follows a page break and is commented on further below, p. 697.

The paragraphing and line-spacing could of course be erroneous at any point, reflecting an authorial, scribal, or compositorial slip rather than authorial intention. But the reasons for the presence or absence of paragraphing or line-spacing at any given point are so subjective as to make editorial intervention unwise in most cases.

There is, however, one category of potential line-spacing problems that editors must consider: whether any intended line-spaces coincide with page breaks and are thereby concealed. In practical terms (for there is only one exception), this problem limits itself to pages that begin with paragraph indentations or the beginnings of indented lyrics, any of which could have been intended to follow a line-space. There are forty-six pages that begin with paragraph indentations[33] and three that begin with the first lines of indented lyrics (the lines are 2.39.108, 3.25.85, and 4.15.66). A strong case can be made that three of the page breaks in the first category and all three in the second conceal line-spaces. Of the former, 2.1.57 and 2.1.230 begin the descriptions of two of the pilgrims, and in this canto most of the individual descriptions are separated by line-spaces; and 3.20.25 follows a lyric of eight spaced stanzas. Of the three indented lyrics, all have line-spaces following them and thus seem clearly to require line-spaces preceding them as well, given the consistent pattern elsewhere: lyrics are not always indented, but, when they are, there are always line-spaces preceding and following them. The present edition therefore incorporates line-spaces at these six points.[34] It does not provide line-spaces preceding the other forty-three instances of paragraph indentations at the tops of pages; although line-spaces

33. The following indented lines fall at the tops of pages in the first edition: 1.3.119; 1.8.26; 1.28.48; 1.42.83; 1.44.32; 2.1.57, 230; 2.4.69; 2.9.32; 2.10.123; 2.11.62; 2.23.56; 2.27.102; 2.29.20, 124, 159; 2.34.10; 2.35.33; 3.5.137; 3.6.136; 3.10.19; 3.11.121; 3.12.135, 169; 3.13.84, 115; 3.16.182; 3.19.19; 3.20.25; 3.21.42; 3.23.53; 3.25.118; 3.27.51, 86; 3.28.56; 3.30.69; 4.2.66; 4.5.68; 4.9.21, 90; 4.10.126; 4.12.32; 4.16.7; 4.26.275; 4.27.29; 4.33.25. There are also five pages that begin with the second (and thus indented) part of a verse line made up of two part-lines (1.30.100; 2.13.100; 2.30.47; 4.1.127; 4.21.121); this category of indented lines can perhaps be dismissed from further consideration because at only one other place in the book does a line-space come between two part-lines (2.13.10), and at that point the compositor gave the second part-line the ordinary indentation for a paragraph opening, as if it were a full line. The consistency on this score is remarkable, whether it reflects Melville's manuscript or the printer's practice.

34. These spaces are not emendations to the copy-text but the result of editorial interpretation of page breaks: the editors consider these six line-spaces to be present in the copy-text but concealed by page breaks.

could conceivably have been intended at any of those places,[35] the matter is too uncertain to warrant including the spaces in the text.[36] There are two further situations—both unique—in which the present edition incorporates line-spaces in the text at first-edition page breaks. First, the lyric at 3.17.21–58 includes italicized and centered speech headings, indicating which of four "Voices" sing each line or group of lines, and two of these speech headings occur at the tops of pages (the headings preceding 3.17.37, 50); the typographic pattern of the lyric consistently employs line-spaces both above and below such speech headings, and they obviously belong at these two points as well. Second, the lyric at 3.32.56–64 has a line-space preceding it and a page break following it, with the first line on the next page *not* indented; clearly there should be a line-space at the end of the lyric, matching the one at the beginning, even though the next line is not indented, for a few verse paragraphs do apparently continue after spaced lyrics (see p. 695 above).

35.   There is one special case. In the first edition, 2.9.31 is at the bottom of a page and ends with a semicolon; 2.9.32, at the top of the next page, begins with a paragraph indentation. One must either remove the indentation or change the semicolon to a period; the matter could be argued either way, but the Northwestern-Newberry editors conclude that the semicolon, rather than the indentation, is the more likely compositorial error, and the semicolon is emended to a period.

36.   In three instances (2.29.124; 3.16.182; 3.30.69), the preceding type page is one line longer than usual, apparently to prevent a widow (a final line of a paragraph appearing at the top of a page). Widows are not, however, always avoided; but in all fourteen places where full-line widows occur they are never followed by line-spaces (1.11.33;   1.16.175;   2.14.23;   2.21.117;   2.26.93;   3.1.89;   3.3.32;   3.21.77;   4.7.65; 4.10.195; 4.14.11; 4.26.102; 4.28.124; 4.30.98). (Obviously a stranded part-line at the top of a page has some white space below it because of the indentation of the second part-line, as at 1.14.61, 2.22.45, and other places; but in no instance is there a line-space between such part-lines.) If one could conclude from these facts that the three anomalous pages mentioned here resulted from a particular effort to avoid any widows that would be followed by line-spaces, one would have grounds for incorporating line-spaces at these three points. But this is not a conclusion that one can have much faith in, and the line-spaces are not incorporated into the present text. (A related line-spacing matter may be mentioned here: the double line-space preceding 2.11.55 in the first edition was apparently inserted to make the paragraph 2.11.55–61 fill out the page, so that the first line of a new paragraph would not have to be stranded at the foot of the page—though at 2.13.64 an opening line of a paragraph at the foot of a page was allowed to stand even though preceded by a line-space. That space is standardized in the present edition to a single line-space: variable as the usage of line-spaces is, the intention throughout seems to be to use only one at a time, not to create breaks of varying sizes.)

One other spacing matter deserves notice. Lyrics that are set off with line-spaces also generally observe an indented left margin;[37] but in seven instances such lyrics are not indented (1.2.109–22; 1.41.106–15; 3.13.106–27; 3.17.21–35; 3.26.30–63; 3.29.41–79; 3.32.56–64),[38] and in one instance the left margin of a lyric is to the left of the regular margin (3.14.69–76). The former category does not call for emendation, since one cannot know whether Melville thought of these passages as "lyrics" analogous to the indented passages; in any case, the variability throughout in the means of designating quotations suggests that he was not concerned with consistency in this matter. The other category, in which a lyric extends into the left margin, does, however, result in emendation: that lyric is printed here so that its left margin is the same as the established left margin of the book as a whole. That the placement in the first edition was a compositorial decision (occasioned by the long lines) seems more likely than that Melville intended this one brief lyric to establish the outermost left margin, in effect making all the rest of *Clarel* indented.

One final question relating to accidentals arises from Melville's copying out of one of the lyrics (3.4.1–21), under the title "Ditty of Aristippus," in 1888. (For an account of this manuscript, see RELATED DOCUMENTS, pp. 867–70.) His copy varies from the first edition only twice, aside from his adjustment of the indentation of the second line (see the end of footnote 40 below). Both variants are in the last line, one in spelling and one in punctuation: "revelers" in the book becomes "revellers" in the manuscript, and the end punctuation is an exclamation point in the book and a period in the manuscript. An editor must consider whether these manuscript readings, in Mel-

---

37. That is, even when the lines of lyrics display intricate patterns of indentation (as at 3.4.1–21), the lines that begin farthest to the left maintain a margin that is indented from the regular margin of the book as a whole.

38. The fourth of these examples consists of the first fifteen lines of a chant in which different speakers are designated in speech headings, as in the printed text of a play; the remaining twenty-three lines are shorter and are indented. One further instance of an unindented lyric might seem to fall in this category—the "Dirge" at 4.31.1–19. But because this lyric constitutes the entire canto, it is in a class by itself; furthermore, indentation in such a situation would serve no real purpose, and no emendation need be considered. There is also an instance (2.26.1–14) in which the first eight lines of a lyric are indented and the remaining six are not; although this shift of margin could be a compositorial error, a break in the lyric does occur at this point, and Melville may have intended the arrangement of lines as printed, to distinguish the "doggerel" from the "after-cry" (lines 16–17).

ville's hand, should replace the readings of the first-edition text. The spelling "reveler" or "revelers" occurs four other times in the first edition (3.11.211; 3.12.29; 3.14.136; 3.25.97), and "reveller" or "revellers" does not appear at all. It is possible that by 1888 "revelers" had become Melville's habitual spelling, but it is equally possible that he used both spellings and was not making an intentional change in writing the word in this form. In any case, since the first-edition spelling consistently uses one "l", there is a strong likelihood that "revelers" was the form present in the manuscript used by the Putnam compositors and the form intended by Melville in 1876. As for the variation in punctuation, Melville's final period in 1888 may simply be the result of haste in copying; even if it was intended, this isolated change after twelve years would not supersede his intention of 1876. The exclamation point in the 1876 edition, matching the one at the end of the first stanza, seems more likely to reflect printer's copy than to be a compositorial error. Therefore neither of these variants in Melville's 1888 copy of the Aristippus lyric is incorporated into the present text.

EDITORIAL APPARATUS

THE BASIC EVIDENCE for textual decisions in the present edition is given in the preceding sections of this NOTE and in the two lists that follow it and complete the TEXTUAL RECORD. (Since there was only one edition of *Clarel* during Melville's lifetime, those alterations in Copy B—along with two in the "Ditty of Aristippus" manuscript—are the only known variants from his lifetime; and since all the alterations in Copy B, except the erased one, are adopted and thus reported as emendations, the LIST OF EMENDATIONS is also a record of variant readings—except for the erased one in Copy B, which is discussed above on p. 683, and the two in accidentals, not adopted here, in the "Ditty of Aristippus," discussed just above. All the alterations in Copy B and the "Ditty of Aristippus" are in any case recorded in RELATED DOCUMENTS, pp. 854–57, 867–70.)

DISCUSSIONS. The majority of these discussions identify Melville's allusions and sources. But a number of them take up textual questions, treating any reading (whether a copy-text reading or an emendation) adopted in the Northwestern-Newberry text that seems to require discussion or explanation beyond the general guidelines already stated. Certain instances of decisions not to emend, as well as some actual emendations, are commented upon.

LIST OF EMENDATIONS. This list records every change made in the copy-text for the present edition, accidentals as well as substantives. The left column gives the Northwestern-Newberry readings, the right column the rejected copy-text readings. When an emendation comes from Melville's annotation in Copy B at Harvard rather than from the editors, it is followed by the symbol HM instead of NN.[39] Items marked with an asterisk are commented on in the DISCUSSIONS.

As this list indicates, 163 emendations have been made in accidentals, 30 in substantives. Of the emendations in accidentals, 24 are corrections made by Melville in Copy B at Harvard, and the other 139 have been made by the present editors; of the emendations in substantives, 15 come from Melville and the other 15 from the present editors. No emendations of any sort have been made silently; using the LIST OF EMENDATIONS and its headnote (which describes the editorial decisions regarding line-end hyphens and page-end line-spaces), one can reconstruct the copy-text in every detail.[40]

39. The presence of an NN symbol signifies only that the reading does not occur in the Putnam edition or in Melville's annotations; it does not imply that no one has ever thought of it before.

40. That is, every *textual* detail: features of the typographic styling or design of the edition containing the copy-text are of course not recoverable from this list. In addition to the typeface used in the main body of the text, the following are regarded as features of styling and therefore nontextual: the form and content of the title page, half-title page, divisional title pages (here eliminated), table of contents (here changed from two listings to a single one, with new entries added for the end matter in the present volume), and running titles; the typography and end punctuation of the dedication and of the part and canto numbers and titles (the numbers here changed from roman to arabic), both in the table of contents and at part and canto heads (as well as the typography and end punctuation of other headings or closings, such as the speech headings at 3.17.21–55 or indicators like "End of Part First"); the placement and typography of the prefatory note; the typography of the punctuation surrounding italic letters (here consistently italic); the design of breaks between cantos (the decorative rules here eliminated); the use of marginal line numbers on text pages (present here but not in the first edition); the display capitalization of canto openings, the full capitalization of first words of cantos, and the paragraph indentation of opening lines of cantos (here printed flush left); the exact amount of indentation of verse lines and part-lines (though the *pattern* of indentation of full lines *is* a textual matter); the height of line-spaces and the width of spaces after marks of punctuation (here standardized); and the placement of opening quotation marks in spaced lyrics (here consistently standing clear). Although the part and canto titles in the first edition were set in capitals at part and canto heads, they are set in upper and lower case here in conformity with the styling of the Northwestern-Newberry Edi-

With the information presented here readers can examine and reconsider for themselves the textual decisions for the present edition and in the process see more clearly the relationship between the text of *Clarel* available during Melville's lifetime and the one that is offered here as a more faithful representation of his intentions.

---

tion; the capitalization of these titles has been derived from that in the tables of contents of the first edition (except for 4.18, where "Hill-Side" appears as one unhyphenated word in the table of contents).

Since the Northwestern-Newberry Edition does not use display capitals at canto openings (except for the first canto of each part), it can print opening quotation marks when cantos begin with quotations. Such quotation marks are not present in the original edition because the design of that edition called for display capitals and the omission of any quotation marks that would precede them. (In one instance, at the beginning of 4.24, there is no display capital, presumably because it would interfere with the pattern of indentations in the lyric that opens this canto [but cf. 3.4.1–2, discussed in the next paragraph]; in this one case, an opening quotation mark is present at the beginning of a canto.) The present edition inserts quotation marks at the beginnings of twenty-eight cantos, where the existence of quotations is made evident by the presence of closing quotation marks later. These insertions are not textual emendations but rather adjustments necessitated by a difference in typographic design between the present and the original editions. They are therefore not included in the LIST OF EMENDATIONS; but, for the record, their locations are noted here (by part and canto numbers): 1.9, 1.15, 1.34, 2.2, 2.4, 2.13, 2.19, 2.25, 2.26, 2.30, 3.3, 3.4, 3.7, 3.11, 3.13, 3.14, 3.16, 3.20, 3.27, 3.28, 3.31, 4.3, 4.9, 4.17, 4.19, 4.20, 4.21, 4.27. For comments on the instances where " 'Tis" is the opening word of a canto, see the discussion at 3.19.1.

An example of a further problem created by the display capitals is illustrated by 3.4.1–2, where the second line of the opening lyric is indented farther than the first because of the display capital in the first; it is clear from the other two stanzas, however, that the first two lines of each stanza are to be indented the same amount, and they are so printed in this edition (again an instance of design, not textual emendation). (Melville, when he copied out this lyric in 1888, observed the proper indentations in the opening lines; see RELATED DOCUMENTS, pp. 867–70.)

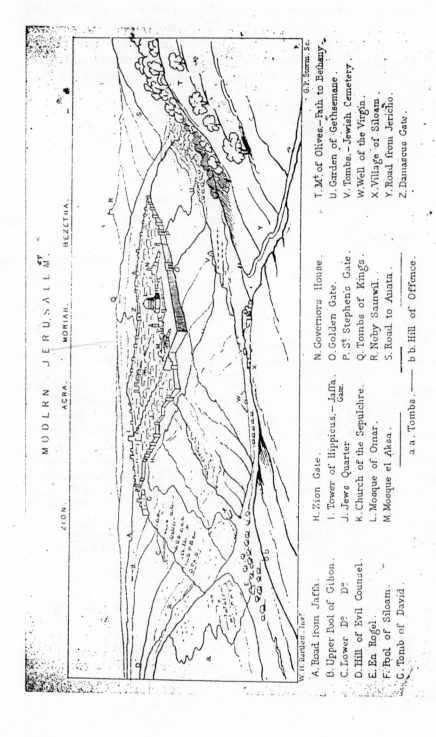

MODERN JERUSALEM.

ZION.   ACRA.   MORIAH.   BEZETHA.

W. H. Bartlett. Inv.   G. P. Storm. Sc.

A. Road from Jaffa.
B. Upper Pool of Gihon.
C. Lower Dº   Dº
D. Hill of Evil Counsel.
E. En Rogel.
F. Pool of Siloam.
G. Tomb of David.

H. Zion Gate.
I. Tower of Hippicus. — Jaffa. Gate.
J. Jews Quarter
K. Church of the Sepulchre.
L. Mosque of Omar.
M. Mosque el Aksa.

N. Governors House.
O. Golden Gate.
P. St Stephen's Gate.
Q. Tombs of Kings.
R. Neby Sanwil.
S. Road to Anata.

T. Mt of Olives. — Path to Bethany.
U. Garden of Gethsemane.
V. Tombs. — Jewish Cemetery.
W. Well of the Virgin.
X. Village of Siloam.
Y. Road from Jericho.
Z. Damascus Gate.

a a. Tombs. ——— b b. Hill of Offence.

Discussions

S INCE MELVILLE was a learned amateur with an extraordinary memory, the majority of these discussions identify his biblical and classical allusions, demonstrate his use of sources, and provide cross-references to his *Journals* and, when especially relevant, to other Melville writings and biographical data; other discussions comment on emendations and decisions not to emend (for commentary on special classes of textual decisions, see the NOTE ON THE TEXT, pp. 680–99). The discussions are preceded by a list of abbreviations and short titles of frequently cited works, a chronology of the pilgrimage, and two maps: Jerusalem and Environs (Map A, p. 707) and Route of the Pilgrims (Map B, p. 709).

Unless otherwise specified, all quotations from Melville's writings (and page references cited) follow the Northwestern-Newberry (NN) Edition (e.g., Volume 15, *Journals*). All quotations are presented *literatim* (except for the silent correction of typographical errors in secondary sources); any variation between a document as transcribed in the works listed below and as printed here is based on an examination of the original. Illustrations (some reduced) are drawn mainly from nineteenth-century books cited in the discussions.

ABBREVIATIONS AND SHORT TITLES

Bartlett, *Forty Days*	W[illiam]. H[enry]. Bartlett, *Forty Days in the Desert.* New York: Scribner, [186–?]. Sealts 48.
Bartlett, *Walks*	W[illiam]. H[enry]. Bartlett, *Walks about the City and Environs of Jerusalem.* London: Virtue, [second ed., revised, 186–?]. Sealts 50.
Bercaw (followed by entry number)	Mary K. Bercaw, *Melville's Sources.* Evanston: Northwestern University Press, 1987.
Bezanson	Walter E. Bezanson, "Herman Melville's *Clarel.*" Ph.D. dissertation, Yale University, 1943.
Bezanson, "Arnold's Poetry"	Walter E. Bezanson, "Melville's Reading of Arnold's Poetry," *PMLA,* LXIX (June, 1954), 365–91.
Chateaubriand	F. A. de Chateaubriand, *Travels in Greece, Palestine, Egypt, and Barbary, During the Years 1806 and 1807.* Trans. F. Shoberl. [London: Colburn, 1811–12]; New York: Van Winkle & Wiley, 1814.
Copy B	*Clarel,* a custom-bound copy of the first edition with revisions in Melville's hand; now in the Houghton Library of Harvard University. See pp. 849–63 below.
Curzon	Robert Curzon, *A Visit to Monasteries in the Levant.* New York: Putnam; London: Murray, 1849.
HCL-M	Melville Collection (Harvard College Library) of the Houghton Library of Harvard University
Index	A Critical Index of the Characters (in the present volume, pp. 613–35).
Kitto	*The Cyclopædia of Biblical Literature.* Ed. John Kitto. 2 vols. [Edinburgh: Black, 1845]; New York, 1845, and later printings from the same plates, with the same pagination, various publishers.
Log	Jay Leyda, *The Melville Log: A Documentary Life of Herman Melville, 1819–1891.* New York: Harcourt, Brace, 1951; Gordian Press, 1969. 2 vols. [Forthcoming: *The New Melville Log,* ed. Jay Leyda and Hershel Parker. New York: Gordian Press].

Murray	*A Handbook for Travellers in Syria and Palestine.* 2 vols. London: Murray, 1858.
NN	Northwestern-Newberry Edition
Sealts (followed by entry number)	Merton M. Sealts, Jr., *Melville's Reading.* Revised and Enlarged Edition. Columbia: University of South Carolina Press, 1988.
Stanley	Arthur Penrhyn Stanley, *Sinai and Palestine in Connection with Their History.* New York: Redfield, 1857; reprinted from the same plates, New York: Widdleton, 1863 [Sealts 488], 1865.
Thomson	William McClure Thomson, *The Land and the Book; or, Biblical Illustrations Drawn from the Manners and Customs, the Scenes and Scenery of the Holy Land.* 2 vols. New York: Harper, 1858; reprinted 1859 [Sealts 523].
Warburton	Eliot Warburton, *The Crescent and the Cross; or, Romance and Realities of Eastern Travel.* [London: Colburn, 1844]; New York: Wiley & Putnam, 1845; later printings 1848, 1849, 1850, 1859.
Wright	*Early Travels in Palestine.* Ed. Thomas Wright. London: Bohn, 1848.

View of the Dead Sea from the W. of Mt. of Olives.

MODERN JERUSALEM

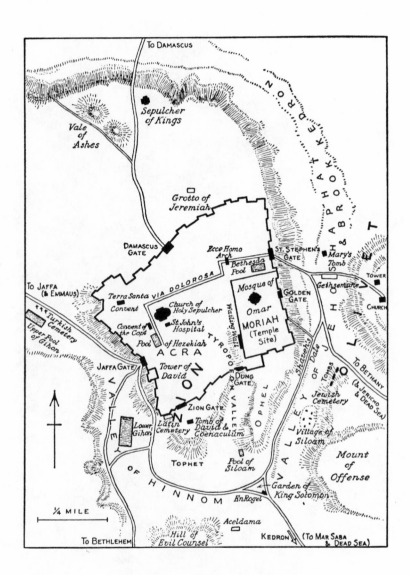

(A) JERUSALEM AND ENVIRONS

DEAD SEA FROM THE TOP OF OLIVET.

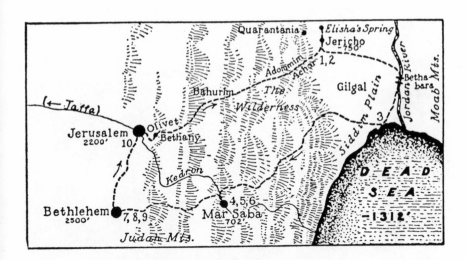

(B) ROUTE OF THE PILGRIMS

CHRONOLOGY OF THE PILGRIMAGE

Days
1, 2   The pilgrims leave Jerusalem on the morning of Candlemas (February 2) and spend the first night at the Crusaders' Tower near Jericho. The second day is given to explorations and talk.

Day 3   On the third morning the pilgrims head for the Jordan and spend that night by the Dead Sea.

Days
4, 5, 6 They travel up the Judah mountains and reach Mar Saba at evening; the night is given to revels and evaluations. The fifth day is a holy day at the monastery with ceremonials that reach into the night. They watch the dawning of the sixth day from Saba's tower and then turn to individual explorations of the monastery.

Days
7, 8, 9 At dawn of the seventh day the pilgrims leave Mar Saba, traveling to Bethlehem and spending the night at the Latin monastery by the Church of the Nativity. They watch the eighth day break and are still in Bethlehem at twilight. The ninth day dawns in Bethlehem also, and they remain to watch the rites of the monks. Late at night they take saddle for Jerusalem.

Day 10   The pilgrims reach the city gates at the dawn of Ash Wednesday.

MOUNT ZION – JAFFA GATE.

PART 1

1.1.0   THE HOSTEL] The opening scene is a room in what is evidently the Mediterranean Hotel, in Jerusalem, like the one in which Melville stayed from January 6–18, 1857, except for a three-day excursion to the Dead Sea (*Journals*, pp. 79–80).

1.1.10   Vigil of Epiphany] January 6, a church festival celebrating the coming of the Magi to visit the baby Jesus at Bethlehem. Since the pilgrims leave Jerusalem on Candlemas, February 2 (1.44.2), Part 1 covers a time span of four weeks minus one day. Melville's use of holy days as a backdrop for Clarel's problem and passion, here and especially at the end of the poem (4.29–34), gives dramatic irony to the narrative. Melville apparently had no specific year in mind by referring to these holy days: in the poem's time scheme, Ash Wednesday falls on February 11, ten days after Candlemas, but it did so in no actual year between 1850 and the publication of the poem.

1.1.24   Siloh's oracle] The Pool of Siloam (Map A, p. 707), the site of Jesus' miracle of the healing of the blind man, John 9.1–7 (see also the discussion at 1.28.96). Milton's invocation at the opening of *Paradise Lost* comes to mind: "Siloa's brook that flow'd / Fast by the Oracle of God" (1.11; Melville owned the *Poetical Works* [Boston: Hilliard, Gray, 1836; Sealts 358b]; see also the NN *Moby-Dick*, pp. 957–58).

1.1.28   Off Jaffa] The usual port of entry for tourists and pilgrims going to Jerusalem. Ships had to anchor a mile from shore in the open roadstead, while small boats beat through dangerous surf and rocks to land passengers (the illustration opposite is from Rev. James Aitken Wylie, *The Modern Judea* [Glasgow: Collins, 1841], facing p. 329). Jerusalem, about forty miles to the southeast, could be reached only by horseback across the coastal Plain of Sharon (line 38). From the little town of Ramleh (line 41), nine miles inland, there was a view of the Ephraim Mountains (line 46), stretching north of Jerusalem. Melville took this route in 1857 (see *Journals*, p. 79); the Jaffa Gate by which he entered the city is pictured opposite, from W. H. Bartlett's *Jerusalem Revisited* (London: Hall & Virtue, 1855), frontispiece.

1.1.39   her titled Rose] The famous "rose of Sharon" named in the Song of Solomon 2.1. Controversy as to its species and color was common, and is reflected here and in the 1856–57 journal: "A delightful ride across Plain of Sharon to Jaffa. Quanities of red poppies. (Rose of Sharon?)" (p. 80). The answer to Melville's question is "No" (*Journals*, p. 423).

1.1.44   dazing] This word has the meaning "glittering" in the 1848 Webster's and is presumably what Melville wrote, though perhaps it is an error for "dazzling".

1.1.58   Louis] Chateaubriand, pp. 464–65, tells what Louis IX and his Crusaders encountered at Carthage in 1270: "the Moors raised the burning sand by means of machines, and scattering it before the southern breeze, they exposed the Christians by this fiery shower to the effects of the *Kamsin*, or terrible wind of the desert."

1.1.64   Salem to be no Samarcand] The theme is that of many passages in Melville's 1856–57 journal, particularly the following: "No country will more quickly dissipate romantic expectations than Palestine—particularly Jerusalem. To some the disappointment is heart sickening. &c" (p. 91). Salem, the ancient name for Jerusalem (Gen. 14.18), is used frequently in the poem. Samarkand, an ancient city of Central Asia, conquered by Alexander and once Tamerlane's capital, here symbolizes Romance.

1.1.87   my countryman] The remarks of "my countryman" are such as Melville himself might have made to a young traveler, and serve as early warning against confusing the mature Melville with the young Clarel.

1.1.108   Vesta] Roman virginal divinity, goddess of the hearth, the symbol of home.

1.1.125–26   He sought . . . warm stone,] In Copy B of *Clarel* (HCL-M) Melville put a check beside these two lines; his intention is not clear (see pp. 854 and 858 below).

POOL OF HEZEKIAH.

1.1.134   the view] Exactly this view (Map A, p. 707) from a roof terrace above the Pool of Hezekiah (lines 146–47), looking east toward Olivet (line 139), may be seen opposite, from Thomson, II, [523]. Acra (line 135) was the northwest section, the Christian Quarter, of Jerusalem. The Coptic Convent (line 161) was just north of the Mediterranean Hotel, toward the Church of the Holy Sepulcher. Melville's room in this hotel in 1857 had a similar view: "Hotel overlooks on one side Pool of Hezekiah (balconies) is near the Coptic Convent. . . . From platform in front of my chamber, command view of battered dome of Church of Sepulchre & Mount Olivet" (*Journals*, p. 79; this passage he marked with a large red-pencil crosshatch—see the textual note at 79.19). Elsewhere he noted that the minarets of Constantinople "gleam like lighthouses" (*Journals*, p. 74; cf. line 162).

1.1.167   the Kaatskills] The old Dutch spelling (used by Washington Irving) for the Catskill Mountains of east-central New York.

1.2.3   a slim vial] A tube containing the mezuzah, a parchment with passages from the Law (Deut. 6.4–9; 11.13–30) inscribed on it. The parchment was rolled so that the word "Shaddai" (Almighty) showed through a hole in the vial. Melville's 1856–57 journal describes his room in the English Hotel at Jaffa: "In the right lintel of the door is a vial masoned in, & visable, containing some text of Jewish scripture—a charm" (*Journals*, p. 81; see also p. 426, which explains line 5: the innkeeper told a contemporary traveler he had put vials on the lintel of every door; but "Frenchmen, who did not read the Bible, sometimes mocked at it, and this led to angry discussion, so that from many of the doors it was now removed").

1.2.7   the Black Jew] See ABDON (Index) for Melville's source and the idea that he came from Cochin (line 32).

1.2.38   Esdras saith] In the Apocrypha (2 Esd. 13.40–45).

1.2.45   scholars various notions] The mystery of the Lost Tribes fascinated the nineteenth century. Of the original twelve tribes of Israel (Gen. 49), which included Judah and Benjamin (line 48), ten "disappeared from history during and after the Babylonian captivity," according to Kitto, II, 893, and occasioned "so many volumes that it would be difficult to condense the contradictory opinions advanced in them." But Clarel's "deeper mystery" (line 47) would seem to be: how has Jewish culture survived all this time?

1.2.50   Amazon] The fresh waters of the river carry two hundred miles into the sea, so great is its volume.

1.2.69   Under Moriah] Many Jews returned to be buried in the Valley of Jehoshaphat, beneath the shoulder of Moriah, which was the site of the ancient Temple (Map A, p. 707).

THE HOLY SEPULCHRE.

1.2.87 an amulet] Presumably the phylactery; strips of parchment inscribed with four biblical passages were folded into a small leather box and attached by leather straps to the forehead and left arm, in accordance with the Law (Deut. 6.8). Kitto, II, 532, says "they were also regarded as amulets." The leathern "scroll" here (line 89) and in line 17 may be the parchment.

1.2.101 JUDÆA] The poem by this title which follows first asks for gifts from "Sychem" (Shechem: line 110), one of the most fertile and beautiful towns of Palestine, 34 miles north of Jerusalem. Then it names Mt. Tabor (line 111), further north, whose slopes ("which the Eden drapes" [line 111]—i.e., Eden-like) are verdant with oaks, bushes, and pistachio trees. Finally it cites Sharon (see the discussion at 1.1.39). But these three beautiful sites are in Samaria and Galilee, not Judaea. Their grapes, garlands, and roses contrast with the dusty "palms" (line 121) of the second stanza and set the theme of desolate Judaea, site of *Clarel*.

1.2.102 paper lining of the tray] Writing to his brother Tom, May 25, 1862, Melville told of having sold off a batch of "doggerel . . . at ten cents the pound" to a trunk-maker: "So, when you buy a new trunk again, just peep at the lining & perhaps you may be rewarded by some glorious stanza stareing you in the face & claiming admiration."

1.2.122 Since . . . me."] NN inserts a line-space after this line, marking the end of the lyric, because in the first edition there is a line-space (actually a smaller space than the usual line-space) after line 107, marking the beginning of the lyric. The spaces in the first edition after lines 107, 108, 115, and 116 are all smaller than the usual line-spaces but are clearly intended as such; NN regularizes them to a standard size as a matter of design.

1.2.134 Katahdin] A mountain in central Maine; its complete lack of supernatural associations, as contrasted with the hallowed slopes of Olivet, sounds again the "naturalistic knell" (line 23) of the opening canto.

1.3.0 THE SEPULCHRE] The church and Melville's frequent visits there are described in the HISTORICAL AND CRITICAL NOTE, pp. 517–18, and in *Journals*, pp. 79, 85, 87–89 (this last lengthy passage—heavily revised—was later marked through in pencil, probably after use in *Clarel*). Melville read and marked up Stanley's account of the church, pp. 451–66; the canto reflects Stanley's point that, authentic or not, the site is of great historical interest (lines 112–14), and notes the merchant-like activities on holy days (lines 125–32), the specific comparison of the open dome with the Pantheon (lines 169–70), and other bits on Godfrey and Baldwin (see the discussion at line 177 below), Golgotha, the chapels, etc. The site was widely discussed and pictured in Holy Land literature; the illustrations on pp. 714–15 here are from Bartlett's *Walks*, facing p. 168, and Thomson, II, [562]. Pictured opposite is the sepulcher itself, from *Walks*, p. 175.

CHURCH OF THE HOLY SEPULCHRE.

1.3.1   In Crete] Mt. Ida in Crete was sacred above all other places to Zeus (here "Jove," the Roman name); there he was born in a secret cave and there, some claimed, was his tomb.

1.3.41   The Druid priest Melchizedek] King of Salem and "the priest of the most high God," Melchizedek brought bread and wine to the valley of Shaveh (line 39) and blessed Abram for driving out the enemy after the Battle of the Kings (Gen. 14). This "earliest authentic record of Canaanite history" as Stanley, pp. 282–83, calls it, is used by Melville as a "primeval" (line 38) scene of Druidic rites to set the tone for contemporary rituals. Here and elsewhere in the poem Melville places Shaveh in the Kedron ravine (Valley of Jehoshaphat) alongside Jerusalem; Stanley argues (pp. 246–47) that it was actually east of the Jordan, but in Melville's copy of Stanley the two leaves containing pp. 245–48 are not completely opened.

1.3.94   power . . . subdue] Cf. Wordsworth's "Tintern Abbey," lines 32–33: ". . . of ample power / To chasten and subdue." In his annotated copy of the *Complete Poetical Works* (Sealts 563a; see p. 646n. above), Melville heavily checked the title of this poem in the table of contents but did not mark these lines.

1.3.108   a'Becket's slayers] Tradition has it that the knights who slew the Archbishop of Canterbury were required to serve fourteen years under the Templars of the Holy Land, in penance; also that they were buried in the porch outside the church of the Templars (now the mosque El Aksa, on Moriah: line 111). On this spelling of "a'Becket", see the NOTE ON THE TEXT, p. 686, footnote 21.

1.3.123   pedlars versed in wonted tricks] Melville had described the courtyard before the Church of the Holy Sepulcher in his 1856–57 journal as "A considerable area, flagged with venerable stones, upon which are seated a multitude of hawkers & pedlers of rosaries, crucifixes, toys of olive wood and Dead Sea stone, & various other amulets & charms" (p. 89; this passage marked with a small "x" in red pencil—see the textual note at 89.3).

1.3.152   like Ludovico] The villain in Richard Sheil's *Evadne: or, The Statue* (1819; New York: Berford, 1847), first played in Covent Garden in 1818 with Macready as Ludovico, and playing in the Bowery in 1847. The setting for act 5: "A vast Hall in Colonna's Palace, filled with Statues.—The Moon streams in through the Gothic windows, and appears to fall upon the Statues. A Chamber-door at back." Ludovico has arranged the murder of the king of Naples, and believes him dead, when suddenly the king comes forward from behind the statues. Ludovico:

> What do I behold? is not my sense
> Mocked with this horrid vision,
> That hath started up
> To make an idiot of me?—is it not
> The vapour of the senses that has framed
> The only spectacle that ever yet
> Appalled Ludovico?

1.3.163   pride's Smyrna shawl] Possibly as in Hawthorne's "Lady Eleanore's Mantle," in *Twice-Told Tales* (vol. II, 1837); not marked in Melville's copy (Boston: Munroe, 1842; Sealts 260; Bercaw 341).

1.3.168   Golgotha] Hebrew for skull, and the site of the Crucifixion (Matt. 27.33). Melville noted in his 1856–57 journal that the dome of the church was "battered," "damaged," and "ruined" (pp. 79, 87); the parallel with the Pantheon (line 170) at Rome is of course ideological as well as archaeological.

1.3.177   Godfrey and Baldwin] Bartlett, *Walks*, p. 177, notes that near "the rock of Calvary" in the church "are the tombs of Godfrey of Bouillon, leader of the Crusaders, the first Latin King of Jerusalem, and his brother Baldwin" (later destroyed). Godfrey (ca. 1060–1100, r. 1099) was the hero of Tasso's *Jerusalem Delivered* (1581), an allegorical epic of the siege and capture of Jerusalem in the First Crusade; Baldwin (1058?–1118) was crowned his brother's successor on Christmas Day, 1100. In 1857 Melville saw Tasso's birthplace near Naples, his tomb in Rome, and his prison in Ferrara (*Journals*, pp. 104, 110, and 117). See also the discussions below at 1.4.5 and 2.16.80.

1.3.181–82   fancy ... / Imagination] The pointed distinction here is Coleridge's, in *Biographia Literaria* (second ed., New York: Wiley & Putnam, 1847 or 1848; Sealts 154; Bercaw 147). Note how Rolfe is linked to imagination through the word "earnest"; see the HISTORICAL AND CRITICAL NOTE, pp. 589–90.

1.3.186   the three pale Marys' frame] Mary the mother of Jesus, Mary Magdalene, and "the other Mary" (Matt. 27.61); all three were at the Crucifixion. The "she" of the next line is Imagination, and "the eclipse" refers to Luke's account of the Crucifixion: "And the sun was darkened ... " (Luke 23.45).

1.3.200   The floral Easter holiday] Compare with "Easter" (4.33).

1.4.5   wherefore did they doff the plume] In Tasso's *Jerusalem Delivered* (see the discussion at 1.3.177) occurs the stanza (canto 3.7, trans. Wiffen) describing the Crusaders at the moment of sighting Jerusalem (from contemporary reports):

> Each, at his Chief's example, lays aside
> His scarf and feathered casque, with every gay
> And glittering ornament of knightly pride,
> And barefoot treads the consecrated way.
> Their thoughts, too, suited to their changed array,
> Warm tears devout their eyes in showers diffuse,—
> Tears, that the haughtiest temper might allay. ...

The stanza is quoted in Bartlett, *Walks*, p. 120. Note the relation of the third line to Melville's line 32, and of the last two lines to Melville's lines 17–19.

1.4.7   to quote Voltaire] As Gibbon did in the passage (chap. 58) describing first the "promiscuous massacre" which the Crusaders engaged in for three days after capturing Jerusalem; then—"Bareheaded and barefoot, with contrite hearts and in a humble posture, they ascended the hill of Calvary, amidst the loud anthems of the clergy, kissed the stone which had covered the Saviour of the world, and bedewed with tears of joy and penitence, the monument of their redemption. This union of the fiercest and most tender passions has been variously considered by two philosophers— by the one as easy and natural, by the other as absurd and incredible." Quoted by Bartlett in *Walks*, pp. 124–25. Footnotes in Gibbon indicate that it was Hume who accepted, Voltaire who was appalled by, the sudden shift from slaughter to piety (for Voltaire see also the discussion at 2.1.92; also

4.18.144). Melville owned an unidentified set of Gibbon (Sealts 223b). See also the discussions at 1.4.22, 1.25.55, 1.31.111, and 4.20.45.

1.4.14   the Calabrian steep] Melville saw the Calabrian mountains of southern Italy (*Journals*, p. 100).

1.4.22   more concern than Tancred knew] In another part of the passage quoted in the discussion at 1.4.7, Gibbon notes: "Of these savage heroes of the cross, Tancred alone betrayed some sentiments of compassion." Tancred, a Norman leader of the First Crusade, is one of the heroic figures of Tasso's epic (see the discussion at 1.3.177).

1.5.4   in sculptured stone] "Much elaborate sculpture once graced what is now visable of the original facade; but Time has nibbled it away, till it now looks like so much spoiled pastry at which the mice have been at work." So Melville described the facade of the church in 1857 (*Journals*, p. 89). A large engraving of the facade is in Bartlett, *Walks*, facing p. 168 (reproduced on p. 714 above). Neither Melville's 1856–57 journal nor the engraving records that the sculpturing over the doors was of the triumphal entry, though Murray, I, 160, substantiates it. For the "golden and triumphal" gate of line 8 see the discussion at 1.10.74.

1.5.9   Palm Morn] Compare with Clarel's experience in the canto "Passion Week" (4.32).

1.5.17   Nisan's festal month] The first month of the Hebrew civil year and the time of the annual feast of the Passover, celebrating the deliverance of the Jews from Egyptian bondage. Jesus was twelve when his parents took him to Jerusalem for the Passover (Luke 2.41–50).

1.5.34   starry watchers] Luke 24.4.

1.5.60   The Scala Santa] When he was in Rome, Melville recorded this scene in his journal: "To St. John Lateran . . . Scala Santa—(5 stairs) pilgrims going up—penitents" (pp. 108–9; see also p. 475, with an illustration). These holy stairs of the cathedral church were reputed to be the ones that Christ ascended going into the Judgment Hall (Pilate's house); they had been brought from the Via Dolorosa in Jerusalem by Constantine.

1.5.71   Scripture, here recalled] John 19.41–42; 20.15.

1.5.111   St. Paul] Acts 27 tells of Paul's encountering storms and shipwreck on the way to Rome; see the allusion in *Moby-Dick*, chap. 2, p. 10.

1.5.117   Tyre] Melville did not visit Tyre, but he marked Stanley's eloquent account of the desolation of Tyre and Sidon, pp. 264–68.

1.5.131   In gliding turn of dreams] Clarel's dream-vision (lines 132–209) presents four pilgrimage groups: Greek Christians coming to the Holy Sepulcher, Levantine Moslems headed for Mecca, Indian peasants on the way to

Brahman temples, and Chinese pilgrims crossing the Himalayas to Buddhist shrines. The theme that emerges—"The intersympathy of creeds" (line 207)—is in harmony with early popularizations of comparative religion in the 1870's in America. James Freeman Clarke, the famous Boston Unitarian minister from whom Melville's wife received communion on her wedding day, August 4, 1847 (*Log*, I, 255), had written articles on the subject in the *Atlantic Monthly* (1869); in 1871 he published *Ten Great Religions: An Essay in Comparative Theology* (Boston: Houghton Mifflin), in which he attempted "to do equal justice to all the religious tendencies of mankind" (p. 3). The idea of the Mecca pilgrimage may have grown from roughly similar lines (1–21) in Arnold's "Resignation," which Melville read with great admiration in *Poems* in 1862 (Boston: Ticknor & Fields, 1856; Sealts 21; Bezanson, "Arnold's Poetry," pp. 375–76). Details, however, are clearly borrowed from Bartlett's *Forty Days*, pp. 152–62, in which he marked several passages. Compare lines 132–41 with: "A burst of tom-toms, a rude sort of Arab drum, and a denser crowd, now indicated the approach of the central and most important part of the procession, viz., the Mahmal, or camel selected to carry, under a costly canopy, the copy of the Koran sent to Mecca" (p. 156); and further with: "The Mahmal, (seen in the centre of our view,) borne on the back of a fine camel, selected for the purpose, and exempted for the rest of its life from ordinary labour, consists of a square wooden frame, terminating in a pyramidal form, covered with dark brocade, and highly ornamented with gilt fringes and tassels. Mr. Lane states that in every cover he has seen, was worked a view of the Temple of Mecca, and over it the Sultan's cypher" (pp. 157–58). Clarel's vision of "Curveting troops" (line 146) as well as of poor families on donkeys (lines 153–54) both derive from Bartlett, pp. 154–55. Compare lines 155–77 with Bartlett's description of "their ignorance of the way and blind reliance on the providence of Allah. . . . They inquired for Akaba, . . . supposing it always just at hand; and were astounded when we told them they had nearly three days' journey to accomplish" (pp. 154–55); with Bartlett's speculations on the dangers ahead of the pilgrims—"the Bedouins of the Great Desert [Melville's 'desert of the Word'], the fearful Simoom [a hot, dry, violent wind laden with dust]" (p. 161, marked with Melville's marginal line); and with Bartlett's imagining a "broken-down straggler, whom the departing host has heartlessly left behind to perish, to dig with his expiring strength his own shallow grave in the sand, and await the passing of the angel of death" (pp. 161–62).

1.5.132 Damascus' gate] The two famous pilgrimages to Mecca, birthplace of Mohammed, were from Damascus, the capital of Syria, and Cairo, in Egypt. In the next verse paragraph the scene apparently shifts to a Cairo pilgrimage.

1.5.149   Feiran's palms] Feiran is an oasis high up on the Sinaitic table-land. Stanley, p. 73, writes: "The palm-groves of Feirân I saw only by the clear starlight; yet it was still possible to see how great must be the beauty of the luxuriant palms and feathery tamarisks."

1.5.176   the desert of the Word] Identified in the Bible only as "that great and terrible wilderness" of the Israelite wanderings (Deut. 1.19; 8.15), this northern wasteland of the peninsula of Sinai was known in the nine-teenth century by the Arabic name of El (or Et) Tîh (line 177). Melville checked the section in Stanley (pp. 7–8) on "The Plateau on the Tîh"; the last sentence reads: "Its one interest now is the passage of the Mecca pilgrim-age." He also underlined the phrase "plateau of the Tîh" (p. 93).

1.5.191   Compostel or brown Loret] Figurative allusions (truncated to fit the meter) to two famous European pilgrimage spots: (Santiago de) Compostella, Spain, reputed burial-place of the apostle James, and Loreto, Italy, principal shrine for devotion to the Virgin Mary.

1.5.202   Mongolian Fo] Gautama, the founder of Buddhism. "Fo" is a Chinese term for a buddha.

1.5.218   tempest-tossed,] In the first edition, there is no hyphen linking these two words, and a dash follows "tossed". Melville apparently wished to revise the punctuation here, for in Copy B at Harvard (see pp. 854 and 858 below) he placed a check mark in the right margin, following this verse line; and, within the line, he entered a caret between "tempest" and "tossed" and marked a slash through the dash. In the other instances where Melville en-tered a caret in the text (1.6.1; 1.7.15; 2.16.107), he indicated the correction in the margin; here he did not complete his marking, or else he felt that the correction was obvious, and he simply called attention to the spot by a marginal check mark. Presumably he meant to insert a hyphen between "tempest" and "tossed". His intention in marking the dash is less clear, however. It seems unlikely that he wished to delete it without substituting another mark of punctuation, because some punctuation seems called for, and Melville himself added punctuation at a number of line-ends in Copy B. On the assumption, therefore, that Melville wanted a less intrusive break than a dash, NN prints a comma here.

1.6.0   TRIBES AND SECTS] Though Clarel felt a sympathy among the var-ious religions, he now finds "feud" within Christianity. Stanley, p. 456, points out the "Diversity of sects" at the Holy Sepulcher, and Murray, I, 83, says they "appear to agree in little else but a cordial hatred of each other." The Georgians (line 8) lost their wealthy Jerusalem holdings as their national power declined and had now dwindled to a handful. The Maronites (line 8), a heretical sect of the seventh century, had 82 wealthy convents in Lebanon and a small outpost in Jerusalem. The Armenians (line 9), separated from the churches of the East and West in the fifth century, were a wealthy church throughout the Turkish empire; their convent on Mt. Zion was the richest in the city. The Greeks (line 9) were native Arabs, members of the "Holy Orthodox Church of the East," and the largest Christian group in Palestine; they held eight convents and five nunneries within the city; four beyond the city included Mar Saba and the Convent of the Nativity at Bethlehem. The Latins (line 10) were Arabic-speaking seceders from the Greek Church. The Abyssinians (line 12) had minor joint holdings with the Copts (Egyptians). The Holy Sepulcher had become a babel of tongues and competing rituals. See *Journals*, pp. 87–88 and 438–39.

1.6.10   The Latin organ] An exact duplicate of this organ provided accompaniment for John Banvard's Holy Land panorama, shown before Queen Victoria and then, in 1853, at the Georama, 596 Broadway, New York. *Description of Banvard's Pilgrimage to Jerusalem and the Holy Land . . .* (n.p., 1853).

1.6.28   To Lot's Wave by black Kedron] Rising a mile northeast of Jerusalem, the Brook Kedron (biblical Kidron, also Cedron), which Stanley, p. 171, calls "The Black Valley," defiled into the wilderness past Mar Saba and drained into the Dead Sea (the site of Sodom, where Lot lived until the city was destroyed). Melville owned an engraving on which he wrote "Gorge of Cedron"; reproduced as fig. 8 in Robert K. Wallace, "Melville's Prints and Engravings at the Berkshire Atheneum," *Essays in Arts and Sciences*, XV (June, 1986), 59–90, and p. 814 below.

1.6.29   by Mount Seir, through Edom] The ravaged wilderness south of the Dead Sea. The force of the malediction lies in Ezekiel's long and dire prophecy against Seir and Idumea (Edom), concluding: "thou shalt be desolate, O mount Seir, and all Idumea, even all of it: and they shall know that I am the Lord" (Ezek. 35).

1.7.1   a silence reigns] On the "*Interior of Jerusalem*," the 1856–57 journal reads: "Silence & solitude of it" (p. 89; marked by a large crosshatch in red pencil—see the textual note at 89.12–13). The theme of silence dominates lines 1–24, and among other examples we have the "Wild solitudes" of 1.16.26.

1.7.20   truth's forecasting canticles] The Revelation of St. John the Divine, in the chapter envisioning the fall of Babylon: "And the voice of harpers, and musicians, and of pipers, and trumpeters, shall be heard no more at all in thee; and no craftsman, of whatsoever craft he be, shall be found any more in thee; and the sound of a millstone shall be heard no more at all in thee; And the light of a candle shall shine no more at all in thee; and the voice of the bridegroom and of the bride shall be heard no more at all in thee . . ." (Rev. 18.22–23).

1.7.26   Jaffa Gate] The main western gate (see p. 710). Half a mile out the Jaffa Road, Clarel passes the Turkish Cemetery (Map A, p. 707).

1.7.39   Luke's narration] The account (Luke 24.13–35) of Christ's appearance after his death and burial to two disciples on the way to Emmaus, a town midway between Jerusalem and Jaffa.

1.7.68   Paul's evidence] "Now faith is the substance of things hoped for, the evidence of things not seen" (Heb. 11.1).

1.7.84   poet pale] Keats. Melville knew the anecdote from the painter Benjamin Robert Haydon's *Life . . . from His Autobiography and Journals* (ed. Tom Taylor [New York: Harper, 1853]; Sealts 262): on his deathbed "Keats made Ritchie promise he would carry his *Endymion* to the great desert of Sahara and fling it in the midst" (entry for December 28, 1817). The Scottish explorer Joseph Ritchie met Keats through Haydon during his preparations for an expedition to the Sudan in 1819; he died on the return trip.

1.8.5   Narraganset's marge] Narragansett Bay, Rhode Island. Melville knew it from at least one boyhood visit to his aunt Mary and uncle John D'Wolf in Bristol, on the bay (see *Log*, August, 1828).

1.8.22   pointed by St. John] His vision of the heavenly Jerusalem (Rev. 21.10–27). Melville is in error on one detail: though beryl was one of the twelve precious stones in the city's foundations, the twelve gates were pearls. This same apocalyptic vision of the New Jerusalem later leads Nehemiah to his death by drowning (2.38).

1.8.27   Zion restore] The 1856–57 journal: "Be it said, that all these movements combining Agriculture & Religion in reference to Palestine, are based upon the impression . . . that the time for the prophetic return of the Jews to Judea is at hand, and therefore the way must be prepared for them by Christians, both in setting them right in their faith & their farming—in other words, preparing the soil literally & figuratively" (p. 93).

1.8.35   he of Tarsus roved] Paul, in his three missionary journeys, visited many Mediterranean countries.

1.8.38   Smyrna's mart] Smyrna was a seaport city of Asia Minor where Melville had twice stopped (*Journals*, pp. 69–70, 98). "Joppa's [Jaffa's] stair" (line 39) refers to the rocky ledge extending from Jaffa's edge into the sea; Melville had rowed out to explore it (*Journals*, p. 82).

1.8.43   fire-flakes of the Pentecost] Acts 2.1–13: on the day of Pentecost (the fiftieth day after the feast of the Passover) the eleven apostles were sitting together when "there appeared unto them cloven tongues like as of fire, and it sat upon each of them."

1.8.48   *"Time and times and half a time"*] A representative invocation of various millennial groups, stemming from Daniel's visionary prophecies, as in Daniel 7.25: "and they shall be given into his hand until a time and times and the dividing of time." Deacon Dickson said to Melville outside Jaffa: "The fact is the fullness of Time has come" (*Journals*, p. 93).

1.8.54   Ravens] Elijah was fed by ravens (1 Kings 17.4–6).

1.8.71   A *Santon* held him] The 1856–57 journal describes one in a more violent and ironic tone: "Trying to be serious about St. John when from where I stood figure of Santon a Arab holy man came between me & island—almost naked—ludicrous chaced away gravity—solemn idiocy—lunatic—opium-eater—dreamer—yet treated with profoundest respect & reverence—allowed to enter anywhere.—Wretched imbecile! bare & beggarly Santon, miserable stumbling-block in way of the prophecies, since saint though thou art thou art so far from inheriting the earth that thou dost not inherit a shirt to thy nakedness!" (p. 98).

1.9.13–14   Beulah dear / And New Jerusalem] Evangelical symbols for heaven, derived from Isaiah 62.4 and Revelation 21.2.

1.10.0   RAMBLES] Melville recorded in his 1856–57 journal several days of "roaming over the hills" and "roaming about city" (pp. 79–80).

1.10.3   serial wrecks on wrecks] This persistent theme of the poem (repeated, e.g., in 1.16.35–39) has its first statement in the 1856–57 journal: "There are *strata* of cities buried under the present surface of Jerusalem. Forty feet deep lie fragments of columns &c" (p. 90). The Hospitalers (line 7) were the famous Knights of St. John of Jerusalem; their cloisters were built near the Holy Sepulcher. According to Murray, I, 170: "But, alas! how fallen and degraded! It is now the cesspool of a neighbouring tannery, and apparently the public dunghill of the whole quarter." The remaining sequence of ruins were all on Mt. Moriah, site of Solomon's Temple. "Fatimite palaces" (line 9: Fatima was the favorite daughter of Mohammed; the first edition's "Fatamite" is here emended) probably refers to the mosque on Moriah built by Omar when he took Jerusalem in A.D. 636. Earlier, Herod (line 10) had rebuilt the Temple ca. 20 B.C. Earlier still, Judas Maccabeus (line 11) had rebuilt it in 165 B.C., and earlier still was Solomon's original Temple, begun four years after David's death (ca. 1012 B.C.) on the threshing floor of Ornan the Jebusite (line 14) where David (line 13) had planned it (2 Chron. 3.1). Part of Melville's source for such material could have been Kitto, II, 834–42.

1.10.16   Glenroy's tiers of beaches] Glen Roy (or "Glenroy") is a valley in northwestern Scotland (further north than Melville visited in 1856), along the sides of which run a series of roads or terraces, once thought to show successive water levels of ancient lakes.

1.10.20   on Moriah] Magnificent gardens and walks surrounded the Mosque of Omar and the Dome of the Rock on the great stone platform of Moriah where the Temple had once stood. They were first opened to non-Moslems in 1856, but at a price of one pound. Melville seems not to have visited them, but they were visible, of course, from rooftops and Mt. Olivet.

1.10.29   The chapel of our Dame of Grief] Notre Dame des Douleurs, a small exterior chapel of the Church of the Holy Sepulcher, marking the spot where the Virgin Mary stood during the Crucifixion. For Baldwin (line 28), see the discussion at 1.3.177.

1.10.30   Ophel's winding base] The sloping shoulder of the southeast corner of the city, outside the walls; between Ophel and the fountain of En Rogel lay the so-called Garden of King Solomon (line 33; Map A, p. 707).

1.10.38   Adonijah, Adonijah] By the stone of Zoheleth, near En Rogel, Adonijah feasted in celebration of his expected succession to King David; hearing trumpets, he learned from a messenger that Solomon had just been anointed king at Gihon (1 Kings 1).

1.10.56   This field] Aceldama (line 65), the famous "field of blood" described in the New Testament (Matt. 27.3–10; Acts 1.16–20), so called because it was purchased with the thirty pieces of silver for which Judas betrayed Christ. A place "to bury strangers in," Aceldama was the site of a massive charnel house of masonry backed against a rock; from inside one looked down into a great pit where for centuries the bodies of pilgrims and other strangers had been thrown. The 1856–57 journal soundingly records: "And smote by the morning, I saw the reddish soil of Aceldema, confessing its inexpiable guilt by deeper dyes" (p. 87); see Map A, p. 707 above.

1.10.71   Christ's resort] Luke 21.37.

1.10.74   the Golden Gate] Pictures of the famous sealed Golden Gate may be seen in Bartlett, *Walks*, pp. 158, 159. Melville's 1856–57 journal is the source here: "The Beautiful, or Golden, Gate—two arches, highly ornamental sculpture, undoubtedly old, Herod's Time—the Gate from which Christ would go to Bethany & Olivet—& also that in which he made his entry (with palms) into the city. Turks walled it up because of tradition that through this Gate the city would be taken.—One of the most interesting things in Jerusalem—seems expressive of the finality of Christianity, as if this was the last religion of the world,—no other, possible" (p. 86). For the triumphal entry, see Matt. 21.1–11.

1.11.0   LOWER GIHON] One of two ancient reservoirs frequently referred to in the Old Testament as Gihon; here Solomon was anointed (1 Kings 1.32–40). Both the Upper Pool and the Lower Pool (of Gihon) are in the

Valley of Hinnom, west of the city (Map A, p. 707). Bartlett, *Walks*, facing p. 56, has an engraving of Lower Gihon.

1.11.19   three demoniacs] The incident is built on Christ's miracle of casting out devils from the naked man who lived in the tombs of the Gadarenes (Luke 8.26–36). "What have I to do with thee, Jesus, thou Son of God most high?" the man cried out in a loud voice before he was healed. Melville had made the cryptic entry in his 1856–57 journal: "*Wandering among the tombs*—till I began to think myself one of the possessed with devels" (p. 84). That Celio, the "stranger" (line 12), should be found among demoniacs is an augury of his own inner bedevilment.

1.11.66   By David's Tower] They are just outside the Jaffa Gate, overlooking Hinnom (Map A, p. 707). Melville's 1856–57 journal sets the scene: "For daily I could not but be struck with the clusters of the townspeople reposing along the arches near the Jaffa Gate where it looks down into the vale of Gihon, and the groups always haunting the neighboring fountains, vales & hills. . . . I looked along the hill side of Gihon over against me, and watched the precipitation of the solemn shadows of the city towers flung far down to the haunted bottom of the hid pool of Gihon" (pp. 86–87). A woodcut of the Tower of David is in Thomson, II, 475, reproduced on p. 728 below.

1.11.83–84   this glen / Of Moloch] Tophet, in the Valley of Hinnom, where the Jews had sacrificed children by fire to Moloch, the god of the Ammonites (2 Kings 23.10).

1.11.89   Return he will over Olivet] Nehemiah is literally referring to the sun (line 83), but the language here echoes the common belief of Zionist millenarians, based on the prediction that the supposed place of the Ascension should also be the site of the Second Coming (Acts 1.10–12). The 1856–57 journal reports that Deacon Dickson, one of the prototypes for Nehemiah, was seen "going about Jerusalem with open Bible, looking for the opening asunder of Mount Olivet and the preparing of the highway for the Jews. &c" (p. 94).

1.12.4   Terra-Santa's wall] Latin convents in the Holy Land were regularly designated La Terra Santa (the "prefix dropped"—line 5—here is the definite article) and were staffed by Franciscans. The "warden" (line 7), an Italian appointed for three years by the pope, resided at the Convent of St. Salvador in the northwest section of the city (Map A, p. 707).

1.12.43   Absalom's locks but Æsop's hump] Absalom's perfect beauty and magnificent hair are described in 2 Samuel 14.25–26. In one of the villas outside Rome (Melville said in his lecture on "Statues in Rome") is found "a bust of Æsop, the dwarfed and deformed, whose countenance is irradiated by a lambent gleam of irony such as plays round the pages of Goldsmith" (NN *Piazza Tales* volume, p. 407).

TOWER OF DAVID.

Arch of the Ecce Homo.

1.12.70   St. Peter's balcony] When in Rome, Melville recorded many impressions of St. Peter's (*Journals*, pp. 103–13).

1.12.122   Santa Croce's base] Santa Croce in Gerusalemme, Rome (not mentioned in Melville's 1856–57 journal). The "earth of Jewry" (line 123) said to be under the floor was brought to Rome not by medieval Crusaders (line 124) but by St. Helena in the fourth century (see the discussion at 1.31.111). "Trajan's hall" (line 125) is presumably the great Forum Trajanum in Rome.

1.12.127   Titus' Arch] A marble relief on the Arch of Titus in Rome depicted a procession of Roman soldiers carrying the seven-branched candlestick, the table of shewbread, and silver trumpets, plunder from the emperor Titus's capture of Jerusalem, A.D. 70. Bartlett, *Walks*, p. 49, has a small woodcut of this relief. Melville alludes to the seven-branched candlestick in two discussions of sculpture in the 1856–57 journal; see *Journals*, pp. 111, 158, and 482.

1.12.141   her] In Copy B at Harvard (see pp. 854 and 859 below), Melville wrote "her" in the left margin preceding this verse line, without indicating where (or whether) it was to be inserted. If he did mean to insert it, the only place he can have had in mind, however, is preceding "colony." Possibly he meant for "her" to replace "or" in order to maintain the strict meter ("Her appanage, her colony."). But the matter is not clear enough to justify such an emendation, and NN more cautiously inserts the "her" without making any other alteration. (For a discussion of the rationale for accepting as emendations all of Melville's marginal notes, see the NOTE ON THE TEXT, pp. 681–83.)

1.13.0   THE ARCH] The Ecce Homo Arch (line 24) was one of many stations along the Via Dolorosa (or Via Crucis, line 20, as Melville calls it; see the illustration on p. 838 below). This narrow lane, the supposed route to the Crucifixion, zigzagged from the governor's house near the Gate of St. Stephen across town to the Church of the Holy Sepulcher; the arch spans the way near the northwest Temple corner (Map A, p. 707). "*Behold the Man!* [Ecce homo]" Pilate cried (line 36), presenting Jesus to the mob (John 19.5). Melville caught the ironic collision of values here in a journal entry: "Leads from St. Stephens Gate up towards Calvary. Silence & solitude of it. The arch—the stone he leaned against—the stone of Lazarus &c. City like a quarry—all stone.—Vaulted ways—buttresses (flying) Arch (Ecce Homo), some one has built a little batchelor's abode on top. *Talk of the guides* 'Here is the stone Christ leaned against, & here is the English Hotel.' Yonder is the arch where Christ was shown to the people, & just by that open window is sold the best coffee in Jerusalem. &c &c &c" (p. 89). The woodcut of the arch pictured opposite is from George Williams, *The Holy City* (London: Parker, 1849), II, 429.

1.13.47   *My God, my God, forsakest me?*] "And about the ninth hour Jesus cried with a loud voice, saying, Eli, Eli, lämä sabachthani? that is to say, My God, my God, why hast thou forsaken me?" (Matt. 27.46; cf. 3.7.1).

1.13.74   How long] "And Jesus walked in the temple in Solomon's porch. Then came the Jews round about him, and said unto him, How long dost thou make us to doubt? If thou be the Christ, tell us plainly" (John 10.23–24).

1.13.95   the Medusa shield] The aegis which Athena carried for Zeus or wore as a breastplate blazed brightly, was fringed with gold, and displayed in the center the Gorgon's snaky head, the sight of which turned men to stone.

1.13.103   He turned] Celio's movements in this and the next canto are symbolic. Going west along the Via Dolorosa he comes to the scene of the Wandering Jew (line 112), whose story is later dramatized by the monks of Mar Saba (see the discussion at 3.19.0); shaken by its relevance he reverses his steps and goes back through the arch and out the eastern Gate of St. Stephen (line 121; see the illustration on p. 761 below). Melville was well aware of the gate's connotation of martyrdom, as in his 1856–57 journal: "And in the afternoon, I would stand out by St: Stephen's Gate, nigh the pool likewise named after him, occupying the spot where he was stoned" (*Journals*, p. 87; see also p. 438, and Acts 7.59). That is, if Celio is now cursed, like the Wandering Jew, he also merits "the martyr's leaf" (1.14.5). His night alone in Jehoshaphat (line 122) is thus both an excommunication from the city (the locking of the gates at sundown, a routine matter, is not to be so understood here), and a testing of his nerve and purpose.

1.14.1   Savonarola's zeal] Girolamo Savonarola (1452–98), the fearless Dominican of Florence, was hanged and burned on order of Pope Alexander VI, whose infallibility he denied.

1.14.3   Leopardi, stoned by Grief] Count Giacomo Leopardi (1798–1837), Italian lyric poet and pessimist. In the copy of Antoine Valery's *Historical, Literary, and Artistical Travels in Italy* (Paris: Baudry, 1852; Sealts 533; Bercaw 729) which Melville, aged 37, purchased in Florence, he checked on p. 354 a passage with Leopardi's name and double-checked another passage and underlined in it: "died at Naples of the *cholera*, on the 28th of June 1837, *aged forty years*" (Melville's underlining italicized). Marking up Schopenhauer's *The World as Will and Idea* (London: Trübner, 1888; Sealts 448) over thirty years later, Melville made a check mark beside the sentence with Schopenhauer's comment that Leopardi's "theme is everywhere the mockery and wretchedness of this existence . . ." (III, 401). St. Stephen (line 4) was a man "full of faith and power" (Acts 6–7).

1.14.22   three tombs] As Melville wrote in his 1856–57 journal: "Side by side here tombs of Absolom, Zachariah & St: James. Cut out of live rock in Petra style. St: James a stone verandah overlooking the gorge—pillars" (p. 86; see also pp. 433–34, 436, with illustration). The Petra image (line 25) is understandable in terms of a later canto (2.30). The "tradition" (line 31), as told by Murray, I, 146–47, was that St. James hid here after the Crucifixion and took a vow not to eat or drink until he should see Christ arisen. The setting for Celio's night exile is thus highly calculated.

1.14.37   off Tamura] Peninsula in Siberia extending into the Arctic Ocean, variously spelled "Taimyr," "Tamara," "Taimur," "Taimir," "Taymyr," etc.

1.14.42   From the high gate] The journey of the Terra Santa monks (to line 125) is as follows (Map A, p. 707): out the Gate of St. Stephen, down the path into the Kedron ravine, a brief pause beside the Tomb and Chapel of the Virgin, another brief stop by the adjacent Garden of Gethsemane, and then on up the Bethany Road over Olivet to Bethany. The traditional tomb of Lazarus (line 90) was a deep, narrow vault, partly excavated in rock, with stairs leading to a small chamber (where Celio apparently stays) and more stairs leading down to the inner vault. Here, according to John 11.1–46, Christ raised Lazarus from the dead and presented him to his weeping sisters, Mary and Martha. As the monks chant the famous phrase from Paul's letter to the Corinthians— "O death, where is thy sting? O grave, where is thy victory?" (1 Cor. 15.55)—Celio retorts dramatically and flees.

1.15.1   "Lo, shoot the spikes] Celio is talking as he watches the sun break (line 6) over Olivet, on whose summit stands the small-domed Church of the Ascension (see the discussion at 1.35.4). His theme, which contrasts so with Nehemiah's (1.11.80–93), comes from the 1856–57 journal: "The mind can not but be sadly & suggestively affected with the indifference of Nature & Man to all that makes the spot sacred to the Christian. Weeds grow upon Mount Zion; side by side in impartial equality appear the shadows of church & mosque, and on Olivet every morning the sun indifferently ascends over the Chapel of the Ascension" (p. 85).

1.15.12   gliding] Melville may have written "gilding", using the conventional image of the sun as gilding what it shines on (cf. "The Gilder," chap. 114 of Moby-Dick), but here the stress seems to be on the transitory nature of the sun's touch as the "tinging gleam" moves, and "gliding" is retained.

1.15.23   the muezzin's cry] "Wearily climbing the Via Dolorosa one noon," Melville wrote in his 1856–57 journal, "I heard the muezzin calling to prayer from the minaret of Omer" (p. 89). Here Clarel hears the morning call of the same muezzin, rolling down the Valley of Jehoshaphat past the Pool of Siloam (line 30; see the discussion at 1.28.96) and the fountain of En Rogel (line 29), and rounding the Hill of Zion (line 32: Map A, p. 707). Bartlett's engraving (*Walks*, facing p. 94) of this scene (reproduced opposite) shows the walls, the deep gulf, and the minaret. For the rule that only the blind might serve in this post (lines 40–49), cf. Curzon, chap. 4.

1.15.30   Siloa] Siloam; for this spelling, see the discussion at 1.1.24.

1.15.37   the Crescent rides the Cross] The phrase was made a byword of the century by Eliot Warburton's immensely popular book, *The Crescent and the Cross* (see p. 705 above).

1.15.59   the Ezan] The Mohammedan call to prayer, also "azan."

1.15.64   a jealous God] The second commandment warns: "for I the Lord thy God am a jealous God" (Exod. 20.5).

1.16.2–3   from Moriah . . . / Slips Kedron] An unfounded myth, probably an offshoot from Ezekiel's vision of the holy waters flowing from the Temple down Kedron and on through the wilderness to the Dead Sea (Ezek. 47.1–12). Beneath the "temple" (line 6), however, were mammoth subterranean vaults and passageways, believed to have been cisterns serving the Temple area in ancient times. Jerusalem had often been attacked through its underground warrens (line 22).

1.16.24   the glades of cactus trees] The 1856–57 journal reports: "Inside the walls are many vacant spaces, overgrown with the horrible cactus" (p. 90; underlined with dashes in red pencil—see the textual note at 90.1–2).

1.16.28   the hand-mills] Two small grindstones turned by women to grind corn make "the sound of the grinding," as they did in the time of the Preacher (Eccles. 12.4).

1.16.34   Dark quarries where few care to pry] The image is archaeologically sound as well as psychologically telling. As the 1856–57 journal notes: "Part of Jerusalem built on quarries—entrance from North wall" (p. 91). Cuttings from these quarries near the Damascus Gate went into buildings since demolished.

1.16.79   The Hebrew quarter] Jerusalem was roughly divided into quarters: the Christian at the northwest, the Mohammedan at the northeast, the Armenian at the southwest, and the Jewish at the southeast between Zion and Moriah, but not including the Temple area.

Mount of Olives from the Wall

Jews' Place of Wailing, Jerusalem

1.16.80   Wailing Day] Murray, I, 121, warns that trying to find the Place of Wailing without a guide would be useless. The secluded area was a small paved quadrangle facing a section of the southwest wall of the old Temple foundations. The lower five courses of stone were massive beveled blocks—"an Ararat" (line 88), as it were, in size and significance (referring to the seventeen-thousand-foot mountain on which Noah's ark came to rest). Here every Friday for centuries Jews from all over the world had come to bewail the Dispersion, to remember the great days of "Judah's prime" (line 113), and to wait "until Shiloh [line 116: the Messiah] come" (Gen. 49.10). The illustration on p. 733 is from Bartlett's *Walks,* facing p. 140.

1.16.103   Levite trains] The Levites were charged with minor sacerdotal offices, including the guarding of the Temple. They were not priests, however, like the sons of Aaron, and so did *not* wear the ephod with bells and pomegranates along its hem (Exod. 28.31–35; see also the discussion at 2.5.55).

1.16.120   the Black Jew] Abdon (1.2).

1.16.122   stern Shaddai] Earlier name (from Abraham to Moses) for Jehovah, the Almighty God. The first edition's "Shaddei" is emended as a misreading of Melville's hand.

1.16.131   Man's . . . latest strain] Nathan, an American.

1.16.132   Behind the master Moslem's back] The Mohammedans controlled the entire Temple site (Moriah), allowing the Jews only this piece of back wall for performing ancient rituals such as reading Moses' laws (line 133).

1.16.183   features finely Hagarene] Like Hagar, the Egyptian concubine of Abraham and the mother of Ishmael (Gen. 16). Ruth's mother is Agar, the New Testament name for Hagar (Gal. 4.22–25). See also 2.27.44.

1.17.0   NATHAN] Henry W. Wells, in *The American Way of Poetry* (New York: Columbia University Press, 1943), p. 86: "This section of only ten pages constitutes a really remarkable epitome of no small part of America's social and intellectual history."

1.17.10   emigrants which inland bore] For the imagery of the plains that follows, see the account of Melville's journey to Illinois in 1840, in John W. Nichol, "Melville and the Midwest," *PMLA,* LXVI (September, 1951), 613–25.

1.17.18   Esdraleon] The major open area of central and northern Palestine. Melville did not visit Esdraelon (as it is normally spelled), but he read chap. 9 in Stanley, "Plain of Esdraelon" (with map). The first-edition spelling, necessary for the meter, is retained.

1.17.38   Saco's mountain wilds] Both the Saco River and the Ammonoosuc (line 83) rise in the White Mountains (line 82) of New Hampshire, scene of the Willey Slide (line 88; see the discussion below).

1.17.51   *her* sake part] In this condensed phrase "part" means "partly" or "in part."

1.17.56–60   Indian mounds / . . . Pyramids] Possibly Melville saw Indian mounds during his visit to Illinois in 1840 (see the discussion at 1.17.10). He saw the Egyptian pyramids in 1856 (*Journals*, pp. 72–79).

1.17.88   the Slide! the Slide!] Exactly the same words occur at the dramatic center of Hawthorne's story "The Ambitious Guest," in *Twice-Told Tales* (1837); Melville wrote "The Slide" under the title in his copy (see the discussion at 1.3.163) and marked some passages. In both instances the scene is Crawford Notch—"one vale he would [wanted to] forget" (line 42). There on the night of August 28, 1826, began the fiercest and most destructive storm in White Mountain history, during which a slide detached itself from the mountain above the Willey homestead and descended. Its downward course was split by a ledge of rock so that it parted on either side of the cabin. By an irony which has made the event dramatic in New England history and folklore, Mr. and Mrs. Willey, their five children, and two hired men were all destroyed when they fled the cabin seeking safety. The site is still visited. Melville had passed through the White Mountains on his honeymoon in 1847, and spent part of his 1870 vacation in North Conway, near Crawford Notch.

1.17.103   A dusty book] Probably *The Age of Reason* (1794–95) by Thomas Paine, who could be the "Deist" of line 145 and who is cited later (3.23.38).

1.17.165   Favonius] The west wind.

1.17.177   Ceres] Goddess of the fruits of the earth.

1.17.203   Nerea's amorous net] Not sexual wiles, as of this Greek sea-nymph, attracted Nathan, but rather the prophetess-like quality of a Miriam (line 204), the sister of Moses and the leader of the women in the wilderness (Exod. 15.20–21). Cf. "nereids" (3.29.60) and "the tangles of Neæra's hair," *Lycidas*, line 69 (for Melville's copy of Milton see the discussion at 1.1.24; he marked lines nearby but not this one).

1.17.208   Rephaim and the Rama plains] There was a Plain of Rephaim just southwest of Jerusalem; by "Rama" (also at 4.29.111) is probably meant the Ramah of Samuel, possibly near Bethlehem; it was not a plain, but a town or hill (see Matt. 2.18: "In Rama was there a voice heard, lamentation, and weeping . . .").

1.17.215   rear-ward] The first-edition reading "rear-wall" can be taken metaphorically to provide an adequate, if strained, sense, but it seems more likely that what Melville wrote was "rear-ward" (with the third "r" peaked), parallel to "backward" two lines earlier. The word "rearward" is used memorably in *Pierre* (see especially bk. 9, p. 166).

1.17.224   fame] The first-edition reading "fame" seems somewhat askew and may be a misreading of another word, such as "same", or possibly "fane". Neither of these possibilities alleviates the problem sufficiently to warrant making an emendation.

1.17.304   Armed husbandmen] Melville noted in his 1856–57 journal that "All who cultivate the soil in Palestine are Arabs. The Jews dare not live outside walled towns or villages for fear of the malicious persecution of the Arabs & Turks" (p. 94). Nathan's fate (1.42) is thus nearly inevitable.

1.17.305   Pequod wilds] The Pequod (or Pequot) Indians, a warlike tribe of the Algonquians in Connecticut, killed a number of settlers and consequently were exterminated as a tribe in 1637. (In *Moby-Dick*, chap. 16, the *Pequod* is said to be named for the "celebrated tribe of Massachusetts Indians, now extinct as the ancient Medes"; see pp. 69, 839). Those of the Hittites (line 306) "whom the children of Israel also were not able utterly to destroy" were put in bondservice by Solomon (1 Kings 9.20–21).

1.18.3   Damascus' plain] Melville did not visit beautifully located Damascus, seven days to the north, but Stanley, p. 402, gave him the images for minarets (line 7), fruit (line 14), water (line 16), and Mt. Hermon snow (lines 21–22); he also quotes Mohammed's judgment that it was a "Paradise" (line 35).

1.18.8   St. Sophia] Melville had been greatly impressed by the dome of St. Sophia, in Constantinople, preferring it to St. Peter's (see *Journals*, pp. 59, 67, 106, 158).

1.18.18   Abram's steward] "The steward of my house [in Canaan (line 21: Palestine)] is this Eliezer of Damascus," said Abram (Gen. 15.2), in the only biblical mention of Eliezer (line 19).

1.18.29   Thy wall, Angelico] Fra Angelico (1387–1455), the great Florentine painter, whose frescoes Melville probably saw in Florence in 1857, although he did not mention them in his journal.

1.18.72   Abdon under *talith*] The tallith is a tasseled shawl worn over the head or around the shoulders during morning prayers.

1.19.29   faith's receding wave] The dominant image of Arnold's "Dover Beach" in *New Poems* (Boston: Ticknor & Fields, 1867; Sealts 20), which Melville read but did not mark in his surviving copy (Bezanson, "Arnold's Poetry," p. 390).

1.20.0   VALE OF ASHES] North of the Damascus (Ephraim) Gate (line 2), and near the so-called source of the usually dry Kedron (line 5). According to Murray, I, 101, here were "three large white mounds, which have latterly attracted attention in consequence of a theory propounded by somebody, that they are composed of ashes, and that the ashes are those of the sacrifices offered up in the temple!" (cf. line 21). Murray prefers the older assumption that they come from the city soapworks. See Map A, p. 707.

1.20.10   Joel's wild text] Joel 3 predicts that final judgment shall be made in the Valley of Jehoshaphat, which the narrator here calls "hollow of Melchizedek" (line 14; see the discussion at 1.3.41). Here too will be Clarel's "valley of decision" (4.30).

1.20.26   remote from Celio's mound] Celio's grave, we learn in 1.40, is south of the city in the Latin Cemetery on the slopes of Mt. Zion.

1.21.14   Haggard as Horeb] A part of (or the same as) Mt. Sinai, the great barren mountain in the wilderness where the Law was given to Moses; pictured in Bartlett's *Forty Days*, facing pp. 73, 81.

1.21.15   Hermit, antler of Cape Horn] Hermit Island is ten miles northwest of the Horn. See the discussion at 2.30.68. For Melville's three passages of the Horn, see *Journals*, p. 532.

1.21.30   Emim Bey the Mamaluke] Bartlett's *Forty Days*, pp. 187–90, tells his story in detail, as does Warburton, I, 47–48. In 1811 Mehemet Ali massacred hundreds of the Mamelukes, his political rivals, by inviting them to a feast at the Citadel of Cairo. Only Emim Bey escaped; on horseback he leaped the Citadel wall to a pile of rubbish and fled, eventually reaching Constantinople. At Cairo, Melville saw "the spot where the Memlook saved himself by leaping his horse" (*Journals*, p. 74).

1.22.19   Prediction and fulfillment] As in Isaiah 6.11–12: "Then said I, Lord, how long? And he answered, Until the cities be wasted without inhabitant, and the houses without man, and the land be utterly desolate, And the Lord have removed men far away, and there be a great forsaking in the midst of the land."

1.22.29   The beams] A precise example of Melville's reworking of a detail from the 1856–57 journal. At Jaffa (not Jerusalem) he had noted: "The main beam crossing my chamber overhead, is evidently taken from a wreck—the trenail holes proving it" (p. 81).

1.22.39   Uz] A deserted ancient region of the Edom wasteland.

1.22.61   this raven] See 1.8.54.

1.22.98–99   the angel . . . / Of Peter dungeoned] The "angel of the Lord" who released Peter from prison (Acts 12.1–19).

1.22.111   Eliphaz the Temanite] One of the three friends who came to comfort Job. He confessed: "In thoughts from the visions of the night, when deep sleep falleth on men, Fear came upon me, and trembling, which made all my bones to shake" (Job 4.13–14).

1.23.37   robe with mystic hem] The fringe that God commanded the children of Israel to wear "throughout their generations" as a reminder of the commandments and the duty of holiness (Num. 15.37–41).

1.24.3   Moriah and Zion] The two hills, west and east, on which the southern section of Jerusalem was built. Zion extends southward well outside the walls. In the wall between them lay the Dung Gate (line 11: Neh. 2.13). At Rogel (line 10) was the Well of Job (Map A, p. 707).

1.24.21   Rome's port Esquiline] An ancient Roman gate near rubbish and pauper burial grounds. In the 1856–57 journal, Melville later penciled "Port Esquiline of the Universe. (For Note)" as a general commentary on the "*Barrenness of Judea*" (see *Journals*, textual note at 83.38).

1.24.35   the man] Margoth; he reappears in 2.19.

1.24.58   *Lamentations* say] "All that pass by clap their hands at thee; they hiss and wag their head at the daughter of Jerusalem, saying, Is this the city that men call The perfection of beauty, The joy of the whole earth?" (Lam. 2.15); the first edition's citation of the "fourteenth" (line 60) verse is here corrected (see the NOTE ON THE TEXT, p. 684).

1.24.68   by arid gullies bare] The mood, though not the detail, of these lines is found in the 1856–57 journal: "Hill-side view of Zion—loose stones & gravel as if shot down from carts. . . . Weeds grow upon Mount Zion" (p. 85).

1.24.77–78   the gate / Of David] Zion Gate in the south wall (Map A, p. 707).

1.25.0   HUTS] The lepers' huts just inside the Zion Gate had horrified Melville, as they did most travelers: "*Village of Lepers*—houses facing the wall—Zion. Their park, a dung-heap.—They sit by the gates asking alms,—their whine—avoidance of them & horror" (*Journals*, p. 84). No source has been located for Melville's detailed account of the famous rituals at the medieval lazarettos or leper houses (estimated to have been over nineteen thousand in number) by which inmates were proclaimed dead to the world of men (lines 23–50, 64–72).

1.25.11   lava glen in Luna's sphere] A famous ring crater of the moon, named after Tycho Brahe, the eminent Danish astronomer (1546–1601).

1.25.15   Than] Although the first-edition reading "Then" is an obsolete form of "Than", there seems less likelihood that Melville wished to use an archaism here than that "Then" is simply a compositorial error. NN therefore emends it to "Than".

1.25.55   Julian's pagan mind] The emperor Julian (331–63), a nephew of Constantine, brought up as a Christian but famous for his apostasy. Gibbon (chap. 23) examines his pagan mind in considerable detail (for Melville's use of Gibbon see the discussions at 1.4.7 and 1.4.22).

1.25.57–63   *"He lives forbid; / . . . rejected."*] A reworking of Isaiah's prophecy of Christ's low estate and sufferings: ". . . he hath no form nor comeliness; and when we shall see him, there is no beauty that we should desire him. He is despised and rejected of men . . . and we hid as it were our faces from him . . . we did esteem him stricken, smitten of God, and afflicted . . . and he was numbered with the transgressors" (Isa. 53.2–4, 12).

1.25.79   Sybella] Queen Sibyl (d. 1190), the sister of Baldwin IV of Jerusalem; he died at the age of 25 from leprosy. On the spelling of her name, see the NOTE ON THE TEXT, pp. 688–89.

1.25.82   St. John Almoner] In the eleventh century two hospitals were founded near the Holy Sepulcher by Franks: one for women, dedicated to Mary Magdalene, and one for men, dedicated to St. John of Jerusalem, the almsgiver. Thus began the famous Knights of St. John, or Knights Hospitalers, whose grandmaster, according to one tradition, at one time had to be a leper. See the discussion at 1.10.3.

1.25.93   Faith, Reverence, and Charity] A variant on Paul's famous "faith, hope, charity" (1 Cor. 13).

1.26.27–28   the hill / And gate Davidic] Zion was the site of the City of David, and of David's palace and tomb. The view described is traditional. The Mount of Offense (line 34), the southernmost hill of Olivet, was the presumed "hill that is before Jerusalem" (1 Kings 11.7) on which Solomon worshiped Chemosh and Moloch. The "Crag of Evil Council" (line 35) was the high hill south of Jerusalem on which it was supposed the priests and elders took counsel to destroy Jesus (Matt. 26.59); "Council" is retained here as an acceptable spelling of "Counsel"—the word refers to evil advice, not to an evil group of men dispensing advice. Near the top of this hill, Murray wryly relates (I, 105), "stands a solitary tree of a peculiar shape and blasted look, to which the monks have assigned the honour of having been the gallows of Judas [Iscariot: line 36]." Melville's 1856–57 journal reads: "On the Hill of Evil Counsel, I saw the ruined villa of the High Priest where tradition says the death of Christ was plotted, and the feild where when all was over the traitor Judas hung himself" (p. 87; in a marginal note written later in ink on the same page, possibly while writing the poem, he also used "Council"). The pit of Tophet (line 44) lay between Zion and Evil Counsel; it was part of the Valley (Ge) of Hinnom (Ge-Hinnom: Gehenna) where human sacrifices were thought to have been made (2 Kings 23.10) and where continual fires burned the city rubbish and offal. Tophet gave the Hebrews their image of Hell. The "Cœnaculum" (line 48) was the room on the second floor of a white building topped with a minaret which was believed to be over the tombs of the kings of Judah; this upper room (line 49) was thought to be the scene of the Last Supper (line 51), where Christ gave the farewell talk to his disciples reported only by John (line 53: John 14–16). Melville's topographical analogy of the Coliseum (line 32) recalls a journal entry: "Coliseum like great hollow among hills" (p. 106).

1.27.23   Rabboni] "My great master"; Hebrew title of even greater respect than "rabbi."

1.27.33   gaberdine] The medieval Jewish gown or mantle.

1.27.51   Naomi ere her trial] Before the death of her husband, Elimelech (Ruth 1.3). The Agar-Naomi comparison foreshadows the death of Nathan.

1.27.62   IF I FORGET THEE, O JERUSALEM!] Ps. 137.5.

1.27.86   'Tis a bad place] Of a missionary family whom Melville met in Jaffa he wrote in his 1856–57 journal: "Their little girl looks sickly & pines for home—but the Lord's work must be done" (p. 92).

1.28.24   The rifled *Sepulcher of Kings*] The huge rock-hewn sepulcher, half a mile north of the Damascus Gate (Map A, p. 707), was the most remarkable ancient tomb at Jerusalem. At one edge of a sunken, unroofed court, ninety feet square, was the broken portico entrance to the main vestibule of the tomb (here Vine is seated). From inside this vestibule a secret hinged rock door lifted vertically, leading into an elaborate series of underground vaults and crypts. The deeply carved frieze along the cornice of the vestibule portico—clusters of fruit, vine-leaves, and tryglyphs (Kitto, I, 361–62, and Murray, I, 148–49)—gave Melville his trope: the gay frieze at the entrance to the dark vaults was like a line from the idyllic poet Theocritus (line 30) threading Joel's dire prophecy (line 31) on the terrible judgments of God. Melville's attribution of the tomb to the Herods was only one of half a dozen current theories (Murray, I, 150–51). Bartlett's *Walks*, pp. 127–30, has four small woodcuts of the tomb, including the friezed entrance and a rifled sarcophagus, plus a "Plan" (map) on p. 129. Thomson, II, 487, also shows the entrance. The illustration opposite is from J. T. Barclay, *The City of the Great King* (Philadelphia: Challen, 1858), facing p. 192.

1.28.37   But who is he] Vine. The view that Vine is a portrait of Hawthorne is presented in the HISTORICAL AND CRITICAL NOTE, pp. 593–604 (sect. 8).

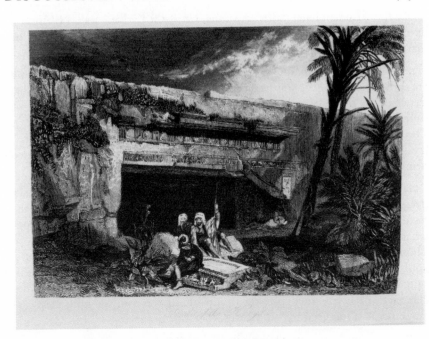

TOMBS IN THE VALLEY OF JEHOSHAPHAT.

1.28.41   Lydian hair] Soft, sensuous. Cf. "soft Lydian airs"—*L'Allegro*, line 136 (for Melville's copy of Milton see the discussion at 1.1.24; he marked lines nearby but not this one).

1.28.53   Moriah's walls] They have come down the Kedron ravine and are somewhere near the southeast angle of Moriah. Clarel recalls the magnificence of the third Temple, rebuilt by Herod (line 55) with marble columns supporting the cedar roofs of surrounding halls (see the discussion at 1.10.3). The "valley Tyropœon" (line 59), largely filled in with rubbish and debris, lay between the Temple area and David's original City of Zion, the two being connected by a great arched bridge (Map A, p. 707).

1.28.61   Across Jehoshaphat] Toward the ancient village of Siloam (Map A, p. 707) was a collection of ruined tombs and huts part way up the eastern slope. The "tombs in row" (line 64), viewed from the exact spot where Clarel and Nehemiah stand, may be seen on p. 741 above, from Thomson, II, [479]. In his 1856–57 journal, Melville recorded: "Siloam— pool, hill, village. (Here, at narrow gorge begins Vale of Kedron &c. Village, occupying the successive terraces of tombs excavated in the perpendicular faces of living rock. Living occupants of the tombs—household arrangements. One used for an oven. Others for granaries.—" (p. 85).

1.28.72   angle of King David's wall] Presumably the southeast corner of the Temple platform. Bartlett's *Walks*, facing p. 110, has a view from the village of Siloam which shows the high jut of the wall from here, and speaks of "the steep precipice of Moriah, surmounted by the angle of the temple wall, of which the remarkable ancient masonry is here very conspicuous." "Franconian land" (line 76) is Franconia Notch in the White Mountains of New Hampshire, site of the famous Old Man of the Mountain, an extraordinary natural profile when seen from one particular spot in the Notch. The 1856–57 journal notes: "The South East angle of wall. Mosque of Omar— Solomon's Temple. Here the wall of Omar rises upon the foundation stones of Solomon, triumphing over that which sustains it, an emblem of the Moslem religion, which at once spurns that deeper faith which fathered it & preceded it. &c" (p. 85).

1.28.96   Siloam] See the discussion at 1.1.24. Bartlett's *Walks*, facing p. 68, has a large engraving of the steps and grotto (reproduced on p. 744 below), speaks of it as "a delicious shelter from the burning noon-day beams of a July sun" (p. 68), and mentions Bethesda (line 111; p. 69). Melville's reference to "Science" (line 108) is to the dramatic research of Edward Robinson (1794–1863), America's most eminent sacred geographer and the author of *Biblical Researches in Palestine* (1841). By crawling underground— north through 800 feet of narrow passageway from where the water entered Siloam's arch, and then south for 950 feet from the Fountain of the Virgin—

he showed the two were joined, and so explained the intermittent flow of Siloam. It was a daring triumph for the new science of exact archaeology, and was widely reported. See 2.10.143, where the Elder repeats Robinson's work.

1.28.111   Bethesda's pool] Where another miracle occurred—Jesus' healing of the impotent man (John 5.1–9). It was a pool of five porches, where "an angel went down at a certain season . . . and troubled the water: whosoever then first after the troubling of the water stepped in was made whole of whatsoever disease he had." That Melville followed the monkish tradition placing Bethesda (or "Bezetha") near St. Stephen's Gate (Map A, p. 707) is elsewhere clear (2.3.6), though the standard guidebooks did not. His comment in the 1856–57 journal—"The so-called Pool of Bethesda full of rubbish—sooty look & smell" (p. 91; see also p. 440)—suggests the gap between ancient vision and present fact (he later boxed this sentence in red pencil—see the textual note at 91.10–12).

1.28.116   Ammon's in the Libyan wild] The famous temple and oracle of Ammon, Egyptian counterpart of Zeus and Jupiter, in the Libyan desert.

1.28.118   a jostled pebble] Superb exemplum of the tiny, crucial difference between the supernatural and the natural worlds throughout the poem; like the psychologist's drawing of a stairway that can be seen as ascending or descending, but cannot be seen both ways at the same time, Siloam is either the miraculous pool, or "a rural well" (line 121).

1.29.5   mistletoe] See the discussion at line 58.

1.29.20   Admetus' shepherd] Apollo, the most favored of the Greek gods, tended the sheep of Admetus in Thessaly for nine years.

1.29.26   angels round Cecilia] St. Cecilia, martyred ca. 230 at Rome, became the patron saint of music. She is the occasion of "The Second Nun's Tale" by Chaucer and a "Song" and an "Ode" for St. Cecilia's Day by Dryden, and also of famous paintings including Raphael's St. Cecilia in Ecstasy, which Melville saw at Bologna (Journals, p. 116). Melville's source for the details of this passage (e.g., "that perfumed spell / Of Paradise-flowers invisible," lines 24–25) is unlocated; but the Paradise roses with which her guardian angels crowned her left such a smell (see 2.24.25–27). For Melville's print of St. Cecilia see Wallace (cited in the discussion at 1.6.28), pp. 63, 83, fig. 9. Of interest is Melville's letter of December 9, 1872, to his cousin Catherine Gansevoort Lansing: "Do you know much about the Natural History of Angels? Well, there is one variety known by this: in the place where they may have tarried for a time, they leave behind them a fragrance as of violets."

Pool of Siloam

The Garden of Gethsemane

1.29.30   swart Vesuvian wine] Probably Lachryma Christi, the famous red wine produced in the region (mentioned at 3.25.98—see the discussion).

1.29.38–39   Carthusian / Tho' born a Sybarite] Carthusians belong to one of the strictest Catholic orders, noted for austerity and long periods of individual isolation; whereas the residents of ancient Sybaris were voluptuaries.

1.29.51   an Ariel unknown] Tricksy, a shape-shifter, like Ariel in Shakespeare's *The Tempest*. Melville owned a seven-volume set of Shakespeare (Boston: Hilliard, Gray, 1837; Sealts 460; Bercaw 634); see the NN *Moby-Dick*, pp. 955–70.

1.29.58   the Sibyl's Golden Bough] The Sibyl of Cumae told Aeneas where to find the sacred bough, glowing and golden in the dark groves, which served him as talisman in the descent into the underworld in search of his father. In Dryden's translation, which Melville owned (New York: Harper, [18—], vol. XII; see Sealts 147 and p. 224), the bough is described as Aeneas seizes it:

> Through the green leaves the glitt'ring shadows glow;
> As, on the sacred oak, the wintry mistletoe,
> Where the proud mother views her precious brood,
> And happier branches, which she never sow'd.
> Such was the glitt'ring; such the ruddy rind,
> And dancing leaves, that wantoned in the wind.
>
> (6.297–302)

Virgil's simile of the mistletoe provides the imagery with which Melville opens (lines 4–6), as the golden bough closes, the glowing description of Vine. For Melville's framed engraving of J. M. W. Turner's *The Golden Bough* see Wallace (cited in the discussion at 1.6.28), pp. 59, 68, 86.

1.30.0   THE SITE OF THE PASSION] The Garden of Gethsemane, in the Kedron Valley between St. Stephen's Gate and Olivet (Map A, p. 707), was, at the time Melville visited Jerusalem in 1857, a grove of eight ancient olive trees ("survivors," line 25) enclosed in 1847 by the Franciscans (Latins) with a high white wall. For a gratuity a monk showed visitors the presumed sites connected with the Passion, such as the "rock" (with body imprints) where James and Peter fell asleep (line 73) and the "grotto of the Bitter Cup" (line 102). The engraving reproduced opposite is from Bartlett, *Walks*, facing p. 98 (before the wall was raised).

1.30.24   In olives, monumental trees] "The olive tree much resembles in its grotesque contortions the apple tree—only it is much more gnarled & less lively in its green. . . . It is a haunted melancholy looking tree (sober & penitent), quite in keeping with Jerusalem & its associations" (*Journals*, p.

89; later marked by a pair of dashed lines in red pencil—see the textual note at 89.29–32).

1.30.30   Dathan] One of the rebels against Moses who joined Korah and was swallowed up in a miraculous cleavage of the earth (Num. 16).

1.30.35   the chapter in St John] John 18.1–14.

1.30.48   the fraud foreknown] "Jesus therefore, knowing all things that should come upon him . . ." (John 18.4).

1.30.73   James and Peter fell asleep] In the copy of the New Testament (New York: American Bible Society, 1844; Sealts 65) which Melville took around the Horn with him in 1860, he underlined Matthew's version of Jesus' words, "Sleep on now, and take your rest . . ." (Matt. 26.45); then he wrote a commentary: "This is ironical." Luke (line 77), on the other hand, says Jesus "found them sleeping for sorrow, And said unto them, Why sleep ye? rise and pray, lest ye enter into temptation" (Luke 22.45–46).

1.30.112   Paul Pry] An inquisitive man, as defined in dictionaries of colloquial speech, proverbs, slang, and household words. For example, the following definition is given in *Brewer's Dictionary of Phrase and Fable*, 8th rev. ed. (New York and Evanston: Harper & Row, 1963): "an idle, meddlesome fellow, who has no occupation of his own, and is always interfering with other folk's business. The term is from the hero of John Poole's comedy, *Paul Pry* (1825)." The obvious "Paul Pry" in this passage is the "Inquisitive Philistine" (line 105) tourist with his guidebook (in contrast to Nehemiah's Bible), intruding into the sacred precincts of Gethsemane. His irreverent attitude is like those of Glaucon, Derwent, and Ungar in the canto "By the Garden" (2.3) and of Glaucon in Bethlehem and in the vale of Tempe (2.5; see the discussion at 2.5.46). It has been argued that Vine's expression of "freakish mockery" (line 109) makes the naively sensitive Clarel unhappy to see not only the tourist but Vine himself as a Paul Pry. But, whether or not this interpretation is right, the dictionary definitions show that "Paul Pry" is too common a colloquial epithet to lend convincing support to the argument (used as evidence that Vine portrays Hawthorne) that here it is an allusion to Hawthorne's early tale "Sights from a Steeple," in which the narrator, presumably Hawthorne's spokesman, says that "the most desirable mode of existence might be that of a spiritualized Paul Pry." The sketch is in *Twice-Told Tales* (vol. I, 1837), a copy of which Hawthorne inscribed to Melville in 1851 (Boston: Munroe, 1845; Sealts 259); Melville did not mark the passage, I, 261. For the Hawthorne allusion argued see Henry A. Murray's introduction to *Pierre* (New York: Hendricks House, 1949), pp. lxxviii, 476, and Hershel Parker, "The Character of Vine in Melville's *Clarel*," *Essays in Arts and Sciences*, XV (June, 1986), 91–113.

1.31.3   A second stranger] Rolfe. The view that Rolfe is a partial self-portrait by Melville is developed in the HISTORICAL AND CRITICAL NOTE, pp. 586–89.

1.31.12   Sunium by her fane is crowned] Cape Sounion (or Colonna, ancient Sunium Promontorium) at the southern tip of Attica, magnificent site of the ruined columns of an ancient temple of Poseidon.

1.31.32   Baalbec] The ancient ruined city in Lebanon famous for its great temples. Melville did not visit it. Stanley, p. 399, mentions it briefly.

1.31.66   by Christ's belfry] Beside the square tower of the Church of the Holy Sepulcher stood a minaret (line 67: the "Saracen shaft" of line 73), as can be seen in the view of the Pool of Hezekiah reproduced on p. 712 above. The "Norman tower" (line 73) was a three-story remnant of the massive five-story campanile of the Crusaders. The 1856–57 journal, describing the church from the front, comments: "To the left is a high & venerable tower, which like an aged pine, is barked at bottom, & all decay at top" (p. 89).

1.31.82   The story's known] In Stanley, p. 455, Melville underlined the part of this passage italicized here: "*the minaret of Omar beside the Christian belfry*, telling its well-known story of *Arabian devotion and magnanimity*. . . ." In a footnote to this Stanley wrote in part: "The minaret is said to stand on the spot where Omar prayed, as near the church as was compatible with his abstaining from its appropriation by offering up his prayers within it." According to Murray, I, 172, Omar had been told by the patriarch of the Church of the Sepulcher that he might pray right there, but refused: " 'If I had prayed in any of these churches,' he said, 'the Muslems would undoubtedly have seized upon it the moment I left your city on my way homeward.' "

1.31.101   Long afterward] Omar took Jerusalem in 636; the "butchery" (line 103) by the "Christian knights" (line 102) refers to the Crusaders (see the discussion at 1.4.7).

1.31.111   Queen Helena] St. Helena (ca. 247–327), wife of Constantius I. By one set of traditions she was at the age of 79 divinely directed in finding the true cross, locating the sacred spots attached to it, and building the Church of the Holy Sepulcher. An earlier tradition, according to Murray, I, 156–57, attributes this work to Constantine, her son and emperor of Rome (324–37). Rolfe first advances the earlier theory, calling her a "second Mary" (line 108), but soon gets skeptical. The whole problem of Constantine's motives in his famous conversion to Christianity is examined by Gibbon (chap. 20; see the discussion at 1.4.7).

1.31.125   the fair De Maintenon] Madame de Maintenon (1635–1719), second wife of Louis XIV, made the founding of St. Cyr, a school-convent for indigent young girls of fine families, the passion of her later years. Her religious and educational motives may have been touched with personal vanity.

1.31.138 Last time 'twas burnt] The major conflagration of 1808, mentioned by Stanley, p. 458, described by Murray, I, 159. The phrase "now some three score years ago" (line 160), i.e., about sixty years, would place the writing of this passage around 1868.

1.31.161 Lima's first convulsion] In 1746 much of the city was destroyed: Melville had been ashore in Lima about January 1, 1844, as a member of the crew of the frigate *United States*; there are repeated references to Lima in his works; see especially "The Town-Ho's Story," *Moby-Dick*, chap. 54, pp. 242–59.

1.31.182 The priest, I said] Rolfe uses the term in the generic sense indicated in the 1856–57 journal, where Melville refers to the Pyramids as the creation, not of Nature or Man, but of "that supernatural creature, the priest." For "out of the rude elements of the insignificant thoughts that are in all men, they could rear the transcendent conception of a God" (p. 78).

1.31.199 Tyrrhene seas] The "eerie hue" of Rolfe's eyes is compared to the blue of the overcast Mediterranean around southern Italy; the phrase appears in Dryden's translation of the *Aeneid* (e.g., 7.8), which Melville owned (see the discussion at 1.29.58).

1.31.208 Phylæ] The whole passage (to line 230) demonstrates the impact of comparative religion on the faith-doubt problem. Phylae (or Philae) was the sacred island of ancient Egyptian religion, on the Nile just above the first cataract. Melville had not visited it when he was in Egypt, but he read Stanley's account, pp. xliv–xlv, which concludes: "The mythological interest of the Temple is its connection with Isis, who is its chief divinity, and accordingly the sculptures of her, of Osiris, and of Horus, are countless. The most remarkable, though in a very obscure room, and on a very small scale, is the one representing the death of Osiris, and then his embalmment, burial, gradual restoration, and enthronement as judge of the dead." He read also Bartlett's *The Nile Boat* (New York: Scribner, [186–?]; Sealts 49, annotated) in which pp. 210–12 discuss Philae as one of the fabled burial places of Osiris, and point out that Osiris, in his role as sacrifice to Typho, after which he rose to new life as judge of the dead, provides a "very remarkable analogy to the office sustained by our Saviour." The implications of Osiris for the American mind at this time are suggested by Emerson's sacramental visit in 1872 to see the tomb of "him who sleeps at Phylae," described by Ralph L. Rusk, *The Life of Ralph Waldo Emerson* (New York: Scribner's, 1949), pp. 457–71 (Rusk cites the quoted passage in Emerson's *Journals* [Boston: Houghton Mifflin, 1904], X, 405). Python (line 211), here symbolizing

Greek religion, was the great serpent that came from the earth-mud after the deluge of Deucalion, and lived in the caves of Parnassus until slain by Apollo. Rolfe's emphasis is on the way Egyptian religion gave way to Greek (the Greek Ptolemies, in Stanley, pp. xliv–xlv) on the one hand, and on Osiris as a prototype for Christ (line 219) on the other. Rolfe's reference to Hosea (line 222) is to the verse: "When Israel was a child, then I loved him, and called my son out of Egypt" (Hos. 11.1), and to St. Matthew (line 221): "When he [Joseph] arose, he took the young child and his mother by night, and departed into Egypt: And was there until the death of Herod: that it might be fulfilled which was spoken of the Lord by the prophet, saying, Out of Egypt have I called my son" (Matt. 2.14–15). Stanley, p. xxvii, in the opening paragraph of his introduction, notes that "the Evangelist emphatically plants in the first page of the Gospel History the prophetical text which might well stand as the inscription over the entrance to the Old Dispensation—'Out of Egypt have I called my Son.' " Clarel's reply to Rolfe (lines 226–27) was the standard conservative interpretation of the problem; but Rolfe clearly would go beyond it.

1.31.231   To Cicero] Melville had acquired a volume of Cicero as early as 1849 (New York: Harper, [18—]; Sealts 147). Outside Rome he had a "View of Tusculum (Cicero) from top of hill, at end of long avenue of olives" (*Journals*, p. 112).

1.31.252   Numa's Jove] Numa Pompilius, legendary second king of Rome, revered by the Romans as the establisher of their whole religious system.

1.31.284   Kidd's doubloons] The legendary buried treasure of the privateer-pirate Captain William Kidd (ca. 1645–1701), long sought by various means, including the divining rod or "wand" (line 285). See *Redburn*, chap. 1, p. 8, and *Pierre*, bk. 7, p. 132, and bk. 17, pp. 253–54.

1.32.0   Of Rama] The epic hero of the Indian *Ramayana*. When mankind was being tyrannized over by Ravana, a great demon, Vishnu the Preserver came forward and offered to be born as a man in order to subdue him. Rama is thus the avatar or incarnation who appears on earth to do battle with Ravana without himself knowing his divine origins. The *Ramayana* treats him as both human (bks. 2–6) and divine (bks. 1, 7). Melville's knowledge and frequent use of Indian and Middle Eastern materials are explored by Dorothee Metlitsky Finkelstein in *Melville's Orienda* (New Haven and London: Yale University Press, 1961) and by H. Bruce Franklin in *The Wake of the Gods: Melville's Mythology* (Stanford: Stanford University Press, 1963). Maunsell B. Field, in *Memories of Many Men* (New York: Harper, 1874), p. 202, reports a conversation at Arrowhead during the 1850's between Melville and Oliver Wendell

Holmes on "East India religions and mythologies . . . which was conducted with the most amazing skill and brilliancy on both sides." Melville may well have known *The Poetry of the East* (Boston: Whittemore, Niles, & Hall, 1856), William Rounseville Alger's collection of specimens of Hindu, Persian, and Arab fragments preceded by a long prose introduction. Here, for example, Alger gives a summary of the *Ramayana* and offers a translated fragment (pp. 29–37). The same book, incidentally, carries many poems which in imagery or setting touch *Clarel*. Melville owned and annotated another of Alger's books, *The Solitudes of Nature and of Man* (second ed., Boston: Roberts, 1867; Sealts 11).

1.32.56   in the verse, may be, he is] Though the narrator is coy about identifying his Rama-like character, it must be either Vine or Rolfe. The case for Rolfe is easily the stronger. Rolfe dominates the preceding and following cantos; it is his modes of thought and action which are at stake at this point. Though some of the attributes of lines 12–31 fit Vine, only Rolfe, whose rebellion against conventional glosses is everywhere stressed, and who is later called "An Adam in his natural ways" (3.16.181), has the attributes of lines 32–48. Except for the concluding couplet, the canto stands as a separate poem and, like other passages, may well have been an insertion.

1.33.3   Prediction of Our Lord] Across the Kedron Valley from the Temple area, according to Bartlett's *Walks*, p. 97, was "a small building on the point whence Christ is said to have predicted the ruin of the city." "Luke's words" (line 23) begin: "And when he was come near, he beheld the city, and wept over it . . ." (Luke 19.41–44; cf. lines 21–22). This famous view of Jerusalem from Olivet, both in the round and in the very popular keyed skeleton-view, may be seen in *Walks*, facing p. 100 and after p. 54 (reproduced on p. 702 above).

1.33.15   Pale as Pompeii] Melville visited Pompeii in 1857 (*Journals*, pp. 101–2).

1.33.32   the plain of Troy] Melville in 1856 saw the general plain southeast of the entrance to the Dardanelles from shipboard (*Journals*, p. 68), and also Mt. Ida (Gargarus: line 34) above it. Heinrich Schliemann's famous excavations, begun in 1870 and known about 1872, fixed the exact site, and may be reflected in the phrase "verifying Homer's sites" (line 35).

1.33.46–47   the gate / Which overlooks Jehoshaphat] St. Stephen's Gate.

1.33.58   The hat goes round the world] The old Chaluka system by which Jews were maintained in Palestine. Murray, I, 83, notes the poverty, idleness, and dependence of the Jerusalem Jews, as do others.

1.33.62   Patagonian beach] The southern end of South America, toward the Horn.

1.33.68 *Woe, we depart!*] The woes against wickedness are everywhere in the Old Testament. Father Mapple rings the changes on them at the climax of "The Sermon" (*Moby-Dick*, chap. 9).

1.33.83 the brood without the hen] This reference and Nehemiah's following speech (lines 84–89) draw on Jesus' words: "O Jerusalem, Jerusalem, which killest the prophets, and stonest them that are sent unto thee; how often would I have gathered thy children together, as a hen doth gather her brood under her wings, and ye would not!" And again: "If thou hadst known, even thou, at least in this thy day, the things which belong unto thy peace!" (Luke 13.34; 19.42).

1.34.1–2 How solitary . . . / Sitteth the city] Vine's "text" (line 12) is the opening lines of the Lamentations of Jeremiah, who was born in Anathoth (lines 10–11): "How doth the city sit solitary, that was full of people!"

1.34.19 Zion, like Rome, is Niebuhrized] A major theme of the poem and of Rolfe's point of view (though he laments it)—that the Holy Land is no longer part of divine history but has become just another chapter in the natural history of man. Barthold Niebuhr (1776–1831), the famous German historian, is used here as a symbol of the critical spirit of the age; his *Roman History* (1827–32) sought to winnow out factual history from the long accumulations of myth and legend. Melville in a moment of bitterness had once confided to his 1856–57 journal: "Heartily wish Niebuhr & Strauss to the dogs.—The deuce take their penetration & acumen. They have robbed us of the bloom. If they have undeceived any one—no thanks to them" (p. 97).

1.34.25 Atlantis and Cathay] The fabled western island beyond the Pillars of Hercules; and marvelous, faraway China.

1.34.26 Diana's moon] The myth of the moon goddess, Diana, and her love for the beautiful Endymion (line 28). As Melville's brother-in-law John C. Hoadley indicated in his copy of *Clarel* (see the HISTORICAL SUPPLEMENT, p. 664 above), "Affirming it [the moon] a clinkered blot" (line 27) alludes to Martin Farquhar Tupper's "The Moon," in *A Thousand Lines* (Boston: Peirce, 1848), in which the moon, "a giant ash of death," is asked "must I take thee for the blot / On God's fair firmament . . . ?"

1.34.31 Appian to his Capital] The great paved highway from Rome to Brindisi.

1.34.59 Solomon's complaint] The theme of evil is almost everywhere in Ecclesiastes and Proverbs, favorite writings of Melville. The ointment image (line 60) would seem to come from Ecclesiastes 10.1: "Dead flies cause the ointment of the apothecary to send forth a stinking savour." Beelzebub (line 62), from the Hebrew word meaning "fly-lord," is the contemptuous term for Satan frequently used in the New Testament, and for his chief lieutenant in *Paradise Lost*.

1.35.0   ARCULF AND ADAMNAN] Arculf was an eighth-century French bishop who made one of the earliest recorded pilgrimages to the Holy Land. On his return voyage, according to the Venerable Bede (673–735; mentioned in 3.16.180) in his *Ecclesiastical History*, Arculf was wrecked on the island of Iona (line 21), an early center of the Celtic Church in the Scottish Hebrides (line 36). Here was located the monastery which St. Columba (line 26), one of the three patron saints of Ireland, had founded in 563, and which had come under the ecclesiastical rule of the Culdees (line 23), an irregular monastic order then strong in Scotland. The abbot of St. Columba, Adamnan, received the shipwrecked bishop and recorded his pilgrimage. Melville had access to at least three sources for the part of the story he used: *The Miscellaneous Works of Venerable Bede*, ed. Rev. J. A. Giles (London: Whittaker, 1843), III, 223–33; "The Travels of Bishop Arculf in the Holy Land. Towards A.D. 700. Written from his Dictation, by Adamnan, Abbot of Iona," in Wright, pp. 1–12; and Bartlett's fragmentary account in *Jerusalem Revisited* (London: Hall & Virtue, 1855), pp. 118–19. Wright, pp. 5–6, was his probable source: "On the highest point of Mount Olivet, where our Lord ascended into heaven, is a large round church, having around it three vaulted porticoes. The inner apartment is not vaulted and covered, because of the passage of our Lord's body. . . . On the ground, in the midst of it, are to be seen the last prints in the dust of our Lord's feet, and the roof appears open above, where he ascended. . . . In the western part of the same church are eight windows; and eight lamps, hanging by cords opposite them, cast their light through the glass as far as Jerusalem; which light, Arculf said, strikes the hearts of the beholders with a mixture of joy and divine fear. Every year, on the day of the Ascension, when mass is ended, a strong blast of wind comes down, and casts to the ground all who are in the church. All that night, lanterns are kept burning there, so that the mountain appears not only lighted up, but actually on fire, and all that side of the city is illuminated by it." The canto is thus an imagined dramatization of Arculf telling Adamnan one of the wonders of the Holy Land—the annual miracle at the Church of the Ascension on Olivet, in order to contrast their awe and credulity with the uneasy skepticism of Clarel and his friends.

1.35.4   A little plastered tower] A replacement for the famous church (line 18) built on Olivet by St. Helena. The structure is described by Stanley, pp. 446–47, as "a small octagon chapel within the court of a mosque, the minaret of which is ascended by every traveller for the sake of its celebrated view over Jerusalem and the Dead Sea." This view can be seen in the illustration on p. 708 above, from Thomson, II, [465]. The minaret is pictured here, from *Through David's Realm*, by Edward Staats DeGrote Tompkins (Troy, N.Y.: Nims & Knight, 1889), p. 83.

1.35.10   Hakeem's deed] The founder of the Druze, a Mohammedan sect which began in Egypt in the tenth century, was el-Hâkim, the third Fatimite caliph. Murray, I, xli, 91, characterizes him as "a madman" and "a wild and visionary fanatic." His fierce persecution of the Christians included the destruction of Helena's original Church of the Holy Sepulcher (line 14), and perhaps her Church of the Ascension on Olivet.

1.35.36   Patmos] The island in the Aegean where St. John was favored with his apocalyptic visions (Rev. 1.9) and which Melville found so haunting yet disillusioning (*Journals*, pp. 71, 72, 97, 98); see also 4.2.21–22 and "Parallel Passages," p. 872.

1.35.39   Omar's prime] The caliph Omar took Jerusalem in the year 636, built his famous mosque (the Dome of the Rock), and instituted two centuries of relative peace for Jews and Christians.

1.35.45–48   Glad tidings . . . *the Lord*] A variation on Luke 2.10–11.

1.35.86   Vesuvius' plume of fire] As Melville's ship approached Naples at night in February of 1857, he saw the "Dim mass of Vesuvius" (*Journals*, p. 101) but no "plume of fire / Redden the bay, tinge mast and spire," as here. He ascended Vesuvius the same day and saw the "flare of flame" in its crater (*Journals*, p. 101).

1.35.88   Ascension Eve] The Thursday forty days after Easter is Ascension Day.

1.35.105   The Pictish storm-king] An image of primitive, pre-Christian forces threatening the Christian ideal. The aboriginal Picts and invading Aryans once controlled all of Britain.

1.35.109–15   The legends . . . Science now] On "Saturday in Easter Week / 1877" Melville wrote to his brother-in-law John C. Hoadley: "Your legend from Marco Polo I had never previously met with. How full of significance it is! And beauty too. These legends of the Old Faith are really wonderful both from their multiplicity and their poetry. They far surpass the stories in the Greek mythologies. Dont you think so? See, for example, the life of St. Elizabeth of Hungary."

1.36.0   THE TOWER] See the discussion at 1.35.4.

1.36.11   the wanderer] Nehemiah.

1.36.13   Images he the ascending Lord] Off Cyprus, Melville noted in his 1856–57 journal: "From these waters rose Venus from the foam. Found it as hard to realize such a thing as to realize on Mt Olivet that from there Christ rose" (p. 95).

1.36.22   the print to view] Stanley, p. 447, writes: "Within the chapel is the rock which has been pointed out to pilgrims, at least since the seventh century, as imprinted with the footstep of our Saviour. . . . Here there is nothing but a simple cavity in the rock, with no more resemblance to a human foot than to anything else." The almost casual improvisation of this site, particularly when the New Testament located the Ascension in Bethany (Luke 24.50–51), had made it controversial; here, the pilgrims "mark it, nor a question moot" (line 24), and go climb the minaret.

1.36.29   the city Dis] Dante's Nether Hell in *The Inferno* (bk. 8ff.); see also the discussion at 3.25.43. On his 1849 trip, Melville had thought London seen from a bridge "a city of Dis (Dante's)" (*Journals*, p. 14) and he later wrote a chapter about London in *Israel Potter* entitled "In the City of Dis" (chap. 25). Melville's annotated copy of Dante is Cary's translation (London: Bohn, 1847; Sealts 174).

1.36.31   bewrinkled mezzotint] Warburton, II, 60, likens the appearance of Jerusalem, approached from the west, to "an immense mezzotint engraving."

1.36.37   the son of Kish] The wrathful and melancholy King Saul was the son of Kish (1 Sam. 9.1–2).

1.36.53   Hope's hill descries the pit Despair] The fundamental allegory of the poem—geographical, theological, psychological—here emerges in Bunyan-like terms. From the traditional site of the Ascension and Second Coming, the pilgrims have turned east and for the first time looked down across the Judah wilderness to the dull, narrow gleam of the Dead Sea (line 40). Rolfe's instantaneous response to its baleful quality and Vine's "wordless look intent" (line 46) anticipate what lies ahead. Clarel is caught by their mood. Only Nehemiah, in his dreamworld of the New Jerusalem, fails to see; his proposed journey to Bethany (line 59), the pastoral town of Jesus a mile east of Jerusalem (Map B, p. 709), marks his inability to share the sea's ominous forewarning, though he will die in it (2.39). A view, "Dead Sea from the Top of Olivet," is in Thomson, II, [465], reproduced on p. 708 above.

1.37.0 A SKETCH] See NEHEMIAH (Index). The canto is an adaptation of the experiences of Captain George Pollard, whose whaler, the *Essex*, was sunk in the Pacific in 1820 by two smashing blows from an 85-foot whale. Rather than risk cannibals on nearby Tahiti (a mistaken apprehension, as Rolfe hints in line 56) the crew took to whaleboats and ventured the two-thousand-mile trip to South America ("the Spanish Main": line 52). The subsequent tragic voyage—which led to cannibalism on their own part (the point of lines 63–65)—was a moving sea-saga which took tremendous hold on Melville. The *Essex* story was summarized in *Moby-Dick* (chap. 45, p. 206) as a major affidavit for the coming catastrophe of the *Pequod*. "Being returned home at last," Ishmael concludes, "Captain Pollard once more sailed for the Pacific in command of another ship, but the gods shipwrecked him again upon unknown rocks and breakers; for the second time his ship was utterly lost, and forthwith forswearing the sea, he has never tempted it since." Melville knew of the *Essex* disaster through forecastle talk aboard the *Acushnet*; then through a shipboard gam with William Chase (whose father had been second mate aboard the *Essex*), after which he borrowed from the son the father's book: Owen Chase, *Narrative of the Extraordinary and Distressing Shipwreck of the Whale-Ship Essex of Nantucket* (New York: Gilley, 1821); and finally through his own copy of this rare book, found for him by Thomas Macy of Nantucket shortly before *Moby-Dick* was in its flurry (Sealts 134). Further, Melville wrote, and had bound into his copy of Chase, eighteen pages of memoranda still extant in it (reproduced and transcribed in the NN *Moby-Dick*, pp. 971–95). The striking event for *Clarel* was Melville's visit to Nantucket in July, 1852: "I—somewhere about 1850–3—saw Capt. Pollard on the island of Nantucket, and exchanged some words with him. To the islanders he was a nobody—to me, the most impressive man, tho' wholly unassuming, even humble—that I ever encountered" (pp. 987–88). Henry F. Pommer, in his "Herman Melville and the Wake of the *Essex*," *American Literature*, XX (November, 1948), 290–304, suggests that in this canto Melville made certain changes in the original Pollard story for effect: he put the chance running aground first and the more ominous staving in by a whale ("Of purpose aiming," line 83) second; he changed the whaling voyage to a sealing voyage to heighten the whale's malice; he made Pollard the sole survivor of the first disaster; etc. Pommer also notes that Pollard died in 1870; this suggests that lines 21–23, and perhaps the whole canto, may have been written after that date, but Melville habitually made late local insertions in his works. Toward the end of one of his 1856–57 journal notebooks, Melville at some time made the cryptic entry: "Cap. Pollard. / of *Nant.*" (p. 154).

1.37.31   Calvin's or Zeno's] That is, Christian or classical. John Calvin (1509–64) formed a "creed" (line 102) stressing predestination; Zeno (d. ca. 264 B.C.) was the Greek philosopher who developed doctrines of Stoicism.

1.37.105   Silvio Pellico] Italian poet, prose writer, and patriot, Pellico (1789–1854) was condemned to death for high treason by the Austrians, but instead was imprisoned for ten years (1820–30). The first edition's "Sylvio" has been emended. The story of his imprisonment is told in *Le mie prigioni* (1832), translated by Mrs. Andrews Norton as *My Prisons* (Cambridge, Mass.: Folsum, 1836). Melville devoted a poem to Silvio: "Pausilippo (In the time of Bomba)," stressing that the "enthusiast" was "quelled," and "Unmanned, made meek through strenuous wrong" (in *Timoleon*; NN *Published Poems*, pp. 297–99). See Hans-Joachim Lang, "Silvio Pellico, Melville's 'Dungeoned Italian,' " *Melville Society Extracts*, No. 58 (May, 1984), 4–6.

1.37.115   Laocoon's serpent] Melville said in his lecture on "Statues in Rome": "In a niche of the Vatican stands the Laocoön, the very semblance of a great and powerful man writhing with the inevitable destiny which he cannot throw off. Throes and pangs and struggles are given with a meaning that is not withheld. The hideous monsters embrace him in their mighty folds, and torture him with agonizing embraces. The Laocoön is grand and impressive, gaining half its significance from its symbolism—the fable that it represents. . . . the Laocoön represents the tragic side of humanity and is the symbol of human misfortune" (NN *Piazza Tales* volume, pp. 403–4). Melville had visited the Vatican twice in March of 1857, but he did not mention this statue in his journal (see *Journals*, pp. 110, 112). Hawthorne in *The Marble Faun* comments at length on the artistic power of the Laocoön group: "a type of the long, fierce struggle of man, involved in the knotted entanglements of Error and Evil, those two snakes, which, if no divine help intervene, will be sure to strangle him and his children in the end" (chap. 43).

    NN retains the first-edition form of the name, without the diaeresis on the last "o", because the meter of the line requires that the word be pronounced in three syllables, not four. Cf. "aërial" at 1.41.3 and "Sabaïtes" at 3.27.61, where the diaereses do indicate that the double vowels are not to be pronounced as diphthongs. (Diacritical marks are occasionally used in *Clarel*, as in "Señor" at 4.19.25, but nineteenth-century American practice—supported by contemporary dictionaries—often regarded them as dispensable.)

1.38.0   THE SPARROW] The image relates both to Nehemiah's loneliness and Clarel's search for a mate (next canto). The "Psalmist's" (line 21) cry had been: "I watch, and am as a sparrow alone upon the house top" (Ps. 102.7). Thomson, I, 53–54, comments on sparrows being "snared for mar-

ket" (line 17) in Palestine: "These birds are snared and caught in great num-
bers, but, as they are small and not much relished for food, five sparrows
may still be sold for two farthings." He also notes biblical allusions and
shows a woodcut of a sparrow.

1.40.0   THE MOUNDS] This canto, exploring the problem of deathbed
rites, may well have been prompted by Arnold's "The Wish," a poem on
this theme which Melville marked up in a newspaper clipping in 1867 and
again in *New Poems* (see the discussion at 1.19.29) in 1871 (Bezanson, "Ar-
nold's Poetry," p. 384). The scene of the canto is the Latin and English
cemeteries on Zion hill (Map A, p. 707). Melville's 1856–57 journal records:
"I would stroll to Mount Zion, along the terraced walks, & survey the tomb
stones of the hostile Armenians, Latins, Greeks, all sleeping together" (p.
87). The key word here for the canto is "hostile." Another entry reports: "I
often passed the Protestant School &c on Mt Zion, but nothing seemed
going on. The only place of interest there was the Grave Yard" (p. 92). The
idea of "mistimed zeal" (line 13) could have been suggested by Bartlett's
complaint, in *Walks*, p. 75, against the "bad taste" of a gravestone inscrip-
tion in the same Latin Cemetery: it tells of an American turned Catholic in
his last hours, while ill at the Terra Santa Convent (Celio's), "savouring
more of the joy of the proselyte seeker than the sorrow of the friend."

1.40.47   Job's text] Job 19.25.

1.40.79   Burckhardt] Johann Ludwig Burckhardt (1784–1817), famous
Swiss explorer and travel writer (e.g., *Travels in Syria and the Holy Land*,
1822), had adopted the disguise of a Turkish native, mastered the languages
and mores of an alien civilization, and so gained access to Mohammedan
holy places no European had seen before. For his discovery of Petra see
2.30.8 and the discussion at 2.29.78–79 below. His burial as a Mohammedan
is told by Bayard Taylor, *Cyclopædia of Modern Travel* (Cincinnati: Moore,
Wilstach, Keys, 1856), p. 226.

1.41.0   ON THE WALL] Probably the wall by the Jaffa Gate. The canto
title has a double meaning (line 148).

1.41.27   Lazarus in grief] Luke 16.19–31 set the prototype of poverty: "a
certain beggar named Lazarus."

1.41.51   Jaffa's stair] See the discussion at 1.8.38.

1.41.58   *Nil admirari*] To wonder at nothing (Horace, *Epistles*, 1.6.1).

1.41.79   The Fathers] Here, the Old Testament, as "The Evangelists"
(line 81) are the New Testament.

1.41.98   Cristina of Coll'alto] Melville's reference is to some actual or
legendary person (perhaps from a "romance," line 96), but this woman
"built up in wall" is unidentified.

1.41.109   rabble-banners] The pejorative revolutionary imagery of this poem by "B. L." (line 143; unidentified) foreshadows a major political theme of *Clarel*: intense distrust of French revolutionary politics in the nineteenth century, and of radicalism generally. These evoke throughout *Clarel* such political-religious epithets as "Atheists," "Vitriolists," "Red Caps," "Communist," "Red Republic," etc., from Rolfe, the Dominican, Mortmain, and Ungar. No one, including the narrator, offers a defense of revolutionaries. In some passages it is not entirely clear which of three major revolutions is being referred to, the sense often being collective—1789, 1848, or 1871. Melville of course knew of Bastille days (see also the discussion at 2.35.1) through general historical reading (and perhaps through Carlyle) and from his visit to Paris in 1849 (see *Journals*, pp. 30–34 and 330–47); of the February Revolution (in 1848) through newspaper reports as well as vivid letters from George Duyckinck to the young New York group of which he was then part; and of the 1871 Paris Commune through his daily papers. The fact that the red flag was flying over Paris from March 18 to May 24, 1871, while he was writing *Clarel*, certainly accounts for this recurrent theme.

1.41.133   Started from Strauss] David Friedrich Strauss (1808–74), leader of the higher criticism on the Continent and popularly known for later editions and translations of his *Das Leben Jesu* (1835–36); the translation by George Eliot, *Life of Jesus* (1846), caused a crisis in her life. Strauss took a mythical view of Jesus. His major counterpart in France was Ernest Renan (1823–92), learned philologist and historian, author of *La vie de Jésus* (1863); Renan was heretic, idealist, scholar, and revolutionary at various times: he suffered many disenchantments. Pierre Joseph Proudhon (1809–65) was a philosophical anarchist and predecessor of the syndicalists (line 137). He hurled himself into the 1848 revolution as a Paris journalist, but had to flee to Belgium.

1.41.143   St. Mary's Hall] Magdalen College, which Melville visited in 1857 (see *Journals*, pp. 128, 156). For "B. L." see the discussion at 1.41.109.

1.42.5   To Siddim] The Siddim Plain beside the Dead Sea. Map B, p. 709, shows the journey route here proposed.

1.42.19   John's wilderness] The Judah wilderness of Part 2, where John the Baptist, that "voice of one crying in the wilderness," stayed "in the deserts till the day of his shewing unto Israel," and then "came into all the country about Jordan, preaching the baptism of repentance for the remission of sins" (Luke 1.80; 3.3–4).

1.43.0   A PROCESSION] The Armenian funeral Clarel encounters somewhere here in the back streets of Jerusalem is a clear instance of transposition. In Constantinople Melville recorded in his journal: "Armenian funerals winding through the streets. Coffin covered with flowers borne on a bier. Wax candles borne on each side in daylight. Boys & men chanting alternately. Striking effect, winding through the narrow lanes" (p. 62). This passage Melville later underlined in red pencil and marked in the margin, probably when composing *Clarel* (see the *Journals* textual note at 62.25–28).

1.43.17–18   the Golden Bowl / And Pitcher broken] "Or ever the silver cord be loosed, or the golden bowl be broken, or the pitcher be broken at the fountain, or the wheel broken at the cistern" (Eccles. 12.6).

1.43.23   Her groom that Blue-Beard, cruel Death] The folk-tale killer of his successive wives. The joint image here of death and marriage (cf. Hawthorne's story "The Wedding-Knell," in *Twice-Told Tales*, vol. I [not marked in Melville's copy; see the discussion at 1.30.112]) becomes obsessive with Clarel and recurs several times in the coming journey (2.17; 2.29; 4.16; 4.32). The narrative function of this recall is to create ominous premonitions as to Ruth's future—amply fulfilled in the resolution (4.30). The psychological effect is to suggest Clarel's unconscious wish to escape marriage. The moral implication is that any hope that love can solve the "complex passion" (1.5.217) is foredoomed.

1.44.2   the morn of Candlemas] February 2, the feast commemorating the purification of the Virgin Mary; the day when altar candles are blessed.

1.44.5   Mount Acra's cope] See the discussion at 1.1.134.

PART 2

2.1.1   the Dolorosa Lane] See the discussion at 1.13.0.

2.1.7   Chaucer's Tabard Inn] The analogy with *The Canterbury Tales* (Sealts 138–41) is here made explicit, and the rest of the canto parallels the format of Chaucer's "Prologue." As the poem develops, various sketches or personal histories given by the pilgrims slightly imitate the ancient storytelling tradition of oriental literature, of Ovid, Boccaccio (line 241), and Chaucer. Yet as the narrator says, this is "Another age," and it is the "unfulfilled romance" (lines 12–13) of modern man and the contours of a new sensibility which are Melville's real theme.

2.1.9   Kent . . . Canterbury] In 1849 Melville got acquainted with both when he landed at Deal, strolled and rode by rail through Kent, and stayed overnight at Canterbury (see *Journals*, pp. 12–13).

2.1.30   the Templar old] The Knights Templars, who with the Knights of St. John (see the discussion at 1.25.82) were the two great religious and military organizations that evolved from the Crusades. For a satirical portrait of their fall from grace to graciousness (relevant to Derwent) see Part 1 of Melville's story "The Paradise of Bachelors and the Tartarus of Maids" (NN

Piazza Tales volume, pp. 316–23). At Oxford in 1857 Melville noted of scholars like "Old Burton" that "As knights templars were mixture of monk & soldier, so these of monk & gentleman" (*Journals*, p. 129, also p. 156).

2.1.41   Jonathan] Common nineteenth-century personification of the United States, or of a Yankee.

2.1.60   Like Talus] A mythical bronze giant of Crete. Allusions to Talus (as a character in Spenser's *Faerie Queene*, 5.1.12) occur in the "Extracts" in *Moby-Dick*, p. xx, and in "The Bell-Tower," NN *Piazza Tales* volume, p. 184. Melville owned Child's edition of Spenser (Boston: Little, Brown, 1855; Sealts 483).

2.1.63   Grampian kirk] The Scottish Church (alluding to the Grampian Mountains). Sixteenth- and seventeenth-century Presbyterians signed covenants opposing the imposition of episcopacy in Scotland.

2.1.92   the fag end of Voltaire] Voltaire (1694–1778) was among other things a founder of modern historical (anti-fabulist) methods. See also the discussion at 1.4.7.

2.1.104   a banker] For Melville's own visit to Thessalonica and to the country estate of the wealthy Abbott family there, see *Journals*, pp. 55–56, 392; see also Ekaterina Georgoudakis, "Djékis Abbot and the Greek Merchant in Herman Melville's *Clarel*," *Melville Society Extracts*, No. 64 (November, 1985), 1–6.

2.1.114   Paul's plea] Paul's two epistles to the Thessalonians, exhorting them to godliness.

2.1.146   By gorgons served] A joking reference to the three mythical and hideous maidens, including Medusa. "Duennas" (line 147) are governesses in Latin families. "Argive" (line 149) means Greek.

2.1.156   Smyrna] See the discussion at 1.8.38 above.

2.1.167   Beyrout] Melville spent several days at Beirut, a Syrian seaport, in 1857 (*Journals*, p. 95).

2.1.186   Of rigorous gloom] In Copy B at Harvard, Melville underlined the reading of the first edition, "Austerely sad"; and the words "rigorous gloom" appear in his hand in the left margin of p. 160 and in his list of alterations (see pp. 851, 855, and 860 below). The word "Of" is necessary if Melville's marginal substitution is to be accepted. The reasons for accepting all of Melville's annotations in Copy B are set forth in the NOTE ON THE TEXT, pp. 681–83.

2.1.203   The white cross gleamed] The same image of "the jointed workings of the beast's armorial cross" occurs in the final lines of Melville's sketch of "Norfolk Isle and the Chola Widow" in "The Encantadas"; there the scene of the ass ridden by the stricken Hunilla evoked tears from Lowell (see the NN *Piazza Tales* volume, pp. 162, 605–6).

2.1.214   vernal Easter caravan] The annual pilgrimage of thousands of Greek Christians from all over the Levant who assemble in Jerusalem and under the protection of Turkish guards go down to Gilgal (line 215: the plain west of the Jordan [line 209]) and so reach the Palmers' Beach (line 218) on the river. Here at the site of Christ's baptism by John (Matt. 3.13–17) they bathe, dip shrouds, and bring back staves. Melville did not see this but Stanley (pp. 308–10) did.

2.1.240   the phantom knight] In Boccaccio's *The Decameron* (eighth novel, fifth day). A violent, expiatory tale of a knight who committed suicide for love, and of his contemptuous lady who joyed in his death. Daily they reenact their punishment: he pursues her through the Ravenna pine wood, disembowels her, and feeds her heart and other entrails to pursuing dogs. A young man overcomes the resistance of his own hardhearted beloved by causing her to witness the scene.

2.2.2   Libertad's on the Mexic coin] From 1824 through the nineteenth century, Mexican silver coins had on the reverse a liberty cap with the word "Libertad" on it. Melville could have seen them in circulation on ships in the Pacific. See Frank W. Grove, *Coins of Mexico* (Lawrence, Mass.: Quarterman, 1981), pp. 194–257.

2.2.12–13   the wishing-cap / Of Fortunatus] The cap enabled Fortunatus, a European folk hero, to be transported wherever he might wish. Dekker's comedy *Old Fortunatus* (1600) is mentioned in *White-Jacket*, chap. 41, p. 168. See Bercaw 199.

2.3.0   BY THE GARDEN] See the discussion at 1.30.0.

2.3.6   from Bethesda's Pool] Map A (p. 707) shows the pool (see the discussion at 1.28.111), St. Stephen's Gate (line 10), the Virgin's Tomb (line 8: see Murray, I, 175–76), and Gethsemane (line 15). The pilgrims both leave and return to the city by St. Stephen's Gate, also called the Martyr's Gate or, by Latins, the Gate of My Lady Mary (line 9), pictured above from Tompkins, *Through David's Realm* (cited in the discussion at 1.35.4), p. 96.

2.3.60   the *'King of Terrors.'*] Melville twice uses this phrase in his moving account of the death of the young seaman during his 1860 *Meteor* voyage (*Journals*, pp. 134–35). The phrase occurs in Job 18.14.

2.3.76   Tivoli] Melville saw the "fine site" of Tivoli outside Rome in 1857, on the way passing Lake Tartarus, and made the cryptic notation "From *Tartarus to Tivoli*" in the margin of the entry for that day and in the back of that journal notebook (*Journals*, pp. 113, 154, and textual note at 113.10).

2.3.98   sounding brass] Paul's famous characterization of those who "have not charity" (1 Cor. 13.1).

2.3.108   *Terra Damnata*] Melville took the phrase, which he checked and underlined, from Stanley, p. 450.

2.3.120   The bitter cup] When Peter drew his sword to defend Jesus in the Garden of Gethsemane, Jesus said, "Put up thy sword into the sheath: the cup which my Father hath given me, shall I not drink it?" (John 18.11).

2.3.146   crucify] The cry of the mob to Pilate: "Away with him, away with him, crucify him" (John 19.15).

2.3.170–71   Bel shall bow / And Nebo stoop] Isaiah 46.1: "Bel boweth down, Nebo stoopeth . . . ," declaiming against these false gods of the Babylonians (Bel) and the Chaldeans (Nebo).

2.4.4   your new world's chanticleer] That is, Rolfe's America. Melville's "Cock-A-Doodle-Doo!" exploits the image fully (NN *Piazza Tales* volume, pp. 268–88). The first edition of *Walden* quoted from its own first chapter on the title page: "I do not propose to write an ode to dejection, but to brag as lustily as chanticleer in the morning." (See Bercaw 711.)

2.4.29   This Psalmanazer] George Psalmanazar (or "Psalmanazer," ca. 1679–1763) was the pseudonym of a never-identified French adventurer whose *Memoirs* were published in 1764. He was also an imposter, but it is not clear that that connotation is at stake here.

2.4.31   an Arcadian] Mortmain succumbed to the pastoral or "innocent" view of experience.

2.4.32   *Peace and good will*] Luke 2.14.

2.4.40   a decade dim] Europe in the 1840's was on the edge of deep social conflicts which suddenly burst wide open in 1848, in general resulting in the fall of "kings" (line 99), some new constitutions, and then new rulers.

2.4.97   weaves] In Copy B at Harvard, Melville wrote "weaves" in the left margin next to lines 96 and 97 of this canto, without indicating what word in the printed lines it was intended to replace (see the reproduction on p. 861 below). Walter E. Bezanson, in the Hendricks House edition, p. 591, mistakenly says that Melville wrote the word "weaves" twice in the margin; and he substitutes the word twice, first for "ebbs" (in 2.4.95) and then for "Floods" (2.4.96), producing the reading "The flood weaves out—the ebb / Weaves back". Since Melville actually wrote "weaves" only once, this reading is implausible; and in any case it is not apparent why Melville would have wished to alter his double use of "flood(s)" and "ebb(s)", each appearing once as a noun and once as a verb. The position of "weaves" in the margin suggests that it was intended to replace a word in lines 96 or 97, not 95, and the most likely word is "wears", which could easily have been a compositorial misreading of "weaves". The sense supports this conjecture, since "wears" is the one word that does not seem appropriate here: despite the fact that "wears and tears" is a common idiom, just how the shuttle "wears" the web is not clear. NN therefore substitutes "weaves" for "wears".

2.4.124   Micah's mind austere] Among Micah's austerities: "and what doth the Lord require of thee [not "thousands of rams, or . . . ten thousands of rivers of oil"], but to do justly, and to love mercy, and to walk humbly with thy God?" (Micah 6.8).

2.4.133–34   bale / Medean] The enchantress Medea, among other wicked acts, murdered her two children. See the discussion at 2.36.91.

2.4.142   Fair Circe] In the *Odyssey* (trans. Chapman; London: Smith, 1857; Sealts 278) the island sorceress (also mentioned at 2.28.12) who turned Ulysses' men into swine, but with whom he afterwards shared bed for a year; with her advice he sailed safely by the sea-nymph Sirens (line 144), bound to the mast. (Melville's poem "In a Bye-Canal" describes a Venetian encounter, with the same allusion [in *Timoleon; NN Published Poems*, pp. 292–93].) A Fury (line 144) of mythology was one of the serpent-haired, dog-headed, bat-winged, and bloody women who carried scourges and punished murders, disobedience toward parents, etc. The whole passage (lines 131–44) is most intense psychologically, as of course the Greek myths are themselves, and seems to cluster around violences of love and punishment as Rolfe and the narrator (line 145) struggle to explain Mortmain. In his own trance-like monologue by the Dead Sea, Mortmain himself is driven to name Medea again, and two other wicked women, Tofana and Jael (2.36.91–93). The retraction both times of the Medea image is not quite persuasive.

2.5.14   of Homer spake] Smyrna (line 15) was one of the seven cities contending for the honor of Homer's birth.

2.5.28   Bethlehem] Famous among travelers for its pastoral setting and pretty girls. In 1834, following a town revolt, Ibrahim Pasha (line 31; see the discussion at 2.7.17) wiped out the Mohammedan quarter.

2.5.46   Tempe's Vale] The lovely valley of the Greek poets, where Apollo purified himself after killing the Python. At Thessalonica (line 47) Melville had recorded in his journal in 1856 that an Englishman there "Said he had been *a day's shooting in the Vale of Tempe*—Ye Gods! whortleberrying on Olympus, &c" (see *Journals*, pp. 55, 393). Analogously profane was Glaucon's shooting both there and at Nazareth (line 45), the town where Jesus grew to manhood.

2.5.55   ephod on the festa] The outer garment of the high priest, worn at the rituals of feast days (see also the discussion at 1.16.103).

2.5.65   flower-girl of Florence] This song (lines 54–69) reflects Melville's own experience in Florence in 1857, when he wrote in his journal "Something good might be written on . . . the flower-girls" (p. 115; see also p. 495). See also GLAUCON (Index).

2.6.0   THE HAMLET] Melville had thought Bethany, less than two miles from Jerusalem, a "wretched Arab village" (*Journals*, p. 82), and here makes clear it was not like an American farm village (lines 9–10). But it was also the pastoral town so often visited by Jesus, coming out the shepherds' gate (line 24: Golden Gate) and walking to visit the "sisters" (line 32), Mary and Martha (line 14). It was Mary who had anointed Jesus "and wiped his feet with her hair" (John 11.1–2; line 34). At this period Jesus had declared himself "the Son of God" (line 30; John 10.36). Stanley, p. 186, describes the "mountain-hamlet" of Bethany. The illustration here is from Tompkins, *Through David's Realm* (cited in the discussion at 1.35.4), p. 87.

2.6.7   Three trees] Kitto, I, 497, describes "the tradition . . . that the true cross consisted of three kinds, cypress, pine, and cedar, or of four kinds, cedar, cypress, palm, and olive."

2.6.16   Carmel's beauty] Mt. Carmel, the promontory by the Bay of Acre, was a favorite of the Hebrew poets and prophets. Stanley, p. 344, refers to it as "the Park" of Palestine.

2.6.19–20   the face / Of meekness] The face of Nehemiah.

2.7.14   a Druze of Lebanon] See DJALEA (Index).

2.7.17   Ibrahim's time] Ibrahim Pasha (1789–1848), son of Mehemet Ali, was the brilliant, brutal Egyptian general who held Syria from 1832 to 1841. See also 2.5.31, 3.5.26, and 3.16.237.

2.7.60   Palmyrene] From Palmyra, Roman name for the biblical "Tadmore" (line 61), Solomon's ancient city northeast of Damascus (1 Kings 9.18).

2.7.69   the Amalekite] The warlike nation, south and east of Palestine, with whom the Hebrews often battled; here, nomadic Arabs (Bedouins).

2.7.75   Carmel's prophets of the cave] "The large caves, indeed, which exist under the western cliffs . . . may have been the shelter of Elijah and the persecuted prophets" (Stanley, p. 345).

2.7.86   Politic Mahmoud] Mahmoud II, sultan of Turkey (1808–39), in 1826 butchered the Janissaries, since the fourteenth century the standing army of the Ottoman Empire. Byzantium (line 89) had been capital of the earlier empire, on the site of Constantinople. Melville's spelling "Artmedan" (line 88) has not been located (he does not mention the circus in his 1856–57 journal account of his visit to Constantinople); Thomas Hope's *Anastasius* (London: Murray, 1836; Sealts 282) gives the Turkish name as "At-Meidan, or place of horses" (I, 161). For NN treatment of Middle Eastern spellings, see the NOTE ON THE TEXT, p. 689.

2.7.96   Osmanli] The name Turks prefer.

2.7.101   An Aga's] Belonging to a commander of the Janissaries.

2.7.117–18   Solomon, / Prolific sire] In his account of Arabian horses, Warburton, II, 120–23, mentions that some of the choice Arabians "are said to derive their blood from Solomon's stables."

2.8.23   who tricked me of late] Melville noted in his 1856–57 journal: "How it affects one to be cheated in Jerusalem" (p. 85). This passage demonstrates how parallel in his mind ran the Christian and classical traditions. Argos (line 24) was the Peloponnesus (or a town in it) where many mythical events occurred.

2.8.32–33   Pericles? / Plato . . . Simonides] Respectively statesman, philosopher, and lyric poet in the Golden Age of Greece.

2.9.0   THROUGH ADOMMIN] Normally spelled "Adummim," mentioned twice in the Old Testament and assumed to be the scene of Christ's parable of the Good Samaritan (Luke 10.30–37), retold here. Stanley, pp. 416–17, discusses the parable, its setting, and the dangers of Adummim in the nineteenth century.

NN retains the first-edition spelling here and at 2.9.18 and 2.10.117 because the "-in" ending is required for Melville's rhyme in the latter two appearances of the word. (The "o" could result from a misreading of Melville's handwritten "u"; but the fact that it occurs three times suggests that it may not be a misreading. And the "o" need not be regarded as an error in light of the NN policy of retaining the first-edition spellings of Middle Eastern names when they approximate the intended pronunciation; see the NOTE ON THE TEXT, p. 689.)

2.9.2   Through Bahurim] As King David, fleeing Absalom, passed through Bahurim (generally assumed to be in this region), Shimei (line 3) of Saul's family appeared on the rocks above, hurling stones and curses (line 5) at David as a "bloody man" (2 Sam. 16.5–14).

2.9.10   Acheron] Virgil's river approaching Tartarus, the first of several references equating the Siddim Plain with the underworld. In his 1856–57 journal, Melville wrote: "Where Kedron [Melville's error] opens into Plain of Jericho looks like Gate of Hell" (p. 83).

2.9.37   I've just been reading] Luke 10.30–37 tells the parable of how the Good Samaritan (line 42) cared for the stricken traveler after a Levite and a priest (line 85) had passed him by—at this spot.

2.10.0   A HALT] The halting first forty lines of this rocky canto are quarried from an essay-like entry of more than a page in Melville's 1856–57 journal. In part it reads: "Stones of Judea. We read a good deal about stones in Scriptures. Monuments & stumps of the memorials are set up of stones; men are stoned to death; the figurative seed falls in stony places; and no wonder that stones should so largely figure in the Bible. Judea is one accumulation of stones—Stony mountains & stony plains; stony torrents & stony roads; stony walls & stony feilds, stony houses & stony tombs; stony eyes & stony hearts. Before you, & behind you are stones. Stones to right & stones to left" (p. 90; later marked through by diagonal strokes in pencil—see the textual note at 90.8–23). In composing the canto Melville probably used a concordance or Bible dictionary. Biblical sources for the more specific references are: Jacob at Bethel (line 5: Gen. 28.10–22); Absalom buried near Ephraim (line 15: 2 Sam. 18.6–17); Naboth stoned (line 20: 1 Kings 21.1–14); Stephen stoned (line 21: Acts 7); Christ threatened with stones (line 22: John 8.59); and Cain as murderer (line 65: Gen. 4.8).

2.10.41–48   "Not . . . two."—] NN retains the punctuation of the first edition, in which the stanzas of this lyric begin with quotation marks to show that it is part of Glaucon's speech, but the two stanzas are not individually enclosed in additional single quotation marks to show that each is spoken by a different person, the first by Helen (line 45) and the second by Paris (line 43). Since there is no regular practice in the first edition for the use of quotation marks and since at certain other places the spacing of stanzas serves in itself to indicate quotations, the NN editors see no compelling argument for adding further quotation marks here.

2.10.43   Paris] The Trojan prince who seduced Helen (line 45) and precipitated the Trojan wars.

2.10.68   on far island-chains] Melville's explorations of the rock altars and carved gods in the Valley of the Taipi, Nuku Hiva (Marquesas Islands), are recounted in *Typee* (chaps. 21–24, pp. 153–79); the tone of malediction is missing there.

2.10.70   the shittim Ark] The ark of the covenant, made of shittim wood and veiled within the tabernacle (Exod. 25.10; 26.33).

2.10.108   land of Eblis] Hell; Eblis is the prince of apostate angels in Mohammedanism (prominent in William Beckford's *Vathek* [1786], and mentioned in *White-Jacket*, chap. 73, p. 306).

2.10.115   Paul's courtesy] Paul regularly concluded his epistles with the wish that "the grace of our Lord Jesus" be with his correspondents.

2.10.143   Measuring the sub-ducts] See the discussion at 1.28.96.

2.10.145   the Tomb's old fane] The Church of the Holy Sepulcher. The question of whether it was the legitimate site of the Crucifixion and burial (lines 158–60) was a classic dispute of the time; Melville marked nearly fifty lines in Stanley's discussion, pp. 451–55, of the location of the church in relation to Herod's wall (line 160). Jesus was crucified "without the gate" (Heb. 13.12).

2.10.153   Castor and Pollux for a sign] After being wrecked on Melita, Paul headed for Rome in an Alexandrian ship "whose sign was Castor and Pollux" (Acts 28.11); these sons of Zeus were worshiped as the protectors of sailors, among other attributes.

2.10.190   Flinging aside stone after stone] The episode further characterizes Nehemiah as deluded. In his 1856–57 journal Melville wrote: "In many places laborious attempt has been made, to clear the surface of these stones. . . . But in vain; the removal of one stone only seems to reveal three stones still larger, below it" (p. 90; cf. lines 193–94). Nehemiah is taking literally various biblical admonitions, such as Isaiah 40.3: "Prepare ye the way of the Lord, make straight in the desert a highway for our God." In the 1856–57 journal Melville mentioned a historical basis for so dramatizing Nehemiah's delusion: "There is some prophecy about the highways being prepared for the coming of the Jews, and when the 'Deputation from the Scotch Church' were in Judea, they suggested to Sir Moses Montifiore the expediency of employing the poorer sort of Jews in this work—at the same time facilitating prophecy and clearing the *stones* out of the way" (p. 90; Montefiore is identified on p. 442).

2.10.226   Nehemiah's conceit about the Jew] See the discussion at 1.8.27.

2.10.242   On Syracusan coin] Quite possibly a coin shown in Sir William Smith's *A Concise Dictionary of Greek and Roman Antiquities*, ed. F. Warre Cornish (New York: Holt, 1898), plate I, opp. p. 178: coin no. 13 has an extremely attractive female head surrounded with dolphins, between which are the Greek capital letters for Syracuse, famous city of Sicily.

2.11.0   Of Deserts] Melville's major source for the beauties and horrors of the desert and for caravan images was Bartlett's *Forty Days, passim*: e.g., he checked a passage on the Gate of Victory (lines 33–34: p. 5), lined several passages on the Cairo-to-Mecca caravan (lines 32–36: see the discussion at 1.5.131), and lined a description of a pyramid "casting an immense shadow over half the boundless Libyan Desert" (lines 56–61: p. 196). Stanley, pp. 67–68, describes a sandstorm near the Red Sea and compares it to a storm at sea (lines 36–48). Such reading refreshed Melville's own strong responses to the Libyan Desert, seen from Cairo and the Pyramids (*Journals*, pp. 74–78). Compare the canto with Melville's short poem "In the Desert" (in *Timoleon*; NN *Published Poems*, p. 314).

2.11.12–13   Darwin quotes / From Shelley] In chap. 8 of *Journal . . . of H. M. S. Beagle* (New York: Harper, 1846; Sealts 175; Bercaw 191), Darwin quotes these lines (75–77) from Shelley's poem "Mont Blanc" (1816): "None can reply—all seems eternal now. / The wilderness has a mysterious tongue, / Which teaches awful doubt." For Darwin see also the discussion at 2.21.24.

2.11.26   Tantalus] Very specific here, as desert mirages resemble Tantalus's receding lake in which he stood with a raging thirst.

2.11.52   Josephus saith] In *The Antiquities of the Jews* (trans. Whiston), bk. 3, chap. 5: ". . . nay, indeed, it [Mt. Sinai] cannot be looked at without pain of the eyes: and besides this, it was terrible and inaccessible, on account of the rumour that passed about, that God dwelt there."

2.11.65   Erebus] The dark spaces leading into Hades.

2.11.73   Kedron] All scholars, including Stanley, p. 171, agree that Kedron means "black"; it does flow (but only when there is storm water) from near Gethsemane (line 77) to Mar Saba and so to the Dead Sea (line 76).

2.11.91   John, he found wild honey] Mark 1.6.

2.12.5   Lethe] River of oblivion in Hades; here also "sleep."

2.12.30–31   Holbein's . . . Claude] Rolfe's sophisticated metaphor draws on Melville's own interest in art. Claude Lorrain (1600–1682) was a mild-mannered landscape painter famous for his serene landscapes, sunlit Arcadian scenes of woods and ruins, and harbor views; many of these were widely circulated as engravings. Hans Holbein the Younger (1497?–1543) did a famous series of 49 woodcuts, "The Dance of Death," in each of which, typically, the grimacing skeleton prepares to drag off Pope, Emperor, Old Man, Miser, etc., with gleeful violence. In Italy in 1857 Melville saw various works by both artists (see *Journals*, pp. 108–9, 111, 113, 475, 476, 478). Claude figures in his unpublished poem "At the Hostelry" (in the NN volume *BILLY BUDD, SAILOR and Other Late Manuscripts*).

2.12.52   Lord, now Thou goest forth] From the song of Deborah and Barak: "Lord, when thou wentest out of Seir, when thou marchedst out of the field of Edom, the earth trembled . . ." (Judg. 5.4).

2.13.8   St. Louis] Louis IX, who died of a plague outside Carthage during his Crusade. Chateaubriand, pp. 465–68, recites the moving account of his death, and quotes the holy instructions he left for his son. At his own request Louis lay on a bed of "ashes" (line 2). See the allusion at 4.10.111.

2.13.25   the dreary Hecla] One of several Arctic areas, or more probably southwestern Iceland (see the discussion at 2.34.10).

2.13.37   The beast] Compare 4.16.44.

2.13.47   A mounted train] Melville had greatly enjoyed a 45-minute ride from Ramleh to Lydda (returning to Jaffa) in the train of a governor's son (line 93) escorted by armed horsemen: "Fine riding. Musket-shooting. Curvetting & caracoling of the horsemen. Outriders. Horsemen riding to one side, scorning the perils. Riding up to hedges of cactus, interrogating & firing their pistols into them" (*Journals*, p. 80). The train's "tulip plight" is an example of Melville's deliberate use of archaisms: "tulip" derives from the Arabic word for "turban" (cf. lines 69 and 74); and "plight" here means "attire" (listed as rare in the *OED*).

2.13.79   Giaour] Turkish word for infidels or non-Moslems, especially Christians. "Franks" (line 90) is the Levantine word for Europeans.

2.13.95   Lebanon to Ammon's steeps] The one north of Palestine, the other across the Jordan to the east. "Hauran" (line 98: Ezek. 47.16) was a tract of land near Damascus; the first edition's "Houran" is emended as a misreading of Melville's hand.

2.14.0   BY ACHOR] In this canto William H. Shurr, in *The Mystery of Iniquity: Melville as Poet, 1857–1891* (Lexington: University of Kentucky Press, 1972), pp. 71–73, sees echoes of Browning's "Childe Harold to the Dark Tower Came." For Achor see the discussion at line 28.

2.14.2   how far above the sea] See Map B, p. 709, for elevations.

2.14.28   authentic text] The dramatic story of Joshua's defeat at Ai (line 29), the revelation of Achan's thievery (line 31), and the stoning and burning of him and his family here in the Valley of Achor, is told in Joshua 7.

2.14.56   Quarantania's sum of blights] Traditionally imagined to be the "exceeding high" mountain (line 96) where the devil took Jesus, after his forty days (line 55) in the wilderness, and offered him the world if Jesus would worship him (Matt. 4.1–11). Melville's 1856–57 journal comments: "Mount of Temptation—a black, arid mount—nought to be seen but Dead Sea, mouth of Kedron—very tempting—foolish feind—but it was a display in vision—then why take him up to Mount?—the *thing itself* was in vision" (pp. 82–83). Stanley, p. 130, makes the point strongly that this event was only "in vision." The illustration here is from Tompkins, *Through David's Realm* (cited in the discussion at 1.35.4), p. 175.

2.14.67   mounts of Moab] A trans-Jordan range (Map B, p. 709). On the long ridge, Abarim (line 79), Moses stood on Pisgah (line 84: apparently a peak of Mt. Nebo) and saw the Promised Land before he died (Deut. 34.1). Peor (line 79) may have been in the same range (Num. 23:.28).

2.14.70   trail,] NN inserts a comma here, for even in the rhetorical style of punctuation a pause would be required to prevent "mortcloths" from being taken as the object of "trail".

2.14.82   palms in Memphian row] Stanley's account, p. 301, of Jericho makes much of the disappearance of the palms and guesses they must have looked like the magnificent groves then at Memphis, Egypt. See also the discussion at 2.20.79.

2.14.89–90   Balboa's ken / . . . Darien] An allusion to Keats's sonnet "On First Looking into Chapman's Homer," with the historically correct substitution of "Balboa" for "Cortez."

2.14.98   an iceberg] See Melville's short poem "The Berg," in *John Marr;* NN *Published Poems,* pp. 240–41.

2.15.0   THE FOUNTAIN] Elisha's Fountain, where he "healed" the waters miraculously (2 Kings 2.19–22).

2.15.8   Hymned Pison] Gen. 2.10–11: "And a river went out of Eden to water the garden . . . and became into four heads. The name of the first is Pison: that is it which compasseth the whole land of Havilah, where there is gold."

2.15.49–51   A reed . . . / In wilderness?] A reference to Jesus' words about John the Baptist: "What went ye out into the wilderness for to see? A reed shaken with the wind? . . . A prophet? Yea, . . . and much more than a prophet" (Luke 7.24–26).

2.15.72   Nor Zin, nor Obi] Zin is one of the biblical deserts southwest of the Dead Sea. Obi is not biblical; it may be the Obi (or Ob) River, a vast Siberian river system which travels through swamp lands and empties into the Arctic; or perhaps Obi is a misreading for Gobi, the great sandy wasteland of central Asia, thus completing a triad of deserts.

2.16.0   NIGHT IN JERICHO] The scene of the pilgrimage now holds steady for seven cantos. Jericho had long since been destroyed, and only dirty villages and ruins remained. Melville's Crusaders' Tower (line 9) is probably Murray's " 'The House of Zacchæus.' It is a half-ruinous square building, about 30 ft. on each side and 40 high, now occupied by the Turkish garrison . . . . The view from the top is commanding . . ." (I, 194–95). Melville's 1856–57 journal records: "Tower with sheiks smoking & huts on top—thick walls—village of Jericho—ruins on hill-side" (p. 83). Stanley describes the biblical Jericho, pp. 299–304.

2.16.18   Nebo far away] See the discussion at 2.14.67.

2.16.28   Ammon] See the discussion at 2.13.95.

2.16.31   O haunted place] Beyond Gilgal, after crossing the Jordan by dividing it, Elijah (line 32) "went up by a whirlwind into heaven" in a chariot of fire (2 Kings 2.1–11). And by the Jordan, John the Baptist (line 37) preached, dressed in "raiment of camel's hair" (Matt. 3.4). Against these two great mythical figures Rolfe places three moderns: (1) line 38, C. F. Volney (1757–1820), the brilliant young skeptic of the Enlightenment who set himself up against "imagination" and "illusion" in his *Voyage en Égypt et en Syrie* (1787), translated as *Travels through Syria and Egypt, in the Years 1783, 1784, and 1785* (1787); (2) line 41, the Vicomte de Chateaubriand (1768–1848), whose *Le génie de Christianisme* (5 vols., 1802), translated as *The Beauties of Christianity* (1813) and as *The Genius of Christianity* (1856), was a romantic eulogy and defense of Catholicism against the atheistic revolutionaries of his time, and who also published his *Itinéraire de Paris à Jérusalem* (1811; translated that year as *Travels*—see p. 704 above) and a historical novel, *Les martyrs*

(1809), with scenes in Jerusalem and at the Jordan and Dead Sea; (3) line 50, Alphonse de Lamartine (1790–1869), who recorded his trip of 1832–33 in his romantic *Voyage en Orient* (1835), translated as *A Pilgrimage to the Holy Land* (1835), and then, moving from poetry to politics, served as minister of foreign affairs in the provisional government of 1848 only to have his bourgeois idealism smashed; see the allusion in *Journals*, p. 9; see also p. 256. See also MORTMAIN (Index).

2.16.47   Septemberists] Parisians who took part in the massacre of royalists and prisoners, September 2–6, 1792. This spelling, ordinarily "Septembrists" (in French, "Septembriseurs"; in Carlyle's *French Revolution*, "Septemberers"), may be Melville's adaptation to fit the meter. See *White-Jacket*, chap. 11, p. 11. "Vitriolists to-day" (line 48) probably refers to 1871, but possibly 1848. See the discussion at 1.41.109.

2.16.66   Prince Sigurd] In Wright, from which Melville probably took his story of Arculf (see the discussion at 1.35.0), we find: "The Saga of Sigurd the Crusader. A.D. 1107–1111." The brief account of Sigurd in Jerusalem (pp. 56–58) describes him as landing at Acre, but a footnote (p. 62) says it was Joppa (line 67: Jaffa); perhaps this confirms Wright as a source.

2.16.73   Knight of the Leopard] A figure from the early pages of Sir Walter Scott's *The Talisman* (1825), who wandered about in this area; the fountain was fictional, as was most of Scott's Eastern geography.

2.16.80   Tasso's Armida] In *Jerusalem Delivered* (see the discussion at 1.3.177), Armida is the beautiful enchantress in the service of the devil who for a time woos the heroic Rinaldo (line 83) away from reason and his purpose of conquering Jerusalem (bks. 10, 14–16); she had a palace in the midst of the Dead Sea. See also 2.37.30.

2.16.87   Rahab] Joshua 2 tells the story.

2.16.90   Like Arethusa under ground] The mythical fountain at Syracuse, Sicily, presumed to run underground from Greece.

2.16.96   At Easter] See the discussion at 2.1.214.

2.16.114   Who so secure] Compare Rolfe's defense of Mortmain with Melville's letter to his friend Evert A. Duyckinck, April 5, 1849, about a friend, Charles Fenno Hoffman, who has gone mad; especially, "And he who has never felt, momentarily, what madness is has but a mouthful of brains."

2.16.139   Ashtoreth] Biblical term for the moon goddess (1 Kings 11.5), also known as Astarte (mentioned at 2.37.8). The first-edition spelling "Ashtaroth" (the plural form) requires emendation because a singular is called for, and the singular ending is "-eth"; the error could have resulted from a misreading of Melville's handwriting. Although the "a" would not have to be altered to "o" under NN policy (see the NOTE ON THE TEXT, p. 689, and the discussion at 2.9.0), it, too, could be a misreading of handwriting. Since NN must emend the ending, it emends the middle vowel as well, assuming the standard spelling is what Melville intended.

2.17.22   a fountain sealed] Song of Sol. 4.12: "A garden inclosed is my sister, my spouse; a spring shut up, a fountain sealed."

2.17.33   Sargasso's mead] The great mass of floating seaweed in the North Atlantic, known as the Sargasso Sea. The first-edition spelling "Sargossa" is emended as either a misreading of Melville's hand or his unintentional error; he used the correct "Sargasso" in "Tom Deadlight" (*John Marr;* NN *Published Poems,* p. 215).

2.18.0   THE SYRIAN MONK] The basis of the canto is the biblical account of Christ's temptation and Melville's own speculations on Quarantania (see the discussion at 2.14.56). An earlier germ is a phrase that occurs among notes Melville made in 1849 in a volume of his Shakespeare set (Boston: Hilliard, Gray, 1837; Sealts 460): " 'How was it about the temptation on the hill?' &c" (see the NN *Moby-Dick,* p. 969). The monk's account is full of oblique biblical allusions which have not been documented here.

2.18.21   De Gama's men] Lines 21–23 are apparently a confused allusion, possibly involving the "Spirit of the Cape" (see *Billy Budd, Sailor,* chap. 8), to Camões's *Lusiads* (Bercaw 111), where no such scene appears. Cf. Melville's unpublished poetic vignettes on Camões's life (in the NN volume *BILLY BUDD, SAILOR and Other Late Manuscripts*).

2.18.40   perceived, untold, by Vine] See 2.14.103–8.

2.18.56   Dengadda] "Between Jericho and that sea is the land of Dengadda," explains Mandeville in Wright, pp. 178–79; the name does not occur in other sources examined.

2.18.61   mazed Gehennas] See the discussion at 1.26.27–28.

2.18.158   Jonah in despair] Especially his agonized prayer, Jonah 2.

2.19.1   Easter barque] Kitto, II, 824, tells of palms specially grown in a valley near Genoa, blessed at Rome for Palm Sunday ("Green Sunday," line 9), and distributed to the cardinals and other dignitaries.

2.19.2   Leon's spoil] Juan Ponce de León (1460–1521) found great treasure in Cuba. Melville's truncated reference to him as "Leon" was perhaps induced by metrical demands; the first edition had "Spanish" and he made the change to "Leon's" in Copy B at Harvard (see pp. 855 and 862 below).

2.19.7   Calpe's gate] Classical name for the Straits of Gibraltar.

2.19.22   Christ's flower, chrysanthemum] The symbolism is uncommon, or perhaps in error; the Greek roots mean flower of "gold," not of "Christ."

2.19.44   I've met that man] See 1.24.

2.19.53   Hegelized] Georg Hegel (1770–1831), German philosopher. Though Hegel was appropriated for dialectical materialism, he was actually an idealist, radically hostile to natural science—as Rolfe seems not to know.

2.19.85   Bare] The first-edition form "Bare", the old preterite of "bear", may be an archaism that Melville intended; but it might also be a misreading of "Bore" in his hand. NN makes no emendation.

2.19.86   True Rock of Ages] A play on a basic Old Testament image of God as the *rock*. The phrase is an alternate translation of Isaiah 26.4, and title of the famous hymn "Rock of Ages" (1775) by Augustus M. Toplady.

2.20.1   From Ur] Abraham, founder of the Hebrew nation, was born in Ur and buried in Mamre (line 10).

2.20.29   crumbled aqueducts] Murray's mention, I, 194–96, of ruins, aqueduct arches, and an old Roman road in this area and the illustration here, from Tompkins, *Through David's Realm* (cited in the discussion at 1.35.4), p. 143, substantiate Melville's analogy with Caesar's chief British port, Richborough, in Kent (lines 35–36: near Canterbury), where there are extensive Roman ruins which Melville visited in 1849; see *Journals*, pp. 12, 259–60.

2.20.46   Esau's hand] Two likely connotations are "hairy" (which Esau's name meant), or the hand of one deprived (like him) of his birthright (Gen. 25–27).

2.20.52   the Phlegræan fields] The mythical site of the great battle between the gods and the Titans, variously located but most commonly at Solfatara (line 55) outside Naples, the site of a dormant volcano with escaping steam and gases. The 1856–57 journal records: "Went to the Solfatara—smoke—landscape not so very beautiful.—Sulphurous & aridity, the end of the walk" (p. 102).

2.20.60   Old clo'!] Probably the street cry of the (Jewish) "Houndsditch clothesman" to whom Derwent later refers (2.22.25).

2.20.79   last late palm] Stanley makes much of the royal palms of Jericho (see also the discussion at 2.14.82), and twice mentions, pp. 144, 301, that the last of them went down in 1838; so Montezuma II (line 80; r. 1502–20), last of the Aztec emperors, went down before Cortés.

2.20.99   Mambrino's helmet] The famous barber's basin of brass which the ingenuous hero of *Don Quixote* takes for the enchanted and golden helmet of Mambrino (or Malino); see pt. 1, bk. 3, chap. 7, and bk. 4, chap. 18, in Melville's annotated edition (trans. Jarvis; Philadelphia: Blanchard & Lea, 1853; Sealts 125; Bercaw 122).

2.21.3   a Saurian] Here, a prehistoric monster.

2.21.24   Darwin is but his grandsire's son] Charles Darwin (see also the discussion at 2.11.12–13) was the grandson of the physiologist Erasmus Darwin (1731–1802), who was also a poet of science, as in his *The Botanic Garden* (1791), and this is Rolfe's real point. Rolfe offers the very modern view that physics (line 19) is conceptual, like Platonism or Hinduism, and that Newton's system (line 25) was not absolute. Whereupon Derwent names him a Pyrrhonist (line 31) or absolute skeptic, in accordance with doctrines of Pyrrho (ca. 365–275 B.C.).

2.21.53   Dancing Faun . . . Faun with Grapes] If Melville had two specific statues in mind (as "shapes" suggests), perhaps the first was the bronze statuette found in Pompeii, which gave its name to the House of the Faun, and which Melville probably saw in Naples in 1857 (*Journals*, pp. 102–3). The second may have been any of several such figures; however, if Derwent's phrase "Fine mellow marbles" (line 55) applies, Melville's reference may be general.

2.21.63   Whither hast fled] Note the several parallels between Rolfe's speech here and the more anguished broodings of Celio (1.13.36ff.).

2.21.71   even in a Magdalen] The Mary Magdalene of all four Gospels, healed by Jesus of evil spirits (Luke 8.2); traditionally a harlot and type of repentant sinner, she followed him and stayed by him in his final agonies (Luke 7.36–50; Mark 15.40–41).

2.21.74   Cana] Cana in Galilee, the scene of several of Christ's miracles (John 2, 4). See also 3.11.154.

2.22.0   CONCERNING HEBREWS] On March 25, 1877, Edward Sanford wrote to Melville's cousin Catherine Gansevoort Lansing: "I have been reading 22 chapter of 2d part of 'Clarel—Concerning Hebrews—I like the book very much, how did Friend Melville know so much about the Jews—" (*Log*, II, 760). The canto is an intricate consideration of Jewish belief and apostasy; at the same time it serves to point up Derwent's mild historical relativism and denial of anything "mystic" (line 31), Rolfe's respect for free thought and commitment to "self-hood" (line 103), Clarel's bewilderment before such alternatives (lines 129–30), and Vine's boredom with the whole tendency to get away from the motivations of Margoth and into generalized argument (lines 4–6, 104, 143). Melville's notation on a rear leaf of his 1856–57 journal ("Spinoza, Rothschild, &c. &."; p. 154) may be related to this canto.

2.22.19–20   the breastplate bright / Of Aaron] Aaron, as the first high priest, wore the brilliantly colored breastplate, set with precious stones (Exod. 28); contrasted later (lines 48–49) with the "Genevan cloth" garb of Protestant ministers (influenced by John Calvin of Geneva).

2.22.21   Horeb's Moses] The Moses of Mt. Sinai; "rock" could refer to the tablets of the Law (Exod. 24) or the rock from which he drew water by smiting it with his "rod" (Num. 20); "closeted alone" (line 22) is Moses in the tabernacle talking with God (Exod. 33).

2.22.25   Houndsditch] A ghetto section in the East End of London. See the discussion at 2.20.60.

2.22.42   Holland] Amsterdam, especially, had a large and learned Jewish community, including many refugees from Spain and Portugal. Talmudic volumes (line 44) deal with the body of Jewish civil and canonical law.

2.22.47   keep] Melville presumably intended this use of the subjunctive here. For other instances, see "leave" at 3.27.172 and "speak" at 4.22.67.

2.22.63   Uriel Acosta] Acosta (1585–1640), philosopher and theologian, was a Portuguese Jew brought up a Catholic. In Amsterdam he was excommunicated by the synagogue for dissent and skepticism, rejoined and was again excommunicated, rejoined and committed suicide.

2.22.66   Heine] Heinrich Heine (1797–1856), lyric poet and critic, renounced Judaism for Christianity. His mask of mocking amorality shocked many contemporaries, as did his violent illness in his last years. Pictures of his original simple tomb in Paris in Monmartre Cemetery show the rail, tomb, and wreath of lines 73–74. See Bezanson, "Arnold's Poetry," pp. 385–87, for Melville's marking of Arnold's "Heine's Grave" in his copy of *New Poems* (see the discussion at 1.19.29).

2.22.77   Eclectic comfort] The famous Neoplatonic School at Alexandria (A.D. 300–400) attempted to reconcile the Hebraic-Christian traditions with Greek philosophy.

2.22.84   Moses Mendelssohn] Mendelssohn (1729–86), philosopher and theologian, was a German Jew in the rationalist tradition who tried to reconcile Jewish and Gentile cultures. The source of the attributed quotation in lines 89–91 has not been located.

2.22.96   Neander] Johann Neander (1789–1850), a major historian of Christianity, was the son of a Jewish peddler, Emmanuel Mendel (*not* Mendelssohn); he changed his name to Neander at seventeen when he was baptized. The uncertainty of both Rolfe and Derwent here (unless Mendelssohn is a pun) may arise because Moses Mendelssohn did have a famous grandson who turned Christian: Felix Mendelssohn, the composer.

2.22.110   Spinosa's starry brow] Baruch Spinoza (also "Spinosa," 1632–77), the great philosopher and another Amsterdam Jew who was excommunicated. He worked humbly as a lens grinder, but meanwhile in his great *Ethics* (1677) put the case for the intellectual love of God. Rolfe's phrase "Pan's Atheist" (line 121) plays on the common designation of Spinoza as a Pantheist. For Melville's further views on Spinoza and Heine see Bezanson, "Arnold's Poetry," pp. 385–87, and Sealts, "Melville and the Platonic Tradition," *Pursuing Melville* (Madison: University of Wisconsin Press, 1982), pp. 322–23. See also the discussion at 2.22.0 for a mention of Spinoza at the end of Melville's 1856–57 journal.

2.22.118   informing guests of Abraham] The three angels who visited Abraham at Mamre and foretold the birth of Isaac (Gen. 18).

2.23.27   Balaam on the ass] Numbers 22 tells the story of Balaam, the diviner, riding an ass that saw ahead an armed angel of the Lord that Balaam did not see, and so saved his master from being slain in a narrow place.

2.23.33   Caracas] The chief city of Venezuela (and a mountain adjacent) which was almost completely destroyed by earthquake, March 26, 1812.

2.23.45   Suspicious ground] This encounter with the trans-Jordan Arabs (to the end of the canto) is an elaboration from an experience recorded in the 1856–57 journal: "every creature *in human form* seen ahead—escort alarmed & galloped on to learn something—salutes—every man understands it—shows native dignity—worthy of salute—Arabs on hills over Jordan—alarm—scampering ahead of escort—after rain, turbid & yellow stream—foliaged banks— beyond, arid hills.—Arabs crossing the river—lance—old crusaders—pistols— menacing cries—tobacco.—Robbers—rob Jericho annually—&c" (p. 83).

2.23.82   Midian's screen] The Midianites are evil enemies in the Old Testament, given to idolatry; the immediate image is perhaps that of the Midianite woman and the Israelite man slain in intercourse by Phineas (Num. 25.6–8).

2.23.145   Don John] I.e., the great lover Don Juan. Melville knew Byron's *Don Juan* (London: Murray, 1837; Sealts 108; and in *Poetical Works*, Boston: Little, Brown, [1853?]; Sealts 112; Bercaw 105) and quoted it in a letter to his brother Thomas, May 25, 1862. Evidently he had seen Mozart's *Don Giovanni*, to which he alluded in *White-Jacket*, chap. 90, p. 377.

2.23.159   Richard's host] Richard the Lionhearted (1157–99), who in the Third Crusade captured Acre (line 160) in July, 1191.

2.23.167   I, Ishmael] The biblical Ishmael is to the Arabs and Bedouins progenitor and spiritual father, as Abraham also is to them, as well as to the Jews.

2.23.193   The halcyon Teacher] Jesus, baptized here in the Jordan by John the Baptist (Matt. 3.13–17).

2.24.0   THE RIVER-RITE] Now begin three cantos which provide a unit on Catholicism comparable to the recent sequence on Judaism. The scene is Bethabara (line 6), near where John did his baptizing (John 1.28) and from the days of medieval pilgrims a ritual site (the illustration opposite is from Wylie's *The Modern Judea* [see the discussion at 1.1.28], facing p. 217). Melville had Chateaubriand, p. 269, freshly in mind: "I fell upon my knees on the bank. . . . Having forgotten to bring a bible, we could not repeat the passages of scripture relating to the spot where we now were; but the drogman, who knew the customs of the place, began to sing: *Ave maris stella* [cf. line 13]. We responded like sailors at the end of their voyage: Sire de Joinville could not have been more clever than we. I then took up some water from the river in a leather vessel: it did not seem to me as sweet as sugar [cf. line 70], according to the expression of a pious missionary. I thought it on the contrary, rather brackish." "Hail, Thou Star of Ocean" was a famous medieval hymn, anonymous and dating back to the ninth century, in seven short quatrains, of which the first and "last" (line 50) are

> Ave maris stella,
> Dei mater alma
> Atque semper virgo,
> Felix coeli porta.

> Sit laus Deo Patri,
> Summo Christo decus,
> Spiritui Sancto:
> Tribus honor unus!

2.24.27   Cecilia] See the discussion at 1.29.26.

2.24.30   St. John's convent] St. John in the Desert, one of the fourteen Latin convents in Syria. This explanation (lines 24–30) of the provenance of Rolfe's hymnal, the gift of "friar Benignus Muscatel," is perhaps a takeoff on Curzon's *A Visit to Monasteries in the Levant*, in which Curzon manages to buy or otherwise obtain a precious ancient book from almost all the monasteries he visits.

2.24.75	the Jordan's fall] Stanley, pp. 276–77, describes the Jordan's three stages: to Lake Merom (line 76; also called Lake Hula), to the Sea of Galilee, and to the Dead Sea; the 27 rapids after Galilee caused a fall of a thousand feet, exceeded only by the Sacramento in California.

2.24.84	The chief of sinners] Paul wrote that "Christ Jesus came into the world to save sinners; of whom I am chief" (1 Tim. 1.15). See also 1.7.93.

2.24.94	The Thessalonian] The Greek Banker, 2.13.101–2.

2.25.0	THE DOMINICAN] A member of the order created by St. Dominic (ca. 1170–1221), which became a powerful agent for propagation of the Roman Catholic Church, the eradication of heresy, and the promotion of morals. Members wore a white robe (line 18), but preached in a black mantle (cf. 2.26.181). See the allusion in *Moby-Dick*, chap. 54, p. 249.

2.25.56	Thou Paul! shall Festus] Acts 25–26 tells how Festus gave Paul fair chance to be heard, then told him "much learning doth make thee mad," which Paul promptly denied. Cf. Melville's letter to Hawthorne, November 17?, 1851.

2.25.73	The foolish, many-headed beast] The blasphemous beast with seven heads that John saw rising out of the sea (Rev. 13).

2.25.100	Melancthon] Philipp Melanchthon (or "Melancthon," 1497–1560), close associate of Luther (line 101) in the Reformation, urged a concilia- tory position on the issue of breaking with the Church.

2.25.107	Red Republic] France, probably 1871; see the discussion at 1.41.109.

2.25.108	Scarlet Dame] John's vision of "THE MOTHER OF HAR- LOTS AND ABOMINATIONS OF THE EARTH" (Rev. 17).

2.25.158	Abba Father] "Abba" is a child's term for "father" in Aramaic. Christ in his agony at Gethsemane cried out to "Abba, Father," to whom "all things are possible" (Mark 14.36; Rom. 8.15; Gal. 4.6). In contrast the "Artifi- cer" (line 159) is the deist God, rationally apparent by the argument from design (His works in Nature), and limited by natural law.

2.25.180	Abaddon's cradle] Again in John's vision, the nightmarish lo- custs that rose out of the bottomless pit had a king named Abaddon, or Apollyon (Rev. 9; cf. 3.8.17).

2.25.182	Charlemagne's great fee] Christendom.

2.26.9–10	pix, / Paten and chalice] Container, plate, and cup used in the Eucharist (sacrament of the Lord's Supper).

2.26.14	Pope Joan] A folk figure, a girl reputed to have dressed as a man and risen to be cardinal, to have been elected Pope John VIII (ca. 855–58), and then to have died in childbirth during a public procession!

2.26.32   St. Dominick] As here, Melville chose to use the old spell-
ing "Dominick" in the ship's name in "Benito Cereno" (NN *Piazza
Tales* volume, p. 49; see also p. 583). For St. Dominic, see the discussion
at 2.25.0.

2.26.35   Papal nuncio] An official representative of the pope at a foreign
court.

2.26.39   To Hildebrand's an appanage] That is, he would make the
modern age like lands set aside for his younger children by a prince—here St.
Gregory VII (originally named Hildebrand), who as pope from 1073 to 1085
established a strong papacy in church and state. Cf. 1.12.141.

2.26.65   a Bayard knight] Like the Chevalier de Bayard (ca. 1473–1524),
"sans peur et sans reproche." He died as his fathers had for two centuries—in
battle, and exhibiting extraordinary bravery.

2.26.92   Like Dorian myths] The myths from early Greece which served
later Greek and Roman writers.

2.26.130–31   Frederick / The cynical] Frederick II ("the Great") of Prus-
sia (1712–86), given to epigrams in his old age. This particular "curse" (lines
131–32) has not been located.

2.26.169   Vine evangelic, branching out] The image is from Christ's
words in John 15.1–8: "I am the vine, ye are the branches. . . ."

2.27.20–21   John's baptistery: / May Pisa's] The Jordan compared
with the building Melville saw in Italy: "*Baptistery* like dome set on
ground. Wonderful pulpit of marble" (*Journals*, pp. 113–14; see also p.
489).

2.27.44   Hagar] Mother of Ishmael (Gen. 16), who fled into the wilder-
ness. See also the discussion at 1.16.183.

2.27.49   Nimrods] Like the mighty hunter of Genesis 10.8–10.

2.27.76   the Book of Job] Nineteenth-century commentaries carry im-
mense speculations on the sources and nationality of this ancient poem, one
of Melville's favorite biblical books.

2.27.80   At Lydda late] A small village which Melville visited on the
way from Jerusalem to Jaffa in order to see the picturesque ruins of the old
Crusaders' church (*Journals*, p. 80).

2.27.85   one of Sydney's clan] A true "nobleman," in the image of Sir
Philip Sydney (or "Sidney," 1554–86), English poet and soldier who died in
battle and was reputed to have passed a cup of water to a wounded soldier,
saying, "Thy necessity is greater than mine."

2.27.90   Ararat] See the discussion at 1.16.80.

2.27.153   descended erst the dove] Luke 3.21–22.

2.27.162   the oil of gladness] Ps. 45.7: "Thou lovest righteousness, and hatest wickedness: therefore God, thy God, hath anointed thee with the oil of gladness above thy fellows."

2.28.0   THE FOG] With the move from Jordan to Siddim the pilgrims enter the underworld—"Pluto's park" (line 1) surrounded by the hateful "Stygean" river (line 6: the Styx). With the blighting of the willow-palms by the "bitter mist" and "rack" off the Dead Sea (lines 39, 48) they have moved from light into a darkness where companionship gives way to separateness, hope to despair, life to death. From here to the end of Part 2 the mood is the sea's, the moment is Mortmain's. Geographical and psychological aspects of the scene are discussed in the HISTORICAL AND CRITICAL NOTE (sects. 1, 7).

2.28.10   Pippins of Sodom] Murray, I, 243, describes the famed apples of Sodom: "The fruit resembles a large smooth apple, hangs in clusters of two or three, and has a fresh, blooming appearance; when ripe it is of a rich yellow colour, sufficiently tempting to the thirsty traveller. But on being pressed or struck it explodes like a puff-ball, leaving nothing in the hand except the shreds of the thin rind and a few dry fibres." The apples grew on trees from ten to fifteen feet high. Melville mentions them twice in his 1856–57 journal (pp. 82, 83).

2.28.12   Circe] See the discussion at 2.4.142.

2.28.18   by Achor's rim] See the discussion at 2.14.28.

2.28.27   Genesis] Gen. 14.10: "And the vale of Siddim was full of slimepits; and the kings of Sodom and Gomorrah fled, and fell there. . . ." Stanley, p. 282, has a paragraph on the Battle of the Kings.

2.28.34   Milcom and Chemosh] 1 Kings 11.5–7. Solomon, in his period of idolatry, turned to the worship of "Milcom the abomination of the Ammonites" and "Chemosh, the abomination of Moab." The pilgrims are now in the "lee" (line 35) of the Moab Mountains, which rear across the Dead Sea.

2.28.44–47   "Though . . . here."] NN follows the first edition in printing only a single set of quotation marks around this stanza, rather than two sets, one to show that Nehemiah is speaking and another to indicate that the words are a paraphrase of Psalm 23.4. The practice throughout in marking paraphrases, spaced lyrics, and quotations that incorporate lyrics is so variable that the usage here cannot be considered anomalous.

2.29.8   Fair Como would like Sodom be] In his 1856–57 journal, Melville wrote of the Dead Sea: "Mountains on tother side—Lake George—all but verdure" (p. 83). But later (presumably after he had spent a day at Lake Como, *Journals*, pp. 121–22) he crossed out "George" and penciled in "Como".

2.29.16   charred or crunched or riven] Compare with the 1856–57 journal on the "*Barrenness of Judea*": "crunched, knawed, & mumbled" (p. 83).

2.29.27   Libanus] Lebanon. Stanley, p. 287, also describes "trunks and branches of trees, torn down from the thickets of the river-jungle by the violence of the Jordan, thrust out into the sea, and thrown up again by its waves." See the illustration on p. 788 below.

2.29.34   hitherward by south winds] The narrator, under the spell of the mountainous desolation about the sea, now chants in Miltonic style the names of ancient biblical sites to the south: the salt hills of Usdum at the southernmost tip of the sea, and, beyond, Bozrah's site, the destroyed capital of the Edom wastes (line 35); then, far up the east shore, Karek's castle, the great fortified citadel on the very top of a mountain (line 37), and another ancient city, Aroer, on the bank of the precipitous river Arnon that plunges down a chasm to the sea through lands where "robbers often waylay travellers" (lines 38–39: Murray, II, 301); then, halfway down the east shore, the Cascade of the Kid (line 45: which Stanley, p. 289, calls "the spring of the wild goats, or gazelles") at En-Gedi, a high and beautiful oasis; and just south of En-Gedi, the Maccabees' Masada (line 53). The epic of Masada was not a Bible story but was recorded by Josephus in *The Wars of the Jews* (trans. Whiston), bk. 7, chaps. 8–9; it told how Eleazer (line 55), leader of 967 Jews locked up in the great fortress built by Jonathan Maccabeus (line 53), and hopelessly besieged by massive Roman forces under Flavius Silva ("Flavian arms," line 54), persuaded the garrison of men, women, and children (all but seven) to make a mass suicide rather than be captured. The story is related by Murray, I, 239–42.

2.29.58   Mariamne's hate] Matthew 14 attributes the death of John the Baptist to the hatred of Herodias, the wife Herod Antipas took from his brother; but there are several Mariamnes of Judaic history related to the Herods. John was imprisoned in the castle at Machaerus, a fortress on the east shore of the Dead Sea.

2.29.67   In] Possibly this word should be "On", for the two words are often indistinguishable, except by context, in Melville's manuscripts. But the "In" is possibly idiomatic, and NN retains it.

2.29.73   Mount Hor] Numbers 20.22–29 tells how Aaron (line 75) was not allowed to enter the Promised Land but went up on Mt. Hor and died there.

2.29.78–79   prohibited Seir / In cut-off Edom] The whole passage (to line 102) centers in a historic debate. Edom (Greek Idumea; also known as Mt. Seir) was a mountain region, some one hundred miles long and twenty miles wide running north and south about halfway between the Dead Sea and the Gulf of Akaba. A *terra incognita* until the nineteenth century, it was taken to be impassable because of God's several curses upon it and the command that "none shall pass through it for ever and ever" (Isa. 34.10). Alexander Keith (line 101) in his *Evidence of the Truth of the Christian Religion Derived from the Literal Fulfillment of Prophecy* (New York: Harper, 1839), pp. 135–68, stated the rigid case that no man ever would go through Edom because of the prophecy; first published in Edinburgh in 1838, the book went through over thirty English and American reprintings and revisions in twenty years. Nehemiah accepts this position. Margoth is correct however; in 1812 Burckhardt (see the discussion at 1.40.79) went through Edom, discovering Petra, and soon others followed. The American traveler John Lloyd Stephens went through "braving the malediction of Heaven" and melodramatically refuting the school of Keith all the way (*Incidents of Travel in . . . the Holy Land* [New York: Harper, 1837], II, 35, 85, 110). Still another work discounts Keith's prophecy on the ground that a literal interpretation of the Bible is impossible in view of its orientalism (line 97): Rev. James Aitken Wylie, *The Modern Judea* (Glasgow: Collins, 1841), p. 472.

2.29.81–82   The satyr to the dragon's brood / Crieth] Isaiah 13.19–22 prophesies the desolation of Babylon "shall be as when God overthrew Sodom and Gomorrah. . . . It shall never be inhabited . . . and satyrs shall dance there. And the wild beasts of the islands shall cry in their desolate houses, and dragons in their pleasant palaces."

2.29.116   Ah, look] For Melville's 1856–57 journal comment on a rainbow over the Dead Sea see the discussion at 2.39.131. Iris (line 123) was the Greek goddess of the rainbow. Margoth's wry comment on the "covenant" with Noah (line 150) is a double misreading of Genesis 9.8–17 (a misreading which Melville seems also to have preferred): the covenant was that "*all* flesh" would not be destroyed by a flood; and Sodom and Gomorrah were destroyed not by flood but by "brimstone and fire" (Gen. 19.24).

2.30.0   Of Petra] Petra was the ancient fortress-city of the Edom waste (see the discussion at 2.29.78–79) whose discovery by Burckhardt in 1812 was a major event. Uninhabited and "lost" for centuries, Petra proved an archaeological spectacle. The chief approach lay through a winding defile a mile long with narrow sides one to three hundred feet high, the cut rock gorgeously hued in dull crimson with accents of purple, black, yellow, and green, and fringed with oleanders. Temples, tombs, and even a Greek theater open up in the defile, they too being cut out of the rock face. (See the illustrations opposite, from Bartlett, *Forty Days*, engraved title page and facing p. 136.) Melville had not seen Petra, though when leaving Palestine he had met "the *Petra Party*" at Jaffa (*Journals*, p. 80). His source for the present canto, however, was a section on Petra in Stanley, pp. 88–92, 97–99. In this section he made eight careful markings of various sorts, and as a reminder he wrote on the title page of Stanley: "The Red City. 91." Every specific detail about Petra in the canto has its source in Stanley (examined in detail in Bezanson, pp. 118–22). The three main themes also start with hints from Stanley, but are peculiarly Melville's: that the charm of expectation surpasses fulfillment, that art is an ordered form on the rim of the abyss, and that all solicitations for final meanings remain unanswered. The canto itself is an episodic intrusion and may have been added at any time.

2.30.7   Jason] Leader of the Argonauts, who found the golden fleece, guarded by dragons, in Colchis (line 28); see also 2.38.26–27. For Burckhardt (line 8) see the discussion at 1.40.79.

2.30.17   Esau's waste] Edom, where Esau lived (Gen. 32.3).

2.30.20   Horite] One of the Horim, who preceded the Edomites. Melville marked two passages on this word in Stanley, p. 89.

2.30.31   prospect from Mount Hor] The only spot from which any part of Petra is visible from the outside world, Stanley explains, p. 98, is the peak of distant Mt. Hor. From there, and beyond an intervening peak, one can see only El Deir (line 39: Arabic for "The Convent"), an elaborately sculptured but crude Christian temple (illustrated on p. 785 above).

2.30.49   Along ravine] After digressing to the view from Mt. Hor, Rolfe has returned to journeying in the flume. Beyond the fane (line 19) the defile comes upon a gigantic stairway leading up through rock clusters to the high site of El Deir. Further back (Rolfe scrambles the details) were a Street of Tombs and the Greek theater: "Puck's platform" (line 53).

2.30.59   Sinbad's pleasant] The seven wonderful adventures of Sinbad (or Sindbad) the Sailor are among the stories told in *The Arabian Nights' Entertainments* (Bercaw 18). Melville's early reading and use of this work are discussed by Dorothee Metlitsky Finkelstein in *Melville's Orienda* (cited in the discussion at 1.32.0), pp. 26–41. See also 3.12.1.

2.30.60   Pæstum] The deserted site of an ancient Greek colony in Italy whose temple ruins were discovered in 1745.

2.30.68   yon rock] A buried image of Cape Horn, foreshadowed in the "haggard" Horeb-Horn complex of 1.21.14–15, echoed later in two images, both associated with Rolfe (3.29.8–23; 4.4.40–47). Here Rolfe's haggard crag recalls two of Melville's journal entries aboard the *Meteor* in 1860: "Horrible snowy mountains . . . hell-landscape," and, "in a squall, the mist lifted & showed, within 12 or fifteen miles the horrid sight of Cape Horn— (the Cape proper)—a black, bare steep cliff, the face of it facing the South Pole . . . awful islands & rocks—an infernal group" (pp. 133–34). The whole imagery cluster is complex: Nehemiah's sleeping under the rock recalls Pierre under the Memnon Stone (bk. 7); Derwent's "queer" (line 68) recalls Stubb's many uses of the word in *Moby-Dick*; the hell images of the *Meteor* account reinforce the sense of Siddim as underworld. In the next canto Rolfe likens the Slanted Cross to the Southern Cross constellation and there the Cape Horn image emerges fully (2.31.37). Just as Melville, the day after seeing the Horn, witnessed the death and burial at sea of a young sailor (amid gales and sleet, the reading of prayers, a shotted hammock, a sloped plank) so the pilgrims the next morning bury Nehemiah, with this imagery repeated (2.39.115–20).

2.31.66   Orion's sword] After his death the "Giant" (line 68) and hunter of Greek mythology was placed in the sky with girdle, sword, lion's skin, and club.

2.31.97   hammer huge as Thor's] The Norse god of thunder was armed with a magic hammer (emblematic of the thunderbolt) that returned to him when thrown.

2.32.41   Lot and his daughters twain] Gen. 19.15–30.

2.32.88   St. Francis] Not St. Francis of Assisi (1182–1226), founder of the Friars Minor, but St. Francis of Sales (1567–1622), who reconverted the province of Chablais after it had gone Calvinistic and who directed the founding of the Order of the Visitation for the ill or physically weak.

2.32.91   wise as serpents] Christ's commission to the apostles, Matt. 10.16: "be ye therefore wise as serpents, and harmless as doves." Cf. the brooch worn by the Reverend Mr. Falsgrave in *Pierre*, "representing the allegorical union of the serpent and dove" (bk. 5, p. 102).

2.33.16   a palm-shaft green] Stanley, p. 143, mentions "the trunks of palms washed up on the shores of the Dead Sea,—preserved by the salt with which a long submersion in these strange waters has impregnated them." The illustration on p. 788 below is from W. F. Lynch, *Narrative of the United States' Expedition to the River Jordan and the Dead Sea* (Philadelphia: Lea & Blanchard, 7th ed., rev. 1850), facing p. 276.

2.33.27   asphaltum] By "jewel" Margoth is probably referring to trinkets carved from the shiny black stones and asphaltum found here that were sold in Jerusalem, according to Murray, I, 201.

2.33.33   Stone-of-Moses] A nineteenth-century geographical survey of the region describes it: "At the northern extremity of the Dead Sea is found the stink-stone, whose combustible properties are ascribed by the Arabs to the magic rod of Moses [Exod. 5.17]. These stones are laid on fires made of camels' dung, to increase the heat" (F. R. Chesney, *The Expedition for the Survey of the Rivers Euphrates and Tigris . . . In the Years 1835, 1836, and 1837 . . .* [London: Longman, Brown, Green, & Longmans, 1850], pp. 567–68). The stinkstone is a sedimentary rock that emits a fetid odor (from the decomposition of organic matter) on being struck, broken, or rubbed.

2.33.47   All's mere geology] The materials of the debate here between Rolfe and Margoth on whether the valley was struck by natural or supernatural forces are in all contemporary literature, including Stanley, pp. 281–85, and Murray, I, 200–203. Cf. Murray's "the cavity of the Dead Sea was coeval in its conformation with the Jordan Valley" with line 65.

SHORE OF THE DEAD SEA

2.33.67 A hideous hee-haw] In *Oriental Acquaintance* (New York: Dix, Edwards, 1856), p. 93, J. W. De Forest gives the reaction of "John Jackass" to the Jordan pilgrim throng: " 'Here you are, all but me, trotting straight to a fool's Paradise. I shan't be there myself, perhaps; but go ahead and don't wait, bretheren; here's my blessing. Ee—aw! ee—aw! ee—aw!' " In his 1856–57 journal, Melville commented on donkeys and donkey boys in Egypt (p. 77).

2.33.90 Moses' God is no mere Pam] The God of Exodus 3.14 ("And God said unto Moses, I AM THAT I AM . . ." [cf. line 91 and Melville's "The Great Pyramid," in *Timoleon*; NN *Published Poems*, pp. 315–16]) is compared to "Pam / With painted clubs" (lines 90–91): "the knave of clubs, esp. in the game of five-card loo, in which this card is the highest trump" (*OED*, citing Alexander Pope's "The Rape of the Lock": "Ev'n mighty Pam, that Kings and Queens overthrew" [3.61]).

2.34.10 Hecla ice] Ice and ashes from the massive and often active volcano in southwestern Iceland. See 2.13.25 and the NN *Moby-Dick*, p. 833.

2.34.20 brook Cherith] Where Elijah hid and was fed by ravens until the brook dried up (1 Kings 17.1–7).

2.34.33 pause of the artillery's boom] Probably after the Treaty of Frankfurt, May 10, 1871, ending the Franco-Prussian War.

2.34.40 *Vox Clamans*] The "Voice Crying" of "Mad" John the Baptist, "he that was spoken of by the prophet Esaias, saying, The voice of one crying in the wilderness [*vox clamantis in deserto*], Prepare ye the way of the Lord . . . ," and who in this same area preached, "Repent ye: for the kingdom of heaven is at hand" (Matt. 3.1–3). Mortmain's clamor against "Anti-Christ," "Atheist," and "Anarch" (lines 37–38) either recollects the revolutions of 1848 or more likely acknowledges the new violences surrounding the Paris Commune of 1871 (see the discussion at 1.41.109).

2.34.63 Marah] Exod. 15.23: the Israelites in the wilderness "could not drink of the waters of Marah, for they were bitter."

2.34.67 gall] Lam. 3.19: "Remembering mine affliction and my misery, the wormwood and the gall." This links the Dead Sea to the star of 2.36.22–23 (see the discussion).

2.35.1 Piranesi's rarer prints] Giovanni Battista Piranesi (1720–78) was primarily famed for his magnificent large engravings of Roman ruins. The first-edition spelling, "Piranezi", is emended as a misreading due to Melville's often indistinguishable "z" and "s" (see the NOTE ON THE TEXT, pp. 688–89). Here the narrator's "Bastiles" (line 6) and "rarer" (line 1) show that Melville had specifically in mind the sixteen *Carceri* (*Prisons*) of Piranesi: technically superb, monumental views of imagined colossal arches and gigantic stairways in fantastic prisons peopled with dreamlike figures; these

Second State.

prisons Piranesi "saw" in the delirium of fever. They serve here as striking analogues for the depths of man's mind. No Piranesi prints owned by Melville are known (see Wallace, cited in the discussion at 1.6.28). Reproduced here is plate I (of 16), the title page, in its second state (1761), reduced from its original 54.5 by 41 cm (approx. 16 by 21 in.). By courtesy of Dover Publications it is taken here from THE PRISONS [Le Carceri], by Giovanni Battista Piranesi, with a new introduction by Philip Hofer (New York: Dover, 1973). A broadside with this plate (original size) and the Piranesi passage from Clarel (2.35.1–37) was printed by the Gehenna Press, Northampton, Massachusetts, and the Meriden Gravure Company in December, 1969, and issued (twelve hundred copies), as a New Year greeting, for the 150th anniversary of Melville's birth, August 1, 1819. In writing the passage, Melville may have had this title-page plate before him, not just in mind, because it is the only one of the sixteen plates to contain all of the images he itemizes in the passage. "Rhadamanthine chains" (line 12) are those imposed by Rhadamanthus, the relentless judge of the Greek underworld.

2.35.24   Paul's "mystery of iniquity:"] A favorite phrase of Melville's (2 Thess. 2.7), again called on (twice) when in Billy Budd, Sailor he struggled to define Claggart's malice.

2.36.10   the Cities Five] See the discussion at 2.37.0.

2.36.22–23   the star / Called Wormwood] From St. John's vision of the plagues that followed the opening of the seventh seal (Rev. 8.10–11): "And the third angel sounded, and there fell a great star from heaven, burning as it were a lamp, and it fell upon the third part of the rivers, and upon the fountains of waters; And the name of the star is called Wormwood: and the third part of the waters became wormwood; and many men died of the waters, because they were made bitter."

2.36.64   Burker] William Burke was hanged in Edinburgh in 1829 for smothering victims to get bodies to sell for dissection.

2.36.90–91   wive's wine, / Tofana-brew] A poisonous solution of arsenic concocted in the mid-seventeenth century by an Italian woman named Tofana (Toffana, Toffania, Tofagna) and used by numerous young Roman wives to murder their husbands (see, for example, Penny Cyclopædia, s.v. "aqua tofana").

2.36.91   O fair Medea] She killed her brother, murdered her two children, and killed her rival for Jason (cf. 2.4.133–34). Jael (line 93) drove a nail (a tent pin) through the head of Sisera, fastening it to the ground, while he slept under her presumed protection (Judg. 4.18–21). Leah (line 93) was the "hated" but fruitful wife of Jacob, given to him in deception (Gen. 29.15–30).

2.36.118   Zoima] Probably a coined name, based on the root meaning "life" or "life-force."

2.37.0   Of Traditions] Melville is chiefly improvising here, with help
from "The Book of Sir John Maundeville. A.D. 1322–1356," in Wright, pp.
127–282. There, pp. 178–79, he found the names (line 5) of "the five cities,
Sodom, Gomorrah, Aldama [Melville's "Aldemah"], Seboym, and Segor,"
the last three of which in the King James Bible and travel literature are
usually Admah, Zeboim, and Zoar (Gen. 14.2; 10.19); the oddly phrased bit:
"About that sea groweth much alum and alkatran [line 23: probably bitu-
men]"; and the hint that Segor "was saved and kept a great while, for it was
set upon a hill, and some part of it still appears above the water; and men
may see the walls when it is fair and clear weather" (lines 24ff.).

2.37.9   Terah's day] Genesis 11.24–32 tells of Terah, the father of Abra-
ham. For Astarte (line 8) see the discussion at 2.16.139.

2.37.30   Armida] See the discussion at 2.16.80.

2.37.32   King Nine] I.e., Ninus, semi-mythical king of Assyria, of
which Nineveh was the capital.

2.37.65   Dismas the Good Thief] The traditional name (not in the Bible)
for the one of the two thieves crucified with Jesus who asked forgiveness and
was told by Jesus: "To day shalt thou be with me in paradise" (Luke 23.32–
43); the name is used by Mandeville (Wright, p. 131).

2.37.68   the Last Supper] Matt. 26.20–25.

2.37.76   Simon Magus] Simon the Magician, who appears in Acts 8.9–
24 trying to learn the new powers of Christianity; many medieval legends
grew up about him. Melville saw the painting *The Fall of Simon Magus* in
Rome (*Journals*, p. 112).

2.38.3   Pentateuchal] Relating to the first five books of the Bible.

2.38.15   the city rose] All the symbolic details of Nehemiah's dream—
city, bride, jeweled streets, rivers, Fleece (the Lamb), throne—are directly
from John's vision of the New Jerusalem, Rev. 21–22; lines 29–30 are a
paraphrase of Rev. 21.4; the use of Fleece (line 27) enables the contrast be-
tween Jesus and Jason (line 26; see the discussion at 2.30.7).

2.38.25   Saint Martin's sun] An allusion to "St. Martin's summer," a
season of fine November weather (the saint's day is November 11).

2.39.68–69   *Resurget . . . / In pace*] He will rise again—in peace.

2.39.77   Orcus] Roman god of the underworld, later identified with
Greek Pluto (line 78); the word also stands for Hades. Rolfe may be describ-
ing an ossuary urn (olla) here.

2.39.102   reminded of the psalm] Ps. 23.4; see 2.28.44–47.

2.39.115   As some hard salt at sea] See the end of the discussion at
2.30.68.

2.39.131   And came a rush] Part 2 closes with the double symbol of the avalanche and its "counter object" the "fog-bow" (lines 150, 154). The 1856–57 journal makes no mention of an avalanche; this would seem an invention extending the entry: "Thunder in mountains of Moab—Lightning. . . . Rainbow over Dead Sea—heaven, after all, has no malice against it" (p. 83). The reader may decide how much ironical intention the comment bears, and whether the massive violence of the avalanche is held in balance by the slim pencil of light—"how frail" (line 151).

2.39.147   El Ghor] The "sunken plain," Arabic name for the great valley reaching from Lebanon to the Gulf of Akaba, described by Stanley, pp. 277, 285.

PART 3

3.1.15   St. Teresa] The question here is whether the immortality accorded such a one as the Spanish nun, mystic, and writer (1515–82) would be granted a Leopardi (line 16; see the discussion at 1.14.3) or an Obermann (line 16). Melville knew the fictional narrator of Étienne Pivert de Sénancour's *Obermann* (1804) through Arnold's two poems ("Obermann" in *Poems* and "Obermann Once More" in *New Poems*; see the discussions at 1.5.131 and 1.19.29) about his spiritual agonizings, both of which he marked carefully (Bezanson, "Arnold's Poetry," pp. 376–78, 387–88).

3.1.47   Ere,] NN adds a comma here as required, even in Melville's rhetorical punctuation, to show that "Ere" is not to be associated with "enlocked"; no additional comma is needed after "bound", however, in Melville's system (as it would be in a syntactical system).

3.1.65   the calcined mass] The image of burnt rock comes from the "whitish ashes—lime-kilns" of the 1856–57 journal (p. 83), and occurs more explicitly in the "lime-kilns" passage of lines 122–25.

3.1.95   But twice a year] See the 1856–57 journal: "rain only two or 3 days a year" (p. 84).

3.1.99   Joshua met the tribes] His victories in Joshua 10–12.

3.1.109   the Maldives'] Of the group of coral atolls in the Indian Ocean.

3.1.129   text of Scripture] Gen. 19.28: "And he looked toward Sodom and Gomorrah, and toward all the land of the plain, and beheld, and, lo, the smoke of the country went up as the smoke of a furnace."

3.1.141   Kadesh Barnea] Biblical city and region in the larger desert area of Zin (line 142), south of the Dead Sea.

3.1.144   God came from Teman] Mortmain's splendid outburst, recalling the revolution of which he had once been a part (2.4.40ff.), is drawn directly from the magnificent prayer of Habakkuk (line 169) to the terrible majesty of God coming out of Teman and Paran (lines 144–45) and making the Midians (line 168) tremble (Hab. 3).

3.1.156   the red year Forty-eight] See the discussion at 1.41.109.

3.2.18   tale by Rolfe narrated] See 1.37. The story of the carpenter is reminiscent in tone of Ishmael's tale of the blacksmith (*Moby-Dick*, chap. 112, pp. 484–86). Cf. similarly motivated withdrawals by the title character in "Jimmy Rose" (NN *Piazza Tales* volume, pp. 336ff.) and by Charlemont in *The Confidence-Man* (chap. 34, pp. 184ff.).

3.3.0   OF THE MANY MANSIONS] John 14.2 provides the text and title. The paraphrase of Jesus' words (line 5) comes from Matthew 11.28. The Sermon on the Mount (line 22) is in Matthew 5–7. The "Jew" (line 36) is not biblical, but is the Wandering Jew of tradition, whose story is dramatized in 3.19. "Job's pale group" (line 62) are the three friends who when they saw his condition sat "seven days and seven nights, and none spake a word unto him" (Job 2.13). Rolfe's whole argument that the Christian heaven differs from other imagined centers of bliss (lines 6–7) in its idea of recompense for suffering, and that this has dangerous social implications, is an important extension of Celio's more personal argument (1.13.36ff.).

3.3.6   Fortune's Isles] The Fortunate Isles, or Isles of the Blest, the happy otherworld of Greek and Roman mythology. "Tempe's dale": the lovely valley in Greece between Olympus and Ossa (cf. 2.5.46). "Araby the Blest" (line 7): Arabia Felix, the "happy" flourishing area beyond Arabia Deserta; also loosely the source of the wealth of India.

3.3.24   Python] The frightful monster that guarded the caves at Parnassus; here, apparently, primitive evil.

3.3.50   Herr von Goethe] Mortmain's view extends Melville's criticism of Goethe written beside Arnold's poem "Obermann" (see the discussion at 3.1.15): "Of Goethe it might also be said that he averted his eyes from everything except Nature, Intellect, & Beauty" (Bezanson, "Arnold's Poetry," p. 376). The whole lyceum movement (line 49; see also the discussion at 3.28.7) in America was dedicated to the appropriation of "Nature" to the uses of the "World" (line 42).

3.4.1   Noble gods at the board] This "hymn of Aristippus" (line 68) Melville liked sufficiently well to copy out by hand and send to Edmund Clarence Stedman when the latter wrote him on January 20, 1888, asking for "one of your best known shorter poems, in your own handwriting" and a portrait, both for inclusion in a copy of Stedman's *Poets of America* (1885) that he was extra-illustrating. Melville copied it almost exactly and titled it "Ditty of Aristippus"; that original manuscript copy, now in the American Antiquarian Society, Worcester, Mass., is the only known part of *Clarel* in Melville's hand (reproduced and discussed in RELATED DOCU-MENTS, pp. 867–70). The light poem's view of the gods as resting after their labors, oblivious to mortals, though willing to answer prayers if they could but take the time from their revels, ironically attributes to them the hedonism of Aristippus (435–386 B.C.); he advocated virtue and happiness through the pursuit of pleasure and the exercise of prudence in avoiding pain (cf. Part 1 of "The Paradise of Bachelors and the Tartarus of Maids," in the NN *Piazza Tales* volume, pp. 316–23). This poem anticipates the coming revels at Mar Saba and also starts the interesting series of rose images (beauty, love, life) that partly counter the recent aura of sin and death.

3.4.30   what Delian] Either Apollo, among other things god of song and music, and known as the Delian because he was born on Delos; or any Delian, member of the famous military confederacy of 477 B.C. formed to resist the Persians. Orpheus (line 36) went down into Hades to rescue his beloved Eurydice, enchanting the damned with his harp; here the Cypriote descends into Siddim. Allusions to Orpheus occur in *Redburn*, *White-Jacket*, *Pierre*, "The Fiddler," *The Confidence-Man*, "The Armies of the Wilderness" in *Battle-Pieces*, and *Billy Budd, Sailor*.

3.4.50   Phrygian cap] A close-fitting, conical cap represented in Greek art as worn by Orientals.

3.4.88   Azrael's scroll] In both Jewish and Mohammedan angelology Azrael separates the soul from the body at the moment of death.

3.4.98   I chance to know] Melville found this in Stanley, p. 310, who says Easter pilgrims bathed in white dresses which were then "kept for their winding-sheets."

3.5.1   Where silence] The sixteen-line simile is drawn from Stanley, p. 46, where he has an account of the Convent of St. Catherine and its neigh-boring chapel, on Mt. Sinai (Horeb); italics indicate words used by Melville: "Another (which has not found its way into books), is the *legend* in the *convent* . . . of the *sunbeam*, which on *one day* in the year *darts* into the *Chapel of the Burning Bush* from the Gebel-ed-Deir. It is only by ascending the mountain that the origin of the legend appears. Behind the topmost cliffs, a narrow *cleft* admits of a view, of the only view, into the convent buildings, which lie far below, but precisely commanded by it, and therefore necessari-ly lit up by *the ray*, which once in the year *darts* through that especial crevice."

3.5.26   Ibrahim's wild infantry] See the discussion at 2.7.17.

3.5.36 Ormuzd involved with Ahriman] William Rounseville Alger, *The Poetry of the East*, pp. 134–36 (see the discussion at 1.32.0), has a poem called "A Zoroastrian Myth":

> Ormuzd and Ahriman; Devotion's dazzling child,
> And Doubt's demoniac son, false, filthy, black, and wild.
>
> The moment they were born, creation they began:
> Ormuzd all good things made; all evil, Ahriman.

3.5.40 old Gnostic pages] The Gnostic heresy, which rose in the first century, flourished in the second, and had faded by the sixth. Combining Greek and oriental philosophy and religion with Christian, it stressed knowledge over faith and claimed to penetrate the mysteries. The narrator sees it as a forceful dualism, and ends by comparing it with the mild God and epicene Christ of the nineteenth century. Melville alludes to the Gnostics in *White-Jacket*, chap. 38, p. 156, and critics have discerned a Gnostic element in *Moby-Dick*.

3.5.68 Galileo] The scientist's advocacy of the Copernican system was branded heretical and forced his recantation before the Inquisition in 1616.

3.5.75 petrified] Cf. Hawthorne's "The Man of Adamant," in *The Snow-Image* (1851); not marked in Melville's edition, acquired in 1871 (Boston: Ticknor & Fields, 1865; Sealts 255).

3.5.89 Saint Denis] In the cathedral of St. Denis in this northern suburb of Paris are buried, with four exceptions, not only the Capets of the third dynasty (987–1328) but all the later kings of France, through the mid-nineteenth century—not all of them Capets as Melville says, probably figuratively, but kings during more than the "Eight centuries" he specifies (line 91); see the NOTE ON THE TEXT, p. 684. As to leaving the coffin "On steps that led down into vault" (lines 92–96), Melville's unlocated source told of the same burial custom as a later English account: "Another part of the crypt became the burial place of the Bourbon family. . . . The day of the funeral the body was placed in the vault '*sur des barres de fer, devant une statue en marbre de Nostre Dame.*' There it remained for a year, after which it was deposited in the tomb of the sovereign's ancestors. This curious arrangement became a custom by pure accident. Henri IV. [d. 1610] not having signified any desire as to his place of burial, was left in this vault, '*le caveau des cérémonies,*' while his widow and *les Etats* discussed the question of erecting a monument; and thus, by force of habit, the succeeding Bourbons, being placed by the side of Henri, the '*caveau*' became the mausoleum of the family" (S. Sophia Beale, *The Churches of Paris from Clovis to Charles X* [London: W. H. Allen, 1893], pp. 72–73).

3.5.103   The Sibyl's books] The Sibylline Books were oracular utterances on religious worship and law, reputedly obtained from the Cumaean Sibyl and preserved in Rome until A.D. 405.

3.5.133   when the Tartar took Pekin] If it actually suggested that the inhabitants of the city "Knew not the fact" (line 135) of the conquest, Melville's unlocated source supplied dubious anecdotal history, which would be surprising if true (note Melville's skeptical aside, "If credence hearsay old may win" [line 134]). The story probably stemmed from those early European accounts which favored the Tartar (i.e., Manchu) conquerors and therefore minimized the carnage and devastation that attended the conquest (1644) and the end of the Ming dynasty. The fall of Pekin, soon after an internal usurpation and the suicide of the last Ming emperor, was by all European reports too devastating an event to go unnoticed by very many of the large city's people. See Edwin J. Van Kley, "News from China: Seventeenth-Century European Notices of the Manchu Conquest," *Journal of Modern History*, XLV (December, 1973), 561–82.

3.5.140   Roman A. U. C.] *Anno urbis conditae*—from the founding of the city (Rome), 753 B.C.

3.5.197   Sidon] Melville read Stanley, pp. 265–66, on Tyre and Sidon.

3.5.201   Endor's withered sprite] The witch whom Saul consulted (1 Sam. 28.7–14).

3.6.29   roseace] A rose-window (usually "rosace"), to which Mortmain likens Derwent for the "rosy" light of his views. NN retains the first-edition spelling because the *OED* lists variants with "e" in most derivatives of "rose" (though not specifically this one).

3.6.47   cheerful Paul] 1 Thess. 5.16: "Rejoice evermore."

3.6.62   Durham's prelate] Joseph Butler (1692–1752), bishop of Durham 1750–52, in his famous work *The Analogy of Religion* (1736) sets aside the inquiry whether God can be proved benevolent and argues that he is righteous and moral in his government of the world, rewarding the righteous and punishing the wicked (pt. I, chap. 3).

3.6.81   modern be] Derwent's thesis that the gods are anthropomorphic was a standard thesis of the new writers on comparative religion. For the epic *Ramayana* (line 88) see the discussion at 1.32.0.

3.6.90   lumped his limbs] The verb "lump" makes sense here when taken as "to drop down like a lump" (*OED*), though possibly "lumped" is a misreading for "humped"; see line 50: "A hump dropped on him," and lines 44–45 of "Chattanooga" in *Battle-Pieces*: "his back / Heaps slowly to a hump" (NN *Published Poems*, p. 67).

3.6.96   favorite theory] Derwent's little lecture suggests five influences on Jewish theology: the native strain, darkened by the Egyptian captivity ("Nile": line 98) and the forty years in the wilderness (line 99); the Greeks (line 107), whose influence on the New Testament was immense; the Magi (line 114), an occult group who were originally a class of priests among the Medes and Persians, and whose theology was much like that of the Hebrews, perhaps because of the Babylonian captivity; "Hillel's fair reforming school" (line 116), a group of the scribes led by the tolerant and genial Hillel, born 112 B.C., and since he lived to be 120 perhaps one of the doctors before whom Jesus went in the Temple; and the Essenes (line 124), who at the time of Jesus lived in isolated communities along the Dead Sea and elsewhere and who minimized the Law for emphasis on ideal purity, self-denial, and spiritual aspiration.

3.6.139   Shaftesbury] Anthony Ashley Cooper (1671–1713), third earl of Shaftesbury, English moralist and author of *Characteristics of Men, Manners, Opinions, Times* (1711), notable for its deistic and mild notions of virtue. (See Bercaw 633.)

3.6.147–48   Ceres' child / In Enna] Proserpina, lovely daughter of Ceres, wandered too far picking narcissus and was carried off by the god of the underworld (Pluto: line 149); the Latin poets placed the scene of the rape at Enna, in Sicily. Melville's image of her dropping a flower at the sight of Pluto's "pale brow" occurs in neither the relevant passage in Ovid's *Metamorphoses*, 5.385–401, nor the one in *Paradise Lost*, 4.268–72, both of which he knew (New York: Harper, [18—]; Sealts 147; and Boston: Hilliard, Gray, 1836; Sealts 358b). In *Pierre*, bk. 3, p. 59, he alludes to "Pluto stealing Proserpine."

3.7.1   ELOI] Mark 15.34: "And at the ninth hour Jesus cried with a loud voice, saying, Eloi, Eloi, lama sabachthani? which is, being interpreted, My God, my God, why hast thou forsaken me?" (cf. 1.13.47).

3.7.14   David in Adullam's lair] When David fled for fear of Saul he hid in "the cave Adullam" (1 Sam. 22.1). The first-edition spelling here ("Adullum") is emended as a misreading of Melville's hand; cf. "Adullam" at 4.28.65.

3.7.18   the Cenci portrait] Admiration was general in the nineteenth century for this supposed portrait (then attributed to Guido Reni) of Beatrice Cenci, who was executed for incest with her father, and for murdering him; yet she seemed the very type of innocence. Shelley's *Cenci* (1819) made the incest theme famous (Melville alludes to the work in *White-Jacket*, chap. 89, p. 376). In *Pierre* (bk. 26), before seeing the original painting, Melville called the picture "that sweetest, most touching, but most awful of all feminine heads" because of her blonde beauty and black crimes—"the two most horrible crimes (of one of which she is the object, and of the other the agent) possible to civilized humanity—incest and parricide" (p. 351). The 1856–57 journal indicates that Melville was offered a copy of the picture for four dollars in Rome and that he went expressly to the Palazzo Barberini to see the original: "Expression of suffering about the mouth—(appealing look of innocence) not caught in any copy or engraving" (*Journals,* p. 108; see also pp. 106, 154, and 474, with a reproduction of the painting). Melville owned an engraving of the painting. Hawthorne's fascination with the picture if anything exceeded Melville's: Mrs. Hawthorne's abridged *Passages from the French and Italian Note-Books* (Boston: Osgood, 1872), which Melville acquired in 1872 (Sealts 252) but marked only slightly, included part of Hawthorne's first description of the painting (February 20, 1858) but omitted his second one (May 15, 1859), made when he went for "a farewell look at the Beatrice Cenci, which I have twice visited before" (*The French and Italian Notebooks,* ed. Thomas Woodson [Columbus: Ohio State University Press, 1980], p. 520; see the complete earlier entry, pp. 92–93). In the excerpt Melville saw (but did not mark) in *Passages,* Hawthorne thought it "the most profoundly wrought picture in the world"; in his second description, omitted by Mrs. Hawthorne and therefore not seen by Melville, he called it a picture "resolved not to betray its secret of grief or guilt. . . . The mouth is beyond measure touching; the lips apart, looking as innocent as a baby's after it has been crying." He ended up "perplexed and troubled . . . not to be able to get hold of its secret." Drawing on his two entries, Hawthorne made the picture significant in *The Marble Faun* (Boston: Ticknor & Fields, 1860) and the subject of chap. 7; Melville acquired that novel in 1860 and read and marked it (but not this chapter) on his *Meteor* voyage that year (Sealts 247). In summary, Melville and Hawthorne shared the fascination of their era with the picture and agreed strikingly that its major attributes were femininity, weakness, suffering, inaccessibility, and that it betrayed *either* innocence or dark criminality.

3.7.32   alb] A white full-length ecclesiastical vestment.

3.7.51   the blast from Roncesvalles] Ambushed and hopelessly beset there, Roland sounded his magic horn, whose blast Charlemagne heard many miles away but ignored because of Ganelon's treachery.

3.8.0   TENTS OF KEDAR] A famous phrase of the Bible, occurring for example in Psalm 120 and in the Song of Solomon 1.5 (cf. lines 86–88): "I am black, but comely, O ye daughters of Jerusalem, as the tents of Kedar, as the curtains of Solomon."

3.8.4   With gluey track] From the 1856–57 journal: "Crossed elevated plains, with snails, that tracks of slime, all over" (p. 84). Melville later underlined the last part in pencil, probably when composing *Clarel.*

3.8.17   Apollyon] Angel of the bottomless pit, also called Abaddon (Rev. 9.11; cf. 2.25.180).

3.8.61   Ebal's hill] Ebal and Gerizim (line 62) are two mountains about thirty miles north of Jerusalem. God set the choices of "a blessing and a curse" before the Hebrews, according as to whether they obeyed or disobeyed his commandments; and the blessing was "upon mount Gerizim, and the curse upon mount Ebal" (Deut. 11.26–32).

3.8.71   Theocritus divine] This famous poet of the third century B.C. in his idylls writes charmingly of pastoral scenes; previously contrasted with the grim Joel (1.28.30–31).

3.8.82   in faintly greenish hollow] From the 1856–57 journal: "Arab-Bedouin encampment in hollow of high hills—oval—like two rows of hearses" (p. 84). Melville later circled in pencil the last four words; see the *Journals* textual note at 84.3–4.

3.8.115   Ibrahim's way] See the discussion at 2.7.17.

3.8.161   Japhet, Shem, and Ham] The three sons of Noah: "and by these were the nations divided in the earth after the flood" (Gen. 10.32).

3.9.0   OF MONASTERIES] Melville may have read Curzon's *A Visit to Monasteries in the Levant* (see also the discussions at 2.24.30 and 3.16.236–37), though of the seven monasteries in the canto only two fall within the scope of his book. St. Bernard (923–1008, line 4), the Apostle of the Alps, founded the Hospices of the Little and Great St. Bernard Passes (see also the discussion just below). "Nitria's sand" (line 7), near the Nile Delta, is the site of several convents of the Copts (Egyptian Christians); described in Curzon (chaps. 7–10). "Spermos" (line 14) may be correct, or may refer to Hagios Stephanos, which Curzon (chap. 19) says looks away to Mt. Olympus (line 12). The "Grand Chartreuse" (line 19) is near Grenoble and is where St. Bruno of Cologne founded the Carthusian (line 26) order in 1084; Arnold's "Stanzas from the Grande Chartreuse" in *New Poems* (see the discussion at 1.19.29) was familiar to Melville (Bezanson, "Arnold's Poetry," pp. 388–90). Vallambrosa (line 29) refers to a Benedictine monastery on the wooded hillside above a shady valley near Florence. Though Melville did not visit it in 1857 he may have remembered the passage in *Paradise Lost* reminiscent of Milton's visit in 1638–39: "Thick as autumnal leaves that strow the brooks / In Vallombrosa, where th' Etrurian shades / High overarch'd imbow'r . . . " (1.302–4; not marked in Melville's copy of Milton—see the discussion at 1.1.24). Montserrat (line 30) is a jagged mountain near Barcelona which has the ruins of a famous ninth-century monastery on it. For Saba (line 33) see the HISTORICAL AND CRITICAL NOTE (sect. 2), Murray, I, 204–6, and Curzon, chap. 15.

3.9.3   stone hospice] This description of the St. Bernard Pass (see the preceding discussion) may be another instance of transposition: Melville in

1857 had crossed the Alps by the San Gotthard Pass: "Houses of refuge. Discussion of the gods &c. . . . Summit. Hospice. Old stone warehouse. Scene there. Men in comforters, frozen horses. . . . Like coming out of the clouds" (*Journals*, pp. 124–25).

3.9.41   samphire-gatherers] Gatherers of herbs on the cliffside; here and in *Moby-Dick* (chap. 47, p. 216) the image comes from *King Lear*, 4.6.14–15 (for Melville's edition see the discussion at 1.29.51). A later notation added to the 1856–57 journal records: "St. Saba—Samphire gatherers—monks dreadful trade" (see *Journals*, textual note at 83.38).

3.9.54   Saint Basil's banner] Basil the Great, fourth-century father of the Greek Church; the "brede" (line 53) is embroidery or braid. Stanley, p. 462, mentions "a long procession with embroidered banners, supplying in their ritual the want of images." Melville marked the passage.

3.10.0   BEFORE THE GATE] Some of the details of this canto come from the 1856–57 journal: "*St. Saba*—zig-zag along Kedron, sepulchral ravine, smoked as by fire, caves & cells—immense depth—all rock—enigma of the depth . . . wall of stone on ravine edge—Monastery (Greek) rode on with letter—hauled up in basket into hole—small door of massive iron in high wall—knocking—opened—salaam of monks—Place for pilgrims— divans—St Saba wine—'*racka*'—comfortable" (p. 84). Portions of this passage were later circled and underlined in pencil, probably during composition of *Clarel;* see *Journals*, textual notes at 84.5 to 84.13–14. The illustration on p. 802 of the monastery and the Kedron gorge is from Thomson, II, [434]. For other views of Mar Saba see pp. 813 and 814 below.

3.10.1   Kedron] The usually dry brook which begins at Jerusalem takes its course through the Judah wilderness past Mar Saba on its way to the Dead Sea.

3.10.16   Uriel, warder in the sun] An allusion to the archangel of Milton's *Paradise Lost* (from Rev. 19.17): "the same whom John saw also in the sun" and who, after Satan encountered him on duty there, watched Satan's descent to earth and warned Gabriel of his presence (3.621ff., 4.555ff.; the first passage is marked and annotated in Melville's copy of Milton—see the discussion at 1.1.24).

3.10.36   Perizzite] Member of an ancient biblical nation in Palestine before the Jews; here, local Bedouins.

3.10.45   Pico Rock] A volcanic peak in the Canary Islands.

3.10.57   The voucher from their Patriarch] Travelers wishing to stay at one of the Greek monasteries had to secure a letter from the resident patriarch in Jerusalem.

CONVENT OF SANTA SABA.

3.10.74   Saba's wine] The brief 1856–57 journal entry: "St Saba wine—
'*racka*'—" (p. 84), refers to raki, a brandy wine made there.

3.11.0   THE BEAKER] The all-night revels and the heart-searchings that
follow (cantos 11–16) apparently had no counterpart in Melville's experience
there. After the descent to Kedron in the evening of his one night's stay (see
the discussion at 3.25.32), the 1856–57 journal records: "Good bed & night's
rest" (p. 84).

3.11.26   In Mytilene] Melville's impression of this Greek island (Lesbos)
is found in the 1856–57 journal: "Steered in between Mytelene & the main.
A large & lovely island, covered with olive trees. They make much wine.
The whole island green from beach to hill-top—a dark rich bronzy green, in
marked contrast with the yellow & parched aspect of most other isles of the
Archipelago" (p. 68). The poet Sappho (fl. ca. 600 B.C.), rejected by Phaon
(line 27) the boatman, here leapt into the sea from the Leucadian rock.

3.11.36   An Arnaut] See The ARNAUT (Index). His descent is from
Pyrrhus (line 39), king of Epirus, who defeated the Romans at Heraclea and
Asculum in the third century B.C. Scanderbeg (line 42) was the Albanian
national hero who held off the Turks in the fifteenth century. Arslan (line
43), or Alp-Arslan ("Courageous Lion"), was an eleventh-century Seljuq
Turkish sultan who conquered Georgia, Armenia, and much of Asia Minor.

3.11.50   his *Labarum*] Ecclesiastical banner.

3.11.61   for the garb] Melville took the details of his Arnaut's dress
(lines 61–72) from Warburton, I, 220 (italics added): "their dress is the most
picturesque possible. A *red tarboosh*, with a purple silk *tassel*, covers their
long flowing locks that stream down the shoulders like those of the Cava-
liers; an embroidered *jacket* of scarlet, or dark *blue cloth*; a very voluminous
white kilt, reaching to the knee; *greaves*, or a sort of embroidered gaiters,
upon their legs, and red slippers, constitute their dress. A brace of long
pistols and a *dagger* are stuck in a large *silken sash* that girds their bodies; a long
silver-mounted musket is slung at their backs, and a *curved sabre* at their side."

3.11.62–67   sword-hilt: / . . . weaves;] In this series (introduced by
"garb:"), three items are followed by colons (after "sword-hilt", "rows",
and "leather") and three by semicolons (after "stains", "thonged", and
"weaves"). Although Melville's colons and semicolons could easily have
been misread and he might perhaps have intended the same mark of punctu-
ation after all these items, there is also the possibility—given his rhetorical
style of punctuation—that he was thinking of different kinds of pauses. If all
these marks but one had been identical, one might more readily conclude
that consistency was intended (as at 4.34.27); but under these circumstances
it is not at all clear that Melville would have preferred identical punctuation
at each of these spots, and NN does not emend.

3.11.154   At Cana] John 2.1–12 tells of Jesus performing his first miracle here, the turning of water into wine. See also 2.21.74.

3.11.177   a bit of song] A Mufti (line 178) is an official expounder of Mohammedan law. The "Rabbi in Prague" of the second quatrain comes from Stanley, p. 163: "the grapes of Judah still mark the tombstones of the Hebrew race in the oldest of their European cemeteries, at Prague."

3.11.189   armed Og] King of Bashan, that "remnant of giants" who had an immense iron bedstead (Deut. 3.11).

3.11.212   this ditty wee] In subject and tone this song and some of the others resemble Melville's "Weeds and Wildings, with a Rose or Two," a collection of verse dedicated to his wife Elizabeth in 1891, but not published (included in the NN volume BILLY BUDD, SAILOR and Other Late Manuscripts).

3.11.227   Ahab's court] Suddenly into the evil court of Ahab came Elijah the Tishbite (line 228), who prophesied violent drought and then retreated to live by the brook Cherith (1 Kings 17). Mortmain is the one here compared to Elijah (see the discussion at 2.34.20). Cf. Moby-Dick, chap. 19.

3.11.254   wine of Xeres] Handy rhyme for "wearies"; also the old name of Jerez, in Spain, famous for its sherry.

3.12.0   THE TIMONEER'S STORY] The story that begins at line 57 has in it many details—cabin arms, pursuing birds, spinning compass, corposants (see the discussion at line 93)—recalling Moby-Dick. See also Melville's poems "The Haglets" (John Marr; NN Published Poems, pp. 218–25) and "The Admiral of the White" (in the NN volume BILLY BUDD, SAILOR and Other Late Manuscripts). The 1856–57 journal reports that at Thessalonica the ship's captain "told a story about the heap of arms affecting the compass" (see Journals, pp. 56, 393).

3.12.1–2   Sinbads . . . Decameron] Like Sinbad (or Sindbad) the Sailor in The Arabian Nights' Entertainments and the Florentines in the Decameron, the company assembled here will tell their tales. See the discussion at 2.30.59.

3.12.7   Godfrey's sword] Curzon (chap. 13) mentions "the sword and spurs of Godfrey de Bouillon" (see the discussion at 1.3.177) kept in the sacristy by Latin monks and used by the Reverendissimo to confer the order of Knight of the Holy Sepulcher.

3.12.16   Antar's rhyme] Antarah ibn Shaddad was a sixth-century Arab warrior and war poet; he wrote The Romance of Antar.

3.12.69   Wahabee] Member of a Mohammedan reform sect.

3.12.93   Corposants] Occasional flaming discharges of electricity at yardarm ends in stormy weather. Melville recorded his first seeing them on his 1849 voyage to England (*Journals*, p. 6) and made dramatic use of them in *Moby-Dick*, chap. 119, pp. 507–8.

3.12.144   The incident] Murray, I, 205, warns of the dangers below Mar Saba.

3.12.146   the Cyclades] Greek islands in the Aegean.

3.13.6   Cybele] A nature goddess of Asia Minor, often worshiped by orgiastic rites (see the discussion at 3.16.66).

3.13.15–17   With . . . flung] In the first edition, these three lines (which are the last three lines of a page) are printed uniformly with a left margin to the left of the one followed by the preceding lyric, yet not as far left as the regular left margin (as established by the concluding lines of the preceding canto at the top of the page). This slight indentation (less that the usual paragraph indentation) of these three lines is clearly a printer's error, for the following lines (3.13.18ff.), on the next page, observe the normal left margin. A more significant problem here is the fact that line 15 is not indented farther than the two following lines, and thus no paragraph opening is indicated. The editors have concluded that the practice throughout necessitates the insertion of a paragraph indentation here (see the NOTE ON THE TEXT, pp. 694–95); and the emendation therefore consists of giving line 15 the usual paragraph indentation and moving lines 16 and 17 flush left.

3.13.28   Such influences] Here Rolfe cites a random cluster of ancient and modern Mediterranean peoples and places of which the less familiar are: Medes and Elamites (line 29) from ancient Babylonia; Cyrene (line 32), an ancient Greek city in northern Africa: Smyrna (line 34), in western Turkey; Stamboul (line 35), part of Constantinople; and Fez (line 35), a city in northern Morocco.

3.13.55   Chang and Eng] The death of this famous congenitally linked pair (the "Siamese Twins") in 1874 may have brought them to Melville's mind. During Melville's residence in New York from 1847–50 he probably saw them on exhibition there in P. T. Barnum's American Museum. In *Moby-Dick*, chap. 72, p. 320, the monkey-rope is "an elongated Siamese ligature" joining Ishmael and Queequeg; see also *The Confidence-Man*, chap. 21, p. 108.

3.13.71   Hafiz] Either the fourteenth-century Persian poet or simply a title of respect for anyone who knows the Koran by heart. "Didymus" (line 72) is fictional here but is perhaps named in allusion to the disciple Didymus, or Thomas, later known as "Doubting Thomas" because he was skeptical of Christ's Resurrection until he saw the physical evidence (John 20.24–29).

3.13.104   Methodius] The chaplain was named after St. Methodius, ninth-century missionary of the Greek Church to the Danube area.

3.14.8 Euroclydon] The "tempestuous wind" of Acts 27.14 that wrecked Paul. See *Moby-Dick*, chap. 2, p. 10.

3.14.18 The fair young Earl] James Radcliffe, third earl of Derwentwater (1689–1716), at the age of 27 was beheaded on Tower Hill, February 24, 1716, for treason. Northern lights were specially bright that night near Dilston Hall (line 17), the family castle, and are still known locally as "Lord Derwentwater's Lights."

3.14.54 Your Koran bars] For a possible source, see the HISTORICAL SUPPLEMENT, p. 669 above.

3.14.56 Ramadan] Ninth month of the Moslem year, when fasting is required.

3.14.66 The Anak] Numbers 13.33 tells of Anak whose sons "come of the giants" and make other men "as grasshoppers." Here, the Arnaut. "Mahone" is an archaism for Mohammed.

3.14.69 Bey, the Emir, and Mamalook lords] Eastern terms for a Turkish governor, an Arabian prince, and Egyptian military men; used loosely here.

3.14.79 Bazra blade] Belex's scimitar is from Basra (or Bassorah), the river port at the head of the Persian Gulf below Baghdad, then in Asiatic Turkey, now Iraq.

3.14.110 Theseus] The legendary hero of Attica, slayer of the Minotaur; he was believed to have returned to aid the Athenians at Marathon.

3.14.120 Off Chiloe] Large island close to the coast of Chile; its western shores have steep rocky masses up to three thousand feet. The White Whale was said to haunt that area (*Log*, II, 799).

3.15.24 Brinvilliers'] Of the French marquise, a notorious poisoner, beheaded 1676; subject of a poem in *Timoleon* (NN *Published Poems*, p. 285).

3.15.35 the sweet Sabæa] Sheba; see Jeremiah 6.20 for the "incense from Sheba," and also, for a Miltonic influence in this whole passage, Henry F. Pommer, *Milton and Melville* (Pittsburgh: University of Pittsburgh Press, 1950), pp. 32–33.

3.15.78 Druze initiate] See DJALEA (Index).

3.15.82 Lady Esther] Lady Hester Stanhope (1776–1839), the brilliant and eccentric niece of William Pitt the Younger. From 1810 she lived as a kind of wealthy prophetess in the Lebanon Mountains, where she was visited by many famous travelers, including Kinglake and Lamartine. Alexander Kinglake's *Eöthen* (1844; New York: Wiley & Putnam, 1845), chap. 8, pp. 62–83, describes her as a Sibyl, the niece of Pitt (cf. line 84: "Pitt's sibyl-niece"), one who "trusted alone to the stars for her sublime knowledge" (cf.

line 85) and who believed "the Messiah was yet to come" (cf. line 89). See also Thomson, I, 110–15.

3.15.90–91   veil / Of Sais] Saïs is a temple city in Egypt. Melville acquired in 1849 and took on the *Meteor* in 1860 a copy of *The Poems and Ballads of Schiller* (trans. Bulwer Lytton; Leipzig: Tauchnitz, 1844; Sealts 439); he marked "The Veiled Image at Sais," about a youth who raised the veil, though warned not to, and so lost happiness but passed "through guilt to truth." Melville alludes to the poem in *Moby-Dick*, chap. 76, p. 338.

3.15.115   No God there is but God] In his 1856–57 journal, Melville reports the ship was in a fog off Constantinople: "Old Turk ('Old Sinope') I said to him 'This is very bad' he answered 'God's will is good, & smoked his pipe in cheerful resignation" (p. 58).

3.15.118   Pallas' statue] No episode of iconoclasm involving a statue of the Greek goddess Pallas Athena, or of her Roman counterpart Minerva, has been located, and perhaps the reference is figurative.

3.16.0   THE EASTER FIRE] The celebration of Greek Easter at the Church of the Holy Sepulcher in Jerusalem was a favorite subject of Eastern travelers. Melville had not seen it, but he marked three passages in Stanley's account, pp. 459–65. Since Rolfe's account is a broken one (lines 44–83, 103–8, 124–40, 221–48), the main elements of the story follow. Greek pilgrims from all over the Levant gather to watch the receiving from heaven of the Holy Fire. For hours before, the men race and leap around the Sepulcher in a wild ritual which Stanley compares to "a mixture of prisoner's base, football, and leapfrog" (and which Rolfe compares to Greek and Polynesian games, lines 226–30). Then comes a bannered procession of the priests, chanting, and the Turkish guards are forcibly ejected in a ritual battle. The bishop enters the Chapel of the Sepulcher, closes the door, and an awful silence descends. Suddenly a flame appears at an aperture—"the light, as every educated Greek knows and acknowledges, kindled by the Bishop within—the light, as every pilgrim believes, of the descent of God Himself upon the Holy Tomb." In a frenzy of excitement the pilgrims struggle to light their own torches from the flame until there is a blaze of thousands of them. The bishop is carried out in an assumed faint, and wild panic descends on the pilgrims. The sacred fire is carried by horsemen to the Greek convent in Bethlehem (Melville marked this bit and transferred it to Mar Saba, lines 101–8). Details of Melville's borrowings are in Bezanson, pp. 128–33.

3.16.12   Toll-taker at the Sepulcher.] The Turkish guards inside the Church of the Holy Sepulcher, often commented upon by travelers, had been noted by Melville in his 1856–57 journal: "At the entrance, in a sort of grotto in the wall a divan for Turkish policemen, where they sit crosslegged & smoking, scornfully observing the continuous troops of pilgrims entering & prostrating themselves before the anointing-stone of Christ" (p. 87). The period in all examined copies of the first edition makes this line an incomplete sentence, and perhaps a comma was intended, to make the line in apposition to "he" in the next line. But as punctuated the line makes enough sense as an elliptical response to the question in the preceding line.

3.16.29   El Cods, Jerusalem] This variant of el Kuds (the Holy), an Arabic name for Jerusalem, occurs, for example, in Chateaubriand, p. 247.

3.16.66   ecstasy of Atys' scath] Driven to madness by the goddess Cybele (3.13.6), the Phrygian shepherd Atys (or Attis) castrated himself at the foot of a pine tree, and violets grew from his blood. Catullus deals with the story in his poem "Attis." Priests of the Atys cult had to undergo emasculation. A spring festival on Mt. Dindymus (line 71) involved carrying a pine tree and violets up the mountain to Atys's tomb, and a violent three-day "search" for him, accompanied by wild rites.

3.16.72   Christian fakirs] Fakirs are religious ascetics in Mohammedan or Hindu religion; the wordplay here is obvious.

3.16.180   Venerable Bede] The great seventh-century English churchman, perhaps the most learned scholar of Western Europe in his day (see also the discussion at 1.35.0). Rolfe as Adam (line 181) should be compared with 1.32.46.

3.16.192   Scriptures say] Ps. 117.2: "the truth of the Lord endureth for ever."

3.16.199   Comte, Renan] Auguste Comte (1798–1857), the founder of positivism and the man who coined the term "sociology"; a major leader of new thought. For Renan see the discussion at 1.41.133.

3.16.228   slain Patroclus] In Homer's *Iliad* (trans. Chapman; London: Smith, 1857; Sealts 277; Bercaw 367), the friend of Achilles, slain by Hector by the walls of Troy (near the Hellespont, line 227). Funeral games were celebrated in his honor.

3.16.236–37   the narrative receive / Of Ibrahim] This facet of Rolfe's narrative is not in Stanley, but is in Curzon, chap. 16. Curzon was there during the 1834 Easter, which turned into a wild massacre; Ibrahim Pasha (see the discussion at 2.7.17), then governor of Jerusalem, was in the church and was nearly killed; "He fainted more than once in the struggle" and his soldiers had to cut a way out for him. Curzon went to the pasha afterwards and pleaded to have the celebration discontinued, but he refused: "The interference of a Mahometan in such a case as this would only have been held as another persecution of the Christians."

3.16.251   some story of his line] In *Pierre*, such "decline / Of all his spirits" (lines 249–50) comes upon Pierre when he hears—and believes—Isabel's story that she is his father's illegitimate daughter.

3.17.0   A Chant] The four-voiced chant is Melville's own, but is based primarily on Jeremiah 32–39. The first part tells of Jeremiah (line 22) thrown into prison for his prophecies of the fall of Jerusalem; the coming of the Chaldean army (line 25); the blinding of King Zedekiah (line 27) before the Chaldeans carried him off to captivity. But in the second part (beginning at line 42) God's promise of a gracious return (Jer. 32) becomes cause for joy.

3.17.10   Saint Cosmas' canticle] One of the songs by Cosmas of Jerusalem, famous hymnologist of the Greek Church and, until A.D. 743, a monk at Mar Saba. The first-edition spelling, "Cosmos", is emended as a misreading of Melville's hand.

3.17.34   Nergal and Samgar, Sarsechim] Jeremiah 39.3 names these conquering princes of Babylon.

3.17.41   A sword without] Ezek. 7.15: "The sword is without, and the pestilence and the famine within."

3.18.0   The Minster] Curzon (chap. 14) has good descriptions of the buttresses, library, and church of the opening lines. The 1856–57 journal records only: "Went into chapel &c" (p. 84).

3.18.20   Urim and Thummim] Mysterious and never described parts of the breastplate of the high priest (Exod. 28.30); they mean "lights" and "perfections" respectively, and were probably sacred jewels or stones.

3.18.22   Semiramis] A great and ancient Assyrian princess, ca. 800 B.C., perhaps founder of Babylon, according to Greek myth.

3.18.26   Septuagint] The Greek version of the Old Testament used in the Eastern Church.

3.18.39   Greek cross] A cross with all four arms of equal length (like the modern Red Cross).

3.19.0   The Masque] The legend of the Wandering Jew is medieval in origin; told by Matthew Paris in the thirteenth century, it has often been elaborated since, by A. W. Schlegel, Eugène Sue, etc. One form uses the name Cartaphilus (line 8) for a servant of Pilate, reputed to have given Jesus a blow as he was led out to execution; for this he received the sentence, "Thou shalt wander on the earth till I return." See 1.13.110–16 for Melville's version of his offense. The actual scene of the masque, the Kedron gorge, here stands for the Valley of Jehoshaphat (line 10) beneath the Jerusalem wall. The whole alienation theme of the poem—continuous echoes of being "cut off"—here reaches climax. See Bernard Rosenthal, "Herman Melville's Wandering Jews," in *Puritan Influences in American Literature,* ed.

Emory Elliott (Urbana, Chicago, London: University of Illinois Press, 1979), pp. 167–92.

3.19.1   'Tis] In the first edition there is no apostrophe preceding the "T", although "'tis" (or "'Tis") is regularly spelled with the apostrophe in that edition (e.g., 1.11.23; 1.18.91, 100; 3.10.1; 3.14.31; 3.15.24; 3.23.1; 3.24.74; 4.10.83; 4.15.37). Since quotation marks never appear before the display capitals at the beginnings of cantos in the first edition, one might assume that apostrophes would not be used with display capitals either. But in two other instances "'Tis" is the first word of a canto (3.10.1; 3.23.1), and in both places the apostrophe is present. Its absence at 3.19.1 is therefore considered simply a compositorial error (perhaps induced by the display capital), which NN corrects.

3.19.38   Shaveh's dale, in Joel's court] Here, synonyms for the Valley of Jehoshaphat, Joel's "valley of decision," Joel 3.14 (and Clarel's: 4.30).

3.19.71   Elymas] The sorcerer of Acts 13.8.

3.19.148   Absalom's Pillar] Famous landmark in the Valley of Jehoshaphat; Murray, I, 146, seems the source for lines 148–53: "Its lower part is now buried to some depth in a mass of stones, thrown at it by Jews, who, believing it to be really the pillar of Absalom mentioned in Scripture, have been in the habit from time immemorial of showing their horror at his rebellious conduct by casting a stone and spitting as they pass by. Most of them, however, might save themselves the trouble if they would only reflect on the words of our Lord: 'He that is without sin among you, let him first cast a stone.' " See also Journals, pp. 433 (illustration), 436.

3.19.170   Bismillah!] Belex, the Bethlehem guard, here gives the Moslem invocation "In the name of God!"; to which Mortmain, from a point high above (the Matterhorn, line 179, is an Alpine peak—see the discussion just below), replies with the opening words of a famous medieval hymn sung in the mass for the dead: "The day of wrath, that dreadful day" (line 172). (Conceivably—from the context—Melville may have mistaken "Dies iræ" to mean "God of wrath.")

3.19.179   the Matterhorn] This simile in which Mortmain is "Fitful revealed" (line 176) may owe something to Melville's passage through the Alps in 1857; though he did not mention the Matterhorn in his journal he did cross Lake Maggiore about 35 miles away (Journals, p. 124) and could possibly have seen the mountain in its "cragged austerity."

3.20.1   Seedsmen of old Saturn's land] Saturnus, a mythical king of Italy, who brought agriculture, civilization, and a golden age, and whose name may be derived from the root of the Latin verb sero, "to sow."

3.20.6   Soldan] Sultan.

3.20.35   the lesson Joel taught] See the discussion at 1.28.24; again, the Hebraic-Greek contrast, with Titian (1477–1576), famous for his superb rendition of flesh, adding a Renaissance dimension to the Greek mythological creatures with goat's feet, pointed ears, and wineskins (line 37). For Melville's acquaintance with Titian's works in Italy in 1857 see *Journals*, pp. 109, 111, 115, 118, 119, 122, 483–84, 493–94, 504, 506.

3.21.72   Achor's glen] See 2.14.

3.21.80   old Duns Scotus] The great thirteenth-century theologian, who countered Thomism with Scotism.

3.21.201–2   Bacon . . . / In one ripe tract] Sir Francis Bacon's *De Sapientia Veterum* (1609), translated as *The Wisdom of the Ancients* (1619), a study of 31 Greek myths which are "explained" in terms of Bacon's own philosophical views.

3.21.240   blanks] Of all the corrections and revisions entered by Melville in Copy B at Harvard (see pp. 849–63), this substitution of "blanks" for "banks" is the only one marked in the copy of *Clarel* Melville inscribed to his wife (Copy D at Harvard; see pp. 865–66): in that copy, the "l" and a slash are entered in the right margin of p. 395, next to this line.

3.21.253   The Stoic] The great school begun by Zeno about 310 B.C., in which a severe philosophy of wisdom, virtue, and self-control takes the place of religion.

3.21.279   by Nile] Melville's visit to the Nile near Cairo in 1857 is the source of his comment "From waste to garden but a stile" (line 280): "Line of desert & verdure, plain as line between good & evil. An instant collision of the two elements. A long billow of desert forever hovers as in act of breaking, upon the verdure of Egypt. Grass near the pyramids, but will not touch them—as if in fear or awe of them. . . . The Sphynx. back to desert & face to verdure" (*Journals*, p. 76).

3.21.294   Joined Werter's] Refers to Goethe's *Die Leiden des jungen Werthers* (1774), the most famous early Romantic document of self-torture, followed by the stormy and unconventional works of Byron (line 293) and Shelley (drowned near Pisa in 1822; see *White-Jacket*, chap. 65, p. 271)—all now gone by and out of fashion, says Derwent, as are the views of Rolfe and Vine—like prints struck from well-worn plates. The variant spelling "Werter" occurred in some early editions and in *The Confidence-Man*, chap. 4, p. 19.

3.22.8   Chapels and oratories] The 1856–57 journal notes "Went into chapel &c—little hermitages in rock" (p. 84; "little hermitages" later underlined in red pencil). No written source has been located for either the chapel or the medallion described in this canto.

3.23.39   worse than Arian] The famous heresy of Arius in the fourth century that Christ was not divine.

3.23.61   The Fathers] St. John Chrysostom, St. Basilius (or Basil), and St. Athanasius were all fourth-century fathers of the Greek Church. The first edition's "Athanese" is here emended as a misreading for the standard French form of the name, "Athanase" (line 63), which Melville probably used to suit the meter.

3.23.102   These dry bones] Ezek. 37.1–5: "The hand of the Lord was upon me . . . and set me down in the midst of the valley which was full of bones . . . and, lo, they were very dry. And he said unto me, Son of man, can these bones live? . . . Thus saith the Lord God unto these bones; Behold, I will cause breath to enter into you, and ye shall live . . . ." 2 Kings 13.21 tells of a man who came to life when he was buried in Elisha's tomb and touched his bones (lines 119–21).

3.24.17   The long-sword Cid] The Cid (1040?–99), great national hero of Spain during the Moorish wars, was first buried in the monastery of San Pedro (line 16), later in nearby Burgos. The epic *Poema del Cid* (ca. 1140), and many legends, plays, songs, poems, and an opera have idealized him.

3.24.92   Die—to die!] This phrase and the next line are an obvious play on Hamlet's most famous soliloquy, in 3.1 (for Melville's edition see the discussion at 1.29.51).

3.25.30   St. Saba's fount] Among the miracles attributed to St. Saba (also "Sabas" or "Sabbas," 439–532), the anchorite who founded the monastery, was the creation of a fountain "in a narrow cave in the bottom of the glen below the convent walls" (Murray, I, 205). See also the discussion at 3.25.59.

3.25.32   Down, plummets down] The descent of Derwent and the Lesbian has a parallel in the 1856–57 journal: "At dusk went down by many stone steps & through mysterious passages to cave & trap doors & hole in wall—ladder—ledge after ledge—winding—to bottom of Brook Kedron—sides of ravine all caves of recluses—Monastery a congregation of stone eyries, enclosed with wall" (p. 84).

3.25.43   to Avernus] Here, a mock descent into hell, with a later reference to Virgil (line 80), who served Dante (line 81) as guide in *The Inferno* (*Hell* in the Cary translation Melville owned—see the discussion at 1.36.29). In 1857 Melville took a tour through an Augustan tunnel linking Lake Avernus with another lake: "Curious they should have fabled hell here. . . . Descent to infernal regions, guide said . . . Infernal enough.—What in God's name were such places made for, & why?" (*Journals*, p. 104; see also p. 461).

Peter Toft, *The Holy Palm, Mar Saba, Palestine.* Courtesy of the Berkshire Athenæum.

Thomas Allom, *The Monastery at Santa Saba*. Courtesy of the Berkshire Athenæum.

3.25.47–60   "'Tis . . . believer?"] Since no speaker is directly assigned to these two speeches, it is difficult to tell that it is the Lesbian who, most likely, offers his cup (lines 47–48) and certainly comments on his own aversion to water (lines 49–60). Although it is possible that Derwent offers the cup and the Lesbian responds, the first-edition reading (which, with a colon at line 49, suggests there is no change of speaker) makes good sense, and in any case no feasible emendation would clearly identify the speaker.

3.25.57   Terrace on terrace] From the 1856–57 journal: "numerous terraces, balconies" (p. 84; later underlined in red pencil).

3.25.59   Our famous palm] This central symbol of Part 3 in the remaining cantos is mentioned briefly in the 1856–57 journal: "solitary Date Palm mid-way in precipice" (p. 84; later underlined in red pencil). Chateaubriand, p. 259, was greatly struck by its "verdure" in the midst of "such dreary sterility," and Curzon (chap. 14) was told it was "endowed with miraculous properties." The tradition of the monastery was that it had been planted by St. Saba himself (line 64; see the discussion at 3.25.30). The artist Peter Toft, a friend of Melville's later years (see *Log*, II, 799, 801, 820), painted a large brush and ink watercolor in shades of brown on a beige ground (11 by 15 in.), with his title "The Holy Palm, Mar Saba, Palestine"(reproduced on p. 813). In the same brown ink as his title are his notation in the lower left "Mar Saba / P. Toft / 82", which may be his postdating of the work, and his inscription at the lower right "In memoriam of Herman Melville", which he must have made after Melville's death in September, 1891. Perhaps Toft presented the picture to Mrs. Melville in 1892 with two slips of paper (now in HCL-M) bearing his copy of Vine's soliloquy to the Palm and signed "P. Toft, New York, '92, Denmark". This watercolor and three others by Toft which Melville owned are now in the Berkshire Athenæum, Pittsfield, Mass. Also in this collection is an engraving owned by Melville (reproduced opposite) on which he wrote "Gorge of Cedron." For this and the works by Toft see Wallace (cited in the discussion at 1.6.28), pp. 76–78, 86, and figs. 8 and 11.

3.25.65   Indeed] The four lines beginning here are Derwent's only commentary on the Palm. Henry W. Wells, in *The American Way of Poetry* (New York: Columbia University Press, 1943), p. 84, commends the final cantos of Part 3 as the "most sustained passage" of "metaphysical and symbolical expression" in the poem, noting that five major characters successively confront the Palm: Derwent (here), Vine (3.26), Mortmain (3.28), Rolfe (3.29), and Clarel (3.30). The device is an interesting parallel to chap. 99 in *Moby-Dick*, "The Doubloon."

3.25.73   the *laura*] Curzon (chap. 15) explains in his section on Mar Saba: "The word laura, which is often met with in histories of the first five centuries after Christ, signifies, when applied to monastic institutions, a number of separate cells, each inhabited by a single hermit or anchorite, in contradistinction to a convent or monastery, which was called a coenobium, where the monks lived together in one building under the rule of a superior."

3.25.98   *Lachryma Christi*] "Tears of Christ": the famous red or white wine from the slopes of Vesuvius (see the discussion at 1.29.30). Cyril plays with the words.

3.25.120   A great bird] Shortly before his death, Ahab's hat was stolen by a "black hawk"—"one of those red-billed savage sea-hawks" (cf. 3.27.9)—who then dropped it "from that vast height into the sea" (*Moby-Dick*, chap. 130, p. 539).

3.25.140   these eagles-gier] The gier eagle which has stolen Mortmain's cap (cf. Agath: 3.27) is probably an Egyptian vulture; the gier eagle is twice mentioned in the Bible, as unclean for eating.

3.26.2   terce, sext, nones] In monastic life, the third (9:00 A.M.), fourth (noon), and fifth (3:00 P.M.) periods of the day, canonical hours set aside for devotions; vespers (line 3) is the early evening sixth period.

3.26.11   Achmed with his hundred brothers] The allusion is unlocated.

3.26.41   on Delos] Apollo was born on the island of Delos, and his temple was there.

3.26.53   Talassa's year] Unlocated; cf. "thalassa," Greek for "sea."

3.26.63   the Seraphim] Celestial beings hovering about the throne of God in Isaiah's vision (Isa. 6).

3.27.9   a big bird, red-billed and black] See the discussion at 3.25.120.

3.27.54   Your friend there] Mortmain.

3.27.61   Sabaïtes'] I.e., of Saba-ites—dwellers at Mar Saba.

3.27.71   bankrupt man of Uz] Job 1.1. For line 73 see the discussion at 2.25.56.

3.27.113   these writings on the wall] Lines 123–27 recall Satan's lament in *Paradise Lost* (4.75–78; for Melville's edition see the discussion at 1.1.24):

> my self am Hell;
> And in the lowest deep a lower deep
> Still threat'ning to devour me opens wide,
> To which the hell I suffer seems a heaven.

Lines 129–32 relate to Melville's unpublished poem "The American Aloe on Exhibition" (in the NN volume *BILLY BUDD, SAILOR and Other Late Manuscripts*). Lines 135–38 are perhaps an oblique reference to the story of Samson killing the young lion and returning to take honey from the carcass (Judg. 14). Lines 149–50 slightly resemble the inscriptions over the gateway to hell in canto 3 of *The Inferno* (for Melville's edition see the discussions at 1.36.29 and 3.25.43).

3.27.133   Nostradamus] Celebrated French astrologer of the sixteenth century, author of the book of prophecies entitled *Centuries* (1555). The first edition's "Nostrodamus" is emended as a misreading of Melville's hand.

3.27.162   ninth part] I.e., small fraction, an expression possibly suggested by "I'll cavil on the ninth part of a hair" (Shakespeare, *1 Henry IV*, 3.1).

3.27.166   Og] The Arnaut; see the discussion at 3.11.189.

3.27.172   leave] For other examples of the subjunctive, see the discussion at 2.22.47.

3.27.185   the dervishes] Members of Moslem ascetic sects famous for their dancing, spinning, whirling, or howling. In Constantinople Melville noted in his 1856–57 journal: "the Dancing Dervishes. Saw their convent. Reminded me of the Shakers" (p. 62).

3.27.190   danced before the Ark] 2 Samuel 6.12–16 tells how David "danced before the Lord with all his might" when the ark of the covenant was brought into the city. The "cheeses" (line 188) are low curtsies; "pigeon-wings" (line 192) are particular figures in American folk dancing.

3.28.1   "See him] Mortmain is watching the Lesbian's dance across the gulf that separates them. He does not see the Palm until line 50.

3.28.7   *Knowledge is power*] Mortmain scorns Francis Bacon's apothegm, which was taken as a motto of the American lyceum movement (see also the discussion at 3.30.50). That "true lore / Is impotent for earth" (lines 8–9) is the Plinlimmon theme from *Pierre* (bk. 14). The italicized quotation (lines 9–10) is a paraphrase from Luke 23.35–37 of the jeers and taunts hurled at Jesus on the cross.

3.28.35–36   the hand / Gnawed in the dream] See 3.15.17–20.

3.28.58–59   Gabriel bore / To Mary] The angel's visit to Mary is in Luke 1.26–38; the lily-rod (line 58) is probably from one of the famous Annunciation paintings.

3.28.91   thou Paraclete] The Holy Spirit as intercessor.

3.29.0   ROLFE AND THE PALM] The canto is of extreme interest as a late commentary on Melville's Marquesan adventure of 1842. The details compare closely with the account in *Typee*: the dangerous descent into the valley, the being taken as a god (cf. "Of Rama," 1.32), the bathing girls, the peaceful life, the effort to prevent escape, the escape. The Eden reference (line 46) parallels the Paradise-Pacific theme stated at the end of the 1856–57 journal (see "Miscellaneous Entries," *Journals*, p. 154), with the open admission that Rolfe is still haunted by the experience.

3.29.11   Mother-Cary's bird] Mother Cary's (or Carey's) chicken, sailor term for the small (stormy) petrel. Melville may have seen such birds nestled in the waves thus on his own three passages of Cape Horn in 1841, 1844, and 1860. Here, this Cape Horn image, one of the poem's most elaborate Homeric similes, leads nicely into Rolfe's remembrances of a Pacific-island adventure.

3.29.26   Man's work or nature's] Murray, I, 204, reports: "the other buildings are so dispersed along the whole side from the summit to the bottom of the ravine, that it is almost impossible to tell how much is masonry, and how much nature."

3.29.38   Bandusia fount] The *Bandusia Fons* in Apulia, celebrated in Horatian odes. See Shurr's *Mystery of Iniquity* (cited in the discussion at 2.14.0), pp. 95–96.

3.29.42   Soolee] Perhaps the Sooloo (or "Sulu") archipelago, an island group of the Philippines, or perhaps an invented Polynesian place name.

3.29.43   Indian Arcady] From Pacific Edens Rolfe slips into his favorite classical vocabulary: Arcadia (toward India), symbol of pastoral beauty; "Hesperian orchards" (line 54), the fabled western garden of golden apples; Iris (line 56), goddess of the rainbow; nereids (line 60), lovely sea nymphs;

and Pan (line 81), god of pastoral life. The canto is thus a classic threnody (line 81) to a retreating dream. If the Palm means the hope of heaven to others, to Rolfe it means the memory of paradise lost.

3.29.47   old Mendanna's sea] Alvaro Mendaña de Neira, the sixteenth-century explorer who discovered and named the Marquesas Islands. Melville alluded to his voyages familiarly in *Typee*, chap. 1, p. 5, and chap. 25, p. 183, also in *White-Jacket*, chap. 76, p. 323, *Moby-Dick*, chap. 57, p. 271, and obliquely in "Benito Cereno," NN *Piazza Tales* volume, p. 74.

3.29.62   Puck's substantiated scene] A coming-true of the dreamworld manipulated for Oberon, king of fairyland, by Puck, the folk imp in Shakespeare's *A Midsummer Night's Dream* (for Melville's edition see the discussion at 1.29.51).

3.30.23–24   ledge-built balcony / Inrailed] The 1856–57 journal contains the germ of this phrase and the canto: "balustrade of iron—lonely monks. black-birds—feeding with bread" (p. 84; later underlined in red pencil—see the textual notes). The Reverend Andrew Thomson, *In the Holy Land* (London and New York: Nelson, 1874; later printings 1875, 1876, 1883), p. 197, says the monks "were able, by a familiar whistle, to bring up [birds] from the neighbouring gorge. One beautiful creature, as large as a thrush, with black plumage and yellow wings, perched on the fingers of one of the monks and fed there." Thomson's book has a frontispiece engraving of the Saba tower and gorge.

3.30.50   above the Plato mind] For this estimate of Plato, see Merton M. Sealts, Jr., "Melville and the Platonic Tradition," *Pursuing Melville* (Madison: University of Wisconsin Press, 1982), p. 332. Cf. 4.20.96–99.

3.30.62   Mary, to fulfill the law] Luke 2.22–24 tells how Mary brought a pair of turtledoves to the Temple as a sacrifice in the purification rites following the birth of Jesus; this was the Law according to Leviticus 12.

3.30.67   where Enoch roves] Gen. 5.24: "And Enoch walked with God: and he was not; for God took him."

3.30.69   Nor myrtle here] Again the classical-Christian contrast. The myrtle, held sacred to Venus (line 65) in ancient times, is played against the highly symbolic Palm (line 69) of Christendom.

3.30.75   Fomalhaut] First magnitude star; identified as part of the Southern constellation Piscis Austrinus by Melville's brother-in-law John C. Hoadley in his annotated copy of *Clarel* (see p. 664 above).

3.30.106   old hermit-rhyme] The manuscript was written by a Greek-Christian ("Thebæan": line 108) in the third century (time of the emperor Decius: line 107). An ascetic tract on woman-as-trouble, it cites: "David's son" (line 109), David and Bathsheba's illegitimate child, who died as their punishment (2 Sam. 11–12); "he of Dan" (line 109), the son of Jacob by his wife Rachel's handmaid (Gen. 30.4–6); "him . . . that fled the bride" (line 110), unidentified; "And Job" (line 111): "Then said his wife unto him, Dost thou still retain thine integrity? curse God, and die" (Job 2.9). Slight wonder the good monk wished "The rib restored to Adam's side" (line 113: Gen. 2.21–24).

3.30.135   Bethel-stair of ledges] The image (it comes back twice in the next canto) is triple: Bethel is on a steep ridge; Bethel is where Jacob saw the "ladder set up on the earth, and the top of it reached to heaven: and behold the angels of God ascending and descending on it" (Gen. 28.12); and Bethel means "The house of God." Henry W. Wells, in *The American Way of Poetry* (New York: Columbia University Press, 1943), p. 85, notes that at this moment Clarel "perceives in the sweep of a single glance both the palm itself and the three persons really seriously concerned with it. . . . Even in many pages it would be impossible to analyze in this fugue-like passage the nuances of the poet's symbolism."

3.30.150   as David sings] 2 Sam. 1.26: "I am distressed for thee, my brother Jonathan [line 151]: very pleasant hast thou been unto me: thy love to me was wonderful, passing the love of women."

3.31.1   (if Luke attest)] Luke 1.28: "And the angel came in unto her, and said, Hail, thou that art highly favoured, the Lord is with thee: blessed art thou among women." This completes a cycle of three recent references to Mary touching on the annunciation, purification, and now immaculateness (cf. 3.28.58–60; 3.30.62); they prepare for Bethlehem. "HOLIDAME" (line 6), applied to Mary, by folk-etymology, is a variant of "Halidom": holy place or holiness.

3.31.22   turn the cheek] Luke 6.29: "And unto him that smiteth thee on the one cheek offer also the other."

3.31.35   the Founder's words] Matt. 22.30: "For in the resurrection they neither marry, nor are given in marriage, but are as the angels of God in heaven," said Jesus.

3.32.5   white shreds of shroud] Completing the cycle that began when Mortmain first looked from Achor down across cloud-swept Siddim (2.14.69–72).

3.32.15–16   the Gileadite / In Obadiah's way] 1 Kings 18.7: "And as Obadiah was in the way, behold, Elijah met him: and he knew him, and fell on his face, and said, Art thou that my lord Elijah?"

3.32.37–38   palm-boughs sway / In Saint John's heaven] Rev. 7.9: the multitude about the throne of the Lamb, "clothed with white robes, and palms in their hands."

3.32.64   healing hills of Gilead] Cf. Jer. 46.11: "Go up into Gilead, and take balm . . . and in vain shalt thou use many medicines; for thou shalt not be cured."

3.32.69   without the walls] Mortmain is buried as he had lived—in alienation; the serenity that surrounded his death gives way to savagely Darwinian images.

PART 4

4.1.3   Three mitered kings] The unnamed wise men of Matthew 2.1–12. Mandeville says (Wright, p. 163): "and the Jews call them in Hebrew Appelius, Amerrius, and Damasus. These three kings offered to our Lord gold, incense, and myrrh; and they met together by a miracle of God, for they met together in a city in India called Cassak." Though Bethlehem was 53 days away, the wise men reached there in 4—"and that was a great miracle." No source has been located for Melville's spellings of their names.

4.1.51   Pisa's Tower] Melville had seen the famed Leaning Tower in 1857 (*Journals*, p. 114); for a mention of the adjacent baptistery see also the discussion at 2.27.20–21 above.

4.1.70   Chiron] The most celebrated of the Centaurs, who were half horse and half man.

4.1.99   fair] Why the "South-West" should be called "fair" in this context is not clear; possibly the word is a misreading of "far" (meaning "far-away") in Melville's hand.

4.1.106   the Epirot] The Arnaut.

4.1.141   the Moor's Tower] The minaret of the twelfth-century Moorish mosque became the tower (known as La Giralda) of the fifteenth-to-sixteenth-century cathedral of Seville; within is a spiral ramp to the platform at an elevation of seventy meters, which commands a famous view.

4.1.151   palmer-worm] An American pest that skeletonizes apple leaves; here it plays also on the word "palmer."

4.1.157   Naaman in his leprous plight] 2 Kings 5.9: "So Naaman came with his horses and with his chariot, and stood at the door of the house of Elisha"; after protest he did as Elisha told him, and was cured of his leprosy.

4.1.160   the Promethean ledge] The great ledge to which Prometheus was bound while vultures daily ate out his liver; this for stealing fire from the gods.

4.1.187   the wreck—Jerusalem!] This major culmination of the theme of the Ruined City, here and in the opening lines of the next canto, was twice recorded in the 1856–57 journal: "On way to Bethelam saw Jerusalem from distance—unless knew it, could not have recognized it—looked exactly like arid rocks" (p. 84). An added note at the back of that journal notebook reads: "Jerusalem seen from Bethalem Road" (p. 154)—which was later lined through in black pencil, possibly after using here.

4.2.17   city St. John saw] Rev. 21: sardonyx (line 18) was one of the twelve foundations; ruby (line 18) was not (see the NOTE ON THE TEXT, p. 684). Monte Rosa (line 19) is the second highest peak of the Alps. For Patmos (line 21) see the discussion at 1.35.36.

4.2.27   The Illyrian bold] The Arnaut, sweeping about like "Prince Charlie's men" (line 30) in the ballad.

4.2.51   A crucifixion in tattoo] This first tattoo puts Agath in the company of two other old sailors in Melville's writings. Jarl, the taciturn sea-Viking of *Mardi*, had on his arm a blue and vermillion tattoo of "our Saviour on the Cross" (chap. 47, p. 147). Another old sailor, the title character of "Daniel Orme," one of Melville's final portraits, bore on his chest an indigo and vermillion tattoo of the "cross of the Passion, . . . often found tattooed on the sailor, upon the fore-arm generally, sometimes . . . upon the trunk" (in *BILLY BUDD, SAILOR and Other Late Manuscripts*).

4.2.68–69   The *Ensign* . . . Jerusalem's] Evidently this tattooed "Ensign" (whether taken from a flag, coat of arms, or other symbolic insignia) held some unusual significance for Melville, because he not only devoted this entire canto, titled "The Ensign" to it, but also (presumably) called for it to be on the covers of his subsidized book, and supplied the variant ensign that appeared there (see p. 674 above). Despite extensive library research and consultation with various experts, the sole verification so far found that the palm-leaves, cross, star, and crowns constitute the Jerusalem Ensign occurs (in reference only to tattoos) in John W. Carswell, *Coptic Tattoo Designs*, second ed. (Beirut: American University of Beirut, 1958), where the same design as on the covers of *Clarel* is discussed and shown in three illustrations of tattoo designs centuries old, one (fig. 1, p. xxv, reproduced below) showing both the ensign on a left arm and a crucifixion on a right arm (see the preceding discussion). The editors have been unable to confirm Rolfe's assertion (line 70) that the ensign was "Coeval with King Baldwin's sway" (1100ff.; see the discussion at 1.3.177) or the specific reference of each symbol as pointed out by Derwent in lines 131–35. Furthermore, the ensign as described in the canto has curious differences from the one pictured here and on the front covers of the first edition: first, the symbols are described in "upside down" order in the canto (lines 54–58), and second, the "equi-limbed small cross" in the canto (line 56) does not match this variation

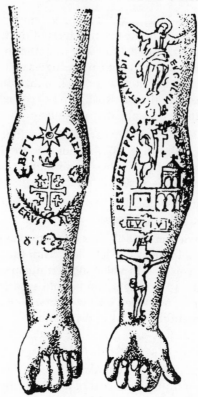

Fig. 1 Tattooed arms of 17th.
century pilgrim from Hamburg.

of the well-known Jerusalem cross, which has smaller equi-limbed crosses in each angle of the central equi-limbed cross, making five crosses in all. It would appear that while writing this canto Melville cannot have had before him, or clearly in mind, the same ensign that appears on the covers of the book, and he did not revise the canto to fit that variation of the ensign. Unquestionably, Melville knew the description and one meaning of the Jerusalem cross, apart from the whole ensign. In his 1856–57 journal, he made a later notation in pencil: "See page 124 of Saunders for curious description of Jerusalem. (Jerusalem Cross 5 Wounds) P. 124" (see *Journals*, textual note at 84.28). As R. S. Forsythe discovered—and reported in his review of Raymond Weaver's *Journal Up the Straits* for *American Literature*, VIII (March, 1936), 93—"Saunders" was in fact George Sandys. Melville may have been first directed to Sandys by Bayard Taylor's *The Lands of the Saracen* (New York: Putnam, 1855), p. 350. The following passage appears (with slight variations) on p. 124 of the editions of 1652, 1658, 1670, and 1673 of Sandys's

A Relation of a Journey Begun An: Dom: 1610: "They bare five crosses gules [red], in form of that which is at this day called the *Ierusalem* crosse; representing thereby the five wounds that violated the body of our Saviour." The tattooing of pilgrims is reported, for example, by the seventeenth-century traveler Henry Maundrell: "pilgrims . . . have their arms mark'd with the usual ensigns of Jerusalem" (*A Journey from Aleppo to Jerusalem at Easter A.D. 1697* [1810; reprinted with introduction and notes by David Howell, Beirut: Khayats, 1963], p. 100) and by Thackeray: "Some worthies there are who drive a good trade by tattooing pilgrims with the five crosses, the arms of Jerusalem; under which the name of the city is punctured in Hebrew, with the auspicious year of the Hadgi's visit. Several of our fellow travellers submitted to this queer operation, and will carry, to their grave, this relic of their journey. Some of them had engaged a servant, a man, at Beyrout, who had served as a lad on board an English ship in the Mediterranean. Above his tattooage of the five crosses, the fellow had a picture of two hearts united, and the pathetic motto, 'Betsy, my dear.' . . . The beads and tattooing, however, seem essential ceremonies attendant on the Christian pilgrim's visits; for many hundreds of years, doubtless, the palmers have carried off with them these simple reminiscences of the sacred city. That symbol has been engraven upon the arms of how many Princes, Knights, and Crusaders!" (*Notes of a Journey from Cornhill to Grand Cairo*, by M. A. Titmarsh [London: Chapman & Hall, 1846], pp. 213–14). See *Journals*, p. 432, the discussion at 84.28, with the mistaken statement that the Timoneer in *Clarel* bears such a cross.

4.2.74   Java-Head] At the northwest corner of the island of Java, at the approach to the "narrow straits of Sunda," is "that bold green promontory, known to seamen as Java Head" (*Moby-Dick*, chap. 87, p. 380).

4.2.112–13   Temple round / In London] Melville's 1849–50 journal records: "to the Temple Church to hear the music. Saw the 10 Crusaders— those who had been to the Holy Land, with their legs crossed" (p. 16; see also pp. 281–82, with illustration). See also Part 1 of "The Paradise of Bachelors and the Tartarus of Maids," NN *Piazza Tales* volume, pp. 316–23.

4.2.181   Valhalla's hall] Here went the souls of Norse heroes slain in battle.

4.3.0   THE ISLAND] See Sketch Fourth of "The Encantadas" for a further description of Narborough, the volcanic island in the Galápagos to which Agath here refers (NN *Piazza Tales* volume, pp. 139–41). The first two sketches (pp. 125–33) there are eloquent on "the monstrous tortoise drear!" (line 61).

4.3.11   It burns by night—by day the cloud] Exod. 13.21: "And the Lord went before them by day in a pillar of a cloud, to lead them the way; and by night in a pillar of fire, to give them light. . . ."

4.3.44   in his calenture] Delirious fever.

4.3.55   old skulls of Anaks] See the discussion at 3.14.66.

4.5.47   Varus' legions] Publius Quintilius Varus, governor of Germany under Augustus, who with his three legions was utterly destroyed by the barbarians in a three-day battle.

4.5.53   Parsee] Sun-worshiper. A Parsee becomes a major character in *Moby-Dick*, from chap. 48 forward (see p. 871 in that volume).

4.5.77   Bridge of Sighs] In Venice, between the Doge's palace where prisoners were sentenced and the prison to which they were led over it; Melville saw it in 1857 (*Journals*, p. 119).

4.5.87   A paper pact] The Constitution of the United States.

4.5.98–104   That Pamphylian / . . . earth.] These lines give a quite loose version of Socrates' "fable" of Er the Pamphylian in Book X of Plato's *Republic*. (The name is rendered "Erus" in both the Taylor-Sydenham translation Melville used in *Mardi* and the Bohn Classical Library translation by Charles Davis he probably acquired in 1850 or 1851 and quoted in *Billy Budd, Sailor*; see Sealts, "Melville and the Platonic Tradition," cited in the discussion at 3.30.50 above, pp. 293, 299.)

4.5.127   Mary-Land] Named after "heaven's gracious Queen" (line 126), the Virgin Mary, Queen of Heaven; and "Britain's princess" (line 127), Queen Henrietta Maria (1609–69), wife of Charles I. The ships *Ark* and *Dove* (line 116) arrived in the spring of 1634. George Calvert (1580?–1632), first baron Baltimore, had won the charter for the new colony (line 128).

4.5.131   under Tilly's great command] Johann Tserclaes, count of Tilly (1559–1632), was a German general of the Thirty Years War. Melville wrote this phrase (without an accompanying page number) in his list at the front of Copy B at Harvard (see pp. 851 and 856 below). Since there is no difference between Melville's inscription and the printed text of this phrase, the reason for Melville's noting this phrase is not clear. Perhaps the note was to remind him that he wished to think further about the wording; or perhaps he meant to check on the dating of Tilly's command.

4.5.148   holding slaves] Ungar's version of where the "iniquity" (line 149) lies agrees with Mortmain's (2.36.76ff.).

4.5.178   Rizpah] 2 Samuel 21.1–11 tells of her steadfastness in guarding the seven hanged corpses of Saul's sons (two born of Rizpah) from the birds by day and the beasts by night.

4.6.1   Over uplands now] The 1856–57 journal notes: "Over lofty hills to Bethalem.—on a hill" (p. 84), which keys the opening line and Derwent's "What other hill?" in line 29. The illustration opposite of Bethlehem is from Thomson, II, 504.

VIEW OF BETHLEHEM.

4.6.20   terraces, which stair by stair] Murray, I, 207: "The terraces . . . sweep in graceful curves round the ridge, regular as stairs."

4.6.37   Mary with the spikenard] John 12.3: "Then took Mary a pound of ointment of spikenard, very costly, and anointed the feet of Jesus, and wiped his feet with her hair: and the house was filled with the odour of the ointment."

4.6.48   Nehemiah's proffer] 1.36.58ff.

4.7.5   Grim abbey on the wave afloat] Whereas in "Benito Cereno" the ship-as-monastery is the image, here it is the monastery-as-ship. See the NN *Piazza Tales* volume, p. 48 and *passim*.

4.7.18   the girt Capuchin] Distinguished by the long pointed cowl; Capuchins, a branch of the Franciscans, controlled the Latin monastery in Bethlehem.

4.7.39   Mary found no room] Luke 2.7.

4.7.86   The compline service] Last liturgical prayers, after vespers; the seventh canonical hour.

4.7.96   Job's chambers of the South] Job 9.8–9. Possibly a constellation, or the vast spaces of the southern hemisphere. Job asks how man can contend with God "which alone spreadeth out the heavens, and treadeth on the waves of the sea. Which maketh Arcturus [line 95: a first magnitude star], Orion, the Pleiades, and the chambers of the south."

4.8.2   old Sylvanus (stories say)] Sylvanus was the Roman wood god. Henry F. Pommer, in *Milton and Melville* (Pittsburgh: University of Pittsburgh Press, 1950), p. 136, has the key: Milton's account of the exiling of pagan deities in "On the Morning of Christ's Nativity." Melville's copy of Milton (see the discussion at 1.1.24) confirms Pommer's point: cf. line 3 here ("The oracles adrift were hurled") with line 173 of the poem ("The oracles are dumb"), which Melville marked with an "x" and annotated: "Plutarch on the cessation of Oracles".

4.9.22   The Valley of the Shepherds] Melville's name for the scene of Luke 2.10 (line 36). The shekinah (line 46) in Jewish theology is the radiance surrounding the divine presence; cf. the last stanza of "In the Desert" (*Timoleon*; NN *Published Poems*, p. 318):

> Holy, holy, holy Light!
> Immaterial incandescence,
> Of God the effluence of the essence,
> Shekinah, intolerably bright!

4.9.48   a little St. John boy] Dressed like John the Baptist.

4.9.67   Lot and Abraham] The speech that follows (lines 69–79) is from Genesis 13.8–9, 11, almost verbatim.

4.9.86   Eden's placed not far] Eden's site was much disputed in the nineteenth century; scholars generally agreed it was probably in Palestine, though not necessarily near Bethlehem.

4.9.112   *As cruel as a Turk*] A recurrent theme for several cantos, and one that Melville had used in his 1860 lecture "Traveling" (NN *Piazza Tales* volume, p. 422): "The Spanish Matador, who devoutly believes in the proverb, 'Cruel as Turk,' goes to Turkey, sees that people are kind to all animals; sees docile horses, never balky, gentle, obedient, exceedingly intelligent, yet *never beaten*; and comes home to his bull-fights with a very different impression of his own humanity." Cf. lines 105–7.

4.9.133   How many Hughs of Lincoln] Legendarily, in Lincoln a boy named Hugh was kidnapped, tortured, and crucified by Jews. Chaucer used the legend in the tale told by the Prioress.

4.10.7   an ancient monument] No description has been located in travel literature.

4.10.27   Shearer . . . dumb] Cf. Isaiah 53.7.

4.10.64   Toward Mecca] In his 1856–57 journal, Melville wrote: "(Passed over Bethalem hills—where shepherds were watching their flocks, (as of old) but a Moslem with back to Jerusalem (face to Mecca) praying" (p. 84).

4.10.76   the humble publican] Luke 18.10–14 gives the parable of the self-righteous Pharisee and the humble publican.

4.10.93   The ship in manifest] A list of ship's cargo, signed by the master, for the information and use of a customs inspector such as Herman Melville.

4.10.111   Louis plied the rod] See the discussion at 2.13.8.

4.10.114–23   Charlemagne? / . . . ceremonial clings] Charlemagne was crowned emperor by Pope Leo III in Rome on Christmas Day, A.D. 800, though only legendarily with the crown described in lines 117–21, which is the actual tenth-century imperial crown now among the treasures of the Neue Hofburg, Vienna. In the sixteenth century Dürer executed an idealized portrait of Charlemagne wearing it. Melville's source for details in this passage is unlocated.

4.10.168   once in York] Melville's 1856–57 journal mentions leaving York on a rainy day (*Journals*, p. 50).

4.12.0   OF POPE AND TURK] The canto stems from contemporary interest in the Crimean War (Melville reached Constantinople only seven months after the 1856 treaty ending it, and his 1856–57 journal notes several military sights; see pp. 52, 57, 69, 79, 390, 394–95); from "The Turkish Question" in general; and from his own interest in real, as distinct from stereotyped, ethics. See Murray, I, xlvi–xlvii, for a discussion of Turkish character. When he was in Smyrna in 1856 Melville "Heard a good deal about the commerce of England with Turkey" (*Journals*, p. 70).

4.12.29   Dismembered Poland] The third partitioning of Poland among Russia, Austria, and Prussia, in 1795, which left Poland broken for a century; the insurrection of 1831 (line 45) was protested by the pope because of announced Russian hostility to Catholicism.

4.12.38   Urquhart's vanity] David Urquhart (1805–77) conducted several crucial diplomatic missions to the Middle East for England. A critic of his government's stand on the Crimean War, in his books he argued for Turkish autonomy.

CAVE OF THE NATIVITY.

4.12.72   Ormus] In *Paradise Lost* Satan sat upon a throne which "Out-shone the wealth of Ormus and of Ind" (2.2; this line not marked in Mel-ville's annotated copy—see the discussion at 1.1.24); once one of the world's richest cities, Ormus (now "Ormuz" or "Hormuz") went to ruins. Here the term may be generic for Persia. Selim (line 74) was the name of a series of Turkish sultans up to the nineteenth century: perhaps here generic for Turkey.

4.13.0   THE CHURCH OF THE STAR] Melville's brief jottings at Bethlehem in the 1856–57 journal mention the "monk" (line 15), the "lamps" in the place of Nativity (lines 113–15), "Constantine's mother" Helena (line 144), and the tombs of the saints Paula and Jerome (4.16.1–6): "old chapel of Helena. . . . In chapel, monk (Latin) took us down into cave after cave,—tomb of saints—lights burning (with olive oil) till came to place of Nativity (many lamps) & manger with lights" (p. 84). Detailed descriptions of the church are in Stanley, pp. 433–37, and Murray, I, 209–11; the illustration opposite is from Thomson, II, [507].

4.13.38   This Isaac] The child Isaac (Gen. 22.1–14) was about to be sacri-ficed by his father Abraham at the command of Jehovah, who called off the deed at the last moment.

4.13.45   the deep Dodona grove] The grove of beeches in Epirus, scene of the most ancient oracle of Greece (with Delphi); the parallel is one of meaning as well as chronology.

4.13.48   (if ye recall)] Rolfe's "Dead Man's Inn" of 2.15.39.

4.13.70–71   and thought / Of Baldwin] For Baldwin and Godfrey (line 72) see the discussion at 1.3.177.

4.13.105   Archimago's cave] In Spenser's *The Faerie Queene* this great enchanter has no cave; possibly Melville had in mind either the "darksome hole" of Errour (1.1.14), or, more likely, the house of Morpheus "amid the bowels of the earth" (1.1.39; for Melville's edition see the discussion at 2.1.60). The Persian Sibyl (line 107) is one of the several sibyls vaguely and darkly mentioned by ancient writers.

4.13.114   Pleiads] Commonly Pleiades: a cluster of stars in the constella-tion Taurus.

4.13.166   The first Franciscan] St. Francis of Assisi (1182–1226) becomes a central topic in these cantos. The Tuscan monk's dress has already been described (lines 17–24), and now Rolfe explains its meaning. In the next canto Salvaterra recalls Angelo Tancredi (4.14.45), a cavalier convert of Francis's who afterward wrote the saint's life. The discussion then culminates with a long tribute from Rolfe (4.14.63–82), who has probably been reading the *Little Flowers of St. Francis*, the semi-legendary fourteenth-century narrative about his deeds and disciples.

4.13.192   In Latin text] HIC DE VIRGINE MARIA JESUS CHRISTUS NATUS EST. "*Salvator Mundi*" (line 202) means "Savior of the world."

4.14.33   Ignatius] Ignatius of Loyola (1491–1556), Spanish soldier crippled for life at Pamplona, who founded the Order of the Jesuits. St. Martin (line 34) was a fourth-century French bishop who had reluctantly served in the army in youth.

4.14.96   Machiavel] The central drift of the brilliant writings of Niccolò Machiavelli (1469–1527) is a rejection of the divine concept of state or man for a harshly realistic one.

4.15.20   a Poor Clare] Member of the Order of Poor Clares founded by the friend of Francis, St. Clare of Assisi (1194–1253). The "Cordelier" (line 22) is a Franciscan (with a knotted girdle of rope). The "passion-flower" (line 29) is the genus *passiflora*, with corona taken as crown of thorns, stamens and pistil as nails, five sepals and five petals as the ten faithful apostles.

4.15.39   Hid organ-pipes] Bartlett's *Walks*, p. 209, reports an ecstatic listening to matins, hymns, and the organ here.

4.16.0   THE CONVENT ROOF] Melville had noted in his 1856–57 journal: "View from roof of chapel &c" (p. 84).

4.16.3   Paula] The tombs of Paula and Jerome near the Manger are discussed in Murray (I, 210): Paula (347–404) went to the East in 385 with the great scholar and church father, Jerome (340–420: line 6). She is considered the model of Christian widows by the Church; she came from one of Rome's first families ("Scipio's heir": line 4).

4.16.80   St. Mark's Square] In 1857 Melville had seen this great square in Venice (*Journals*, p. 118).

4.16.92   Boaz' seat] How Ruth (line 93) gleaned after the workers of Boaz in Bethlehem is told in Ruth 2.

4.16.133   thou mayst recall] But Rolfe doesn't; the masque occurred in 3.19, but the "balm-wind from Sabæa" (line 140) was on the night of the revels (3.15). Rigel and Betelgeuse are brilliant first magnitude stars (line 139), such as interested the Chaldean magi (line 138), famous for their oracular astronomy.

4.16.167   Rome's wide campania] This district outside Rome was dangerously "malarial" (line 170).

4.16.172   the broidered maniple] An ornamental band worn on the left arm near the wrist when serving at the Eucharist.

4.16.190   Pera] A suburb of Constantinople, where Melville lodged for several days in 1856 (see *Journals*, pp. 58ff., 402, and map, p. 399). The cluster of Persian elements in the following lines includes an "Astracan" (now "Astrakhan") hat (line 191), made of curly young lamb's wool, and a reference to Saadi (line 194), the Persian poet (1184–1291), whom Melville had been reading (London: Kingsbury, Parbury, & Allen, 1822; acquired 1868, annotated; Sealts 434; Bercaw 597). It culminates superbly in the abdication of Mithras ("Mythra": line 210), Persian god of the sun, light, and wisdom.

4.17.29   Prospero] A wise and good magician, like the character in Shakespeare's *The Tempest*. See Melville's 1849–51 note in a volume of his Shakespeare set (Boston: Hilliard, Gray, 1837; Sealts 460) on the contrast of goetic (black) and theurgic (white) magic (transcribed in the NN *Moby-Dick*, p. 970).

4.17.69   An Ethan Allen] Ethan Allen (1738–89) was captain of the "Green Mountain Boys" and famous for bold military operations; he was also a noted deist. See *Israel Potter* for an elaborate picture of him as folk hero. Edward Herbert, first baron Herbert of Cherbury (1583–1648), was also a distinguished soldier and deist (line 70).

4.18.4   About the fane] Helena's basilica, the Church of the Nativity, is attached to the three convents; the whole mass looms like Ehrenbreitstein (line 7), the great fortress on a rocky hill in Rhenish Prussia, which Melville saw in 1849 (*Journals*, p. 37) and alluded to in both *Moby-Dick* (chap. 8, p. 39) and *Pierre* (bk. 4, chap. 2, p. 69).

4.18.12   legendary grot] The Milk Grotto, in Murray, I, 211; its legend is as much a fairy tale as are fauns, cherubs, genii, and Oberon (line 19), king of the fairies.

4.18.36   Tahiti's beach] With this image the Pacific-Palestine themes are brought into direct opposition. On a rear leaf of his 1856–57 journal Melville wrote (possibly while composing *Clarel*): "J. C. should have appeared in Taheiti" (p. 154); see also the discussion at 3.29.0 above. "Ver" (line 39) is Latin for the season of spring, or the springtime of life. In *Omoo* Melville mentions Omai (line 43), who was taken from a neighboring island to London, feted there, and brought back (1775, 1777), and repeats like Rolfe the long-held erroneous notion of "no tides" (line 40) at Tahiti (chaps. 18, 27). Howard C. Horsford's speculations (in his 1955 edition of Melville's 1856–57 journal) on how Melville's mind may have worked in this canto are of interest (Princeton: Princeton University Press, 1955, pp. 263–64).

4.18.88   Argo] Rolfe here once again presses analogies between Homeric sites and myths and Christian traditions.

4.18.105–7   water-spout / . . . pistol-shot] Allusion to this piece of sea-lore also occurs in *Moby-Dick* (chap. 40, p. 176).

4.18.144   Voltaire] See the discussions at 1.4.7 and 2.1.92.

4.19.26   Aquaviva] Although Melville's use of "Spanish" in this non-Spanish (Italian) name, in forms of address (pairing "Señor" with "Don"), and in some words (e.g., "excellenza" at 4.19.151) is incorrect, it seems calculated for humorous effect and is in any case mostly unemendable.

4.19.33   *The Cock*] Melville's 1849–50 and 1856–57 journals indicate at least three visits to the famous old London tavern (see *Journals*, pp. 19, 41, 127).

4.19.113   imp of Semele] Since Semele was the mother of Bacchus, this may be taken as wine, and Raleigh (line 114) as tobacco.

4.19.137   great Diana of ill fame] Diana, or Artemis, had a great temple at Ephesus, showing her image with many breasts; her worship by the Ephesians (line 136) is the subject of Acts 19.23–41.

4.19.148   Cotopaxi] Volcano in Ecuador.

4.20.1   the still small voice] So God spoke to Elijah (1 Kings 19.11–12), rather than in wind, earthquake, or fire.

4.20.45   Aurelius Antonine] Marcus Aurelius Antoninus (121–80), Roman emperor (r. 161–80), whose *Meditations* express his Stoic philosophy. He is praised in Melville's poem "The Age of the Antonines" *(Timoleon;* NN *Published Poems*, pp. 286–87), which idealizes the era (96–180) as a "summit of fate" and "zenith of time, / When a pagan gentleman reigned." Melville reported in a letter of March 31, 1877, that the poem, written some time earlier, was "suggested by a passage in Gibbon (Decline & Fall)" (evidently in chap. 2 or 3). For Gibbon, see the discussion at 1.4.7.

4.20.89   them Immanuel fed] Matt. 14.13–21.

4.20.96   others] The next seven lines seem a jab at the Transcendentalists and their Neoplatonic notions; cf. the comment at 3.30.49–51. See Merton M. Sealts, Jr., "Melville and Emerson's Rainbow," *Pursuing Melville* (Madison: University of Wisconsin Press, 1982), pp. 250–77; and Harrison Hayford, "Melville's German Streak," in *A Conversation in the Life of Leland R. Phelps* (Durham, N.C.: Duke University Center for International Studies, 1987), pp. 1–16.

4.20.117   the long Tuileries] The Palais des Tuileries, formerly the royal residence, near the Louvre. Melville saw it in 1849 (*Journals*, p. 31, with illustration on p. 340); the main wing was burned in the revolution of 1871. It was seized in the first revolution, but in 1792 not 1789. The episode Melville had in mind seems somehow garbled here, and his source has not been located. The Cathedral of Notre Dame (line 124) is just upriver.

4.21.30   How profits it] "Therefore they [the wicked] say unto God, Depart from us; for we desire not the knowledge of thy ways . . . and what profit should we have, if we pray unto him?" (Job 21.14–15). Joshua made the sun stand still at Ajalon (lines 35–36) on the day of the great slaughter (Josh. 10.12–15).

4.21.51   excellence] Melville apparently thought of altering this word to "rectitude", and wrote "the rectitude of man / left to himself / Part IV." on the divisional title page to Part 3 in Copy B at Harvard. This notation was later erased; unlike many of Melville's annotations in this copy, it is not an obvious or necessary revision, and Melville himself may have erased it. NN therefore does not emend the first-edition reading. (See the NOTE ON THE TEXT, pp. 693–94.)

4.21.83–84   theme. / . . . extreme,] The first-edition punctuation marks (a comma after "theme" and a period after "extreme", leaving the following sentence beginning with a parenthetical clause) are emended thus as required to restore the obvious sense of the passage. See the NOTE ON THE TEXT, p. 690 and footnote 22.

4.21.86   an old thought] What American historians of the Frederick Jackson Turner school later called "the safety valve theory" of the frontier.

4.21.140   America!] This anomalously isolated exclamation seems best construed as the collective thought of Rolfe, Vine, and Clarel in response to Ungar's tirade, in which the phrase "your vast plains" (line 138) is addressed to them. Alternatively, the exclamation may be taken as the narrator's reflection. Conjecturally, the exclamation was meant to be the last word of Ungar's foregoing speech ("your vast plains, . . . America!"—cf. "Rome!" at 2.26.8 and "Jerusalem!" at 3.19.34), but this reading would require changes that cannot reasonably account for the first-edition punctuation and spacing.

4.22.41   *Be born anew*] John 3.7: "Ye must be born again."

4.24.25   Unkenned] The unknown singer is the Prodigal of a later canto (4.26).

4.25.54–59   And now . . . strung] The purport of this rather cryptic passage seems to be that the ensuing episode of the Prodigal Lyonese with his love songs is not designed in a wanton mode but in that of a tragicomic (satyric) afterpiece to the (perhaps tragic?) "piece / Which in these cantoes finds release" (lines 56–57). Melville may have drawn the contrast from Gibbon's *Decline and Fall*, chaps. 23 and 24, where both the wanton "grove of Daphne" (line 55) outside Antioch and the nature of "the Greek *satyrs*, a dramatic piece, which was acted after the tragedy," are discussed (see also the discussion at 1.4.7).

4.26.0   THE PRODIGAL] The next three cantos are complicated. (See the preceding discussion for their mode.) The Lyonese Frenchman with Spanish associations is somewhat prodigal in his sexuality as well as being a "prodigal son" in refuge from his Judaism. While persistently celebrating female love and beauty, he also voices his emotional response to Don Rovenna (line 95), with whom he was "Locked friends" (line 51)—"dear Rovenna" (line 147). Clarel, the night they share a room, marks his "Rich, tumbled, chestnut hood of curls," leading the narrator, in a surprising figure, to liken him to a Polynesian girl eloping with her lover to feed "on berries and on love" (lines 248–53; cf. *Omoo*, chap. 46, p. 180)—though Rolfe is the man of Polynesian memories. Clarel's ambiguous dream that night involves "clasping arms" (line 309), but whether they are Ruth's or the Lyonese's we are not told. The next morning Derwent speaks to Clarel of "the sweet shape" of Bacchus (4.27.24), and his comment on the Prodigal's "warm / Soft outline" brings "a stare / Of incredulity" to Clarel's eyes (4.27.18–20). It is possible that Clarel is afraid to return to Ruth because she may be dead, but also because she may not be. It will be recalled that Ruth had blossomed wonderfully during the courtship, but that Clarel, who had never known a mother or sister, felt fully the "charm" of Agar, but an "unrest" toward Ruth (1.39.17ff.). In his own mind this is due entirely to the problem of religious doubt, which is real; but his sexual confusion seems as great, and the two are interwoven. The death of Nathan gives him the excuse he wants, and with a full rationalization but deep sense of guilt he sets off. His fantasies about the Armenian funeral procession during the pilgrimage have no basis for being related to Ruth except as unfulfilled wish. Its fulfillment in 4.30 is thus a complex disaster.

4.26.76–77   the bier / Of Jacob] Following his father's wish, Joseph brought the body of Jacob up out of Egypt and made a seven-days mourning at the "threshingfloor of Atad [line 78], which is beyond Jordan" (Gen. 50.1–13).

4.26.81   Jephthah's daughter] Jephthah, before sacrificing his only daughter to fulfill a vow, gave her two months; and she went up and down the mountains, bewailing her virginity (Judg. 11.29–40).

4.26.98   *saya-manto* in Peru] Properly "saya-y-manto [*or* manta]": petticoat and veil; probably contracted for the meter. Cf. "Benito Cereno": "a Lima intriguante's one sinister eye peering across the Plaza from the Indian loop-hole of her dusk *saya-y-manta*" (NN *Piazza Tales* volume, p. 47); and "Crossing the Tropics (From 'The Saya-y-Manto')" (*John Marr*; NN *Published Poems*, p. 239). See the note at 176.10 in *Pierre*, ed. Henry A. Murray (New York: Hendricks House, 1949), p. 466.

4.26.116   Isaiah's dark burden] The Prodigal reveals considerable biblical background in this speech (to line 135). Damascus in the nineteenth century was still a magnificent city, and there is point to his mockery of Isaiah's malison—three separate prophecies of the sure destruction of the city (Isa. 7.8; 8.4; 17.1). He recalls too most of the details of the Damascene leper, Naaman, who replied to Elisha when told to wash seven times in the Jordan: "Are not Abana and Parphar, rivers of Damascus, better than all the waters of Israel?" But he did wash, and was healed (2 Kings 5).

4.26.153   dame Judah here] The Prodigal's jaunty discourse draws its main details (italicized here) from Stanley, pp. 162–63: "The elevation of the hills and table-lands of *Judah is the true climate of the vine* . . . . It was from the Judæan valley of *Eschol*—'the torrent of the cluster'—that *the spies* cut down *the gigantic cluster of grapes. . . . The 'vine' was the emblem of the nation on the coins of the Maccabees*, and in *the colossal cluster of golden grapes which overhung the porch of the second Temple.*"

4.26.171   Solomon's harp] The Song of Solomon (7.4; 2.16; 2.5; 7.3) provides the citations for lines 174–78. The argument over the meaning of the Canticles—whether it is a love song or a theological piece (lines 182–83)—is discussed by Kitto, I, 381–87. St. Bernard (line 185) is mentioned there, though not as prime interpreter; and so is Hafiz (line 194). That lush Persian poet of the fourteenth century was also theologically construed—by the Bonzes (line 194), Buddhist monks in China or Japan.

4.26.217   Ahasuerus] How this king chose Esther (line 218), without knowing she was a Jewess, to replace the proud Vashti as queen, and what followed, is the theme of the Book of Esther. Her concealed race is especially relevant. Nero (line 219), after divorcing, banishing, and finally murdering his first wife, married his mistress Poppaea Sabina (line 221). Josephus says Poppaea "was a religious lady, and perhaps privately a Jewish proselyte" (*Antiquities of the Jews*, trans. Whiston, bk. 20, chap. 8).

4.26.231   Urbino's ducal mistress] Melville in 1857 at the Uffizi in Florence was "charmed with Titian's Venus"—probably the one known as *The Venus of Urbino* and thought to be a portrait of a mistress of one of the dukes of Urbino (see *Journals*, pp. 115, 493–94). See also the discussion at 3.20.35 above.

4.26.236   Bathsheba] The account of David's seduction of Bathsheba in 2 Samuel 11 gives no hint that she was looking for the trouble she got. See also the discussion at 3.30.106.

4.26.288   Shushan] Ancient capital of Persia, and setting for the Book of Esther.

4.26.306   the Tuscan] Salvaterra (4.13).

4.28.2   the man of scars] Ungar.

4.28.24   For Hebron bound] About twenty miles southwest of Bethlehem, and site of Abraham's famous "oak" (line 29) beneath which he dwelt.

4.28.64   The well of Jesse's son] David's Well (line 0) supplied the water which three of his mighty men brought him when he was confined in Adullam's cave (2 Sam. 23.15–17).

4.28.69   He stood:] Whether these words are part of Clarel's speech is complicated by the fact that no ending quotation mark is present in the first edition to close the speech that begins in 4.28.61–62. In any case an ending quotation mark needs to be provided in 4.28.84; and if that is the only emendation made, the "He" of "He stood:" refers to "Jesse's son" (line 64). Possibly, however, "He" was meant to refer to Clarel, and emendation would require two quotation marks to exclude "He stood:" from the quoted matter. But since the first-edition reading makes good sense, it is retained.

4.29.0   THE NIGHT RIDE] Melville wrote in his 1856–57 journal: "Ride to Jerusalem—pressing forward to save the rain" (p. 84). Perhaps there was an urgency here that was transposed into Clarel's climactic anxiety as he sets out for Jerusalem on Shrove Tuesday (line 2), the last preparatory day before Lent.

4.29.101   Cursed Manes and the Manichee] Manes (216–76) was the founder of Manichaeism, a dualistic religion that stresses the darkness and power of evil which light confronts.

4.29.113   Rachel wailing] Jeremiah 31.15 tells of the voice heard in Ramah ("Rama" in Matt. 2.18: line 111), "Rahel [Rachel] weeping for her children . . . , because they were not."

4.29.115   Cistern of the Kings] Time for one last site—and the last image of the star of Bethlehem (line 120).

4.29.133   By Jeremy's grot] The Grotto of Jeremiah, mentioned in the 1856–57 journal, p. 89, and pictured here from Tompkins, *Through David's Realm* (cited in the discussion at 1.35.4), p. 56. It lay just north of the city

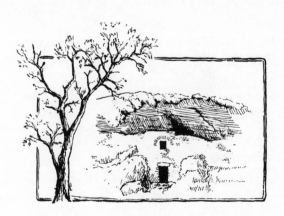

walls outside the Damascus Gate. The route the cavalcade takes (lines 135–48) from where the Bethlehem Road enters Hinnom to St. Stephen's Gate (see the illustration on p. 761 above)—past Zion, Rogel, Ophel, the village of Siloam, and Shaveh's Dale—can be followed on Map A, p. 707. The fiction of an Ottoman camp barring the north route is of course a device for confronting Clarel with the coming scene in the Jewish Cemetery.

4.30.0　　THE VALLEY OF DECISION] Joel 3.14: "Multitudes, multitudes in the valley of decision: for the day of the Lord is near in the valley of decision." See also *Journals*, pp. 433–34.

4.30.9　　Coquimbo's ground] A province in Chile.

4.30.107　　Mad Korah] He was mad with rebellion (Num. 16).

4.30.145　　Ash Wednesday] First day of the penitential season of Lent.

4.31.8　　Shun Orcus] See the discussion at 2.39.77. For Azrael (line 11), see the discussion at 3.4.88.

4.32.0　　PASSION WEEK] Holy Week, the week before Easter: Palm Sunday (line 54) is the first day of Holy Week, commemorating the triumphal entry; followed by Holy Thursday (line 74) and Good Friday (line 81).

4.32.90　　Mortmain, pallid as wolf-bone] Cf. 3.15.20.

4.32.104　　The Comforter] Jesus' promise: "And I will pray the Father, and he shall give you another Comforter, that he may abide with you for ever" (John 14.16). Erebus is the son of Chaos.

4.33.1　　BUT ON THE THIRD DAY] Luke 24.7.

4.33.6　　the Stabat] The liturgical *Stabat Mater*, "The Mother was standing." "Tenebræ" (line 7): hymn of the shadows which fall as candles are extinguished during Wednesday, Thursday, and Friday of Holy Week.

4.33.57–58　　Thammuz' . . . Joel's] The bereaved heart is assuaged neither by the seasonal resurrection of nature in spring and glade, as celebrated in that of the Syrian deity Thammuz or Tammuz (explained, for example, by Kitto, II, 825, as a sun god affecting vegetation, akin to the Phoenician Adonis and the Egyptian Osiris), nor by Old Testament prophecy, like that of Joel (3.2–16) that the day is near when the Lord will judge the heathen in the valley of decision (Jehoshaphat) but "will be the hope of his people and the strength of the children of Israel." See 1.31.223–28 (and the discussion at line 208), linking Osiris with Christ, and, for other classical-Christian contrasts, 1.3.1–5 and the discussions at 1.17.203, 1.28.24, 1.37.31, 2.8.23, 3.20.35, 3.30.69, and 4.18.88.

4.33.65　　*Christ is arisen*] Matt. 28.6: "He is not here: for he is risen, as he said."

VIA DOLOROSA

4.34.0   VIA CRUCIS] The germ of this final scene of the poem lies in the 1856–57 journal: "*Thoughts in the Via Dolorosa*—women panting under burdens—men with melancholy faces" (p. 84). The passage was later marked through with a wavy pencil line, probably after using here. "Via Crucis" (Way of the Cross) is the Via Dolorosa, pictured opposite, from Bartlett's *Jerusalem Revisited* (London: Hall & Virtue, 1855), facing p. 108.

4.34.10   part] In his list at the front of Copy B at Harvard (see pp. 849–57), Melville corrected the first-edition reading "In parts suggests" to "in part suggest" (though he obviously did not intend for the line to begin with a lowercase letter). The change from "parts" to "part" is clearly an improvement; but the elimination of the final "s" of "suggests" must be an oversight (perhaps induced by the deletion of the "s" from "parts"), since the subject ("lane") is singular and requires the form "suggests". NN therefore emends only "parts" to "part".

4.34.22   'Tis Whitsun-tide] The seventh Sunday after Easter, when the apostles were visited by cloven tongues of fire from heaven (Acts 2.1–14).

4.34.51–52   far under sea / They talk] President Buchanan and Queen Victoria exchanged greetings by the newly completed Atlantic cable, August 5, 1858; it ceased functioning on September 1. By 1868 a new cable was working. Clarel's comment here (his final speech) contrasts pointedly with Emerson's enthusiasm for the new telegraph, in stanza 8 of "Ode Sung in the Town Hall, Concord, July 4, 1857":

> And henceforth there shall be no chain,
>   Save underneath the sea
> The wires shall murmur through the main
>   Sweet songs of liberty.
>   (*Complete Works* [Boston: Houghton Mifflin, 1904], p. 200).

4.35.25–26   at the last, / . . . heaven] This couplet, at a penultimate moment, echoes the famous motto *Denique Coelum* (Heaven at Last). Since it is an old Crusaders' cry, it sends reverberations back through the winding corridors of this massive historical poem. Melville knew the motto: *Denique Coelum* appears in *White-Jacket* (chap. 93, p. 396), where it has become the "family crest and motto" of the Lieutenant of Marines. A further resonance: this was the Melville family motto (Raymond M. Weaver, *Herman Melville: Mariner and Mystic* [New York: Doran, 1921], p. 34; *Log*, I, xvii). (The arms of the earls of Melville were quartered with those of the earls of Leven. The Melville arms in the shield pictured below are—in nontechnical terms— those in its upper right and lower left quarters. The illustration is from *The Scots Peerage*, ed. James Balfour Paul [Edinburgh: Douglas, 1909], VI, facing

p. 75.) Thus, on the last page, Melville encoded into his long, essentially disconsolate poem a thread of hope for Stoics like himself. The concluding octet which follows offers a much wider hope, not for the narrator, but for the young seeker, Clarel.

Leven and Melville

List of Emendations

I N THIS LIST of changes made in the first-edition copy-text by
the present editors, the following abbreviations are used to desig-
nate the sources of readings:

    HM   Melville's annotations in Harvard Copy B

    NN   Northwestern-Newberry Edition

For further comment on this list, see p. 700 above; for discussions of
the emendations marked with an asterisk (*), see the DISCUSSIONS
(where the entries are not always keyed to the same words as here,
because more than one crux may be taken up in a single discussion).
Citations of readings in the table of contents are to page and line (and
thus contain only one period, separating the two elements, the first of
which is a roman numeral); citations of readings in the text of the
poem itself are to part, canto, and line (and thus contain two periods,
separating the three elements, all of which are arabic numerals). The
wavy dash (~) stands for the word cited in the left column and signals
that only a mark of punctuation is emended. The caret (ʌ) indicates
the absence of a punctuation mark (but does not necessarily imply the
presence of a space). Empty brackets ([ ]) indicate space where a
letter or mark of punctuation failed to print.

There are two categories of textual decisions not entered in this list because they do not involve emendations; but they do require editorial judgment as to what readings the copy-text in fact contains. (1) *Line-end hyphens.* Relatively few verse lines in the first edition of *Clarel* run on to a second type line, and of those that do only six break a word at the end of the first line. In four instances there is no question of retaining the line-end hyphen ("ex-/pand" at 2.21.95; "Me-/thinks" at 2.31.74; "sam-/ple" at 3.13.94; and "trem-/bler" at 3.28.41); and in one instance it is nearly as obvious that the hyphen should be retained ("ill-/resigned" at 4.35.27). The only line-end hyphen that necessitates an editorial decision is "over-/night" at 3.21.49; NN prints the word in unhyphenated form because it occurs that way at three other places (2.25.29; 2.39.13; 4.28.5)—although it appears as two separate words at 1.5.97. (Two other line-end hyphens appear in the front matter: one—"PUBLICA-/TION"—in the dedication, and one—"before-/hand"—in the prefatory note. Clearly neither hyphen should be retained.) There are no line-end hyphens in the text of the present edition (except for two in the prefatory note that should obviously not be retained in quotation). (2) *Page-end line-spaces.* The NN editors have decided that at nine places the end of a page in the first edition coincides with an intended line-space, and they therefore provide line-spaces preceding 2.1.57, 230; 2.39.108; 3.17.37, 50; 3.20.25; 3.25.85; 3.32.65; and 4.15.66. For discussion of this matter, see the NOTE ON THE TEXT, pp. 696–97. No line-spaces coincide with the ends of pages in the present edition.

It should also be noted here that as a matter of design NN begins cantos (except for the first canto of each of the four parts) with regular capitals, not display capitals as in the first edition, and therefore supplies opening quotation marks at the beginnings of the twenty-eight cantos where in the first edition they did not appear because the design of that edition called for their omission preceding display capitals. See the NOTE ON THE TEXT, p. 701, footnote 40.

	NN READING	COPY-TEXT READING
xi.5	*Night in* NN	Nightin
xii.35	*Shepherds'* NN	Shepherd's
1.1.35	[*indentation*] NN	[*no indentation*]
1.1.75	mind, NN	~.

	NN Reading	Copy-Text Reading
1.1.101	[*no indentation*] NN	[*slight indentation*]
1.2.116	"The NN	∧~
*1.2.122	[*line-space follows*] NN	[*no line-space follows*]
1.3.168	Golgotha, NN	~∧
1.5.63	step. NN	~:
*1.5.218	tempest- HM	~∧
*1.5.218	tossed, HM	~—
1.6.1	stood: HM	~∧
1.7.15	fanned, HM	~∧
1.8.15	thence, NN	~∧
*1.10.9	Fatimite NN	Fatamite
1.12.23	known, NN	~∧
1.12.27	heart, NN	~∧
1.12.113	old, HM	~∧
1.12.114	rolled: HM	~∧
*1.12.141	her HM	[*not present*]
1.13.74	doubt?" HM	~?∧
1.15.6	"He NN	∧~
1.15.15	gate, NN	~∧
1.16.8	walls∧ NN	~.
1.16.50	where, NN	~∧
*1.16.122	Shaddai NN	Shaddei
1.16.136	ill-content, NN	~∧
*1.17.215	rear-ward NN	rear-wall
*1.24.60	fifteenth NN	fourteenth
*1.25.15	Than NN	Then
1.25.95	needs NN	need
1.28.29	death NN	dearth
1.31.94	'Me NN	"~
1.31.95	merciful!' NN	~!"
1.31.157	chill, NN	~∧
1.31.161	"In NN	∧~
1.31.175	north, NN	~∧

	NN Reading	Copy-Text Reading
1.31.203	inference HM	influence
1.34.63	[*indentation*] NN	[*no indentation*]
1.37.17	history. NN	~:
*1.37.105	Silvio NN	Sylvio
1.41.116	blur:— HM	~⅄⅄
1.42.82	Jericho. NN	~ˌ
2.1.14	[*indentation*] NN	[*no indentation*]
2.1.182	[*indentation*] NN	[*no indentation*]
*2.1.186	Of rigorous gloom HM	Austerely sad
2.1.218	true: HM	~ˌ
2.1.221	herein. HM	~ˌ
2.2.31	here," HM	~ˌˌ
*2.4.97	weaves HM	wears
2.5.47	know, NN	~ˌ
2.9.31	command. NN	~;
2.9.70	By NN	In
2.10.155	shrine?' NN	~?"
2.12.36	books can HM	volumes
2.13.25	Hecla NN	Hela
*2.13.98	Hauran NN	Houran
2.13.124	spell— NN	~–
2.13.129	"Rather NN	ˌ~
*2.14.70	trail, NN	~ˌ
2.16.89	[*indentation*] NN	[*no indentation*]
2.16.107	overmuch, HM	~ˌ
*2.16.139	Ashtoreth NN	Ashtaroth
*2.17.33	Sargasso's NN	Sargossa's
*2.19.2	Leon's HM	Spanish
*2.20.99	Mambrino's NN	Malbrino's
2.21.64	best, NN	~ˌ
2.21.79	'world' NN	"~"
2.22.41	deceive: HM	~.
2.23.162	cheered: NN	~.

	NN Reading	Copy-Text Reading
2.24.96	spake. NN	~,
2.26.9	pix, NN	~∧
2.26.23	"Nay NN	∧~
*2.26.130	Frederick NN	Frederic
2.27.138	bar?— HM	~?∧
2.29.52	site), NN	~).
2.29.97	display HM	play
2.30.69	[*indentation*] NN	[*no indentation*]
2.31.70	we?'∧ NN	~?' "
2.33.64	make: HM	~∧
2.34.27	sail?" NN	~?∧
*2.35.1	Piranesi's NN	Piranezi's
2.39.75	Nor hopeful HM	All hopeless
3.1.23	reign, NN	~∧
*3.1.47	Ere, NN	~∧
3.1.100	through NN	though
3.1.109	child? NN	~.
3.1.135	stare, NN	~∧
3.2.8	heart, NN	~∧
3.3.30	plea, NN	~∧
3.3.64	view? NN	~∧
3.4.129	"With NN	∧~
3.5.103	Sibyl's NN	Sibyls
3.5.107	clear-eyed, NN	~∧
3.5.135	town, NN	~∧
3.6.25	Days?" NN	~?∧
3.6.53	part. NN	~:
3.6.135	optimists NN	optimists
*3.7.14	Adullam's NN	Adullum's
3.7.32	shrinking∧frame NN	~-~
3.10.40	sign-manual NN	sign-manuel
3.11.38	heroic, HM	~∧
3.11.245	Vine, NN	~∧

	NN Reading	Copy-Text Reading
3.12.14	And HM	The
3.12.57	see: HM	~—
3.12.129	[indentation] NN	[no indentation]
*3.13.15	[indentation] NN	[slight indentation]
*3.13.16,17	[no indentation] NN	[slight indentation]
3.13.38	become HM	became
3.13.76	"Signior NN	∧~
3.13.82	Greek. NN	~:
3.14.69,70, 73,74	[lines begin flush left] NN	[lines begin to left of regular margin]
3.14.77	[indentation] NN	[no indentation]
3.14.113	thou! HM	~∧
3.16.66	Atys' NN	Aty's
3.16.134	no: HM	~.
*3.17.10	Cosmas' NN	Cosmos'
*3.18.20	Thummim NN	Thummin
3.18.56	go." NN	~.∧
*3.19.1	'Tis NN	∧~
3.19.34	"Jerusalem NN	∧~
3.19.132	clime, NN	~∧
3.19.144	[indentation] NN	[no indentation]
3.19.144	glen, NN	~∧
3.19.160	"But NN	∧~
3.20.4	"Golden NN	∧~
3.20.7	"Venus NN	∧~
3.20.10	"Big NN	∧~
3.20.13	"Sweet NN	∧~
3.20.16	"Glum NN	∧~
3.20.19	"Thrill NN	∧~
3.20.22	"Back NN	∧~
*3.21.240	blanks HM	banks
3.21.290	unfold— HM	~∧
3.22.26	dinted HM	dented

	NN READING	COPY-TEXT READING
3.22.59	holy— HM	~∧
3.23.7	archimandrite NN	archimandrate
*3.23.63	Athanase NN	Athanese
3.25.112	nervously. NN	~,
3.26.39	"But NN	∧~
3.26.44	"Thou NN	∧~
3.26.50	"Tropic NN	∧~
3.26.55	"But NN	∧~
3.26.63	[*line-space follows*] NN	[*no line-space follows*]
3.27.126	'There NN	"~
*3.27.133	Nostradamus NN	Nostrodamus
3.27.135	'. . . *testimony* NN	. . . '~
3.28.56	"Envoy NN	∧~
3.28.86	not NN	no
3.29.38	Bandusia HM	Bandusa
4.1.3	Amerrian, NN	~∧
4.1.177	"Wreck NN	[]'~
4.2.191	mint∧ HM	~.
4.3.41	who, NN	~∧
4.3.41	him, NN	~∧
4.8.23	[*indentation*] NN	[*no indentation*]
4.9.115	the NN	the the
4.11.41	ease), NN	~)∧
4.16.2	prayer, NN	~.
4.16.26	now?" NN	~?∧
4.16.207	Zoroastrian NN	Zoroastian
4.19.1	chant, NN	~∧
4.19.33	'The Cock' NN	"~~"
4.19.107	hey! NN	~?
4.19.151	Good, NN	~∧
*4.21.83	theme. NN	~,
*4.21.84	extreme, NN	~.
4.23.19	do. NN	~,

	NN Reading	Copy-Text Reading
4.26.35	Lyons NN	Lyon's
4.26.178	roes.' " NN	~.∧"
4.26.257	part? HM	~∧
4.26.302	[*indentation*] NN	[*no indentation*]
4.26.310	such NN	each
4.27.19	stare NN	scare
4.28.84	grain?" NN	~?∧
4.29.113	wailing. NN	~∧
4.30.86	thou, NN	~∧
4.30.118	It HM	Still
4.32.87	Wan HM	White
4.33.1	Christ NN	christ
4.33.37	[*indentation*] NN	[*no indentation*]
4.33.67	[*indentation*] NN	[*no indentation*]
4.33.75	[*indentation*] NN	[*no indentation*]
4.34.7	[*indentation*] NN	[*no indentation*]
*4.34.10	part HM	parts
4.34.22	[*indentation*] NN	[*no indentation*]
4.34.27	staves; NN	~,

Melville's Annotated Copy of Clarel

O NE SET of the sheets printed from the Putnam typesetting of *Clarel* demands particular attention because it contains annotations by Melville indicating some forty possible textual corrections and revisions. Copy B in the Houghton Library at Harvard (*AC85M4977.876c(B)), a copy in a single-volume custom binding (not in the publisher's two-volume binding), is labeled in pencil on the front free endpaper in the hand of Melville's wife, Elizabeth Shaw Melville: " 'Revised' sheets – / Herman's corrections / Index to 3^d & 4th parts wanting" (reproduced on p. 857 below). An editor's decision regarding the adoption of any or all of Melville's "corrections" in this copy does not necessarily depend on knowing the precise status of these "sheets"; but determining whether the sheets are some prepublication form of the book could have a bearing on ascertaining when Melville made the annotations, and thus possibly on whether they (or some of them) were finally rejected in favor

This RELATED DOCUMENT was prepared by G. Thomas Tanselle.

of the printed readings or were intended to supplant them. If the sheets do represent prepublication material, Melville could (though need not) have made the annotations at an earlier time than would have been possible if they are simply the sheets of an ordinary published copy. Examination of Harvard Copy B has not settled this matter; a description of the copy will make clear what the problems are.

Harvard Copy B brings together in a single volume the leaves containing the 565 pages of the printed text of the poem, preceded by the title leaf and the table-of-contents leaves for Volume I. The copy therefore lacks the dedication leaf of Volume I and the two preliminary leaves (title and table of contents) of Volume II.[1] The sheets thus constituted are bound in smooth, light yellowish brown cloth, with white wove endpapers and an additional white wove binder's leaf at front and back; the sheets are trimmed to 17.2 x 12.3 cm. Following the binder's leaf at the front is a leaf (reproduced opposite) on which Melville entered twenty-three page references to the pages of Volume I (pages on which, with three exceptions, he had made annotations), followed by sixteen page references to Volume II, with the accompanying alterations noted (and one further notation without a page number).[2] This leaf appears to be of the same paper stock (laid pattern, with chainlines 30 mm apart; .089 mm thick) as that of the

1. Melville's wife not only called attention on the front free endpaper to the absence of the table of contents for Volume II; she also noted on a slip pasted between p. 300 and the divisional title page for Part 3, "Table of Contents / for 3^d [altered from 2^d] & 4th parts / missing here" (reproduced on p. 857 below). Surprisingly, she did not note the absence of the dedication. The possibility that the dedication had not yet been printed at the time she wrote would seem to be ruled out by the fact that her note on the endpaper was certainly written after the present binding was completed; and since this binding was not undertaken until after Melville had gone over the printed text and made his annotations (or at least some of them), it seems unlikely that the binding could have been completed before the dedication was printed. Besides, the title page in Copy B includes Melville's name, as do the title pages in the published copies, and the decision to use his name was linked to the creation of a dedication (see p. 540 above). The absence of the dedication leaf from Copy B may simply result from a binder's error, since in the published copies the leaf is not conjugate with another leaf and had to be inserted. This possible explanation for its absence does not, however, explain why Melville's wife failed to call attention to its absence.

2. There are four additional places, all in Volume I, where Melville marked a page of text but entered no number on this leaf.

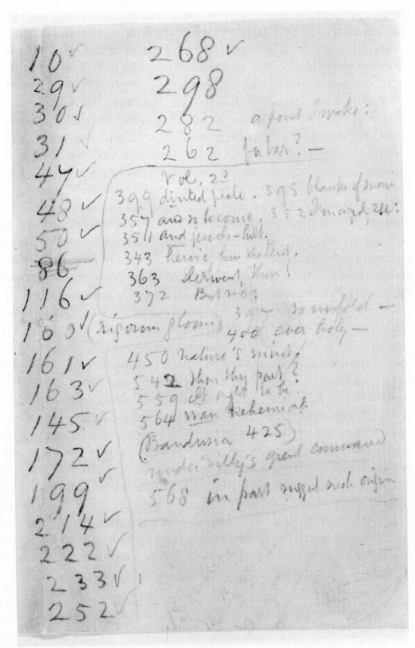

Melville's list of alterations in Copy B.

binder's leaves in the ordinary copies in publisher's binding, which in those copies are inserted at front and back next to the free endpaper and are of a different paper stock from that used for the printed sheets. In Copy B the printed sheets are gathered in eights, as in the ordinary published copies; and the last four leaves of Part 2, as in the regular copies, form a gathering, with the two preceding and the two succeeding leaves stuck in. The first of those succeeding leaves—the divisional title leaf for Part 3—bears traces in its upper left corner of a pencil annotation in Melville's hand, now erased but still legible, referring to a passage in Part 4. These printed sheets seem identical to those in ordinary copies, with two categories of exception: (1) some sheets are carelessly folded, producing excessively wide (and sometimes tapering) gutters on some pages and correspondingly narrow ones on the companion pages on conjugate leaves (an example is the wide gutter on page 213 and the narrow one on page 220);[3] (2) many pages in the last two gatherings (indeed, all of them but pp. 548, 550, and 551) display marks, usually vertical black lines at the margins, suggesting that improperly locked-up formes allowed the printer's spacing material and furniture to work up and leave an inked impression. The paper does not appear to be distinguishable from that in regular copies; the last two gatherings seem, on first inspection, to have a smoother finish and not to have a laid pattern, but there is in fact a faint trace of a chain-line pattern in them, and some sheets of the regular copies have laid patterns equally difficult to discern.

Two conclusions that can be drawn from these facts are, first, that the sheets of Copy B, being printed on both sides and imposed for folding, are not likely to be ordinary proof sheets (though they could be trial copies of the final sheets pulled for inspection); and, second, that—even if they are early—they are not early enough to have been imposed for gathering in twelves, according to the printed signatures, since they are gathered in eights, like the published copies. Beyond that, the evidence does not lead clearly in a single direction. That Melville listed his corrections and revisions on the recto of what appears to be the binder's leaf from a published copy suggests that he was using a

3. Although gutters are difficult to measure in bound books, the combined width of the uneven gutters on two companion pages is approximately the same as the combined width of the even gutters on the same pages of other copies. There is no reason to suppose, therefore, that these sheets reflect different impositions and thus different printings.

copy in publisher's binding;[4] but the faulty printing of the last two gatherings, not present in those gatherings in examined copies of the published book, suggests that at least some of the sheets date from a time preceding the regular print run. Conceivably what Melville used was a copy of Volume I in the publisher's binding (though perhaps an early or trial copy, in which the dedication leaf had not been inserted and some of the sheets were carelessly folded) and a copy of Volume II in the form of unbound gatherings. (Perhaps he stopped by Put-nam's, which—at 182 Fifth Avenue, near Twenty-third Street—was close to his house on Twenty-sixth Street, and picked up what was available.) Such a possibility might account for his listing on the front binder's leaf of Volume I the page numbers for the pages on which most of his annotations occur in that volume, and then adding, for Volume II, the actual revisions as well as the page numbers[5] (with no markings on the pages themselves in Volume II, except for the one, now erased, on the divisional title page for Part 3).[6]

4.   This possibility is supported by the fact that Mrs. Melville wrote at the foot of the recto of this leaf, below Melville's annotations, "To the Binder: Retain this page" (and called attention to the instruction with a pointing hand). (This inscription was later erased and may not show at all in the reproduction.) If the binder had been given Volume I in the form of a copy in publisher's binding and if Mrs. Melville's note had not been present, he would in all probability have eliminated this leaf in rebinding, along with the original endpapers; binders routinely supply new end-papers, and often additional leaves as well, and do not normally try to reuse such material, particularly if it had been used as note paper. If, on the other hand, the binder had been given Volume I (as well as Volume II) in the form of unbound (or disbound) gatherings and if the leaf with Melville's annotations accompanied them, a note indicating that the leaf was part of the material to be bound would have been superfluous.

5.   Three of the Volume I references also have accompanying annotation (as described above, p. 681).

6.   This annotation follows the same principle as the others for Volume II in not appearing on the actual text page referred to. The divisional title page for Part 3 would have been the first of two loose leaves at the top of a set of unbound gatherings for Volume II, if that set excluded (as Copy B does) the general title and the contents leaves for that volume. (That Melville's annotation refers to Part 4 yet appears on the divisional title page for Part 3 is further indication that this divisional title page was on top.) If Melville did have a bound copy of Volume I and an unbound copy of Volume II at the time of his annotations, one can only speculate whether Melville's wife (or Melville himself) would have been likely, at some later time, to have had Volume I disbound and the sheets of both volumes then bound together rather than having just the sheets of Volume II bound (and thus creating an unmatched set).

Whatever the history of the sheets that now make up Harvard Copy B, that copy as annotated is clearly one of the documents that must be taken into account in editing *Clarel*. The considerations involved in deciding the status of Melville's proposed alterations to the text are discussed above, pp. 681–83. Melville's list of alterations and all of the annotations in Copy B (those by Melville's wife as well as those by Melville) are reproduced here (slightly reduced), courtesy of the Houghton Library of Harvard University. For convenience of reference, the list below reports Melville's annotations in tabular form, providing (in order) page references to the first edition, part-canto-line references to the present edition, the readings of the first-edition text at the points of Melville's annotations, and descriptions of his markings (with transcriptions). Brackets around page numbers indicate that Melville did not enter those numbers in his list. The entries are given here in numerical sequence, though many of them are out of order in Melville's list. Items marked with asterisks are commented on further in the DISCUSSIONS.

Volume I

10	1.1.125–26	He . . . stone,] *check mark in margin to left of these lines*
*29	1.5.218	tempest] *followed by caret*
*29	1.5.218	tossed—] *slash through the dash; check mark in right margin*
30	1.6.1	stood] *followed by caret; colon and slash in right margin*
31	1.7.15	fanned] *followed by caret; comma and slash in right margin*
47	1.12.113	old] *followed by comma*
47	1.12.114	Two . . . rolled] *colon and slash in margin to right of this line*
*48	1.12.141	Her appanage or colony.] *the word* her *and check mark in margin to left of this line*
50	1.13.74	"How . . . doubt?] *ending double quotation mark and slash in margin to right of this line*
86	1.22.103–1.23.14	All . . . rows] *nothing marked on page; page number canceled in Melville's list*

116	1.31.203	influence] *underlined; slash and the word* inference *in left margin*
145	1.41.116	"What . . . blur] *colon and dash followed by slash in margin to right of this line; also an erased line under the word* this *in mid-line*
*160	2.1.186	Austerely sad] *underlined; the words* rigorous gloom *in left margin and in list on binder's leaf; trimmed-off edge of sheet possibly carried slight additional penciling*
161	2.1.218	The . . . true] *colon and slash in margin to right of this line*
161	2.1.221	It . . . herein] *circled period in margin to right of this line*
163	2.2.31	"A . . . here,] *ending double quotation mark and slash in margin to right of this line*
*172	2.4.96–97	Floods . . . web.] *slash and the word* weaves *in margin to left of these lines*
[176]	2.5.70	I] *circled (presumably because it is the wrong font in the first edition)*
[193]	2.10.219	the] *the letter* e *circled (presumably because it does not print properly)*
199	2.12.36	volumes] *underlined twice; the words* books can *in right margin*
[209]	2.15.59	wait,] *circled (presumably because the letter* a *and the comma do not print properly)*
214	2.16.107	overmuch] *followed by caret; slash and comma in left margin*
222	2.19.2	Spanish] *underlined; slash and the word* Leon's *in left margin*
233	2.22.41	Signs . . . deceive·] *colon and slash in margin to right of this line*
[240]	2.23.91	The] *circled (presumably because the letter* T *is the wrong font in the first edition)*
252	2.26.0	OF ROME.] *underlined; check mark in left margin*
252	2.26.8	Rome!] *underlined; check mark in left margin*
262	2.27.138	for bar?] *nothing marked on page; in list on binder's leaf, Melville wrote* for bar?— *(adding a dash)*

268	2.29.97	For . . . play] *check mark in margin to left of this line; the word* display *and a circled question mark to left of lines 94–95 beside a long slash (and obviously a possible substitution for the word* play *at the end of line 97)*
282	2.33.64	A point I make] *nothing marked on page; in list on binder's leaf, Melville wrote* a point I make: *(adding a colon)*
298	2.39.74–75	They . . . return.] *the words* Nor hopeful *written in margin to left of these lines, with left stem of the* N *cut off by trimming (obviously a possible substitution for the words* All hopeless *at the beginning of line 75)*

Volume II [*From this point on, all of Melville's notes, transcribed here, appear in his list, not on the text pages—with one exception, taken up at the end of the present list. The periods at the ends of some of Melville's entries were obviously intended to mark the ends of those entries, not to indicate the addition of periods to the text.*]

343	3.11.38	heroic from the tent] heroic, from the tent.
351	3.12.14	The jewels . . . hilt.] <u>And</u> jewels–hilt.
352	3.12.57	I'm aged, see—] I'm aged, see:
357	3.13.38	and so became] and so become.
363	3.14.113	Derwent, thou] Derwent, thou!
372	3.16.134	But no·] But no:
*395	3.21.240	banks of snow] blanks of snow
397	3.21.290	so unfold] so unfold—
399	3.22.26	dented plate] dinted plate. *(with the letter* i *underlined)*
400	3.22.59	ever holy] ever holy—
425	3.29.38	Bandusa] Bandusia *(the whole entry, with the page number following the word, in parentheses)*
450	4.2.191	Nature's mint.] Nature's mint *(followed by a period with a slash through it)*
*[461]	4.5.131	under Tilly's great command] under Tilly's great command *(not altered)*
542	4.26.257	thou thy part] thou thy part? *(the page number altered from 544)*

559	4.30.118	Still *ought* to be!"] It ought to be.
564	4.32.87	White Nehemiah] Wan Nehemiah
*568	4.34.10	In parts suggests such origin.] in part suggest such origin

[*The following annotation, now erased, appears in the upper left corner of p. [301], the divisional title page for Part 3.*]

| *[523] | 4.21.51–52 | the excellence of man / Left to himself,] the rectitude of man / left to himself / Part IV. |

Elizabeth Shaw Melville's label on the front free endpaper (above) and her notation on a slip before the divisional title page for Part 3 (below) in Copy B.

Against the utterance demurred
And failed him. With infirm intent
He sought the house-top. Set of sun :
His feet upon the yet warm stone,
He, Clarel, by the coping leant,
In silent gaze. The mountain town,
A walled and battlemented one,
With houseless suburbs front and rear,

Yes, sympathies of Eve awake ;
Yet do but err. For how might break
Upon those simple natures true,
The complex passion ? might they view
The apprehension tempest tossed—
The spirit in gulf of dizzying fable lost ?

30   *JERUSALEM.*

VI.

TRIBES AND SECTS.

HE turned to go ; he turned, but stood
    In many notes of varying keys,
From shrines like coves in Jordan's wood
Hark to the rival liturgies,
Which, rolling underneath the dome,

Athwart the way, and key in hand
Noiseless applies it, enters so
And vanishes. By dry airs fanned
The languid hyssop waveth slow,
Dusty, on stones by ruin rent.
'Twould seem indeed the accomplishment
Whereof the greater prophet tells

Melville's annotations on pp. 10, 29, 30, and 31 of Copy B.

Nay, nay ; your future's too sublime:
The Past, the Past is half of time,
The proven half.—Thou Pantheon old,
Two thousand years have round thee rolled
Yet thou, in Rome, thou bid'st me seek
Wisdom in something more antique
Than thou thyself. Turn then : what seer,
The senior of this Latian one,
Speaks from the ground, transported here
In Eastern soil ? Far buried down—

48   *JERUSALEM.*

Whose sway occult can so command ;
Make even Papal Rome to be
Her appanage or colony.
Is Judah's mummy quite unrolled ?
To pluck the talisman from fold !

Nature and thee in vain we search :
Well urged the Jews within the porch—
"How long wilt make us still to doubt ?
How long ?—'Tis eighteen cycles now—
Enigma and evasion grow ;
And shall we never find thee out ?

Intense he spake, his eyes of blue
Altering, and to eerie hue,
Like Tyrrhene seas when overcast ;
The which Vine noted, nor in joy,
Inferring thence an ocean-waste
Of earnestness without a buoy :
An influence which afterward
Acquaintance led him to discard
Or modify, or not employ.
       Clarel ill-relished.
                         Rolfe, in tone

inference

Melville's annotations on pp. 47, 48, 50, and 116 of Copy B.

If Atheists and Vitriolists of doom
Faith's gathering night with rockets red illume—
So much the more in pathos I adore
The low lamps flickering in Syria's Tomb."—

"What strain is this?—But, here, in blur
'After return from Sepulcher:
B. L.'"—On the ensuing day
He plied the host with question free:
Who answered him, "A pilgrim—nay,
How to remember! English, though—
A fair young Englishman. But stay:"

Viewing those Levantines in way
Of the snared lion, which from grate
Marks the light throngs on holiday,
Nor e'er relaxes in his state
Austerely sad; rode one whose air
Revealed—but, for the nonce, forbear.
Mortmain his name, or so in whim
Some moral wit had christened him.

In vernal Easter caravan,
Bound unto Gilgal's neighborhood.
Nor less belief his heart confessed
Not die he should till knees had pressed
The Palmers' Beach. Which trust proved true
'Twas charity gave faith her due:
Without publicity or din
It was the student moved herein

"Hallo, what now? They come to halt
Down here in glen! Well, well, we'll vault."
His song arrested, so he spake
And light dismounted, wide awake.—

"A sprightly comrade have you here,
Said Derwent in the senior's ear.
The banker turned him: "Folly, folly—
But good against the melancholy."

Melville's annotations on pp. 145, 160, 161, and 163 of Copy B.

That is not lackey to the moon
Of fate.   The flood ebbs out—the ebb
Floods back ; the incessant shuttle shifts
And flies, and wears and tears the web.
Turn, turn thee to the proof that sifts:
What if the kings in Forty-eight
Fled like the gods ? even as the gods
Shall do, return they made; and sate
And fortified their strong abodes;
And, to confirm them there in state,
Contrived new slogans, apt to please—

weaves

"My friends stand by; and, 'There!' she says—
An angel arch, a sinner:
I grudge to pay, but pay I must,
Then—dine on half a dinner !—

"Heigh-ho, next month I marry : well!"
With that he turned aside, and went
Humming another air content.

What other element for thee ?
Whales, mighty whales have felt the wound—
Plunged bleeding thro' the blue profound;
But where their fangs the sand-sharks keep
Be shallows worse than any deep."—
Hardly that chimed with Derwent's bell:
Him too he left.

THE BANKER.   **199**

To face a skull.   That sachem old
Whose wigwam is man's heart within—
How taciturn, and yet can speak,
Imparting more than volumes win ;
Not Pleasure's darling cares to seek
Such counselor: the worse he fares ;

books can

Vine watches; and his aspect knows
A flush of diffident humor: "Nay,
Me too, me too let wait, I pray,
On our snubbed kin here;" and he rose.

Melville's annotations on pp. 172, 176, 193, 199, and 209 of Copy B.

And fell the silence unreleased
Till yet again did Rolfe round peer
Upon that moonlit land of fear:
  " Man sprang from deserts : at the touch
Of grief or trial overmuch
On deserts he falls back at need ;
Yes, 'tis the bare abandoned home
Recalleth then. See how the Swede
Like any rustic crazy Tom,
Bursting through every code and ward

222   *THE WILDERNESS.*

XIX.

AN APOSTATE.

Leon's

BARQUE, Easter barque, with happier freight
    Than Spanish spoil of Inca plate ;
Which vernal glidest from the strand
Of statues poised like angels fair ;
On March morn sailest—starting, fanned

                        " Jews share the change,"
Derwent proceeded: " Range, they range—
In liberal sciences they roam ;
They're leavened, and it works, believe ;
Signs are, and such as scarce deceive·
From Holland, that historic home
Of erudite Israel, many a tome
Talmudic, shipped is over sea

240   *THE WILDERNESS.*

Djalea waits. The mare and man
Show like a stone equestrian
Set up for homage. Over there
'Twas hard for mounted men to move
Among the thickets interwove,
Which dipped the stream and made a snare.

Melville's annotations on pp. 214, 222, 223, and 240 of Copy B.

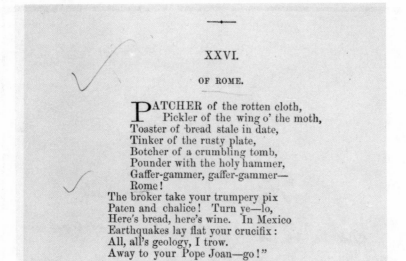

XXVI.

OF ROME.

PATCHER of the rotten cloth,
    Pickler of the wing o' the moth,
Toaster of bread stale in date,
Tinker of the rusty plate,
Botcher of a crumbling tomb,
Pounder with the holy hammer,
Gaffer-gammer, gaffer-gammer—
Rome!
The broker take your trumpery pix
Paten and chalice! Turn ye—lo,
Here's bread, here's wine. In Mexico
Earthquakes lay flat your crucifix:
All, all's geology, I trow.
Away to your Pope Joan—go!"

But changing, and in formal way—
"Admitted; nay, 'tis tritely true;
Men pass thro' Edom, through and through.
But surely, few so dull to-day
As not to make allowance meet
For Orientalism's play
In Scripture, where the chapters treat
Of mystic themes."
              With eye askance,
The apostate fixed no genial glance:
"Ay, Keith's grown obsolete. And, pray,
How long will these last glosses stay?

298   *THE WILDERNESS.*

Warm tears, cold odors from the urn—
They hearsed in heathen Rome their dead
All hopeless of the soul's return.
Embracing them, in marble set,
The mimic gates of Orcus met—
The Pluto-bolt, the fatal one
Wreathed over by the hung festoon.

Melville's annotations on pp. 252, 268, and 298 of Copy B.

This copy is specially
presented to my wife, without
whose assistance in manifold ways
I hardly knew how I could have
got the book (under the circumstances)
into shape, and finally through
the press.   Herman Melville

June 6, 1876
    New York.
104 E. 26 St.

Melville's inscription in the copy of *Clarel* he presented to Elizabeth Shaw Melville. Courtesy of the Houghton Library of Harvard University.

Elizabeth Shaw Melville's
Copies of Clarel

O F THE FOUR copies of *Clarel* in the Melville Collection of
the Houghton Library of Harvard University, the most im-
portant is obviously Copy B, in which Melville entered
some forty annotations (see above, pp. 849–63). Two of the other
copies are of particular interest, however, because they belonged to
Melville's wife, Elizabeth Shaw Melville.[1] One of them, Copy C
(*AC85M4977.876c(C)), in the publisher's binding of light grayish
reddish brown cloth, has her signature and her Eighteenth Street
address—the address to which she moved in 1892—on the front free
endpaper of Volume I. This copy, the gift to the Harvard College

This RELATED DOCUMENT was prepared by G. Thomas Tanselle.

    1. The remaining copy, Copy A (*AC85M4977.876c(A)), presented to the
Harvard College Library by Eleanor Melville Metcalf, is in the publisher's binding of
dark yellowish green cloth. The only markings it contains, in an unidentified hand,
are a check mark in the right margin of p. 79 following the twelfth line (1.19.43) and
a question mark on p. 432 after the word "HOLIDAME;" (3.31.6).

Library of Mrs. E. Barton Chapin, a granddaughter of Melville, contains no other markings.

Copy D (*AC85M4977.876c(D)) is of greater interest, for it is the copy Melville presented to his wife. It is in the same color publisher's binding as Copy C and bears on the front free endpaper of Volume I a seven-line presentation inscription, signed by Melville and dated June 6, 1876: "This copy is specially / presented to my wife, without / whose assistance in manifold ways / I hardly know how I could have / got the book (under the circumstances) / into shape, and finally through / the press." (See the reproduction on p. 864 above.) The only other marking in this copy is on p. 395: in the twenty-third line (3.21.240), there is a caret between the first two letters of "banks"; and in the right margin, in Melville's hand, there is the letter "l" and a slash (see the reproduction below, courtesy of the Houghton Library of Harvard University). This correction of "banks" to "blanks" is also among the alterations Melville listed on the binder's leaf in Copy B (see pp. 851 and 856 above). This copy was given to the Harvard College Library by Eleanor Melville Metcalf, a granddaughter of Melville.

From Clarel naught.
Derwent went on: " For lamp you yearn—
A lantern to benighted thought.
Obtain it—whither will you turn ?
Still lost you'd be in banks of snow.
My fellow-creature, do you know
That what most satisfies the head
Least solaces the heart ?   Less light
Than warmth needs earthly wight.
Christ built a hearth: the flame is dead
We'll say, extinct ; but lingers yet,
Enlodged in stone, the hoarded heat.
Why not nurse that ?   Would rive the door
And let the sleet in ?   But, once o'er,
This tarrying glow, never to man,
Methinks, shall come the like again.
What if some camp on crags austere

The "Ditty of Aristippus" Manuscript

T HE ONLY SEGMENT of the text of *Clarel* known to exist in Melville's hand is in a manuscript at the American Antiquarian Society, Worcester, Massachusetts, headed "*Ditty of Aristippus*". The paper, measuring 23.8 x 20.3 cm, is folded once, cutting the longer dimension and producing two leaves measuring 20.3 x 11.91 cm; it has a laid pattern, and in the first of the two leaves (i.e., the one Melville used first) a watermark is visible, in the form of an escutcheon with a diagonal bar, surrounded by scrollwork, with a fleur-de-lys and the letter "F" beneath. Melville wrote the first two of the three seven-line stanzas of this lyric on the recto of the first leaf and the third stanza and his signature on the recto of the second leaf; he did not write on the two versos. The lyric corresponds to the first twenty-one lines of Part 3, canto 4, of *Clarel* (called "hymn of Aristippus" at 3.4.68). The text of the manuscript is identical to that in the first edition of *Clarel* except at three points: (1) Melville indented the second line exactly the same amount as the first line, corresponding to the pattern of indentation in the other stanzas, whereas in the

This RELATED DOCUMENT was prepared by G. Thomas Tanselle.

Ditty of Aristippus

Noble gods at the board
Where lord unto lord
Light pushes the care-killing wine:
Urbane in their pleasure,
Superb in their leisure —
Lax ease —
Lax ease after labor divine!

Golden ages eternal,
Autumnal, infernal,
Deep mellow their temper serene:
The rose by their gate
Shall it yield unto fate?
They are gods —
They are gods and their garlands
keep green.

Ever blandly adore them;
But spare to implore them:
They rest, they discharge them
                    from time;

Yet believe, light believe
They would succor, reprieve —
            Nay, retrieve —
Might but revellers pause
                    in the prime.

Herman Melville

printed text the display capital at the beginning of the first line necessitates a greater indentation of the second line; (2) in the last line Melville wrote "revellers" in the manuscript, whereas "revelers" appears in the printed text; (3) Melville placed a period at the end of the last line in the manuscript, whereas in the printed text an exclamation point appears there. (The lyric is in quotation marks in the printed text because it is sung by a character, the "Cypriote"; but Melville naturally did not place quotation marks around the poem in the manuscript, since no text is present there except the lyric.) For further discussion of these variants, see the NOTE ON THE TEXT, pp. 698–99.

This manuscript can be dated 1888 because it was produced in response to a request from Edmund Clarence Stedman in January of that year. Stedman (1837–1908), the prominent anthologist, was about to include selections from Melville's work in the seventh volume (1889) of *A Library of American Literature*, coedited with Ellen M. Hutchinson, and wrote to Melville asking permission to do so on January 24, 1888. Melville replied on January 27, "Of course you are at liberty to make the extracts." A few days earlier, on January 20, Stedman had written asking Melville for "one of your best known shorter poems, in your own handwriting" and for information about a portrait, to be used in "illustrating and extending" his own copy of his earlier book *Poets of America* (1885)—a critical study that mentions Melville in passing as one of a group of poets whose lyrics display "native fire" (p. 49). Melville sent the Aristippus lyric to Stedman on January 29, with a note (written on the same stock of paper as the lyric) that began, "I accede with pleasure to your request. Accordingly you will find enclosed a short Piece" (both letters to Stedman are at Yale; see *The Letters of Herman Melville*, ed. Merrell R. Davis and William H. Gilman [New Haven: Yale University Press, 1960], pp. 285–86, and the Northwestern-Newberry *Correspondence* volume).

The manuscript of the Aristippus lyric came to the American Antiquarian Society as the gift of Charles H. Taylor, Jr., on June 1, 1926. According to a note by Clarence Brigham penciled on the verso of the first leaf, it had been bought for Taylor by the dealer P. K. Foley at the Stedman auction on January 19, 1911. The first stanza was reproduced by Jay Leyda in 1951 in *The Melville Log* ([New York: Harcourt, Brace], II, 905), and a full transcription appeared in the Davis-Gilman *Letters* (p. 286). The present reproduction (approximately original size) is published courtesy of the American Antiquarian Society.

Parallel Passages in Clarel and Melville's 1856–57 Journal

F OR FURTHER information, including fuller excerpts from the journal and Melville's markings of these journal passages, possibly while composing *Clarel*, see the accompanying discussions (indicated here by asterisks). See also the HIS-TORICAL AND CRITICAL NOTE, pp. 511–23 above. Passages are arranged in the order in which they appear in the journal; parenthetical references in the first column are to the Northwestern-Newberry edition of *Journals*, ed. Howard C. Horsford with Lynn Horth (1989).

1856–57 JOURNAL	CLAREL
Melville talks with an Englishman who had been *"a day's shooting in the Vale of Tempe—*Ye Gods!" (p. 55).	Glaucon, young blade, says: "Fine shot was mine by Nazareth; / But birding's best in Tempe's Vale" (*2.5.45–46).

This RELATED DOCUMENT was prepared by Walter E. Bezanson, originally for his "Herman Melville's *Clarel*" (Ph.D. dissertation, Yale University, 1943), here revised and supplemented by Alma A. MacDougall.

1856–57 JOURNAL

CLAREL

Two comments on Captain Tate's story of arms affecting the compass (p. 56; later notation in pencil, textual note at 56.25–26).

Greatly expanded as major incident in "The Timoneer's Story" (*3.12).

Ship in dangerous fog off Constantinople; old Turk smokes: "God's will is good" (pp. 57–58).

The Druze, Djalea, calmly smokes (pipe his symbol); says: "No God there is but God" (*3.15.115).

"Striking effect" of Armenian funerals winding through the lanes of Constantinople; bier, candles, chanting, flowers, etc. (p. 62).

"A Procession" (*1.43): elaborate description of same funeral in Jerusalem. Becomes a recurrent symbol of disaster to Clarel (see the discussion at line 23).

Sees the convent of the Dancing Dervishes in the Constantinople suburb of Pera (p. 62).

Derwent describes visiting the dervishes (*3.27.185–92).

Island of Mytilene described: "large & lovely . . . green from beach to hill-top—a dark rich bronzy green" (p. 68).

The island described: "Sappho and Phaon's Lesbos green, / . . . his [the Lesbian's] lax Paradise, / An island yet luxurious seen, / Fruitful in all that can entice" (*3.11.26–30).

Description of camels in Smyrna: "a most ungainly creature . . . crain-like neck, . . . he seems stalking along on four mops. . . . Has a way of turning his head so that his face & tail face you together" (p. 69).

"Camels . . . / Stalk through the street" (1.21.8–9); "The camel too / Her crane-like neck swerved round to view" (2.13.32–33).

In Smyrna "Heard a good deal about the commerce of England with Turkey," etc. (p. 70).

"Of Pope and Turk" (*4.12): business ethics of East and West compared.

Patmos a "disenchanting isle"; "to look upon the bleak yellow of Patmos, who would ever think that a god had been there" (pp. 71, 72).

"To Patmos now may visions steal? / Lone crag where lone the ospreys wheel!" (4.2.21–22).

Description of the Greek as a "natural dandy" (p. 71).

The Lesbian a development of this type (see Index, p. 624).

1856–57 JOURNAL	CLAREL
Melville sees spot in Cairo where Emim Bey escaped (p. 74).	Incident of the escape told dramatically (*1.21.30–39).
At the Nile struck by contrast of "desert & verdure, plain as line between good & evil" (p. 76).	". . . by Nile— / From waste to garden but a stile" (*3.21.279–80).
Account of Cairo donkeys and donkey boys: "Donkey is one of the best fellows in the world. . . . Tipe of honesty" (p. 77).	The Ass developed extensively as a symbolic figure (see Index, p. 616).
"Sea & sky molten into each other" off Alexandria; "A daub of Prussian blue" (p. 78 and textual note at 78.6; see also p. 82: same phrase used for sea off Jaffa).	Agath tells of sailing from Egypt, "the sky there, always blue, / And blue daubed seas so bland" (3.12.59–60).
Melville lands at Jaffa, rides to Jerusalem, stays at Mediterranean Hotel, view from balcony, etc. (p. 79).	Clarel does the same (1.1; see the discussions at lines 0, 28, and 134).
Cunningham's dragoman, the Druze, Abdallah (p. 80).	Probable source of character Djalea, a Druze (see Index, p. 622).
Melville stays at Greek convent in Ramleh with "Letter from Greek Patriarch" (p. 80); at Mar Saba the comment "Monastery (Greek) rode on with letter" (p. 84).	Pilgrims use "voucher from . . . Patriarch" to get into Mar Saba (*3.10.57).
Rides to Lydda in train "of Governor's son" with "mounted escort . . . all armed." "Horsemen riding . . . up to hedges of cactus, interrogating & firing their pistols into them" (p. 80).	The Greek Banker and Glaucon depart with the "mounted train" the pilgrims encounter. The horsemen, guarding "their prince, a fair youth," "in nooks of blight / Discharg[e] shots" (*2.13.47–63).
In the Plain of Sharon "Quanities of red poppies. (Rose of Sharon?)" (p. 80).	"The breath of Sharon's prairie land! / And was it, yes, her titled Rose, / That scarlet poppy oft at hand" (*1.1.38–40).

1856–57 JOURNAL	CLAREL
"Found the *Petra Party* at Jaffa" (p. 80).	"Of Petra" (2.30)—but direct source is Stanley's *Sinai and Palestine*, pp. 88-92, 97-99.
Wreck-beams in Jaffa hotel (p. 81).	Transferred to Nehemiah's room in Jerusalem (*1.22.29–31).
Vial [mezuzah] masoned into lintel in Jaffa hotel (p. 81).	Transferred to Clarel's room in Jerusalem (*1.2.3–7).
Keeper of hotel in Jaffa a Jew (p. 81).	Abdon developed from this character? (see Index, pp. 612–13).
Section entitled *"From Jerusalem to Dead Sea &c"* (pp. 82–83).	Part 2, "The Wilderness," based on this section.
Sees "trees of apple of Sodom" (p. 82).	Expanded symbolically to develop character of Margoth, who picks one (*2.28.4–15).
Mount of Temptation. Melville speculates on its meaning: "a black, arid mount—nought to be seen but Dead Sea, mouth of Kedron—very tempting—foolish feind—but it was a display in vision—then why take him up to Mount?—the *thing itself* was in vision" (pp. 82–83).	Random speculations by the pilgrims (2.14.53–64, 94–111). "The Syrian Monk" (2.18): whole canto fictionalized; of a monk who stayed on Quarantania. Highly developed material.
Melville camps on Plain of Jericho (p. 83).	Pilgrims do same (*2.16).
"Thunder in mountains of Moab" (p. 83).	Roaring avalanche in the Moab mountains (*2.39.131–47). Developed symbolically.
Encounters trans-Jordan Arabs with "lance—old crusaders." Their "native dignity" (p. 83).	Encounter fully described (2.23; see the discussion at line 45); the Arab's "poor lance . . . like some crusader's pole / Dropped long ago" (lines 154–61). Vine develops their "chivalry"—"of Sydney's clan" (2.27.70–101).

1856–57 JOURNAL	CLAREL
Dead Sea like Lake George or Lake Como—"all but verdure" (p. 83 and textual note at 83.18).	"Fair Como would like Sodom be / Should horror overrun the scene . . . " Developed for several lines (*2.29.8–19).
Dead Sea described. Terrible sensitivity to its meaning: "bitterness of life—thought of all bitter things . . . " (pp. 83, 158).	Part 2, *passim*; becomes strongest symbol in the poem.
"Rainbow over Dead Sea—heaven, after all, has no malice against it" (p. 83).	Very high symbolical development of rainbow as balancing agent to the sea's evil (2.29.116–23; 2.39.150–61; see the discussion at 2.39.131).
Section on *"Barrenness of Judea"* (pp. 83–84); includes the material on Mar Saba and Bethlehem (passage heavily marked in red pencil—see the accompanying textual notes).	Basis of Part 3, "Mar Saba," and Part 4, "Bethlehem."
Horrible barrenness detailed from the Dead Sea to Mar Saba (p. 83).	"In the Mountain" (3.1; see the discussion at line 65): same area, same tone, many of the same details. See also the discussion at 2.29.16.
Random note at foot of page describing route from Dead Sea to Mar Saba: "Port Esquiline of the Universe. (For Note)" (textual note at 83.38).	Port Esquiline in Rome compared with Dung Gate in Jerusalem (*1.24.18–22).
Random note on Saba monks as "Samphire gatherers" (textual note at 83.38).	Simile developed (*3.9.39–43).
"Crossed elevated plains, with snails, that tracks of slime, all over" (p. 84).	"In Indian file they gain / A sheeted blank white lifted plain— / A moor of chalk, or slimy clay, / With gluey track and streaky trail / Of some small slug or torpid snail" (*3.8.1–5).

1856–57 JOURNAL	CLAREL
"Arab-Bedouin encampment in hollow of high hills—oval—like two rows of hearses" (p. 84).	"Tents of Kedar" (3.8; see the discussion at line 82): "in faintly greenish hollow / An oval camp of sable hue." "The oval," says Rolfe, "seems his [Lot's] burial-plot" (lines 82–83, 90).
Kedron ravine (between Mar Saba and Jerusalem) described: "sepulchral, . . . smoked as by fire, . . . enigma of the depth" (p. 84).	Seven-line description of it (3.10.1–7).
Rain "only two or 3 days a year" (p. 84).	"But twice a year the waters flow" (3.1.95).
Arrival at Mar Saba, the small door, letter of admission hauled up in basket, etc. (p. 84).	"Before the Gate" (*3.10): same details, amplified.
"St Saba wine—'racka'" (p. 84).	Revels at Mar Saba (3.10–3.20; see the discussion at 3.10.74): talk, drinking, singing, etc.
Melville descends by ladders and passages to bottom of Mar Saba—the Kedron ravine (p. 84).	Derwent and the Lesbian do the same (3.25; see the discussion at line 32).
"Went into chapel &c—little hermitages in rock" (p. 84).	"The Medallion" (3.22; see the discussion at line 8): Derwent finds a chapel with a symbolical medallion in it. (Chapel named "Galilee"; no written source located for chapel or medallion.)
Sees monks by a "balustrade of iron" feeding "black-birds" with "bread" (p. 84).	The Celibate feeding the Saba doves from a balcony (*3.30.23–38).
Later notation about the "Jerusalem Cross 5 Wounds" (in Sandys's Relation; textual note at 84.28).	A Jerusalem cross appears as part of the device on the covers of the first edition (see p. 674 above).
Sees "numerous terraces, balconies" (p. 84).	"Terrace on terrace piled. And see / Up there by yon small balcony" (*3.25.57–58).

|

Notices "solitary Date Palm midway in precipice" (p. 84).

First described at *3.25.59–65. Cantos 3.16, 3.18, and 3.19 explore the responses of three major characters: Vine, Mortmain, and Rolfe. Mortmain dies with eyes fixed on the Palm (3.32): highly developed symbol of hope, life, immortality.

"Over lofty hills" to Bethlehem (p. 84).

"Bethlehem" (4.6) begins "Over uplands now . . . ."

"Passed over Bethalem hills— where shepherds were watching their flocks, (as of old) but a Moslem with back to Jerusalem (face to Mecca) praying" (p. 84).

Incident developed in detail (4.10); shepherds with "backs on Bethlehem turned" (line 65).

Guided through the Church of the Nativity by a Latin monk (p. 84).

"The Church of the Star" (*4.13) and "Soldier and Monk" (4.14). Salvaterra possibly developed from the Latin monk (see Index, p. 632).

"View from roof of chapel &c." (p. 84).

"The Convent Roof" (4.16).

"Ride to Jerusalem—pressing forward to save the rain" (p. 84).

"The Night Ride" (4.29): emotion of hurrying carried over into Clarel's desperation to see Ruth.

View of Jerusalem from Bethlehem road—"like arid rocks" (pp. 84, 154).

On the Bethlehem road Agath points and cries, "Wreck, ho! the wreck—Jerusalem!" (*4.1.187). Followed by a description of the view.

Section called "Jerusalem": impressionistic record of sights and thoughts (pp. 84–91).

Part 1, "Jerusalem," and last few cantos of Part 4 take place against this background; minor references to it throughout.

"*Village of Lepers*"; Melville horrified (p. 84).

"Huts" (*1.25): whole canto on lepers with much extraneous material from unidentified sources.

1856–57 JOURNAL	CLAREL
"*Wandering among the tombs*—till I began to think myself one of the possessed with devels" (p. 84).	The three demoniacs (*1.11.19–33).
"*Thoughts in the Via Dolorosa*—women panting under burdens—men with melancholy faces" (p. 84).	"Via Crucis" (*4.34).
Lengthy descriptions of the Church of the Holy Sepulcher, to which Melville went "almost every day" (pp. 85, 87–89).	Four cantos (1.3–1.6) on Clarel's visit (see the discussion at 1.3.0). History of the church (1.31.74–179). Ridiculed by Margoth (1.10.145–50). Its treasury mentioned (3.12.8). "The Easter Fire" (*3.16). Sects at the church (3.21.97–103). Celebration of Easter at the church (4.33).
Sun "indifferently ascends" over Olivet (p. 85).	"'Tis Olivet which thou ascendest . . . Yet how indifferent thy beam!" (1.15.7–9; see the discussion at 1.15.1).
"The old Connecticut man wandering around with tracts &c" (p. 85).	Prototype of Nehemiah (see Index, p. 630).
"Living occupants of the tombs—household arrangements" (p. 85).	Man and child living in tomb (1.28.78–89; see the discussion at 1.28.61).
"Side by side here tombs of Absolom, Zachariah & St: James. Cut out of live rock in Petra style" (p. 86).	"Flanked by three tombs, from base to head / Hewn from the cliff in cubic mass, / . . . And one presents in Petra row / Pillars in hanging portico" (1.14.22–26).
Melville describes and speculates on symbolism of the Golden Gate being walled up (p. 86).	Same details, same attitude (*1.10.74–95).
The "reddish soil" of Aceldama (p. 87).	Aceldama—"that dull reddish soil" (1.10.59; see the discussion at line 56).

1856–57 Journal	Clarel
Turkish guards at the door of the Church of the Holy Sepulcher—"crosslegged & smoking, scornfully observing" (p. 87).	At the church "warders" sit "Cross-legg'd," with pipes; "bored dead apathy" (3.16.15–20; see the discussion at line 12).
In front of the church, "hawkers & pedlers" with relics (p. 89).	By the church "pedlars versed in wonted tricks, / Venders of charm or crucifix" (*1.3.123–24). Some of the same relics named (2.3.26–35).
Sculpture on church: "Time has nibbled it away" (p. 89).	"Dim and defaced" sculpture described (*1.5.3–12).
On "*Interior of Jerusalem*": "Silence and solitude of it" (p. 89).	In the city "a silence reigns" (*1.7.1–25). "Wild solitudes" in the city (1.16.26).
Arch of Ecce Homo mentioned three times (p. 89).	"The Arch" (*1.13): dramatic canto on Celio at the arch.
Hears "muezzin calling to prayer from the minaret of Omer" (p. 89).	The "muezzin's cry" elaborated (*1.15.22–49).
Penitential appearance of the olive trees (p. 89).	Same theme (*1.30.22–27).
"To the left [of the Church of the Holy Sepulcher] is a high & venerable tower, which like an aged pine, is barked at bottom, & all decay at top" (p. 89).	"The tower looks lopped; it shows forlorn— / A stunted oak whose crown is shorn" (1.31.76–77; see the discussion at line 66).
Cactus growing in Jerusalem (p. 90).	Within the walls are "glades of cactus trees" (*1.16.24).
The "*strata* of cities" under Jerusalem (p. 90).	In Jerusalem "serial wrecks on wrecks confound /. . . in stratifying way" (*1.10.3–5). Jerusalem underground described (1.16.1–22).
Long section on "Stones of Judea" (p. 90); almost essay form. Attempts to remove them "like mending an old barn; the more you uncover, the more it grows."	Opening of "A Halt" (*2.10.1–33): same essay kind of treatment. Nehemiah "Flinging aside stone after stone, /. . . While every stone that he removed / Laid bare but more" (*2.10.190–94).

1856–57 JOURNAL	CLAREL
"Part of Jerusalem built on quarries—entrance from North wall" (p. 91).	The city once taken by means of a secret underground passage (1.16.13–22). And: "Dark quarries where few care to pry" (1.16.34).
Section on "Christian Missions &c in Palestine & Syria" (pp. 91–94).	Provided some evangelical qualities for Nehemiah and minor characters.
The Saunders' little girl "pines for home" (p. 92).	Ruth's hatred of Jerusalem as a child (*1.27.84–86).
Deacon Dickson (pp. 93–94).	Prototype for Nehemiah and Nathan.
Arabs and Turks persecute Jews beyond the city walls (p. 94).	Nathan murdered beyond walls (1.42).
Dickson expects "opening asunder of Mount Olivet" (p. 94).	Nehemiah: "Return he will over Olivet" (*1.11.89).
"Heartily wish Niebuhr & Strauss to the dogs" (p. 97).	"Zion, like Rome, is Niebuhrized" (*1.34.19).
Melville sees a "Santon," Arab holy mad-man (p. 98).	Nehemiah held a "Santon" (*1.8.69–75).
"French judge with black cap on" (p. 105); with later notation in pencil, "(Sentencing cap)" (textual note at 105.24).	Possible source for "The Skull-Cap" (2.2): canto on Mortmain's "black cap."
Melville offered a copy of a Guido "Cenci" (p. 106); goes to Cenci Palace (p. 107); sees and describes the original (p. 108); makes note "The Cenci portrait" (p. 155).	The portrait used as a symbol in the analysis of Vine's character (*3.7.16–24).
Sees Scala Santa in Rome: "(5 stairs) pilgrims going up— penitents" (pp. 108–9).	Clarel had once seen the Scala Santa, "watched the knees / Of those ascending devotees" (*1.5.60–61).

       CLAREL

1856–57 JOURNAL	CLAREL
Sees painting of "Fall of Simon Magus" (p. 112).	Legend of Simon Magus (*2.37.76–81).
Twice makes a notation about the trip in Italy "From *Tartarus to Tivoli*" (textual note at 113.10; p. 154).	Derwent's "good spirits made / A Tivoli of that grim glade [Gethsemane]" (*2.3.75–76).
In Pisa sees the Baptistery of the cathedral: "like dome set on ground. Wonderful pulpit of marble" (pp. 113–14).	Compares Jordan as baptistery with building in Pisa (2.27.20–21).
Is "charmed with Titian's Venus [*The Venus of Urbino*]" in Florence (p. 115).	The Prodigal describes this portrait, "Earth's loveliest" (*4.26.228–35).
In Florence meets a "singular young man who . . . presented me with a flower, and talked like one to whom the world was delightful." Speculates that "Something good" might be written on "that 'Henry' & the flower-girls" (p. 115).	Light-hearted Glaucon sings about the flower-girls of Florence (2.5.54–69).
Crosses Alps by San Gotthard Pass: "Hospice. Old stone warehouse" (pp. 124–25).	Description of St. Bernard Pass: "stone hospice" (*3.9.3).
"J. C. should have appeared in Taheiti" (p. 154).	Rolfe: "Tahiti should have been the place / For Christ in advent" (4.18.44–45; see the discussion at line 36; see also the discussion at 3.29.0).
"Palm Sunday—Beautiful Gate" (p. 154).	Clarel at the gate on Palm Sunday (4.32).
"Spinoza, Rothschild &c. &." (p. 154).	"Concerning Hebrews" (2.22): canto on famous Jewish people and their religion.

Melville's relation with Hawthorne counts as one of the tragedies of his life; and it was more than a minor one. Friendship itself must have seemed a mockery, when he found that the dearest friend and closest intellectual companion he had yet encountered was bound tight in the arctic ice, and many leagues away. But he had no sense of the distance between them until he attempted to span it: and it must have been with amazement, with incredulity, that he finally read the story of Ethan Brand, written during the prime year of their friendship, and discovered what in his heart of hearts Hawthorne felt about Melville's lofty pride and his extreme spiritual quests. . . .

We do not know when Melville discovered these words or felt their jagged edges in his bosom: but we can be certain that from that day forth the friendship between the two men sank like a stone in quicksand.

For Melville this was perhaps a last desperate essay at maintaining their friendship; and in spite of Hawthorne's cordial greeting, the meeting was hollow and it had come to nothing. Each had a secret locked in his bosom; and, in a sense, each had lost the key. Yet there was something fine and true between these two men—if only there had not been the reserve and the distance between them, a reserve that Melville's old rollicking ways and easy gipsy friendliness could not break down. One can scarcely doubt that it was about Hawthorne Melville wrote . . . Monody.

Two passages in which Lewis Mumford in his *Herman Melville* (1929, pp. 145–46, 264–65; see p. 884 below) developed the 1920's idea of an "estrangement" in the Melville-Hawthorne friendship, with no evidence but no doubts: (1) by advancing the soon-disproved notion that Hawthorne portrayed Melville in "Ethan Brand," and (2) by asserting, for the first time, the still-possible but unproven notion, now legendary, that Melville wrote "Monody" about Hawthorne.

Melville's "Monody": For Hawthorne?

T HE NOTION that Melville's poem "Monody" is about Hawthorne is quite rightly listed by John Bryant among what he calls "legends" in Melville scholarship. By a "legend" Bryant means "an interpretation or hypothesis that, for some, has acquired the exalted status and immunity from attack of a fact" (*A Companion to Melville Studies* [New York: Greenwood Press, 1986], pp. xxii–xxiii). The document presented here, with a question mark, is only possibly related to *Clarel* because it is only possibly about Hawthorne. It is the sole surviving manuscript of "Monody" in Melville's hand. From it, his wife Elizabeth Shaw Melville made the also extant printer's copy of the poem as published in *Timoleon* (1891). All three versions are reproduced below, pp. 891–93, the first two (at about three-quarters of the original size) by permission of the Hough-

This RELATED DOCUMENT was prepared by Harrison Hayford; the genetic transcription of Melville's manuscript was made by Robert C. Ryan and verified by Hayford.

ton Library of Harvard University, the third (full size) courtesy of The Newberry Library.

Whether "Monody" is in fact related to *Clarel* depends, first, upon whether it is in fact about Hawthorne, as originally asserted by Lewis Mumford in 1929, without documentary evidence or any Melville family tradition (*Herman Melville* [New York: Harcourt, Brace], pp. 264–65). It also depends, second, upon whether the character Vine in *Clarel* is in fact a portrait of Hawthorne, as first argued by Walter E. Bezanson in 1943 (see pp. 593ff. above). Although neither of these hypothetical identifications stands or falls by the other, the two are commonly linked in support of each other, as by Bezanson (p. 602 above). There is not space here to examine the history and rationale of the questionable "Monody"/Hawthorne hypothesis. For such an examination, the reader is referred to a forthcoming article by Harrison Hayford that involves, as it must, the whole matter of conflicting theories about the Melville-Hawthorne friendship, the biographical context in which most references to "Monody" occur.[1] At stake in Melville's biography is the large chapter about their friendship that depends on the validity—or invalidity—of both identifications as autobiography. Unfortunately, no clear-cut yes-or-no answer to the question about "Monody" emerges from Hayford's examination. Mumford's notion that Hawthorne is in the poem, like Bezanson's hypothesis that he is in *Clarel*, can so far neither be proved nor disproved; but the assumptions on which these identifications rest are brought into the open by the examination, which is designed to awaken awareness of the problem, in both readers and writers.

Examination of the only manuscript of "Monody" in Melville's hand, reproduced below in photofacsimile with other documents, likewise leaves a question mark. Nothing in the manuscript either proves or disproves that Melville wrote the poem for Hawthorne; nor does anything scholars have as yet discerned show just when he wrote it.

Physically, the manuscript consists of two segments: (1) a small piece of paper with the first stanza in ink on it, pinned near the top of (2) a larger piece of paper with the second stanza in ink on it, below the first. The inks and the papers are different. The first stanza is

1.   A preliminary version of Hayford's article appears in *Melville's "Monody": Really for Hawthorne?*—a keepsake issued by the Northwestern University Press in December, 1990, to mark publication of this edition of *Clarel*.

inscribed in blue-green ink on the relatively thick (ca. .114 mm) piece of yellow paper cut from a larger piece (trimmed along the stanza's top, left, and bottom edges, with the right edge untrimmed). The clipped-out stanza (14 x 6 cm) is pinned to the thinner (ca. .101 mm) cream-colored full leaf (18 x 14.28 cm—that is, the approximate size Melville used for most of his late manuscripts).[2]

Several inferences relevant to the Hawthorne question can be made from these physical facts about this manuscript.

1. This is not Melville's earliest manuscript of "Monody," or of either stanza. Scholars have found that Melville habitually composed in pencil (not ink), with tortured revisions, through several stages. Here, since he inscribed each stanza in ink, without revisions, we can safely infer that each was copied at a different time, from some earlier, but not necessarily its earliest, draft.[3]

2. We can infer that Melville *inscribed*—not that he *composed*—this clear-copy first stanza of "Monody" at some undetermined time earlier than the second. But we can infer nothing about the time order of what went on in any drafts through which he arrived at the present wording of either stanza. (For all we can tell, for example, the second stanza, though *inscribed* later than the first, may have been *composed* earlier than the first.) We know from the scholars cited above (footnote 2) that in making successive clear working copies as he composed and revised, Melville often clipped and kept (rather than troubled to recopy) passages that were still clearly legible, and then pinned each such "clip" to a new leaf ("mount"). He evidently did so in writing "Monody," and the pin can be seen in the photoreproduc-

2. Manuscripts called "late" in the Northwestern-Newberry Edition are most of the ones Melville left unpublished (and mostly undated) in his desk when he died in 1891. For more about the reasoning and terms used in the following notes, see the descriptions in the following works: the Hayford and Sealts edition of *Billy Budd, Sailor* (Chicago: University of Chicago Press, 1960), pp. 223ff.; Eleanor Tilton's "Melville's 'Rammon': A Text and Commentary," *Harvard Library Bulletin*, XIII (Winter, 1959), 50–91; and Robert C. Ryan's 1967 Northwestern University dissertation on *Weeds and Wildings*, pp. 142–46, 152–53; as well as the Northwestern-Newberry volumes *Published Poems* and *BILLY BUDD, SAILOR and Other Late Manuscripts*.

3. For examples of various manuscript stages, see the Northwestern-Newberry *Confidence-Man* volume, pp. 401ff., and the other editions cited just above. For a clear copy by Melville, see "Ditty of Aristippus," reproduced pp. 868–69 above. For Mrs. Melville's clear printer's copy of "Monody," see below, p. 892.

tion, just below "to be" in the third line. Sometimes Melville later moved such a clip forward again, and perhaps at last made it more secure on its mount with dabs of glue or sealing wax. (Possibly his wife helped with some of these procedures.) In available space above and/or below the "clip" thus attached to its "mount" Melville might then copy passages he had revised too heavily for ready legibility, or he might add new ones. As stated above, Melville had earlier inscribed the first stanza of "Monody" on a leaf, from which he clipped it; the second stanza he inscribed on the "mount."

3. In his attempt to date "Monody" for placement in his 1951 *Log* (New York: Harcourt, Brace), Jay Leyda reasoned as follows. In some of the other late manuscripts, the same two ink and paper combinations occur in the same relationship as in "Monody." From internal physical and textual evidence Leyda was the first to note that the blue-ink-on-thick-yellow-paper combination is the earlier of the two (later scholars agree, though just how much earlier they have not determined). But since (a) the first stanza of "Monody" (which Leyda presumed to be about Hawthorne's death in 1864) and (b) some of the late-manuscript poems about Mediterranean travel (1856–57) share that earlier ink and paper, Leyda inferred that Melville composed and inscribed them (in this form) all at the same period, around or soon after 1860, the travel poems possibly for the book manuscript which he had ready for publication then, but which was not published and is not preserved as such.[4] The closest later student of the problem, Robert C. Ryan, has found no physical or other evidence either to prove or to disprove the validity of this inference, which some other scholars have accepted. Leyda, on this reasoning, placed the composition of the first stanza of "Monody" in 1864 and entered it in his *Log* (II, 664) below the date and entry for Hawthorne's death, May 19, 1864. Above the stanza he supplied the date "May?" and this heading: "*M composes the first stanza of 'Monody'.*" (Here, as all through the *Log*, Leyda's documentary method kept him from explaining his reasons for such placements. He may have had a second reason for printing only the first stanza: the glaring discrepancy between the flowering Maytime of Hawthorne's funeral and the winter landscape of the second stanza.) But this *possibly* early dating is not *proof* that the first stanza of "Monody" (or anything else with the same blue ink and

4. See above, pp. 524, 530, and Melville's memoranda for his brother Allan, May 22, 1860, in the Northwestern-Newberry *Correspondence* volume.

yellow paper) was in fact written that early, as Leyda supposed—only that it may have been—for all that the manuscript evidence can be made to show thus far. At the other calendar end, however, Ryan finds it unlikely that the first stanza of "Monody" and the other manuscripts in question were *inscribed* later than mid-1888 (see Ryan, pp. 142–46, 152–53).

4. One further observation is directly relevant to the Hawthorne question. At some time before his wife, Elizabeth Shaw Melville, made the printer's copy, Melville considered changing his pronoun references to the mourned person from masculine to feminine. This is shown by his penciled, then later erased revision twice in line 1 of "him" to "her". (This tentative revision, like other penciled ones, cannot be verified in the reproduction.) Probably Melville made and unmade this change in pronouns before clipping and pinning the first stanza to its mount, since he did not pencil a third change of "his" to "her" in the first line of the present second stanza, as he might well have done had the present stanza already been there. In any case, since this is not Melville's original draft manuscript, we cannot reliably infer from his tentative rejected change of pronouns whether the poem's original subject was a man or a woman. Melville may or may not from the outset have disguised that person's gender by using an opposite pronoun, writing "him" for an actual "her"—or vice versa. We do, however, know that Melville did not often identify private individuals in his poems, at least in the surviving ones—or the private individuals (if any) portrayed in his prose works. (Well-known public figures are of course named in *Battle-Pieces* and other works, as well as various writers and artists in the poems.) We also know that Melville disguised or post-assigned the personal references of (and in) some of them.[5]

5. Among the few surviving poems identifying private persons are "Epistle to Daniel Shepherd" and "To Tom" (his brother Captain Thomas Melville), neither of them published. Poems of the second kind published in *John Marr and Other Sailors* are, e.g., "Bridegroom-Dick" (with pseudonymous references to his cousin Guert Gansevoort and others), "To Ned" (Toby Green), "To the Master of the 'Meteor' " (brother Tom). Among unpublished works, his dedication of *Weeds and Wildings* to "Winnefred" disguises the reference to his wife Elizabeth. The real woman in "Shadow at the Feast" is known to have been a "Mrs. B. 1847" (Mrs. Morewood's sister Ellen Brittain?) only because after Melville had retitled the poem (from "Lonie") his wife penciled this identification on his manuscript. Similarly, the real woman in "Iris" is identified as Rachel Turner Pond by his wife's varying notations on Mel-

5. An intriguing question arises, but ends in quandary. If Elizabeth Shaw Melville, his wife, knew whom "Monody" is about, why did she never tell? If about Hawthorne, why not tell her daughters, who would have transmitted the tradition? Why not tell J. E. A. Smith and Arthur Stedman, early biographers of Melville? Or Harriette M. Plunkett, a Pittsfield friend whom she helped with a 1900 article reviving Melville's "Hawthorne and His Mosses" and celebrating the friendship? (See Merton M. Sealts, Jr., *The Early Lives of Melville* [Madison: University of Wisconsin Press, 1974], pp. 29ff., 47ff., 78, 217.) Since Elizabeth (presumably after his death) noted on three of Melville's unpublished manuscripts the names of the private persons they were about (see footnote 5 above), why did she not somewhere note—if she knew—the name of the one "Monody" is about? Why not note that Hawthorne, for example, was the man, if she knew that? Or whomever else, man or woman, it was about? Must we be content to suppose she did not know, had never asked her husband, when she copied "Monody" for the printer's copy? Or had she been put off, or told but forbidden to tell? Our only answer is her granddaughter Eleanor Melville Metcalf's response: "There is NO family tradition linking 'Monody' to Hawthorne," when she was asked the direct question (through her husband) by Merton M. Sealts, Jr., at Hayford's request (in December, 1962; Hayford to Sealts, December 7, 1962, and Sealts to Hayford, February 19, 1963).

6. The five observations above leave unanswered whether "Monody" is or is not about Hawthorne. But they show that Jay Leyda's treatment of the first stanza of "Monody" in his *Log* was quite mistaken: (a) in the unexplained acceptance, as fact, of Hawthorne as its subject; (b) in the assumption that its earlier ink and paper justify dating, as fact, Melville's "composing" at least (or only?) its first stanza in "May?" of 1864, after Hawthorne's death on May 19; (c) in printing that first stanza in its final form, from *Timoleon* (1891), as if that were its "composed" form in 1864, or as if its final form had been arrived at already.

Four final observations about the poem's genetic history, though not relevant to the Hawthorne problem, may be made.

---

ville's manuscript and two transcripts. See *Collected Poems*, ed. Howard P. Vincent (New York: Hendricks House, 1947), pp. 276–78, 384–85, 401–3, 407, 480–81, 486, and the Northwestern-Newberry *Published Poems* volume, pp. 201–13, 228, 237–38.

7. Elizabeth Shaw Melville's hand appears on the manuscript in the first line of the second stanza. In pencil her husband had canceled "silent" and written a substitute word above it (perhaps "wintry"); then canceled that word and restored "silent"; then recanceled "silent" and written "wintry". In ink she wrote "wintry" on top of his first substituted word, indicating its place for insertion by a caret and guideline; and then (if not sooner) erased his pencilings.

8. Vestiges of three other revisions are reported and interpreted in Ryan's three bracketed and italicized patches of analysis in his genetic transcription facing the photofacsimile (on which the revisions cannot be verified). This is the gist of his analysis: (a) Another stanza may once have come before the present first one, as indicated by what is left of a large orange-pencil cross-out mark at the upper left corner of stanza one. (b) Melville fussed over the line indentations of his poem. (c) The vestigial two-stage pencil revision ("Aloof from drxx") at the lower left edge of the clip evidently was of the opening words of the then-following stanza (whether or not it was the present second stanza in an earlier version).

9. Melville's penciled foliation "47" at the upper left corner of the mount shows that it then stood as manuscript page 47 in his arrangement of the poems for *Timoleon*, compatibly, according to Ryan, with its appearance on page 34 of the book.

10. In making the printer's copy in ink, Elizabeth Shaw Melville followed the wording of Melville's manuscript faithfully. She omitted most or all of his punctuation marks from it, and after Melville had penciled his desired punctuation marks on her copy she inked them in. The poem as printed in *Timoleon* had only one change in punctuation that caused a change in meaning, from singular to plural: Melville's "fir-tree's" in his manuscript and her printer's copy became "fir-trees'" in the printed poem. Ryan restores "fir-tree's" in the Northwestern-Newberry *Published Poems*, p. 276 (printed in full on p. 602 above), following the textual policy of this whole edition, to follow the copy-text (here the printer's copy) when the source of changes from it is uncertain. (See the NOTE ON THE TEXT, p. 676 above.)

In the bracketed analysis in the genetic transcription below, all words in roman are authorial; all words in italics are editorial. The symbol "xxxx" represents an undeciphered word or series of letters (the number of x's approximates the number of letters involved).

GENETIC TRANSCRIPTION OF
MELVILLE'S MS.

[*The yellow paper of the clip is thick (approximately .114 mm), inscribed with blue-green ink. The cream-colored paper of the mount is thinner (approximately .101 mm), inscribed with gray iron-gall ink.*]

[*on mount: foliated in pencil on upper left corner* 47]

Monody

_____ " _____

[*on clip:*]

[*at the upper left corner of the clip is a diagonal orange pencil mark, at approximately a 45 degree angle to the clip's side; since the top of the clip has a scissored edge, the orange pencil mark may indicate cancellation of lines—perhaps six or more—that earlier preceded what is now the first stanza*]

Tȯ have known him, [*insert in pencil, then erase* her] to have loved him, [*insert in pencil, then erase* her]
  After loneness long;
And then to be estranged in life,
  And neither in the wrong;
And now for death to set his seal—
    Ease [*an erased vertical pencil mark runs from below* After *to a point left of* Ease *and is probably a mark indicating that this line is to be moved to the left and indented only as far as are lines 2 and 4; an erased penciled X and horizontal mark at the left of* Ease *possibly indicate that HM once thought of not indenting this line at all*] me, a little ease, my song!
[*beginning at the lower-left edge of the clip are the erased penciled words* Aloof from drxx *(partly scissored away); before these words were inscribed, however, the pencil-circled penciled words (now mostly scissored away) for which they are a further revision, were inscribed*]

[*on mount:*]
By silent [*pencil cancel* silent *and pencil insert, then erase* xxxxx {= ?wintry} *then restore, then re-cancel* silent *then pencil insert, then erase, and ESM insert (writing on top of the first HM substituted and erased word and with guideline to caret) her copy of his word* wintry] hills his hermit-mound
  The sheeted snow-drifts drape,
And houseless there the snow-bird flits
  Beneath the fir-tree's crape;
Glazed now with ice the cloistral vine
  That hid the shyest grape

_____ " _____

Melville's surviving manuscript of "Monody."

41

Monody

To have known him, to have loved him
After loneness long;
And then to be estranged in life,
And neither in the wrong:
And now for death to set his seal —
Ease me, a little ease my song!

By wintry hills his hermit-mound
The sheeted snow-drifts drape,
And houseless there the snow-bird flits
Beneath the fir-tree's crape:
Glazed now with ice the cloistral vine
That hid the shyest grape.

———— " ————

Elizabeth Shaw Melville's printer's copy of "Monody."

MONODY.

TO have known him, to have loved him
    After loneness long;
And then to be estranged in life,
    And neither in the wrong;
And now for death to set his seal—
    Ease me, a little ease, my song!

By wintry hills his hermit-mound
    The sheeted snow-drifts drape,
And houseless there the snow-bird flits
    Beneath the fir-trees' crape:
Glazed now with ice the cloistral vine
    That hid the shyest grape.

"Monody" as it appeared in *Timoleon* (1891).

COLOPHON

THE TEXT *of the Northwestern-Newberry Edition of* THE WRITINGS OF HERMAN MELVILLE *is set in eleven-point Bembo, two points leaded. This exceptionally handsome type face is a modern rendering of designs made by Francesco Griffo for the office of Aldus Manutius in Venice and first used for printing, in 1495, of the tract* De Aetna *by Cardinal Pietro Bembo. The display face is Bruce Rogers's Centaur, a twentieth-century design based on and reflective of the late-fifteenth-century Venetian models of Nicolas Jenson.*

This volume was set in type by Alexander Typesetting, Inc., of Indianapolis, Indiana. It was printed and bound in paper by Braun-Brumfield, Inc., of Ann Arbor, Michigan, and bound in cloth by John H. Dekker & Sons, Inc., of Grand Rapids, Michigan. The typography and binding design of the edition are by Paul Randall Mize.